"This book, rich as it is in history and sociology, compelling narratives and social studies, will serve as a reliable source for those wondering what the century we are about to leave was like.... [Susan Faludi] identifies so much of what it means to be a man these days, so many of the often opposing forces at work in our lives, the damned-if-you-do and damned-if-you-don't imbroglios. Her observations about a culture now dominated by the mall and the marketplace rather than the factory ... are hard-won and well-woven into the fabric of the male experience.... She sees, in the lives of men and of women, human wonders, human failings, human possibilities. And therein lies the final promise of *Stiffed* because she gets so much so right: There's the hope, still unrealized but maybe just a matter of time, that we might truly 'get it' after all."
                                                                —*Los Angeles Times*

"Faludi masterfully weaves larger essays with case histories and personality profiles. She connects the general to the specific and enlivens her argument with a host of haunted voices ... will be reread decades hence.... *Stiffed* is a pathography of our time."
                                                                —*Washington Post*

"Elegiac.... *Stiffed*, which you could see as the American literary equivalent of the British hit movie *The Full Monty*, is the product of six years of aggressive reporting and an admirable knack for bringing the results to life. No one will ever put this book down for lack of vivid scene setting or compassionate observation."
                                                                —*New York Times Book Review*

"Though Faludi is best known for her feminist polemic *Backlash: The Undeclared War Against American Women*, her new book is no attack on men. It is, instead, a sympathetic account of the lives of men who have been tossed about by forces beyond their control.... Faludi's book is a provocative reminder that both men and women are struggling in the aftershocks of seismic cultural shifts. *Stiffed* may help us move past the politics of blame that has characterized too much of the public conversation."
                                                                —*Atlanta Journal and Constitution*

"Out of her fearless detective work, her searching interviews, her feminist skepticism and her sensitivity to historical change, Susan Faludi has written a compelling interpretation of men's anger as they face the economic and cultural pressures of American society at the end of the twentieth century.... Faludi is unflinching. There will be people who will read this book—sometimes I found myself one of them—as voyeurs; she is not afraid to hang out in the underworld of inner-city crimes, among the producers of pornographic movies, with men who collect guns.... Readers will have their favorite sections, but for me, the book's most compelling ones are the interlocking chapters in which the tragedies of the Vietnam War linger in men's imaginations. Faludi restores Vietnam—and especially the My Lai massacre—to its place in living memory."   —*Chicago Tribune*

"*Stiffed* is much more than a polemic. There are richly poignant stories here of working stiffs and superstars, media movers and porno studs. Faludi weaves these tales together in a style that's threaded with empathy.... It's a new rhetoric to suit a new situation.... There's a greater recognition now that sexism is not just a conscious choice but an artifact of larger economic and cultural forces. In Faludi's hands, this perspective is as subversive as any second-wave feminist tract. After all, to the extent that women and men are fixed on each other's perfidy, they are less likely to see the common source of their misery—and more likely to fall for retail fantasies that give the illusion of liberation. The only way to elude these snares is to speak truth to market power, and this is what Faludi has done.... There is something utterly believable and undeniably tragic about the guys in this book."
   —*Ms.*

"*Stiffed* is an admirable, serious, and humane book. It records the dead-end [that] society has put men into as workers, parents, and citizens. *Stiffed* is blessedly free of jargon and full of telling detail. Its analysis is meant to provoke debate and will continue to do so."   —*Slate*

"Engrossing ... stunning case studies.... Her call for men's liberation is neither naive nor unsupported, and the stark reasoning and thick description in this book merit at least as much public discussion as did *Backlash*. Faludi is warning us, after all, that mass mobilizations like the Promise Keepers and the Million Man March may not have been mere wind-driven ripples on the surface of history, but advance signals of some serious seismic shaking down below."   —*Village Voice*

"This is a tour de force of personal reportage, brilliantly written, immensely compelling, filled with fascinating stories and insights worthy of thorough study."   —*Seattle Press-Intelligencer*

"Remarkable.... If feminism is Faludi's lens and compass, journalism is her splendid trade. She listens like a tuning fork, and picks up unseen vibrations. ... Her ear knows how to listen; her heart is made of sympathy; her mind is always changing; she wants to change the world.... There isn't a subject she touches on—from the space program to Tailhook to Rodney King to S.I. Newhouse—that she doesn't illuminate in prose as graceful as a gazelle.... And there's not a jot of jargon in the whole brilliant book."   —*Newsday*

"Men who read Pulitzer Prize–winner Susan Faludi's masterwork on the betrayal of the American man will find themselves, their fathers, brothers or uncles in its pages. . . . Readers will find men they know in *Stiffed* and never look at them the same way again. . . . Looking through new eyes, *Stiffed* gives both men and women a fresh appreciation for what it means—and more importantly how it feels—to be an American male in search of identity at a time when the definition of manhood is in question. Well-conceived, meticulously researched and well-written. . . . *Stiffed* is a landmark, a remarkable and rare book that will change the way men look at themselves and help women understand them better." 　　　　—*Columbus Dispatch*

"Faludi does a delicious job attacking the rise of today's ornamental culture of masculinity—which objectifies men and imprisons them in the notion that manhood depends on the achievement of a certain 'look,' the accumulation of specific props and, at best, celebrity. . . . It is impossible not to be won by the rigor of her analysis. . . . The cultural moment defined by the arrival of Faludi's book and the omnipresence of men-in-crisis does present a historic opportunity for men and women to come to new terms about what it means to be a man." 　　　　—*Hartford Courant*

"Susan Faludi's *Stiffed* is a book that ought to be read and discussed, not just in classrooms and on TV and radio talk shows but also by friends and families in kitchens and dens and bedrooms." 　　　　—*Fort Worth Star-Telegram*

"In this pathbreaking study of the contemporary 'male crisis,' award-winning journalist and author Faludi solidifies her reputation first gained in *Backlash* as one of our most astute analysts of gender relations. . . . This is brilliant stuff, cutting through nonsense, letting men speak for themselves and taking from their words original and compassionate insight." 　—*Kirkus Reviews*

"Absorbing and provocative. . . . Faludi tracks with care and intensity many events that have capsized the American male's dream boat . . . all fascinating, all revealing, all well told." 　　　　—*Tampa Tribune*

"*Stiffed* is a brilliant book, by a woman who likes us in spite of ourselves." 　　　　—CBS News

"*Stiffed* got some dumb reviews ('Gee, a feminist has something to say for men'), but the brighter reviewers recognized this for the signal service it is. Good for feminists, antifeminists and the Just Confused—a superb and entertaining book of social reporting about Where We Are Now." 　　　　—Molly Ivins

"[*Stiffed*] hits the nail on the head." 　　　　—Arnold Schwarzenegger

Also by Susan Faludi

Backlash: The Undeclared War Against American Women

Stiffed

The Betrayal of the American Man

AMERICAN STOCK

Susan Faludi

HARPER ● PERENNIAL

NEW YORK ● LONDON ● TORONTO ● SYDNEY ● NEW DELHI ● AUCKLAND

HARPER ● PERENNIAL

First Perennial edition published 2000.

Designed by Jane Palecek

Photographic research by Caren Alpert

The Library of Congress has catalogued the hardcover edition as follows:
Faludi, Susan
  Stiffed: the betrayal of the American man / Susan Faludi.
    p. cm.
  Includes bibliographical references and index.
  ISBN 0-688-12299-X
  1. Men—United States—Social conditions. 2. Men—United States—Psychology. 3. Masculinity—United States. I. Title.
HQ1090.3.F35 1999   99-35504
305.31'0973—dc21   CIP

ISBN 0-380-72045-0 (pbk.)

17 ❖/RRD 11

TO RUSS

contents

PART ONE

DEPARTURES

1   **THE SON, THE MOON, AND THE STARS**
The Promise of Postwar Manhood   3

PART TWO

UTILITY MEN

2   **NOTHING BUT BIG WORK**
From Shipyards to Space, the Closing of the American Job   51

3   **GIRLS HAVE ALL THE POWER**
What's Troubling Troubled Boys   102

4   **A GOOD DAWG WILL ALWAYS REMAIN LOYAL**
The Cleveland Browns Skip Town   153

5   **WHERE AM I IN THE KINGDOM?**
A Christian Quest for Manhood   224

PART THREE

EVIL EMPIRES

6   **GONE TO SOLDIERS, EVERY ONE**
The Vietnam War That No One Dodged   291

7   **THE CREATURE IN THE MIRROR**
The Fantasy Cavalry to the Rescue   359

8   **BURNING DOWN THE HOUSE**
The Fire Last Time in Waco, Texas   407

PART FOUR

HOOD ORNAMENTS

9 **MAN IN A CAN**
Moon Walkers, Ghetto Stars, and Cross-Dressers in a Gilded Age 451

10 **WAITING FOR WOOD**
A Death on the New Frontier 530

PART FIVE

DESTINATIONS

11 **PARTING SHOTS**
The Fighter Still Remains 577

12 **REBELS IN THE KINGDOM** 594

ACKNOWLEDGMENTS 609

NOTES 611

INDEX 651

ARCHIVE PHOTOS

PART ONE

DEPARTURES

Ernie Pyle aboard the aircraft carrier USS *Cabot*, World War II.

1

THE SON,
THE MOON, AND
THE STARS

The Promise of Postwar Manhood

WHEN I LISTEN TO THE SONS BORN after World War II, born to the fathers who won that war, I sometimes find myself in a reverie, conjured out of my own recollections and theirs. The more men I talk to, the more detailed this imagined story becomes. It is the story of a boy in bed pretending to sleep, waiting for his father. Tonight, the father has promised to reveal to the son a miraculous inheritance: the transit of an artificial star.

The door opens, and the hall light streams in, casting a cutout shadow man across the bedroom floor. For a moment, from the boy's vantage point, his father seems almost unreal, a flattened spectral image. Then the shadow moves forward into the room, hustling the boy into a jacket over his cowboy pajamas, arming him with a big chrome flashlight, digging out his Keds from under a heap of clothes in the closet. The boy pulls the coat around him and, even though it is August, feels wrapped in a delicious and unexpected comfort, enveloped in his father's hushed exuberance.

Earlier that evening, while his mother was busy scraping dishes in the kitchen, the boy and his father had hunched conspiratorially over the latest issue of *Life* magazine, the father pointing out features of the fantastical orb they were to observe, just the two of them, at an hour later than the boy had ever been allowed to be awake: *Ten stories high! Seven times as bright as the North Star!* His father said the satellite was really more of a balloon, a "satelloon," and told him how it had been clamped down with huge clothespins and folded into an egg-shaped magnesium sphere for the launch; how the shell had hatched open, right on time, when it reached its orbit, a mighty man-made explosion giving birth to a big, shiny beach ball called Echo. His father had said Echo's skin was half the thickness of the cellophane wrap on his cigarette pack; a meteorite could puncture it, even the sun's rays might disturb its course.[1] *It could collapse at any moment!* And it was this that would linger in the boy's mind: that something so powerful could be so fragile.

The boy, clutching his flashlight and his Davy Crockett cap, races after his father along the shadowy upper hallway past the bedroom where his mother lies sleeping, then down the stairs and through the living room where the blank eye of the new Philco TV gazes coolly upon their passage. On a sticky July evening a month ago, he had sat in front of the Philco with his parents and watched a young presidential nominee on a confetti-strewn proscenium turn his face ceremonially to the west and call on the "young men" of a "new generation" to join "a race for the mastery of the sky." It was up to boys like him, the man had said, to save not just the Earth but the "far side of space" from a Communism that had already "penetrated into Asia."[2]

He follows his father through the kitchen, the Frigidaire thrumming in the darkness, out the screen door and down the steps, where the aluminum patio furniture and the shiny globe of the barbecue grill phosphoresce like flying saucers come in for a landing. They are on the black-green quarter acre of clipped lawn now. His father bends, spreading his old navy peacoat like a blanket on the buzz-cut grass. The man and the boy in his raccoon cap kneel on the scratchy wool, two pioneers of the crabgrass prairie, and then the father snaps off the boy's flashlight. All the familiar moorings drop away and they are swept up, a father and a son, into the bright sky. The father touches the boy's shoulder and directs his vision to a faraway glimmer. The boy looks up, knowing that his father is pointing out more than just an object; it is a beacon of pride and secret knowledge, a paternal gift rocketing him into a future his father has helped to launch. At first, all he sees is the blanket of stars spreading out cold and vast between the trees. But then, there it is at last, a pinpoint of light crawling across the firmament, infinitesimally tiny, impossibly bright.

I KNEW THIS BOY. Like everyone else who grew up in the late 1950s and early 1960s, I knew dozens of him. He was Bobby on the corner, who roamed the neighborhood with his cap gun and holster, terrorizing girls and household pets. He was Ronnie, who wore his Superman suit way past Halloween and, sure he could fly, leaped from his living-room stairs one day and cracked his head open on the foyer linoleum. He was Frankie, who blew off part of his pinkie while trying to ignite a miniature rocket in the schoolyard. Even if he wasn't brought out into the backyard and shown an American satellite glinting in the sky, he was introduced to the same promise and the same vision, and by such a father. The fathers of that era often seemed remote, as unreal as those perfect dads on television, though not intentionally so. They were just fathers in the era after the war, living in brand-new suburbs with wives and children they barely knew, working at brand-new jobs on brand-new corporate "campuses," miles from their brand-new aluminum-sided houses. Which is to say that the life of the postwar father was altogether too newly out of the box for him to understand it, much less explain it to his son.

Many of these fathers were veterans of World War II or Korea, but their bloody paths to virility were not ones they sought to pass on, or usually even discuss. Because the fathers offered few particulars about their "baptisms" at Normandy or Midway or Heartbreak Ridge, war was a remote romance that each boy had had to embellish with details culled from Sergeant Rock and his combat adventures in DC comics, or Sergeant Bilko and an endless procession of television war series (*Crusade in Europe, Crusade in the Pacific, Victory at Sea, The Big Picture*), or later, GI Joe and his miniature arsenal.[3] Not that paternal knowledge of the war, even if shared, could have helped those sons, whose male proving grounds were to be on peaceful terrain. This was to be the era of manhood *after* victory, when the pilgrimage to masculinity would be guided not by the god of war Mars, but by the dream of a pioneering trip to the planet Mars. The satellite: here was a visible patrimony. And so Echo, with its reflective shell floating one thousand miles above the earth, became a remote point of triangulation connecting one generation of men to the next, and a visual marker of vaulting technological power and progress to be claimed in the future by every baby-boom boy. The men of the fathers' generation had "won" the world and now they were giving it to their sons. Their nation had come into its own, powerful, wealthy, dominant, in control of the greatest destructive force ever imagined. The fathers had made their sons masters of the universe and it felt, as in the time of Alexander, that what they had created would last forever.

I. The American Century Versus the Century of the Common Man

FOUR DECADES LATER, as the nation wobbled toward the millennium, its pulse-takers seemed to agree that a domestic apocalypse was under way: American manhood was under siege. Newspaper editors, TV pundits, fundamentalist preachers, marketeers, legislators, no matter where they perched on the political spectrum, had a contribution to make to the chronicles of the "masculinity crisis." Right-wing talk-radio hosts and left-wing men's-movement spokesmen found themselves uncomfortably on common ground. MEN ON TRIAL, the headlines cried. THE TROUBLE WITH BOYS, ARE MEN NECESSARY?, MAYBE MANHOOD CAN RECOVER. Periodicals of every political stripe from the conservative *Weekly Standard* (THE CRISIS OF MANLINESS) to *Newsweek* (WHITE MALE PARANOIA) to the progressive *Utne Reader* (MEN: IT'S TIME TO PULL TOGETHER) bannered the crisis on their covers.[4] Newspaper and broadcast journalists raced to report on one young-male hot spot after another: Tailhook, the Citadel, the Spur Posse, South Central gangsters, high-desert skinheads, militiamen blowing up federal buildings and abortion clinics, schoolyard shooters in Arkansas, Mississippi, Kentucky, Pennsylvania, Oregon, and Colorado.

In the meantime, the media's softer lifestyle outlets happily turned their attention to male-crisis-*lite:* the retreat to "gentlemen's" cigar clubs and lap-dancing emporiums, the boom in male cosmetic surgery and the abuse of steroids, the bonanza of miracle hair-growth drugs and the brisk sales of Viagra. Social scientists from right, left, and center pontificated on "endangered" young black men in the inner cities, Ritalin-addicted white "bad boys" in the suburbs, "deadbeat dads" everywhere, and, less frequently, the anguish of downsized male workers. Social psychologists and researchers issued reports on a troubling rise in male distress signals stretching over the last several decades—anxiety and depressive disorders, suicides and attempted suicides, physical illnesses, certain criminal behaviors—and a "mortality gap" that was putting the average man in his grave seven years before the average woman.[5] And by century's end political pundits seemed incapable of discussing anything *but* the president's supposedly dysfunctional masculinity; they contemplated Bill Clinton's testosterone level and manly credentials (Too much or not enough? Office lech or military virgin?) as if his Y chromosome was the nation's greatest blight.

Pollsters investigated the electoral habits of a new voting bloc they called "the Angry White Male" and researched the shopping choices of an emerging men-in-crisis demographic they had dubbed as early as the late eighties "the Contenders" or, less charitably, "the Change Resisters." Marketeers hastened to turn the crisis into entertainment and profits— from TV shows like *Men Behaving Badly* to sporting-goods sales of T-shirts that proclaimed DESTROY ALL GIRLS or WIFE BEATER (a retail phenomenon described in one newspaper headline as CASHING IN ON THE BAD BOY IMAGE) to advertising campaigns meant to salve the crisis-ridden male's wounds like Brut's aftershave slogan for the nineties, "Men Are Back!" And by the hundreds of thousands, men without portfolio confirmed the male-crisis diagnosis, convening in Washington for both the black Nation of Islam–led Million Man March and a largely white, evangelical-led Promise Keepers rally entitled, hopefully, "Stand in the Gap."[6]

If so many concurred in the existence of a male crisis, consensus collapsed as soon as anyone asked the question: Why? Not that there was a shortage of responses. Everyone proposed a favorite whipping boy—or, more often, whipping girl—and blame-seekers on all sides went after their selected culprits with righteous and bitter relish.

As a feminist and a journalist, I began investigating this crisis where you might expect a feminist journalist to begin: at the weekly meetings of a domestic-violence group. Wednesday evenings in a beige stucco building a few blocks from the freeway in Long Beach, California, I attended a gathering of men under court order to repent the commission of an act that stands as the emblematic masculine sin of our age. What did I expect to divine about the broader male condition by monitoring a weekly counseling session for batterers? That men are by nature brutes? Or, more optimistically, that the efforts of such a group might point to methods of managing or even "curing" such beastliness? Either way, I can see now that I was operating from an assumption both underexamined and dubious: that the male crisis in America was caused by something men were *doing* unrelated to something being done to them, and that its cure was surely to be found in figuring out how to get men to *stop* whatever it was. I had my own favorite whipping boy, suspecting that the crisis of masculinity was caused by masculinity on the rampage. If male violence was the quintessential expression of masculinity run amok, out of control and trying to control everything in its path, then a domestic-violence therapy group must be at the very heart of this particular darkness.

In my defense, I wasn't alone in such circular reasoning. Shortly after declaring my intention to investigate American masculinity, I was besieged with suggestions along the same lines from journalists, feminists, antifeminists, and other willing advisers. Women's-rights advocates mailed me news clips about male office stalkers and computer harassers. A magazine editor urged me to explore the subject of men on offshore oil rigs—"a real bastion of retrograde masculinity!" he said with curious enthusiasm. A fellow reporter, also a man, repeatedly called to alert me to horrific acts of male criminality he had spotted in the paper; serial rapists and killers were particular favorites. That I was not ensconced in the courtroom for O. J. Simpson's murder trial struck many of my volunteer helpers as an appalling lapse of judgment. "The perfect case study of an American man who thinks he's entitled to just control everything and everybody," one of them suggested.

But by the time of the Simpson trial, I had already been attending the domestic-violence group for several months—the very group O. J. Simpson was, by coincidence, supposed to have attended but avoided with the promise that he would speak by phone to a psychiatrist—and it was already apparent to me that whatever the crisis was, it did not stem from a preening sense of entitlement and control. The two counselors who ran the group, which was called Alternatives to Violence, worked hard to make "control" a central issue. Each new member would be asked to describe to the group what he had done to a woman, a request that was generally met with sullen reluctance, vague references to "the incident," and invariably the disclaimer "I was out of control." The counselors would then expend much energy showing him how he had, in fact, been in control the entire time. He had chosen his fists, not a knife; he had hit her in the stomach, not the face; he had stopped before landing a permanently injurious blow, and so forth. One session was devoted to reviewing "The Power and Control Wheel," a mimeographed chart that enumerated the myriad ways men could victimize their mates. No doubt the moment of physical contact for these men had grown out of a desire for supreme control fueled by a need to dominate. I cannot conceive of a circumstance that would exonerate such violence. By making the abusive spouse take responsibility for his actions, the counselors were pursuing a worthy goal. But the logic behind the violence still remained elusive.

A serviceman who had turned to nightclub bouncer jobs and pastry catering after his military base shut down seemed to confirm the counselors' position one evening shortly before his "graduation" from the group. "I denied it before," he said of the night he pummeled his girlfriend, who had also worked on the base. As he spoke he studied his massive, callused hands, lying uselessly on his lap. "I thought I'd blacked out. But looking back at that night when I beat her with an open hand, I didn't black out. I was feeling good. I was in power, I was strong, I was in control. I felt like a *man*." But what struck me most strongly was what he said next: that moment of control had been the only one in his recent life. "That feeling of power," he said, "didn't last long. Only until they put the cuffs on. Then I was feeling again like I was no man at all."

He was typical in this regard. The men I got to know in the group had without exception lost their compass in the world. They had lost or were losing jobs, homes, cars, families. They had been labeled outlaws but felt like castoffs. Their strongest desire was to be dutiful and to belong, to adhere with precision to the roles society had set out for them as men. In this respect, they were prototypical modern wife beaters, who, demographic research suggests, are commonly ill equipped to fulfill the requirements of expected stereotypical sex roles, men who are socially isolated, afflicted with a sense of ineffectuality, and have nothing but the gender rule book to fall back on.[7]

There was something almost absurd about these men struggling, week after week, to recognize themselves as dominators when they were so clearly dominated, done in by the world. "That 'wheel' is misnamed," a laid-off engineer ruefully told the counselors. "It should be called the Powerlessness and Out-of-Control Wheel." The men had probably felt in control when they beat their wives, but their everyday experience was of feeling controlled—a feeling they had no way of expressing because to reveal it was less than masculine, would make each of them, in fact, "no man at all." For such men, the desire to be in charge was what they felt they must do to survive in a nation that *expected* them to dominate.

Underlying all the disagreement over what is confusing and unnerving to men runs a constant line of thinking that blinds us—whatever our political beliefs—to the nature of the male predicament. Ask feminists to diagnose men's problems and you will often get a very clear explanation: men are in crisis because women are properly challenging male dominance. Women are asking men to share the public reins and men can't bear it. Ask antifeminists and you will get a diagnosis that is, in one respect, similar. Men are troubled, many conservative pundits say, because women have gone far beyond their demands for equal treatment and now are trying to take power and control away from men. Feminists are "feminazis," in their view, because they want to command every sphere once directed by men, from deportment in the boardroom to behavior in the bedroom. The underlying message: men cannot be men, only eunuchs, if they are not in control.

Both the feminist and antifeminist views are rooted in a peculiarly modern American perception that to be a man means to be at the controls and at all times to feel yourself in control. The popular feminist joke that men are to blame for everything is just the flip side of the "family values" reactionary expectation that men should be in charge of everything. The problem is, neither of these views corresponds to how most men feel or to their actual positions in the world. The year I spent at the domestic-violence group, as it turned out, wasn't a diversion. It illuminated a dynamic in men's lives that indeed causes trouble, but it was the reverse of what I expected. Everywhere men look, even in a therapy session intended to offer men "alternatives to violence," they are told that there is no alternative: they must be at the helm.

The man controlling his environment is today the prevailing American image of masculinity. A man is expected to prove himself not by being part of society but by being untouched by it, soaring above it. He is to travel unfettered, beyond society's clutches, alone — making or breaking whatever or whoever crosses his path. He is to be in the driver's seat, the king of the road, forever charging down the open highway, along that masculine Möbius strip that cycles endlessly through a numbing stream of movies, TV shows, novels, advertisements, and pop tunes. He's a man because he won't be stopped. He'll fight attempts to tamp him down; if he has to, he'll use his gun. It seems to us as if it has always been thus, ever since the first white frontiersman strode into the New World wilderness, his rifle at the ready.

But a look at our history, long since buried under a visual avalanche of Marlboro Men and Dirty Harrys and Rambos, suggests a more complicated dynamic, one in which from the nation's earliest frontier days the man in the community was valued as much as the loner in control, homely society as much as heroic detachment. Even in the most archetypal versions of the original American male myth, a tension prevailed between the vision of a man who stood apart from society and the man who was a part of society; the loner was not the ideal. The "Indian fighter" was ultimately a homesteader. In its genesis, the story of Daniel Boone was not simply a tale of a frontiersman taming the world with his rifle and knife. Essential to the myth of his journey into the wilderness was his return from it to retrieve his family and establish a new community. John Filson, the author who first mythologized Boone's life in the late eighteenth century, was adamant on this point, as frontier historian Richard Slotkin observes: "For Filson, Boone's solitary hunting trips are, not ends in themselves, but means to a social end. Solitude has value in the Boone narrative only insofar as it contributes to the ultimate creation of a better society; hunting is noble only insofar as it clears the way for husbandry." Or, in words attributed to Boone in his as-told-to-Filson autobiography of 1784: "Thus we behold Kentucke, lately an howling wilderness, the habitation of savages and wild beasts, become a fruitful field; this region, so favourably distinguished by nature, now become the habitation of civilization." Conquering "savages" on that uncultivated frontier was only half the story, and not necessarily the important half. "Soon after," Boone recounted of his earliest forays into the hinterland, "I returned home to my family with a determination to bring them as soon as possible to live in Kentucke, which I esteemed a second paradise, at the risk of my life and fortune."[8] The risk only had meaning because it meant something for the future of his family and his society.

Historian E. Anthony Rotundo has observed in *American Manhood* that men of the colonial and Revolutionary eras "especially were judged by their contribution to the larger community. Before 1800, New Englanders saw a close link between manhood and 'social usefulness.'... Men who carried out their duties to family and community were men to admire." A study of heroic male figures in late-eighteenth-century periodicals similarly found that the perceived key to masculinity was "publick usefulness." The hunter in the saddle, untethered from public life, was regarded as only half a man. He was the outrider whose bloodletting served no social purpose, the lone killer who kept on killing because there was nothing else to do. He was the "frontier wastrel," as literary historian Vernon Louis Parrington wrote of Davy Crockett in 1927, "but one of thousands who were wasting the resources of the Inland Empire, destroying forests, skinning the land, slaughtering the deer and bear, the swarms of pigeons and turkey, the vast buffalo herds. Davy the politician is a huge western joke, but Davy the wastrel was a hard, unlovely fact."[9]

In industrializing nineteenth-century America, however, the wastrel would begin to gain a certain renown as an emblem of virility, his rapaciousness evidence of his ambitious, rags-to-riches drive, his heaps of dead pelts the equivalent of the tycoon's consolidated fortunes, his killer instinct compensating for the loss of service to a community. To be a man increasingly meant being ever on the rise, and the only way to know for sure you were rising was to claim, control, and crush everyone and everything in your way. "American manhood became less and less about an inner sense of self, and more and more about a possession that needed to be acquired," Michael Kimmel has observed in *Manhood in America*. Davy Crockett was elevated to the masculine pantheon, along with Wild Bill Hickok, Jesse James, and Captain Carver, the last famed in his time for slaughtering more buffalo in one day than any other man ever had — and leaving miles of carcasses behind him. Long forgotten was the final appeal to God by the Quaker-bred Daniel Boone in his autobiography, to "banish the accursed monster, war, from all lands, with her hated associates, rapine and insatiable ambition."[10]

Even as the ethic of solo ambition gained ground, social utility remained a competing index of American manhood. The federal government would call on it in times of national emergency, and the quality of "publick usefulness" would continue to be longed for, however quietly, in the hearts and imaginations of individual men. At the tail end of the Gilded Age, novelist Frank Norris critiqued the prevailing culture in *McTeague*, the story of a giant-size, inept dentist driven by a predatory "ambition"—"to have projecting from that corner window a huge gilded tooth, a molar with enormous prongs"—who meets his demise in Death Valley chained to the corpse of the rival he has murdered. Norris expressed what many believed privately about the new ideal of Darwinian manhood—that it led to a sterile and self-destructive violence, that the "survival of the fittest" when applied to modern man might mean the survival of no one.[11]

But such critiques were in the minority, and later in our century would be nearly drowned out by images of virility generated by the overpowering new mediums of film and television. In his incarnation as a cleaned-up Walt Disney television character in 1955, Davy Crockett would eclipse Daniel Boone for good. His "appearance" in a three-part series on the popular program *Disneyland* set off a real-life mass slaughter, as the marketplace raced to meet the runaway demand for raccoon hats by doing in much of the continent's raccoon population. In the popular imagination, Boone had dissolved into Crockett; actor Fess Parker would portray them both for Disney, each in a coonskin cap, oblivious to the fact that the real-life Boone had declined to wear what he viewed as the haberdashery of the uncivilized brute.[12] The new King of the Wild Frontier would rule his era along with his advertising doppelgänger, the Marlboro Man, who was likewise no settler, just a mute icon presiding over an emptied-out Western landscape. In the new mass-marketed wilderness, a cast of heroic outriders triumphed over and over against the backdrop of Death Valley and Monument Valley and all the other never-to-be-populated valleys of the Wild West. They were men judged by their ride out into the wasteland, not their return; they were measured by the control they achieved over their environment through gunplay, not husbandry. The essential question to be resolved, in episode after episode, sequel after sequel, was not whether our hero had been socially engaged and useful, but whether he had maintained control and survived.

And so modern debates about male angst are invariably diverted by that old issue of control in the wilderness. What gets discussed is how men are exercising or abusing their control and power, not whether a lack of mooring, a lack of context, is causing their anguish. ARE MEN REALLY THAT BAD? was how *Time* magazine sniffily defined the central question in a 1994 cover story, memorably illustrated by a man sporting a business suit, a wedding ring, and a pig's snout for a face.[13] While the image indicted a swinish wallowing in dominance, it left unexamined the American man's more common experience of fear at losing the job that requires the business suit, the family for whom he wears the ring, any context in which to embed his life. If men are the masters of their fate, what do they do about the unspoken sense that they are being mastered, in the marketplace and at home, by forces that seem to be sweeping away the soil beneath their feet? If men are mythologized as the ones who *make things happen,* then how can they begin to analyze what is *happening to them?*

More than a quarter century ago, women began to suspect in their own lives "a problem with no name." Even the most fortunate woman in postwar, suburban America, maneuvering her gleaming Hoovermatic across an expansive rec room, sensed that she'd been had. Eventually, this suspicion would be expressed in books—most notably Betty Friedan's *The Feminine Mystique*—that traced this uneasiness back to its source: the cultural forces of the mass media, advertising, pop psychology, and all the other "helpful" advice industries. Women began to free themselves from the box in which they were trapped by feeling their way along its contours, figuring out how it had been constructed around them, how it was shaped and how it shaped them, how their reflections on its mirrored walls distorted who they were or might be. Women were able to take action, paradoxically, by understanding how they were acted upon. "Women have been largely man-made," Eva Figes wrote in 1970 in *Patriarchal Attitudes.*[14] What had been made by others women themselves could unmake. Once their problems could be traced to external forces generated by a male society and culture, they could see them more clearly and so challenge them.

Men feel the contours of a box, too, but they are told that box is of their own manufacture, designed to their specifications. Who are they to complain? The box is there to showcase the man, not to confine him. After all, didn't he build it—and can't he destroy it if he pleases, if he is a *man?* For men to say they feel boxed in is regarded not as laudable political protest but as childish and indecent whining. How dare the kings complain about their castles?

Women's basic grievances are seen as essentially reasonable; even the most blustery antifeminist these days is quick to say that, of course, he favors equal pay and equal opportunity. What women are challenging is something that everyone can see. Men's grievances, by contrast, seem hyperbolic, almost hysterical; so many men seem to be doing battle with phantoms and witches that exist only in their own overheated imaginations. Women see men as guarding the fort, so they don't see how the culture of the fort shapes men. Men don't see how they are influenced by the culture either; in fact, they prefer not to. If they did, they would have to let go of the illusion of control.

Today it is men who cling more tightly to their illusions. They would rather see themselves as battered by feminism than shaped by the larger culture. Feminism can be demonized as just an "unnatural" force trying to wrest men's natural power and control from their grasp. Culture, by contrast, is the whole environment we live in; to acknowledge its sway is to admit that men never had the power they imagined. To say that men are embedded in the culture is to say, by the current standards of masculinity, that they are not men. By casting feminism as the villain that must be defeated to validate the central conceit of modern manhood, men avoid confronting powerful cultural and social expectations that have a lot more to do with their unhappiness than the latest sexual harassment ruling.

The very paradigm of modern masculinity—that it is all about being the master of your universe—prevents men from thinking their way out of their dilemma, from taking active political steps to resolve their crisis. If they are the makers of history, not the subjects of historical forces, then how can they rise up? Even those most sympathetic to men's anguish recoil from seeing their problems politically. Herb Goldberg's 1977 book *The Hazards of Being Male* was among the first in the men-in-distress genre to acknowledge that men lead their lives "in harness." Nonetheless, Goldberg typically rejected any solution that would snap the harness. "There could be no movement for men like the women's movement," he wrote in a foreword to the tenth-anniversary edition. To hold out hope "that men's problems could be solved with external answers and solutions," he warned, was just "fueling fantasies."[15]

Goldberg, like others, assumed men's problems to be internal. Yet clearly masculinity is shaped by society. Anyone wondering how mutable it is need only look at how differently it is expressed under the Taliban in Kabul or on the streets of Paris. Witness men walking with their arms wrapped around each other in Istanbul or observe the Mexican immigrant to Los Angeles whose manhood is so linked to supporting a family that any job, even a busboy's, holds a masculine pride. As anthropologist

David D. Gilmore demonstrated in *Manhood in the Making,* his comprehensive cross-cultural survey of masculine ideals, manliness has been expressed as laboring-class loyalty in Spain, as diligence and discipline in Japan, as dependence on life outside the home in the company of men in Cyprus, as gift-giving among Sikhs, as the restraint of temper and the expression of "creative energy" among the Gisu of Uganda, and as entirely without significance to the Tahitians. "Manliness is a symbolic script," Gilmore concluded, "a cultural construct, endlessly variable and not always necessary."[16]

It should be self-evident that ideas of manhood vary and are contingent on the times and the culture. Despite that, contemporary discussion about what bedevils men fixes almost exclusively on the psychological and the biological. Whatever troubles a man must be an essential aspect of that individual, a problem of testosterone surges, sperm counts, Ritalin dosages, or the scars of inadequate mothering. To alleviate his distress, he need only get a prescription for Viagra or a lifetime gym membership or reconnect with the Wild Man "lying at the bottom of his psyche" or "The King Within," as two popular books that typify the fare in the new "men's studies" sections instruct. (The coauthors of *The King Within,* a therapist and a Jungian psychoanalyst, even advised male readers that to remasculinize themselves they should collect pictures of Egyptian pharaohs and "imagine yourself inside the pyramid, or imagine it inside of you, perhaps in the chest area.")[17] The man in crisis need only picture himself a monarch, pump up, armor himself, go up against the enemy, and prove that he's in control.

Women faced their problem-with-no-name by breaking their isolation and organizing. The solutions offered to men generally require them to see themselves in ever more isolated terms. Whatever troubles the American man, the outlets of mass culture from Hollywood to pop psychology to Madison Avenue tell him, can be cured by removing himself from society, by prevailing over imaginary enemies on an imaginary landscape, by beating a drum in the woods until he summons the "deep masculine," by driving ever faster on an empty road. Instead of collectively confronting brutalizing forces, each man is expected to dramatize his own struggle by himself, to confront arbitrarily designated enemies in a staged fight—a fight separated from society the way a boxing ring is roped off from the crowd. It is a fight that society watches and may applaud but does not participate in and has no influence over.

Popular accounts of the male crisis and male confusions are almost unrelievedly ahistorical. The conditions under which men live are ignored and men themselves are reduced to a perennial Everyman—as women were a century ago, when the phrase "the Woman Question" was invoked to refer to their perplexing sex in the ethereal singular. How would men's problems be perceived, though, if we were to consider men as the subjects of their world, not just its authors? What if we put aside for a time the assumption of male dominance, put away our feminist rap sheet of men's crimes and misdemeanors, or our antifeminist indictment of women's heist of male authority, and just looked at what men have experienced in the past generation? God is the only being who has no history. Even the most "powerful" man has had at least as much happen to him as he has made happen.

――――――

WHAT DID HAPPEN to the men of postwar America?

Ernie Pyle might have told us. He was the World War II journalist whose stories from the front turned the GI for a time into an American male ideal. If the French revolutionaries of the 1790s cast their struggle in iconographic terms that were essentially maternal—Marianne as Liberty in Delacroix's later painting, breast bared and bearing her standard into battle—Americans of the 1940s sexed their icons the other way. A band of marines struggling to erect a flagpole in the flinty ground of Iwo Jima would become the supreme expression of the nation's virtue. A team of anonymous, duty-bound young men successfully completing the mission their fathers and their fathers' fathers had laid out for them, defeating a vile enemy and laying claim to a contested frontier—this would be the template for postwar manhood. The United States came out of World War II with a sense of itself as a *masculine* nation, our "boys" ready to assume the mantle of national authority and international leadership. The nation claimed an ascendancy over the world, men an ascendancy over the nation, and a male persona of a certain type ascendancy over men.

There was nothing fancy about that type, not in the beginning at least. Ernie Pyle chose to sing not of the silk-scarfed fighter pilots but of the unsung infantrymen, "the mud-rain-frost-and-wind boys," as he called them in his daily columns, which, more than any of the other wartime dispatches, determined how Americans saw and remembered the Second World War. The appellation was made visual in Bill Mauldin's wartime cartoons of Willie and Joe, his "dogface" soldiers, characters for whom, as the artist noted, "the bags under their eyes and the dirt in their ears are so similar that few people know which is Willie and which is Joe." Mauldin, himself an infantry "doggie" during the Italian campaign, "loved to throw hooked cartoons" at the glamorous image of the Air Corps "flying boy."[18] In his classic World War II memoir, *To*

Hell and Back, Audie Murphy, the most decorated soldier of the war, recalled how he and his GI buddies literally threw hooks (of the left and right variety) at a group of drunken airmen they encountered in a café in Rome, after mocking them with a serenade of their version of "Junior Birdman":

> And when they make a presentation,
> And hand out those wings of tin,
> You too can be a Junior Birdman—
> If you'll send those box tops in.[19]

For Ernie Pyle, though, something more than home-team chauvinism inspired his praise of the men on the ground. "Goddamn all big shots," he once said to a friend, summing up his view of men who call attention to themselves, who make public spectacles out of their individual "achievements." Prewar, Pyle wrote what was probably the nation's first aviation column in the *Washington Daily News,* and even then he was suspicious of macho displays: his daily air-flight reports eschewed the antics of stuntmen and speed-demon record breakers for the quiet dedication of the men who braved storms and poor navigational equipment to deliver the mail. Pyle also loathed writing about Hollywood. "It's all I can do to face a movie star," he told a friend. "They make me sick." During the war, he refused to dote on airborne Hollywood-esque heroes. Let the rest of the media go gaga over the glittering "flyboy." For Pyle, the mud-caked private was more man than any pilot would ever be. "War makes strange giant creatures out of us little routine men who inhabit the earth," Pyle wrote, speaking of himself as much as of the men with whom he marched. "They live and die so miserably and they do it with such determined acceptance that your admiration for them blinds you to the rest of the war."[20]

Pyle's view became the official one. Government radio propaganda dubbed the conflict the "little guys' war." At war's end, General Dwight D. Eisenhower pronounced: "All in that gigantic fighting machine agree in the selection of the one truly heroic figure in that war. He is GI Joe.... He and his platoon leaders have given us an example of loyalty, devotion to duty, and indomitable courage that will live in our hearts as long as we admire those qualities in men." By Eisenhower's voice and Pyle's typewriter, the foot soldier was elevated into a masculine emblem—a man who proved his virility not by individual feats of showy heroism but by being quietly *useful* in conducting a war and supporting the welfare of his unit. "We are all men of new professions out in some strange night caring for each other," Pyle wrote. Each "little routine man" was part of a team that shared a common mission, his manhood coming from contributing to something bigger than himself. "The men didn't talk any," Pyle wrote of the 9th Infantry Division as he accompanied the unit during its assault on the port city of Cherbourg, north of the Normandy beachheads. "They just went. They weren't heroic figures as they moved forward one at a time, a few seconds apart. . . . They weren't warriors. . . . They were American boys who by mere chance of fate had wound up with guns in their hands. . . . They were afraid, but it was beyond their power to quit. They had no choice. They were good boys."[21]

In the forge of his daily columns, Ernie Pyle took these frightened good boys and made them, in the eyes of the nation, into men. The template for this man-making process was Pyle's most famous column, "The Death of Captain Waskow," a tribute to a beloved, paternal company commander. "After my own father," Pyle quoted one of his sergeants as testifying, "he came next."[22] The prevailing narrative fashioned from the battlefronts of World War II, laid out in countless columns, newsreels, and movies, was a tale of successful fatherhood and masculine transformation: Boys whose Depression-era fathers could neither provide for them nor guide them into manhood were placed under the benevolent wing of a vast male-run orphanage called the army and sent into battle. There, firm but kindly senior officers acting as surrogate fathers watched over them as they were tempered into men in the heat of a heroic struggle against malevolent enemies. A father-son rupture in the nation had been healed: the boys, saved and molded into men, would return to find their wives, form their families, and take their places as adult men in the community of a nation taking its place as a grown-up power in the world.

This was the story America told itself in dozens of war movies in which tough but tenderhearted commanding officers prepared their appreciative "boys" to assume their responsibilities in male society. It was the theme of the 1943 film *Guadalcanal Diary,* where the boys ship out, tussling playfully with one another like a bunch of mismatched kittens, and then shed their differences in a marine family presided over by a fatherly captain and a fatherly Father. "Great bunch of kids, Father," the captain says proudly to the priest. "They'll do all right." It was the theme behind the 1949 film *Sands of Iwo Jima,* with John Wayne as Sergeant Stryker, a stern papa molding his wet-behind-the-ears charges into a capable and adult fraternity. "Before I'm through with you, you're gonna move like one man and think like one man," he tells them. "If I can't teach you one way, I'll teach you another, but I'm gonna get the job done." And he does, fathering a whole squad of youngsters into communal adulthood.

It was the dream of a male society to minister to its boys in the context, ironically enough, of war, and turn them into men through tenderness, not brutality. A nation that had been birthed by metaphorically orphaned Sons of Liberty, and a nation in which, more recently, a generation of unemployed fathers had been unable to provide for their families, emerged from World War II with the conviction that it had at last forged a father-son bond strong enough to prove a foundation for the domestic peace to come.

The transition was celebrated on August 14, 1945, V-J Day, when the war ended in victory over Japan. President Harry Truman declared a two-day holiday. Across the country, joyous citizens welcomed returning troops with impromptu parades, spontaneous street dancing, and christenings of shredded-phone-book confetti, champagne, and water. Women raced to shower the GIs with "kissing from coast to coast," as *Life* put it in a famous two-page photo spread on "the osculatory gamut." In Manhattan, two million celebrants crammed into Times Square, while in Brooklyn, Italian-American mamas and papas set up tables on the street and plied their young heroes with food and wine. "We are faced with the greatest task we've ever been faced with," the president declared from the lawn of the White House to cheering throngs. He called on the nation's returning men to tackle the responsibilities of rebuilding a free nation and world. "It is going to take the help of all of us to do it. I know we are going to do it."[23] Was there ever such a national moment of masculine certainty, so ringingly recognizing the American boy's transport into a state of manhood—a state where his passage was cheered, his contribution called essential, the nation's faith in his ability to keep on "doing it" boundless?

By lionizing the grunt, Ernie Pyle inadvertently became an architect of what many hoped postwar manhood would become. The promise was that wartime masculinity, with its common mission, common enemy, and clear frontier, would continue in peacetime. By 1950, a quasi-militarized peacetime economy and a national security state had arisen in America. Within the context of the cold war, the postwar man, too, seemed to share with his cohorts a common mission of prevailing in a struggle against Communism on the battlements of Europe, throughout Asia, at home, and even on the frontiers of outer space. Like GI Joe, he would be judged not on his personal dominance but on his sense of duty, his voluntary service to an organization made up of equally anonymous men. The dog soldier would continue to have his day.

WORLD WAR II, HOWEVER, would prove not the coronation of this sort of masculinity but its last gasp. The model Ernie Pyle limned in his columns he had crafted during the Great Depression, while touring small-town and rural America chronicling the quiet struggles of Alabama sharecroppers and Mississippi shrimp-cannery workers, Oklahoma ditch-diggers and Great Plains Dust Bowl farmers trying to survive the nation's economic devastation. In fact, Pyle's vision owed more to the New Deal than it did to the Normandy invasion. Before he praised the GIs he was praising peacetime grunts like "the CCC boys," the young Civilian Conservation Corps workers who were showing "what man can do with mountains." The literary figure he emulated was John Steinbeck, and, long before World War II, President Franklin Delano Roosevelt was his hero for the war he waged on poverty and on his own polio-paralyzed body. Observing one day in Rapid City, South Dakota, as the visiting president lifted himself into his leg braces on "his powerful arms," an emotional Pyle wrote, "I have never seen a man so straight."[24]

The idea of a manhood embedded in and useful to an embattled society seeking to foster social welfare and equity was promoted by a New Deal America and brought to life in such mammoth efforts as the federal Works Progress Administration, which invested billions of dollars in massive projects: building schools, constructing waterworks and sewage plants, electrifying rural areas, controlling floods, reforesting the distressed land. The WPA also employed small armies of artists, writers, actors, playwrights, and musicians, whose legacy is still with us in extraordinary murals on public buildings, literate regional and state guides, and classic plays and music. The New Deal's masculine ideal was the selfless public servant whose "satisfaction derived from sinking individual effort into the community itself, the common goal and the common end," Roosevelt's attorney general Francis Biddle wrote at the time. "This is no escape from self; it is the realization of self." And the realization of a manly self. As an artist with the Public Works of Art Project, a prototype for the WPA, wrote to President Roosevelt, this was the era when American art finally "took on a virility," because of "this golden opportunity to do our best work for our fellow countrymen." New Deal historian Arthur Ekirch, Jr., has observed, "No longer was competition considered superior to cooperation and association." The New Deal's master builder himself spelled out this newly minted masculine conception in a 1932 speech. "The man of ruthless force had his place in developing a pioneer country," Roosevelt declared, but now he is "as likely to be a danger as a help"—a danger because "the lone wolf . . . whose hand is against every man's, declines to join in achieving an end recognized as being for the public welfare."[25]

This ethic was promoted most strongly by Roosevelt's secretary of agriculture and, later, vice president Henry Wallace, an Iowa agrarian who spun a progressive dream for the nation's future around the heroic figure of the "Common Man." Wallace imagined an army of ordinary workingmen who, if given a shot at decent educations, jobs, and housing, could be a force on "the new frontier" for expanded production, well-being, and democracy not only in the nation but throughout the world. The "Century of the Common Man," as Wallace dubbed it in a famous speech in May 1942, was to include both sexes, but he defined it in quintessentially masculine terms. Wallace saw America as "a boy of eighteen" who could no longer "avoid becoming a man by wearing short pants" and who could mature into a "grown-up United States" by stoically "shouldering our responsibility," by contributing to the needs of the world rather than simply aspiring to dominate it.[26] America's mission, he said, only half jokingly, should be to ensure "that everybody in the world has the privilege of drinking a quart of milk a day." He was guided, as historian John Morton Blum has written, by "his belief in the possibility of brotherhood and the inherent virtue of husbandmen."[27]

It was this faith in the dignity and moral decency of Common Men who would shoulder responsibility for one another—not just respond to the war cry of "Kill Krauts and Japs!"—that Ernie Pyle was struggling to keep alive first on the European and then on the Pacific front, and was hoping would survive the war. "We have won this war because our men are brave, and because of many other things," he wrote at the end of the European conflict. "We did not win it because destiny created us better than all other peoples. I hope that in victory we are more grateful than we are proud. . . . The dead men would not want us to gloat."[28]

On April 18, 1945, in the final months of the war, Ernie Pyle made the mistake of poking his head out of a trench on Okinawa for a quick reportorial look around; a Japanese machine-gun bullet pierced his left temple. The "slightly used secondhand man," as Pyle referred to himself, was dead.[29] The day he died could well have been the day Ernie Pyle's stoical man died and the Century of the Common Man was stillborn. Only nobody knew it yet.

Toward the end of the war, two visions of postwar America vied for attention on the national stage in a battle over the nation's future that has long since been forgotten. One contender was Wallace's Common Man century; the other was Henry Luce's American Century. The fate of the world, broadcaster Edward R. Murrow wrote in August 1942, hinged on whether the vision of Henry Wallace or Henry Luce would become "the forerunner of the American policy of tomorrow."[30] Luce, the founder and editor of *Time* and *Life* magazines, saw America as a masculine nation whose manifest destiny was to loom like a giant on the global stage. He proposed the average man acquire a grander sense of himself by association with a nation that would dominate the world through unapologetic force. If Wallace's manly ideal was all about parental care and nurturance, Luce's was all about taking control—and, even more important, displaying it.

"The fundamental trouble with America," Luce asserted in a classic 1941 call to arms to policy makers, which he published in *Life* and called "The American Century," was that its citizens had "failed to play their part as a world power." Luce's argument had its merits in a nation reluctant to respond to Hitler. But Luce's "cure"—"to exert upon the world the full impact of our influence, for such purposes as we see fit and by such means as we see fit"—would prove a postwar prescription for aggression. The price for failing to flex the national muscle, he warned repeatedly, would be a terrifying loss of virility: "the virus of isolationist sterility" would infect America, he wrote; we must dominate the world "or else confess a pitiful impotence."[31]

Wallace responded to Luce's call for a domineering America with his own warning: "Force is important—but it is not enough. Force without justice would sooner or later make us into the image of that which we have hated in the Nazis." Already, he observed in the early forties, such a mentality was taking its toll: "The symbols of collective security are being used to build collective aggression, the unity of the great nations against fascism is becoming a unity of the nations against communism, the ideals of the defeated have been taken over by the victors." Would we, he asked plaintively, enter a "century of blood or milk"?[32]

This question had been lingering in the wings since at least the early nineteenth century. Did an American man establish his merit by nursing his nation's people or by goring the world's? Was he Daniel Boone come home to tend to his community's affairs or Davy Crockett sallying forth to take his pelts? The years following World War II were not, of course, to usher in a "century of milk" and Henry Wallace himself would be one of the first victims of the rising appetite for blood. As his campaign to create sixty million jobs, support labor and civil rights, and challenge big business ran afoul of a conservativizing "get tough" Congress, Wallace would be dumped from the vice presidential ticket and replaced by Harry Truman in 1944. Four years later, after Wallace mounted an ill-advised, disastrous third-party bid for the presidency, he was deemed a Communist dupe and promptly retired to the slag heap of suspect, out-of-touch progressives.[33]

At first, the American Century would masquerade as a blood brother of the Century of the Common Man; it would appear to be designed to help a new generation of men become the caring good fathers that Wallace and Pyle had envisioned—and that the men themselves yearned to be. The veterans of World War II were actually more inclined toward a continuation of a common-man ethic than was the general public; they were eager to embrace a masculine ideal that revolved around providing rather than dominating. Their most important experiences centered on the support and comfort they had given one another in the war, and it was this that they wished to preserve. "Rather than being militarized by their war experience," historian Paul A. Carter observed in *Another Part of the Fifties*, "the GIs to a remarkable extent had civilianized the armed forces in which they served."[34] As artilleryman Win Stracke told oral historian Studs Terkel in *The Good War*, he came back from the war "primarily concerned with making a living to support my new family" and bearing this most cherished memory of his service overseas: "You had fifteen guys who for the first time in their lives were not living in a competitive society. . . . There's a job to be done and everyone pitches in, some more than others. For the first time in their lives, they could help each other without fear of losing a commercial advantage. Without cutting each other's throat or trying to put down somebody else through a boss or whatever. . . . I had realized it was the absence of competition and boundaries and all those phony standards that created the thing I loved about the army."[35]

The men who had bought into the Ernie Pyle ideal of heroically self-less manhood, the fathers who would sire the baby-boom generation, would try to pass that experience of manhood on intact to their sons in the 1950s and 1960s. The "routine little men" who went overseas and liberated the world came home to the expectation that they would liberate the country by quiet industry and caretaking. Their chances of that had already been greatly reduced with President Truman's abandonment of the Democrats' "New Bill of Rights," which would have guaranteed, among other things, full employment and equal access to food, health care, education, and housing. But the vets made the most of what remained, the GI Bill of Rights, by which unprecedented numbers of them acquired college degrees, job skills, and homes. The vets threw themselves into their federally funded educations, and later their defense-funded corporate and production-line jobs, and their domestic lives in Veterans Administration–financed tract homes. White men from midwestern small towns and black men from the rural South moved west toward the promising oasis of southern California military-backed jobs and affordable home ownership. They were hopeful that their dedication, their anonymous service, their humble loyalty to the team would add up to something larger, something sturdy and generative that they could pass on to their sons.

More than a century earlier, Alexis de Tocqueville had puzzled over a singularly American paradox. The nation's citizenry seemed "eaten up with longing to rise, but hardly any of them seem to entertain very great hopes or to aim very high."[36] Now it seemed that American men would all rise together, with the greatest of hopes and the highest of aims. When, in 1961, the nation's helm was taken by a young president, a World War II vet, the nation's aims seemed to rise as high as the moon. Men were buoyant with the expectation that the American Century would be their century. They were eager to show their sons how the postwar bounty would one day soon be theirs. They made a promise to their boys and they planned to make good on it. Like Sergeant Stryker in *Sands of Iwo Jima,* they vowed: "If I can't teach you one way, I'll teach you another, but I'm gonna get the job done."

II. The Unpassed Torch

THE AMERICAN PERIOD OF SOARING EXPECTATIONS that followed the close of World War II is conventionally known as the "baby boom" era, as if its defining traits were the nesting and diapering habits of young mothers. But truly it was the era of the boy. It was the culture of *Father Knows Best* and *Leave It to Beaver,* of Pop Warner rituals and Westinghouse science scholarships, of BB guns and rocket clubs, of football practice and lettered jackets, of magazine ads where "Dad" seemed always to be beaming down at his scampy, cowboy-suited younger son or proudly handing his older son the keys to a brand-new tail-finned convertible. It was a father-son Eden showcased in *Life* with pictorials like the one where Dad shows Bill, nine, and Rob, eleven, "how to remove an old stoker motor from the furnace in the cellar."[37] It was a world where, regardless of the truth that lay behind each garden gate, popular culture led us to believe that fathers were spending every leisure moment in rounds of roughhouse play and model-airplane construction and backyard catch with their beloved boys.

In the aspiring middle-class suburb where I came of age, there was no mistaking the belief in the boy's preeminence; it was evident in the solicitous attentions of parents and schoolteachers, in the centrality of coaches and Cub Scouts and Little League, in the community life that revolved around boys' contests and boys' championships and boys' scores—as if these outposts of tract-home America had been built mainly as exhibition rings for junior male achievement, which perhaps they had. It was evident in the periodic rampages of suburban boys that always seemed to go unchecked, the way they tore up the lawns with their minibikes or hurled rocks at newcomers with impunity or tormented the girls at the public swimming pool; inherent in their behavior was the assumption that this was their birthright—to be imperial bullies over their miniature dominions. To grow up as a girl in this era was to look on with envy, and to see the boy as being automatically entitled and powerful. Surely when we were grown, he would have the control. He would dispense the gifts. The boys believed that, too.

The speech that inaugurated the shiny new era of the 1960s was the youthful John F. Kennedy's address to the Democratic National Convention, a month before the launch of Echo. The words would become, along with his inaugural oration, a haunting refrain in adolescent male consciousness. He spoke not of the populace at large but principally of "young men"—"young men who are coming to power," "young men who can cast off the old slogans and the old delusions." What Kennedy implicitly presented was not so much a political platform as a new rite of passage for an untested male generation. "[T]he New Frontier of which I speak is not a set of promises," he told them. "It is a set of challenges." Kennedy understood that it was not enough for the fathers to win the world for their sons; the sons had to feel they had won it for themselves. If the fathers had had their chance to be GI Joes, then Kennedy would ensure that at least a few of the sons would have their shot at being Green Berets. If the fathers had their Nazis and "Nips," then Kennedy would see to it that the sons had an enemy, too. He promised as much on Inauguration Day in 1961, when he spoke vaguely but unremittingly of Communism's threat, of "the prey of hostile powers," of the "hour of maximum danger," of "a long twilight struggle," and most memorably of a country that would be defined by its readiness to "pay any price" and "oppose any foe." The fight was the thing, the only thing, if America was to retain its manhood. "And let every other power know," Kennedy decreed in his inaugural address, "that this hemisphere intends to remain the master of its own house." What Kennedy was selling was a government-backed program of man-making, of federal masculinity insurance. As author Norman Mailer observed at the time: "The President has commissions and commissars and bureaus and agents and computer machines to calculate the amount of schooling needed to keep America healthy, safe, vigorous, proof against the Russians. To keep America *up* [his emphasis]. Virility is the unspoken salesman in American political programs today."[38]

The promise the president made to his nation of young men was the one the father made to the boy, the aerospace corporations made to their gray-flanneled male employees, the mission-control officials made to their astronauts, the expanded armed forces made to their cold warriors, the *Boys' Life* editors made to the readers they addressed as "space conquerors" and "rocket riders," the aeronautical-engineer dad Fred MacMurray made on TV to his three sons, the Mattel toy makers made to the young buyers of their water-powered, two-stage plastic missiles. The promise was of a spectacular ascension, a vertical demonstration of prowess that would concentrate all of the masculine force and beauty of battle into one breathtaking explosion of exploratory power and muscle. At the same time, the promise was supposed to reprise Ernie Pyle's war, in which the anonymous work of dutiful men would add up to one glorious and visible victory on a faraway frontier, a victory that would belong to all men. Admittedly, no army of GI brothers would fight on that frontier. "But in a very real sense, it will not be one man going to the moon," President Kennedy declared. "We make this judgment affirmatively—it will be an entire nation, for all of us must work to put him there."[39] Just to get astronaut John Glenn into orbit for the first time, *Time* reminded its readers in 1962, required "nearly 35,000 people": "Besides his fellow astronauts and a staff of 2,000 at Cape Canaveral, 15,000 men stood by for recovery or rescue operations on ships stretched across the Atlantic, 500 technicians manned 18 tracking stations on four continents and two oceans, and 15,000 scientists, technicians and factory workers who had labored for nearly four years on the space program left their imprint on the flight."[40]

The promise was a mission to manhood. It borrowed its blueprint from the time-tested tenets of what might be called the national male paradigm, which had four aspects: the promise of a frontier to be claimed—the American Wild West and the wartime fronts would now become the frontier of space; the promise of a clear and evil enemy to be crushed—instead of an Indian or a Nazi, the enemy would now be a Communist; the promise of an institution of brotherhood in which anonymous members could share a greater institutional glory—in place of an army of foot soldiers it would now be a brotherhood of organization men, engineers, middle managers, and bureaucrats, as typified by the National Aeronautics and Space Agency; and finally, the promise of a family to provide for and protect—for the working war wives had now become housewives who waved from train platforms as their husbands shipped off, not for the front, but for their offices.

It took some preparation to convert the World War II model to a peacetime setting, but it was done: the federal money that had poured into airpower to win the war now poured into rocket power to win the peace; the government that financed construction and roads to support its male military force now underwrote suburban construction and highways to support its male bureaucratic workforce (and to transport cold-war troops and evacuate cities in the event of a nuclear attack).[41] That the peacetime model was intended to convey a wartime urgency was evident in the name the government assigned to the domestic road-construction program: "The National System of Interstate and Defense Highways." The peacetime GI was issued an education, a swatch of land and a house in strip developments like Levittown, New York, and Lakewood, California, and, often enough in an ever-expanding defense industry, a subsidized job. Rosie the Riveter, the wartime woman worker, was demobilized and sent home to become an aspiring consumer who would depend on and spend the demobilized soldier's postwar wages. Their sons would be made educationally combat-ready thanks to the National Defense Education Act, which promised $634.4 million worth of science and math training to create a generation of rocket and missile warriors.[42] And every new recruit on the cold-war domestic team would learn how to cheer on his side from the bleachers of the many brand-new, government-subsidized football stadiums. Implicit in all of this was a promise of loyalty, a guarantee to the new man of tomorrow that his company would never fire him, his wife would never leave him, and the team he rooted for would never pull up stakes.

These, then, were the cold warriors representing the most powerful country in the world with the strongest economic pulse recorded in all history. Wouldn't a boy in such a world have every faith in his father's patrimony, his father's promise? Wouldn't he take for granted that he, too, would be in charge of his own destiny—and his nation's?

————

WHEN I TALK WITH MEN WHO GREW UP DURING THE BABY BOOM, this mission to manhood shows up in their minds not as promises met but as betrayals, losses, and disillusionments. It is as if a generation of men had lined up at Cape Kennedy to witness the countdown to liftoff, only to watch their rocket—containing all their hopes and dreams—burn up on the launchpad. There had been so much anticipation, so much excitement, so many assurances that nothing could possibly go wrong. But somehow, it all had.

The initial disillusionment was with the frontier. In 1957, the Russians orbited Sputnik, the first satellite, and in the United States panic ensued.

It was a "crisis," a showdown between superpowers for the control of the heavens that was supposed to have all the gravity of the Second World War. This stratospheric confrontation, the "father of the hydrogen bomb," Edward Teller, told a TV audience, was "a battle more important and greater than Pearl Harbor." *The Reporter* magazine insisted that Sputnik "is to Pearl Harbor what Pearl Harbor was to the sinking of the *Maine*." A *Life* magazine editorial went even further, equating Sputnik with "the shot heard round the world" at Lexington. The most powerful U.S. senator at the time, Lyndon B. Johnson, went verbally airborne in his declaration of high noon in the heavens. "Control of space means control of the world," he intoned. "From space the master of infinity would have the power to control the earth's weather, to cause drought and flood, to change the tides and raise the levels of the sea, to divert the Gulf Stream and change temperate climates to frigid. That is the ultimate position: the position of total control over earth that lies somewhere in outer space."[43]

Space, however, turned out to be a place not much worth conquering. What the promoters of space exploration did not or chose not to understand was a frontier's role. It was not simply an empty field where men left behind civilized comforts and faced danger; it was a place where men faced peril for a reason. They were there to claim territory to be occupied by a domestic population that would follow. This "return to primitive conditions on a continually advancing frontier line," as Frederick Jackson Turner put it in his famous lament over the closing of the West in 1890, created the conditions for a "perennial rebirth"—a rolling rite of passage in which male pioneers become settlers and pillars of new communities.[44]

But space was a sterile environment, not a place where women and children could or would want to settle. To explore space was to clear the way for no one, to be cut off from a society that had no real investment in following. Nor was space a place of initiation, of virile secrets, of masculine transformation. There was no one there to learn from or to fight. It was a void that a man moved through only passively, in a state of almost infantile regression. The astronaut was a dependent strapped to a couch in a fetal position, bundled in swaddling clothes. He made it through space only by never breaking the apron strings of mission control back on Mother Earth. An astronaut returned from space unchanged by the experience, because there was no experience. No wonder that, for all the promotional effort expended on space, by the time Neil Armstrong stepped on the moon, Americans were already suppressing a yawn over the adventures of their new heroes.[45]

When the boy got older, he was at last presented with his own war, in Southeast Asia, but it was hardly the crucible of courage against a clear and visible enemy that his father had faced. There was nothing clear about any of it, not the nature or the identity of the enemy, not the mission, not where they should be shooting or who was shooting at them, and certainly not the meaning of victory. Nor was this a "masculine" war in the World War II mode. There were no landings, no front lines, no ultimate objectives. It was essentially a war against a domestic population, against families, where huts were burned with Zippo lighters, cattle slaughtered, children machine-gunned—a war in which the most remembered grunt leader was not a benevolent Captain Waskow but Lieutenant William Calley, a callow young man known only for going on a murderous rampage of monstrous proportions at My Lai. It was a war in which the most remembered pronouncement was a U.S. major's explanation for the obliteration of Ben Tre: "It became necessary to destroy the town to save it."[46]

Then the boy came home—whether from Saigon or Kent State—to the domestic continuation of a guerrilla war. Now the contested village was his own, the village he thought he was defending. He was greeted on his return by women not blowing kisses but indifferent or even hostile to his efforts. These women did not leave their jobs upon his arrival; many of them didn't accept or accepted only resentfully a renewed dependency upon him, because about the time the men were off trying to prove their manhood by liberating an "oppressed" people or clashing with the National Guard, their wives and girlfriends had decided to liberate themselves. The loved one whom the man imagined himself supporting and protecting was often doing just fine on her own, and she didn't much appreciate his efforts to assert his authority. In fact, sometimes his wife now saw *him* as the oppressor.

And finally, as the boy grew older, the institutions that had promised him a masculine honor and pride in exchange for his loyalty double-crossed him. In truth, the fix was in from the start: corporate America's promise to continue the World War II GI's wartime experience of belonging, of meaningful engagement in a mission, was never authentic. The massive bureaucracies of postwar "white collar" employment, especially the defense contractors fat on government largesse, were replete with make-work jobs with inflated titles. Their vast middle managements were filled with functionaries who often didn't even know what they were managing, who suspected they weren't really needed at all. What these corporations were offering was a secure job, not a vital role. And ultimately even that would prove a lie. There was to be no lifetime security at McDonnell Douglas or Lockheed or IBM or even in the military itself. There were to be no iron-clad union protections. The postwar grunts' submission to the national-security state would, after a prosperous period of historically brief duration, be rewarded with insecurity and pink slips, with massive spasms of downsizing, restructuring, union-breaking, contracting-out, and outsourcing. The institutions that men had identified with no longer identified with them. Even hometown sports teams repaid their fans' devotion by hurriedly packing up and racing to other cities dangling brand-new, deluxe, and rent-free stadiums and a 100 percent take on tickets and concessions.

The frontier, the enemy, the institutions of brotherhood, the women in need of protection—all the elements of the old formula for attaining manhood had vanished in short order. The boy who had been told he was going to be the master of the universe and all that was in it found himself master of nothing. How had this happened in such a brief period of time?

III. The Violent and the Perfumed

IN 1957, THREE YEARS before boys across the country watched as Echo passed overhead, another small American male was caught in the act of musing on the heavens. He was the lead character in a sci-fi film released in the year of Sputnik's launch. In *The Incredible Shrinking Man,* Scott Carey has a good job, a suburban home, a pleasure boat, a pretty housewife. His is the quintessential life envisioned by the GI Bill of Rights and underwritten by the beneficence of a brotherly corporation—in this case, literally so; Scott Carey works for his brother. And yet, after he passes through a mist of atomic radiation while on a boating vacation in the Pacific, something happens. As he tells his wife in horror, "I'm getting smaller, Lou, every day."

As Scott Carey quite literally shrinks, the promises made to him are broken one by one. The employer who was to give him lifetime economic security fires him. His wife, Louise, becomes his protector until he gets lost in the cellar of their house and she presumes he's been gobbled by their house cat. He is left with only feminine defenses—to hide in a dollhouse, to fight a giant spider with a sewing pin. And it turns out that the very source of his diminishment is implicitly a military atomic test by his own government. His only hope, his brother tells him as he lays him off, is to turn himself into a celebrated freak and sell his story to the media. "I'm a big man!" Scott Carey says with bitter sarcasm. "I'm famous! . . . One more joke for the world to laugh at." In the end, the shrinking man finds himself, like the boy in my reverie, beneath a vault of stars, gazing into the galaxy. But he is alone and the firmament he beholds is empty, without evidence of man's technological promise. No blip of man-made light blinks reassuringly across the night sky. "What was I?" the shrinking man beseeches the silent heavens. "Was I still a human being? Or was I the man of the future?"

The more Scott Carey shrinks, the more he strikes out at those around him. The tinier he gets, the greater his combativeness becomes—and his desire for a combatant to defeat. His obsession with regaining dominance turns him into, as he puts it, a "caricature" of a man. "Every day I became more tyrannical," he comments, "more monstrous in my domination of Louise." It's a line that would ring a bell for any visitor to the Alternatives to Violence group and for any observer of the current male scene. As the male role has diminished amid a sea of betrayed promises, many men have found themselves driven to more domineering and some even "monstrous" displays in their frantic quest for a meaningful showdown.

If few men would do what Shawn Nelson did one evening in the spring of 1995, many could relate. A former serviceman whose career in an army tank unit had gone nowhere, a former plumber who had lost his job and whose tools had been stolen, a former husband whose wife had left him, the thirty-five-year-old Nelson broke into the National Guard armory, commandeered a fifty-seven-ton M-60 army tank, and drove it through the streets of San Diego—flattening fire hydrants, crushing forty cars, downing traffic lights and enough utility poles to cut off electricity to five thousand people. He was at war with the domestic world that he once thought he was meant to build, serve, and defend. His world had turned inside out. He was going to drive that tank he had been meant to command if it killed him. And it did. The police shot Shawn Nelson to death through the turret hatch, even though his tank had ground to a halt, stuck on a three-foot-tall concrete highway divider, even though he was unarmed. The police explained to the press later that if he had gotten the tank under way again, traffic would have been "endangered."[47]

If a man could not get the infrastructure to work for him, he could at least tear it down. If the nation would not provide an enemy to fight, he could go to war at home. If there was to be no brotherhood, he would take his stand alone. Shawn Nelson's sense of desperation, if not his actions, were shared by many men of his generation. Like the incredible shrinking man, they could feel their stature dwindling along with their spheres of influence—any day now, they feared, they would wake to find themselves misplaced in the cellar. If so many men seemed to be seeking an enemy to subdue, it was because they could conceive of no other path that might lead them up and out of their present mess. All the pillars of the male paradigm had fallen, except the search for the enemy.

From the start, that search had been at the heart of Luce's American Century. It was, ultimately, what the American Century was all about. By century's end, it had turned into a search for someone to blame for the premature death of masculine promise. The longer the search went on, the more frantic and desperate the searchers became. What began in the 1950s as an intemperate pursuit of Communists in the government bureaucracy, in the defense industries, in labor unions, the schools, the media, and Hollywood, would eventually become a hunt for a shape-shifting enemy who could take the form of women at the office, or gays in the military, or young black men on the street, or illegal aliens on the border, and from there become a surreal "combat" with nonexistent black helicopters, one-world government, and goose-stepping U.N.-peacekeeping thugs massing on imaginary horizons. A handful of men would attempt to gun down enemies they imagined they saw in family court, employee parking lots, McDonald's restaurants, the U.S. Congress, the White House, a Colorado schoolhouse, and, most notoriously, a federal office building in Oklahoma. A far greater number would move their destruction of the elusive enemy from the real world to the fantasy realm—to a clear-cut and controllable world of action movies and video combat, televised athletic tournaments and pay-per-view ultimate-fighting bouts.

But none of it would satisfy, because the world and the fight had changed. In Ernie Pyle's terms, the real fight was no longer between the GIs and the Nazis, but between men on the same side—the mud-caked soldiers and the glamorous pilots. And this fight hadn't turned out the way that Pyle would have liked.

Pyle's legacy includes a film about his exploits that lives on in the American consciousness, *The Story of G.I. Joe*. The journalist to whom (as his editor once said) "the very word 'Hollywood' meant fraud" would be celluloided.[48] During wartime, Pyle found his rising celebrity back home a horrible burden. The mobs of autograph seekers and photographers, the offers of lecture tours and radio programs, the prying questions of *Time* editors preparing a cover story about the man they called "a sort of prose Charlie Chaplin," the demands to endorse cigars, sit for sculptors, and pose for layouts in women's beauty magazines, the whole "frenzied goldfish life" sent the man who owned only one suit and rolled his own smokes fleeing back to the army.[49] In front of the spotlight, he felt strangely depleted. But soon after his burial, the man who hated Hollywood became a Hollywood icon.

Originally, the movie based on Pyle's collected columns (for which Arthur Miller was hired to write the screenplay's first draft) was supposed to honor the grunts who the army contended had been slighted in Hollywood's depictions of wartime heroics.[50] The grunts—even the grunts in the movie—were aware of being shortchanged. "The flyers are the guys you guys always write about, right?" a GI observes caustically to Pyle as the movie opens. "The Hollywood heroes. We're just the lumps along for the ride. That's all, just for the ride." While they appreciate Pyle's attentions and understand him to be a grunt sympathizer, they also know that he is a journalist and so a new kingmaker, a celebrity anointer whether he wants to be or not. And this is the story the movie unintentionally tells. As the grunts trudge by, they call out to Pyle, "Hey, how do I get my name in the paper?" They look to him as a bridge to the world of recognition, but also fear that the bridge is not for them. When Pyle wins the Pulitzer Prize for his coverage, the soldiers' kudos have an acid aftertaste. They crumple up the congratulatory telegram and toss it at him, then bow down and address him mockingly as "our hero." They sense that he is becoming one of the flyboys, that they will lose him to the world of glamour. *The Story of G.I. Joe* turned out to be less about the fight between Allies and Axis than about the postwar battle to come over who would be the Man of the Century, the grunt or the flyboy, the Common Man or Superman, anonymous men expecting the mantle of masculine honor for their loyalty to a common cause or a few glamorous men who understood intuitively that in the coming media and entertainment age the team of men at work would be replaced by the individual man on display.

The handful of men plucked arbitrarily from the anonymous crowd and elevated onto the new pedestal of mass media and entertainment glamour were unreachable. That wasn't because they were necessarily arrogant or narcissistic, though some would surely become so; they simply existed in a realm from which all lines to their brothers had been cut. In this sense, the astronaut was emblematic, the most celebrated postwar flyboy. He was supposed to be the representative man, experiencing space for all his brethren. But the many men who supported him would no more share the experience or the limelight than would the "organization men" whose company loyalties turned them into wallpaper, unseen backing for the corporation's real star: its brand name. The space shot would launch only a handful of big shots into the media heavens; the rest would fall off the monitors of mission control, consigned to the outer space of noncelebrity.

The fathers had led the sons to believe that space exploration would hold up a mirror into which any American man could look and see himself reflected in enlarged form. Echo, like its namesake, the nymph of Greek mythology who fell in love with Narcissus, was supposed to glorify them by beaming around the globe their every word. Like the other technological achievements of NASA, McDonnell Douglas, and military-industrial America in general, the satellite and the rocket were supposed to magnify the average man's presence in the world. Some of the sheen from the huge new machines put out by huge new institutions was supposed to make him feel huge, too. But the images in those mirrors turned out to have a televisable life of their own and the best that any man could do was try to reflect them. The night the boy had watched the satellite arc over his backyard, his father had told him that Sputnik was the enemy—an enemy America would vanquish. But decades later, as the grown son gazed out his window into his own backyard, where a beached satellite dish brought him ninety-nine channels and no opportunities for stardom, a more likely scenario began to take shape in his mind: perhaps Echo had vanquished *him*.

If the failure to find a new frontier or a clear enemy or women in need of protection was devastating, it was accompanied by yet another problem for which the grunt fathers had never prepared their sons. The men of the new generation had not simply lost a utilitarian world; they had been thrust into an ornamental realm, and the transformation had proved traumatic. I'm not speaking simply of the economic shift from industry to service, which is a shift from heavy-lifting "masculine" labor to "feminine" aid and assistance, nor about a shift from a society organized around industry to one set up around electronic technology. And I'm not speaking simply about the irony of men supporting a massive military-industrial effort to produce machines—computers, robots, smart bombs—that ultimately would replace them, lifting them into space while making them increasingly expendable on the ground. Those changes were only surface symptoms, for we have changed fundamentally from a society that produced a culture to a culture rooted in no real society at all. The culture we live in today pretends that media can nurture society, but our new public spaces, our "electronic town squares" and "cyber-communities" and publicity mills and celebrity industries, are disembodied barrens, a dismal substitute for the real thing. Where we once lived in a society in which men in particular participated by being useful in public life, we now are surrounded by a culture that encourages people to play almost no functional public roles, only decorative or consumer ones. The old model of masculinity showed men how to be part of a larger social system; it gave them a context and it promised them that their social contributions were the price of admission to the realm of adult manhood. That kind of manhood required a society in order to prove itself. All of the traditional domains in which men pursued authority and power—politics, religion, the military, the community, and the household—were societal.

Ornamental culture has no such counterparts. Constructed around celebrity and image, glamour and entertainment, marketing and consumerism, it is a ceremonial gateway to nowhere. Its essence is not just the selling act but the act of selling the self, and in this quest every man is essentially on his own, a lone sales rep marketing his own image with no paternal Captain Waskows to guide him. In an age of celebrity, the father has no body of knowledge or authority to transmit to the son. Each son must father his own image, create his own Adam.

Ornamental culture has proved the ultimate expression of the American Century, sweeping away institutions in which men felt some sense of belonging and replacing them with visual spectacles that they can only watch and that benefit global commercial forces they cannot fathom. Celebrity culture's effects on men go far beyond the obvious showcasing of action heroes and rock musicians. The ordinary man is no fool: he knows he can't be Arnold Schwarzenegger. Nonetheless, the culture reshapes his most basic sense of manhood by telling him as much as it tells the celebrity that masculinity is something to drape over the body, not draw from inner resources; that it is personal, not societal; that manhood is displayed, not demonstrated. The internal qualities once said to embody manhood—surefootedness, inner strength, confidence of purpose—are merchandised to men to enhance their manliness. What passes for the essence of masculinity is being extracted and bottled—and sold back to men. Literally, in the case of Viagra.

It is not, as conventional media wisdom would have it, that contemporary men are vain or the products of a "self-absorbed" sixties generation that didn't appreciate their fathers' war-forged discipline and sacrifice, but rather that the culture they live in has left men with little other territory on which to prove themselves besides vanity. The culture they are stranded in was birthed by their fathers' generation. What gets left out of the contemporary nostalgia of baby-boom men for their World War II fathers—evidenced in the huge appetite for the film *Saving Private Ryan* and books like Tom Brokaw's *The Greatest Generation*—is what those fathers did *after* the war. When *Dateline NBC* produced a special documentary based on Brokaw's book, celebrating the World War II "tougher than tough" heroes, especially relative to their pampered sons, the troubling and perhaps unintentional subtext was how devastatingly *un*fathered those sons were, how unnourished and how inadequately prepared for manhood they felt they were by the "heroic" men who were their fathers. One of those sons in the documentary, Frank Kilmer, moved across the country and into a Buddhist monastery, trying desperately to blaze his own way to manhood, eventually becoming a plumber, but he was still haunted by the knowledge of the patrimony denied him by a "distant" father: "To be brutally honest, I have been a major disappointment to him," he said of his father.[51] Left implicit was how deeply his father may have disappointed him.

The younger Kilmer's disappointment was presaged in, of all places, a John Wayne film, *Sands of Iwo Jima,* made, like many of the actor's war films, in the years *after* the war. At closer inspection, the character repeatedly played by Wayne personifies less the World War II officer than the *postwar* father figure: remote, unreadable, an enforcer of conformity, a cold-war man. As Garry Wills astutely observed in *John Wayne's America,* Wayne's on-screen persona may have appealed to so many postwar boys both because he's an implacable authority figure and because "an affective link" is formed between Wayne and his young costars "precisely from the refusal to show affection." Silence supposedly conveys love, his films suggest. "Wayne was both an alternative to that parent and an excuse for him," Wills wrote.[52] And unlike many of their fathers, Wayne often dropped his guard and revealed a touch of humanity in the final frame. When Wayne's Sergeant Stryker dies in the closing scene of *Sands of Iwo Jima,* his grunts find in his pocket an unfinished letter to his son. It is the beginning of a paternal confession: as a father, Stryker testifies in the note, "I've been a failure in many ways." These are the words that real postwar sons like Frank Kilmer so needed to hear.

In truth, despite all their wartime heroics, the fathers abandoned their sons, however inadvertently, in an image-based, commercial-ruled world that they had largely created in their postwar haste to embrace the good life. The fathers had their reasons—years of deprivation in the Depression followed by the brutal hardships of World War II—but what they bestowed was a culture where the sons could not exercise the sorts of traditional manhood that the fathers so judgmentally endorsed. Symbolically speaking, what the fathers really passed on to their sons was not the GI ethic but the GI Joe "action figure," a twelve-inch shrunken-man doll whose main feature was his ability to accessorize.

The fathers did give the sons a New Frontier, but it was a land made sterile by the onrush of mass consumerism. The more productive aspects of manhood, such as building or cultivating or contributing to a society, couldn't establish a foothold on the shiny flat surface of a commercial culture, a looking glass before which men could only act out a crude semblance of masculinity. And what act could be more crudely and stereotypically masculine than a show of violence? But while violence uses all the visible aspects of male utility—strength, decisiveness, courage, even skill—its purpose is only to dismantle and destroy. Violence stands in for action but is also an act of concealment, a threatening mask that hides a lack of purpose. In a way, our culture replicated Davy Crockett's wilderness, where a man had nothing to do but consume (in Crockett's case, wild animals), and no way to make that consumption seem masculine except to present it as an aggressive triumph. Crockett, too, was putting on a show; his boasts—105 bears killed in a year! Hand-to-fin combat with a twelve-foot-long "monstratious great Cat-Fish"!—were propaganda in an early image war.[53]

As early as 1963, Norman Mailer observed glimmerings of the new desperado mandate. "[I]t was almost as if there were no peace," he wrote, "unless one could fight well, kill well (if always with honor), love well and love many, be cool, be daring, be dashing, be wild, be wily, be resourceful, be a brave gun. And this myth, that each of us was born to be free, to wander, to have adventure and to grow on the waves of the violent, the perfumed, and the unexpected, had a force which could not be tamed. . . . Indeed a quarter of the nation's business must have depended upon its existence."[54] As men's utilitarian qualities were dethroned, as their societal roles diminished, violence more and more came to serve as the gang leader for a host of rogue masculine traits.

By the end of the American Century, every outlet of the consumer world—magazines, ads, movies, sports, music videos—would deliver the message that manhood had become a performance game to be won in the marketplace, not the workplace, and that male anger was now part of the show. An ornamental culture encouraged young men to see surliness, hostility, and violence as expressions of glamour, a way to showcase themselves without being feminized before an otherwise potentially girlish mirror. But if celebrity masculinity enshrined the pose of the "bad boy," his rebellion was largely cosmetic. There was nowhere for him to take a grievance because there was no society to take it to. In a celebrity culture, earnestness about social and political change is replaced by a pose of "irony" that is really just a sullen and helpless paralysis.

The images produced by the culture, however, still promote the model of an American man who dominates his world. If anything, such images have been inflated as superstars prevail, again and again, on athletic courts, the battlefields and cityscapes of giants. For the ordinary man, however, there is less and less to control beyond his remote-control device, and ever fewer venues in which he can harness the energies of his masculinity productively. He is still expected to dominate, but when mastery of a trade and mastery over one's life fade as possibilities, all that may seem to be left is raw dominance. The urge to control, unharnessed and unmoored, soon spins out of control. Without a society, Daniel Boone would have been just a killer. It was this dead end that faced not only the many men who got shoved aside by celebrity culture but the few who were elevated in it. Boxer Mike Tyson equated that elevation with imprisonment. As he remarked from the penitentiary after he had been convicted of raping Desiree Washington: "Maybe I don't think I want to be a big star no more.... I don't like living where—which I found out here—everybody is a potential enemy."[55]

It's often been observed that the economic transition from industry to service, or from production to consumption, is symbolically a move from the traditional masculine to the traditional feminine. But in gender terms, the transition is far more than a simple sex change and, so, more traumatic for men than we realize. A society of utility, for all the indisputable ways that it exploited men's health and labor, and in an industrial context broke the backs and spirits of factory workers and destroyed the lungs of miners, had one saving grace: it defined manhood by character, by the inner qualities of stoicism, integrity, reliability, the ability to shoulder burdens, the willingness to put others first, the desire to protect and provide and sacrifice. These are the same qualities, recoded as masculine, that society has long recognized in women as the essence of *motherhood*. Men were publicly useful insofar as they mastered skills associated with the private realm of maternal femininity. Like mothers tending selflessly to their babes, men were not only to take care of their families but also their society without complaint; that was, in fact, what made them men. Masculinity as "a nurturing concept" was one of the few continuities anthropologist David Gilmore found in his cross-cultural study.[56] A maternal conception of manhood was precisely what Henry Wallace had in mind when he compared the Common Man who served in World War II to "a she-bear who has lost a cub."[57]

In a culture of ornament, by contrast, manhood is defined by appearance, by youth and attractiveness, by money and aggression, by posture and swagger and "props," by the curled lip and petulant sulk and flexed biceps, by the glamour of the cover boy, and by the market-bartered "individuality" that sets one astronaut or athlete or gangster above another. These are the same traits that have long been designated as the essence of feminine *vanity*, the public face of the feminine as opposed to the private caring, maternal one. The aspects of this public "femininity"—objectification, passivity, infantilization, pedestal-perching, and mirror-gazing—are the very ones that women have in modern times denounced as trivializing and humiliating qualities imposed on them by a misogynist culture. No wonder men are in such agony. Not only are they losing the society they were once essential to, they are "gaining" the very world women so recently shucked off as demeaning and dehumanizing.

The old American male paradigm can offer no help to a man competing with ghostly, two-dimensional armies of superathletes, gangsta rappers, action heroes, and stand-up comedians on television. Navigating the ornamental realm, much less trying to derive a sense of manhood from it, has become a nightmare all the more horrible for being virtually unacknowledged as a problem. At the close of the century, men find themselves in an unfamiliar world where male worth is measured only by participation in a celebrity-driven consumer culture and awarded by lady luck. There is no passage to manhood in such a world. A man can only wait to be discovered; and even if he lucks out, his "achievement" is fraught with gender confusion for its "feminine" implications of glamour and display.

The Ernie Pyle movie was right. The man of the future was to be the flyboy, not the grunt. Ernie Pyle's model of manhood would not hold past the Eisenhower presidency. Eisenhower would be replaced by a PT-boat captain who had sought duty on a vessel where he could be the lone star, rather than service on a big ship where he would have been anonymous. Kennedy's one wartime "rescue" mission would be repackaged to market the first Hollywood-style glamour candidacy, but that was only the beginning of the transition.[58] By 1980, the new president would be Ronald Reagan, a man who only went to war in the movies. By 1996, Bob Dole, a candidate who had been GI Joe incarnate, would lose the presidential race to a man who famously didn't go to war at all. That election was not an embrace of a man's considered decision to refuse military service, for which Bill Clinton was excoriated, but a rejection of the foot soldier as a serviceable model of American manhood. By the waning of the nineties, despite all the celebrity encomiums to the Private Ryans and their "greatest generation," it was patently evident that this exemplar of masculinity would have no place in the century to come. Bob Dole was consigned to shilling erectile-dysfunction cures. Few could deny now what John Kenneth Galbraith had asserted three decades earlier in his book *The New Industrial State:* "By all but the pathologically romantic, it is now recognized that this is not the age of the small man."[59]

IV. Cause Without a Rebel

A QUESTION THAT HAS PLAGUED FEMINISTS like myself is the nature of male resistance to female change. Why are so many men so disturbed by the prospect of women's independence? Why do so many men seem to begrudge it, resent it, fear it, fight it with an unholy passion? The question launched my inquiry. But in the end, much to my surprise, it was not the question that most compelled me. It is not the question, finally, that drives this book. Because the more I explored the predicament of postwar men, the more familiar it seemed to me. The more I consider what men have lost—a useful role in public life, a way of earning a decent and reliable living, appreciation in the home, respectful treatment in the culture—the more it seems that men of the late twentieth century are falling into a status oddly similar to that of women at mid-century. The fifties housewife, stripped of her connections to a wider world and invited to fill the void with shopping and the ornamental display of her ultrafemininity, could be said to have morphed into the nineties man, stripped of his connections to a wider world and invited to fill the void with consumption and a gym-bred display of his ultra-masculinity. The empty compensations of a "feminine mystique" are transforming into the empty compensations of a masculine mystique, with a gentlemen's cigar club no more satisfying than a ladies' bake-off, the Nike Air Jordan no more meaningful than the Dior New Look.

And so my question changed. Instead of wondering why men resist women's struggle for a freer and healthier life, I began to wonder why men refrain from engaging in their own struggle. Why, despite a crescendo of random tantrums, have they offered no methodical, reasoned response to their predicament? Given the untenable and insulting nature of the demands placed on men to prove themselves in our culture, why don't men revolt?

Like many women, I was drawn to feminism out of a desire to challenge the silence of my sex. It has come to seem to me that, under all the rantings of men seeking to drown out the female voice, theirs is as resounding a silence. Why haven't men responded to the series of betrayals in their own lives—to the failures of their fathers to make good on their promises—with something coequal to feminism? When the frontier that their fathers offered them proved to be a wasteland, when the enemy their fathers sent them to crush turned out often to be women and children trembling in thatched huts, when the institutions their fathers claimed would buoy them downsized them, when the women their fathers said wanted their support got their own jobs, when the whole deal turned out to be a crock and it was clear that they had been thoroughly stiffed, why did the sons do nothing?

The feminine mystique's collapse a generation earlier was not just a crisis but a historic opportunity for women. Women responded to their "problem with no name" by naming it and founding a political movement, by beginning the process of freeing themselves. Why haven't men done the same? This seems to me to be the real question that lurks behind the "masculinity crisis" facing American society: not that men are fighting against women's liberation, but that they have refused to mobilize for their own—or their society's—liberation. Not that traditional male roles are endangered, but that men themselves are in danger of not acting.

Many in the women's movement and in the mass media complain that men just "don't want to give up the reins of power." But that would seem to have little applicability to the situations of most men, who individually feel not the reins of power in their hands but its bit in their mouths. What's more likely is that they are clinging to a phantom status. A number of men I interviewed, as they argued for the importance of having a male head of the household, tellingly demoted that to an honorary post: it's important, they would say, that every home have a "figurehead." But even the natural reluctance to give up a position of putative superiority, no matter how compromised, is not enough to explain a deeper male silence.

To understand why men are so reluctant to break with the codes of manhood sanctioned in their childhood, perhaps we need to understand how strong the social constraints on them are. It's not just women who are bombarded by cultural messages about appropriate gender behavior. In the past half century, Madison Avenue, Hollywood, and the mass media have operated relentlessly on men, too. The level of mockery, suspicion, and animosity directed at men who step out of line is profound, and men respond profoundly—with acquiescence. But that is not a wholly satisfying explanation either, for haven't women, the object of such commercial and political manipulation, kicked over these traces successfully?

If men do not respond, then maybe it is because their society has proposed no route for them to venture down. Surely the culture has not offered an alternative vision of manhood. No one has: not the so-called men's movement, which clings to its dusted-off copies of *Grimms' Fairy*

Tales and its caveman clichés; not conservative or liberal political leaders who call for a remilitarized model of manhood with work camps and schools run by former generals; not the Promise Keepers or Nation of Islam ministers, whose programs of male contrition and resurrection are fantasies of past fantasies; not a gay culture, which, as it gets increasingly absorbed into the larger commercial culture, becomes increasingly muted in its challenge of masculine roles; not even the women's movement, which clamors for men to change but has yet to conceptualize that change. But then, did feminists wait upon men to craft their revolution for them? Didn't the women's movement make its own way, without any assistance—no, with much resistance—from the dominant culture? So why can't men act? The ultimate answer has deep ramifications not only for men but for feminists. Eventually I came to believe that, far from being antagonists, they were each poised at this hour to be vital in the other's advance. But that answer came at the end. First I had to begin.

V. Ground Zero

AT THE START, guided by the most visible flares of troubled masculinity, I visited and eventually moved to southern California. In the early 1990s it seemed like the epicenter of "toxic masculinity," to use a phrase then much favored in the press. And it proved a good place to be, just not in the way I had initially imagined.

When I first arrived in southern California, the economy was in tatters. The downsizing in the region was harsher than in many other areas of the United States. The recession was deeper and had gone on longer in an economy dependent on a relatively small number of enormous defense-related corporations. California's trials were useful exaggerations, as were other signals from the margins of male experience, whether the rage of deserted Midwest football fans or the militia vengefulness over the immolated Branch Davidian compound in Waco, Texas. One man consumed with that latter event, a self-described "patriot" and avid fisherman, once explained this societal dynamic to me in terms of a river: "If you want to see what's happening in the stream called our society, go to the edges and look at what's happening there, and then you begin to have an understanding—if you know how a stream works—of what's going on in the middle," he said. "You have to be very careful not to mischaracterize what you're witnessing as 'fringe elements,' thus assuring the listener that he's okay because it's not about him, which is bullshit." And so the stories of the underemployed, contracted-out, and laid-off men of southern California, and their counterparts in other regions I visited, illuminated more general male losses, losses that the later "boom" economy would to some extent conceal, but not cure.

The economic improvement spelled little relief for the men I had come to know at job clubs, "retraining" agencies, family-service centers on military bases, and outplacement offices set up by aerospace companies like McDonnell Douglas. It was little relief even for those men who finally found jobs. Something had been broken inside them, and it wasn't going to be made right by a boom based on inflated stock-market prices and temporary personnel—a boom that yielded great wealth to the already affluent and deeded to the average man an insecure job, a rise in status anxiety, and a mound of credit-card debt (which, by 1998, had contributed to a sevenfold increase in the rate of personal bankruptcies since 1980).[60] A categorical shift had occurred and it threatened bedrock concepts of American manhood. A social pact between the nation's men and its institutions was collapsing, most prominently but not exclusively within the institutions of work. Masculine ideals of loyalty, productivity, and service lay in shards. Such codes were seen as passé and their male subscribers as vaguely pathetic. Loyalty meant you were too slow or too stupid to skip out on the company before it skipped out on you. Productivity was something corporations and their shareholders now measured not by employee elbow grease but by how many employees the company laid off. And service meant nothing more than consumer assistance, exemplified by a telemarketer trapped in a cubicle, a phone glued to his ear, his have-a-nice-day conversations preformulated and monitored. Such a profound and traumatic transformation affected all men, whether they lost their jobs or simply feared losing them, whether they drowned or floated in the treacherous new currents. In the course of my travels, I would meet men amply rewarded by the quicksilver, image-based new economy, men who, nonetheless, felt, as they would say to me time and again, "emasculated" by the very forces that elevated them.

I didn't, however, move down to Los Angeles to interview unemployed adult men. What actually brought me there and preoccupied me initially was the misbehavior of boys. The adults, their fathers, were almost a curious afterthought, even if an inevitable one. You could say that I stumbled on the fathers by way of the sons. At first, the fathers were like the unmentioned missing persons in boys' adventure tales. The sons I met seemed to exist in a strange self-generated bubble. The fathers, when enlisted for comment, seemed more often like baffled onlookers than interested parties. It was as if they were passing some horrible wreck on their way to work. The fathers and sons appeared to be living in parallel universes. And because our image and media culture is fascinated with youth, the sons' universe was the one that attracted the camera crews.

Judging by the headlines, Los Angeles was the prime exporter of carcinogenic young manhood, from the sexually predatory Spur Posse to the parent-killing Menendez brothers, from teenage gang warriors to the youthful-looking ski-masked bank robbers who blazed away with AK-47s on a North Hollywood shopping strip.[61] Sometimes, the "bad boy" was seen as a literal L.A. export. YOUTH GANGS FROM WEST COAST BECOME ENTRENCHED IN NEW YORK, the *New York Times* warned its readers in the summer of 1997; the Bloods were "slowly but surely . . . migrating eastward," using the city's jails "as a beachhead," and had already committed "at least 135 random slashings on the city streets as part of their initiation rite." (Six months later, the paper admitted to a false alarm: "Police officials, sociologists and gang experts say there is no real gang presence in the city," the *Times* reported, attributing the hysteria to mysterious "widespread rumors.")[62] But the bad boy was just as frequently a shipment wrapped in celluloid and airbrushed in advertising campaigns, where what had just been demonized about him could now be glamorized, his exaggerated criminality repackaged for profit, the sexual predator made sexual object. The media's nightmare visions of "wilding" boys with Mac-10s would become the commercial daydreams of Hollywood and Madison Avenue, as snarling young gangsters and rapists re-formed into long-lashed Tupac Shakur matinee idols and sulky-lipped Marky Mark pinups. The Nike-shod thug with his predatory "attitude" and the bare-chested Calvin Klein poster boy with his gigantic tented underwear rivaled the Marlboro cowboy's spurs for preeminence along the Sunset Strip's billboard gulch. The perfumed junior hoodlum became the prevailing male icon, lord of the unzipped flies.

A legion of media reports titillated readers with overwrought tales of bad-boy marauders. *Time*'s September 1994 cover story WHEN KIDS GO BAD presented an apocalyptic portrait of a system overwhelmed "by pint-size drug runners and by 16-year-old gunmen." One such pipsqueak, unidentified, posed for another *Time* cover story, A BOY AND HIS GUN, clutching a firearm, his face covered by an outlaw bandanna. *Newsweek* beat the same drum with a cover story, WILD IN THE STREETS, warning of "a virtual 'epidemic' of youth violence." A *U.S. News & World Report* cover story, KIDS WHO KILL, gasped at "the stone-hearted ethos of an astonishingly large segment" of teenage boys. The story would be the same no matter what newspaper or magazine you read it in. A Fort

Lauderdale *Sun-Sentinel* headline intoned, THE MISBEHAVIOR OF BOYS HAS TURNED INTO A SCARY NATIONWIDE CRISIS, while Cleveland's *Plain Dealer* deplored "a generation that some dub 'the young and the ruthless' " and Long Island's *Newsday* served up ROUGH BOYS, a feature article filled with youngsters who offered such quotes as, "It's 'like I'm a beast.' "[63]

Boys preoccupied politicians. Federal hearings were convened to denounce the lawless behavior of young men. Congress pursued military solutions, doubling the number of junior ROTC programs in high schools and pumping millions of dollars into boot camps for dropouts and mini–military academies on inner-city campuses.[64] State legislators drafted paddling bills; government officials backed curfews and "get tough" policies that made possible the prosecution of teenage boys as adults.[65] And Los Angeles led the way, with its city attorney at one point seeking a dusk-to-dawn curfew and even a "pass law" for juveniles, and its cops swooping down on the streets as part of Operation Hammer, a dragnet that, between 1988 and 1991, in combination with similar efforts by the sheriff's department, picked up tens of thousands of young minority men. The arrests were often for dubious reasons: in at least one sweep, after the media departed, the police released more than 90 percent of their "suspects" without charges.[66]

In his 1994 State of the Union address, President Bill Clinton singled out the beastly boy as a prime source of national moral decline. "We cannot renew this country," he said, "when thirteen-year-old boys get semiautomatic weapons to shoot nine-year-olds for kicks." In public-opinion polls, Americans expressed a conviction that the greatest cause of crime and violence was young men; a majority called for the execution of teenagers convicted of homicide.[67]

While youth crime was indeed on the rise, it was hardly at the "epidemic" levels or of the vicious quality that the media had claimed. Juveniles were arrested for less than 15 percent of the murders and about 18 percent of violent crimes in the 1990s; and in spite of massive press coverage of schoolyard shootings, FBI statistics showed no actual increase in children arrested for murder.[68] As social scientist Mike Males found in *The Scapegoat Generation*, arrests of teenage boys were rising far more than their actual crimes, and the increase in crimes was actually a function of increasing poverty, not youth. In the eighties and nineties, young people disproportionately suffered the most dramatic rise in poverty.[69] Yet the public fathers were determined to crack down on their "criminal" sons. Recrimination seemed the last abiding tie in a time when the worlds of fathers and sons were drifting apart like separating continents, when an entire generation of male elders seemed to have little to bequeath their boys in the way of masculine skill and mastery and community leadership, when the fathers were alone in the new world, too, and knew only that they were expected to dominate.

While boys may not have been the murderous monsters painted by media's demonologists, they were clearly in some sort of trouble and anxious to admit their transgressions in the confessionals of the press. What lay behind these transgressions, however, was barely examined. The economic and social roots of young male pathology were largely overlooked by a media that preferred other culprits: testosterone, drugs, "permissive" or neglectful working parents (which, either way, almost always meant Mom), or, increasingly by the decade's end, feminism. The women's movement was a favorite target when the press and its pundits turned their attention to the troubles of *white* boys. (Black and Hispanic boys, by contrast, were generally seen as a gun-and-crack-dealing army assaulting an innocent nation.) "With all the attention devoted to our daughters over the past decade, are our sons falling by the wayside?" *Newsweek* fretted in a cover story, BOYS WILL BE BOYS. The *New York Times* invoked the same bugaboo in HOW BOYS LOST OUT TO GIRL POWER. The problem, the article concluded, may well be that "the wrong sex is getting all the attention in school." The media found plenty of "expert" witnesses to support this view among the bumper crop of books published on the bad-boy crisis in the late nineties. By provoking mothers to denigrate their sons, feminist attitudes can "create boys that are either murderous or suicidal," maintained Don and Jeanne Elium, coauthors of the popular *Raising a Son*.[70]

The Eliums were right in one regard, anyway—the problem of *what boys were doing to the world* was rooted in *what the world was doing to boys*. I realized this myself as I dutifully followed the restless searchlight of the nineties media casting its powerful beams on one male trouble spot after another. The men were always young, their troubles always with girls, drugs, or guns. The location was, more often than not, southern California. I attended a weekly "gang prevention" class at Millikan High School in Long Beach, about twenty miles south of Los Angeles, where kids sat in a portable unit (what passed for a classroom facility in the financially strapped public-school system) and watched videos about the baneful influence of graffiti artists and street cliques. I rode with the truancy police as they chased down young male fugitives from the barbed-wire locked compounds of Los Angeles public schools, pseudo-cops who liked to impress me with Polaroids they carried of scowling adolescent thugs, their versions of the Nation's Most Wanted posters. (One such wanna-be G-man carried his snapshots in a family-style photo album.) I sat in on a Los Angeles County "Youth Summit," held in the banquet room of a woefully underfunded community hospital, where a panel of impoverished male adolescents—and no adults—discussed how to combat the threat that the older society said they posed.

As elsewhere, boy trouble was just the surface manifestation of boys in trouble. That trouble wasn't simply indulgent or neglectful parents or harridan feminists, but a culture that had the boys *and* their elders by the throat. The injuries borne by successive generations looked different, but they were inflicted by the same trauma.

The common burden of fathers and sons struck me as I found myself in the fall of 1993 at what any newspaper would have called ground zero of the American masculinity crisis: in a town a few miles east of Long Beach called Lakewood, seated in a molded plastic chair at a chain restaurant, chilled air and Muzak flowing through the vents, talking to Billy Shehan, the sex-"points" champ of the nationally notorious bad-boy pack called the Spur Posse. A half year past his media fame, Billy was trying to figure out where his young life had taken such an unsavory turn, and he was beginning to make a connection that had eluded his many journalist interviewers. They largely wrote off the Spurs as arrogant high-school athletes who had let all the glory go to their heads. But Billy Shehan suspected that sports was just the most visible sign of a deeper problem, one that had less to do with high-school trophies and more to do with history. "The parks are here because of [the aerospace corporation] McDonnell Douglas," he said to me. "Pop Warner's here because of Douglas. So we have to be products of our society somehow, don't we?"

So they do, and so do their fathers, and all the men who have been buffeted by the collapse of that society's promise. This is the story of a feminist's travels through a postwar male realm, a journey that began in Los Angeles but led through an America deeded by the fathers, inhabited by the sons, but belonging in the end to neither. It is also a reflection of my own mental journey as I struggled to understand the perilous voyage to manhood undertaken by the men I once knew as boys—boys who were shown a satellite, and understood in its transit that the world would soon be theirs.

PART TWO

UTILITY MEN

Long Beach Shipbuilding and Drydock, Navy Department, 1944.

2

NOTHING BUT
BIG WORK

From Shipyards to Space,
the Closing of the American Job

I FIRST APPROACHED THE LONG BEACH NAVAL SHIPYARD in 1996
by way of Hollywood. The town built on artifice is connected to the
industrial port by about thirty miles of freeways. As I drove these roads,
I became aware that I was traversing a generational as well as geographic
terrain. To travel south from Hollywood to Long Beach is to clamber
down the tree of the postwar economy to its root.

The uppermost branches of that tree, its new, bright layers of growth,
are hung with the tinsel of shopping emporiums, glossy multiplexes and
pastel minimalls, home electronics stores and espresso franchises. As the
5 freeway passes south, it passes directly through the shadow of the
Citadel Mall, a designer discount palace whose hulking Assyrian turrets
and crenellated walls formerly housed a Uniroyal tire plant. Uniroyal,
along with the area's other large manufacturers—General Motors, Bethlehem Steel, Chrysler, Firestone, BF Goodrich, Norris Industries, and
Goodyear—fell before the recessionary body blows of the late seventies
and early eighties (blows that, nationwide, cost 11.5 million workers their
jobs in plant shutdowns and relocations).[1] With the demise of the Los
Angeles area factories also died the livelihoods of anywhere from forty
thousand to eighty thousand mostly male heavy-industrial workers, men

whose weekday grapple with heavy machinery had hoisted them into the ranks of the unionized middle class.[2]

The freeways then enter an area of economic decimation of more recent vintage as they pass through towns like Torrance and Lakewood, a famed stretch known as "Aerospace Alley." This region once claimed the nation's largest and most concentrated share of cold-war defense contracts, garnering nearly a fifth of all federal defense dollars; the aerospace industry was the biggest employer in southern California.[3] On the day I drove down, it looked more like it had taken a hot-war hit; it resembled a huge bombed-out back alley. The parking lots that once served a massive aerospace bureaucracy were noticeably vacant. The cinder-block storefronts of unemployment agencies showed more activity than the sleek, depopulated offices of the weapons makers and all the ancillary businesses they supported, many now plastered with FOR LEASE signs. The collapsing aerospace industry in Los Angeles County shed at least half of its jobs by the mid-1990s, and it would contribute to a broader regional crisis: a quarter million manufacturing jobs and a total of more than a half million jobs were lost in the county.[4]

In the mid- to late nineties, I'd travel this route often and I'd witness two tragic and contrasting stories of modern masculinity. One was a cautionary tale involving McDonnell Douglas, a downsizing aerospace giant, the nation's largest arms maker. The other, less publicized but crucial in the lessons it contained about manhood, was the one I discovered when I reached the end of the road.

The 110 freeway terminates at the port — and at the taproot of southern California's midcentury industrial growth: the Promethean workshops wherein ships were built and repaired. As I rounded the freeway's final bend that first morning, the sky banked wide and high over the harbor, and it seemed as if I would ascend right into the heavens as my car climbed the dauntingly steep arc of the Vincent Thomas Bridge. At last the bridge crested to reveal its destination below: Terminal Island, a flat, jagged spit of semimarshland as irregularly shaped as a jigsaw-puzzle piece. Stamped on its surface was the crisp, monumental geometry of the Long Beach Naval Shipyard. Even as I descended and drew closer, the landscape remained all clean lines and right angles, the scrubbed, unadorned contours of a utilitarian world. Nothing was for embellishment; every spool of wire and coil of rope had a purpose and a place. The yard's no-frills asceticism held an essential beauty — the boiled-down purity of a world that was exactly what it was and hid nothing.

The Long Beach Naval Shipyard rose to prominence at roughly the same moment as the great Douglas factory complex (later merged with

McDonnell Aircraft) to its north in Aerospace Alley. At their height, the combined industries of aircraft construction and shipbuilding and repair employed hundreds of thousands locally and accounted for three-quarters of the manufacturing in the Los Angeles area, including hundreds of smaller plants machining aluminum, molding synthetic rubber, making machine tools and ordnance.[5] Here, as in Norfolk, Boston, and other cities along the nation's coasts, the aerospace and maritime industries seemed to share an identical mission, forging monumental works in record time to serve the aims of war. Nevertheless, one represented America's industrial past, the other its corporate future.

Dead Soldiers, All Piled Up

PRESIDENT THEODORE ROOSEVELT'S "GREAT WHITE FLEET" first steamed into Long Beach harbor in 1908, and the navy has been a presence ever since. During World War II, Terminal Island, an old rumrunners' hideout, was converted into a mammoth facility boasting the Moreell, one of the nation's biggest dry docks. That war made shipbuilding and repair the nation's largest nonagricultural occupation, and the Long Beach Naval Shipyard southern California's second-largest employer, with sixteen thousand workers laboring around the clock.[6] The yard worked in concert with private shipbuilders in the port — among them Calship, Todd Shipyards, Craig, Consolidated, and Bethlehem Shipbuilding — which were rolling out record numbers of destroyers and transports and PT boats and landing and supply craft from their frenzied wartime assembly plants. On Terminal Island, Calship was completing a dozen Liberty ships a month; at the war's height, its fifty-five thousand full-time employees finished a ship a day. When these new men-of-war limped home from battle in the Pacific, the Long Beach Naval Shipyard nursed them back to health in record-breaking time. Celebrated as "the Workshop of the Fleet" for its prodigious speed and miracle cures — it turned around as many as twenty war-wounded vessels a month — the yard was an essential support system for the nation's fabled victory at sea.[7]

At war's end, America's shipyards and its fleet were hailed as embodiments of the nation's new robust economy. They were also at the heart of its masculine ethic. On October 27, 1945, President Truman presided over Navy Day, a national holiday. Christening an aircraft carrier the USS *Franklin D. Roosevelt,* he reviewed a seven-mile-long parade of men-of-war on the Hudson River; a million people gathered in Central Park to hear his speech and millions more listened in by radio. Americans must never forget, Truman said, that the country's might rested on

Roosevelt's "constant battle for the forgotten man" and on his guiding spirit as the navy's "father," a man "who rolled up his sleeves" and got down to work on a shared national task. It was a spirit most honorably expressed by the many workers "in the shipyards of the nation who in the last five and a half years built carriers like this one, and over a hundred thousand other ships."[8] By such an ethic of grit and duty, the president assured his national audience, would America steer triumphantly into a new age.

The shipyard that greeted me fifty years later was a realm of staggering proportions. Overhead, gantry cranes towered, their arms rising and falling like the heads of gigantic horses. The tallest of them all—374 skyscraper feet high and capable of lifting more than four hundred tons (it once hoisted Howard Hughes's "Spruce Goose," the biggest airplane ever built)—was the Titan, the world's largest self-propelled floating crane, known affectionately to the men laboring in its shadow as Herman the German. America's largest war trophy, Herman was captured from the Germans in 1945, partly dismantled, and hauled by barge through the Panama Canal. Below the massive crane gaped its apposite, the gigantic maw of the Moreell dry dock, capable of floating any of the navy's largest aircraft carriers on fifty-six million gallons of seawater.[9]

The size of the machinery, however, was the secondary spectacle. The secret of the place lay in the dependency of such immense machines on men's mastery. Herman the German was no robotic superman; its operation required twelve to fifteen men with the skill and precision of surgeons. For all the dry dock's pumps and valves and vents, maneuvering a ship into its berth was no mechanized process; the yard's men spent weeks making the razor-thin calculations necessary to position ridiculously tiny keel blocks on the dry-dock floor. That a group of men through skill, experience, and gumption could make a mammoth carrier balance on such child's blocks was one of the astonishments of the yard.

Admiral Ben Moreell, the "King Bee of the Seabees," after whom the dry dock was named, had led the World War II Naval Construction Battalions in a frenzy of overseas building—nine hundred shore installations, airfields, ports, and roads through jungles. These were spectacular engineering projects that provided the wartime infrastructure for military mobilization. It was the productivity of Moreell's soldiers that the dry dock's baptizers vowed to honor—and emulate.[10] In the years to follow, the shipyard would make good on that vow. As many as forty ships at a time jammed its harbor. Its thirteen and a half miles of railroad tracks and thousands of feet of piers were thronged with welders and riggers and electricians and boilermakers. "Everywhere was the hustle and bustle of moving busy workers, trucks, plate lifts, yard cranes, electric mules, the blue flashes of arc welders, brighter than the noonday sun," wrote Chester Himes in *If He Hollers Let Him Go,* a novel set in the shipyards in San Pedro (next door to Long Beach), where the author worked as a shipwright's helper during World War II. "And the noise, always loud, unabating, ear-splitting. I loved it like my first love."[11]

The shipyard represented a particular vintage of American masculinity, monumental in its pooled effort, indefatigable in its industry, and built on a sense of useful productivity, of work tied to service. "The creed of the shipyard will be 'not for us, but for others,'" declared the yard's commander, Captain Emmett E. Sprung, at a rechristening ceremony in 1951. Like the Seabees, the shipyard's men grounded their own worth and identity not in the masculine model of the warrior but in that of the builder. Being a man was not about "killing Krauts," but collectively creating something tangible that was essential to a larger mission. In 1993, a Los Angeles television personality, Huell Howser, toured the Titan for a show on California history. He was baffled to find on the crane, untouched, its fifty-year-old German insignia. "So this was just like it was?" Howser asked his guides, two retired shipyard workers, and he sounded amazed. Why hadn't they expunged all signs of its previous operators, now that it was "ours"? The former workers just shrugged. What was most significant to them about Herman the German was not that they had conquered it, but that they knew how to make it work.[12]

Three years after Howser's filming, the crane was leased and towed away to Panama. The shipyard was being dismantled. A budget-trimming Pentagon had given it two years to shut itself down and close its gates.

On one of my visits to the shipyard in the summer of 1996, it was immediately made clear to me that the world of ship work was still at the center of a "battle" over manhood—though not one President Truman would have envisioned. Among the first people to greet me was a government marriage-and-family therapist named Terri Rosenthal. Well, she told me with a small pained smile, I had certainly come to the right place to observe American men. "It's the last bastion of white male dominance."

I wasn't sure what to make of her assessment, except that it held the weight of official authority. She was one among a phalanx of healing professionals who had conquered the shipyard seemingly overnight. The beachhead these "career transition" counselors had established was in a corner of Building 300, a tinted-glass, cubelike edifice on a hill that had once housed the shipyard's administrative, planning, and engineering offices. The yard workers called it "the Black Box" because its internal processes seemed so mysterious to them: it was the only building in the yard not devoted to hands-on production. The counselors were efficient refurbishers. Quickly, they set up their beige and green cloth-covered office dividers and posted sign-in sheets for "interview skills training" and "stress management" classes. A calendar of upcoming lectures — "Surviving a Layoff Financially," "Making Transition Work for You" — was illustrated with happy-face cartoon figures; one character, a man treading water, was inexplicably grinning from ear to ear as a huge wave crashed down upon his head.

Terri Rosenthal had been assigned by Long Beach's Employment Development Department to salve troubled minds in the shipyard's final days. Rosenthal's last duty post had been at an "outplacement center" near McDonnell Douglas's Long Beach plant, about eleven miles up the road. The center's counselors hadn't placed many ex–aerospace engineers, but they had their hands full managing the animus and bile in the psychic aftermath of McDonnell Douglas's massive layoffs. Rosenthal expected no less from her shipyard clientele; in fact, she had already decided, given their "last bastion of white male dominance" profile, it would be worse.

One morning in August 1996, Terri Rosenthal expelled a sigh of frustration as she plopped her coffee container on a laminated desk and herself in a just-out-of-the-wrapper swivel chair. "There's a lot of parallels with the aerospace men. Only here, you are talking about a population of men with extremely limited skills — social skills, work skills, communication skills." The indictment she ticked off sounded like a caricature of blue-collar men. "They don't emote. It's a culture totally based on false pride, alcoholism, and violence. This is the distillation of the male ego in its coarsest form." As evidence, she recalled a recent foray to what remained of the base's recreation center. "You should see the bar in the bowling alley. It's this surrealistic scene, all dark, this dark abyss with metaphorically silent figures, each of them staring straight ahead and each of them with a bottle of beer in front of them." She shot me a knowing look. "These men have *no* tools for living in the *real* world."

I would return to the shipyard often as, over the next year, it went about the ornate rituals of shutting down, but I was never sure what Terri Rosenthal meant by her diagnosis of the place as "the last bastion of white male dominance." For starters, the shipyard she described as "white" was 60 percent black, Hispanic, and Asian. But she was right about one thing: the shipyard was a "last bastion," for the men who worked there were surely among the last to embody a certain kind of masculinity.

When I drove through the shipyard gate on an early visit, Ernie McBride, Jr., was waiting for me under a big, years-old banner that read THE SHIP, THE YARD, THE TEAM, and a newer one that said CLOSURE WITH PRIDE. He had a creased face and the most work-worn hands of any public-relations man I'd ever met. Until July 22, 1996, McBride had spent thirty years as an electronics mechanic, radar specialist, and combat electrical systems expert. Then he was appointed the public-affairs officer of the moribund shipyard. I was his only customer.

"Welcome to the shipyard!" McBride greeted me ceremonially, if a bit shyly, extending one of those leathery hands and presenting me with a hard hat. The hat seemed wishful thinking at a "work" site where head protection was no longer necessary. Still, he had even gone to the trouble of printing my name and title—AUTHOR—on the bill.

McBride led the way to his new office on the top floor of the Black Box, his first office with a view, although it was no longer a view bustling with industry. Outside stretched the abyss of the Moreell, devoid of ships, tools, men—a black hole. The most recent ship to be repaired—and the dry dock's last—the USS *Kinkaid*, had just sailed. With its departure most of the remaining thousand employees were, like McBride, "working out of trade," that is, at something other than their usual task. If they were lucky, they got a shot at using their craft in reverse, to disassemble their tools and machinery. The others picked up trash and swept the piers.

Two such "working out of trade" men were hovering in the corridor, and when McBride opened his door, they came in and gathered by the big picture window to examine the view. Only I saw an empty pier. The men saw the ghostly outlines of their last lost hope, the destroyer *Kinkaid*.

"The *Kinkaid* was a big job," McBride murmured, following their gaze. "Eleven months of work and two of shipping sea trials."

His reminiscence was picked up by the visitors: Marty Hernandez, a pipe fitter and mechanic who had been an assistant project superintendent on the *Kinkaid*, repairing its main shafts (and was now an "environmental specialist" stripping asbestos out of deserted buildings), and Bob Thomas, the assistant project superintendent in charge of the *Kinkaid*'s vertical launch system. "That ship had got nothing but big work on it," Thomas said, and from the way he said it, I could tell that there was no higher compliment. "See, a ship is like an enclosed little universe. Everything's connected. Just to do the vertical launch system affects every other system on the ship—radar, electronics, habitability, fresh water, even the rest rooms. You start on one system on a ship, you're affecting everything."

The ship wasn't the only interconnected universe on the men's minds. Later that morning, Marty Hernandez walked me out to the Moreell dry dock. We stood on the massive caisson separating the cement chasm from the immense pressure of the sea and he showed me the plug in the wall that kept the ocean at bay. He pointed out what had once been the ball field, the bar and grill, all the support buildings, now vacant. "Everything was here," he said softly. "Everything you needed. And it was such a sheltered harbor. In storms, it was like nothing."

In McBride's office, the men talked about the craziness of the government's decision. Long Beach had been one of the best-performing shipyards nationwide for nearly a decade. It won the navy's highest award for cost savings, work quality, and safety. In 1989, the shipyard produced something rare for a government installation: $26 million worth of profit. In four years, the shipyard saved the government nearly $100 million and became the only public yard in the nation to operate in the black. And a federal government audit from 1989 to 1991 found Long Beach outperformed the private ship-repair firms, which often ran months behind schedule and more than 30 percent over budget.[13]

But its performance earned it only enemies. "The private people just hated that here was this public shipyard that was not only doing a good job but turning a profit," Long Beach city councilman Ray Grabinski told me. The private Port of San Diego Shipyard Association even hired a former federal base closure attorney to lobby for the mothballing of the shipyard, promising him a $75,000 bounty if he killed his prey.[14] But as the only shipyard on the California coast with a dry dock big enough to handle an aircraft carrier, the shipyard survived the first two rounds of cuts by the federal Base Realignment and Closure Commission, and the men had been optimistic about the third and final round; they received the news of their death in June 1995 at a champagne reception they'd arranged as a victory party.[15] "I cried," Louis Rodriguez, a mechanical-engineering technician and union local president who'd led the fight to save the shipyard, told me. "Everyone was crying. We felt we had been stabbed by our own government, by the country we served."

On this particular morning, one bitter explanation for their defeat in the form of a recent *Los Angeles Times* article sat on McBride's desk. Southwest Marine, a San Diego–based firm that was the navy's largest private West Coast ship-repair contractor, had been the yard's biggest foe, and it was in the news again for questionable business practices. That firm, along with other San Diego–based private contractors and with the aid of San Diego politicians, had successfully lobbied the Long Beach shipyard out of existence. A number of these firms had poured cash into federal politicians' coffers, hired retiring top navy officials to cushy posts on their executive staffs, and showered key congressmen with golfing expeditions, dinners, and gifts, sometimes illegally. In 1992 the chief executive of Pacific Ship Repair and Fabrication pleaded guilty to, among other things, making illegal congressional campaign contributions and was sentenced to eighteen months in jail.[16] Now, Southwest Marine was battling charges of using fraudulent tactics to win a five-year navy contract worth up to $150 million. As the *Los Angeles Times* article on Ernie McBride's desk revealed, the government was investigating allegations by a former executive that the company had stolen navy property and greatly inflated ship-repair costs. (The federal government never brought charges.) Arthur Engel, the firm's multimillionaire chief executive at the time, was a major political contributor who evidently didn't like his commands to be flouted. The *Los Angeles Times* reported that he even demanded a refund from a congressman who had decided to support the Long Beach Naval Shipyard's effort to stay open.[17]

The political clout had apparently worked. Now there was talk of the government spending two billion dollars to build a new dry dock in scenic San Diego while the perfectly good ones in gritty Long Beach sat vacant. "All because the navy brass wanted to be sipping their mint juleps on their balconies in San Diego instead of Long Beach," Councilman Grabinski said to me bitterly.

But for all that, the shipyard men were curiously unvengeful. Wasn't it hard to throw yourself into your work on the *Kinkaid* after the way the government had treated you? I asked the men in McBride's office. After all, stories of work slowdowns and sabotage were legion among downsizing workforces. The men were mystified by my question. "Oh no," Bob Thomas said. "The guys took it on themselves to say, 'Hey, this is our job. Let's do the work like we always do.' The resolve everybody had was fantastic." Marty Hernandez added: "We couldn't go out any other way. We decided to close with pride. Because this is who we *are*. This is our identity."

Kurt Leonard, head of operations at the shipyard and the man in charge of the *Kinkaid* overhaul, told me that his toughest problem had been "getting my people off the ship." No one wanted to leave. And none of the foremen could bear sending "their people" to Excess Labor, the building formerly for those who were injured or between jobs but now the headquarters where men mobilized for their sweeping-up chores. "If there was a blemish, we'd redo it. By the time we got done, it looked like a brand-new ship." Leonard had himself once turned down a plum post in the Pentagon to stay at the shipyard because he wanted to be able to "see what I create." Now, he finally had to order the men on the *Kinkaid* to disembark. "I was one of the guys who had to go around and tell everybody, 'You've got to go. It's time for you to move on.'" The supervisors pooled their money and threw a barbecue on the pier. One by one, the men passed through the project office for the last time, dropping their hard hats on the table. "I left my hat there," Leonard recalled. "And the shipyard commander left his hat there, too. That table was full of dead soldiers, if you will. Dead soldiers, all piled up."

The day after the *Kinkaid* sailed, the men were instructed to turn in their equipment. A few weeks later, Ben Francisco, a boilermaker turned Excess Labor supervisor, showed me a thick list of men and the tools they still had in their possession—drills, grinders, chisels, clamps, sanders, torches, gauges. "And this is just the list of men in Shop Eleven," he said, sighing. "They just want to hold on to their tools till the last day, like a security blanket." Doyce Scoggins, the head of Excess Labor, went over to the piers to collect equipment to turn into scrap metal, and found one of the supervisors "clinging to this very expensive valve," he recalled. "He thought he needed it to support his crew. I had to say, 'Look, you don't need this. You can't use it for anything else but ships. And the ship is gone and it's not coming back.'"

But why did they work so hard? Why hadn't they thumbed their noses at the government that put them out of business? I asked Kurt Leonard. "No, no. Because we don't see it that way," he said. "We were helping the ship." His explanation didn't make much sense to me, not then, anyway. But virtually all the men I talked to in the yard would explain themselves in similar terms.

As I listened, I wondered where such men fit into an era in which the best-known downsizing tales were of former post-office employees shooting their supervisors. (Homicide had, in fact, become the leading cause of workplace death in many cities hit by downsizing in the eighties, and the second-largest cause of workplace fatalities nationwide by the nineties. That was particularly the case for women, 42 percent of whose deaths on the job were the result of murder, compared with 12 percent of men's.)[18] The deindustrialization and "restructuring" of the last couple of decades had scythed through vast swaths of industrial America, shuttering steel and auto plants across the Midwest, decimating the defense industry, and eliminating large numbers of workers in corporate behemoths: 60,000 at Chrysler, 74,000 at General Motors, 175,000 at IBM,

125,000 at AT&T.[19] Though "going postal" was an extreme reaction, downsizing was a violent dislocation, often violently received. Yet these prototypical workingmen in the "last bastion" of a traditional male workplace were taking their bitter disappointment with remarkable gentility. What was the plug in the dike, I wondered, that miraculously kept their anger at bay?

No Way You Can Feel Like a Man

I'D SEEN THE DEVASTATION OF A DOWNSIZING, eleven miles up the freeway and some years up the tree of Los Angeles's economic development. The McDonnell Douglas Outplacement Center occupied a storefront behind a Der Wienerschnitzel fast-food franchise with a red enamel roof in what had once been a minimall retail strip. The strip had bustled back when it seemed that the defense dollars would rain down on Aerospace Alley forever. Now it was empty, except for a state unemployment office and the center. It had no sign to advertise the center's existence or to reflect the fact that the McDonnell Douglas layoffs in Long Beach—nearly thirty thousand between 1990 and 1994—were on such a grand scale that the government, with the company's assistance, had to set up this satellite office just to handle the army of castoffs from the nation's master builder of military aircraft.

On my first visit in the spring of 1994, I had made my way through rows of battered cars with the uneasy feeling of being watched. It was late morning, the sun was high, the streets were busy. I turned and scanned the lot. In a half dozen of the cars, men sat. They didn't lurk; they weren't quite loitering. They were just sitting, watching, and waiting—for what or whom, they could no longer say. Some had been waiting literally for years.

The "career transition center," as McDonnell Douglas and the city's Employment Development Department would have it, was supposed to have been a sort of human retooling shop where laid-off aerospace workers would be "processed" through an assembly line of "résumé development" classes, "interview-skills training," "skills transference workshops," and "stress management" sessions, until they emerged shiny and spanking new, ready to face the brave new world of the temporary-service economy. But inside, the center seemed less a revitalization spa than a nursing home for men. McDonnell Douglas had laid off plenty of women (mainly from its clerical and administrative staffs, where most of its female workforce was employed), but they had moved on more easily to other equally low-paying jobs, while the men gathered here like war refugees, uprooted, disoriented, and bitter. Their faces tense with confusion and anger, they all asked the same question: What enemy had done this to them?

Inside the center's glass door, a sign-in book by a receptionist's desk greeted visitors. A bulletin board displayed in-house news. Beyond the lobby, a front room contained a line of cubicles with short dividers, each with a phone — TIME LIMITED TO 10 MINUTES PER PERSON, a sign advised. A second back room had three worn tables pushed together to approximate a workspace, and two hand-me-down IBM typewriters, one with a BROKEN sign pasted on its keys. After taking a cursory glance at the wall adorned with job listings, which on this day was full of openings for manicurists, receptionists, and croupiers, the men gravitated to the back room. I noted that a Las Vegas casino offered the most openings, including one for "pit clerk," described thusly: "Ability to work from a standing position for extended periods of time; visual ability to work with computer and do paperwork in a dimly lit environment; perform reaching, stooping, crouching motions repeatedly. . . ."

Perhaps because the jobs seemed so distant from the men's homes and experience, so "out of trade," the talk around the table only occasionally involved job tips. Mostly I heard disjointed accounts of betrayal or despair, offered up to everyone and no one in particular. The men sat in an atmosphere of unconvincing cheer, attended by a handful of determinedly chipper combat nurses — the center's counselors and "reemployment specialists." At the front desk, Dolores "Dee" Smaldino, herself a laid-off McDonnell Douglas employee, kept the coffee urn and pastry basket full and dispensed occasional back rubs and a steady stream of pep talk. She tried to interest the men in the job postings, but it was tough going.

For the typical McDonnell Douglas man — middle-aged, college-educated, a homeowner, a family provider; a man from the company that had conquered the skies, rained bombs on the Axis, and built the beloved DC plane series as well as the feared F-15s and F/A-18 jet fighters — to gaze upon the postings for casino pit clerks felt like sudden death; they were in free fall and it was a long way down. "I'm kind of losing my grip," Ron Smith, an ex–McDonnell Douglas planner who had been out of work nearly two years, said to me as he perused the listings. "I'm like the guy who's hanging from the cliff. I'm starting to lose my grip."

For many of the men, the outplacement center was the only safe ledge on this particular cliff. Some of them spent a full day "working" there, from the time the doors opened at 8 A.M. until Dee locked up at

4:30 P.M. Some spent the night out in the parking lot as well. A handful slept in their old vacation trailers; the less fortunate, in their cars. At one time, three former McDonnell Douglas men pooled their money, bought a motor home, and parked it in the lot. "We have men here," center director Shirley Judd said, "who have not told their families. They get dressed and come in here every day." One man had been engaged in that charade for five months. "A lot of them have not yet come to grips with the loss of McDonnell Douglas," added job counselor Sally Ghan. "They take part-time jobs because they're waiting to be called back . . . just waiting to go back to Douglas."

Of all the drifting, in-limbo figures who belonged to this crash scene, none lumbered more haltingly or wincingly than Don Motta. A large man whose weight had only risen since his layoff, he leaned on a cane as he shuffled past. He was only forty-eight, but his hair had already turned gray around the edges. Behind thick glasses with old-fashioned black plastic frames, his eyes were wide pools, and he blinked anxiously as he eased his weary body into one of the chipped, rocky-on-its-legs chairs that McDonnell Douglas had donated to the center.

For twelve years, during the heyday of Reagan administration defense spending, Don Motta had worked as a military-contracts negotiator. McDonnell Douglas was pleased to have his insider's expertise: the previous thirteen years he had worked on the other end of the negotiating table as a senior auditor for the Defense Contract Auditing Agency. You could say, given the largely federally funded nature of McDonnell Douglas's work, that Don Motta had spent a lifetime drawing his paycheck from the government—with all the predictability, stability, and security that implied, or used to.

For the last quarter of his tenure at the company, Motta had watched the layoff spasms, ever more frequent and acute, closing in. In mid-1990, "the first wave" hit the Long Beach facility, pushing out 20 percent of its employees—eight thousand people. By the end of '92, another ten thousand slots had been emptied. "What I should've done is gone to another area of the company," Motta said, replaying his moves again and again. "But I had loyalty to my boss . . . which was probably a mistake." For men of Motta's generation, corporate loyalty wasn't supposed to be a mistake; it was supposed to be a meal ticket to lifetime employment.

The day came, Don Motta said, planting his meaty hands on the worn office desk to steady himself as he spoke—for already his voice was shaking—when a senior manager summoned him to his office. "I'm sorry to inform you," Motta recalled him saying, "that you are an R.I.F.

[Reduction In Force] candidate." The speech was so short and so euphemistic that Motta wasn't sure it had actually happened. He had two weeks to exit.

What Motta dreaded most was what came next—the telephone call to inform his wife, Gayle. He reached her at home, but no words came out. "I just, I just couldn't." For the next two weeks, in fact, Motta came home from work as if nothing had happened. It was not until his very last day that "I said, 'This is my last day.' I don't think she believed me."

The weeks and months to follow streamed by like an endlessly unreeling bad dream. He shipped out one hundred résumés and got four interviews. None led to a job. "Then came the question of how to make the house payment." It took three unemployment checks—$230 a week—to make his monthly mortgage. He refinanced the house. He gave up his health insurance so that he could cover his wife: $353 a month. At this point, he said, beads of sweat appearing on his forehead, his savings were nearly gone; no more than a month's living expenses remained.

His fears that an R.I.F. at work might mean an R.I.F. at home proved founded. "Gayle got the impression that I wasn't looking for work. She felt like I lost my own job. I said I didn't have any control over it."

Gayle Motta would later tell me that while it might have been unfair to blame him, fear of ruin and abandonment drowned out kinder instincts. "I felt hurt, like I couldn't trust him anymore. I just felt that maybe it was him who goofed up, even though the whole department was laid off."

A few months after the layoff, Don Motta came home to find another man settled on the living-room couch. "He found me attractive *and* he supported me" was Gayle's comment on her new boyfriend; he gave her four hundred dollars a month, she said. And he soon met the third requirement of traditional husbandly performance. One day, Don came home and threatened her, she told me. The boyfriend jumped in and pummeled him. Such a protective display, ugly as it was, gave Gayle a feeling of reassurance.

Just the week before, Motta said, his wife had thrown him out of the house. She had locked the screen door—not much of an impediment, but breaking down doors was not Don Motta's idea of manhood, despite his occasional resort to threats. "I'm not into that macho image, as you can see," he commented, looking woefully down at his expansive body. His definition of masculinity, one widely shared by the men of McDonnell Douglas, involved buying new screen doors, not yanking them off their hinges. That he was no longer able to do so was a matter of vast, unspeakable shame.

"There is no way you can feel like a man. You can't. It's the fact that I'm not capable of supporting my family.... When you've been very successful in buying a house, a car, and could pay for your daughter to go to college, though she didn't want to, you have a sense of success and people see it. I haven't been able to support my daughter. I haven't been able to support my wife.

"I'll be very frank with you," he said slowly, placing every word down as if each were an increasingly heavy weight: "I. Feel. I've. Been. Castrated."

Motta was exceptional among the outplacement denizens, but not for his family woes. Many of the men there had tales only slightly less horrific to tell. Motta was unusual for tying his sense of emasculation directly to downsizing. For most of the men, the designated culprit was another sex, another nationality, another race. An anti-immigration referendum, Proposition 187, was on the California ballot that fall of 1994 and the center was full of talk of "illegal aliens who are taking our jobs away," talk that expanded inevitably into broadsides against job-poaching "minorities" in general. Stories abounded of men like the fifty-two-year-old white "senior material support analyst" who made fifty-four thousand dollars a year until he was laid off in 1993. He had barged into a retraining center for McDonnell Douglas workers at California State University–Long Beach and "began insulting every minority in my office," recalled the center's director, Paul Bott. He called the Asians in the office "sneaky" and "inscrutable" and claimed that he couldn't understand Susan Huh, the center's second in command, a Korean woman who spoke flawless, unaccented English. "He was flushed, beet red, blood vessels sticking out of his head and throbbing, like some primordial monster," Bott said.

In fact, minorities, who had never had a great presence in the white-collar end of McDonnell Douglas, were estimated to have suffered slightly more than half of the aerospace cuts in the early 1990s.[20] Some of the white men at the center freely admitted the irrationality of their words. But anger must flow somewhere and this target, at least, seemed conveniently remote. "I mean, I don't think there are any planners and engineers coming across the border," ex-planner Ron Smith told me one afternoon. "But it hurts when you go to an interview and you know damn well you can do the job, and you know they are looking at you and thinking, 'Forget it.'"

Lest I mistake this admission as an easing of his usual vituperation,

Smith looked over his shoulder, lowered his voice, and started up about the "peter power" of Mexicans and how it made him yearn for what he called, variously and approvingly, a "police state," "a dictatorship," or a "controlled environment," a state in which the old "system" would be reimposed, his status restored, and the reins of authority returned to a benevolent but firm white male management. The racial attitudes that he shared with others at the center buttressed a masculinity based on exclusion and privilege.

With the exception of its lower-rung jobs, McDonnell Douglas had, in fact, been a remarkably white institution, the long-term result of aerospace's fiercely maintained segregationist policies (in spite of World War II federal orders to integrate). Congressional hearings in 1941 found that the entire southern California aircraft industry employed only four black production workers.[21] But race was only one aspect of the exclusiveness the company offered its middle managers. Ron Smith and other laid-off employees felt their positions at McDonnell Douglas had endowed them with an upper-echelon status that had raised them above the common run of men. Their animosity for the despoiling ranks of Mexicans, blacks, and women came, in part, from remorse over the loss of a white-collar status that wasn't just income-based. Though the white-collar men at McDonnell Douglas didn't make all that much more than many of their blue-collar counterparts, they were intent on staying on one side of a new masculine divide erected by the postwar economic ethic, one that elevated affiliation to a glamorous, brand-name corporate giant over meaningful participation in a giant collective project.

He Took Care of His People

BY CONTRAST, THE LONG BEACH NAVAL SHIPYARD I encountered in its closing days was an institutional expression of an ethic of inclusion and community. Beyond its obvious ethnic significance, the shipyard's integration held an extra, hidden benefit. It created an environment where every male worker regardless of race could embrace a type of masculinity based neither on exclusivity nor dominance. You were not elevated into this type of manhood; you were enlisted into it. Even the yard's hierarchy stressed inclusivity. The white-collar administrators had largely risen from the blue-collar shops, and it was a point of pride that the work they supervised was work they'd actually done. Bob Sabol, a thirty-one-year employee and a contracting officer who had traded a prospective career as an attorney after law school for a dry-dock apprenticeship at the shipyard, expressed typical satisfaction in working for a place where "people from production moved all the way up the ladder and retired at the top grade," and where the top and bottom were never that far apart. The top civilian officer at the shipyard, he pointed out, made $98,000, while the lowest-paid employees, the helpers and laborers, made $25,000, which often rose to at least $35,000 with overtime. At the private ship-repair firms, the workers were paid on average only a third of the pay drawn by their counterparts in Long Beach, while the owners lived in luxury; Arthur Engel, Southwest Marine's founder, lived in a $3 million house, piloted a yacht, and for a while even owned a share of the San Diego Padres.[22]

For the shipyard that inducted blacks and Hispanics into skilled trades, as well as for the minorities who sought the work, ambition and success were defined by the ideal of inclusion. Especially for its black workers, the shipyard had been a way to join the greater community and claim the fundamentals of a particular sort of manhood—mastery over an essential trade and usefulness to others. The resilience of the men now faced with expulsion from those trades and from the yard owed a lot to the type of struggle they'd had to wage to get into them. The shipyard was no holdover from some ancient golden age of guild-and-craft work (and to perceive it as such was to indulge in cheap romance). Its apprenticeship model was inherited from a hard era that had its own great problems and predations. The shipyard's real virtue lay in what its current workers had made of that old model. They had fashioned something better out of vintage cloth, something that was still very much a work in progress as the shipyard entered its final decade. Their finest hour may have been the hour before the yard closed.

One afternoon a couple of weeks after I met Ernie McBride, Jr., we drove over to visit his father at the tidy little bungalow with roses out front on Lemon Avenue that Ernie McBride, Sr., had bought in 1948, after successfully combating racially restrictive covenants in court and in spite of white neighbors who petitioned to keep him out. The house, now in a mostly black neighborhood, was recently designated a historic landmark by the city council, partly because of the courageous NAACP meetings once held inside and partly because, as a city councilman observed, it was not possible to designate McBride himself, even though "he really is the landmark."[23]

I already knew McBride, Sr., by reputation: cofounder of the city's NAACP branch in 1940, mastermind of protests that stopped discriminatory hiring practices at local grocery stores and desegregated local housing, organizer of a picketing campaign that abolished elementary-school minstrel shows and eliminated racist textbooks at the high school. When McBride, Jr., set up his new office as public-affairs officer, he tacked a small notice to his bulletin board, next to a snapshot of the elementary-school team he coached and a photo of his daughter modeling sneakers for a Nike fashion shoot. It was a citation from the January 20, 1995, issue of the *Congressional Record,* which noted his father's role in integrating the Long Beach Naval Shipyard.[24] Ernie McBride, Sr., was, in fact, one of the first black men hired at the yard by a union that had until then barred blacks from its membership rolls. And he had to appeal all the way to the White House to make it happen.

When we pulled up to the house, McBride, Sr., was waiting for us at the door. Eighty-seven years old, he was stooped but unbowed. Behind him, the television set was tuned to a local news report on confrontations between the police and young black men — an issue that deeply troubled him because he saw that none of the tools he had honed in his historic battles seemed the least bit effective in this new struggle. Nor did there seem to be any mustering of men to fight it. "I look out the window and I see young black men facing disaster," he said. "If we don't do anything about it, the black man is gone." And with him, McBride sensed, went a resistance essential to the nation. "The only challenge to America *is* the black male American." He was not, however, referring to the despairing "rebellion" of the 1992 riots that swept through not only Los Angeles but Long Beach; he was talking about the principled challenge that only an adult could mount.[25]

McBride's son gently tried to nudge him toward the subject of the shipyard, but his achievements there seemed very far away. "I did make a contribution and that is the only thing a man can do. I think I'll be remembered for what I did, but . . ." His frail voice dribbled away. He gazed hopelessly at the many plaques and citations on his walls, the various keys to the city he had been awarded over the years. None would unlock the gates of the present nightmare spilling out on television and in the streets around him.

Ernie McBride, Sr., had come to Wilmington, a town close to Long Beach, in 1930 from Little Rock, Arkansas, in a car with five other men, all lured by advertisements for industrial work and a mirage of social equality at the end of the highway. What he found was the same old segregation in a subtler shade — "The only difference was, the signs weren't on the bus" — and the same old economic emasculation, with a cruel twist. "When I came to Long Beach," he recalled, "not only were there no jobs for male black persons, a lot of the office-cleaning jobs, they worked *women.*" He answered an ad in the classifieds that read "Wanted, a woman weighing 200-plus pounds, jet black, good salary paid." He went to the address, which turned out to be a café that was being picketed by its employees. The owner of the restaurant, which did not serve blacks, wanted a black woman to dress up like Aunt Jemima and follow the picketers with a sign that read I'SE A-PICKIN', TOO. McBride confronted the boss, and got a union friend to promise a day's work to every woman who turned the job down.

All around him in Long Beach, he recalled, "the oil industry was jumping. There was a lot of money to be made, and for years, we lived under that," yet locked outside of it. "There were no jobs for black males except for shoeshine." So for almost two years, McBride operated a shoeshine stand, before finding a job at a supermarket.

One night in 1939, McBride told his wife, "There's going to be a war and I'm going to be prepared for it." In the late thirties, 90 percent of black government employees were doing janitorial work; but with the war, he sensed, there would be an opportunity for a change.[26] He enrolled in electrical school at night; he knew that if ever there was a chance of breaking into the white male world of work, this would be it. "Then the war industry began, but no local union would hire blacks." At Douglas, the aircraft company was promoting only one type of job to black men: dishwashing. At the shipyard, Common Labor Union Local 507, the entry point for untrained and semiskilled workers, had added a clause to its contract barring black members, a typical strategy employed by most of the craft unions at the time.[27] In 1943, McBride wrote to the president and his wife, Eleanor Roosevelt, asking that the clause be struck, and then organized a letter-writing campaign. Shortly thereafter, McBride received a personal letter from the president thanking him for calling the injustice to his attention. The union heard from FDR, too, a letter informing them that there would be no government hiring through the union with the ban in place.

Still, McBride and Nathan Holley, a friend with a degree from Tuskegee Institute, were shunned. "Holley said, 'We're going to straighten this out if it takes all night.' So we went back to the union hall and Holley said to the two men in there, 'There are two of us, and two of you,' and one of them says, 'I think we are man enough.' Then Holley holds open the door to the hall and says, 'You are not man enough to throw us out.' " A near fight ensued, with the men "nose to nose" with the union officials who were screaming that the letter was all a lie. Finally, one of them retreated to his desk and phoned union headquarters. Told that the presidential order was real and had to be followed, he reluctantly informed McBride and Holley that they could become union members, but it would cost twenty-five dollars each. Between them, the two men barely had enough for one membership; it took them a week to borrow the rest, but they did.

In 1943, McBride became one of four black men hired as first-class electricians, and the only black man in the highly skilled motor-generating department. As one electrician from Chicago who came to the shipyard told him, "I know how to hook the wires up, but you know *why*." Soon, McBride also became chair of the grievance committee of the electricians' union local.

When news reached the shipyard that President Roosevelt had died, McBride recalled, he was standing at the dry dock. "All we black union men went to crying because we knew what was going to happen." And it did. The day Truman was sworn into office, every black union official was fired, he said, "except for me. When I heard they intended to fire me, I quit before they could." McBride was the last to leave the union hall.

Even on that gloomy day, he knew that the racists would not prevail. He had helped usher in the opening of skilled ship work to young black men, and in a matter of years, blacks would hold a higher percentage of well-paid craft jobs in shipyards than in any other large industry.[28] "Two things I never feared," he said. "As my dad used to say it, if you know how to use your hands and your head, you can get by in America." He looked down at his hands, gnarled and palsied on the dining room's lace tablecloth. On the television set, a young black man was spread-eagled against a police car, his hands cuffed, his head buried in the hood. McBride turned to look at the image. He said nothing. There was nothing to be said, only to be feared.

The terra firma of work to which a man might anchor himself if he could use his hands and head was being washed away, and McBride had been an early witness to its erosion. When the shipyard union forced him out, he went on to ply his trade in a variety of places, but he eventually wound up driving delivery trucks and tow trucks at a local Ford dealership. In the late seventies, the dealership decided to save money and ordered McBride, who was nearly sixty-five and had worked at the company for fifteen years, to assume an additional job for no extra pay— as a janitor. After getting the news, McBride drove halfway to work, turned around, and came home. He called in his resignation. "And you can keep the rest of my money," he said. They did.

Ernie McBride, Jr., put a gentle hand on his father's. He had to get back to work, he explained. McBride, Sr., walked us out to the front yard. He was still standing on his stalklike legs, swaying slightly among the roses, as we pulled away. After a block or two, his son said, in a tight voice all the more wrenching for its lack of inflection, "If it hadn't been for what my dad did, I wouldn't have had the opportunity."

The love of fathers is one of the most palpable emotions in the yard, particularly among the men whose fathers, like McBride's, were pioneers there. Rick Meza's father was one of the first Hispanic men to rise to a top management position. José "Joe" Meza began in 1942, picking up nails on the pier, one of the few jobs then deemed suitable for Mexican-Americans. Eventually he worked his way into welding, and became the first Hispanic group superintendent of a shop. "I recall as a kid getting in the Ford," Rick Meza said to me as we whiled away one slow after-noon in the decommissioning yard, "and I would drive in with my mother with these burritos wrapped in foil for my father for lunch. We'd drive through the gate, gate number three, where the marines used to hang out. Back then, all this was dirt." He waved at the macadam utility roads. "And we'd walk up to a ship, carrying these burritos. And my father would pop out of a porthole on the bottom of the ship's hull where he was welding. And he'd be so dark from oil and dirt I wouldn't recognize him. I'd just look at him and all I could think was, He works so hard. My father works so *hard*." His voice held admiration and sorrow; his father had died a couple of years earlier. "It's like from a camera, that image. That image never goes away."

Rick Meza came into the shipyard a generation later as a draftsman, far from his father's shop. Like a number of men who followed their fathers into the yard, he kept his employment a secret from his father as long as he could—in Meza's case, almost a year. "I wanted to make it on my own." He shrugged and gave a sheepish grin. "I don't know, it's a man thing." In the world of the shipyard it was also a man thing to find a father figure who could foster your talents, help you to acquire the community connection that would confer a tangible competence. Merit in the shipyard was not about becoming a solo performer, a star. Working alone was rarely possible. If a vengeful foreman wanted to see a man fail or break his neck, the most reliable strategy was to send him off to work by himself. Flourishing in the shipyard meant embracing a kind of dependency and learning to see that as a sign not of weakness but of strength, as a way of becoming a man.

"Oh, there's Vaughn!" Marty Hernandez exclaimed as we crossed the parking lot and eagerly hustled me over for an introduction. "He's like a father figure to me," he later explained. His actual father had worked at the shipyard for more than a decade, but it was operations officer Vaughn Garvey who "made me a man." "He's the one guy who saw the potential in me," he said, his eyes suddenly tearing up. "I was a pipe-fitter supervisor, and on the USS *Wadsworth* he made me an assistant project superintendent and recommended me for an award. Vaughn took a chance on me. He gave me a chance to expand. He's one of the best men I know."

As in so many blue-collar jobs and union environments, old-style paternalism could easily become an exclusionary despotism. But such a system also held a capacity for nurturance through apprenticeship and it was on this that the shipyard workers came to base a viable and encompassing work life. Each successful man in the shipyard had a "father," a more experienced older man, not a relative, often not even of the same race, who had recognized his abilities and cultivated them.

Perhaps no one at the shipyard was more recognized as a good father than Dennis Swann. His own father had worked at the shipyard in the 1950s, the first black electrician and general foreman in his shop. "You could say I followed in his footsteps," Swann said, but he meant only that, like his father, he was the first black man in *his* shop, "gyro," where navigational equipment was repaired. His first year in gyro, 1963, was a horror. "They had me sweep and mop the floors. They had me wash windows till I was afraid the glass would wear out." This was not what a trained instrument mechanic with skills honed during four years in the air force should have been doing. Finally, a man named Charlie Spohn came in to supervise the gyro shop. "And from that point on," Swann said, "my life changed. If it hadn't been for Charlie Spohn, I wouldn't be here." Spohn, who was white, "recognized my talents." He handed Swann a gyro compass to overhaul, which is a complex, highly technical and difficult job—"one of the elites," as Swann put it. He pulled the job off handsomely, "and after that, everybody accepted me. Suddenly I was leadoff mechanic, and I'd take others out there and *they'd* assist *me*." Repeatedly, Spohn put Swann in a position where he could excel, promoting him to instrument foreman (the first black instrument foreman in *any* naval shipyard), and eventually appointing him the first project superintendent in the shipyard. "If there was something in you, Charlie would pull it out of you and put it to good use."

When Swann married, Charlie Spohn was his best man. Three and a half decades later, with Spohn long retired, the two men still talked on the phone regularly. Swann fondly referred to him as "Dad."

Such relationships became generational. Swann became the father of Joe Solis, who had recently been named Hispanic of the Year. Swann and Solis were so close that they were referred to as the "father-and-son" team around the yard, and Solis rose to become assistant project superintendent. "I did the same thing for him that Charlie Spohn did for me," Swann said. "I saw he was eager to learn. I saw he produced. If you don't produce, you're not on my good-boy list. I don't care what color you are. None of that walking up to me and saying, 'Hey brother!' with your fist up in the air. Uh-uh. That doesn't get it. You gotta produce."

And likewise Ike Burr, who had served under Joe Meza, the first Hispanic shop superintendent, and who became one of the first black men to break into upper management: Ike Burr would go on to mentor Meza's son, Rick. "My father, he took care of his people," Rick told me, but it was Ike, he said, who took care of him. "Ike's the best boss I ever worked for," he said with a kind of awe. "He took me under his wing, but not to protect me. If you do a good job, he backs you." Burr recommended him for a $250 award for a cost-saving invention, an award that was not, as is so common in corporate settings, for vaguely defined "excellence" in attitude or management. Rick Meza had come up with a method to stop huge sheets of aluminum from warping when they were cut with hot plasma in the shipfitters' shop, an expensive and time-consuming problem to correct.

To be a shipyard "father" in the later years was to have command not over men but over a body of knowledge — and to be capable of transmitting that knowledge to a younger man who would, through his mastery, become a teacher himself. The more knowledgeable man was the "father" not simply because he had authority but because he was willing and able to confer some of that authority upon another. The shipyard had devised a model of a father-and-son relationship based on work, skill, and usefulness, not on the monopoly and control of power. It was a model not much in evidence in the world beyond its gates.

"There's a lot of lip service to the principle of taking care of your people and a lot less action than used to be the practice," the shipyard commander, Captain John Pickering, said to me in his office one day, with barely contained anger. It upset him whenever he thought of the many politicians who had promised to save the shipyard from closure and then had sat on their hands. Here, he said, taking care had a very specific meaning. "Taking care of your people doesn't mean being nice to them. It means teaching them what they need to know."

Now, with the shipyard closing, what kind of authority could the "fathers" confer upon their adopted "sons"? That was a question that weighed heavily on men like Dennis Swann. As project superintendent on the *Kinkaid*, he had mapped out the plan of attack for the overhaul and made sure that everyone was working in concert. He also spent his

time, even his evenings at home, hunting down job leads for his men
and helping them compile their résumés, especially the laborers, whose
work didn't translate easily into any other job. He saw to it that ten
applications were driven over to Barstow and Bakersfield, six hours round
trip. And when he was on the ship, he found himself drawing the men
out, "getting down to the deck plates," as he called it. "I'd go out and
talk to them, and not necessarily about work. It was more, 'How's your
wife?' 'When are you going to have that baby—and where's my cigar?'
We'd have little barbecues on the pier." He stopped and laughed. "I bet
I bought close to a million doughnuts on that job!"

Such efforts at communal support baffled the career-transition counselors in the Black Box. "If one guy qualifies for some money [to retrain],
then right away he wants all the other guys to have it," Allison Renshaw,
a counselor, told me with a go-figure shrug. "And then we'll get flooded
with calls the next day," Kim Slany, another counselor, put in, "and every
one will be, 'My friend said I should ask you . . .'" One man found a
truck-driving job—and told all his friends to apply. A supervisor came
in looking for jobs for everyone but himself. A boilermaker found an ad
for a boilermaker, and told the rest of the men in his shop. "I said to
him, 'Don't you think you shouldn't share that?'" Kim Slany recalled.
"And he said, 'Let the best man win!' It's like they all want to protect
each other."

In a perverse way, closing the shipyard would call on the capacity that
underlay all their technical skills. "You've got a shipyard that's the best
at what it does," Kurt Leonard, operations officer–cum–human-resources
director, said to me one afternoon. "You've got a shipyard that has now
refocused on helping people. And we intend to be the best at *that*."

Behind those words it was impossible not to hear the deeper conviction: if they could do that, they could go out as men.

What Is It Really That I Do?

LIKE THE SHIPYARD WORKERS, the workforce at Douglas Aircraft had
had a clear and monumental mission when their plant joined the "arsenal
of democracy" in 1941, and like the shipyard, Douglas fulfilled its wartime
mandate with heroic vigor in what a local historian would rightly describe
as "one of the great home front performances of the war."[29] Douglas's
Long Beach plant, the nation's largest wartime civilian employer, with a
total of 175,000 workers, became the first in the world to build $1 billion
worth of aircraft over the course of the war: 9,441 planes, or about 11 a
day. Eisenhower called Douglas's DC-3 design, which was turned into
the C-47 military transport and used by all the Allies, essential to winning

the war; and the British and the Russians credited Douglas's A-20 planes with winning, respectively, the Battle of Britain and the Battle of Stalingrad.[30]

Ernie Pyle dubbed the wartime aircraft workers who poured in from the south "Aviation Okies," and surely their effort was in the valiant tradition of the Dust Bowl men who set their muscle behind the New Deal's vast civil projects and the GIs who slogged through the mud of Europe and Asia. Except for one small detail: at Douglas Aircraft, 87 percent of the wartime workers were women.[31] The Long Beach plant, as McDonnell Douglas spokesman John Thom put it to me, was where "Rosie the Riveter was practically invented." Women produced Douglas's greatest moment in the sun.

When Douglas retooled for peace, its first step, replicated by purges throughout the war industries, was a mass firing of its female factory workers.[32] Restaffed with men, Douglas continued to produce, along with commercial aircraft, the bombers, jet fighters, and rockets that the military and government had decided they would need to wage the cold war—if not to defend the nation from attack, then at least to offer a massive display of airborne dominance. Male veterans, many armed with technical training or college degrees earned with GI Bill funding, flooded the plant gates and moved en masse into Lakewood, the brand-new federally subsidized suburb next door. There, the veterans didn't even need a down payment, thanks to federally guaranteed loans, and fifty dollars covered a monthly mortgage.[33]

The postwar Douglas man had a home of his own, a decent wage to provide for his family, and secure membership in what the company chieftains proclaimed and its employees soon agreed was the "Douglas family." Douglas was known for the value it placed on length of service, on loyalty. And when the company merged with McDonnell Aircraft Company in 1967 to become one of the world's largest military suppliers, the men felt even more confident that they had signed on to a dynasty; they were told they had a guaranteed place at the Douglas family table— and, because of it, a secure place at the head of the family table at home.

Aerospace was one of the nation's biggest manufacturing employers by 1968, and the men pouring into the industry had faith in the mission and its promise—a promise that the former men of McDonnell Douglas still cling to.[34] Seated at the outplacement center's hand-me-down "boardroom" table, Ron Smith recalled with relish the thrill of being part of "something big." When he joined, "it was like you were on top of the world. I thought to myself, Wow, I'm going to be here the rest of my life." Glenn Wisniewski, an electronics engineer laid off in 1990, felt both elevated and anchored in the knowledge that he was "part of a system" that was "like a family," a system where they were "all in it together." The way these men understood it, the aerospace system was an extension of the New Deal, only bigger and better, guaranteed to boost men into a higher economic orbit. The postwar nation was becoming more white collar, less industrial, and it seemed as if the change could only be salutary for the men "rising" into the government-supported white-collar ranks.[35] James Lawrence, a former McDonnell Douglas systems engineer, told me, "The aerospace system was set up the same way as the work programs of the thirties and forties, as the WPA was set up by the Democrats—to set up jobs. All they did is take a blue-collar network and restructure it to advance a white-collar one. That is what aerospace is."

"Back in the fifties," Lawrence summed it up, "a man was able to be a man—and the government supported that."

But if McDonnell Douglas was a "family," then who did the men in the family imagine themselves to be? What was their relationship to each other? Did they see themselves, as in the case of the shipyard, as fathers and sons, or were they "family" relations of an entirely different sort?

Even in that first sunny postwar decade, an uneasiness nightwalked on the creaking floorboards of the corporate dream house. Doubts prowled beneath the presidential encomiums and the commercial testimonials and the press tributes to a young, vibrant nation of men moving ever upwards. Even the men who so wanted to believe, whose very ability to be men was riding on that belief, were beginning to suspect that the postwar passage to manhood through the bureaucratic corridors of corporate and defense America was not all it was cracked up to be; that the emerging national security state seemed to be producing a host of unexpected insecurities for the men who worked inside its garrisons. In the 1950s, such anxieties would find expression in a sudden spurt of popular books about the "soft" and nervously "other-directed" corporate man, most famously William Whyte's *The Organization Man,* David Riesman's *The Lonely Crowd,* and, more radically, C. Wright Mills's *White Collar.* "Today the man is the shadow of the firm," Riesman wrote in 1950. In the new work institution, Whyte observed, "not specific work itself, but the managing of *other* people's work is to be the goal," and ambition was channeled into glad-handing and the seeking of approval. This "new Little Man," as Mills dubbed the postwar white-collar worker in 1951, deluded himself that he was ascending the corporate ladder when he was just one of many "assistants of authorities." "He is always somebody's man, the corporation's, the government's, the army's," Mills wrote, "and he is seen as the man who does not rise."[36]

The prevalence of such qualities in modern business life were not, of course, new; the employee whose future is dictated more by "personality" than craft surfaced within the organizational fiefdoms of the industrial nineteenth century, and the eager-to-please junior executive was a familiar fixture of early-twentieth-century Babbittry; Bruce Barton's bestseller of the mid-1920s, *The Man Nobody Knows,* even envisioned Jesus as a corporate comer who got ahead on charm alone. Still earlier, Theodore Dreiser's late-Victorian novel *Sister Carrie* described such emergent types as the retail manager—whose success depended on his capacity to "greet personally with a 'Well, old fellow'" the many men he didn't actually know—and the "drummer"—a salesman for whom "good clothes, of course, were the first essential, the things without which he was nothing."[37] Nonetheless, the postwar social critics weren't wrong to suspect that working life in corporate America had reached a watershed, and you didn't have to be white collar to suffer the effects.

Richard Matheson came home from World War II in 1945, discharged with a 50 percent disability. He had slogged across Europe in the 87th Acorn division, the "trench foot division," as he called it because of the large numbers of men whose feet were devastated by icy marches in broken-down boots. Matheson nearly lost his feet. He was eighteen. After his discharge, he returned home to Brooklyn, but with the gearing up of the cold war, he moved to California. By 1951, he was working for Douglas Aircraft. "I cut out airplane parts," he recalled as we sat in his pleasant San Fernando Valley home in a foliage-cloaked gated community, surroundings made possible by a writing career that Matheson embarked on after aerospace. "It was like cutting cloth for skirts." He had no particular training. "They were so busy, they'd hire anyone. It's amazing Douglas didn't crash, because no one knew what they were doing. It was all these amateurs." Nor did they know where what they were doing fit into the larger project. "You never saw anything close to an airplane, just a bolt or a piece of metal. You never even saw the constructing of the little parts."

Matheson found a way to create his own custom product, in his head. "I wrote an entire short story under my [welding] mask," he recalled. A year later, he quit and moved to Long Island to work for his brother. In his spare time, he began work on a story "about a man living alone, isolated in a world where a virus had turned everyone to vampires," which would eventually become his 1954 novel *I Am Legend.* A few years later, as he was sitting in his cellar one day, another novel began to take shape. He thought about his father, a Norwegian merchant marine who knew how to "pitch sails in a storm," who came to the United States, found himself installing tiles, deserted his family when Matheson was very young, and died when his son was sixteen—a man "I barely knew." Matheson thought about men like his father, "diminished as men because they couldn't practice their craft" and about the war that had brought women into the workforce and, in his view, "began the social diminishment of men." He remembered a scene in a movie comedy with Aldo Ray and Jane Wyman, where a man puts an oversized hat on his head and it slips down below his ears. And as he sat in his basement and watched a spider weave a web in a shadowy corner, the plot for a novel emerged. He called it *Shrinking Man*. Gold Medal, his pulp publisher, added a "The" to the title. "They didn't want it to apply so generally," he recalled wryly, arching an eyebrow. "They weren't looking for philosophy at Gold Medal." Then Hollywood tacked on the adjective "Incredible," as if to reassure viewers that this was science fiction, not something that would apply to any moviegoers personally.

To Matheson, though, there was nothing incredible about the story. "My characters," he said, "are always about me." An anguished "me." In a futurist short story he published in 1952, "Brother to the Machine," his hero ruminates on a life spent working beneath the supervision of managers hovering overhead in "control ships": "To be a man, he thought. No longer is it a blessing, a pride, a gift. To be brother to the machine, used and broken by invisible men who kept their eyes on poles and their fists bunched on ships that hung over all their heads, waiting to strike at opposition. When it came to you one day that this was so, you saw there was no reason to go on with it."[38]

In a 1989 introduction to an anthology of his short stories, Matheson would observe of his 1950s work: "During this period, my stories were deeply imbued with a sense of anxiety, of fear of the unknown, of a world too complicated which expected too much of individual males. . . . Add to this another aspect of my paranoic leitmotif: the inability of others to understand the male protagonist, to give him proper recognition."[39]

The queasy sense of having too much expected of you as an individual man while being expected to conform, of being monitored and manipulated by "invisible men" yet not understood by them, was prevalent at McDonnell Douglas, as at many of the new technocratic and bureaucratic institutions that came to dominate the postwar workplace. "The boss as an influence disapppears as a person," sociologist Richard Sennett wrote of this managerial sea change in his book *Authority;* the employees find themselves "reacting to blankness on the faces of those in control."[40]

On the surface, said Richard Foster, who came to McDonnell Douglas in the late sixties to work on the NASA space lab, life as an aerospace man seemed to offer the ultimate in masculine freedom and self-sufficiency. "It was idyllic," he told me. "All these little green lawns and houses all in a row. You could drive the freeways and plan your life out." But as time went on, he came to feel that it had all been planned without him, that he was expected to take the initiative in a game in which he was not even a player. "You began to feel so isolated," he said. Like the rest of the managers, he "belonged" to the company in only the most tenuous way. In the end, his individual performance proved of no consequence to the institution. He would wind up being a casualty of corporate "cost reduction" programs five times, his salary plunging in those multiple layoffs from $80,000 to $28,000 to zero. Which was why he was sitting in a vinyl banquette in a chain restaurant in the shadow of McDonnell Douglas's blue-glass tower in the middle of the afternoon, talking to me. "The next thing you know," he said, "you're standing outside, looking in. And you begin to ask, as a man, what is my role? What is it, really, that I *do?*" By the mid-nineties, he was working for a leasing company that financed office equipment: "I sell money," he said, and his face flushed with discomfort.

However little control old-fashioned factory workers had over company policy, they at least knew that their work was tangible, their skill connected to the company's fortunes. In the cold-war world of aerospace, that connection was often severed. Profit was indexed to overly generous government contracts and predictable cost overruns more than to elbow grease. For many years, the lack of competition and inflated overhead charges to the federal government assured aerospace companies like McDonnell Douglas predetermined profits in the range of 12 percent and upward over their costs, and if the workmanship didn't measure up, all the better: the government would give the company a repair contract, letting it draw a profit twice.[41] It was hard for a man to feel essential when man-hours were just another billing tool.

"You'd have a large number of the workforce standing around," said Douglas Griffith, the president of United Auto Workers Local 148, the largest union at the Long Beach plant, in an unusually frank interview with a local newspaper in 1990. "And they're not goofing off. For the most part, they're waiting for job assignments, because management has not empowered them to go over to the next job, which they should be able to do themselves. . . . Half the time they're waiting for supervisors to tell them something that they already know. It's the craziest system I've ever seen in my life."[42]

McDonnell Douglas was an exemplar of the new ethic of managerial monitoring: it had eleven layers of management, filled with men whose primary tasks seemed to be, like that of the futuristic managers in Matheson's "control ship," all about surveillance.[43] They spent their days evaluating and correcting employees on the basis of criteria that were rarely disclosed or explained. "There was more information withheld at McDonnell Douglas than any company I've ever worked for," a former employee at the outplacement center asserted one afternoon as a group of us sat around the boardroom table, and the other men nodded in pained agreement. As former McDonnell Douglas communications director G. J. Meyer recalled in his memoir *Executive Blues,* the company's employees found themselves "shuffling from one day to the next in a kind of low-grade depression governed by an immense body of obscure rules. There were rules about everything, but most of them were invisible until you collided with them." (One of Meyer's collisions occurred while jogging along the company drive; security men swooped down and upbraided him for two violations: running on McDonnell Douglas property and wearing short pants.)[44]

To lessen the resentment of men who sensed that all control rested in the hands of faceless authorities, the company engaged in periodic, increasingly touchy-feely "employee empowerment" campaigns whose hollowness served only to escalate resentment. These began with the "I'm Involved" program of the 1970s, which amounted to the solicitation of worker contributions to a high-school-style suggestion box. "Five Keys to Self Renewal" followed. It was supposed to promote ethical management but functioned largely as a corporate loyalty test for employees.[45] Such efforts culminated in the late 1980s in Total Quality Management, that Holy Grail of postwar management philosophy that grew out of ideas developed by management guru W. Edwards Deming to improve productivity by eliminating fear and intimidation from the corporate environment and by junking phony corporate sloganeering. Deming's ideas were originally applied in Japan. As reenvisioned by American corporate executives in the 1980s, however, Total Quality Management often became a mystifying and fear-inspiring cult in which slogans about "empowerment" substituted for real authority and advancement.[46]

In February 1989, chief executive John McDonnell, the founder's son, unveiled a McDonnell Douglas Total Quality Management System, or TQMS, hailing it as a program to give employees more of a sense of "authority," to view themselves as "teammates" rather than subordinates, and to "get everybody at McDonnell Douglas to act like an owner." The company had an odd way of underscoring this emphasis on teamwork. It promptly summoned fifty-two hundred managers to a paint hangar to tell them they had lost their jobs and would have to reapply for them by proving their team-playing abilities to a panel of judges after engaging in two weeks of role-playing sessions. Half of management at Long Beach lost their jobs this way, among them strategic planner James Douglas, the son of Douglas Aircraft's founder, Donald Douglas, who was laid off after thirty years of service. He sent a letter to John McDonnell, asking him to reconsider. "He never wrote back," Douglas said. Less than a year after advertising that it was eliminating fear from the workplace, McDonnell Douglas announced a mass layoff. Amid the chaos spawned by TQMS, positions sat vacant for months, production lagged, jobs fell behind schedule, and losses mounted. Over the next two years, McDonnell Douglas lost $344 million.[47] Around the company, TQMS became known as "Time to Quit and Move to Seattle" (an allusion to the location of Boeing's corporate headquarters). By 1991, the company had discontinued any notion of TQMS "teamwork" and fallen back on its old manager-heavy organizational style. Executives announced that TQMS had failed because managers had been too "permissive" — and a crackdown ensued. Complaints proliferated about "repressive" and "militaristic" bosses. "Douglas essentially is operating under an authoritarian form of management," the trade magazine *Aviation Week & Space Technology* concluded at the end of 1991.[48]

Authoritarianism was just the other side of paternalism's coin. Whether the manager played permissive pop or martial commander, the problem remained the same: the men who managed had nothing real to offer the men they managed. They had nothing to teach; they could only threaten or coddle. The men I interviewed from McDonnell Douglas never talked about their superiors the way the shipyard men did — most never talked about them at all. Their supervisors had been middle managers with no real authority and no real body of knowledge to impart, a problem that extended all the way down to the factory floor. "Many of the supervisors who are today trying to look over somebody's shoulder to see how to shoot rivets," UAW local president Douglas Griffiths observed, "don't have the vaguest idea of how to shoot a rivet."[49] The managers weren't "fathers"; they were hall monitors — or worse. McDonnell Douglas, G. J. Meyer concluded in *Executive Blues,* was a "gulag" with "generously compensated inmates."[50] If the company was a "family," then the relationship between managers and managed men most closely resembled the relationship between a controlling, remote husband and his alternately cosseted and corseted wife.

The men deprived of mastery were compensated with titles and ersatz status. The company, like the Wizard of Oz, would fish up from its black bag fancy titles and arbitrarily bestow them on its supplicants. Its all-purpose honorific, dispensed as indiscriminately and meaninglessly as so many of the service medals were in Vietnam, was "engineer." There were, of course, actual McDonnell Douglas engineers, particularly in the plane-assembly plants, but they were vastly outnumbered by men whose engineering duties seemed less applied than appliquéd.

Outplacement center job counselor Jean Berry delicately broached this subject one morning in a "skills transference" class, as she passed around the *Dictionary of Occupational Titles* and asked the men to look up their skills and see what their position would be called in "the real world." If they were to find work, she said, they must first relinquish the inflated titles that McDonnell Douglas had conferred upon them. "So many people were walking around in three-piece suits calling themselves engineers at Douglas," she said, "because Douglas called them engineers. 'Engineers' without an engineering degree. So a lot of people were crushed in 1990 when they started looking around and they found out 'I'm not an engineer.' "

At the outplacement center, the middling ranks of McDonnell Douglas—the planners, the engineers, the managers—rarely spoke of their lost work. They talked to me of their lost paychecks, their lost cars, the lost square footage of the split-level ranches they once owned, but not of what they had contributed to the company's fortunes. When I asked electronics engineer Glenn Wisniewski what he valued most about his years at McDonnell Douglas, he launched into a detailed description of his house: $425,000 with a view! Four bedrooms! Three garages! A swimming pool *and* a spa! After the layoff and a fruitless job search, the $425,000 dream house "was auctioned right out from under me," Wisniewski said bitterly. The "engineers" skirted around the subject of their actual duties at McDonnell Douglas, as if to shine a light there too brightly was to reveal a man much smaller than the one they imagined would be driving a BMW and living in a four-bedroom house. Their résumés were full of impenetrable, hollow verbs: they "expedited" and "coordinated" and "facilitated." Yet they never seemed to have conducted an actual task. They maintained their usefulness with an indignant vehemence, but they could not say for sure what it amounted to—

and whether it vanished into thin air the moment they took off their company badges.

With their value to the company in doubt, making clear the distance between themselves and their blue-collar peers became all the more important. They didn't "make" anything, but they did make more money, even if the line was often paper thin and, since 1990, subject to evaporation. The term "mass layoff" made the McDonnell Douglas men cringe; their middle-class status should have lifted them above "mass" anything, distinguished them from the laboring mob. When I asked systems engineer James Lawrence if he was planning to attend a mandated retraining session, he protested, "I'm not a blue-collar, on-the-job type guy. I don't understand the applicability. Unless the whole point of this program is to take high-level people like me and put me down with the workers." He leaned forward to push the words into my face: " 'You're going to be a worker, like it or not!' It's systematic. They're breaking our backs, morally, financially, every which way. . . . In another two decades, there will be no middle class in America."

In place of a master-apprentice relationship, the engineers of McDonnell Douglas had a trademark relationship with their employer. They clung to their corporate identity, their McDonnell Douglas tie pins and the miniature silver airplanes they wore on their lapels with Masonic devotion. They often seemed, as the outplacement counselors observed, more strongly affiliated with the "Douglas Family" than with their own, but it was an affiliation grounded in consumption, not production.

Allegiance to a purchased and decorative identity was a concept inculcated by the company itself. John McDonnell spent lavishly on a marketing firm to buff the company image in the midst of its late-1980s meltdown; the effort centered on the remodeling of the corporate logo. McDonnell Douglas also dangled a vast array of logo-ized trinkets before its employees in its well-stocked company store or as performance rewards. Performance itself was conflated with image enhancement. In 1988, the company urged employees to participate in its latest public-relations campaign: coming up with ways to cut the federal deficit. For their contribution, employees received "Modern American Patriot" certificates, lapel pins, and medallions with a facsimile signature of President Ronald Reagan.[51]

McDonnell Douglas, like much of the aerospace industry, like much of corporate America, was notable for its image-consciousness, especially as the company's problems became more publicly visible. After an engine fell off a DC-10 and 273 people plunged to their death in 1979,

McDonnell Douglas summoned a horde of reporters to the Imperial Ballroom in Chicago's Sheraton Center with the promise of "a major announcement concerning the DC-10 jetliner." It turned out to be the unveiling of a "multimillion-dollar communications campaign," which featured, as its showpiece, a commercial in which astronaut Charles "Pete" Conrad sang the plane's praises.[52]

"The importance of a company's image," Douglas president Robert Hood said, "cannot be overestimated.... The 'investment' a company has made in its image bank can be critically important." That "investment" did not, however, always come out of the company's pocket; McDonnell Douglas dunned the government millions of dollars for its publicity consultants and campaigns. In 1985, the company was even caught billing the Pentagon for the "communications campaign" it launched after the Chicago crash.[53] In the fall of 1993, as Douglas was laying off tens of thousands of employees to cut costs, government auditors disclosed that the company had billed taxpayers at least $55 million over five years for banquets, cocktail parties, horseback-riding expeditions, golf outings, entertainment, movies, orchestra tickets, and souvenir coffee mugs. The company even billed taxpayers $28,000 for the entertainment and drink charges it racked up at the navy's notorious 1991 Tailhook convention in Las Vegas.[54] Nonetheless, the company continued to wheedle for the corporate equivalent of pin money. Even as it was about to overrun the C-17 transport-plane program by more than $1 billion, it still managed to charm improper early payments from its everindulgent husband, the air force.[55]

The Pentagon pin money, like the coffee mugs and other promotional trinkets, was the hard currency of an ornamental existence that was strangely reminiscent of the "kept" status of the 1950s housewife—and of the many wives of its ornamental "engineers." A creation of the new suburban middle class, the company man's wife was typically a woman who had worked during the war and then quit. She had been bombarded by one of the nation's great peacetime propaganda campaigns to convince vast numbers of women that their newly won employment defiled their femininity, while buffing the living-room furniture enhanced it. Many marriages were made in haste between virtual strangers in those years of nesting fervor, particularly in the defense-industry-created suburbs across the country where everyone and everything was so strange and new. The newlyweds walked out of just-built churches into just-built "communities," unsure of whom they had on their arm or what sort of society they were entering, unsure of anything except the guarantee of a chance to play house in the sort of no-money-down tract house that a white-collar aerospace husband could afford on his company salary.

The housewife was an integral part of the aerospace formula, which began at the top, with the government-husband eager to display a glittering stable of fighter jets and missiles. It was a global version of conspicuous consumption meant to demonstrate just who wore the pants — and the six-guns — in any possible cold-war showdown on the world "stage." Just as the government's largesse supported the aerospace company in the style to which it had grown accustomed, just as the company supported its employees with honorary titles and take-home bonuses, so the McDonnell Douglas man played keeper to his newly dependent wife. She had an essential role at the end of the food chain of dependencies: her magnified helplessness was a crucial counterweight to her husband's helplessness on the job. She returned to him the manhood he lost at the office, and he bestowed on her the mantle of bourgeois, idle femininity. The stay-at-home wife could, however, confer only an ornamental masculinity on her husband, while he could only hand over to his shopping-happy spouse his paycheck for immediate expenditure on kitchen and laundry-room appliances. On the frontier of 1950s suburbia, the "real man" sought not to be home on the range but to put his wife in a home with a range. The couple engaged in the same tacit deal that the husband struck with his employer: her lifelong loyalty in exchange for his promise of lifelong economic security. She displayed her till-death-do-us-part commitment on her ring finger the way the McDonnell Douglas lifer wore his corporate wedding band — that tiny silver airplane — on his lapel. Like the marriage at the office, this was another relationship "for keeps" — as long as the paychecks kept rolling in each week.

That the aerospace wife was far more likely to be a full-time housewife than her shipyard counterpart was another indication that the shipyard and McDonnell Douglas stood on either side of a divide — between a utilitarian and an ornamental existence. The contest between utility and ornament was an age-old and blurry one. Certainly utility existed at McDonnell Douglas sufficient to produce airplanes, and it had been challenged by insurgent ornamentality even in some of the grimmest of Depression-era industries. But in a battle where difference in degree could become difference in kind, crucial changes were occurring.

As an ideal of manhood, utilitarian masculinity traditionally required that a man wrest something out of the raw materials of the physical world. "My own notion is that men need this direct connection with nature in work," the author Sherwood Anderson wrote in *Perhaps Women*, his 1931 jeremiad over the crippling effects that the rise of the machine was having on masculinity. "They need to touch materials with their hands. They need to form materials, need to make things with their own hands out of wood, clay, iron, etc. They need to own tools and handle tools. Not doing it, not being permitted to do it, does something to men. They all know it." With that utility, they possess "a certain power"; without it, Anderson wrote, "they become no good for women." Or as Willy Loman put it so succinctly in *Death of a Salesman,* "A man who can't handle tools is not a man."[56]

Another important aspect of such a masculinity was the importance of commanding the inner skills to work with materials. Workmanship generated a pride founded in the certainty that what you did bespoke a know-how not acquired overnight. "I was good at it" was a frequent statement that the shipyard men made to me about their work, a remark offered without inflection or posturing, just as a matter of unassailable fact, a truth on which a man's life could be securely founded. Out of that security grew authority—an authority based, as in the root meaning of the word, on having *authored* something productive.[57]

For all that, though, manhood of this sort rested on something more than tools, productivity, or authority: it wasn't the handwork that was essential so much as the whole idea of having skills that could be transferred to work critical to society and acknowledged for its public value. By this version of manhood, making things and serving the community were one and the same. This old utilitarian connection between handicraft and human-craft, between competence and community, was what allowed the shipyard men to apply their proficiency at industrial tasks to the social task of closing their base. The McDonnell Douglas middle managers had no such connections, no such abilities, and were imbued with no such confidence.

While he was still punching the clock at Douglas Aircraft in 1951, Richard Matheson, the author of *The Shrinking Man,* published a short story called "Clothes Make the Man." The protagonist was a publicist at an ad agency who refused to take off his suit, hat, or shoes because, he maintained, "Man isn't a man without his coat." When a fellow employee steals his hat, he finds he can no longer function. His condition quickly degenerates and ultimately he is replaced altogether by his suit, which assembles itself and goes off to work without him. His wife then leaves him for the suit, "telling all her friends the damn thing has more sex appeal than Charlie ever had."[58]

Many of the laid-off McDonnell Douglas men would have recognized the painful truth in this parable. After the company broke its vows to the company man, the dominoes of dependency continued to fall. As Mike Mulk, a senior industrial engineer at McDonnell Douglas, bitterly told the other members of the outplacement center's Job Club one afternoon, his twenty-year marriage was just the final casualty of his layoff. "My marriage fell apart like my relationship to management. I look back at that vow, it said rain or shine, in sickness and in health. I don't remember it saying not without a job. But I guess it did, because when the job fell off, so did she."

In the year that I visited at the outplacement center, most of the men I met would tell similar tales of abandonment. "She complained about stress from the layoff," Owen Benson said of his wife, who had divorced him after it became clear he couldn't find a replacement engineering job. "She complained about having to deal with uncertainty." She eventually got a job of her own, where she met another man. The end of the marriage plunged Benson into a pit of uncertainty that had no bottom. He quickly depleted his savings. He was now looking at what he called, delicately, "a shortage of food." For $4.75 an hour, he had worked for a while on the graveyard-shift assembly line at Pride Plastics, a factory that made plastic video cases. "My job was to close them up and put them in a box," he recalled, "but they would come out so fast, they would fall all over the floor and the guys would be yelling at me, like a scene from a Lucille Ball movie. My hands just didn't go fast enough." After that, he had drawn a paycheck as Mister Peanut. Dressed in a big brown-and-yellow shell, he handed out roasted-nut samples at grocery-store openings. "I enjoyed being Mister Peanut. At least I was able to give something to people."

Still and all, Owen Benson wasn't inclined to blame his former employers for his catastrophe. "I feel bad that there's not anything for us," he told me, "that there isn't any clear place for us to go. But I don't feel bad about aerospace."

In seeking the face of the elusive enemy who was bombing their lives to smithereens, the men at the outplacement center preferred to look anywhere but up. Top management (excepting, sometimes, the particular manager who had fired them) was regarded as a roaming husband who, any day now, would return to the hearth—and like Odysseus' Penelope, the ex–company men would still be here, loyally spinning and waiting. Whenever there were rumors that the company might get a new government contract, the men talked excitedly about being "taken back." Glenn Wisniewski was a regular fixture before the fax machine, forever sending out his résumé in response to classified ads he'd clipped, some so old the paper was yellowing. Watching him one day, Owen Benson told him that he'd heard it was wise to fax applications to job ads in the Sunday paper at once, because "the first one they get off the pile, that's who they look at."

Wisniewski shrugged. "I'm just updating them about my whereabouts, my address and all." He was just keeping busy, he said, "in this period of waiting."

With corporate management off limits and with the chain of dependence in tatters, the McDonnell Douglas men constructed a reverse chain: of blame. Unlike management, the women who had once depended on them and had now left their sides were not absolved. They were the traitors—even the ones who had stayed but slipped into their work shoes or, for that matter, any woman out there clasping a paycheck. As McDonnell Douglas ex-employee Bill Gersel announced at an outplacement-center group session one afternoon, he felt most humiliated by the fact that his wife was supporting the family now, operating a child-care business at their home. "Instead of getting up in the morning and putting my legs in my trousers, now I go to put my leg in and my wife's already there."

Most shaming to the company men were the women still holding down jobs at McDonnell Douglas. In the period of mass layoffs, federal labor officials reported a breathtakingly high level of sexual harassment and discrimination complaints pouring in from the company's Long Beach plant; more than 330 complaints had been filed in five years. Women reported that they were groped, leered at, even laid off for being pregnant. A federal judge in 1995 found "overwhelming evidence" of unwanted sexual advances and "significant evidence" of a hostile work environment.[59]

The men were anxious to lay down a clear line between themselves and the other sex, much as they sought to draw a thick boundary marker between themselves and their working-class colleagues. "They have all this resentment toward women," the center's director, Shirley Judd, said. They resented women abstractly for "taking their jobs away," and they resented individual women personally—wives, girlfriends—for having abandoned them. And while the resentment bred verbal tirades and physical violence, below the resentment lay a deeper well of shame and fear. So, on the one hand, the battered-women's shelters were reporting an increase in domestic violence, which they attributed in large part to the massive layoffs in the area's leading industry. On the other hand, what the outplacement center's staff saw was the men's fear. "This one guy," Shirley Judd recalled, "he was so scared of his wife and what she would do when she found out he was laid off, he actually moved here in his motor home. 'She'll do bodily harm to me,' he told me. He showed me this picture of her and she was tiny. But he said, 'Rest assured, Mrs. Judd, she's vicious.'" One woman, upon hearing of her husband's firing, threatened to toss him in the street. "She said he had to get out unless he found a job," Judd recalled. The only job he could find was cleaning offices and bathrooms in the middle of the night. He took it. A few weeks later, Judd ran into him at the center and he said, "My wife loves me again. I'm working."

The men's domestic worries sometimes seemed overdrawn to the outplacement center's staff. But more often than not, their worst fears of rejection were realized. "Many families split up," Judd said, "and usually, it's not the husband who leaves. In fact, I can't think of one." Neither could I.

The center played an unexpected role in this gender struggle, as a sort of demilitarized zone where it was safe for men to reveal their hostile feelings toward the opposite sex. "They are amazingly open with us about their anger over women," Judd said, even yanking away their job applications if they learned that the center's counselors were submitting a woman's application as well, as if this somehow constituted betrayal. "And yet," Judd said, "so many of them are coming to the center for female contact."

I encountered this contradictory state of mind in my conversations with James Lawrence, who was among the most eager of the men to lay his troubles on women, most especially on the women's movement. That he was speaking to a woman—and a feminist—didn't seem to faze him. Instead, he was gracious and solicitous, expressing heartfelt gratitude for my having "listened" to him and having allowed him to "open up." It was hard to fit this polite and apologetic man to his virulent words. But by "listening," nodding, and writing down those words, I had, I suspected, inadvertently adopted the role (as had the center's female staff) of the "right" kind of woman, the woman who would set his world right by reinstalling him in the manly position of the voice of authority.

"It's been a complete role reversal" was the first thing he said on sitting down at the center's boardroom table with me one afternoon. "One of the reasons I've been unemployed as long as I have is because I am not willing to give in to that." What his resistance to feminist advancement had to do with his lack of employment I didn't know, and I got little satisfaction in pressing him on the point. "The male gender has taken a backseat—across the board," he said, and that, in a fashion he couldn't explain, had somehow cost him his job. "Women have taken a very masculine role in American society. The way they dress, the way they wear their hair ..." He made chopping motions to signify a butch cut. Then he paused, offered a half apology: "Perhaps my vernacular comes across sometimes more denigrating than I mean it to be." But, that said, he picked right up with the denigrations: "The feminist movement has destroyed what was a perfect society with a few infractions. I'm just tired of being emasculated."

When I asked him how feminism has "emasculated" him, he answered by telling me about his marriage, which had recently ended in divorce. "All of a sudden, my wife became—I don't want to say the breadwinner, but the focal point of earning our living. She was serving both roles. And all of a sudden I'm trying to justify what my purpose is—and I couldn't. I'm trekking down this traditional path and she is taking a divergent path.... She was becoming more progressive and I was becoming more traditional. And she just found it easier to file for divorce."

Lawrence's qualms about his "role" in the face of his wife's working were made worse by the fact that she was working at McDonnell Douglas. When he lost his engineering job in 1991 and accepted another with Grumman, in Melbourne, Florida, she didn't want to give up her job or her life in California, so they lived separately for two years. He returned to California, hoping to revive the marriage, but when his new position at a flight school evaporated, his wife chastised him, he said, for not having gotten the job in writing; he began to drink "a little more beer," she accused him of being verbally abusive, "and the marriage went downhill from there." By the time she filed for divorce, he was facing bankruptcy. And somehow, he had fit together all of these pieces of his personal puzzle into a map of his life in which he could draw a straight line from feminism to divorce to bankruptcy. He had an engineer's preference for linear explanations.

"There is nothing for me," he told me one day. I had coaxed him out of the center for lunch, and we were sitting at a nearby golf-course restaurant. As he talked, we watched retired men in kelly-green trousers parking their golf carts, smoothing their Izod shirts, glancing at their reflections in the window with the satisfied air of those who have followed all the rules and been rewarded. It must have been a discomfiting sight for Lawrence and, though the location had been his choice, I was sorry we had come. "There is no move left," he told me, pushing around the remains of a lunch plate he was too young for, a retiree's meal of cottage cheese and stewed fruits. "Foreclosure is inevitable. Bankruptcy is inevitable. I feel a bit like Custer must have felt. My last stand ... There is no place for me to go."

Later that week, I was standing by the center's fax machine with

Glenn Wisniewski, watching the feeder consume each of the sheets on his tall stack, when Don Motta wandered by. I asked him how he was faring. "Not so good," he said. He had lost a temporary job "working with retarded people"—after one week. The city program had run out of funds. His wife had readmitted him to the house when he got the job, he said, and evicted him once more when he lost it. "She was mad because I wouldn't pay to have the house termited. But I don't have the money. My benefits run out next week." So she termited him.

After Don drifted on, one of the job counselors caught my eye. "You know about what happened with Don and the box?" she asked, lowering her voice. When I shook my head, she filled me in. Gayle Motta and her new boyfriend had pulled up in front of the center one day, wheels screeching as their van lurched to a halt. Gayle had leaped out, in her arms a small cardboard box. She yelled Don's name, heaved the box onto the curb, and jumped back into the van, which careened out of the lot. Inside the box, the staff found portraits of Don's parents, both of whom had died when he was young, and Don's dirty laundry. When I asked Gayle about this incident later, she explained that as humiliating as her appearance at the center must have been to her husband, she had been driven more by despair than cruelty: "I just kept looking at his dirty sheets and the dirty towels he uses over and over and over, and I just couldn't stand it anymore." When I asked her what else she had placed in the box, it turned out the counselor had forgotten to mention one proud possession of Don's: his McDonnell Douglas coffee mug.

People Need to Get Down to the Deck Plates

IN THE LATE 1980s, at the very time when McDonnell Douglas was in the throes of its last government-sponsored spending binge, the Long Beach Naval Shipyard was trimming its sails. Realizing its peril in a downsizing military (Long Beach city officials who met with the under-secretary of the navy reported back that the shipyard would only survive if it became "a lean, mean, producing machine"), and inspired by a new commander, Captain Larry Johnson, the shipyard launched its own pro-ductivity experiment, called "project management." It was a home-grown effort, planned by the men themselves, and it could not have been further from the Total Quality Management plans rampaging through corporate America. Power in the yard was reorganized around work tasks instead of occupational titles and categories. "We went from a hierarchy to a product-oriented structure," Kurt Leonard, then head of operations, recalled.

On each job, the heads of the shops, hitherto largely old-fashioned patriarchs who sometimes had ruled with iron fists (the "little gods," as the shipyard men had called them), ceded control to "project managers" whose mission was simply getting the job done, ship by ship—without defects, on time, and under budget. The project managers were chosen for their industrious past track records, their willingness to pitch in and do the dirtiest jobs in the ship's bowels, and the respect they drew from the other men. Power shifted downward, and the gap between labor and management narrowed substantially. Essentially, project management institutionalized the longstanding father-son dynamic undergirding the shipyard's professionalism and custom-tailored it so that the most dedicated fathers got elevated. Soon thereafter, the shipyard began to turn a profit.

In 1987, the shipyard commander selected the first project manager: Ike Burr, the former shipfitter and "father" to Rick Meza. Burr had recently been production head of the overhaul of the USS *David R. Ray*, where he was generally the first one down the hatch, crawling into the ship's dankest reaches with his men. The *Ray* had been finished in record time at a record low cost and Kurt Leonard, the repair officer for the project, had presented Burr with a handmade plaque, inscribed, "You said it could be done, and it was."

What struck me on first meeting Ike Burr was how he embodied his workplace. His aspect was unadorned, utilitarian, and laconic. His frame was tall and spare, his head shaved, and his words and movements pared to a point; his eyes warned off idle chatter. "I don't much care to get into people's inner zone," he told me more than once. "I'm pretty much of an authoritarian." By that, he didn't mean he relished domination, though I doubt many crossed him without trepidation; his look suggested a man who did not suffer fools. When I asked him if by "authoritarian," he meant being in control, he said: "For a man to feel he's in control of a certain situation, he has to know he *knows* certain things. It's not being 'in control' or 'not in control' of people. It's having a hand in what takes place."

As reluctant as Burr was to probe the "inner zone" of personal affairs, he could be voluble about the inner workings of a project. If you asked Burr to share how he "felt" when he first joined the shipyard, he would answer with the physical specifics of a job. "The *Bon Homme Richard* was my first ship," he told me, when I asked just that question. "I went in with the mechanic. I was in charge of putting in the cooling-element foundations, which were four feet wide by six feet long by four feet deep." His hands shaped the air as he spoke. He was recalling measurements from 1965.

"What was great about the *David Ray* was it was my first opportunity to run something," he told me the day we met, as we sat in his spit-polished office, "to have a vision of how something should be built that no one else had and then to go ahead and build it. When I said to management, 'Do you have any idea how you want to get this done?' they said, 'You tell us.' Big difference."

So when the shipyard commander asked Ike Burr to lead the trans-formation to project management at Long Beach, and later, when Burr was summoned to navy yards on both coasts to help them adopt the principles he had pioneered, this was a "big difference" for a man who had spent most of his work life relegated to the lesser-status shipfitting shop; especially big for a man whose boyhood in inner-city Los Angeles was plunged so deeply into hardship and disenfranchisement that, until his parents took him to visit Compton one day, "I didn't know blacks owned houses." Burr measured the distance he had come this way: "When I was raised, we had a house with a front door, a back door, and a bathroom door. Now I have a house and every room has a door on it."

Burr's deliverance came when he was eighteen, had started college but was struggling, and thought his future had hit a blank wall. "I was stand-ing on the street corner of Vernon and Broadway," he said of the for-tuitous encounter that led to a lifetime career. "A man was handing an application to his son. And because I was standing next to him, he gave another one to me."

The application was to take a math and physics test to qualify for an apprenticeship at the shipyard. About seven thousand men took the test; sixty-seven passed, and Ike Burr was one of them, ranking in the top group, which should have given him first pick of the trade of his choice. But when he asked to be trained as an electrician, he was told that the apprenticeship program was full. They then admitted several white elec-tricians the next day. Next he asked for welding—and again was turned down. "The apprentice instructor said, 'I think you'd be better as a ship-fitter.' " A year and a half later, a group of black shipyard workers filed a grievance against the instructor over the longstanding practice of bar-ring blacks from welding. After the complaint was filed, Ike Burr was suddenly approached and asked if he would like to become an electrician or a welder. "I said, no, I would stay where I'm at." He didn't like the way the apprentices in these trades were "treated like the help"; in ship-fitting, even though its heavy steel structural work was often backbreak-ing, "you were seen as smart" and had more "authority." His first year as a shipfitter's apprentice, he was "put in charge of all the air-conditioning foundations on an aircraft carrier."

Burr's hiring date was timely. The mid-1960s through the early 1970s was an era of racial transformation at the yard, motivated by worker discrimination complaints and a new shipyard commander committed to promoting minorities. The change would clear the way for men like J. B. Larkins, a shipfitter who had crusaded against racism in the yard, to rise to production superintendent and president of the Shipyard Employees Association; and it would open the door for men like Derrick May, a flat-broke postal worker who answered a shipyard ad for boiler-maker trainees. (When May's ailing car gave out the day of the job interview, he climbed on his bicycle and pedaled the thirty-five miles, arriving covered in sweat but with his tie still knotted.)

Ike Burr climbed steadily from foreman to general foreman to project superintendent. On his shipyard wages, he bought a house with a "non-functioning" swimming pool out back that he rebuilt himself. He supported two children and his wife, who left her job at May's department store. When his wife decided she wanted a degree in early child development, he paid her tuition at UCLA. When crime began encroaching, the couple moved their family twice, eventually buying a house in the suburbs far from Los Angeles; Burr's two-hour commute now began at 4 A.M.

"Everything you ever dreamed existed is here," Ike Burr told me one afternoon, in a rare loquacious moment. He wasn't, however, referring to the dream house in the suburbs, or the swimming pool out back. He was talking about the work itself. "Everything you ever dreamed of is *here*. The shipyard is like a world within itself. Most items are one-of-a-type items, done once and not to be repeated. There's satisfaction in it, because you start and complete something. You *see* what you've created. The world of custom-made is finished — except here."

With the rise of project management, the men who did the work rose with it. At the shipyard, that meant men like Ike Burr and Dennis Swann and Henry Cisneros, men who knew the guts of the ships better than anyone else because, delicious irony, that was the place to which their skin color had once consigned them. Henry Cisneros, who could weld inside curved pipes by looking in a series of mirrors and who was known in his shop as "The Hammer" (because "he always hammered it home"), got the top supervisory welding job on the USS *Tarawa* — where he continued to work "in the trenches with my team," and became the first supervisor in his field to get the job done under cost. His approach was typical. "Bottom line," as Dennis Swann described to me his own supervisory style, "you can't manage from the deck, not in a production world. People need to get down to the deck plates."

In a direct repudiation of modern corporate management theories, the men eliminated the occupational perquisites of general foremen, who had previously been denoted on the job by their distinctively colored hard hats. "Used to be, some general foremen wanted you to 'sir' them," Swann said. "Used to be, you'd see a general foreman, you'd run and hide!" Put in charge of the overhaul of the USS *Barbey,* Swann summoned the men into a meeting without their hard hats and said, "Look around. There are no hats in this room. When we get out there, it will be like there are no hats. And there will be no difference between the trades." He told them, "I wouldn't ask anybody to do something I wouldn't do." Swann wasn't sure how this would go over with the foremen or with the unions, but as it turned out, he said, still sounding a little amazed, "It worked." The repair of the USS *Barbey* miraculously made money for the government.

In 1988, Louis Rodriguez was elected union president of the International Federation of Professional and Technical Engineers, Local 174, which represented six hundred men, and he took as his mission the shipyard's rescue. Under the banner of "SOS," for "Save Our Shipyard," Rodriguez and his fellow workers went door to door all over southern California, collecting four hundred thousand signatures to present to Congress. He also went to Washington a half dozen times to go door to door in Congress and the Pentagon. He even secured an interview with Vice President Dan Quayle, who greeted him with "Well, what do you have to say, young man?" (Rodriguez was then in his mid-forties), and whose sum donation to the cause was an autograph for Rodriguez's daughter Chelsea and two vice presidential tie clips, which Rodriguez put to use: he wore one whenever he went to visit a Republican congressman.

As the threat of closure grew more dire, the men in the shipyard drew noticeably closer. The community feeling of the yard had traditionally been maintained within each shop or union local or ethnic enclave through an array of thriving social clubs—the Black Heritage Committee, the Hispanic Heritage Committee, and the Asian Pacific Islander Heritage Committee, to name a few. This was a tradition that stretched back to the 1940s, when wartime shipyard workers created mutual-aid "friendly societies" to tend to one another's financial, medical, and social needs.[60] Increasingly in the yard, each ethnic club's events drew a shipyard-wide attendance. "Originally, if you'd go to a black affair, it was all black," said Dennis Swann, who chaired the Black Heritage

Committee for three years, "and if you'd go to a Hispanic affair it was all Hispanic, and so forth. But the last few years, it became mixed. And everybody liked it so much more that these affairs became huge." Charlie Spohn, Swann's old mentor, became the first white worker to be honored by the Black Heritage Committee. The shipyard's final soiree, a Pacific Island luau, sold out all five hundred tickets, and the organizers chose a non-Islander shipyard employee to be their "Samoan princess." "What happened was that the ethnic groups became about honoring *other* groups," Elizabeth Crockett, the "princess," said, observing that this was at the heart of the shipyard's modern ethic. Even with the announcement that the shipyard's efforts at survival were for naught, that ethic prevailed. "My dad said to me, 'Always put yourself in a position where you are needed, not where you are in need,'" Louis Rodriguez told me. "I sit here and what keeps me going is I focus on other people's problems in the union. The shipyard has been a second family to me. When I get out of here, I'm really going to be lost as a whole. I will have lost my family."

One day I was shown around the adjacent (and also shuttered) naval base by a twenty-eight-year-veteran ship designer. Conservationists in Long Beach had been upset that the base's buildings, designed by the eminent black architect Paul Revere Williams, were to be bulldozed for a container terminal. The ship designer took me over to see them, but he wound up talking more about the plight of some herons that had set up nests in the trees around the imperiled buildings. "Black-crowned night herons, I think they are," he said. "They sit all day in front of Building One. If you take their homes away, they won't have anyplace to go." The shipyard men saw taking care of the herons as their responsibility, too, just as they took care of the giant mechanical cranes in the yard. "This past year," he said, "we had a problem with babies falling out of the nests. Some people went around and picked them up—and they were big babies!—and put them back in the nest."

Thinking of those birds and those men, something occurred to me about the differing "family" dynamics at the shipyard and at McDonnell Douglas. McDonnell Douglas had encouraged its male workers to base their manhood on a dependency that resembled a certain type of femininity: ornamental femininity. The company had issued them glittery titles and fancy nameplates and jewelry in the shape of jet fighters. And it had all turned to tin when they found the pink slips on their desks. At the Long Beach Naval Shipyard, the men had chosen to embrace a very different male ethic that also had a feminine counterpart: mothering. The shipyard was an expression of a sort of maternal masculinity.

They had taught each other how to be men by nurturing a society known as the shipyard, and in spite of the way the culture outside the yard's gates had insulted and betrayed them, they had endured as men in no small measure by relying on that talent for nurturance. Their manhood was pitched on an unassailable mother rock.

I'm Selling Myself Lower

I RETURNED TO THE MCDONNELL DOUGLAS outplacement center after a four-month hiatus in the fall of 1994, just before Halloween. I arrived too early, 7:45 A.M., but Glenn Wisniewski was already waiting for the doors to open. I knew he would be one of the last to leave when the doors closed that night. Wisniewski had been absent from the center for only one extended period in 1993, after he dislocated his shoulder trying to push his broken-down car—a car he was reduced to living in at one desperately low point. The resulting nerve damage left his arm hanging uselessly at his side, placed him on disability, and caused his temporary expulsion, because workers on disability weren't eligible to use the center's facilities. For Wisniewski, it was as if he had been laid off all over again, until one day over a year later Shirley Judd spotted him walking home from the Cerritos Mall and stopped to give him a ride. "She told me that they missed me, that a lot had changed . . . and that it was okay to use the center." He returned at once. On this morning, he showed me the thirty-four résumés he planned to fax today. "I'm selling myself lower," he said. He had dropped his final McDonnell Douglas salary by $10,000. He had had nine interviews over the summer. Only a couple were in aerospace. None produced jobs.

With the doors open, other familiar faces filtered in. It occurred to me that the center might well have less turnover than the average nineties corporation. The counselors were all still there, and still decorating for the season: a Halloween cardboard skeleton dangled over the fax machine, a noose around its neck. In the back room, the broken typewriter was still broken. The job board listed the same fare. The inspirational message taped over the Xerox machine had not been replaced: "The majority of us lead quiet unheralded lives as we pass through this world. There will most likely be no ticker-tape parades for us, no monuments created in our honor. . . . —Leo Buscaglia."

But some things were different. For one, the lumbering Don Motta was missing. No one wanted to talk about where he had gone, other than to say that he had suddenly vanished several months ago, and that I should ask someone else. The other change was posted over the sign-up sheet by the door. Not that I needed to read it: one after another, the regulars had hastened over to tell me the bad news, their voices edgy with anxiety. The center was moving. McDonnell Douglas wasn't going to support it anymore. The city would run the new facility—relocated, painfully enough, on Donald Douglas Drive—and it would be a career transition center for all displaced workers in Long Beach. After the move, only laid-off workers who could certify that they were victims of the changing job market would be admitted.

McDonnell Douglas's Long Beach spokesman, John Thom, offered me various official reasons for the company's withdrawal from funding the center: the layoffs had tailed off for the time being (it had been almost a year since the last one); at a certain point, a company has no obligations to its former workers, and so forth. But for the center's denizens, it was hard to ignore the timing of the forced exodus. As more than one man said acidly, McDonnell Douglas just didn't want a mournful band of company rejects dampening the enthusiasm of current employees who would soon begin visiting a facility the company was building right next door: a McDonnell Douglas company store. This retail outlet would sell McDonnell Douglas model planes, jackets, and coffee mugs. The construction crew was already outside, measuring, sawing, drilling, a reminder that after the move, the men could come back here only as consumers buying souvenirs emblazoned with a logo no longer theirs.

After several days of inquiry as to Don Motta's whereabouts, I was referred to Steve Williams, Don's closest confidant at the center. But Steve's car had broken down and he was off scraping together the money to have it fixed. When at last he arrived and I asked after Motta, Williams looked down at the floor. "Don's in—well, Don's in jail." He hastened to explain that it wasn't as bad as it sounded. Don had hit another car on a busy street, driven off, then stopped a few blocks later. "Apparently that qualifies as a hit-and-run," said Williams, who was clearly finding it hard to imagine the former PTA dad committing a vehicular crime. The other party had claimed to be injured and summoned the police. Now Motta was serving 180 days. Gayle Motta wouldn't post bail. She told me this had been his third smash-up of the year and she'd just had enough. In any case, between unpaid back taxes and overdue mortgage payments, she didn't think the money would be well spent on her husband's bail. "He's cost me too much already," she said. He was now incarcerated in the L.A. County Jail, Williams told me, "right there with O. J. Simpson," he added, sounding both impressed and horrified. Williams had not seen Don since the day of the arrest, nearly five months before.

I asked him if he wanted to come with me to the jail to visit Motta.

He agreed that he might, but seemed nervous and reluctant. "It's hard to picture Don in there."

Locking Up

IKE BURR POSTPONED FOR SOME TIME his official sign-out date at the shipyard. He had found another position at a southern California military installation, El Toro Marine Corps Air Station, and was always "too busy" to get back to Long Beach to turn in his badge. He was working as facilities manager, a temporary post, since El Toro, too, was closing. Nevertheless, one morning in late January of 1997, he took a day off and arrived at the shipyard to pay his last respects. He dressed sharp for the occasion: double-breasted gray suit, paisley tie and matching pocket hankie, even a hint of cologne. The morning management meeting was under way and he had been asked to stop by. He offered them a few pointers on work that he thought still needed to be done. Then Captain John Pickering, the shipyard commander, stood up and gave an impromptu speech—about how Burr was "a troubleshooter," how he "knew everything there was to know about project management," how he was the kind of guy "you could rely on to get the job done." Then Pickering handed Burr a homemade plaque with a lengthy inscription.

Burr tucked it under his arm, embarrassed by the attention. "I guess I better go get the signing-out business over," he said, his voice bumping over choppy seas. He headed out, his new dress shoes squeaking on the worn floors, to make the rounds and get his termination physical. The shipyard nurse declared him healthy, except for "moderate to severe hearing loss," a product of his years working around rivet guns. As he left, Burr ran into Rick Meza. He had signed up for retraining and was back in school learning computer-assisted design. We followed him upstairs to the computer room to look at the programs he and some fellow shipyard workers had already devised. A demonstration ensued of how you could click on any "building" in the "shipyard" and find what was inside. Ike Burr stood a few paces off, watching with his arms crossed, clearly skeptical. After we left the room, I asked Burr what he thought. "It's just games," he said, his voice clipped. "It's not the same as seeing for yourself." Not that there was anything left to see. All around us, what once had been work was now virtual reality.

By late afternoon, Ike Burr had arrived at his final stop, a small office where he was to sign a form surrendering his code word that gave him access to the yard. Though he burst out laughing as he signed, his words belied the laughter. "I have nothing in my possession," he said. "I have lost everything."

The day was over. Burr stopped at the shipyard employee club for a beer and a farewell. The room was filled with familiar faces. We joined a table where top shipyard executive John Pfeiffer was seated with a handful of old stalwarts. Burr lingered awhile to talk before gathering up his things. He wanted to make one last stop at his office before leaving. We drove over to the Excess Labor shop and made our way down its darkened, deserted passageways, our footsteps clanging like struck gongs. The silence roared around us. Burr snapped on the light in his office, which was now someone else's. He looked around, declared it "messy," pulled open a file-cabinet drawer and rummaged for some papers. He emerged from the depths with several rolled-up blueprints, knelt on the floor, and unfurled one of them. The sheet of paper—a "Flood Effect Diagram" of a battleship, composed, as a stamp at its bottom noted, in March 1944—took up a quarter of the room. "Now, that's something real," he declared as he stooped to inspect its finely drawn lines.

Burr locked up the building and walked me to my car. As I started to say a consoling good-bye, he pulled out a blueprint of the shipyard, perfectly rendered down to its tiniest detail. "Keep this." He thrust it at me, then hurried off to his pickup. Like he said, he didn't "much care to get into people's inner zone," his own least of all.

———

A WEEK BEFORE THANKSGIVING 1994, Steve Williams and I drove down to the L.A. County Jail to see Don Motta. It was a Saturday and the visitors' entrance was mobbed. A half hour in a line outdoors got us into a second line in the lobby, at the end of which we received a number and were told it would take two to five hours before it was our turn. "All these men in jail," Williams murmured, aghast. He became increasingly fidgety and agitated as the time wore on. What condition would we find Don in, he wondered. I wondered, too; I couldn't imagine Don with those sad magnified eyes behind his owlish glasses in such a place. But Williams was also anxious, he confided, about what he would say to Don. What if he "ran out of things to talk about" before the time was up? I realized that while Steve Williams might have been Don's best friend at the center, McDonnell Douglas ties didn't run that deep. I began to feel guilty about having dragged him along.

When at last Don's name was called in a list of names, we surged forward with thirty other visitors and were ushered into a long, narrow room lined with cubicles that faced a soundproof wall punctuated with soundproof windows. In one of these, we took our places for a strictly timed twenty-minute session. Don appeared in the window, carrying a copy of the Bible—and looking better than I'd ever seen him. The phones by which we were to communicate didn't work for five minutes, and so we held up signs, telling Don that he was missed at the center. He smiled and nodded serenely. For once, there were no tears behind the smile. The phones were finally switched on and I asked Don about the accident. But the accident was old news for Don; he was far more eager to tell me about his life in jail, especially his position as a prison trusty. He was working in the clinic and in the cafeteria. He wore a different-colored shirt as a trusty, a cut above the inmate masses. "The deputies say to me, 'We don't know why you're here!' " They "respected" him, he said. "It's not all bad here."

I reluctantly handed the phone over to Steve Williams, who even more reluctantly took it. He peered at his friend through the smudged glass barrier. "Since you saw me last, I have not had a position," Steve began hurriedly. "In fact, I'm looking at poverty in January." Then he hastened onto the common ground of news about the center moving, about who hadn't found a job, and what changes had been made to the decor. "Were you there since they put the new wall in?" Steve asked Don. The inmate shook his head. "Yeah, well," Steve said, "it's a pretty good arrangement. It makes it more like an office."

By the time Steve finished recounting the details of the center's home improvements, our twenty minutes were up and the phone went dead. I scribbled down a last question on a piece of paper and held it up to the window. "Is going to jail worse or better than being laid off from McDonnell Douglas?" Don pointed at "better," smiled, and then vanished.

Later, Don's wife, Gayle, told me that he could have applied for release two months earlier for time served but had declined. "He wants to stay in jail," she said, marveling. In his letters home to her, "he would tell me all about his work there in the cafeteria, how he takes care of guys in the infirmary, what time he reports to work in the morning, how many hours he's worked. It's weird."

But it didn't seem so weird to Steve and me as we drove back toward Long Beach that afternoon. "Don looked really good," Steve commented. I agreed, and we discussed how his face had color, his weight was down, how he had squared his shoulders with a bit of pride. I thought I understood what had changed. Within those walls, he had found an economic security lacking in "the real world." The county jail, in this one respect, served much the same function for Don Motta as the McDonnell Douglas Outplacement Center, only better. At the jail, he could not be locked out, only in. He didn't have to leave when the staff secured the door for the night. Don Motta had found a job.

3

GIRLS HAVE ALL THE POWER

What's Troubling Troubled Boys

IT'S NO COINCIDENCE that the same southern California territory that was producing economic despair for the nation's fathers was also producing turmoil for their sons. To those sons, it must have seemed as if the entire world of their fathers was contracting into the miniaturized "reality" of a computer-assisted software program. All around them, the steaming, clanking apparatus of industry was falling silent; the aerospace armies were decamping from their once sleek, reflective compounds; the abandoned armament of shuttered military bases was corroding like the broken statuary of Babylon. In Los Angeles, the shiniest monument to a rising generation of young men was Twin Towers, the massive new men's jail, built in the heart of the downtown business district.

If the years following World War II had crafted a new image of the American boy as a youth of promise, cocksure and slightly vulgar in his tail-finned convertible yet fueled with all the energy and moral vigor of the postwar moment, then that era also birthed an alternate image—the wholesome teenager's malevolent, unredeemable twin. Literary critic Leslie Fiedler famously dubbed the former "the Good Bad Boy"; his ancestors stretched back to Tom Sawyer and forward to Beaver and Wally Cleaver. He was "America's vision of itself," Fiedler wrote, "crude and unruly in his beginnings, but endowed by his creator with an instinctive sense of what is right."[1] By the early 1950s, though, a darker vision of what America promised began to form around the figure of the Bad Bad Boy. No apple-cheeked rascal following the moral compass of his unflecked soul, he was the subject of alarmist newsreels, magazine and newspaper stories, and TV specials, which painted a lurid picture of the "brutal" criminality and predatory sexuality of this new "juvenile delinquent." Congressional hearings and government investigations decried the alleged rise in his delinquency, which they attributed, variously, to the influence of marijuana, violent horror comic books, or Communism. Public polls rated the delinquent as a greater blight than segregated schools or the open-air testing of atomic weapons.[2]

In fact, the juvenile-crime epidemic of the fifties was largely a product of the public's fevered imagination, the statistical evidence grossly inflated by arrests for "joyriding" as well as curfew and traffic violations.[3] What really threatened was the way the Bad Bad Boy seemed to be hijacking an emerging popular culture and using it to thumb his nose at his father's generation; Marlon Brando's scowl and Elvis Presley's thrusting pelvis appeared to be telling their elders to get lost. "Teenagers, by erecting barriers of fashion and custom around adolescence, had walled off a secret and potentially antagonistic area of American culture," historian James Gilbert wrote in his study of the 1950s youth-crime panic, *A Cycle of Outrage*.[4] Or maybe the culture was walling off the teenagers. Already, merchandisers and movie makers were discovering what a potentially fast-selling ornament the smirking male adolescent could be. In any case, the Bad Bad Boy was becoming a masculine image for a younger generation to emulate, if only by purchasing a leather jacket.

With much fanfare, the fawned-over sons of the postwar generation had been handed the keys to the kingdom, and for a while they reveled in their prosperity. But decades later they would discover that the keys hadn't unlocked much more than the door to the Chevy and the entrance to a shopping mall. If they fortressed themselves in a store-bought world of Jerry Lee Lewis records and *High School Hellcats* movies, in retrospect they would see their kingdom as closer to a commercial prison. Even their rebellions incarcerated them, as their anger was turned into pop tunes and films and fashion even as it was condemned.

By century's end, they would be blamed for seemingly everything that went wrong, even by the culture that transformed their renegade style into profitable commodities. The nation's eyes turned with renewed outrage toward the Bad Bad Boy that the culture had spawned—if America's shiny vision had gone rotten, he was the suspected worm at its core.

We Could've Been Big

IT WAS LONG PAST LUNCHTIME on a weekday in early October, but Kris Belman had been awake for only a couple of hours. The nineteen-year-old with the dazed, shaggy surfer looks had risen, as was his custom, at noon. He had nowhere in particular to go. He had graduated from high school the previous spring—the spring of 1993—though he wouldn't get his diploma until he paid a $44 fine for ripping his football jersey. "I'm only paying it if I get my jersey back," he said. He hadn't been able to find a job, except for "picking up scraps for this guy who hangs dry wall," and that only lasted three days. In Lakewood, a bedroom community built to house tens of thousands of McDonnell Douglas workers, and later workers at aerospace firms like Rockwell (now closed) and nearby Northrop and Hughes (where thousands were being laid off), not to speak of all the companies that once supplied and serviced them, there was little work left to justify getting out of bed.[5]

He was home alone; his father, a salesman for an aerospace vendor whose prime contractor was McDonnell Douglas, was out and his mother had moved out after his parents' separation earlier that year. His older brother was off wandering, probably in search of gambling "action." Kris Belman stepped into a pair of baggy shorts and ventured forth into the flat grid of stucco-over-chicken-wire pillbox houses and browning lawns, looking for signs of life. The sidewalks were empty, shades drawn against the hard, biscuit sun that baked this suburb southeast of Los Angeles. The nearly identical houses, their foundations only a foot deep, dug by a bucket excavator in a mere fifteen minutes, had been thrown up in a hurry to create this virtually all-white town in the early 1950s— as many as a hundred a day, 17,500 homes in under three years, the biggest housing project America had ever seen. On the day the homes went on the market in April 1950, *Time* reported thirty thousand people "stampeded" to lay their claim. Only a few furnished models had been built, but that didn't stop more than six hundred customers that week from buying one of the eight- to nine-thousand-dollar units with automatic garbage disposals, stainless steel kitchens, and picture windows. "The City as New as Tomorrow" was the development's motto. It was a slogan that the city's founders evidently approached with some uneasiness: as Lakewood author and city official D. J. Waldie observed in *Holy Land*, his poetic, ambivalent paean to his hometown, one of the town's first ordinances declared all forms of fortune-telling illegal.[6]

Kris Belman gravitated, as did much of Lakewood's young male populace, toward the parks. As a community, Lakewood had been designed to serve the aerospace sons. A network of small parks was built so that a baseball diamond and football field would be within reach of every boy—and they could walk to them on special service roads shielded from traffic. Park sports leagues were inaugurated in the late 1950s.[7]

The aerospace fathers were at a loss to explain to their sons what they did at work, much less to pass down a "mastery" of such bureaucratic duties. The park was where father-coaches transmitted their knowledge to son-players, and where the sons got the idea that such knowledge would be useful to them on the road past childhood. By the empty bleachers, Kris ran into Jimmy Rafkin and Shad Blackman, buddies from high school; Jimmy was aimlessly swinging a strip of discarded plywood as if at an invisible ball. Kris and Jimmy had played together on the football team. Shad had only made the badminton squad. Kris said he wasn't doing anything and they said they weren't doing anything either, and after a while they decided they might as well do nothing together at the Belman house. The three trooped down the service road and up the drive, all in identical plaid shorts with elastic waistbands—"for easy access," as Shad Blackman liked to say.

Kris headed like a homing pigeon for the television, which he liked to have tuned at all times to the white noise of MTV. Jimmy had a shoebox under his arm. He now placed it lovingly on the couch and opened the lid with a flourish. "Check this out, dude," Shad said to Kris in a rare state of enthusiasm. "Reeboks. Jimmy got 'em for thirty-eight bucks instead of forty-five, because the box was marked wrong." They were all pleased with this minor scam and the story of the mislabeled box had to be repeated several times before it was wrung dry of sweet triumph. Then they were ready for lunch. And lucky for them, since only Jimmy had any money from "working occasionally" at a ship-repair company where his dad was a supervisor, I was buying. Chili's, a fast-food Mexican franchise by the Lakewood mall, was their eatery of choice.

They tumbled into the vinyl banquette, poking and elbowing each other and talking loudly about "whipping out our fake IDs," and how "I may be nineteen but this afternoon I'm twenty-three." An oblivious and chirpy-voiced waitress jotted down their drink orders without comment: three strawberry margaritas.

"She wants me, dude, I can tell," Shad said as the waitress disappeared to get their drinks. "I could hit on her, easy."

Kris leaned toward me. "See, that's what I mean. We can have any girl we want. Girls come daily to my friends; we don't have to *force* 'em. There's a gang of fish in the sea." He shot me a sly look. "There's one sitting right next to me."

"What I don't understand is why girls have so much say, you know?" Shad put in. "They can lie, you know, and just get anybody in trouble. Like you," he said, jabbing a butter knife in my direction. "Right now anything could happen and you could get us in trouble."

"How exactly?" I asked.

"Well, this is just 'for instance,' right? Say, like we're driving and just fooling around or whatever, and say you hated the way we acted or whatever, say you totally despised us. You could go back and publish something like 'They tried to hit on me, blah, blah, blah.' Your say is bigger than ours. You know what I'm saying?"

Their burritos arrived and they dived in like they hadn't eaten in days. "Could we get some more of this cheese and salsa?" Shad asked plaintively. "Or do they charge you extra?" For all their swagger, the boys seemed a bit shaky on the basics of restaurant dining.

Jimmy picked up Shad's point. "Like Kris went out with this girl last night. She could say, 'Oh, he raped me,' or whatever, and no questions asked, automatically—"

"Automatically," Shad jumped in, "they'll throw you in jail just to find out if you did it. Girls can say whatever they want and it's believed. I just don't understand why they have so much pull, you know?"

Kris chimed in: "Girls have the power to have sex with somebody if they want to. They have the power. If you hear a girl scream, are you going to come running? Yep. But if you hear a guy scream, who comes running? Nobody."

Shad fished a maraschino cherry from Jimmy's drained glass. He chewed on the stem, still stewing about the unjust fate of his generation. "My dad did the same thing when he was young, a couple girls, one-night stands. It was no big deal. And now it's—after the Tyson thing, you know, it's been getting worse."

"Wait a second," Kris cut in. "What Tyson did, that's rape, dude. That's what I consider it. But a girl having sex with up to seven guys a night, daily, and then she turns around and—"

Was he talking about an actual girl? I ask.

"I'm talking about this girl who gave it up with seven people a night, I heard," Kris said. "And with her dad right there in the other room."

"I think they just were out to get us," Jimmy said.

"I'm glad to see girls get more authority in the world," Shad said magnanimously. "But it's like they already got enough authority when it comes to, you know . . ." He made a thrusting motion with his butter knife. "Girls are like, I dunno, they're going to start getting up their courage in a couple years and going head to head with the guys. Fighting 'em and shit. And girls are going to have to get knocked out. That's how it's going to be, dude."

Jimmy giggled. Shad's remarks had jogged a memory. "It's funny. This girl, she got in a fight with her boyfriend. And this guy we know, he came by and started beating up her boyfriend. And then she came and started hitting *him* and everything. So he punched her."

"Punched her in the mouth," Shad interjected.

"So what happened?" I asked.

"Nothing for publication," Jimmy said.

Shad jumped back in. "See? There, right there, you can say, 'Oh, they hit girls.' That's your word over our word. And your word wins every time."

We drove back to the Belmans', my car radio blasting as loud as the boys could crank it. "Hey dude, did you taste how she put more alcohol in the second round of margaritas?" Shad said. "That girl definitely liked us. We shoulda hit on her." Kris jerked his thumb out the window at a passing young woman. "There's that girl who hates me."

From the backseat, Shad made obscene grunting noises.

"She called the cops on me and shit," Kris said.

"See," Shad said, leaning over the seat and tapping me insistently on the shoulder. "See what I mean? Girls have all the power."

For several years in the mid-1990s the Belman boys and their teenage friends, a.k.a. the Spur Posse, had given form to America's suspicion that its male culture was misogynistic and violent, and that its boys were running amok. Their reign in the spotlight began on March 18, 1993, when the police showed up at Lakewood High School and arrested eight Spur Posse members (and one more boy over the weekend) on suspicion of nearly twenty counts of sexual crimes, ranging from rape to unlawful sexual intercourse to lewd conduct with a ten-year-old girl. In the end, the prosecutor's office concluded that the sex was consensual and all but one count were dropped. One boy spent less than a year in a juvenile rehabilitation center on the lewd conduct charge; the other eight Spurs were released after only a week.[8] The only serious jail time was served by Kris Belman's older brother, Dana, the founder of the Spurs, but that wasn't for sexual assault. He was sentenced to ten years in state prison on thirteen burglary and fraud convictions, most notably for stealing a young woman's credit card and racking up charges during a gambling binge in the Dunes Hotel in Las Vegas.[9] Nonetheless, the subsequent strutting and bragging of the boys, as they cut as comprehensive a swath through the TV talk shows as they had through their high-school yearbook, earned their hometown the moniker of "Rapewood."[10] They mugged on the front page of the *New York Times;* they posed everywhere from *Newsweek* to *Sassy* to *Penthouse;* and for a while in the spring of 1993, it was difficult to flip the channels without running into one Spur or another chatting up a television personality. The local paper, the *Long Beach Press-Telegram,* ran boxed announcements listing their upcoming television spots, under such headlines as POSSE PREMIERE and THE SPUR POSSE ON TV.[11] Most of the Spurs interviewed on the talk shows weren't the ones arrested, but it didn't seem to matter, as long as they were willing to elaborate on (or embellish) their sexual exploits. And they were.

Tirelessly they repeated the details of a Spur Posse "game" that had riveted the media. It was a sex-for-points intramural contest in which each time you had sex with a girl, which they called "hooking up," you racked up a point. You had to achieve penetration and you could only get one point per girl. "It doesn't count if you have, like, sex with a girl, like one hundred and fifty times, two hundred—that's only *one* point," as the Spurs' Kevin Howard took pains to clarify on *The Jenny Jones Show.*[12] When your points added up to the corresponding number on some sports star's jersey, you could then claim that player's name as your own, and the other Spurs would address you as, say, Dave Robinson of the San Antonio Spurs—the basketball player who had unwittingly inspired the posse's name. (Dana Belman was a Robinson fan, and when the Spurs signed Robinson, Belman and his buddies signed up too in the only way they knew how: they went to a sporting-goods store and bought Spurs caps.) This game had only one real winner, of course, the Spur with the most points. And for four years running that was Billy Shehan, with a final score of 67. He even racked up a point, he crowed on *The Jane Whitney Show,* the night before his television appearance, in the Manhattan hotel where the media had put him up.[13]

Their place in the national eye had transformed the Spurs into permanent celebrities, at least in their own minds. "You'll recognize me," Jeff Howard said as we arranged by phone to meet just before Christmas 1993. "I was on *Maury Povich.*"

When I arrived at Coco's, another of the Spurs' preferred dining establishments when someone else was picking up the bill, Howard had brought along a few of his Spur buddies—all twelve of them. The Spurs, as I was to learn, rarely traveled solo. The waitresses had to drag together four tables, and the Spurs took their places ceremonially as if attending a high-school varsity awards banquet. Only none of them were in high school anymore.

It was, in fact, almost a reunion, as Howard informed me when I first walked in. He pointed out a slight boy, who at sixteen seemed barely pubescent, with scared, shadowy eyes that darted nervously around the room. He was the Spur who had been sent to the Kirby Juvenile Detention Center for lewd conduct with a ten-year-old girl. He had been released for a family visit, supposedly to the custody of relatives. But here he was, parentless in Coco's.

I passed a notebook around so the Spurs could write down their names. The nervous boy of honor perched next to me. I told him I wouldn't be identifying him because of his juvenile record, and he asked if he could go by a pseudonym of his choosing. "You could call me the Lost Boy," he said softly. I could see why. He lacked the brazen cockiness one would expect from the posse's lone decorated war hero, on leave from the juvy-hall front. "They called me 'pretty boy' at Kirby," he said in a low, flat voice. "They thought I was wimpish." He looked around furtively, then stared down at his place mat as I asked him questions. He answered passively but dutifully, in a dull monotone, describing one of his sexual encounters as if it were a story that belonged to someone else.

"She gave me oral copulation," he said bureaucratically. "Then I never saw her again." He stopped, waiting for further direction. Well, how did he happen to be in this girl's room? "I went there with two other guys," he went on in his mechanical tone, "and she sucked one of the guys' dicks and my dick."

"She's a whore," one of the boys shouted across the table.

"I heard she's been picked up for prostitution," the Lost Boy said, and then, as if that weren't outlandish enough, he added, "twice."

"She was seen at parties," Jeff Howard said, then delivered the coup de grâce. "She was seen drinking beer."

The Lost Boy returned to his story. "The girl was giving me oral copulation for twenty minutes. Usually, it takes me only a couple of minutes, but it was—I guess I was feeling good, but—it wasn't..." He struggled to put a word to the particular state of mind he had found himself in that evening. "I was bored," he said finally. "I didn't want to sit there all night." He stopped.

So what finally happened? I asked.

"Ten minutes later, I pulled up my pants and left. I called my oldest brother to pick me up. Dana [Belman], I mean. I call Dana 'my oldest brother.' Another guy kept fucking her."

When I asked him about the incident with the ten-year-old girl that had landed him in jail, he said, "If I didn't admit it, maybe nothing would've happened to me either."

But something *did* happen, I said; he had a sexual encounter with a ten-year-old.

"I didn't know how old she was. She had a body and everything. I just seen her at parties. I didn't even know her name."

"Points" king Billy Shehan, who was the unofficial philosopher of the Spurs, leaned across the table. "These girls are *no-names*. We've got a *name*." He gestured around the table. "That's why you're talking to us. It's all about brand names."

This seemed a strange segue from an appalling account of an appalling sexual episode, but once the subject of developing a "name" was introduced, there was no getting off it. "We could've been big," Kris Belman said. "If we had just got the right contacts."

"We're all into communication," Billy Shehan said.

"I want to be an actor, or a model," Jimmy Rafkin said. "I want fame that way."

"I want to be a DJ at my own station," Kris Belman said. "Or a big-time comedian. When I was little, I wanted to play sports. That was my dream. Now, I want to move to Vegas, crack a joke at some casino and hopefully somebody will hear me. I've seen a lot of those guys on all the shows, like HBO—Eddie Murphy, [Andrew] Dice Clay. I just want to be up there with the big boys. Someday I think I might."

Billy Shehan summed up the exchange. "See, brand names are very important. It's like having Guess jeans on instead of some no-name pair."

The Lost Boy sat very still next to me, soaking up the swirl of voices. He didn't seem to mind their interrupting his story. I asked him why he'd been lewd with a ten-year-old. "There are only so many girls," he replied. "You had to have girls to hook up with. I had started keeping track of my points. So, if it's three girls and three guys, and say I had sex with one, after I finish, I'll say, 'Can we switch off?' and most of the time, the girls say yes. Sometimes they say no. And then you say, 'Can I have a phone number?' I never forced a girl. I looked at myself highly. I looked at it like they are passing up something great." These last remarks were delivered dully into the place mat, as if he were reading from a boilerplate script, auditioning for a character he didn't believe in.

"We tell a girl, we don't want to waste our time," he continued. "We don't want to waste time romancing."

Why have sex with girls you don't want to "waste time with" anyway, girls who leave you "bored"?

He looked directly at me for the first time. "For the points," he said. "You *had* to have the points. I was developing my reputation. I was developing my *name*." It occurred to me that maybe Billy Shehan hadn't changed the subject after all.

The most fun they ever had, the Lost Boy told me, was when they would videotape themselves having sex with one of the girls. "Once, three of us were in the closet spying," he recalled. "We opened the door, and we took pictures and videos. It was funny. We could sell the video, but who would buy it?"

Billy Shehan began a story about the time he and another Spur had a porn movie playing while they took turns having sex with a girl and he began copying the moves he saw in the movie. "It felt like I was *in* the movie," he said, and that sensation was so gratifying that the next night he replayed it, this time with four Spurs in attendance. The night after that, he gathered ten Spurs—and a video camera. "We made a porn film of it," he said. "It was great."

But for all that, there was a strange affectlessness to the way he and other Spurs told their sex stories, a boredom that seemed to drop away only with the introduction of a video camera. Their sexual exploits evidently had less to do with the act itself than with being, themselves, an act.

That night, the boys would reconvene for a party at a Spur home, selected because the parents were away. Spur parties were all the same: a blackjack game in one corner, a stereo blasting rap music (in this case, Public Enemy), and a circle of bodies collapsed around the television. But this party, like the Coco's luncheon, was a special event. They had gathered to watch themselves on *The Tonight Show*. Well, Billy Shehan conceded, they weren't really "on" the program. A few of them had managed to get passes to be in the audience for Howard Stern's appearance on the show. "We got this girl who works for KSLX to get us in. . . . We were yelling so hard, 'Spur Posse loves you, Howard!'" Shehan said. "I think he heard us. I know he did."

A Spur sporting a clash of logos—Spurs cap, Dodgers shirt, and Georgetown athletic shorts—sauntered up to Billy. "Hey dude, how'd you get on Jay Leno?" Billy explained. "And of course," he said, "there's the factor of our sales. It's good for marketability to have us in the audience." Advancing the Spurs "brand name" was the ultimate goal. "You gotta get your image out there. It's all about building that image on a worldwide basis."

Earlier, Kris Belman had filled me in on his fruitless efforts at Spur promotion in Hollywood. "You know Mickey Rourke, the actor? One of his roommates called us up, this guy Kizzy, I don't know his full name.

And we went to visit his loft in Hollywood." (Rourke's publicist told me that while the actor does have a loft, he has no roommate named Kizzy.) "We didn't see Mickey Rourke, but I guess he told Kizzy to call us. Kizzy and some guys took us to pizza a couple of times. He took me and my two older brothers out to this club called Tatou. And he introduced us to some agents for movie deals.

"Then they decided to blow us over," Kris said of the agents and producers who had originally expressed interest in a TV movie about the Spurs. "They wanted to make us out as real bad guys, where we went to the parents' house and beat up the dad and took the daughter, that's what they wanted. We were like, no, that's not how we are." But Kris and his posse buddies quickly assented to the plotline anyway. "They were gonna pay out cash. But then all the shows, all the channels like Fox and them thought we were all *too* bad guys, rapists, and they said we don't want to make these guys rich." Kris suspected that the "female executives" were the ones who killed the project. After that, he said, Kizzy "moved out of that loft, and now we don't talk to him at all." For the first time, an emotion played across Kris Belman's face, and it was anger. "I'd like to get ahold of him, though," he said, slamming a fist on the table, "because he screwed us. He screwed us bad."

At the party that evening, I would witness several such bitter outbursts, always revolving around a media or entertainment personality who had helped advance their "name," but somehow hadn't done enough. "Maury Povich, he *lied* to us," Chris Albert shouted, kicking hard at the leg of the blackjack table. "He made it look like he was offering us a palace. Ten days in New York. Two limos. Povich is a cock-sucking bitch." Why he was so incensed he couldn't precisely say. He got his ten days, after all. In fact, eleven. He rode in a limo. But it had left him with the strong suspicion that he had been ripped off. There should have been something more, though he didn't know what.

With another hour before *The Tonight Show*, Billy Shehan went out back to smoke some dope. Lonnie Rodriguez was sitting on the stoop, idly poking a stick in the grass. They greeted each other like long-lost cellmates. Which they had been, in a way. "Lonnie and I did telemarketing together for, like, oh man, it felt like years," Billy said. They had sat in sterile cubicles in windowless rooms with nothing but a phone on a desk, dialing endless rows of numbers. "It was so stressful," said Lonnie, who had recently served six months in jail for violating probation. ("Assaults mostly," he told me when I asked why he'd been in jail, "that's what I'm known for.") He said he found incarceration at National Promotions more debilitating.

"It sucked," Billy agreed. "But you know, the first week, I was the second seller, at three hundred dollars. The second week, I was first. We'd just pitch to hook people, and we didn't care what happened after that. I would change my voice, like an act. I had ten different personalities. I was being fake with all these people. It was like, in telemarketing, even before the Spurs, we were hooking. We've been hooking for years."

Telemarketing was an important landmark in the Spurs' short history. "That's when we first started keeping track of points," Billy said. They had already been counting their rate of return on customer calls, and it seemed a natural progression to apply the same approach to their sex lives. "It's all about statistics," Billy added. As it was in the larger world they inhabited. Telemarketing and the "points system" were just two expressions of an economy in which ratings and rankings, marketing percentiles and slugging percentages, were what seemed to count most. The men who mattered were the ones who claimed the most points, whose number one ranking in whatever category displayed a controlling dominance. As Billy Shehan told me that night, "I want to get control of the world. Well, not the world, but I want to get where they *see* me because I'm on top, where all heads turn when they say my name."

From the living room came howls of "It's on! It's on!" Billy and Lonnie leaped up and charged inside. On the carpet, the Spurs were jostling for a prime spot before the wide-screen TV, which took up much of the tiny living room. Billy and Lonnie settled in just as the show broke for commercials—Wal-Mart wishing America a very merry Christmas, followed by a promotion for an episode of a tabloid TV show on both the Menendez brothers and Michael Jackson. The guys booed and moaned, barely able to contain themselves. "Get this shit off of there," one yelled. "This is our moment!"

And then, at last, Jay Leno was back, schmoozing with Howard Stern. The room went silent for the first time all evening, breaths held, eyes riveted, necks craned forward. The camera did a quick pan of the audience, nothing. Then another, and Chris Albert leaped up, thrusting his arms into the air, triumphant. "That's me! That's me! That's fucking me on the fucking *Tonight Show!*" Albert did a victory walk around the room, exchanging high fives with his compadres. Now the camera had returned to Howard Stern, and Billy Shehan nudged me. He swore he could see a glint of recognition in Stern's eyes. "See how he looked? Howard's acknowledging us."

The party dwindled after that. A few more rounds of blackjack and then Spurs began streaming out the door into the darkened grid of right-angled streets. I walked out with Billy, Lonnie, and Chris, who was still glowing from his media moment.

"Spurs is how I gained my respect," Lonnie said. "But I'm going to have to get out of it soon." He had fathered an infant son and was about to start a job of sorts, behind the counter at Baskin-Robbins 31 Flavors. "The Spurs will never die down, though," he said. "My son will carry it on. We'll always exist."

"And we *do* exist," Billy said, as if someone had suggested otherwise. "I swear to God, we do exist!" Billy threw back his head and shouted to the impassive black firmament. "Howard Stern knows we exist. They all acknowledged us, all in one night."

I got in my car and headed toward Los Angeles. I would see Billy and Lonnie again, but not Chris Albert. A year and a half later, on the Fourth of July, he went to Huntington Beach to set off firecrackers, got into a street fight, and was shot to death. His passing would be noted in a small Associated Press item. "Albert," the brief obituary stated, citing his only achievement meriting mention, "appeared on several news and talk shows, including *Dateline NBC* and *The Jenny Jones Show*."[14] His existence on *The Tonight Show* went unnoticed.

Women Will Destroy the World

IN THE GLARE OF HIGH-INTENSITY CAMERA LIGHTS—the lights under which the civic life of America is increasingly led—the many young-male crisis zones tended to blend into an endless repetition of drugs, guns, sex, and bad behavior. The scenes I witnessed as I visited those zones in the 1990s were distinct and individual, the lessons they offered were often contradictory, but the differences among them were more likely to be obscured than illuminated by the white-hot media flares. And so I anticipated a seamless continuation of the same old story when I traveled from the Spur Posse's shag-carpeted rec rooms to a military-school campus a continent away, in Charleston, South Carolina. In the media, the Spur Posse and the Citadel seemed to be replays of a single theme—bad boys out of control, fueled by a high-octane mix of testosterone, aggression, and the insulting slap of feminism. The media uttered their names in the same breath, lumping them together in the inevitable, hand-wringing news specials on What's Wrong with Our Boys. There seemed to be only one appreciable variation in their accounts of bad-boy behavior: while the Spurs of Lakewood, California, were preying on girls by the truckload, the cadets of the Citadel Military Academy were ganging up on a lone aspiring female student.

On the morning of January 12, 1994, a driving rain flattened the neatly trimmed grass of the Citadel's parade ground, drenching the earth so fast and so deep that it seemed the 151-year-old campus might return to the rice marsh from which it arose. But Shannon Faulkner passed through the deluge as dry as toast, under a cluster of umbrellas held solicitously over her head by an army of attorneys, relatives, well-wishers, and journalists who were able to elbow their way close enough for a few "exclusive" words. More media brought up the rear, a block-long processional of burly men shouldering television cameras, and shellacked blond newscasters retouching rain-smeared makeup. Shannon Faulkner was on her way to register for spring-semester classes, the first woman to cross the gender line at the Citadel. She was defying a fearsome political, legal, and cultural machine working to keep her out and to keep the school a cloister of male "tradition," but her immediate task was to pick her way across the mud-slick parking lot. Wearing a high-necked, satiny white blouse, a long, pleated white skirt, and a pair of white shoes with white flower medallions, she seemed a vision of bridal brightness in a sea of black umbrellas. Her unwilling grooms hovered at the edges of the scene, shadowy and bedraggled, their dark ponchos clinging wetly to their uniforms.

The media were here to record the showdown in an archetypal battle between the sexes in which the cadets were cast as unrepentant sexual segregationists, but the confrontation was interrupted by the reporters' very presence. Faulkner and her buffering phalanx moved through the gray sea of boys like a homecoming float. As she ascended the steps of the Citadel's academic building, the cadets hung back, onlookers in their own drama. Retreating to the opposite side of the street, they gawked like paradegoers. Rivulets of rainwater spilled over the bills of their caps and streamed down their faces. As one of the attendant journalists, I was struck by the irony of the moment. The Citadel was presumably about to be dragged out of its musty Confederate closet and into the gender-neutral fresh air of the late twentieth century, but the woman who had precipitated all this upheaval was as inaccessible to the cadets, as distant and pedestaled, as any "southern lady" of their chivalric dreams.

The students had come to this Moorish-style gated campus on the banks of Charleston's Ashley River for many reasons, but among them was relief; they saw the school as a refuge from the social and economic changes in the world outside. Chief among those changes was the one that had brought women into every aspect of public life. On a drier morning than the rain-whipped day of the press conference, I wandered across the broad expanse of the parade ground where the cadets conduct

their ceaseless drills. Along the way, I stopped to consider the decommissioned military hardware arranged like so many lawn ornaments on
the clipped grass. A Sherman tank's armor glinted pacifically in the South
Carolina sunlight; a submarine's torpedo-loading hatch lay with its door
swung open, a gazebo in search of a tea party; a menagerie of cannons
tilted idly upward, their mouths stuffed with cement.

The World War II weaponry rusting under the summer sun put me
in mind of the cadets themselves, not the glowering ones in the school's
brochures but the ones I'd seen marching back and forth like toy soldiers
across a checkerboard courtyard, pinless rifles on their shoulders, guarding a barracks that didn't need guarding. The defanged guns and the
mothballed armament led me at first to the wrong conclusion: that this
was a fantasy playground where boys only pretended to "prove" their
manhood. What I didn't understand then was that the cadets *were* getting something out of their time, something they felt was essential to
their psychic survival as men—and as human beings. It didn't matter
that the rifles weren't loaded. Firearms weren't essential to what the boys
learned here. The martial facade, however, was necessary cover as they
pursued their real lessons. The more that facade was challenged, the
more the cadets felt compelled to prove its authenticity, eventually re-
sorting to the very violence the world expected of them.

The Citadel's defenders had long known it was only a matter of time
before someone asked how a state-funded public school could legally ban
women from its ranks. In the early 1990s, Shannon Faulkner, a high-
school senior from Powdersville, South Carolina, had asked that question—and thus began a years-long court battle. The young men on
campus were as outraged at Shannon Faulkner's effort to enter their
preserve as the Spurs had been by the Lakewood girls' attempts to press
charges. A federal judge ordered the Citadel to admit Faulkner to day
classes during the spring semester of 1994 (previously women had only
attended on a nighttime extension basis), and in July of that year, a U.S.
District Court ruled that the Citadel must also admit her to the Corps
of Cadets, the regiment all undergraduate men belong to, which promised, through the rigors of barracks living, harsh discipline, and drill, to
turn boys into "Whole Men." Three weeks later, the Citadel won a stay
of that order pending appeal.[15] And so the legal battle raged.

That this crucible of masculine transformation could be misogynistic
was a vast understatement. As became clear in the testimony at Faulkner's court hearing, "female" was the ultimate insult among the cadets.
Ron Vergnolle, an alumnus and the top-ranking scholar in the class of
1991, was asked, "Approximately how many times over your four years

did you hear the word 'woman' used as a way of tearing a cadet down?"
He answered:

> I could not estimate a number. It occurred so frequently. It was an
> everyday part, every-minute, every-hour part of life there. And if the
> term 'woman' was used, then that would be a welcome relief, compared
> to the large majority of the terms you were called, [which] were gutter
> slang for women. And it goes all the way down to the genitalia, and
> that's where the criticism was. And the point was, if you are not doing
> what you are supposed to do, you are not a man, you are a woman, and
> that is the way you are disciplined in the barracks every day, every
> hour.[16]

"According to the Citadel creed of the cadet," former student Michael
Lake told me, "women have no rights. They are objects, they're things
that you can do with whatever you want to." The only way to maintain
such a worldview, of course, was to keep the campus free of women who
might challenge it. The acknowledged explanation for this policy was
that women were to be kept at a distance so they could be "respected"
as ladies. Several months before the Citadel's courtroom defense of its
all-male admissions policy, I was sitting in the less-than-Spartan air-
conditioned quarters of senior regimental commander Norman Doucet.
He was explaining to me how excluding women had enhanced his gen-
tlemanly perception of the opposite sex. "The absence of women makes
us understand them better. In an aesthetic kind of way, we appreciate
them more because they are not here."

Women who breached the Citadel's borders were, however, not appreciated. Newly arrived female faculty members reported receiving obscene phone calls as well as pornographic messages and drawings. One
female professor wouldn't even put her nameplate on her office door
because of the abuse she knew it would draw. When Jane Bishop, a
professor of medieval history, posted on her door a photocopy of a *New
York Times* editorial supporting coeducation at the academy, she found
it graffiti-riddled in a matter of days. "Dr. Bishop," one scribble read,
"you are a prime example of why women should not be allowed here."
Another notation read "Women will destroy the world."

December Green joined the Citadel in 1988, the first woman the political science department had ever hired for a tenure-track position. She
was twenty-six and attractive—"someone the cadets might fantasize
about," a colleague recalled. She soon began getting obscene phone calls
in the middle of the night. Then obscenities like "pussy" and "you

fucking bitch" began appearing on her office door. Though Green's work at the Citadel was highly praised—she received an award for her teaching, research, and service—she left in 1992, in despair over her inability to contain the cadets' fury.

"A lot of terrible things happened to me there," Green, who was now teaching in Ohio, recalled. The hostility ranged from glowering group stares in the hallway to death threats on the cadets' teacher-evaluation forms. Green had to get an unlisted number and eventually moved to escape the harassment. The male faculty and administration offered little support. The department chairman instructed her to "be more maternal toward the students." (A cadet had lodged a complaint after she challenged an essay he wrote praising apartheid.) When she submitted the written threats she received to the dean of undergraduate studies, he took no action and his office "lost" them, she said. A professor who was a proponent of an all-male Citadel stood by one day while his students heckled Green out his classroom window. "You get what you provoke," another staff member told her. If the cadets chose to use women as their whipping girls, their elders made it abundantly clear that they would not stand in their way.

The cadets also saw the face of the enemy in another group of females they had to deal with: "the dates." Cadet treatment of "the dates" could exceed in hostility even the Spur Posse's predations. Cadets described to me classmates "knocking around" uncompliant girlfriends. At one Citadel party, graduate Ron Vergnolle had seen two cadets hold down a young woman while a third, drunken cadet leaned over and vomited on her. Vergnolle added that bragging about humiliating an ex-girlfriend was a common practice—and the more outrageous the humilation, the better the story. Two such cadet storytellers, for example, proudly spread the word of their exploits on "Dog Day," a big outdoor party sponsored by the senior class. Enraged with their dates, they followed them to the Portosans and, after the women had entered, pushed the latrines over, trapping them inside. A cadet reportedly tacked a live hamster to his "date's" front door, while another boasted that, as vengeance against a date who had rejected him, he had smashed the head of her cat against a window as she watched in horror. "The cat story," Vergnolle said, "that was this guy's calling card."

These attitudes showed up in the ditties the cadets chanted in their daily runs around the parade ground. Many of the cadences were the usual military "Joadies," well known for their misogynistic lyrics. But some were of more recent Citadel vintage, including lyrics about gouging

out a woman's eyes, lopping off body parts, and evisceration. One, sung
to the tune of "The Candy Man," went like this:

> Who can take two jumper cables
> Clip 'em to her tit
> Turn on the battery and watch the bitch twitch
> The S & M man can,
> The S & M man can . . .

The next verse started, "Who can take an ice pick . . ." And so on. This
was the world that Shannon Faulkner had applied to enter.

The day after Thanksgiving, 1993, the phone rang at one-thirty in the
morning in the home of her parents, Sandy and Ed Faulkner, in Powdersville, a tiny community on the outskirts of Greenville, about 250
miles away from Charleston. The caller, a neighbor, said they had better
come outside—a car had been circling their block. Out on their front
lawn, Sandy and Ed at first saw nothing. Then, turning back, they took
in the words BITCH, DYKE, WHORE, and LESBO, painted across the white
porch columns and along the siding of the house in gigantic and, in
Sandy's words, "blood red" letters. Ed got up again at 6 A.M. and, with a
bucket of white paint, hurried to conceal the message from his daughter.

A few days after the judge ordered the Citadel to admit Faulkner to
the Corps of Cadets, morning rush-hour drivers in Charleston passed a
huge portable sign, wheeled out in the night by a group of cadets. It
read DIE SHANNON. In the previous year, instances of vandalism and harassment had mounted at the Faulkner home. Someone had crawled under the house and opened the emergency exhaust valve on the water
heater. The gas tank on Sandy's car was pried open. Someone driving a
Ford Bronco mowed down the mailbox. Another motorist "did figure
eights through my flower bed," Sandy said. Someone with access to
Southern Bell's voice-mail system managed, twice, to tap into their voice
mail and change their greeting to a recording featuring rap lyrics about
a "bitch" with a "big butt."

At school, where Faulkner was taking day classes while awaiting her
admission to the Corps of Cadets, sneering continued in every venue
from the pages of the *Brigadier,* the school newspaper, to the stalls in
the rest rooms. Tom Lucas, a graduate student in the Citadel's evening
program, told me about one bit of graffito in a campus men's room that
stuck in his mind: "Let her in—then fuck her to death."

Faulkner's ordeal as an official cadet would be brief. She lasted less than a week. Physically ill from and psychologically wrecked by the unremitting fury of her peers, she withdrew. The media shots the next day documented the reversal that the cadets had achieved. Shannon was captured weeping, her head hanging down, humiliated. The most widely used photograph of the cadets, on the other hand, showed them victorious and gloating.

The cadets would reenact this battle with succeeding waves of female cadets. Two young women in 1996 withdrew after cadets sprayed kitchen cleanser and deodorant spray in their mouths, then doused one's sweatshirt with nail-polish remover and set her on fire.[17] But the glow of triumph would be brief. The problem was, the women were just proxies for the real war—against a new economy and a new culture that could not be battled with obscenities and violence.

The cadets had long suspected they were up against something larger than Shannon Faulkner. The American Civil Liberties Union was "pulling her strings," they proclaimed; she was a "pawn" of (and possibly on the payroll of) the National Organization for Women. In truth, Shannon made an unlikely feminist poster girl. Eschewing sisterhood, she preferred to call herself "an individualist." After the judge issued his decision to admit her to the Corps, Faulkner told the *New York Times* that she didn't consider the ruling a victory "just for women," but a confirmation of her belief that if you want something, "go for it."[18]

Perhaps this was just what the cadets found so unbearable. Without in any way excusing their extreme and brutal misogyny, there was a piece of their plaint that seemed on target, an area where their suspicion that Faulkner was only the emissary of some larger threat proved on the mark. Even as she was victimized by the cadets, Faulkner was thriving in and being rewarded as an "individualist" by the celebrity culture in which the mass of cadets were drowning.

That the young men were culturally outgunned was apparent on the rainy day Faulkner showed up for admission. Her procession halted at the top step of the academic building, where her attorneys announced that their client would entertain a few questions. Before a tangle of microphones, Faulkner called on journalists with polished aplomb. She already knew some of the newscasters by name and recognized them familiarly. No, Sally, she wasn't worried about the physical rigors of the Citadel—this very morning she had risen at 6:30 A.M. to jog. Yes, John, she was sure she could win the guys over with her "outgoing" personality—"I'll make these guys speak to me." No, she didn't worry about their hostility; they'd lighten up when they got to know her as "an individual."

Yes, she intended to sign up for extracurricular events, maybe even to write for the *Brigadier*.

With a polite but firm smile, Faulkner advised the press corps that they needed to wrap things up; she would take only one more question. This teenage girl, on the verge of her nineteenth birthday, had an unerring gift for media management and for how it (like other seductions) necessitated never saying too much, never being too available. An eager journalist shouted out over the noise of the crowd and the rain: Just what was she hoping to *prove* by challenging the Citadel? Faulkner responded without a second's hesitation: "The only thing I have to prove is to *myself*. I don't have to prove anything to anyone else."

A few journalists broke off from the Faulkner brigade to approach the young men, hoping to coax them into the frame of the story. They soon gave up. The cadets didn't make for good copy; they seemed robotic, as if programmed to parrot a party line: "She's ruining a 150-year-old tradition"; "she's destroying a long and proud tradition"; "she can never experience the bonding of the Citadel experience." Mostly, they didn't want to talk at all. Buried beneath their machinelike recitations lurked a smoldering resentment toward the reporters themselves. "If you haven't gone through it, you can't understand it" was the inevitable hostile response to follow-up questions, and then an abrupt turning away. "We don't want you here" was the silent message left hanging in the air, and the angry reticence toward the media gave me my first clue that I wasn't in Lakewood anymore. Whatever the antiwomen similarities, the battle lines here were somehow different.

Visible and Not Ready to Be Visible

ONE DAY IN THE SPRING OF 1994, I met Billy Shehan at a Lakewood park. He was sitting on a bench watching his old Pony League baseball team practice. The thirteen-year-old boys stood around thwacking their fists in their mitts and adjusting their caps, paying no attention to Billy, the lone observer.

He was brooding about his own truncated athletic career. He had been cut a few weeks earlier from the Long Beach City College baseball team. Before Long Beach, he had played ball for Golden West College until he got into a fight in the outfield, and then at Rio Honda College, where the team was lackluster and he had quit in disgust. His Spur celebrity had made him a standout at Long Beach (a celebrity based on media, not police, attention—Billy was never arrested). "People would call out from the stands, 'Hey, how many points did you score?'" But it also cost him a spot on the roster, or so he had convinced himself. "The coach told me, 'You didn't make the team because you were too much of a distraction. People aren't focused on the game.'" In a fury, Billy had "shredded" his Long Beach City College baseball cap.

It had all been so promising back in Pony League. "I had a good name through Pop Warner, a good image," he said. "Lakewood Pop Warner never loses. My name was getting more recognized. But someone with a bigger brand name came along." That boy, whose batting stats weren't—so Billy told me—as good as his but whose father was a well-liked coach in town, got the slot on the All-Star team that Billy thought was meant for him. "I didn't get on All-Stars until later, and then it was too late. The guys who get drafted early get the brand name. It's like Pepsi."

Billy recognized the Pony League coaches from his own playing days and went over to say hello.

"Where is everybody?" Billy said, gesturing toward the empty bleachers. His question opened up a gusher.

"Oh, I don't know, it's just not as team oriented anymore the way it used to be," Coach Al Weiner said dispiritedly. He took off his cap and ran a hand through his thinning white hair.

"It's with the mothers never being home anymore and all," Coach Art Tavizon commented.

"Naah, it's this thing with the kids," Weiner said. "In the old days, the kids who didn't get on, they would show up to watch. Now, if they're not playing, they won't watch."

"And the girls don't watch anymore," Tavizon said.

Weiner nodded. "The girls aren't interested. They're more into girls' sports now."

Tavizon set his mouth in a thin line at the mention of girls' sports and looked grimly across the field as if he had just spotted a menacing thundercloud on the horizon. "Title Nine changed everything," he said, alluding to the 1972 federal law that prohibited sex discrimination at schools receiving federal money, thereby ushering girls into school athletics much the way Shannon Faulkner was being ushered into the Citadel. "All the big moneymakers—football, baseball—and we've got to give it all to girls' badminton! Coaches are getting out of the business because they have to spend all their time fund-raising because the money's been taken to give to girls' sports."

The coach paused, but only to take a breath. He was just getting started. "We had our weight room taken away because girls needed gymnastics. We had that weight room eleven years. We got pushed outside."

His voice was getting louder, his face redder, and I suddenly realized that Billy had dropped out of the picture. The coach was directing his ire at me, the representative woman. "If the women would sit down and give a little bit, instead of insisting, 'Our half of the pie is fifty-fifty.' If they'd just back off and let the big sports be funded the way they used to be. Title Nine is going to be the destruction of high-school sports."

With that, he stormed back to his thirteen-year-old boy stars. Billy and I watched him go. "That's not the problem with baseball," Billy said, and offered his own more up-to-date diagnosis. "The problem with base-ball is that it's a *dad's* game." And not a glamour game. "Baseball doesn't stand out because they don't have the cheerleaders, so there isn't as much of a star thing like you have with football." I wondered at the ranking of fathers under teenage girls in his version of the sports arena. When had the opinions of the older men who coached the game stopped mattering? Billy's father had devotedly coached Pop Warner for twelve years. So had Kris and Dana Belman's father, Don, who had also been a dedicated coach of Park League, Little League, Pony League, and Colt League.

What's so bad about a "dad's game"? I asked Billy.

"My dad, he was living through me with sports. When I got in trouble, he took it like *I* fucked *him* up. My dad provided anything that produced a championship. Sports is what our dads embedded in us. It was like a disease and it contaminated the whole town." Billy's father, doubtless, wanted only what every father wanted—to pass something along to his son, and in postwar suburbia, that patrimony was athletic achievement. Yet it turned out that the lines of inheritance ran upstream. In a gen-erational reversal, the parents were getting their "name" through their children. As Dottie Belman, Kris and Dana's mother, told a reporter: "We became stars, too. We'd walk into Little League and we were hot stuff."[19] In his gut, Billy Shehan knew that the fathers had nothing to teach him about the way the world worked—but the girls did. The Spur Posse members, after all, prayed for what women had long commanded: the camera's attention. Far more than they ever courted women, they courted women's secret access to enshrinement in the public eye. As Billy Shehan told Jane Whitney on her show, he was just trying to do from Lakewood what she was doing on the studio stage. "We probably have the same concept going here," he said.[20]

The cadets, on the other hand, prayed for the cameras to go away. The day of her entrance into the Corps, Shannon Faulkner arrived with her duffel bags, her hair shorn and her "individuality" retired, and the cadets stood in front of the barracks, screaming. But they weren't screaming at her. They were chanting, "Kill the media! Kill the media!" When a CNN cameraman tripped and fell over some garbage cans, the cadets cheered and caterwauled. Newspaper photos of the cadets bawling and shaking their fists through the campus fence captured the conflict's vitriol. What these pictures didn't show was that Shannon Faulkner wasn't in the vicinity. The cadets were threatening the photographers for snapping their pictures. "There's this incredible hostility to the media," Claudia Brinson, a reporter for the *State,* a South Carolina daily, who was covering the Citadel story, said to me. "Like we *did* something terrible to them."

The most obvious thing the media had done "to them," of course, was criticize the school for its position. But the cadets would have opposed the media even without Shannon Faulkner. The problem wasn't just that they hated the media for documenting Faulkner's entrance, but that they hated her (and, by extension, all women) for ushering the media in. The moment Faulkner registered for class, the administration announced that she would have no media contact without their permission.

"The American focus on civil rights," a graduate of the class of '91 wrote in a letter to the *Brigadier,* "has changed from a healthy concern to a crazed obsession, focused not on freedom but on fame."[21] The Spurs would have envied Shannon Faulkner her celebrity, but the cadets shrank from it. "The Citadel can't stay as stoic as it once was, and the media is the biggest factor in changing the Citadel," cadet Jeremy Forstron told me, shouting to make himself heard over the noise of the Friday night crowd in Big John's, a Charleston bar and Citadel hangout. The place was mobbed with cadets who clumped together talking among themselves, the sophomores identical in their uniforms with the thin black line on the cuffs, the juniors in their blazers, and so forth. "You can tell the class by what they wear," Alan Murphy, a junior in a blazer told me, and he seemed to derive a great comfort from such predictability. A harassed-looking waitress came by with a round of beers ordered half an hour before. "How am I supposed to find you guys?" she complained as she handed out the drinks. "You all look the same." That sameness was what Forstron called "stoicism," an impenetrable wall of silence and anonymity that shielded them from having to reveal themselves, from having to be "an individual," as Shannon Faulkner liked to call herself.

To this anonymity, the media and women represented the same threat. The boys came to the Citadel to escape the prying eye of a punitive world. They could not, they felt, be themselves as long as they were exposed to the female gaze. The cadets told me over and over how "embarrassed" and "ashamed" they would feel if women came to the school, and how the media "just wants to embarrass us" and "hold us up for ridicule."

On the first day of the fall semester of 1993, cadets in a Western Civ class pondering the danger that Faulkner represented kept returning to the threat she posed to their privacy. "If women come here, they'll have to put up window shades in all the rooms," a cadet said. "Think of all the windows in the barracks. That could be eight thousand, nine thousand dollars." He had, in fact, researched and written a report on the window-shade problem. What he left unexplained was why it was necessary to cover all those windows.

"Shame," developmental psychologist Erik Erikson wrote, "supposes that one is completely exposed and conscious of being looked at. . . . One is visible and not ready to be visible; which is why we dream of shame as a situation in which we are stared at in a condition of incomplete dress . . . with one's pants down. . . . He who is ashamed would like to force the world not to look at him, not to notice his exposure. He would like to destroy the eyes of the world."[22] But what were the cadets so ashamed of? Why was privacy so important to them? What did they experience behind the locked barracks gates that they couldn't pursue in the public eye without mortification? I naturally assumed it had to be something repellent to public morality, something the cadets feared society would decry as abhorrent, perverted in red-blooded American males. I wasn't far wrong, but not at all in the way I had imagined.

In the classroom of one of the cadets' favorite instructors, I began to understand the desire for concealment. "If Shannon was in my class, I'd be fired by March for sexual harassment," Colonel James Rembert said to me affably as we headed toward the academic building one afternoon. *Colonel* is not a real military title; it is conferred on Citadel faculty members by a largely ceremonial outfit once known as the South Carolina Unorganized Militia, and still called by the acronym SCUM. Rembert has a ramrod bearing and a certain physical resemblance to Ted Turner (who, incidentally, sent all three of his sons to the Citadel and donated twenty-five million dollars to the school in 1994),[23] but his exaggerated rigidity and courtliness sometimes lent him a Monty Python goofiness. The colonel identified himself to me as one of "the last white Remberts" in South Carolina, the Remberts being a Huguenot family of sufficiently ancient lineage to gain him admission to the St. John's Hunting Club of South Carolina, an all-male society that doesn't hunt, chaired by a Citadel alumnus. After graduating from the Citadel in 1961, Rembert served in the army as a training-company commander and then as a paratrooper with the Special Forces at Fort Bragg. After he got his doctorate at

Cambridge University, he moved back behind the Citadel's walls, where he has taught and lived ever since. He preferred the company of men, he told me, in leisure and in learning. "I've dealt with young men all my life. I know how to play with them. I have the freedom here to imply things I couldn't with women. I don't want to have to watch what I say."

Rembert opened the English class with a facetious tale of a "wound" he sustained in Vietnam (where he had never been), an injury that had "left me chaste, lo these past thirty-five years." The ice thus broken, he turned to the literary work under discussion that day: *Beowulf*. The narrative, Rembert told them, was all about "brotherhood loyalty" and "the bonding of males . . . much like the Citadel." Rembert turned to me with an impish grin: "Women are mentioned, Miss Faludi, if at all, preparing the food." Then he handed back their graded papers on the topic.

"Mr. Rice," Rembert said in mock horror. "You turned in a single-spaced paper." This was a no-no. Rembert instructed him to take a pencil and "pen-e-trate"—he drew the syllables out—the paper with the point. Rembert shook his head with faux gravity. "What a pansy!" he said. "Can't catch, can't throw, can't write." Another student was chastised, in the same tone, for the use of the passive voice. "Never use the passive voice; it leads to effeminacy and homosexuality," Rembert told the class. "So next time you use the passive voice, I'm going to make you lift up your limp wrist." Rembert took great pride in this teaching "technique." When he first explained it to me, it didn't make sense: how could calling a bunch of insecure young men "pansies" help them to relax in the classroom?

Literary pointers concluded, Rembert floated the subject of Shannon Faulkner. The usual objections to women were raised: they can't hack the physical deprivations of the Spartan campus life; they won't be able to meet the fitness requirements; they won't want to get a buzz cut. But then we wandered into more interesting territory, provoked by a cadet's comment that "she would change the relationship between the men here." Just what was the nature of that relationship?

"When we're in the showers, it's very intimate," a senior cadet said. "We're one mass, naked together, and it makes us closer. . . . You're shaved, you're naked, you're afraid together. You can cry." Robert Butcher, another cadet, said that the men take care of each classmate. "They'll help dress him, tuck in his shirt, shine his shoes."

You mean, like a mother-child relationship? I asked.

"That *is* what it is," a cadet volunteered. "It's a family. Even the way we eat is family style." Another added, "Maybe it's a Freudian thing, but males feel more affection with each other when women are not around. Maybe we're all homosexuals."

The class groaned. "Speak for yourself, buddy," several chorused.

I began to understand Rembert's teaching "technique." Anxiety over society's judgment soared every time they approached the notion of intimate relationships between men. Cracks about limp-wristed writing provided both a needed screen and an escape valve for such fears and tensions. The rules imposed upon them, rules enforced not just by the Citadel but by the rest of society, required that, being men, they could not enjoy intimacy without denouncing it at the same time. Private tenderness was allowed only to those who publicly promoted their contempt for homosexual love and who were shielded from the assumedly disapproving gaze of women. As Rembert put it to the class, "With no women, we can hug each other. There's nothing so nurturing as an infantry platoon."

The hooted-down cadet, encouraged by Rembert's observation and the nodding agreement with which it was received by his classmates, weighed in again. "When I used to wrestle in high school, we had this great tradition. Right before the game, the coach, he'd slap us really hard on the butt."

Rembert smiled. He and his skydiving military buddies did that, too, he said, right before they jumped. "First man out gets a pat right there." There was a feeling of relief in the room that the subject of male intimacy had been so directly broached even as it was bolted down to the safe terrain of the athletic fields and the battlefields.

Afterward, Rembert and I went to lunch in the "family style" mess hall, an experience akin to dining in a prison cafeteria run by sadists. Upperclassmen bellowed till they spit at cowering freshmen who had failed to sit properly on the edge of their chairs or square their forkfuls at an exact right angle or adhere to any of a myriad of obscure regulations. Rembert sat happily amid the cacophonous din, taking in the verbal carnage with approval. He returned to the theme of manly nurturance among Citadel men. One of his colleagues, he said, "always kisses me on the cheek. It's like a true marriage. There's an affectionate intimacy that you will find between cadets. With this security, they can, without being defensive, project tenderness to each other."

I heard variations on this theme in many different corners of the campus. One day, the Citadel's academic dean, General Roger Clifton Poole, explained to me why he had thrived under the "fourth-class system"—essentially a yearlong hazing process where freshmen are "broken down" and their old identities erased by upperclassmen who constantly hector them and demand that they "brace," a standing-at-attention posture with their chins tucked into their necks like chickens. After a lot of vague language about "bonding" and "molding boys into men," the general finally said, "I learned I was not alone. I didn't have to depend on just me. I found a home." What could he do in this home that he couldn't do elsewhere in the world? I wondered. "Here," he said, "I have no shame hugging and kissing classmates."

One of the most heated disagreements over the admission of women that I witnessed took place at a meeting of the student-run Afro-American Society. Black cadets are painfully aware of the hostility that still greets them at the Citadel, and the parallels between their sense of exclusion and Shannon Faulkner's are not so easily brushed aside. The argument became quite intense and angry until cadet Robert Pickering, the society's president, said something that immediately united all factions and prompted enthusiastic agreement around the room: "Women won't understand or appreciate what we do here. As a man, I wouldn't cry in front of Shannon Faulkner. But with my roommate Santel, I've seen him shed tears."

I was reminded then of a video I had seen screened in a federal courtroom. It was narrated by the Afro-American Society's most illustrious member, Norman Doucet, the Corps of Cadets' senior regimental commander, the top-ranked member of his class. The Citadel had asked Doucet to produce a day-in-the-life video that caught the school's essence and explained why it must remain an all-male institution. Significantly, what he chose to capture on film wasn't martial assemblies and gun drills, but almost entirely domestic scenes: cadets sweeping the floor, taking out the trash, making their beds. Shannon Faulkner's mother, Sandy, who was sitting next to me in the courtroom that day, turned with a look of exasperated bemusement. "That's what *I* do at home!" she whispered. On the witness stand, Doucet continued his narration. The events on the screen were "like some kind of a ballet or dance that's going on. What they are doing here is the Citadel shirt tuck." The tuck requires that a cadet unzip his pants halfway and fold down his waistband, then stand still while his helper approaches him from the back, puts his arms around the cadet's waist, pulls the loose shirt material firmly to the back, jams it as far down in the pants as he can, and then pulls the cadet's pants up. "If you watch closely right here, this is what the fourth-class system is all about," Doucet continued. "In order to get a proper shirt tuck, you can't do it yourself—you need your classmates to do it for you. There's really a lot of dependence upon your classmates."

After Doucet showed the film, a Citadel attorney asked Doucet to explain to the judge why female cadets would pose a problem. The only issue Doucet raised was the humilation that cadets would feel if women observed their domestic relations; the distress would be particularly acute for the freshmen, or "knobs," as they are called for their shaved pates. He recalled the shame that knobs have experienced when, on occasion, a woman happened to be on the parade ground while upperclassmen were disciplining them. "One of the things that knobs really dread is having to brace and pop off or being stopped in the sally port after a parade when there are all these parents and girlfriends and fiancées and whatnot out waiting on their upperclass boyfriends. It's really— I have seen it happen, and I tried to prevent it whenever I saw it, it's just really something that's very uncomfortable for a fourth-classman." As he spoke, the cadets observing in the courtroom bobbed their heads in confirmation.

It is a sociological commonplace that virtually every adolescent male rite of passage—whether it's a tribal scarification ceremony or a fraternity initiation night—is structured to help young men with the imperative of breaking from a mother's protective realm. That separation is played over and over in ritualized form at the Citadel right up to graduation, when each senior receives a "band of gold" in a Ring Ceremony. Receiving the ring, which is "the biggest class ring of any college," as I was constantly reminded, is a literal sacrament—each ring is blessed by the campus chaplain and given to the cadet after he has stepped through a ten-foot replica of the ring itself, with his mother on one arm. In a sort of reconfigured marriage ceremony, the mother gives the cadet away. He kisses her farewell and then marches under the arched swords of the Junior Sword Drill, a new bride of the Corps. When a cadet marries, tradition dictates that he slide his class ring above his wedding band as a symbol of prioritized loyalties. Indeed, several of the alumni listening in the courtroom, I noticed, had their jewelry so ordered.

Doucet directed the court's attention to "one of the great parts" of a freshman's first day, which he had captured on film: the mothers weeping at the gate as their sons were led away and marched directly to the campus barber for a buzz cut. Doucet lingered over the head-shaving scene. "This is what does it, right here. Mothers can't even tell their sons apart after this."

It wasn't just mothers the knobs were fleeing; it was all women. Listening to Doucet's presentation, I wondered if conventional psychology offered only half an explanation for the cadets' flight from their mothers' grasp. As far as I could tell, these young men had two primary objectives that were contradictory, one proclaimed by the culture, and one that must be hidden. They were compelled to break a basic human tie. But because they were human, they at once sought to reestablish it elsewhere. If they were to thrive, they needed to find an alternative life-support system. It was this second impulse that had to be curtained, protected from the shaming gaze of society, a gaze that emanated most strongly, in the perception of the cadet, from the female eye, from the mother herself and all her younger potential surrogates.

In the media's opinion, the cadets did not want invading women contaminating their warrior culture. Even some cadets maintained that. But the cadets were also young men trying to live out "feminine" roles without being ridiculed by a culture whose stereotype of masculinity held no place for such roles. That stereotype, the cadets felt, was enforced by women. The warrior demeanor was their weapon against the female gaze and the rigid masculinity to which that gaze seemed to confine them.

What they entered at the Citadel was a stage set for warfare, in which the real action went on behind the scenes, in the dressing rooms. Here, the young recruits could safely return to the intimacies of childhood, the tenderness of being bathed and dressed and cared for. Here, the shame of having one's domesticity found out, of being accused of "effeminacy and homosexuality" in their daily dealings, was obscured by the ritual of being called a "pansy" for such sins as single-spaced papers. Here, they could be mothered and, just as important, they could mother. They were seeking a way to express maternal femininity in masculine terms. They were looking for a way to find in peacetime what Ernie Pyle's grunts had found in war: a place where they could receive and give care without fear of being shamed, a place where tending to one another's needs produced not ridicule but pride, a place where such intimacies were a mark of manhood, not its annulment.

The knobs actually enter the Citadel's version of manhood on Recognition Day, when the upperclassmen force them to do calisthenics until they drop, then gently lift up their charges and nurse them with Dixie cups of water. At that moment, for the first time in nine months, the older cadets call the knobs by their first names and embrace them.

Feminist sociologists, considering such rites of passage at places like the Citadel or in all-male fraternities, have typically cast them as attempts at a womanless "rebirth," and often have criticized them for their apparent misogyny. The idea that men can't be men until they are reborn via a man-made canal—whether through a giant ring or a grueling gauntlet—is understandably repellent, and not just to feminist sensibilities. But what if that is not the primary purpose of these rituals? What if the young men are attempting not so much to eliminate women as to find a way to experience a maternal femininity, too, without bringing down upon themselves the boot of social opprobrium? Maybe what they are really seeking is the shipyard male experience—the experience of "taking care of our men." The Citadel's motto, advertised on many an admissions brochure, is "Where Manhood Meets Mastery." The cadets can't actually claim mastery of a body of productive knowledge, but the school's ornate system of conduct and "tradition," voluminously documented in the Corps' encyclopedic manual, is a code of knowledge they can crack, a secret territory they can conquer and pass on to apprentice "knobs."

Following Recognition Day, as the knobs are integrated into the Corps, the relationship between knobs and upperclassmen shifts from the maternal to the matrimonial, the "true marriage" that Rembert described, a bond of "brotherhood." The Citadel yearbooks, year after year, present striking pictorial documentation of these unions; leafing through them is more like perusing a wedding album than a commencement volume. The pages are filled with shots of Citadel men doing little but embracing and kissing. Of course, this impulse is always carefully disarmed with a jokey caption. In the 1992 issue, two cadets kiss hard on the mouth, over a caption that reads "Come here, big boy." On the next page, two cadets clinch to the words "You dance divinely, my dear." On the next page, the Citadel's retired assistant commandant Colonel Harvey Dick and another Citadel administrator hug. The inscription notes that the second official "gets set to plant an old smoocheroo on the Dickster."[24] The intimacy these men seek is physical and sensual, though not necessarily sexual; it is a dream of blissful oneness, a sensuality more closely associated with mother and child.

One afternoon, a group of cadets recounted for me the campus's many "nudity rituals," as cadet T. J. Clancy jokingly called them. There's "Senior Rip-Off Day," a spring rite where three hundred seniors literally rip each other's clothes off, burn them in a bonfire, and hug and wrestle on the ground. There's "Nude Platoon," cadet Ron Eyester said, where a group of juniors "will run around the quad totally nude except for their cross webbing and yell, 'We love the Nude Platoon!'" And there's the birthday ritual, where the birthday boy is stripped, tied to a chair, and covered in shaving cream. And, of course, there's the daily nudity in the communal showers, the most valued and guarded sanctum of cadet life, "the heart of the Citadel experience," as more than one young man put it to me. "I'd never want to give this up to a girl coming in," cadet David Spisso said. "It's like this is your home."

The Citadel provides young men with a way to experience male dependency and conceal it at the same time. The cadets manage to be exposed yet safe in one another's company by draping their naked intimacy in the high seriousness of chivalric mysticism and the locker-room patter about "smoocheroos" and "limp-wristedness." But their most important protective cover is the martial facade the school itself provides, a shield that physically separates them from the rest of the world and projects an image of a group of men who are busy marching, not mashing. The fortified walls are an essential buffer. But what happens when that facade is ripped away—when their efforts to keep the world at bay are overwhelmed by social forces that the Citadel's somewhat feeble bulwarks cannot withstand? If dependency was their secret, then public exposure could only lead to shame. But what would the shame lead to?

The Pop Warner System

THE SPURS WERE PARTIAL TO TAKING THEIR CLOTHES OFF, too, but their disrobing was not something they needed privacy to indulge. In fact, they took off their shirts to *attract* the media glare. Kris Belman posed shirtless and pumped in *People*. His older brother, Dana, did the same, with his fingers pulling suggestively at the front of his shorts, in *Glamour*. And John Weber showed off his shaved pecs and legs in *Rolling Stone*.[25] They didn't seem to find it in the least embarrassing. In fact, when I first met Kris Belman, he wanted me to promise to reprint his pinup shot. Privacy didn't seem to be a big issue either. When I asked Billy Shehan if I could glance at his diary, he handed over a box of personal journals, including one in which he had drawn a picture of a penis, evidently his.

Nor did the Spurs yearn to be part of a monolithic unit or to lose their identity in a group or to mother one another as the cadets did. The media misconceived the nature of the Spurs' "club," which was less like a gang or fraternity than a bunch of casual drinking buddies. "People kept calling us a gang," Kris Belman said to me. "We weren't anything like that. It was just some guys who wore hats. . . . And then, once we got famous, there were all these other guys claiming they were Spurs who we didn't even know." If the core group of Spurs all seemed to wear baggy plaid shorts and their caps turned backward, this was in obeisance more to consumer culture than to group bonding. "We weren't ever a real group," Billy Shehan told me one day. "We were just a few people who liked David Robinson. Once the media grouped us together, *that's* when we became more tight." And then it was for promotional, not emotional, reasons. The Spurs weren't looking for the intimacy of a close-knit group. They were looking for the celebrity that identification with a brand name like David Robinson might provide. Like their elders in aerospace, they had attached themselves not to one another but to a household label. Everybody knew the San Antonio Spurs, as everybody knew McDonnell Douglas—and by extension, they could be "known," too; Robinson's name would be theirs.

"Billy did not even really run with this group of kids," Billy's mother, Joyce Shehan, observed to me. "He went to a different high school [from a lot of the other Spurs]. It was the lure of the media, which was overwhelming for all of these boys." She recalled how it all started, the day the eight Spurs were arrested: "I came home that afternoon and Billy said, 'Gotta go, Mom! *Current Affair* is at the Belmans'!' He felt like destiny was calling him." Joyce pleaded with her son, to no avail. When the door slammed shut, she sat down in her living room and wept. "I felt overtaken."

"Doing sports is up there with sexual activities," Billy Shehan explained to me, as he gave me a tour of his parents' home. The walls of the ten-by-ten-foot bedroom where he still lived then were decorated with posters of the scantily clad Bud Lite woman, Hooters women, and decals asserting BLOW ME, STAY HARD, BAD BOYS CLUB, and PUSSIES AREN'T HEROES. I was having trouble matching these sniggering mud-flap sentiments with Billy, who distinguished himself from the other Spurs by a certain capacity (albeit sometimes lost in a dope-induced fog) for self-analysis. He had been in the accelerated program for gifted students throughout school, had graduated with honors, and was one of the few Spurs in school, although his attendance at Long Beach City College was spotty. He was proud of his high SAT scores (1,410 out of a possible 1,600, he said). For all his weight lifting—he tried to work out every other day at the Family Fitness gym—Billy had a physical softness to him; he retained the loose-limbed downiness and padded gait of adolescence. Aside from the posters, his room could've been a kid's, with its sports pennants and discarded clumps of clothing on the floor.

The tour complete, we returned to the living room, where Billy's uncle Brian Shehan; Billy's new girlfriend, Holly Badger; and Spur Jeff Howard were watching a TV movie about baseball and eating corn chips out of a jumbo bag. "When I'm thinking of attraction to girls, I'm thinking I have to stand out," Billy said. "How else can it be done? Same thing with sports. You try for a hit. It's like a mirror." It was the first time I had heard someone equate playing sports to looking in a mirror, and I asked him what he meant.

"It's what Pop Warner is all about," Billy said, "and Lakewood was built around Pop Warner." Playing football in the Pop Warner league was one of the few continuities a Lakewood boy could count on. The city's fathers established the park sports leagues out of alarm over the vast and idle child population of the new suburb: by 1953, 45 percent of Lakewood was under the age of nineteen.[26] The leagues were supposed to keep the baby-boom progeny out of trouble; they needed something to do. But what the elaborate Lakewood regimen of Pop Warners and Pony Leagues and Colt Leagues and All-Stars became, Billy was saying, was not something to *do* but something to *be*. "Pop Warner is what made me like hooking."

His uncle leaned heavily against the wall, his lined face under a battered Pittsburgh Steelers cap, a beaten version of Billy's. He was visiting from Las Vegas, where one week before Christmas he had been laid off as head cook at a restaurant called Bubba's. He had once been a front-end-loader operator but wound up in the new economy slinging hash and ringing up purchases at Fedco's. "So," he said, almost wearily, "it's the Pop Warner Sex-Orgy System?"

"It *is* a system," Billy said. "In the Pop Warner system, you learn how to stand out, you learn how to get people to recognize you. You wear your hat a certain way. Like I started wearing mine angled with the bangs showing, because it looks cute. And everybody else started doing it. I set a lot of fashion trends."

"Every guy is in Pop Warner to get attention," Holly Badger said, though from the exasperated set of her mouth it was clear she found this truth more pathetic than ennobling.

"Sports is not sports anymore," Billy told his uncle. "It's evolved to this whole other level. It's this gamble of are you going to hit it big."

"Why do you guys like to gamble?" Holly interrupted. "All you *do* is gamble." She turned to me. "Every weekend, these guys are off to Las Vegas."

"It's a rush, a fix," Billy said. "It's like Dana's fixation with stealing."

"Yeah, or like breaking and entering," Holly said pointedly. One of the Spurs arrested for sexual misconduct, she told me, had broken into her house four years earlier when she was in the ninth grade. "He forced himself down on top me and a girlfriend of mine. I kicked him and he called me a bitch. Then he took my ring off my finger and put it on his finger and ran out." Hers was not an isolated story. Some of the Spurs had been known to steal things from girls: credit cards and checkbooks and jewelry, and oddities like gym membership cards, which one of the Spurs even tried to use, in spite of the feminine face laminated on the square of plastic.

"Stealing *is* gambling," Billy said. "Gambling evolves into something else."

"Billy wastes his life pursuing baseball," his uncle told me later that day, as we stood on the front porch. He had as much chance making the pros as hitting the jackpot—and as a Las Vegas resident, Brian Shehan knew how good those chances were. As for himself, Brian said, he was considering becoming a nurse; at least society needed them. He crossed his arms and gazed out at the orderly row of houses across the street. "Baseball and celebrity. Billy promised his dad he wouldn't go on the talk shows, and a few days later, he's flying to New York City."

Holly appeared on the porch, her bag over her shoulder. She was on her way to class at a nearby junior college. Jeff and Billy, their baseball caps on backward—Jeff's said STÜSSY, Billy's said L.A.—kicked their designer sneakers at the concrete stoop and talked about job possibilities. Billy last found work as a box boy at Victoria's Secret, but it had only lasted through the Christmas rush. Holly apprised them coolly: "*I* go to school and *I* work," she said. Billy kept kicking at the stoop and said nothing. Holly leaned over to give him a distracted kiss good-bye and drove off.

We went back inside, and Billy booted up his computer to show me his "movie treatment," in which he starred as "Billy Sherwood," the one with "the most points" who "doesn't accept failure." He had quit writing after the cast list and had typed instead some notes to himself about his girlfriend troubles, in lyric form. Billy and a few Spurs formed a band a while back, and he was the songwriter.

> The girl I used to kiss used to only kiss me
> But she has changed and she is 'ho again.
> She's back to who she was.
> I thought I could make her mine . . .

He had broken off there. Underneath, he had written, "But I realize by the answers to my questions, that I never needed her. What I needed was for her to need me."

Something Mean and Out of Control

THE TRAINING GROUNDS FOR THE SPURS were supposed to be the playing fields of Pony League and Pop Warner, and in a way, they were training grounds for the celebrity age. The young men who flocked to Lakewood's sports leagues certainly learned that they would be expected to climb the star ladder, that fame based on your stats would be the determining factor in modern masculinity. But they also learned how high the stakes were, how few resources they had to win the stats war. Playing ball led to stardom for a very few. For the rest, Pop Warner was ultimately a lesson in how impossible it was to be a masculine "player" today. As Spur Jimmy Rafkin told me: "Growing up, everything revolved around Pop Warner. You try and do your best in sports and try to be the best and try to become the best, but it's like one out of a million make it, by far. So what was the point? What was it all *for*?"

The Citadel had initially been a training ground, too — for the industrial age. While the military academy is fabled now as a repository of antebellum southern male culture, its first pressing mission had been to prepare post–Civil War young men to fight off the Yankees on the new front of manufacturing and mechanization. The keepers of the Citadel myth like to play up its original charter as an arsenal in 1822, a response to a slave revolt planned by the freed Charleston slave Denmark Vesey. But when it reopened in 1882 after a Civil War hiatus, federal Reconstruction officials thoroughly stripped the school of military muscle. Its history as an educational institution more accurately begins here, with an explicit mandate to reinvigorate the masculinity of the South by showing its men how to compete with the business and industrial skills of northern "carpetbaggers," who were believed to be much better prepared than the sons of Dixie to enter the Darwinian fray of modern commerce. John Peyre Thomas, the Citadel's president from 1882 to 1885, wrote of the need to teach spoiled plantation boys the rudiments of self-reliance. "It must be admitted that the institution of African slavery, in many respects, affected injuriously the white youth of the South," he wrote. "Reared from infancy to manhood with servants at his command to bring his water, brush his shoes, saddle his horse, and, in fine, to minister to his personal wants, the average Southern boy grew up in some points of character dependent, and lazy, and inefficient."[27]

The Citadel served this purpose into the late twentieth century. Its vaunted ring was a key that opened doors to higher employment in the new business economy of the South. Hence the cadets' common refrain: "Flash the ring, get a job." For many decades, Citadel alumni populated high positions in South Carolina's commercial and political hierarchy, and they were dedicated in their efforts to reach down and give a leg up to the next generation of their alma mater's graduates. The "fourth-class system" that transformed baby cadets into "upperclassmen" was a metaphor for the elevated class assurances that the postgraduation alumni network provided. But as the economic underpinnings of this hierarchy crumbled, so did the powers of the alumni network. The shift was starkly reflected in the "Distinguished Alumni" roster, a public-relations release that listed the professions of the school's biggest luminaries by class year. The honor roll of the academy's Big Men shrunk and slid precipitously from the founders of giant construction and bridge-building concerns in the early years to the lone representative listed for the class of '84: an executive of a steakhouse franchise.

The files of the Citadel's career-placement office in the mid-1990s bore painful witness to the change. As its director, Barbara Fairfax, told me, alumni ties were now mostly yielding sales and service jobs. Trying to put the best face on bleak prospects, she cheerily emphasized the "management trainee" posts that some graduating cadets had snagged in the past year. It turned out these were posts at Kmart and Wal-Mart. About 20 percent of graduates surveyed in the mid-1990s by the school's career office said they had no job and were unsure how they were going to support themselves. The old default mode for young men without work, particularly young men who had graduated from a military academy, was no longer reliable either. With the downsizing of the military prominently in the news, less than a third of Citadel graduates were enlisting in the services, and only 18 percent were making it a career—a steep drop from the days when half to three-quarters of Citadel graduates routinely took a service commission. They weren't wrong to be leery. In town, news of Shannon Faulkner's court case competed in the local *Post & Courier* with news of the closing of the Charleston Naval Shipyard and decommissionings from local military installations.

The night before closing arguments in Faulkner's suit, I had dinner at the on-campus home of Citadel professors Phillipe and Linda Ross. Phillipe, a biology professor, had just completed his first round of moonlighting as a "retraining" instructor at the Charleston Naval Shipyard. He had been prepping laid-off nuclear engineers to enter one of the few growth industries in the area: toxic-waste management. It had been a dispiriting experience, facing a room filled with frightened, desperate men each week. What had stayed with him was the plea of a middle-aged engineer thrust out of the service after twenty-six years: "All I want to do is work." Linda Ross, an adjunct professor of psychology at the Citadel and a woman of obvious empathy, looked across the table with a pained expression. "That whole idea that if a young man went to college he could make a decent living and buy a house and maybe even a boat just does not hold anymore," she said softly. She recalled a Citadel graduate she had run into recently—working behind the cash register at the local supermarket. "It's very scary," she said, and it wasn't just the men of the Citadel whom she feared for. "This change could be bigger than the industrial revolution, and I think very few of us are ready for what's coming."

Institutions that boast of their insularity, whether convents or military academies, are commonly pictured in the public imagination as static, unchanging abstractions, impervious to the ebb and flow of current events. Certainly, in the case of the Citadel, both the cadets and the invading media presented the school as the product of a century of unbending tradition. Nevertheless, its bricked-off culture had functioned more as a barometer of national anxieties than as a stalwart garrison against them. The violence the cadets exhibited toward women, and toward one another, had not always been a staple of student life. When the nation was caught up in a socially acceptable conflict and its soldiers were seen as providing an essential service, the Citadel actually loosened its militaristic harness or removed it altogether. Thus, during the most "acceptable" war in American history, World War II, the "fourth-class system" of hazing and humiliation was all but discontinued, largely in response to the demands of the real military for soldiers they could use in a modern war. The full-dress parades were suspended and upperclassmen couldn't even order a freshman to assume the stand-at-attention "brace."[28] "The War Department and the Navy Department were asking ROTC to do less drilling, more calculus," said Jamie Moore, a professor of history and a military expert at the school. "The Citadel dismantled its fourth-class system because it was getting in the way of their military training." The changes didn't seem to interfere with the school's production of Whole Men. On the contrary, an extraordinary percentage of the Citadel's most distinguished graduates come from these years, including Senator Ernest ("Fritz") Hollings, Alvah Chapman, Jr., former chief executive of the Knight-Ridder news chain, and South Carolina's former governor John C. West.[29]

The kinder, gentler culture of the World War II–era Citadel survived well into the next decade. Although a new fourth-class system was soon established, it remained relatively benign. "We didn't have the yelling we have today," former Citadel commandant Harvey Dick, ex-marine, class of 1953, recalled. "They didn't even shave the freshmen's heads." Ellis Kahn, class of 1958 and now a Charleston attorney, remembered: "In my four years there, nobody ever touched me in a violent way. It was a time of respect."

The postwar years also brought the admission of women to the summer program, without any of the hand-wringing provoked by Shannon Faulkner's application. WOMEN INVADE CITADEL CLASSES FIRST TIME IN SCHOOL'S HISTORY, Charleston's News & Courier noted in its June 21,

1949, issue—a development that merited notice only on page sixteen. "Most male students took the advent of the 'amazons' in their stride," the paper reported cheerfully. "Only the younger ones seemed at all uneasy. Professors and instructors were downright glad to see women in their classes."[30]

The Vietnam War, needless to say, did not inspire the same mood of relaxation on campus. It was in those years that the Junior Sword Drill began mounting violent nocturnal escapades. "The fourth-class system was very physical," said Wallace West, the school's admissions director, who was an undergraduate at the Citadel during the Vietnam years. "When I was there, there was no true emphasis on academics, or on positive leadership. It was who could be worked to physical exhaustion." Alumni from these years remember being beaten with cypress stumps, coat hangers, broom handles, and rifle butts. "Sweat parties," where freshmen were forced to do calisthenics in overheated rooms until they passed out, were a common occurrence. It was the era that inspired Pat Conroy's novel *The Lords of Discipline*, a tale of horrific hazing, directed with special virulence against the school's first black cadet. "They just tortured us," Conroy recalled. He remembered cadets being forced to hang by their fingers from closets and being stuck with sharp objects in the anus and testicles. "It taught me the exact kind of man I didn't want to be."

In 1968, the administration appointed a committee to investigate the violence. The committee issued a report that concluded, "there have been significant and extensive abuses to the [fourth-class] system." With its strong recommendation that hazing result in expulsion, the report seemed to promise a more pacific future on campus.[31]

A decade later, however, as the nation began to deindustrialize and young men's wages and status began to fall, the chart of violence and cruelty at the Citadel began to spike once more. In 1979, the Citadel selected a new president, Vice Admiral James B. Stockdale, for his status as a military hero: he had survived eight years in a POW camp in Vietnam. He failed to see the point of manufactured adversity, and he was repelled by the rising violence on campus. In an afterword to *In Love and War*, a collaborative memoir by Stockdale and his wife, Sybil, he wrote that there was "something mean and out of control about the regime I had just inherited."[32]

On his first day in the president's office, Stockdale opened some desk drawers and discovered "what turned out to be a Pandora's box. From the top down, what was written on the papers I took out of the desk drawers—and conversations with some of their authors—was enough to break anybody's heart." Characteristic was a letter from an infuriated father who wanted to know what had happened to his son "to change him from a level-headed, optimistic, aggressive individual to a fatigued, irrational, confused and bitter one." He also found copies of memos from the Citadel's staff physician complaining repeatedly of "excessive hospitalization." Stockdale sought to rein in the violence, with little success. The school's governing body overruled his expulsion of a senior cadet who had been threatening freshmen with a pistol. And the attention Stockdale brought to violent behavior only produced more of it. Furious at the president for exposing the pistol-packing upperclassman, a fellow cadet avenged his friend by attempting to firebomb Stockdale's home. A year into his presidency, the former prisoner of war submitted his resignation.[33] The Citadel administration and its cadet regiment "thought they were helping people into manhood," Stockdale told me from Palo Alto, California, where he was a scholar at Stanford University's Hoover Institution on War, Revolution and Peace. "But they had no idea what that meant, or who they were."

For the cadets, the response to not knowing who they were was a violent one. But if the level of violence seemed indexed to the fortunes of America's fighting men, how much more wildly would it fluctuate with the collapse of male fortunes in a consumer culture and the end of the industrial economy the Citadel had been built to serve?

Just a Sixty-Six

LAKEWOOD HAD INTENTIONALLY BEEN BUILT AROUND A MALL, the first suburb in America to choose a shopping center instead of a church or a courthouse as its centerpiece. The highest points in the city for many years were the giant emblems on the mall's anchor department store, May Company; four letter *M*s, each sixteen feet high, could be seen from anywhere in Lakewood. The mall became the blueprint for suburban shopping malls across the country, with its covered pedestrian court surrounded by a vast moat of parking areas and set back three hundred feet from the street, a consumer city on a (figurative) hill.[34] More often than not, when I was coming to Lakewood, Billy Shehan would propose we meet up at the mall. It was his version of the Biltmore clock in Manhattan. It was also where the Spurs killed an inordinate amount of time slouched on benches in the mall's atrium or trying on sneakers in its many sportswear stores. On this particular afternoon in the late spring of 1994, it was a destination. Billy Shehan said he wanted to show me how he "made a connection" with girls.

The economic agonies of southern California in the preceding five years, and the particular agonies of Lakewood, had dulled the sheen of this civic temple. We strolled past FOR LEASE signs on vacant stores and watched the big carousel in the middle of the mall reel around, its painted horses bobbing up and down, their saddles empty. Billy stopped at Foto Shack and chatted up a girl he knew vaguely from school. She listened politely for a while, then told him she had to get back to work. "Are there any job openings here?" he asked. She shook her head. Billy wrote his name and number down on a piece of paper anyway, just in case, and left it on the glass counter for her to pass on to the manager. "See," he said as we returned to the parking lot, "I made a connection."

Billy was intent on buying me lunch for a change. He suggested we drive over to the In-N-Out Burger. After studying the menu, though, Billy realized he couldn't afford two meals, even here. I told him I wasn't really hungry anyway, a drink would be fine. So he bought me a Coke, and dug in his pockets for enough coins to manage a small order of fries. We settled at a cement picnic table bolted to the concrete patio. We were all of ten feet from a major thoroughfare, and a hot wind blew up from the onrush of traffic. Discarded burger wrappers scudded through the air and flapped at our heels.

I asked Billy why Chris Albert had been so angry at Maury Povich. Billy guessed it was because Povich hadn't given some of the Spurs money they had been promised "on time," or that he had promised them six tickets to a Knicks game and only came through with two. But what was truly infuriating was something less tangible. No matter how much the TV shows put up (and *Jenny Jones* and *The Home Show* paid $1,000 to each of their Spur guests), the media junket had not paid off in the way the Spurs had imagined.[35] They had pictured it as a road to somewhere; they hadn't anticipated a circular driveway. Billy tried to figure out where his media ride had dead-ended. "If I had responded on the talk shows like I was a star, then I would've been seen as a star," he said. "Instead, I smoked a joint in the limo on the way over and drank shots."

The media-paid trip that Billy took to New York City with Chris Albert and Kevin Howard started out with many promises from *Maury Povich* and *The Jane Whitney Show*, the two TV programs competing for their attention. "First they said to us, 'New York! For free!'" Billy recalled. "Jane Whitney's producer said, 'We'll give you $1,000, and you don't need to worry about spending money, and you'll have limos every day, and elegant meals, and elegant this and elegant that.' Maury Povich's producer said if we don't go on another show first, they were going to give us three hundred dollars upfront and seventy-five dollars a day for nine days," plus tickets to a Knicks game and, or so Billy thought, the hint of something more. "Povich's producer said he was going to set us up with girls on his staff," Billy said. "The producer put Maury himself on the phone. Maury worked it like he was closing a telemarketing deal. Maury says, 'You gotta come down. We got an all-girl staff, beautiful girls.' I said, 'Do I get my pick?' and he said, 'You have my permission.' He was basically telling me they were going to hook us up." No doubt, neither Povich nor anyone on his staff was offering what the Spurs imagined. But like the targets of a telemarketer's pitch, the boys heard what they wanted to hear.

On the ride from the airport to the hotel, Billy felt like a long-exiled prince come to claim his kingdom. "Here I was in this limo in this giant-ass city, and it was like I owned the taxis and the cars, I owned the buildings and all the girls in the windows in the buildings. I felt like I could do whatever I wanted. I had instant exposure. I had this audience. Ten million people were going to be listening to me. I had their attention."

For the next week and a half, the shows vied for the Spurs' attention and the boys drank themselves into a stupor from the little bottles in the Radisson Hotel's minibars. "For eleven days, these guys were our best friends," Billy said of the TV producers. "They showered admiration on us." One night, Billy said, one of Jane Whitney's senior staffers took them in a limo to a strip bar. It was a club in Queens called Goldfingers. Billy recalled: "It was fifty dollars to get in. He was feeding us with drinks and feeding us tip money. He knew a bunch of the girls there and he was introducing me. I must've spent eight hundred dollars on tip money." (The staffer refused to discuss his handling of the show and referred me to Barbara Borgliatti, the senior vice president of corporate communications for Warner Bros., who told me she did not think the matter warranted a response. "I'm not going to sell my executive down the river for these scumbags," she said, referring to the same young men they had courted so assiduously. "They are not people I'd want to be in the same room with.")

Meanwhile, the *Maury Povich* show wooed the boys by sending them out for the evening with four young women from the program's staff. "The whole staff there was girls," Billy recalled. "It looked to me like you can't get a job there unless you're a woman. It was sexist to guys." Billy was under the impression that the evening with the women on staff was a "date." "They asked us to have drinks. We were having a good time. I thought three of the four girls liked me by the way they acted. And then it was like midnight and all of a sudden they said, 'Oh, we have to go,' like dirty-assed Cinderellas." The Spurs still were up for some late-night prowling and one of the young women, Billy said, recommended the boys take a cab over to Times Square. "I said, 'Is it safe?' " Billy recalled. "And they said, 'Oh yeah, it's safe.' "

They jumped out of the taxi at Times Square. "Everything was a fantasy, like I was in Mauryland. Like the whole city was a talk show." They passed a street full of marquees, then one full of hookers, then the streets began to seem darker and menacing. Billy had his tape recorder out— he had brought it along to record his impressions of the city—and he was talking into it as he walked. Suddenly, two hands reached out from the darkness and collared him. The next thing Billy knew, he had been yanked between two buildings. "He was holding something against me that felt like a gun in my back," Billy said. The man ripped the tape recorder out of his hands, extracted his wallet from his pocket, and fled. So did Billy. He lay in his hotel room all night listening to his heart pound. The next morning, he phoned the *Maury Povich* show and demanded that they reimburse him for the robbery. When they declined, he refused to go on the program. "I felt they owed me something."

Billy did, however, make an appearance on *The Jane Whitney Show,* where he would be much remembered and vilified for his boast about scoring his sixty-seventh point with a girl he lured back to the Radisson Hotel. And then he'd returned home, poorer and without taped memories. "For a while when I got back," Billy said, folding his empty frenchfry bag into a smaller and smaller square, "everybody recognized me because of the shows. But now, I mean, some still do, but . . ." His voice trailed off. We sat and watched the traffic, which was starting to thicken. The sun angled down behind a billboard advertising Virginia Slims, creating a golden aura around its larger-than-life ingenue with her head tossed back saucily, lips parted, laughing, under the big-lettered announcement IT'S A WOMAN THING. Billy cleared his throat. "Uh, you know something sort of funny?" I waited. "I didn't get that point," he said. I looked over at him. He had taken off his cap and was nervously snapping and unsnapping the fasteners on the back strap. "The producer said, 'Act like you got a point on the show.' So I did." He gave a short, bitter laugh. "I even wrote a song about it later: 'Everyone thought I was a sixty-seven when I was just a sixty-six.' "

A Man in a Uniform Is a Kind of Dream

"THE EMOTION OF SHAME is the primary or ultimate cause of all violence," Dr. James Gilligan, the former mental-health director of the Massachusetts prison system, concluded in *Violence,* a thoughtful consideration of the origins of violent male behavior in America. "The purpose of violence is to diminish the intensity of shame and replace it as far as possible with its opposite, pride, thus preventing the individual from being overwhelmed by the feeling of shame." The major sources of shame for American men, Gilligan's examination found, were downward social mobility and unemployment, circumstances that reveal a helpless core, showcasing an emasculating dependency.[36] More generally, he wrote, male shame comes from the suspicion that the world discredits your claim to manhood, finds it useless, even risible. The violent response to this knowledge serves as a kind of tortoiseshell to armor and conceal its vulnerable occupant, a shield to deflect further humiliating internal inspection. It is a reaction to being caught out, exposed as weak and insufficient.

Years before Shannon Faulkner submitted her application and brought the cameras onto the Citadel campus, the cadets were girding for such exposure. The martial facade that sheltered them was already crumbling. They sensed that the "tradition" of the academy was not one they could build on anymore. They saw for themselves that the image of a starched and disciplined soldier no longer led to masculine honors or good jobs in the world outside the academy gates. Their shame over feelings of male insufficiency and helplessness bred violence, which in turn attracted media and public attention, which only intensified their sense of exposure and thus their shame.

In the fall of 1991, the regimental chaplain observed to the soccer team's most promising freshman player, Michael Lake, that the brutal hazing he had recently witnessed on campus was the ugliest in his memory. Lake himself was preparing to leave, after weeks of frightening and bruising encounters with upperclassmen that included being knocked down with a rifle butt and that culminated in a bloody beating in the dark by a pack of cadets. It had been the year for battering star freshman athletes—the school's only celebrities, pre-Shannon. A member of the cycling team had been forced to hang by his fingers over a sword poised two inches below his testicles; a placekicker had his head dunked in water twenty times until he passed out; a linebacker was forced to swallow spat-up tobacco and tormented until, he said later, "I was unable even to speak clearly in my classes."[37]

The torment became so disturbing that, in a school where publicly criticizing the alma mater is virtually an act of treason, several athletes told their stories to *Sports Illustrated*.[38] Rather than putting a stop to the violence, the coverage only exacerbated the rage. The Churchill Society, a "literary" club reportedly containing a white-supremacist faction, was organized on campus. The local chapter of the National Association for the Advancement of Colored People urged a federal investigation into a pair of racial incidents: the appearance of a noose over the bed of a black freshman who had refused to sing "Dixie," and the shooting and wounding of a black cadet by a sniper who was never identified. A leader of the Junior Sword Drill leaped off a five-foot dresser onto the head of a prostrate cadet, then left him in a pool of blood in a barracks hall. A lacrosse-team member returning from an away game at three in the morning stumbled upon the victim's unconscious body, his face split open, jaw and nose broken, mouth a jack-o'-lantern of missing teeth.[39]

This explosion of *Lord of the Flies* bloodlust would follow that novel's script of stranded-boy savagery with impressive precision, all the way to an ultimate act of animal sacrifice. One night at about 2 A.M., high-ranking cadets trapped a raccoon in the barracks and began to stab it with a knife. Beau Turner, son of Ted Turner, was awakened by the young men's shouts. "My roommate and I went out there to try and stop it," Turner told me, "but we were too late." Accounts of the episode vary, but the tormentors may have sliced off the animal's tail and sodomized its anus with a sword. What was most recalled was an accompanying chant: "Kill the bitch. Kill the bitch."

The administration managed to keep some of these incidents under wraps, but enough bad news leaked out locally to become a public-relations nightmare, and the school finally commissioned a committee of Citadel loyalists to assess the situation. Even they concluded in their 1992 report that the physical abuse of freshmen, along with food and sleep deprivation, was out of hand. Though they instituted a few minor ameliorating changes, what was fueling these practices was not a question the committee was interested in considering.[40]

When Michael Lake looked back on the abuse he suffered during his abbreviated freshman year, he could see before him, like the emergence of invisible ink on what had appeared to be a blank piece of paper, the faint outlines of another struggle. He saw a submerged gender battle, a bitter but definitely fixed contest between the sexes, concealed from view by the fact that men played both parts. The beaten freshmen sports stars were the "women," stripped and humiliated; the predatory upperclassmen were the "men," who bullied and pillaged. What was, at its best, a strategy for replicating a mother-child relationship in masculine terms out of view of female inspection was becoming, at its worst, a sadomasochistic relationship in which what was "feminine" had to be brutally crushed.

"They called you a 'pussy' all the time," Lake recalled, or "a fucking little girl." It started the very first day they had their heads shaved, when the upperclassmen stood around and taunted, "Oh, you going to get your little girly locks cut off?" When they learned Lake would be playing soccer that fall, their first response was, "What is that, a girl's sport?" Another cadet, Richard Bryant, recalled that his freshman class was even subjected to a version of domestic violence. The upperclassmen, he said, "would go out and get drunk and they would like to come home and haze. And you just hoped they didn't come into your room." Bryant arrived in 1993 and withstood nearly a year of what he characterized as "continual abuse" until he caught himself contemplating a leap out of a fourth-story window in his barracks and quit. Virtually every taunt hurled in his direction, he recalled, equated him with a woman: whenever he showed fear, they would say, "Bryant, you look like you're having an abortion," or "Bryant, are you menstruating this month?"

A fear of having their domestic proclivities mistaken for femininity may have inspired this cresting wave of antifemale sentiment, but a campus where men played both female and male sides of a gender war was only a step away from a campus consumed with a fascination for and fear of homosexuality. Any threat to the cadets' sense of manhood, whether from the media, invading women, or an inhospitable economy, could push the cadets into a nightmarish realm where the kidding about limp-wristedness became real, and mean. In the spiraling tensions of the late 1980s and early 1990s, the beloved communal showers became a place not only of childlike bonding but of homophobic torment. Freshmen told me that as they ran through the showers, the upperclassmen would knock the soap out of their hands and, when they would lean over to retrieve it, the upperclassmen would scream: "Don't pick it up, don't pick it up. We'll use you like we used those girls."

A former Citadel Halloween tradition, of upperclassmen dressing up— mostly in diapers and women's clothes—and collecting candy treats from freshmen, morphed in this period into "tricks" of considerable violence. One upperclassman told me of cadets who knocked dressers over on candy-dispensing cadets and then walked on top of them. The administration tried, unsuccessfully, to put a stop to the whole affair; too many freshmen were getting injured. The playful pat on the butt that served to usher cadets into the brotherhood had its dark version, which surfaced increasingly under the stresses and intrusions of the nineties, just as it had in the Vietnam years. According to a recent graduate, one company of cadets devised a regimen in which the older cadets tested sophomores nightly with increasingly painful ordeals that proceeded to stompings and beatings. The process, which they dubbed "Bananarama," climaxed on a night in which a banana was actually shoved into a cadet's anus.

A homophobic hysteria vented itself with volcanic force on a few young men who either were, or were perceived to be, genuinely gay. Several were hounded out of the school. The scapegoating reached such ugly proportions that the generally slumbering Citadel counseling center set up a sort of group therapy session for the targeted young men, who were known on campus as "It," as in a game of brutal tag.

Herbert Parker had taken two and a half years off after his sophomore year to serve in the military. He returned to a place of strange and subtle menace. One evening, a cadet spotted Parker lounging, after hours, in the TV room of the student activities center, talking to a janitor. By the next morning, the rumor had spread that he had been caught in a sexually compromising position with the janitor. Parker was bewildered. "I was fully dressed," he told me later. "I was sitting by myself on the couch." His bewilderment turned to horror and humiliation when the rumor led to a year of total isolation—cadets refused to sit near him in the mess hall or in classes or share a room—which escalated to terror: incessant threatening phone calls, people under his window at night screaming at him to get out of town, and eventually death threats. The cadets brought him up before the student Honor Court and tried to have him thrown out. As Parker put it later, "It was like I had murdered someone."

One evening in June 1994, after the closing arguments in Shannon Faulkner's court case, I went over to the Treehouse, a "mixed" bar in town with a gay and straight crowd downstairs and an upstairs nightly drag show on the weekends. My intention was to ask about cadet violence against gay men. I presumed, on a campus where every second epithet was "faggot" and where reputedly gay cadets had been cruelly excommunicated, that such hate crimes were all but inevitable. There were indeed a few such cases, I learned, but the circumstances were not what I had expected. To my surprise, the gay regulars at the Treehouse offered me empathetic insights into the cadets' dilemma.

"The proper terminology for the Citadel," Chris Scott, who was seated at the bar downstairs, told me, "is the closet." Up and down the bar, his assessment was greeted with a murmur of agreement. "They love faggots like me." What he meant by "like me," however, was not exactly that he was gay. While that night he looked like a typical *GQ* magazine male model—sleek black hair and a handsome, chiseled face—on the nights he dressed for a performance, he passed for a woman. Arching an eyebrow, Scott said, "The cadets go for the drag queens."

Chris Scott's observation was echoed in ensuing conversations in two visits to the Treehouse where I could find only two drag queens out of about a dozen who had *not* dated a cadet—and that was only because they found cadets "too emotional." "Holly" had been involved with a cadet for three years. "Marissa," the reigning "Miss Treehouse, 1993–94," had gone out with one cadet, broken up, and was now in the throes of a budding romance with another. And "Tiffany," the drag performers agreed, attracted cadets like flies.

"Kimber Love," the picture of Cher with his wide-set eyes and flowing black hair, said that personally he'd just as soon not get entangled with cadets. "I don't mess with them because of the fake butch attitude. They have this male-chauvinist personality. And it's all fake." There was another good reason to avoid dating the cadets. "You can get the ones who are violent," Chris Scott said. "They think they want it, then afterwards they turn on you, like you made them do it." As we were talking, Lownie (he asked that I not use his last name), whose stage name was Mary Terrorista, wandered in and settled on a bar stool. An aspiring fiction writer, he recited the opening lines of a short story he was working on to the appreciative audience. It was a memory piece about meeting his first beloved—who, as it happened, was a cadet. Lownie said he delighted in the Friday dress parades of the Corps of Cadets. "The parades are a big thing with the queers [in Charleston]. We'll have a cocktail party and go over and watch the boys. It's a very southern 'lady' thing to do."

Lownie arranged covert rendezvous with his lover by exchanging coded messages in little-used books in the Citadel library. Sometimes his lover would stay over and sneak back on campus before sunup, jogging through the Citadel gates in his school sweats as if returning from a predawn run. The only real hardship, Lownie said, was witnessing his lover's emotional distress, generated by hazing rituals. "They're so trapped in there, like caged birds, and he needed to talk so much," said Lownie. "Most of [the cadets] have no lives for themselves. They don't have the capacity to live in the real world." Despite his emotional outpourings to Lownie, the cadet appeared to his fellow corpsmen a model of machismo. He was a Junior Sword Drill member, a regimental officer, and a "hang king" who could dangle by his fingers for long periods from a closet rack, a prized skill at the Citadel. Lownie grinned: "I used to make him wear his shako [the Citadel's military cap] when we were having sex. It's manhood at its most."

Lownie himself had spent four years in the air force, and he came away from the experience with a deep and abiding attachment to military life, for reasons similar to the sentiments expressed by the cadets in Colonel Rembert's class. "The day-to-day aspect of being in a military environment is that you run around in a little bit of clothing and you are being judged as to how good a man you are by doing women's work, pressing pants, sewing, polishing shoes. You are a *better* man if you have mastery of womanly arts. The camaraderie doesn't get any stronger than when you are in the barracks, sitting around at the end of the day in your briefs and Ts and dog tags, like a bunch of hausfraus, talking and gossiping while you are polishing your shoes."

"So you get to play house?" I asked.

"Yes," he said, but of course the cadets don't see it that way. "They are buffing and waxing and shining, but they are not consciously doing a womanly art. They think they are becoming a *Whole Man.*" To Lownie, the Citadel served as an unrecognized escape hatch from social expectations. "You don't have to be a breadwinner. You don't have to be a leader. You can play backseat. It's a great relief. . . . You can act like a human being and not have to act like a man."

Many of the Treehouse drag queens shared the cadets' opposition to the admission of women for a mirror-image reason: if the cadets feared female colleagues would destroy their carefully constructed presentation to the world as archetypal officers and gentlemen, the drag queens were guarding their part in the drama, as debs at the hop. "You know what the cadet I'm seeing now said to me?" Tiffany commented. We were sitting in the dressing room a couple hours before a performance and Tiffany was peering into a Lady Clairol mirror set illuminated with miniature movie-star lights, applying layer after layer of mascara and eyeliner with expert precision. "He said, 'You're more of a woman than a woman is.' And that's an exact quote." Tiffany stood up and struck a southern belle pose by way of illustration. "I overexemplify everything a female is—my breasts, my hair, the way I hold myself." Who better to complete the picture than a fantasy gentleman in uniform?

Marissa, Miss Treehouse, looked up from his labors, painting regimental rows of fake nails with pink polish. "I love how they wear their caps slung low so you can't quite see their eyes," he said. "It's like all of us are female illusionists and they are male illusionists. A man in a uniform is a kind of dream."

Tiffany said, "For Halloween, you know what my cadet boyfriend wanted to dress as? A *cadet.*"

The group of men in a dressing room tenderly helping one another get ready for the evening, an elaborate process of pinning and binding and stuffing, was not very different, in its way, from the cadets in Norman Doucet's video tucking in one another's shirts. As the drag queens conversed, they tossed stockings and Ace bandages and cosmetic bags back and forth. "Has anyone seen my mascara wand?" "Okay, who has the blush?" There was a homey comfort that reminded me of child-hood slumber parties, where we would put big, pink, spongy rollers in each other's hair and screech with laughter at the results. What was going on here was play—a kind of freedom and spontaneity and gentle-ness that, in this culture, only women are permitted. Here, each man was allowed to "act like a human being and not have to act like a man."

No wonder men found their Citadels, their Treehouses, where the rules of gender could be bent or escaped, if only in part and for a time and under the most laborious of conditions. For the drag queens of the Treehouse, the distinctions between the sexes were a goof, to be end-lessly manipulated with fun-house-mirror glee. For the cadets, despite the play set of the Citadel and the dress-up braids and ribbons, the guarding of their treehouse was a deadly serious business. As I sat in the dressing room, I found myself imagining what it would be like if the cadets could have adopted from the Treehouse illusionists the art of self-transformation, could have learned to play the gender game without the war game, could have embraced the nurturing camaraderie that they craved, the physical care and domestic intimacy, without compensating shows of belligerence and brutality.

Like the cadets, the drag queens secured themselves in a safe all-male realm where, buffered from the judgmental eyes of society's masculinity hall monitors, they could let down their hair and allow themselves to enjoy a kind of maternal masculinity. And yet, inside this realm, they were also like the Spurs: they put themselves on display, up on a stage, flamboyantly courting attention. Billy Shehan imagined himself the king of "Mauryland," parading before millions of television viewers; Tiffany and Kimber Love and Marissa imagined themselves the queens of the Treehouse, strutting before their admiring fans.

If the setup the Treehouse performers jury-rigged seemed to work for them, it also showed how impossibly constrained the options were for men outside its doors. Its pajama-party playhouse represented a retreat from the larger society, not an alternate route back in or an alternate vision of where society itself might head. The drag queens could act like mother hens or pinup models only by dressing up as women, jumping the gender divide. This was hardly a solution for the average man, straight or gay, or even for the average drag queen, who slipped back into trousers when he left the refuge of the bar. The drag queens could pull it off only by pretending that they *were* female.

That was the problem. Inside the Treehouse, the drag queens could become more nurturing by welcoming a sort of femininity. In the real world, the "feminizing" of men, whether ushered in by Shannon Faulkner or by Maury Povich, only destroyed the possibility of male nurturance, because it destroyed the group anonymity and utilitarian security within which men could permit themselves to nurture, and replaced those with a celebrity sweepstakes that turned men into predators. No wonder the Spurs and cadets both thought that girls had all the power. The "feminine" world of achievement through glamour was being thrust on them (though not really by women), and neither group had found a way to evade its force. The Spurs were trying desperately to avoid an anachronistic anonymity—that is, by accosting young women, they were trying not to become cadets. The cadets were resisting being swept into a media world where worth was adjudged by glitter points on an appearance meter—that is, by shutting out Shannon Faulkner, they were trying not to become Spurs.

Both would fail.

To hold the line against the new global forces demanding display and entertainment was a Herculean task for any boy just now coming of age. The Spurs seemed to have the easier route to navigate. At least the winds were blowing in the direction they wanted to sail. But as the many men who tried to cross the new ornamental straits would learn, the passage to manhood was chancy and treacherous. More sank than swam in those shimmering, mirrored waters.

———

I WOULD TALK TO BILLY SHEHAN on and off over the next couple of years. In Lakewood, his notoriety lingered, although not in a way that proved useful. "Nobody wants to hire me because of the Spur business," he said. When the glittery media culture spat him back into Lakewood, he found his brush with "fame" had turned him into a toad, not a prince. The last time we met, he said he had applied for work at fifty places in the previous month: the stores in "all the malls," restaurants, gas stations, pizza-delivery joints, secretarial pools. From this résumé blitz, he had garnered two interviews—one at Chili's—and neither yielded a job. I asked him if any of the Spurs had a good job now. Billy racked his brain. He could think of only one, a young man who ran a tiny fish-processing business. "If I hadn't been in this Spur shit," he said woefully, "I'd be working right now."

He had caught the public eye again only once. He and some old Spur friends had tried to force their way into Murphy's Bar in Long Beach during a private St. Patrick's Day party. "The bouncers grabbed me and tried to throw me out," he said. "The bouncers were saying that I threw a basketball from the second floor and could've hurt somebody. One of the bouncers, he followed me outside, he grabbed me and threw me up against the wall of the liquor-store window so hard the glass shattered. Like twenty cop cars showed up." Billy was arrested, but no one pressed charges and he was quickly released. "The cops knew who I was. They said, 'Oh, Billy Shehan, what are you doing in this neck of the woods?' " He didn't mind so much. "I'd rather be known than be some random nobody." The horror of being unknown far outweighed the horror of a night in prison. "That's my worst fear," he said, "that I'll die a nothing. I know that can't happen. I know I was meant to be a brand name. But a very small part of me says, What if nothing happens? What if I'm a common person?"

Billy had a new plan for preventing commonness. He had gone to talk to a man who said he was in the X-rated movie business. Billy was going to get some pictures taken and see if this man could pass them on to porn producers. "I figure, I'm already in the shock category." Didn't he worry about being viewed as a piece of meat? I asked. "Oh, I felt like that my whole life. Everybody should feel like that, unless they're an idiot. We're all meat puppets. You know," he added, "everybody says boys control girls, but it's the other way around. Girls have it a lot easier. They get the jobs easier. Because the jobs now are all about presenting yourself. It's all presentation. Girls have it made."

In his diary, Billy showed me a song he had started writing. It began:

> I want to be naked in a cage
> With a naked bitch.
> I want to be naked in a cage
> With a naked bitch.
> Just feed, breed, smoke a little weed
> We can be like pets.

What inspired that? I asked, not sure I wanted to know.

"I was watching TV one night. It was like three in the morning, and this girl was dancing in a cage. And I was thinking how great it would be to be, like, dancing there and be the pet of this girl who pays me a lot of attention and pets me and feeds me, but yet I'd have her in the cage, too, so she can't escape. That would be my idea of utopia."

A half year later, Billy had moved to Las Vegas in hopes of making a new start. I called around to the various places in that desert oasis where he was said to have crashed recently—his uncle's, his grandmother's, an overcrowded bachelor pad—but no one had seen him. I imagined he was off somewhere in the night, under the artificial glow of a Vegas utopia, dancing in his gilded cage.

4

A GOOD DAWG
WILL ALWAYS
REMAIN LOYAL

The Cleveland Browns Skip Town

AS THE RECESSION OF THE EARLY NINETIES ABATED, it seemed that the woes of discarded corporate men would be an unpleasant but largely closed chapter in the annals of American masculinity. Yet high rates of downsizing quietly continued; between 1995 and 1997, about eight million people were laid off due to corporate restructuring, plant closings, and economic dislocation.[1] The difference was that this time the dislocation was unheralded; the media largely ignored it. The company man was still "falling down," just not on the cover of *Newsweek*. The second time around, he was an old story, and one that conflicted with the new narrative of America's "boom economy."

Left out of that narrative were certain unpleasant facts. Men's real wages continued a seemingly inexorable decline from the 1970s. (A slight improvement in the late 1990s still left men's median weekly earnings below 1979 levels.) Men's job tenure continued to drop, their median years with the same employer falling nearly 20 percent from 1983 to 1998 (even as women's rose 5 percent); and each new group of men entering the workforce fell behind the earning power of their male elders. The "boom" was being built on the busted back of a contingent, temporary, contracted-out, no-or-low-benefits, no-guarantees workforce. Employees laid off in the early-1990s recession were much less likely to get their old jobs back than those laid off in any of the last four national economic downturns, and the employees who did get reemployed were more likely to wind up in part-time jobs. While surface economic conditions were healing, the underlying social pact between companies and their company men continued to hemorrhage. The wound went undressed for a reason that had nothing to do with year-to-year fluctuations in the national economy. Employers didn't want to stem the bleeding. Raising profits by shedding employees wasn't an injury to them, it was a boon. Mass layoffs at companies like AT&T, Xerox, and IBM produced instant leaps in their stock prices.[2] Their interests and the interests of their employees no longer coincided.

The postwar pact between employer and employee had been built on a foundational notion about loyalty, a belief that a bond strengthened over time was the basis for a sturdy masculine identity. (There was no such thing as the "company woman"; while being laid off was agony for a female employee, the one aspect of her life it didn't ruin was her feminine identity.) Men throughout America discovered in the eighties and nineties that the contract they thought they had with their employers was a lie. They had played by the company's rules, even when they secretly found them inane or counterproductive. They had been good soldiers and good sons. Yet they were receiving dishonorable discharges. Each had individually been "used and kicked out like a dog," as a laid-off transportation manager working as a secretary wrote of himself. "I was *someone*. . . . Now I'm nothing, just a temp."[3]

It turned out that in the new economy, loyalty was what you got if you were the one bringing the cash to the table. Like so much else in the era, loyalty had become a commodity. Some of the men at the McDonnell Douglas outplacement center refused to face this brutal truth, but a younger generation would have no choice. They saw that corporate loyalty had gotten many of their fathers nothing but a shame-faced middle age, and they wanted no part of it. The Spurs wanted to be celebrities for the same reason that new computer programmers wanted to be independent operators and new athletes wanted to be free agents. Individual renown, celebrity, was your only protection in a world without loyalty. And to be a celebrity, you had to be a marketable personality, your own brand name, not a loyal member of a team.

The sort of "team" in which a man could lose himself while finding himself as a man no longer seemed to exist. Not in the workplace. Not on a battlefront. Not even on the playing fields.

A King from Massillon

ON THE EVENING OF DECEMBER 17, 1995, Big Dawg staggered through the door, past his wife, Mary, and collapsed on the couch in their tiny living room. An hour earlier, Mary had seen him on television. Now, she described how the cameras moved in for close-ups when he started crying. He shrugged. "I don't mind it," he said, his voice a monotone. All day long, the reporters had been on him. They had "mugged" him in the parking lot and followed him into the bleachers. "There were so many out-of-town reporters," he said. "Gary Myers from HBO, and the *Daily News,* the *New York Times,* the top guys from ESPN. It took me an hour to get a hundred yards." In the stands, three reporters sat with him the entire game, monitoring his every emotion, and wherever he looked, he found himself staring down the barrel of a camera lens. "The reporters' number one question was 'How do you *feel?*' So basically, the story I gave was the way it felt to me." It was a story he had been telling for weeks, ever since he'd heard the awful news. He had settled on a metaphor and he stuck to it: "It was like finding out your best friend had terminal cancer and you had just three times left to visit him." No matter how often he offered up this simile, the media ran with it. "They used me so much, it all got sort of diluted," he said mournfully. But he was reluctant to turn them away. "I didn't want to let anyone down." When they asked for his feelings on this, the final day, he stuck with an appropriately updated version of his trusty reply: "Today, it all ended and my best friend died." This was how Big Dawg, a.k.a. John Thompson, described the final game that his beloved Cleveland Browns were ever going to play in Municipal Stadium.

The football team's owner, Art Modell, was moving the languishing fifty-year-old franchise to Baltimore, where he had struck a sugarplum deal dripping with juicy perks, tax breaks, and government subsidies that guaranteed him an income of thirty million dollars a year regardless of the team's performance or the size of the crowds.[4] The "employees" — the players, that is — would be coming with him. Nonetheless, he had shed his minions as surely as had McDonnell Douglas, and induced anguish that seemed, if anything, more visceral in its expression. He was leaving the fans behind.

Big Dawg was not just any Browns fan. He was the self-avowed leader of the Dawg Pound, a rabid pack of men who had turned the decrepit bleachers by the stadium's east end zone into a barking kennel, a howling Greek chorus accompanying the action on the field. "I like to think that the Dawg Pounders are the twelfth man," Big Dawg liked to say. The

"Big" referred to his weight, which hovered around 385 pounds, setting him apart from "D. Dawg" and "Junkyard Dawg" and "Jam Dawg" and "Sick Dawg" and "Ugly Dawg." The Dawg Pounders were the most fervid and loyal of fans, "bleacher creatures," or, as the team's owner, Art Modell, described them to me, "the people who are perceived as the downtrodden, sitting in the cheap seats." For years, most of these men (and they were almost all men) had presided over every home game in dog masks and floppy, fake-fur dog ears, greeting every play with a brandishing of foam and rawhide bones, raining dog biscuits onto the field, and offering up a perpetual cacophony of woofs and yelps. Displaying "how they *felt*," you might say, was their raison d'être. And this had been their last performance.

"We won the game," Big Dawg recalled later, "but I sat around after like we had lost." He was hard-pressed to put a name to the nature of his particular loss, although he knew that it was irrevocable and, in some strange way, the source of unspeakable personal shame. Because of this, he preferred to stick to sound-bite feelings. "It was kind of a reality hitting me in the face," he would say of the long hours that followed the game as he tried to sleep, staring dully into the darkness. "A reality I didn't want to face." So instead he concentrated on the promise of a new Cleveland team at some future date. "I just want to get a team and go to Baltimore and kick Art Modell's ass." He didn't really know why he was hurting so much, or why the men in the stands had been weeping, their heads in their hands, or why they all spoke of "a death in the family," "open-heart surgery," or "being beaten and stabbed." Big Dawg was certain of only one thing. "I want to win," he said, and he looked up at the ceiling wringing his hands as if imploring some deity on high. "I want to win *so bad*."

Football has been a part of American male ritual since the 1890s. It was first embraced on the college gridiron during the great imperial and masculine anxieties of the turn of the century. Its founding father, Walter Camp, was a clock company executive for whom the new sport represented, according to historian Michael Oriard, "the ideal training ground for a managerial elite" who would run a new business world of trusts and combines.[5] Camp transformed rugby into modern football with one key rule change: a team was assigned possession of the ball *before* play began. (In rugby, the teams grappled in a big mass to claim the ball.) From the start, then, football was about the maintenance of control and dominance, which is undoubtedly why it remained primarily a college sport until the end of World War II, college being in the pre–GI Bill era the preeminent province for the training of a ruling class.

Unlike baseball, where the object was to send a ball careening anarchically through a lineup of functionaries in the field, to disrupt, not uphold, the established system, football was predicated on controlling the ball at all costs and conquering every last inch of your opponent's territory.

But in those prewar days, football had another face as well, one more familiar on the factory floor than in the company boardroom. Pro football, as opposed to college football, was the sport of the steelworker, the ironworker, and the miner, whose faces, long before they were helmeted and smeared with antireflective face paint, had been covered with the soot and sweat of manual labor. This version of the game emerged on the soggy, snowbound fields of America's heavy-industrial belt, in gritty contests between underfunded teams with names like the Ironton Tanks and the Providence Steam Roller.[6] In the imaginations of their fans, the players on these gridirons were right out of WPA murals, monumental stone-faced workers come to life. Pro football players were one domestic equivalent of Ernie Pyle's "mud-rain-frost-and-wind boys," playing out a gruntlike drama on a muddy swath of land under the frosted skies of smokestack America.

In the wake of the Second World War, the athletic field would be mythologized as a heroic wilderness from a masculine past in which "the American is still a frontiersman, still, like his ancestors, pressing on," as sports chronicler John R. Tunis would write in 1958.[7] But the "new frontiersmen" of the gridiron, like the new postwar nation they belonged to, would find themselves caught up in a very different game. The rise of professional football as a popular sport after the war has generally been seen, by both its defenders and detractors, as an expression on the playing field of the country's new preeminence on the world stage. With the American Century upon it, the nation seized upon a game that seemed to be all about triumphal leadership—or, to the less enamored, overweening imperialism. By the mid-1950s, professional football was emerging from the long shadow of baseball; it was thriving while attendance at major- and minor-league baseball as well as at college football slumped.[8] As a metaphor, pro football entered the new imperial language of power and of power holders in America. Not for nothing did football come to be termed the "Establishment Game"; not for nothing was the presidential briefcase holding nuclear missile launch commands called "the football." Our imperial presidents, from JFK to Nixon to Reagan, were entranced with the power of gridiron imagery. Nixon ostentatiously watched football while antiwar protesters marched on Washington. Reagan even clothed his presidency in shoulder pads and helmet, taking as his nom de guerre "The Gipper," after Notre Dame's star player of the 1920s, George Gipp, whom he'd portrayed in the 1940 movie *Knute Rockne — All-American*.

The assumption was that spectators flocked to football stadiums precisely *because* the drama therein celebrated an ascendant American power and authority that they identified with. They were reveling in their nation's empire building, and the more they saw, the more it whet their appetites. At least that was the conventional wisdom from football's critics, who saw the sport as an excuse for testosterone-ridden male fans to indulge their naturally aggressive tendencies, just as the media saw the Spur Posse boys as "arrogant" junior-macho egotists. Cocky aggression on the field was supposedly an incitement to cocky loutishness and bad behavior in the stands — in other words, football gore bred bloodthirsty male fans.

But the fans' relationship to the game was never that conveniently straightforward. For the working-class spectator, "supporting" his team was also a way of fighting against marginalization, a way of clinging to the idea that national destiny was still something played out by common men on a muddy field, even in an era dominated by skyboxes, television, and Astroturf. "One of the great mistakes of superficial observers is to believe that players do all the work while fans merely sit passive and 'vicariously' have things done for them," philosopher and sports devotee Michael Novak has written, describing his own experience watching football as "an ordeal, an exercise, a struggle lived through."[9] Football was a workingman's way of resisting being sidelined, even as he sat in the stands. Here he might still believe himself a central "player" in one of his culture's central dramas. He would be ill-prepared for his ultimate marginalization when the transformation of a sport pumped up by TV and ad revenues, and geared largely to America's sports bars and living rooms, revealed just how passive and insignificant a force he was to his team's fortunes.

The Cleveland Browns were hardly the first team to pull up stakes, but their fans had especially good reasons to dread "The End," as Big Dawg called it. The Browns represented a pro football tradition grounded in loyalty, stoicism, and industry and conceived in the rivalry of two steelworker communities fifty miles south of Cleveland. The American Professional Football Association, the direct forerunner of the National Football League, was organized in a garage in Canton, Ohio, now home to the Pro Football Hall of Fame. Paul Brown, the founding coach of the Browns, was raised in neighboring Massillon, his father a dispatcher on the railroads that hauled the fruits of industrial labor out of town. At Massillon's Washington High School, in the depths of the Depression, coach Brown created a brand of play that would earn him the title "the father of modern pro football." He also created something else at Massillon: the modern football fan.

The meaning of that creation was made clear to me by a sixty-two-year-old Massillonian named Phil Glick. A 1951 Washington High School graduate, Glick had been a lifelong parts-sizer at Timken Roller Bearing Company in Canton until 1992, when he opted for an early retirement buyout offer over the risk of being laid off by the downsizing company. He was also a fan extraordinaire whose devotion to his high-school football team, the Massillon Tigers, led to his election as secretary-treasurer of the Sideliners, one of four booster clubs administering to the high-school football team, and ultimately to the presidency of the clubs' umbrella organization, the Massillon Tigers Football Booster Club. When he was picked to head the Boosters in 1988, Glick could scarcely believe his good fortune. "My wife used to tell me, 'One of these days, you will be president,' and it happened—two years after she passed away," Glick reminisced as we lunched at his usual spot, the AmVets Club in downtown Massillon. Judging by the brick and clapboard mom-and-pop shops with hand-painted signs along the town's main street, and the macaroni-and-cheese fare the club was offering, we could have been having our discussion in 1936. He wore an American flag on his left lapel and a Massillon Tigers football-helmet pin on the right one. The way he spoke left no doubt in my mind that he considered them of equal weight. He pushed aside the Wonder-bread-and-saltines condiments dish and laid a worn hand on the table to show me what looked like an oversized class ring. Somberly, he removed the ring awarded to Boosters' presidents after their one-year terms and handed it over for inspection. With what I hoped was the proper gravity, I examined the inset, an aspic of amber preserving, like a relic, the letter *M*. He sighed. "If only my wife were here to see it." He fished in a coat pocket and pulled out a hand-painted pin of Obie, the team's tiger mascot. It was mine to keep, he said, watching approvingly while, at his suggestion, I pinned Obie to my shirt collar. "Now you will always have a reminder of what it is we are all about."

Phil Glick was an exemplar of a masculine way of life adopted by millions every autumn weekend. What I didn't understand, not then anyway, was that Glick's concept of what it meant to be a fan extended beyond being known as president of the Boosters and wearing what looked like a miniature Super Bowl ring. His boosterism was of an earlier vintage, one that had less to do with spectatorship or the expropriation of the players' fame than with community service—with being known for *doing* something that was useful and supportive. The Massillon boosters weren't "fans" as we now understand the word; they were care providers, and the recipients of their care were young athletes. "It's sort of like Big Brothers, except with a player," Glick explained of Sideliners, the first Massillon booster club he helped guide. Each Sideliner takes on the nurturance of a team member—or, in the group's own parlance, "adopts" a player, becoming a surrogate father who is responsible for the boy's needs and there to help him when he is in trouble. Some Sideliners help with homework; some make sure their players are properly clothed and provided for; others offer postgraduation advice. After each game, the Sideliners are afforded locker-room privileges. "And each week of each game, we eat as a group," Phil Glick said, "at the AmVets, or at the American Legion, or the KFC."

As Boosters president, Glick was expected to give speeches, a nightmarish prospect for a man with a lifelong stutter. "I was petrified at first," he recalled. But miraculously, as he realized his young charges needed what he had to offer as much as he needed their appreciation, his anxiety ebbed and his stutter vanished. "I still get Christmas cards from some of my Sideliner lads. Steve Luke with the Packers, he came back to speak, and he saw some of us Sideliners and he recognized us." He paused to dab at his eyes with a paper napkin. "I get choked up a little bit thinking about it."

Sports fans as paternal providers was Paul Brown's notion. He coached the Massillon Tigers from 1932 to 1940 and in developing such fans was undoubtedly mainly concerned with raising funds for his broke, Depression-era team. In 1932, when he took over as coach, money was so tight that the school year had to be shortened to eight months. The coach's annual paycheck was a measly $1,600, and the school's athletic fund was $37,000 in the red. The team had won only one game the previous season, and the woebegone players ran up and down a rocky field in a dilapidated three-thousand-seat stadium that was never filled.[10]

But worse than empty stadiums were empty bellies. In the fall of 1934, according to a local historical account, a Tigers player was "hit so hard in the stomach that he retched, and nothing but tomatoes came up." When Paul Brown asked about "his curious diet," the boy confessed that his family had no money for meals; all he ate were tomatoes he stole from backyard gardens. Worried about the prospects of leading a team of starvelings to victory, Brown persuaded a school-board member and former player to organize what he called a "booster" club. Its charter: to raise enough money to buy each of his players one meal a day. It was the first high-school booster club in the country and its members, multiplying within two years to one thousand, began delivering food baskets to the players' homes. One of the original hungry boys ultimately went on to Ohio State University, while the boosters continued feeding and supporting his destitute family throughout his college years.[11]

Once the town fathers were invested in the young men's welfare, Paul Brown calculated, they would also be invested in the team's future, and he was right. Brown had given the men of Massillon a special paternal stake in the game. Every Monday night, he would show the Boosters Club films of the previous game and ruminate with them about the upcoming contest. At one point interest in being a part of such prep sessions grew so great that twenty-five hundred fans showed up for an outdoor briefing.[12]

The team, nourished now and meticulously dressed in special reversible coats for rainy weather or special warm-up jerseys with their names stitched on the backs, repaid fan devotion with a legendary record that elevated Massillon to "the capital of high-school football in the nation."[13] In the nine years Paul Brown coached them, the Tigers won eighty games and lost only eight. For six years, the Tigers prevailed in the Ohio state championships, and four times they were named national champions. When Brown finally left in 1940 for a coaching job at Ohio State, it was on the wings of a glorious winning streak, thirty-three uninterrupted victories. The 1940 team was so spectacular it even wiped out winning college teams with which it scrimmaged.[14]

Tigers boosterism had become, in Paul Brown's words, Massillon's "prime industry."[15] With the steel mills shuttered or operating at one-quarter speed during the Depression, and much of the male population out of work or only precariously employed, "working" for the team's fortunes became a new and rewarding vocation. In the severe depression of the 1890s, the town's unemployed workers had turned their energies in a political direction; local firebrand Jacob Coxey had led an army of jobless workers from all over the country to Washington to demand a $500 million public works program; the men marched to the Capitol only to be beaten and clubbed by mounted police, who immediately arrested Coxey and other march leaders—for walking on the grass. "Coxey's Army" became a legend. In 1932, Coxey was elected mayor of Massillon, but it was a sentimental vote, not a mandate for another showdown in Washington. This time, the townsmen were throwing their support behind a battle they could win: football.[16]

In a town of 26,000, an average of 18,200 fans turned out for the games. Most of the fans were adults, not children, a demographic still true today. To accommodate the crowds, in the depths of the Depression, the town elders got the WPA to finance construction of a new 21,000-seat stadium—the result in 1937 was the finest high-school sports arena in the nation. By 1940, the stadium was taking in more than $100,000 annually from ticket sales, more than many local businesses could claim. At one point during World War II, federal conservation officials descended on Massillon, demanding that the town save precious electricity by calling off night games. The town's elders, however, were able to prove—with the help of records from the state's utilities—that the town's electrical load actually dropped during games because everybody was at the stadium.[17]

While the townsmen reclaimed their breadwinning roles with the Depression's end, supporting the team gave them something assembly-line jobs at the steel mills didn't: a sense that they were more than cogs in a corporate machine. To the Tigers Boosters the team belonged to them—its triumphs were legitimately theirs. It put their small town on the map, at a time when national manufacturers, national brands, and national entertainment were beginning to erase small-town identities. "The proprietors in town explain it this way," a local account commented. "Some poor guy might work eight hours a day down the street at the steel mill and be a nobody, but for ten weeks every fall, he's a king because he's from Massillon."[18]

For a man to have a hand in the making of a team's fortunes, at a time when the making of everything else was fast slipping out of his grasp, was at the root of what it meant to be a "fan." He could, in the common parlance of sports fans, help "build a winner." The field became an artisan's workshop where products could still be made locally and custom crafted.[19]

"The romantic movements were important as a corrective to the machine because they called attention to essential elements in life that were left out of the mechanical world-picture," Lewis Mumford wrote in 1934 in *Technics and Civilization*. In modern times, whole "romantic" institutions emerged to compensate for the human losses endured with the rise of the machine. "The chief of these institutions," Mumford wrote, "is perhaps mass-sports. One may define these sports as those forms of organized play in which the spectator is more important than the player, and in which a good part of the meaning is lost when the game is played for itself. . . . [T]he spectator feels himself contributing by his presence to the victory of his side. . . . It is a relief from the passive role of taking orders and automatically filling them, of conforming by means of a reduced 'I' to a magnified 'It,' for in the sports arena the spectator has the illusion of being completely mobilized and utilized."[20]

The modern football fan has sometimes been called (as Big Dawg would call him) a team's "Twelfth Man." In Massillon, the Twelfth Man's ancestral home, the boosters wanted their team to win, and win big, but they saw their role in victory as that of responsible older men guiding and sustaining younger charges. "Fans here, they all see themselves as *coaches*," Tommy James, who played under Paul Brown in high school, college, and then on the Cleveland Browns, said to me with arched eyebrows, as we sat in his memorabilia-filled living room in Massillon. "Actually, they think they are *better* coaches. They think they are the authorities." To this day, the town's boosters are famed for demonstrating their devotion to the team with a telling symbolic flourish: they bestow upon every newborn boy in Massillon hospital's maternity ward a miniature white plastic football decorated with an Obie and the booster club's name.

Such a regime could, of course, make life hell for any Massillon boy who didn't fit the mold of expectations. A plastic football was no inheritance at all for a son who wasn't athletic, just a shaming reminder of his failure to make the grade. If boosterism provided a gratifying bond for men like Phil Glick and their Sideliner "lads," its applications were limited and could just as easily become a weapon against other boys, fueling fears and hatreds. As filmmaker William E. Jones made clear in his 1991 documentary film *Massillon,* growing up gay in such an environment was to feel, at best, invisible and, at worst, a pariah. Likewise for a straight teenager looking for paternal support outside the stadium, this civic prescription could prove stifling and disappointing.

In many respects, the Paul Brown model was more fulfilling for the fathers than for the sons, except for one particular set of "fathers"—those coaches who had the misfortune to follow Brown. They were sometimes driven from their posts by the town's male elders. "The funniest thing about this job," one of them, Mike Currence, concluded without amusement as he packed his bags, "is that I could never truly say it was my team. It's the town's team."[21] By the 1990s, with some steel mills not only laying off workers but pulling up stakes entirely, being able to lay claim to the team could be a great solace. Phil Glick, I noticed, didn't sport a pin, ring, or tie clasp with the Timken company's insignia, in spite of thirty-five years on its payroll.

Massillon had sprung into being in 1826 in anticipation of the Ohio and Erie Canal's opening two years later, and soon became a major grain market and industrial center.²² But to talk to the men of Massillon today, you would think that the town's first settler was Paul Brown, whose picture, *Ohio* magazine noted in 1989, "still hangs in the living rooms of some Massillon homes, like Jesus Christ and JFK." When Brown died in 1991, the local paper treated the news like the Kennedy assassination. The entire town fell into mourning. A front-page editorial in the Massillon *Independent* proposed changing the high school's name from Washington to Brown, reasoning thusly: "What had more to do with the finer aspects of what Massillon has become? Who is a more pertinent example of the ideals that should mold where it goes from here? George Washington? Or Paul Brown?"²³ In the end, Brown's memorial would be the stadium, which was rechristened the Paul Brown Tiger Stadium in 1976. In the late 1980s and early 1990s, the town's fathers drummed up one million dollars in contributions to refurbish the arena, which perches Parthenon-style on an incline overlooking Massillon.

Phil Glick took me up the hill to see the remodeled stadium one afternoon in March of 1996. "I've been sitting right up there since 1962, section three, two rows down," he said, pointing proudly to an empty seat. He showed me the new, soft field cover that is less hard on the boys' legs than ordinary Astroturf. Then he took me to the newest addition, a three-story press box. "This is our pride and joy. It can hold up to one hundred and twenty newsmen," though a lot of nonpress types have bought seats there for the prime view. "To buy a seat in the press box, you had to buy it for ten years. We sold them all." On the way out, we stopped to admire the brand-new scoreboard with its fancy message center. Emblazoned on it is a massive image of Brown's face. Glick gazed up reverently. "Yes," he said, "Paul Brown looks down on us all the time." It was an image that still sustained the Sideliners, all these years later. It was their image, really, the image of themselves as providing and productive fathers, looking down with a protective eye on their sons, the Tigers.

In 1946, Brown took his winning formula to Cleveland and right off attracted the largest gate in league history. The fans of his new team would prove as intensely devoted and ecstatically loyal as those he left in Massillon. Clevelanders, too, came out of an industrial landscape dominated by steel mills and smokestacks and a common-man ethic. (Visiting Cleveland, an editor wrote in 1939, "the impression soon prevails in your mind that Ernie Pyle . . . is the president of the United States.")²⁴ They, too, lived in a town where community engagement was next to godliness; its moniker was "the city of co-operation," and for good reason. As one newspaper columnist observed during its Sesquicentennial in 1946, the year the Cleveland Browns were founded, "Cleveland's zeal for civic and cultural improvement is perhaps its greatest distinguishing mark among American cities." During the Depression, the citizenry's city-boosting zeal poured into a phenomenal number of WPA projects, grand-scale public artworks and parks improvements that still dominate the landscape. In the year of the Cleveland Browns' birth, with the Depression and the war behind them, Clevelanders threw themselves once again into city building without reservation. That year, city voters approved all twenty-four civic programs on the ballot, dedicating $58 million to parks, schools, hospitals, public-service and welfare projects, government buildings, a new central market, and a viaduct. When it came to football, civic enthusiasm knew no limits. More than forty thousand would turn out on a bitter cold afternoon, three days before Christmas, to cheer their brand-new team to victory. A statistical analysis of sports devotees at the time concluded that "Cleveland, in proportion to population, took a greater interest in sports than any other city in the country."[25] The Browns fans seemed to be the natural inheritors of the Massillon booster tradition. But were they?

Men Without Hats

BIG DAWG'S FIRST COMMUNION WITH FOOTBALL came via the television set. "My brothers and I used to fight on Saturdays because my brothers would want to watch the Godzilla movies and I'd want to watch sports." Big Dawg, who was then just John, was the youngest of four children in the Thompson family. Though he was born in Cleveland in 1961 and played in the parks and streets within a few miles of Municipal Stadium, the Cleveland Browns seemed to him less an extension of his community life than a dreamed-of escape from it. In the early seventies, "I'd always bug my father to take me to the preseason games, which is kind of weird because nobody wanted to go to a preseason practice game." His father rarely went to a game. The expense was prohibitive, particularly after his diabetic condition forced him to give up the small deli he owned and move the family to a suburb. Gerald Thompson, whom everybody called Whitey because his hair had gone white while he was still relatively young, wound up accepting a job as a produce manager at a grocery store. John's mother, a seamstress, began to take tailoring orders to supplement his income, but soon her little shop operating out of an addition to their home became the family's prime source of income. The grocery-store employees organized their own baseball team and Gerald Thompson served as umpire, but he did not play any role in his son's athletic pursuits. Big Dawg played just about every sport offered in community leagues: baseball, hockey, soccer, basketball, football, Irish football (a variant of the American sport), and another Irish sport called hurling, which involved sticks and a leather ball. "I always wanted to be an athlete," he said. "I loved sports so much."

The more Gerald's health deteriorated, the more his youngest son became a target of his wrath and bitterness. "He would just get excited and blow up. It went on for a long time, I mean actually his whole life. My father probably went after me the most because I was the youngest, and I was the one who wouldn't take it. I was the prodigal son. I would talk back and he would end up chasing me. He'd get real mad at me and hit me with his cane." Or worse. Big Dawg remembered a number of occasions when his father pursued him wielding a knife. "My sister got married when she was nineteen just to get out of the house." John found a different refuge, in the stands.

"It was a good way to escape from all the problems at home," Big Dawg remembered. As soon as he finished his paper route, he'd jump on the bus and catch a seven o'clock Cleveland Indians game. He still yearned to go to a Browns game, but baseball was affordable. On occasion, though, a classmate's father would pass along two Browns tickets and the boy would take John. It was here that he first got the idea that he could do more than just watch; that he could make a difference in the game. "One year, we were playing the 49ers. It was snowing and there was like about a foot of snow on the ground. It was the last home game of the year, and I remember throwing snowballs down at [San Francisco quarterback] John Brodie and, I'm not sure if it was [Green Bay Packers fullback John] Brockington but I remember it was number forty-two—I mean, it's very, very vivid in my head—and I can remember him pointing up at us. They were motioning to us, like this—" He broke off here to demonstrate: they were flipping him the bird. "It was pretty neat." The gesture was good-natured, he assured me. They were more charmed than irritated by the antics of the two boys in the stands, or at least that's how Big Dawg remembered it. The Browns lost that afternoon, but what stayed with Big Dawg was the attentiveness of the players. "They were pointing at *us*."

Gerald Thompson's health was further ravaged by spinal arthritis and, as his son would understand only much later, schizophrenia. The family's crumbling finances forced them to relocate to an even smaller place. By high school, John's athletic aspirations were vanishing. "I had a lot of problems in school," he recalled. "It had to do with my dad." As his father's violence escalated, John retreated behind a wall of bad grades

and drugs—mostly marijuana but also "window pane" and "blotters."
"That kind of ruined it right there. I'd love to go back to that time now
[to redo it]. But it's gone, it's long gone." But "the biggest problem," he
said, "was I wasn't going to school."

John's truancy, and attendant minor troublemaking, eventually landed
him before a caseworker with Catholic Charities. From their conversation, it dawned on him that there might be other ways to escape his
home. "She gave me the option to go through Catholic Charities and go
into a home type of situation." All he had to do was apply to the courts
to relieve his parents of custody. He did it. "The whole thing was," he
said, "I was going in through the courts on my own, to get away from
my father." The caseworker had told him how "it was real nice there,
this big pool, and they had a football field, a baseball diamond. She said
it's like a resort there. You can play all kinds of sports. She was giving
me all these stories." He bought them and signed the papers. He was
sixteen. "And I went there to find out that it was nothing of the sort."
He had checked into St. Anthony's, known more commonly as "the bad
boys' home." As John soon realized, "ninety percent of the boys there
were sent by the court. They were in there for crimes." The school, he
said, was more like a prison. "You had to earn your way to freedom.
You had a little footlocker on the wall, and it got inspected every Saturday. You weren't allowed off the grounds. And I thought, The hell
with that, I'm used to getting on the bus and going to a Browns game."
He ran away four times in four months. Finally, they gave up and sent
him back home.

John tried one more escape: the navy. The recruiters told him he was
too heavy, but he signed up anyway under a delayed-entry program, determined to trim down in the interim. The military struck him as a place
where he might finally get some helpful guidance and attention from
male superiors. He moved into a boozy animal-house-like milieu close
to town, renting a room with "five guys I knew from Irish football." To
get fit, John took up broom hockey, a poor man's version of ice hockey
played late at night on chipped-up ice, "and you have a broom with
rubber melted over it, and instead of skating, you run."

The evening before John was to report to the navy, at his going-away
party, "I proceeded to get bombed," he recalled, "and I ended up getting
in a fight with a couple of my friends." In drunken pursuit of one friend,
John dove over a bush, dislocated his shoulder, and passed out. "I woke
up in the hospital in traction. My mother and sister were there." He was
horrified. "I had lost all this weight, I was in great shape, but I blew it."

Nonetheless, John checked himself out of the hospital and showed up at the navy depot, with two black eyes and his arm in a sling. "They said to me, 'You're not going anywhere, bubba.'"

Meanwhile, his increasingly ailing father was eventually checked into a Veterans Administration hospital for good. He hung on there for many years. John was in the room the night he died in 1990. There were words that John would have liked to hear, but in all the darkened and silent hours he waited, they never came. Big Dawg turned his face away as he recalled that longest night. "It was kind of tough. It was kind of tough because, you know, I don't think—let's put it this way: I don't think he ever told me once in his life that he loved me."

From his years of visits to the VA hospital, one image lingered, though he was hard put to say why. One winter's morning, he was gazing down at the grounds when he saw one of the mentally ill patients slip-sliding, alone, on the ice-covered lake. Suddenly the man came to a halt, chipped a small hole in the ice, and laid his hat on the chilly water. Then he ran off, climbed a tree, and started screaming. The screams drew a security guard, who spotted the floating hat and called 911. "So next thing you know, there were all these rescue squads and firetrucks coming, and they're all down there, throwing a hook and all this stuff down in the water." Finally the madman climbed down from the tree, chortling hysterically. John found himself "dying laughing," too, a laugh mixed with pain. His father—the older man who was supposed to help him maneuver the thin ice of adult manhood—was a broken figure strapped to a dialysis machine. And down there on the lake were all these male authorities busy with phantom heroics. John was having a great and bitter laugh at the expense of men who were never there when you needed them, yet would turn up in full force to rescue an empty hat.

Big Dawg was rescued by the women in his life. From his mother, not his father, he learned a trade: when she was hired as a seamstress at a clothing store, she finagled a job for her son as well. He pressed the clothes she altered while she taught him tailoring. "When she went over to Kuppenheimer's [a men's clothing store]," Big Dawg recalled, "I went, too. We were like a team." In the years to follow, he would move to New York City to try to break into the carpentry and construction trades with a male friend without success. Some union officials sent the two young Irish-American men to Italian-American job sites. "In other words, it was an easy way for a guy to blow us off." Even the Irish job sites, though, had no work to offer. Finally, Big Dawg was broke, but again he was saved by a woman's intercession. At his brother's wedding, he met his future wife, Mary. She spoke to her uncle, a computer-printer-ribbon salesman, who gave John some contacts that led to a full-time sales job. "Now I've been working with the same guy for eleven years," Big Dawg marveled. He and Mary have been married for ten of them and have twin daughters he adores.

"Mary's been very good for me," Big Dawg said, as his nine-year-olds, Michelle and Megan, in their pj's but not yet ready to face the reality of bedtime, clambered onto the couch and nestled sleepy-eyed on his big shoulders. Mary came in and settled on the other couch, reaching for her needlepoint. He looked over at her with affection. "She got me straightened out."

Mary shrugged good-naturedly, her concentration directed toward her sewing. "I kept him on a tight leash," she said.

Big Dawg nodded appreciatively. "Basically, Mary changed my whole life."

For Mary's help, and for his mother's, Big Dawg was grateful, but it couldn't quite fill the space reserved for masculine guidance. In his thirty-four years, there had been few men who had proved reliable or admirable. With one major exception: the players on the Cleveland Browns. In this respect, Big Dawg's story was typical; virtually every Dawg Pounder I talked to offered a variation on it. Joe "Bubba" McElwain said he never saw much of his father, a remote figure who worked the late shift as a pipe fitter at the gas company; it was his brother Bud "Junkyard Dawg" McElwain who "took care of me"—and introduced him to the Browns. Scott Shantery and Ed Kuderna, two Dawg Pounders who attended Browns games together, both came from divorced homes and rarely saw or spoke to their fathers. "I went to a game with my mother once," Ed offered. Their fathers were absent, present but hostile, or mute and without lessons to impart. I did not come across an instance among the Dawg Pounders I talked to of a man who had inherited his love of the game from his father.

Unlike baseball, a sport that poet Donald Hall describes as "continuous . . . an endless game of repeated summers joining the long generations of all the fathers and all the sons," pro football would become for many a showcase not of the bonds between older and younger men but of the strife and disappointment that divided them.[26] Continuity was breaking down in the postwar years, in ways that even baseball couldn't mend, and football was a bloodier venue. Maybe, as some observers have speculated, football fans were baseball fans looking for vengeance.[27]

For postwar fans, the elders who had let them down were not simply their fathers, though many men would personalize all their betrayals in the visage of the disappointing dad. Behind the failed fathers lay the rubble of a promise made to America's postwar sons by the elder male generation, that they would pass on to the young men a national prosperity and would teach them how to build on it. The sons weren't ready to face the breach in its entirety. Football for them was more than just a forum for expelling resentment. "There's always hope in sports," Seth Task, a former Cleveland Browns mascot and an inveterate fan, said to me one afternoon as he sat surrounded by game videotapes in his compact condo. "Things can always turn around, even when you think it's hopeless." Being a fan could be an act of faith as crazy as the faith that sends Charlie Brown hurtling for the thousandth time toward the poised ball that Lucy, this time, for the first time, might not pull away: it was the hope that they might be a part of the game, some meaningful game, after all.

The hometown fans of the Cleveland Browns started out having a relationship with their team similar in some ways to the paternalism the Massillon fans felt toward their Tigers. But as the years passed, a painful role reversal would take place. It was evident in a large photograph framed and hanging behind the desk of Robert Gries, Jr., who was, like his father before him, a minority owner of the Browns. A passionate Clevelander whose family's philanthropic and civic commitment to the city extends back five generations, Gries, disgusted by the decision to transplant the Browns, divested himself of his holdings in the team rather than profit off the move to Baltimore. While we spoke in his office one afternoon, Gries rose and turned to study a photograph on the wall—a black-and-white shot from 1953 of fans in Municipal Stadium watching a Browns game—as if it held a clue to the betrayal of his beloved city. "This was the first time the stadium was full for a football game. And look at it. What do you see? There's something here that's very different."

The hats? I ventured. Because every man—and the stands were virtually all male—was wearing a fedora, along with a suit and tie.

"Yes, it's the hats," Gries said, eyes still fixed on the photo. "Hats and suits. And this was in the *end zone*," the very seats the Dawg Pounders would eventually lay claim to.

Gries's father was part of the original group of men who first organized in 1936 to bring football to Cleveland. His father's motives, Gries Jr. recalled, were "*civic,* totally *civic*. My father was not a 'fan.' He never played football. He was not inclined toward sports. His idea of a good Saturday was to go out and work in his garden for eight hours. He loved to garden." Nor were his motives fiscal. "There wasn't money in football in those days. . . . It was the idea of *bringing* something to Cleveland."

When the Browns started, Gries said, "I can remember my father running around town and he'd always have tickets in his pocket, giving out tickets. He was always taking two dozen people to the games. It was something to *do* for his community. It was something to *give*."

Much later, a crucial difference between those fedoras and the bill caps of today would strike me. The fedora was the haberdashery of a man in a position to *give*, an adult man with some sense of his value and purpose in a civic society into which he blended seamlessly. The cap was the garb of a boy, a man-child still waiting for his inheritance, still hoping to be ushered in by the male authorities and given a sign, a badge, perhaps a fedora, to indicate his induction into adult society. The Massillon boosters had backed their team with such enthusiasm because it was a way literally to give a boost, a leg up, to the next generation; they had embraced their role as supporters because it allowed them to father a team. A generation later, fans like Big Dawg were seeking exactly the opposite; they were looking for a team to father them. For these new-era fans, the hope was that the team would be *their* boosters.

Father Football

THE RELATIONSHIP BETWEEN THE BOOSTERS and the team had always been mediated by the coach. Between the Massillon boosters and their boys on the field stood the mythical figure of Paul Brown. But in this abiding paternal chain, the coach would prove the weakest link. The coach's weakness was concealed behind a prevailing myth. In the gauzy nostalgia that instantly enveloped football's early history, every successful coach would be remembered as an ideal dad.

The essential cinematic expression of this fantasy can be found in the 1940 film *Knute Rockne — All-American*, starring Pat O'Brien as papa-coach and Ronald Reagan as his agreeable young player-son, George Gipp. Their key encounter takes place not on the field but by a hospital bed, where Gipp lies dying and Coach Rockne vows to carry on the young man's legacy. In a sense, it's a reverse image of Big Dawg's memories of his VA hospital vigil. In the film, it is the son, not the father, who is the patient, and the father, not the son, who hovers anxiously over the deathbed. In the film, the coach really cares — and the son hasn't suffered in vain.

To tell such a story required some serious fabrication. Knute Rockne's mythic relationship with George Gipp was an invention of the 1940 film. The reality, in Knute Rockne's case, was that the coach of that 1920s Notre Dame team was far from Gipp's bedside when the star player gasped his final breath. There was, in fact, no deathbed appeal from Gipp to "win one for the Gipper." (George Gipp never even called himself "the Gipper," and most likely contracted pneumonia not from his exertions on the field but after a three-day drinking binge.) The truth was that Rockne was the kind of "father" who was not above making up sob stories to manipulate his players: before one game, he pretended that his *own* six-year-old son, Billy, was near death in the hospital and read to his players a made-up telegram he supposedly received from the boy that said: "Please win this game for my daddy. It's very important to him." The truth was that as a father, Rockne was generally absent from his actual sons' lives. When his other young son, Jack, was *really* in the hospital battling mortal illness, Dad was not at his side; he was on the field exhorting the team to victory.[28]

Nonetheless, these revelations, detailed by scholar Murray Sperber in *Shake Down the Thunder,* remain dwarfed by shelves of Knute Rockne hagiographies. Football's true believers preferred the myth to the reality, just as Ronald Reagan preferred his fantasy of Knute Rockne, All-American Dad, to the reality of his own broken alcoholic father, a man whose appearance at the film's premiere filled young Reagan with, as he put it later, "chilling fear."[29]

Five years after the first screening of *Knute Rockne — All-American,* Paul Brown began to assemble a group of young men just returning from World War II. It was 1945 and the coach from Massillon had been invited to put together a brand-new football team in Cleveland. The word was that this coach was phenomenally devoted to the well-being and advancement of his "boys," that he intended his players to be well supported — equipped, dressed, trained, and compensated in "high-grade" style, as he phrased it. Brown would even see to it that for away games his players flew first class and stayed in nice hotels. Just as the coach and his boosters had given an assist to the football sons of Massillon, he seemed set once more on helping his boys rise as men: he stipulated in their contracts that the players obtain college educations between seasons, and he gave them a bonus if they graduated. To Brown, it was all part of "raising our own," as he called the process by which he planned to shape his green recruits into mature members of the "dynasty" he aimed to build. "At Ohio State, I asked nothing of my players that I wouldn't have asked of my own sons, and that's the way I planned to run the Browns," Brown asserted.[30]

Developing his approach to coaching at a high school (and later a college) and applying it to real boys, Paul Brown had earned the moniker "Father Football." Now he would transfer his method to a new pro league, the All-America Football Conference.[31] He would be presented, and in some respects present himself, as the postwar reincarnation of the fictional Knute Rockne, committed to the future well-being of his sons. But could the prewar civic fatherhood of small-town football's boosters survive the leap to the postwar professional game?

"It was easier for the fans to relate to us because of the war," said Dante Lavelli, a member of the Cleveland Browns' original 1946 team. He was mulling over his past from the back of the small, cluttered furniture-and-home-appliance store he owns in Rocky River, a suburban section of Cleveland about ten miles from Municipal Stadium. Snow swirled on the other side of the store's frost-coated plate-glass window. Little had evidently changed at Lavelli's in the twenty-eight years since it opened; a fine dust had collected over the chipped counters and the yellowing news clips taped to the walls. Even the motley collection of old TV sets, Maytag dryers, and mattresses resting on their sides seemed lifted from the past. In these modest surroundings, with a water-stained ceiling and duct tape over defective outlets, Dante Lavelli received visitors in a pressed blue blazer and a red-white-and-blue rep tie, and with an old-world courtliness muffled by a gravelly, gruff exterior. His was the demeanor of a man whose sympathies run deep but who distrusts easy sentiment. No one who came through the door that morning was a stranger to him; in Rocky River, Dante Lavelli seemed to know everyone by name, and surely everyone knew him.

This morning, Hugh Gallagher had stopped by, as was his habit, just to check in. A sixty-eight-year-old, ruddy-faced Irishman in a worn tam-o'-shanter, Gallagher had known Lavelli since the forties. "Things between the players and the fans then, they were easier," Lavelli was saying to me. "It was easier because there wasn't that big salary difference. Nobody had it what you called 'made.' "

Hugh Gallagher, nodding vigorously, pulled up a chair. "In them days," he pitched in, "the fans, they were more than fans. They were *friends* of the players, and the players were real down to earth." Gallagher knew whereof he spoke; he got to be friends with Lavelli by being a fan.

"That's because everyone was in the same boat after the war," Lavelli said. "We all got out of the service and we all started over with nothing."

"When you'd be leaving the game," Gallagher recalled, "you'd meet up with the players and go socialize with them, or they might invite you along. They were looking for the same activity. We'd all go to Cavoli's, this family-type restaurant and bar on the west side. Back then, they were human beings who'd associate with you. Now, you try to talk to a player, he'd charge you!"

Lavelli passed him an open box of Dunkin' Donuts, which he had run out and bought as soon as I arrived. "You should have another," he said to me for the third time. "What'sa matter, you don't like the jelly kind? Try a powdered one." We were seated at a round table he had set up toward the back of the store, and as Lavelli served the coffee, surrounded by a hodgepodge of vacuum cleaners and washing machines, he seemed to be presiding over a family kitchen, not a place of business.

"The players used to come into my office and use my desk to write their fan mail," Gallagher recalled, grinning at the memory. His small business that distributed carnival supplies and industrial gifts was near the stadium.

"Yeah, early in the morning," Lavelli remembered, with a half groan. "I'd write back to the fans. Two or three letters at a time."

"See"—Gallagher leaned intently across the table, lowering his voice as if imparting a confidence—"the foundation of the team was built not just on performance but on *association* with the fans. It was a hometown deal. You used to even be able to go *sit* on the field. We were part of the family."

"You should try one of these doughnuts," Lavelli interrupted.

"Nobody blew the other guy off," Gallagher continued. "Players would come out and give speeches at a high school, a parochial school, and they'd stay a couple of hours afterward. There was just a total happiness to be there, together. The players would get twenty-five dollars, maybe fifty for the speech, and some of them would be reluctant to take the money off of you."

"The speeches, that was because of Paul Brown," Lavelli added. "The first ten to fifteen years, a lot of the reason that the players got closer to the fans was because we were sent out to meet the public by Paul Brown. It was in your contract, to go out to the high schools and the men's clubs, to develop the fans."

The owners of the new team had chosen Brown precisely because of his skill at building a fan base. Brown understood that, and many of his early moves, from requiring public appearances to filling 90 percent of the team's slots with Ohio-raised players, were designed to cultivate a mass following.[32] But the relationships with fans that developed were not thereby artificial. Their sustaining egalitarianism had more to do with the war just ended than with the newfound peace. Most of the Browns roster were, literally, GI Joes; Paul Brown had recruited them while he was himself in the service. Drafted at age thirty-five, he was billeted at the Great Lakes Naval Training Center as the base's head football coach. From there, he plucked the cream of the athletic crop as they returned from the victorious European and Pacific fronts to their small towns in the region. Dante Lavelli, who had fought in the bloodbath of the Battle of the Bulge, was returning to the tiny town of Hudson, Ohio, where his father, an Italian immigrant, labored as an ironworker. Lou "The Toe" Groza, for twenty-one years the team's famed placekicker who could boot a football through the goalposts from midfield, was coming home to Martins Ferry, Ohio, from the horrific landing at Okinawa; two days after his discharge from the army, he was drafted into the Browns. From the army, Brown scooped up the aptly named Mac Speedie and many other foot soldiers; from the navy, he enlisted Otto Graham, the team's legendary quarterback, and Marion Motley, an extraordinary full-back, and one of two black Browns players who broke the color line on that inaugural team one year before Jackie Robinson did so in baseball. Motley was glad to forgo his job as a pieceworker at the Republic Steel coke ovens, burning scrap iron with a torch; compared with the scourges of war and steel, football looked like a vacation.[33]

The men who belonged to the Browns' early lineup were, by and large, Ernie Pyle's long-suffering doughboys. That this status would continue was implied in their mud-colored uniforms, not far from standard-issue army fare, and the lack of logos on their helmets. A masculine war ethic of stoicism and productive anonymity would continue to be nurtured on the team for nearly two decades. They were "men who didn't expect to be coddled," wrote Ohio sports columnist Terry Pluto of the 1964 team in *When All the World Was Browns Town*, "men who didn't believe the world should genuflect at the mere mention of their names." They were men like the avuncular linebacker Galen Fiss, "who wore bedroom slippers in the locker room," and the blocking back Ernie Green, "who spent his career taking care of others" on the team.[34] As in an army unit, in football group identity trumped the individual's — and nowhere more so than in the kind of football played by the early Cleveland Browns, where Paul Brown's axiom was "No stars."

If the players were the GIs, then the fans were their support troops, part of the on-field battle as much as hospital and supply units had been part of the war. They braved the same elements in the unprotected arena. The protective cover of their cheers let the fighting men know that they had backup; they offered the tenderness of a mutual love that went by the name of "loyalty." "We had a lot of really good fans then, different from now," Lavelli said wistfully. "They gave their *loyalty*." The one he recalled most fondly was Frankie Yankovic, the "polka king," a minor celebrity of the time. Yankovic, an accordionist, accompanied the team to every game, greeted them at railroad stations when they were on the road, and played afterward at every team party, win or lose. What

Lavelli valued most about the polka king's attentions, though, was that they came from a fellow grunt, a veteran of the war.

Lavelli's father came to watch him every Sunday he played for the Browns, a devotion that Lavelli appreciated. But he wasn't looking to prove himself to his father or to anyone on the playing field. He had already done that on the battlefields of Europe. He had had his formative experience and survived. For him, as for so many veterans, all that followed would be dwarfed by the war and his contribution to it. When you asked members of the original Browns about football, their memories frequently overshot the mark.

"We landed on Omaha Beach," Lavelli began, his eyes locked on the opposite wall, as if its yellowing paint had turned transparent and revealed the battlefield itself. "I went on 'D plus twenty.' I was an infantryman, a replacement. We landed in the English Channel and then we had to climb over the boats on a rope and then you just walked. We walked twenty-six miles to the first town, Carentan. And that's where we stopped to cook some potatoes in a grease can. And then you just kept moving up to the front. You kept walking and you'd get on trucks and ride, walk, ride, walk. We walked across France to the front line." He spoke from so far inside the memory that I half expected him to stand right then and start trudging toward the front.

"Our twelve guys in my squad were the only ones that came out of the Bulge in the first three days," he said of the German counteroffensive that produced 81,000 American casualties and 125,000 German casualties.[35] He fell silent, then started up again. On the second day of the Bulge in December of 1944, he recalled, "we passed by the Massacre of Malmédy. It was snowy, like this." He gestured in the direction of the shop window, where the snow was still falling steadily. "We saw the field where they got shot," he said of the roughly one hundred unarmed GI POWs who had been rounded up and, seemingly without cause, machine-gunned to death by German soldiers.[36] "They lined up their tanks on each side. They had no chance. Just stood 'em there and shot 'em down." Lavelli brooded on this image, then said with sudden impatience, "Young people today, they think these are just things in movies: POWs! Massacres! These things were real. These things *happened*.

"These guys, these guys were—" He broke off, unable to put in words the depths of his feelings for his orphaned squad members. "I got some pictures here," he said finally. He reached into a trouser pocket and, with liver-spotted hands that had once caught a football effortlessly enough to earn him the nickname "Glue Fingers," slowly withdrew his wallet. He eased from behind a plastic compartment three tiny, smudged and battered pictures of Lavelli with two of his squad mates. The faces in each gazed up from a copse of trees in the Hurtgen Forest in the dead of winter, solemn and worn, young men already terribly old. "This guy's name is Wally Brunz. He's from Milwaukee. He used to come to Chicago to watch me play football, after we come back to the States. . . . The little guy's dead." Lavelli studied the photos for a long time without saying anything else, then slid them carefully back into the billfold and returned the wallet to his pocket.

On the walls of his shop were the predictable memorabilia of a fabled career in football, plaques and framed photos of testimonial dinners and of his induction ceremony into the NFL Hall of Fame. But what Lavelli valued most was not on display.

To report to the Browns' training camp in Bowling Green, Dante Lavelli took a bus partway and then hitchhiked. Walk, ride, walk — he was heading for the front. He wasn't alone; virtually none of the players had cars.[37] He arrived at camp in his GI uniform, the only clothes he had. The players all got roughly the same salary — and the same treatment. "Everybody was on an even scale — the quarterback, the linemen — everyone was in the same boat. Paul Brown treated third-team players as first-team players. The same benefits and perks." There were no individual merchandising deals and virtually no endorsements. Once, Lavelli was asked to wear a sweater for an apparel company; the earnings, which were nominal, were shared with his teammates. The evenhandedness appealed to Lavelli; it seemed an extension of the stripped-down equality he had experienced in the infantry and would not find much in evidence in peacetime America. "When we were playing, everybody was like brother and sister," he recalled. "My warmest memory is of that. All the original players, we're friends still. We are 'the original friends.' "

That "everybody in the same boat" status bonded the players to the fans as well. The Browns were the first pro football team to draw spectacular crowds; more than sixty thousand spectators came to their opening game in the fall of 1946, breaking all previous pro football records. And the devotion maintained itself over the years, even during losing stretches. The Browns drew crowds of more than seventy thousand when the team played their biggest rival of the 1940s, the San Francisco 49ers.[38] But the stadium also packed in eighty-three thousand spectators for an *exhibition* doubleheader in 1964, a fund-raiser for the city newspaper's Helping Hand Fund.[39]

The fans compensated the players in a way that their paltry salaries couldn't. They were still drawing soldiers' pay; no player in those early years was getting rich from the game. "The amount of money we made," Lavelli remarked, "couldn't buy a lame cockroach a crutch." Almost all the Browns held off-season jobs selling insurance, cars, or home appliances to make ends meet. Precisely because the players were anonymous foot soldiers, they needed the fans' confirming cheers and exhortations. "The Browns were a popular team not just because they won," Terry Pluto observed, "but also because they truly appreciated the fans' support."[40]

In the months after the move to Baltimore became public, Dante Lavelli had received letters from old fans bemoaning the team owner's disloyalty. Lavelli shuffled through the papers on his desk to show me. The letters were full of personal references that bespoke a longer chain of correspondence and common memories held between friends. Several of them, I noticed, were from his fellow soldiers. "Hi Dante," began a typical one from E. L. "Al" Riggs (on RIGGS' CAR CO. letterhead with the slogan "Remember: If you don't know Cars, know your Car Dealer"). "It has been so many, many years since we corresponded but when I saw the article in the *Sports Illustrated* about the Cleveland Browns moving to Baltimore and saw how you felt about it I thought I would drop a line and express my sympathy. . . . I never hear Cleveland Browns mentioned without thinking of Dante Lavelli and the fond memories it brings to me of our 'good old' days in Europe. . . . Do you keep in touch with any of the others from the 28th Division?"

The front door swung open with an icy blast, and a couple with two little boys trundled in, stamping their snowy boots. Lavelli hustled up to help them, stopping at the counter to pluck two lollipops from a bowl. The couple were looking for a dishwasher. He flipped through the sales book with them. "Here's one I recommend. This one I could get you for four hundred dollars, but I don't recommend it. This one's all right. I can get it for you in a day." His sales pitch, if that's what it was, was unadorned. "Comes in black or white," he said laconically.

The door flew open again and another customer blew in. "Hi, Dante, how you doing? I'm so glad you sold that cabinet for me."

"Yeah," Lavelli said, shaking his head, "it finally sold." He shrugged sadly. "No one appreciates the value of cherry wood anymore."

The couple looking for a dishwasher made their selection and left, and Lavelli and the man who still appreciated cherry wood stood for a while talking about this and that.

When our conversation returned to football, Lavelli said, "Paul Brown stood for what America stood for: hard work, dedication, loyalty." He paused, then considered what he had just said and carefully amended his statement. "Well, I mean what it stood for *then*."

It wouldn't take long after the war for the contract between coach, player, and fan to begin to fall apart, and the new relationship to follow was choreographed by, as much as anyone, Paul Brown.

We Dominated Our Era

THE SPORTS PRESS PLACED THE FOOTBALL COACH in a sentimentalized paternal frame; he was the stern but "devoted" martial pop, exacting discipline for his boys' own good. In the 1950s, the yearning for just such a mythic male icon was palpable throughout popular culture. It was most famously embodied in the fatherly sergeant that John Wayne would play over and over again in John Ford cavalry westerns and World War II movies.

If the myth was suspect, the sports media didn't care and the coaches were only too happy to go along, casting their controlling personalities as proof of their devotion to their "boys." No doubt they were devoted to the advancement of the team and so, in a way, to the players. But whether it was Green Bay Packers coach Vince Lombardi, whose bullying posture and business maxims made him more like an iron-fisted chief executive than a model father, or later Dallas Cowboys coach Tom Landry, with his frosty stare and stony visage, the coaches at the helm of pro football's rising franchises were attuned less to the paternal nurturance of a Captain Waskow than to the paternal domination of the general that Lombardi, among others, idolized: George Patton.[41]

The prevailing ethic of the postwar coach more closely emulated a remote manager's discipline than the affection of an emotionally involved father. Not that Paul Brown and the others had ceased to value, in Lavelli's words, "what America stood for." It was just that such values were being reconfigured in a nation reshaping its work life into new bureaucratic and managerial structures and its civic life into a national-security state. Masculinity defined by hard work, dedication, and loyalty meant something different in this new age. It was the dawn of the national era in which, on and off the gridiron, winning and dominating would subsume everything. Before World War II, almost all pro football teams operated in the red; they were civic services, not profitable enterprises. After the war, that would change, and the terms by which "winning" was measured would be adjusted accordingly.

Paul Brown embodied the metamorphosis. One day, back during Brown's reign in Massillon, a doctor had forced the flu-ridden coach to stay in bed and miss a game. Brown coordinated a phone hookup so he could direct his players from his sickroom and then pled frantically with his doctor to release him, which elicited this remark from the amused physician: "Everybody is useful, PB, but no one is necessary."[42] While the high school's boosters knew the difference, it wasn't clear that the coach did. Even back in Massillon, there were signs of the controlling figure the man on top would later become.

Except for that one time, Brown was present at every Massillon Tigers game, and increasingly, both on and off the gridiron, oppressively present in his players' lives. He laid down detailed rules of conduct: during the season the players were not allowed to date or dance and they had to be in bed by ten every night. On the field, everything went by the book and precise adherence to Brown's "system," as he called it, earned his highest praise. He dictated the players' movement from the sidelines with "a wigwag set of hand signals." It was the birth of the sideline play-calling that he would later impose on the Browns and, by example, on the rest of postwar football.[43]

In their first years, the Browns' players tolerated their coach's "system" with few complaints. "We were required the night before the game to stay together as a unit," Tommy James, who had also served under Brown at Massillon, and at Ohio State in Columbus, recalled, "to eat dinner together, to go to a movie together that Paul Brown picked out. And then we'd have a bed check and go to sleep." The players were more bemused than outraged by the rules. If the restrictions seemed silly, then, as Ernie Pyle once wrote of the GIs, "a certain fundamental appreciation of the ridiculous carried them through"—at least their egalitarianism reinforced the team's military-style cohesion.[44] "Loyalty was the thing," James said. "We always felt that if you played on a team and you could *finish* on that team, that was *something*."

The players sought from football what a lot of returning veterans yearned for in postwar America. Whether men could find a way to bring the camaraderie of the trenches into their peacetime lives, whether they could find a way of being men that wasn't based on hierarchy and mutual suspicion, would prove to be one of the silent dramas of the late 1940s. It would either be a historic turning point for men or a heartbreaking lost opportunity, as it would be for a newly powerful nation pulled between the callings of democratic social welfare and a contest for dominant global authority.

In Massillon, Brown's rules had served as a sort of social welfare, teaching high-school boys to develop self-control and discipline. In Cleveland, his dress codes, his curfews, and his strict study regimen with playbooks, constant lectures, and testing, served a different postwar ethic: it enhanced an image, the image of a well-run organization. His model turned out to be less a throwback to wartime army discipline than a look forward to a new style of corporate control.

"We want you to reflect a special image in pro football," Brown told his players in a speech at the opening of each season.[45] They were not to smoke or drink *in public;* they were to wear jackets and ties, slacks and polished shoes *in public;* they were to display a proper "decorum" and not curse *in public;* if they so much as lounged on the ground during a game, they were fined; above all, they were never to behave in a manner that would make the team look "low class"—in other words, that would remind anybody of the league's origins in the mills and mines.

Brown demonstrated the seriousness of all this at the first opportunity: two days before the new league's first title game, he fired the team's captain, Jim Daniell, after the tackle had a few drinks and got into a minor spat with some local policemen. "I'll take my players high class, cold, deadly," Brown repeated in his seasonal speech. "We don't want any butchers on this team. No T-shirts in the dining hall. Don't eat with your elbows on the table and eat quietly." He told *Time* magazine in 1947, "There's no place on my team for Big Butch who talks hard and drinks hard. I like a lean and hungry look." When a young college lineman whom Brown was planning to recruit arrived at the team's training camp unshaven and "dressed like a laborer," Brown took one look, told him that he had been summoned mistakenly, and dismissed him at once.[46]

"Class always shows," Brown maintained, and what he wanted his men to show was the face of the new, white-collar bourgeoisie. "I didn't want them to look like the stereotype of the old-time pros," Brown said. "College players had a good reputation, but the public perception of the professional football player back then was of a big, dumb guy with a potbelly and a cheap cigar. That kind of person disgusted me, and I never wanted anyone associating our players with that image."[47] What Brown wanted was a managerial look: polished and uniform, college-educated but not effetely so, aspiring but conformist. What he wanted was a team represented by organization men. It was the sort of look he himself exemplified. With his contained demeanor, trim frame, and bland corporate suits, he looked like the archetypal suburban husband about to board the commuter train to his desk job in the city. While Brown was insistent on his men flying first class and staying in fine hotels, it turned out this was not so much for their sake as for the public profile of the team. He was intent on turning pro football into the sort of respectable middle-class occupation that fit with the new white-collar bureaucracies and the rising corporate management ethic of postwar America.

Before the war, the pro football coach was a kind of shop foreman, constructing in the stadium along with his "boys" an edifice to man's productivity and muscle. After, he became a corporate manager, seeing to it that his underlings adhered to the game plan in his highly specialized organizational chart. Before, he was the master builder; after, he was, as many of the Cleveland Browns players would come to dub their coach, "the master organizer."[48]

Prewar, pro football had been a casual, part-time operation. Paul Brown was the first to turn it into a full-time business, with a large year-round staff, a scientific management system, and a degree of specialization that would come to rival that of the defense industry. The team kept business hours. Players were expected to report to a meeting at 9:30 every morning and fined if they were late. In fact, they were fined for every imaginable infraction, from tardiness to forgetting a playbook. Tardiness fines were prorated by the quarter hour. "Everything went by the clock," former player Paul Wiggin recalled. "If the Browns were to practice at 1:27, we'd be on the field and practice would begin at precisely that moment. Nothing else would be done other than what he had on the schedule."[49]

The players were under the constant supervision of Brown's middle management: his regiment of assistant coaches. "I always equated forming a coaching staff with working in a bank," Brown said, and like a bank manager, he saw his staff's main duty as monitoring their underlings and compiling what he liked to call the "data." The surveillance device of choice was a camera: for the first time in football, films of the games were pored over to discover flaws in players' technique. Brown believed that "you won only if you had a system," his biographer Jack Clary observed. Failure to follow Brown's precise instructions could mean incurring his icy wrath. It all added up to what one magazine account at the time deemed "the most intensively coached football team in history."[50]

Paul Brown himself became an increasingly remote figure. While he was still physically present at every practice, he kept a chilly distance from his players. He had never been particularly accessible, but now the man who used to take his Massillon high-school boys up to his dad's fishing cottage made a point of never even having a player over to his house for dinner. In his brand of pro football, success depended on "keeping control," and you couldn't keep control, he maintained, when you were "hobnobbing" with the employees.[51] That authority eventually extended to control over the movements of the players on the field during a game. The tradition of the quarterback calling the plays in the huddle was broken. In 1950, Paul Brown decided that he would try calling the plays from the sidelines and messenger them into the huddle via a running relay of guards. (He even tried to relay his plays via a radio receiver in the quarterback's helmet, but abandoned the idea when other teams claimed they could pick up the signals.) Otto Graham, a creative signal caller in college and one of the most skilled quarterbacks of his generation, was expected never to deviate from his master's orders. For this, he earned the sports-page moniker "Automatic Otto." Graham quietly groused, but Paul Brown was immovable. "A quarterback is an important cog in the machine," Brown wrote, "but still a cog." When, in 1961, quarterback Milt Plum complained to the press about not being allowed to call the plays, Brown quickly traded him.[52]

What started as soldierly camaraderie had turned into an early athletic version of McDonnell Douglas's managerial organization, in which all human endeavor was to be processed and regulated according to the principles of systems analysis. To the players, Brown was as inscrutable and distant as that defense company's unseen memo-writing executives would be. To Brown, the players were as manipulable and compliant as aerospace "engineers" on a dutiful career track. His vision would quickly become the prevailing one in football. Barely into the cold-war era, sportswriters were already grousing about "push-button football" where a coach operated like "an executive . . . in his chalk-striped suit" and "quarterbacks were deprived of the right to think."[53]

Whether the players felt productive, whether they could take pride in their individual contributions to the game, was of little account to Brown, whose prime agenda was maintaining their winning record. In the newborn All-America Football Conference, they were the only real contenders and won the championship game all four years of the league's existence. After three seasons and twenty-nine straight victories, the team finally lost a game. An outraged Brown told the press that unless the players who "fell down on the job" redeemed themselves by the next game, he was "going to sell some of these guys while I can still get something for them."[54] When the conference was disbanded and the Browns entered the National Football League in 1950, the "Cleveland Nobodies," as *Sports Illustrated* would later call them, defied all expectations in their first historic contest as they "roasted, braised and fricasseed the big, bad, two-time defending NFL champion Eagles in a game that needed to be a lot closer just to get filed as a blowout." The Nobodies went on to clinch the championship in their first season. For the next five years, the Browns never failed to make it to the championship game and emerged champs twice. From 1946 to 1971, the Browns had only one season in which their losses exceeded their wins, a record streak. They were the NFL's first "dynasty." "I won't say that we were the greatest team that ever came along," Brown would later say. "But I do think we dominated our era."[55]

The more Cleveland won, the more the imperative to continue winning obsessed Brown. His stance was simple and unchanging: "If we won, that's all that mattered," he said flatly. It wasn't enough for the team to shine; his players had to obliterate everybody else. He told them, "I want you to play for the sheer desire of licking somebody. You must sacrifice something to get to the top." This was a very different aspiration from that embraced by his original players. Otto Graham's words in this regard were typical: "I enjoy winning and I play to win. But to me, winning never has been the most important thing in this world." What mattered to him was "putting forth the effort to win—that is the most important thing. You try your best."[56] By the late fifties, the mentoring that—in Massillon, in Columbus at Ohio State, even in Cleveland in the early years—had been part of the conquering process had gone by the boards. The coach's obsession was the same as cold-war America's: staying on top. So was his dilemma: how to maintain dominance and still inspire loyalty, how to be a bully and still be loved.

The central rule of football—that one can only keep possession of the ball by constantly advancing it—fit precisely the concerns and anxieties of the era. Brown, like postwar foreign-policy makers, was a man wedded to an empire-building offense. He preferred to leave the training of his defensive players to others. The precariousness of always having to be on top produced another familiar cold-war state: constant paranoia. Brown began to suffer an unrelenting suspicion that his training camp's security had been breached, his playbooks rifled, his secret football signals leaked and decoded. Brown was forever looking for the football version of Commies under the bed: rival team scouts infiltrating his training camp.[57]

"He had a fetish about secret practices," former player Bernie Parrish observed, remembering how Brown had a seven-foot-high canvas hung around their practice field to hide their training sessions from potential spies. At Brown's behest, the team's equipment manager, Morrie Kono, "spent hours searching dressing rooms for electronic bugging equipment and chasing innocent bystanders away from holes in the fence," Parrish recalled.[58] Brown himself would periodically scrutinize the canvas for furtively drilled peepholes and even the heavens for spies. "When airplanes flew over the practice field," George Plimpton wrote in *Paper Lion*, Brown "would look up, hands on hips, and the players knew that he suspected scouts were taking aerial pictures of the practice." Nowhere was safe. "In the locker rooms at half-time," Plimpton wrote, "Brown would search the corners and run his hands across the walls for microphones, suspecting that the room was bugged, and even his search could not allay his fears. Talking to the team, drawn in close around him, he would diagram a play on the blackboard, but rub it out quickly with an eraser, its name never mentioned aloud. He would say, leaning in toward his players conspiratorially, 'Now in the second half we're going to throw—' and holding up ten fingers three times, he'd mouth 'thirty passes.' "[59]

The sad irony was that Brown's obsessive need for total control and dominance evidently wasn't shared by the very men whom he had originally been hired to court: Cleveland's fans. As the Browns toted up their numbingly triumphant record, the fans' attention waned. Four straight championship seasons in the All-America conference had sent regular attendance plunging from sixty thousand down to twenty thousand. "I would rather win before ten thousand than lose before eighty thousand," Brown said. The man who invented the modern fan had forgotten why he came to the stadium, or that, as *Collier's* magazine noted in 1949, "the average, noncollegiate, dues-paying fan is inclined to root for the underdog.... He may remember with distaste how Adolf Hitler publicly snubbed the losing German contestants in the 1936 Olympic games."[60]

As it turned out, the fans didn't want their team to be, in Paul Brown's words, "the Yankees of football." He had foisted a white-collar vision of a team on a blue-collar town. Clevelanders had loved the early teams for their dumpiness and pluck, for their plug-ugly brown uniforms, for the big belly of Lou Groza, and for the mismatched legs of Mac Speedie. They loved the Browns exactly because they were the "Cleveland Nobodies" tussling in dirt and slush in one of the league's oldest stadiums, not because they were a "first class" organization run by an efficiency expert. The corporatizing of the players that the Brown system had promoted throughout football distressed fans everywhere. As *Life* magazine noted in 1957, the player "has become a faceless employee." It was hard for the fan to identify him, much less identify with him; thanks to the endless substitutions, "even with a program, the fan could not hope to keep them all straight."[61] The GI Joe–like modesty the players had brought to the original Browns was subtly transformed by Paul Brown's authoritarianism. Harnessed to an imperial imperative, their anonymity now echoed the infantilized interchangeability of the corporate man.

If the players were cogs, the play was predictable. As Bernie Parrish recalled, "Fans would stop us on the street and say, 'What's wrong with Paul Brown? I can tell every play he's going to call.' "[62] They sensed in Brown's approach a certain contempt for the players' intelligence—and by extension, for their own. The man who once gave men like them the power to be "boosters," raising up young men, now gave them a game where they had about as much of a role as schoolchildren dutifully watching NASA's computer technicians fire up Mercury's booster rockets.

This Eager Violence of the Heart

THE MEMBERS OF THE ORIGINAL BROWNS TEAM had entered football older, many of them already experienced in the world of work, not to mention the cauldron of war. They weren't depending on football to be their masculine crucible. Even when Paul Brown's treatment of them was shabby, they tended to shrug it off. "We'd bitch and cuss among ourselves," Tommy James said to me, "but then we'd knuckle down and play the game." Otto Graham wearied of "being treated to a degree like a boy" and retired in 1954, but when Paul Brown asked Graham to return the following season, claiming he couldn't find a substitute, Graham agreed; it seemed like good sportsmanship.[63] When Tommy James learned, from a newspaper article, that Paul Brown had cut him in his ninth year, James recalled, "I just went down and picked up my shoulder pads and shoes and stuff, and said hello to him, and that was all." For a while, "I was mad and hated him and hated the whole Browns' organization, but I came around." After all, it was just a game.

But a younger generation joining the Browns in the late fifties and early sixties had come of age under the shadow of the postwar corporation, and they had a more vulnerable, and so, more uneasy, relationship to a "master organizer." Under Brown's direction, they didn't feel like good soldiers, they felt like impotent yes-men. They came directly from school, not war, and resented Brown's acting in loco parentis. When they were on the road and Paul Brown ordered their food without asking them what they wanted, when he chose the movie they would all see and made them sit in a roped-off special section of the theater together, it felt like he was taking diabolic pleasure in reminding them of their Peter Pan status. That wasn't his intention—he was just pursuing his "system" the only way he knew how. But he was dealing with a new generation who had grown up thinking that athletic heroics were a royal road to manhood. Most of them had arrived at training camp expecting that inside its gates lay the key to adult recognition, which the coach would deliver.

"The most significant thing to me about football that first year was not playing the game itself but gaining the approval and respect of Head Coach Bob Vogt," observed former St. Louis Cardinals player Dave Meggyesy of his high-school coach. Born in Cleveland, Meggyesy had been raised in rural Ohio—like Big Dawg, by an embittered father who took his disappointments out on his son with his fists. "Football quickly became my life, and, in a pattern I was to see repeated time and again, the coach became a sort of substitute father." It took him years to face the truth: the coach was a father who preferred to keep his sons in a state of permanent boyhood. "In pro football, as in high school and college, the only way the coaches can establish their authority is to treat their players as boys," Meggyesy wrote after abandoning football in 1970. "Coaches develop a talent for emasculating a player over and over again without quite killing him. . . . Most coaches—Vince Lombardi was the classic example—give their players a tantalizing hint of what it might be like to be a man, but always keep it just out of reach."[64]

The players reacted with all the rage of sons who had been denied their basic birthright. Of course, most of the athletes didn't care to see themselves that way: they maintained that they were "more sophisticated," as Bernie Parrish put it, than those patsies on the Browns' original roster; they just didn't care to take direction from a has-been coach. "I like to have freedom of expression," as Cleveland's celebrated fullback Jim Brown put it airily at the time; he maintained he was objecting only to "suppression of the individual."[65] They were worldly men, the new players insisted; their predecessors, rubes. But their language betrayed a deeper vein of grievance.

They were alienated by Paul Brown's iciness, all the more enraging because of his initial promise of warmth. "Paul dazzled me with compliments and solicitude," Jim Brown would recall. "But I didn't realize at the time that Paul followed a pattern in his handling of men—a pattern in which, at an almost predictable moment, he would turn off his amiability as decisively as a plumber turns off the warm water with a twist of his wrench." Bernie Parrish reflected the disenchantment of many players in his bitter memoir, *They Call It a Game*. "I was welcomed like the Prodigal Son. Then Paul Brown, the world's greatest football coach, picked me to go to war with him." But in the course of four seasons, "I grew to hate him. . . . By the last year, 1962, in the despair of total frustration, I felt like a heart attack would be too good for him."[66]

Young men who believed they had pledged their loyalty in return for the mentorship of an older man on their passage into a world of adults felt they had been betrayed. Somehow, a connection had been missed.

As Don DeLillo vividly described it in his 1972 novel *End Zone,* in which
a chilly, unseen coach dispatches his orders from a tower and a dutiful
player named Bobby tries to fulfill them, "Coach wanted our obedience
and that was all. But Bobby had this loyalty to give, this eager violence
of the heart, and he would smash his body to manifest it."[67]

If the young player could not give his loyalty, he would pledge his
apostasy; that violence of the heart would turn to treason. Seeing the
coach as tyrant was just the flip side of seeing him as savior. Young
players who had eagerly signed on to serve Paul Brown now denounced
him as "a total dictator" who prevailed over a "fading monarchy." His
highest crime was to display "no father image." But his corporate distance was only half the problem. What angered the players at least as
much was, ironically, that the "total dictator" wasn't delivering the corporate promise of total dominance. Most players had bought into the
same winning-is-everything ethic as their coach. Typically, Jim Brown
complained that the coach "no longer was obsessed with winning the
championship." This suspicion built to paranoiac proportions in the early
sixties, when a number of the players convinced themselves that Paul
Brown was actually intent on the team "finishing second."[68]

The nation's new football players felt they were on a mission, fighting
the equivalent of the cold war on the football field, and understood that
such a task demanded eternal vigilance and victory. A few took that
mission quite literally. Green Bay Packers center Jim Ringo somberly
advised Dave Meggyesy: "Dave, in football, the Commies are on one side
of this ball and we're on the other. That's what this game is all about,
make no mistake about it." These children of the American Century
needed their title season year after year after year, or how could they be
men? "That's the way football is," Parrish wrote. "You must be willing
and able to prove yourself again and again—every game, every week, as
long as you are in it."[69] Lavelli's Battle of the Bulge experience had been
a triumphant enough experience to last a lifetime—and it was the care
of the men in his squad, not just the victory, that sustained him. Parrish's
generation had only victory, which had to be won not once on D-Day,
but every Sunday, over and over and over again on the fragile, ever-
shifting beachheads of total dominance.

So the players rebelled against and eventually overthrew Paul Brown,
and before that parricide was even a fact, adopted a big brother in his
place: Art Modell, who bought the Browns in 1961 for the then unheard-
of price of four million dollars. It wasn't actually his money and
Cleveland wasn't even his town. He was an adman and TV producer
from New York City who raised the funds with bank financing. He was

only thirty-five and his claim to fame heretofore had been producing, in 1948, New York's first daytime television show, *Market Melodies,* which played on TV sets installed in supermarkets to whet the consumer appetites of female shoppers. "I never had been to Cleveland in my life until I came out on that snowy Sunday to see the Browns play the Bears," Modell recalled. " 'Anything outside of New York was Bridgeport.' That was my attitude until I had a chance to buy the Browns." For Modell, the Browns beckoned as an imperial edifice. "This was like having a chance to buy the New York Yankees dynasty," he exulted.[70]

Modell was thrilled to be in the presence of these young American Centurions, and unlike their coach, he was accessible and adoring, more like one of the boys than a father figure. If anything, he was on a search for his own surrogate paterfamilias; the searing and formative event of his youth, as he often told it, was the death of his adored father, a traveling wine salesman and charming, handsome figure, who was found unconscious in a Texas hotel and died eight hours later. Art was fourteen. As an adult, the "fatherless hustler," as he was once described, was evidently still looking for someone to replace his idolized dad. The Browns players recalled that he acted at first around them like a boy with an autograph book—"a goggle eyed fan," as Bernie Parrish put it, "overly impressed with us as players." Modell was particularly drawn to the team's brightest light, Jim Brown, whom the new owner introduced at his first press conference as "my senior partner." Modell saw Jim Brown in Hollywood glitterati terms as the team's "star" and himself as the star's agent and publicist. In that capacity, he broke Paul Brown's prohibition against players accepting media offers—which the coach believed would only lead to disruptive individual showmanship and controversy—and arranged for Jim Brown to host a radio show and pen a newspaper column with a veteran sportswriter. Paul Brown's Calvinistic attitude toward drinking and womanizing also was not shared by the unattached, making-the-scene Modell. Soon the Cadillac-driving owner was inviting players out for drinks and up to his Playboy-perfect bachelor pad, complete with blasting hi-fi speakers and jiggle-prone models. "Art turned a sympathetic ear to our complaints about P.B.," recalled Parrish. "He obviously liked rubbing elbows with us. Listening to our complaints was a way to get involved in the real guts of the team. He wanted to be part of it so badly." Into that sympathetic ear, the players didn't waste much time before pouring all their imprecations against Paul Brown. Emboldened, they even took their complaints to the radio airwaves.[71]

Meanwhile, behind the scenes, Modell undermined Brown's authority, taking over contract negotiations, which had always been the coach's purview, and offering special no-cut deals to favored rookies that the treat-everyone-alike coach would never have allowed. Modell even booted Paul Brown into a smaller office. "The control I had once exercised over our team was disappearing before my eyes," Brown wrote later. The struggle between the two men became a showdown in which only one of them could be "on top" and the other had to be swept entirely off the field. Paul Brown suffered a series of setbacks in the early sixties: an expensive, high-profile trade that ended in disaster when Syracuse University star Ernie Davis was diagnosed with leukemia; a third-place finish in the 1962 season after a new quarterback was injured; and Jim Brown's public threats to quit unless he got a new coach. Art Modell saw his opportunity. He summoned Paul Brown to his office and fired him. Modell's parting words, as Paul Brown recalled them, were, "Every time I come to the stadium, I feel that I am invading your domain, and from now on there can only be one dominant image." The morning after the firing, Paul Brown wrote later, he woke to find on his front porch the contents of his desk, right down to the pictures of his family, tossed together like salad in a cardboard box.[72] The McDonnell Douglas–style manager now found himself in roughly the same position as the fired McDonnell Douglas engineer: Paul Brown had been reduced, on this day anyway, to Don Motta.

A few days later, Modell announced his new coach: Blanton Collier, the team's genteel assistant coach. Modell saw in Collier a man who would not thwart his authority. At fifty-six, Collier, a man of old-fashioned loyalties and a lifelong friend of Paul Brown's, was a soft-spoken courtly gentleman from Kentucky, a grandfatherly figure sporting a hearing aid, thick horn-rimmed glasses, and a fedora. He had joined the navy at thirty-seven, even though he would likely have been exempted from the draft, because he believed it was his duty to fight in World War II. He had refused to take an assistant coaching job with the Browns until he was assured that no man had been pushed out to make way for him. Now he told Modell he wouldn't take the job unless he got Paul Brown's blessing. Brown bestowed it, and Collier became coach, at less than half Brown's salary.[73]

Collier dropped the puritanical code of conduct and discontinued the practice of the coach calling plays, explaining in the press, "I think the boys like to feel they have a part in running the thing." He also gave them the affection that Brown had withheld. "The players are responding to Collier, the quiet man of deep emotion, who sometimes clutches them as they come off the field as if they were sons returning from the wars," the *Saturday Evening Post* observed. He also gave them the championship they wanted, in a "return to glory" 1964 season (although it would turn out to be a onetime aberration in his eight years as coach). The players cheered the appointment. The Cleveland fans, on the other hand, were deeply divided. While glad to see a return to a more spontaneous style of play, many were outraged by the firing of the founding coach and the disloyalty it implied.[74] The fans were so busy debating the respective virtues of the two coaches that they failed to see how moot the debate was.

The man who would betray them was the new owner. As a TV producer, Modell understood that the future of football lay in television, a medium that would eventually command every team owner's loyalties. Modell would become a key player in brokering the ascendancy of football as a televised sport; he chaired the National Football League's television committee for thirty-one years. He helped create *Monday Night Football,* a program crucial to the conversion of football into showbiz; the Browns were, in fact, cast against the glitzy, upstart New York Jets for the show's premiere. He was in on the breakthrough $14 million sale of TV rights to CBS in 1964, managed by his close pal NFL Commissioner Pete Rozelle, a former public-relations man and marketing maven. He helped to open the floodgates through which, in 1977, a $656 million four-year deal with the networks poured into the NFL's coffers. That year was a point of no return—the first time the league made more from television than ticket sales.[75]

The new media culture changed the way the game was played and the relationship not only between the sport and its players but also between the sport and its fans. In the new relationship, the players would be the superstars and fans their wide-eyed idolizers. The players were to become the flyboys, the astronauts, and all that was left for the average fan to do, it seemed, was watch—preferably (from the NFL's point of view) from his living-room couch.

After the long, bland managerial era of Paul Brown, televised football seemed to restore to the players their individuality, but just as their anonymity had been sullied when enslaved to Brown's system, their individuality was corrupted by the purposes of their new master: television. On their way to becoming men, they were turned into personalities. With TV stardom came an immense rise in salaries, perks, and endorsements. The overthrow of the autocratic coach would ultimately be achieved via wealth; the superstar players would earn many times more than their coaches. But their new affluence would not grant them the anticipated bounty of masculine dignity, because their salaries were tied to the fickle realm of entertainment ratings. With star status came the insecurity of being a glamorized object, of maintaining not the team's image but the player's own.

In the process of becoming sports pinups, the players not just in football but in baseball and basketball as well would gain much. No longer could owners keep them for their short careers in a state of near peonage, controlling their every move and their livelihoods. Now, players found themselves in play in a lively labor market where they could bargain and negotiate. They had, in essence, gained the right to trade themselves and had become "free agents" in more than just the legal sense.

Television and ad money had decoupled them from servitude, but also from the very idea of "the team," from any concept of loyalty to anything except perhaps their own agents, their own careers, their own images. This was a new world with many perks, but the freer many of them became, the less independent, the less manly they often felt. To market themselves, after all, they were forced to market images of themselves in a culture where sports was increasingly just that—a series of images played and replayed between all the car and beer ads in the living rooms of America. It was no mistake that the new sports "stars" like Jim Brown would sometimes go on to act in Hollywood movies or would become TV sports announcers and personalities introducing the next generation of stars—and their media-wise quirks—to the public.

To make something of their new status, the players found they had to exaggerate it; many quickly learned that bad-boy temper tantrums earned them the most attention from the media and hence money from owners. Others, though in lesser numbers, continued to act like the loyal, good boys of an older era. But they, too, often found that they were acting an image, one whose payoff came only in relation to the antics of the bad boys all around them, and certainly not through any passage to manhood. This was the case in every sport: it was partly John McEnroe's legendary sulks that Bic was buying when the company signed him on in 1982 as their well-compensated spokesman, just as, later on, it was Dennis "Bad As I Wanna Be" Rodman's Jumbotron-sized histrionics that earned the Day-Glo-haired putative groin kicker movie roles and $9 million in endorsement deals.[76] And so it was that most of the players with the biggest contracts and merchandising packages seemed to be the ones who became the most infantile actors on football's new playing field.

"By the middle of the sixties," *New York Times* sports columnist Robert Lipsyte commented in *SportsWorld,* "there was only one true measure, and that was price. Crowds meant nothing anymore." When Art Modell announced in the seventies that he would pour millions into rebuilding

Municipal Stadium, it turned out that he had allotted much of the money for two purposes: luxury boxes for a luxurious few and the second-largest scoreboard in North America, designed to produce $1 million a year in advertising revenues.[77] To Dante Lavelli, the breach of trust occurred the day Modell "raised the ticket prices without telling the fans about it."

Oh yeah, the fans. Much has been written about how the coming of televised football sliced the game into consumable bits sandwiched between commercials, forced the use of injurious Astroturf because it was prettier to look at, turned the sport into a big-stakes money machine, and so forth. But what did it do to the fans?

At first, the only "fans" who seemed to have a visible role in the coming era of television were the cheerleaders. It was no coincidence that at the same time football began to be televised, the male "yell captains" of college football were replaced for the first time ever with pom-pom girls. By the late seventies, most pro football teams had added a corps of cheerleaders of their own, none so extravagantly unclothed as the Dallas Cowboys', who drew the attention of *Playboy* and became a business institution in their own right, complete with a line of costume jewelry and trading cards. The cheerleaders joined the players in a realm apart from the fans. As sports historian Benjamin Rader noted, "The girls became first and foremost entertainers rather than cheerleaders."[78] The yell captains had served to connect the fans with the action on the field, but the pom-pom girls became an entertainment concession at the service of the cameras. In any event, the new male fans, the ones the advertisers salivated over, were increasingly not in the stands. By the eighties many of them would be huddled at sports bars, gazing up like so many worshippers at the TV pulpit posted over their heads, framed by Bud Lite signs. The boosters were long gone. Reshaped in Modell's own image would be the "goggle eyed fan." Which is to say that, in the end, the fans would be betrayed by one of their own.

The stadiums would increasingly become the preserves of an upper crust as ticket prices rose out of the range of the average working-class salary. The men whom pro football had originally promised to speak for and glorify—the hardworking factory workers of what was now becoming the rust belt—were the ones most shut out and turned off in the transition to an electronic age. Football's television viewers were more white-collar, middle-management, and suburban—more likely to have the wherewithal to buy the high-ticket items being advertised on-screen than the traditional working-class ethnic audience of pro football's earlier history.[79] So, too, were its new managers, handlers, and spin doctors. "Football today," Michael Novak observed in 1967 in *The Joy of Sports*, "is preeminently the sport of the new white-collar and professional class, of the statesmen, bureau chiefs, managers, executives, admen, consultants, professors, journalists, engineers, technicians, pilots, air traffic controllers, secret service men, insurance agents, managers of retail chains, bank officers, and investment analysts."[80] Paul Brown had started out seeking to elevate pro football into a "high-class" realm. From the beginning in Massillon, class transformation had been a tacit part of the program of the boosters who were football's founding fans. But instead of pulling up the working-class community that football represented, the Modells of the sport left those who belonged to that world behind. A few astronauts rocketed into the stratosphere of the televised firmament, but the rocket boosters all fell back to earth. This betrayal of the sports boosters did not, however, come without a fight—especially in Cleveland, where the fans were unwilling to relinquish a longstanding relationship.

Every Dawg for Himself

THE FALL AFTER BIG DAWG MARRIED MARY, he gave up the seat he had occupied in the upper deck of Municipal Stadium for seven years. Its ever-rising price was more than he could manage, and besides, he was hoping to interest Mary in his obsession. So in the autumn of 1985, Big Dawg traded in the seat with the better view for two seats in the bleachers by the east end zone. Those seats were half the price, and for a reason: you couldn't get much of an overview of the action.

Mary, who regarded football as a game best observed over a stiff upper lip, found in the birth of their twin girls an excellent excuse to absent herself from her husband's Sunday stadium worship, and she seized it. Big Dawg had sacrificed his better perch in vain. But that's not how he saw it. "It was exciting," he said, "because the seats were available right in the front row. The end zone was probably ten feet away from where my actual seat was." Not that he was sitting most of the time. He was on his feet for much the same reason that the coaching staff paced the sidelines, shouting their counsel: he was reclaiming the original support-trooper role of the Cleveland Browns fan.

In this, Big Dawg was not alone. In 1985, only two thousand of the ten thousand low-rent bleacher spots were held by season-ticket holders. By 1993, the number had jumped to six thousand.[81] By the thousands, the men came down from the heights where they could see the game to the flats where they could be seen by the players—and where, they anticipated, they could make a difference. They intended to level the playing field. They were set on reviving a more intimate relationship with the players, and, in the process, reviving the team's fortunes. "We were like this whole separate unit," Big Dawg said. A group of fans in the front row even wore World War II helmets.

The team certainly needed help. By the mid-eighties, the Browns were languishing. In a decade and a half, the team had made it into postseason contention only four times—and failed in every instance. The dynasty of Paul Brown was so long gone it seemed like a fable.

The team's decline echoed Cleveland's. It had been a terrible decade for this midwestern model of civic pride and industry. The city's Job-like plagues had started with the 1966 riots that had brought with them devastation, death, and the National Guard. They continued with the loss of more than one hundred thousand manufacturing jobs, the fall of the city's public-school system into virtual receivership, and the collapse of city government into default in 1978, making Cleveland the first major city to suffer such a fate since the Depression. By the late 1970s, Cleveland was no longer a blue-collar town: more than 70 percent of its jobs were in the low-paying service economy. By the eighties, poverty consumed one-fifth of Clevelanders, unemployment hovered near 12 percent, and crime was soaring. A series of embarrassing mishaps, scandals, and disasters soon made Cleveland the punch line to every stand-up comic's crack about the dregs of urban living. The city was a virtual caricature of everything that had gone wrong in the post–Vietnam War nation, from social to fiscal to environmental wreckage. It was $111 million in debt, its books declared "inauditable," its infrastructure in a shambles; half the fish in nearby Lake Erie seemed to be floating belly-up, and both the Cuyahoga River and the mayor's hair had caught on fire. Clevelanders packed and fled at the first opportunity; the city that in 1930 was the sixth-largest in the nation was by 1980, the eighteenth. Cleveland was now known not as the "city of co-operation" but as the "mistake on the Lake."[82]

Big Dawg, like many Clevelanders, was personally traumatized by this decline. He had tried to fight it where it hurt his family most, in the public-school system. He made a stink at school-board meetings about the deteriorating education and tried to rally fellow parents behind a plan to make computers available in the schools. But the situation seemed monumentally hopeless. There was no money in the city coffers to rehabilitate the schools, and the Reaganite federal government intent on dismantling its own Education Department was not about to come to the rescue.

At the stadium, on the other hand, a single ray of light had descended. His name was Bernie Kosar, a phenomenal college quarterback raised in Boardman, Ohio. Kosar's lifelong ambition had been to play with the

Cleveland Browns. He was an old-fashioned fan turned old-fashioned, hardworking athlete; in college, he had led the University of Miami football team to a national championship as a red-shirted freshman, while maintaining high grades. In 1985, he skipped the regular draft so he could join the Browns. "I just wanted to go home," he said. His actions inspired NFL management to create the "Kosar rule," preventing players from handpicking their teams in the future. Not that a flood of players would be descending on the woebegone Browns anyway. Kosar was one of a kind, and a grateful city embraced him as their only begotten son.[83]

The new quarterback was a homely guy who ran funny and actually liked being with his family and going to Sunday mass. "In my era," the former Browns mascot Seth Task said to me, "everybody identified with Bernie because he was like the ugly duckling, like the city of Cleveland." And he cared about Cleveland. "Bernie's appeal was so great, because he wooed us more than we went chasing after him," Cleveland *Plain Dealer* columnist Bill Livingston wrote. When the Browns signed him on in 1985, Art Modell got tears in his eyes as he told *Sports Illustrated,* "It's not an everyday occurrence that somebody wants to play in Cleveland." Modell declared himself Kosar's "surrogate father," and so did the men in the stands.[84]

Big Dawg was one of those proud papas and, unable to contain his excitement until the season began, he headed over to the training camp that summer to see what he could do to help. One day, while he and other fans lined the fence watching their team limber up, cornerback Hanford Dixon barked at some fellow players. "I was just trying to fire up our defensive linemen," he recalled later. If they were going to prevail, he told them, they needed to be "like a pack of dogs chasing a cat." And so the "Dawg Defense" was born, "dawg" in honor of Dixon's Alabama drawl.[85]

At the second preseason game, Big Dawg settled into his bleacher seat only to find the next seat occupied by a dog skull. It belonged to Tom McMahon, a self-employed painter and devout fan who had also witnessed the barking episode and took it as a cue. He had painted his face, half orange and half brown—the team colors—and then had applied the remaining orange to his macabre banner, a canine cranium bobbling on two broomsticks. Where he found it no one in the bleachers dared inquire. "I didn't want to know!" Big Dawg said. "No questions! It was like, no names please! It had teeth and everything and the smell was unbelievable. It was little, like a dachshund, but the skull looked more like a Doberman, and it was on these two broomsticks so he could make the mouth move, so it could bark." But best of all, "the players responded to that skull," Big Dawg said. "They would come over, just to see it."

The day before the next game Big Dawg, contemplating how he could support the Dawg Defense, spotted a costume shop. "I went in and they had all these masks hanging off little nails on the wall, and they had one up there that was this dog. I said, 'How much you want for that mask way up there?'" The storekeeper got up on a ladder to remove it reluctantly. "She thought there was no way I was going to purchase this thing." He laughed. "Eight years it'd been sitting up there. They stopped manufacturing the mask in 1980." It had two tags on it, for ten and twelve dollars, and the storekeeper told him he could have it for the lower price. The following morning, he suited up in his new uniform. The rubbery basset hound with its long whimsical face "got everyone laughing," he said, which was no small feat in a stadium beset with a fifteen-year case of the doldrums. "They were laughing their butts off." And the bemused players responded, too. "They were barking at us during warm-ups. It was kind of like a big thing."

Three games later, bleacher denizens started showing up with boxes of Milk Bones and doggy biscuits to hurl onto the field. When the players would on occasion intercept a biscuit and hurl it back at the stands, the fans in the bleachers were thrilled. Soon there were so many biscuits on the field that the maintenance staff had to haul them away at halftime in a brigade of wheelbarrows. Meanwhile, dog masks of every variety proliferated. Some Sundays, the bleachers looked like a masquerade ball; it was hard to find an uncovered face. Tom McMahon hauled in an entire doghouse, presumably the skull's domicile. Brothers Joe ("Bubba") and Bud ("Junkyard Dawg") McElwain brought the mania to its culmination with the real thing: they arrived with their two St. Bernard pups adorned in Cleveland Browns jerseys. The McElwains themselves, however, were the more dramatic sight. Joe, a tool-and-die maker, and Bud, a laborer, sported head-to-toe dog outfits, Dr. Denton's–style cuddly sleep suits with floppy-eared hoods. "They used to call me Fozzie Bear [a small-eared Muppet], or Ewok [small furry critters in *The Empire Strikes Back*], because the ears were too short on my costume," Bud told me, still a bit chagrined. "It cost me over two hundred dollars to get it tailored right.... A lot of people would see us and go, 'Are you with the team?'" Which, as far as he and Joe were concerned, they were.

The barrier between fans and players seemed to lower dramatically. "The players would come down and wave their hands to get us started," Scott Shantery recalled. He and his friend Ed Kuderna had given up their upper-level seats to join the Dawg Pound, and both agreed it was worth it. "You definitely felt like you were *involved*," Kuderna said. Joe and Bud McElwain took to coming a couple hours early to buck up the players as they arrived. Players would stop to pet the real dogs and to thank the Dawg Pounders for the support. "[Linebacker] Frank Stams even said to us we should call him in the off season and have a beer," Joe McElwain said. McElwain did call, but only to get tickets to some away games. The wall might not have seemed as insurmountable, but it was still there. "What are you going to ask a player to do?" he said. Nonetheless, the players, too, seemed to be making an effort. Running back Tommy Vardell greeted Dawg Pounders by their nicknames, even coming over to the fence to pat a devoted barker on the back and thank him. Cornerback Hanford Dixon wrote a daily "Dawg Diary" for the local paper in which he addressed the Dawg fans, advising them on how best to lend support. From the field, he turned at times and entreated the Dawgs to start barking. The fans were delighted.[86]

The team's management also recognized the Dawg Pound's potential usefulness. The Cleveland Browns had never had a mascot before. With all the barking in the bleachers, why not make it official with a costumed Dawg on the field? A contest for "Rover Cleveland" soon followed. The winner was twenty-five-year-old Seth Task, who heard about the tryouts while working at his door-to-door perfume-sales business. His wife tracked him down with the news. Task, a devoted fan, canceled his remaining appointments and "flew down [highway] 90" on the forty-five-minute trip to Browns headquarters. "Luckily, I was my own boss so I could set my own hours," he recalled. He was last on a long line, many already armed with elaborate props and outlandish signs. "All I had was my enthusiasm," he said. It was a beastly hot day and when Task's turn came, he had to doff his thick eyeglasses because they were fogging up under the big dog head, leaving him nearly blind and worrying that he might crash into Art Modell, who was observing the contestants on the field. He nonetheless launched himself into a chaotic but blissful leap-and-dance number, and was chosen. "I didn't actually work for the Browns. I was an agent." In other words, they gave him $100 a game and no benefits. It was just another "independent contractor" job, not unlike hawking fragrance door-to-door, but at least he was doing "something that I believed in." And fans applauded him for his efforts.

Doing a job that others thanked you for was a large part of the reason Vince Erwin volunteered his services in the Dawg Pound. A front-end-loader driver and coal handler at a Morton Salt factory in Rittman, Ohio, Erwin arrived in the bleachers one day wearing a "rabid-looking" dog mask with huge fangs and a long, pointed nose. It wasn't his first time in a mask. He'd worn one once before as an adult, to a union meeting. For years, he had been frustrated with his union local's passivity. Grievances went nowhere, and when he spoke up in union meetings, he was told he had a bad attitude. Soon after, he stenciled the words "Bad Attitude" on his hard hat. "It wasn't long before they told me I had to take it off." The factory where once "people came up through the ranks" had changed hands repeatedly in a series of buyouts and mergers, and "now it was all accountants and pencil pushers running the place," who thought the best way to raise profits was to cut basic employee benefits. "I got very frustrated seeing the union do nothing." In 1982, after hearing that the key union negotiators were spotted on the golf course with management only a few days before a union meeting to ratify a contract, Erwin lost his composure. "I got this pair of coveralls and an old man's mask and a couple of pie tins and a can of whipped cream." With the meeting under way, Vince Erwin burst through the back door, flung the cream pies in the union president's face and tore out of there. "It was two years before they pinpointed who it was under that old man's mask." The gratification of the moment wore off quickly, however, as the contract was approved without a hitch. Later, he made a successful bid for union president, a position he still held, but it had proved harder to make changes than he had hoped. "Factory work, it's the true dead-end job," he concluded. "You try to buck the system, but . . ." He held his hands out, palms up, empty. In the stands, however, he found a place where a man in a mask might have an effect.

Instead of a pie, Erwin carried a large bell and a three-foot rawhide bone. This close to the field, he discovered, the players "were touchable," and so reachable. They couldn't help but hear Erwin's bell and see the bone he wielded—and the unvanquished devotion and support they represented. To demonstrate that this was the devotion of an old-fashioned workingman, not a beribboned cheerleader, he carried a large shovel and, like Big Dawg and numerous other Dawg Pounders, he wore a hard hat. "This is a blue-collar town and I'm a blue-collar guy," he explained. To introduce his new, devoted dog self, he printed up a business card that announced himself as "Vince 'D. Dawg' Erwin." Under a drawing of a tiny dog face and a big bone, the card bore the inscription, A GOOD "DAWG" WILL ALWAYS REMAIN LOYAL. When security guards ordered the Good Dawg to relinquish his bone at the gate—such a large projectile was deemed a potential hazard—Erwin conspired with another fan to sneak it in, via a forty-foot rope draped over the bleachers' wall. One day, a humorless cop jerked him out of his seat. Erwin found himself escorted to the back, where his bone was confiscated and "put in lockup." As he returned to the stands, boneless and slump-shouldered, something unexpected happened to raise his spirits. "As I came down the steps, everyone started cheering me," he recalled, still gratified by the moral support turned his way. "It was this very uplifting feeling. To know that all these people were backing me."

The Cleveland Browns had always had a huge fan base—the Browns Backers was the biggest football fan club in the nation, with 68,000 members and 379 chapters.[87] But the Dawg Pound was something new: a gathering of men looking not only to back their team but to receive some "backing" themselves. Dawg Pounders typically decried the Browns Backers as too "elitist." They felt shunned by the dues-paying organization, with its official round of luncheons and meetings and its self-important Chamber of Commerce–type members. "I attempted a couple of times to join a Backers' club," Big Dawg told me, "but I always thought I was getting the cold shoulder." The Dawg Pounders knew they weren't part of an elite, and that's not what they were looking for anyway. They were asking to be appreciated for their dogged, humble faithfulness. They took the hard benches with the obscured views because they were looking for a place that still honored the sort of man who proved his mettle and his decency by showing up without fail, rain or snow, a man who could be, if nothing else, counted on. The Dawg Pounders wanted confirmation that somewhere in a world that had "cold-shouldered" them, loyalty was still commended, the dog soldier still loved.

For this reason, the concept of the Dawg Pound was embraced by men who had never been to Municipal Stadium's bleachers. The Dawg Pounders were asking for something that any workingman who labored in an insecure and changeable workplace could understand: the assurance that loyalty mattered, that they were still players, not props, that if they did their part to protect the institution they had sworn fealty to they would, in turn, be protected. The Dawg Pound mania "caught on across the nation," an account of Cleveland Browns history observed with some amazement. "Fans who had never been within an all-day drive of Cleveland suddenly found a team with which they could identify. The emotional outlet of the Dawg phenomenon was unprecedented."[88] In Albuquerque, New Mexico, T. J. Trout, a radio-show "personality," declared himself "The Desert Dawg" on the airwaves, vowing his unwavering devotion to the team because "they're always the underdog" and promising in 1989 that if the Browns didn't prevail at the American Football Conference championship, he would "parade through an Albuquerque mall while wearing a chicken suit and carrying a sign declaring, I'M A LOSER BROWNS FAN, KICK ME. The team didn't win and Desert Dawg took his walk of shame through the mall, but "fortunately a lot of Browns fans showed up to support me. They protected me from Bronco fans who wanted to kick and harass me."[89]

It was as if the Dawg Pounders—or the Hogettes exhorting the Washington Redskins or the Cheeseheads abetting the Green Bay Packers—were attempting to transfer all of the long-term ties that had unraveled in other spheres of their lives to the stadium. The anger over broken ties at work and at home reemerged there as an emotional intensity and attachment to the one game that still seemed to follow the rules. "There have always been rabid fans," Jerry Lewis, a Kent State University sociologist who studied fan behavior in Ohio and elsewhere, remarked, "but this is a whole new category. What's so unusual about the superfan is that this is a person who makes a long-term, season-after-season commitment. . . . There is no doubt in their minds that their actions are stimulating other fans, which stimulates their side to do better. . . . [T]his is their weekend job."[90]

The Dawg Pounders had reason to believe that their endeavor was a productive one. "Ever since [the Dawg Pound] started, the Browns have been in the playoffs," Big Dawg pointed out happily. The team that had been limping along for some years racked up five consecutive playoff seasons in the last half of the eighties and headed off to the American Football Conference championships three times (where, however, visions of glory dead-ended in the Denver Broncos). Whether the spell had been lifted by the commitment of the fans or a change in coaching staff and players was not a matter one would have wanted to debate with the Dawg Pounders. "Absolutely," Big Dawg said when I asked him if the Dawg Pound had influenced the team's fortunes. He pointed to a 1986 home game against the New York Jets that went into double overtime. "It was freezing cold that day, and it was because of the fans we really won that game. Because we harassed [Jets defensive end Mark] Gastineau. The Browns had the ball on our own seven or eight yard line," right by the Dawg Pound, and Gastineau and his fellow Jets became distracted by all the howls. "You had ten thousand people yelling 'Gastineau sucks!' That makes a difference." Seth Task recalled a game that Cleveland was losing to the Bears until, "for absolutely no reason, the stadium started to erupt [with cheers]," he recalled. "The fans pulled that game out for the team. Cleveland finally was rising from the ashes. And the entire nation saw that."

Their contribution was based on sacrifice. It was important to the

Dawg Pounders that they were present even in the worst weather and did not take refuge in the enclosed loges, even when, on occasion, a wealthy ticketholder offered them temporary shelter. The McElwains, who always made a point of walking the eight miles from their home to the stadium, recalled with pride one ice-cold vigil before the ticket office. "We sat a whole night for playoff tickets," Bud said. "There were a thousand people waiting, and it was very cold. There were fires in barrels but it didn't do much good. My mother brought us soup." His brother Joe added, "The thing I hated was fair-weather fans. We stood by 'em, from thick and thin."

However, as the team entered the nineties, signs began to surface that the fairest of fair-weather friends were on the field, not in the stands. The players seemed to lose interest in the Dawg Pound and their performance slumped once more. When Big Dawg won an "Insiders" fan contest on the radio in 1990, he was allowed, as his prize, to attend a closed practice. He was shocked at what he saw. "Players were just B.S.-ing on their cell phones and lounging on the blocking dummies. And they didn't even try to hide it. In fact, the coach was there." Signs that the players were lapsing in other ways had been surfacing for several years. The grapevine was buzzing with rumors about who was checking into the "Inner Circle," a secret drug program set up by the Browns to rehabilitate addicted players, and by the last half of the eighties, the press was reporting on rampant drug abuse on the team.[91] "A lot of the players were forgetting about the fans and that the fans pay their wages," Bud McElwain said. "Like [safety Eric] Turner. I used to wear his number, and when I saw him in a bar, he'd talk to us. Then he got real big and he wouldn't talk to you anymore." By "real big," McElwain referred to a contract renewed at more than $8 million over three years with a $2.75 million signing bonus. The fans' distress rose with the soaring contracts and focused in particular on free agent Andre Rison, who became the NFL's highest-paid receiver in 1995, with a $17 million contract and a $5 million signing bonus, and whose perceived snootiness became a symbol to fans of the changed climate. The Browns had one of the highest payrolls in the NFL, and were second only to the Dallas Cowboys in the amount they poured into signing bonuses in the 1995 season.[92] Meanwhile, fans were feeling snubbed from another quarter: the new coach, Bill Belichick, who arrived in 1991. An often chilly figure who shunned the press, Belichick seemed to have little interest in what he regarded as the dubious contribution of the Dawg Pound.[93] "Belichick exhibited a complete arrogance toward the fans," Les Levine, a longtime Cleveland sports journalist and host of the talk radio show *Guys in the*

Know, said to me. The rift between coach and fan became a chasm two years later when Belichick jettisoned native son Bernie Kosar. Even Big Dawg, who was one of Belichick's few defenders in the Dawg Pound, said, "When Belichick let Bernie go, that was the fall of the city."

The fans were particularly upset because Belichick didn't even bother to trade Kosar; the coach just fired him, then compounded the humiliation by insulting his manhood in a press release that spoke of "a diminishing of his physical skills." The men in the stands seized upon that phrase in outrage. Many a Dawg Pounder brought it up in conversation with me, years later, spitting out the words "diminishing skills" as if the coach had spoke it of them. The way Kosar was fired was an unwanted reminder of the way many Dawg Pounders were used to being treated in the modern workplace, a reality they had come to the stadium to forget. The Browns were supposed to be a throwback to a time when men had other roles to occupy between superstar and sloughed-off dog. As Rocky DiCarlo, a distraught fan of twenty years who gave away his season tickets in protest, told reporters, Kosar "may not have been the greatest quarterback who ever lived. But he was a good quarterback, and a good person. He didn't deserve this." At a more intimate level, it seemed like another paternal betrayal. "Modell said, 'Bernie's like a son to me, he'll always be here,'" Dawg Pounder Ed Kuderna recalled bitterly. Modell offered only a mealy-mouthed explanation to the press at the time about how he "loved" Bernie but had to stand by his coach.[94]

In the aftermath of Kosar's firing, the Dawg fans turned rabid. A mob of nearly a thousand hounded Belichick from the stadium in a scene out of Nathanael West's apocalyptic novel *The Day of the Locust.* "They were yelling obscenities, really hateful stuff," Big Dawg remembered. "The mob was so vicious. They would've torn him apart if they could." Back in the safety of "the interview room," the coach shrugged off the furious fans, who could still be heard through the thick walls screaming "Bill Must Go!" "You listen to the fans," he observed acidly, "and you'll be sitting up there with them."[95] To be "sitting up there," he was saying, was to be decommissioned, consigned to the dress circle of workingman's hell. The coach had put into words the suspicion the Dawgs had been trying to bury for years: the fan was beside the point.

In the weeks that followed, the fans' rage began to fix on another target: new quarterback Vinny Testaverde. Smoldering resentment toward the men on the field, who seemed wedded more to their endorsement deals than to their boosters and who increasingly performed only for the eye of the camera, had burst into flame. A new venomous tone crept into their language. "Lest the dotard [Bill Belichick] has any doubts," fan Peter Carden wrote in a letter to the fan periodical *Browns News Illustrated,* "his customers despise Vinnie Notesticleverde." He related the words of another fan: "If he walked in this bar," the fan had said, "I'd beat him worse than [serial killer] Jeffrey Dahmer."[96] What bothered the fans most about Bernie's replacement was the seeming shift from scruffy workingman to glamour-puss. "Belichick wanted a guy who *looked* like Vinny Testaverde," Vince "D. Dawg" Erwin said to me disgustedly.

The fans who had donned dog faces and hard hats found themselves face-to-face with a truth they had been desperately trying to dodge. The battle now, the one that fans and players alike were caught up in, was really for the camera's attention. The show of hard hats, of dog suits, of toughing it out in the rain and the snow, in the end, became exactly that—a show, a beauty contest of sorts, where the object was to attract the camera with bizarre caricatures of working stiffs. To the extent that they were anything, they, too, had become just more entertaining images for the real fans of this new age, the consumers watching the game on TV.

The men on the field and the men in the stands had entered a world where what mattered, what brought you attention and gave you momentary value, was how you looked. In a celebrity culture, the so-called "male gaze" was no longer where power was located. As betrayed fan and sportswriter John Underwood wrote in his broadside *Spoiled Sport,* the athlete was now more "like the beautiful woman who has been 'taken care of,' until her beauty wanes or her dumbness manifests itself."[97] The Browns players were not the on-field equivalent of steelworkers, representing their blue-collar town. They were ogled models, advertising themselves; they were selling a product. Their supporters weren't D. Dawg and Big Dawg; they were being "taken care of" now by sneaker and beverage companies. The fans were there simply to enhance their appeal to advertisers, to show that the team was a much-desired consumer item. They were no different from game-show studio audiences, supplying the requisite applause and laughter. They were props for the players, a backdrop to the action, and the more outlandishly clothed or made up among them served as a useful momentary stopping spot for the ever-restless camera's eye, a joke on the very idea of the rabid football fan for the viewer back home. As Dawg Pounder Dan Harasyn put it in an outburst to a reporter: "They'll take a sport like this and turn the fans into background for the cameras. And if they can do it to us, they can do it to anyone."[98]

Rising violence would become the fan phenomenon of the late eighties and nineties: suddenly, it seemed, fans were throwing punches at players, firing flare guns across the field, breaking bones in the stands. The Philadelphia Eagles brought in police dogs and mounted police officers and set up a makeshift courtroom in the basement of the stadium to try proliferating lawbreakers on the spot. The media attributed fan misbehavior, variously, to excessive drinking, an increase in "delusional disorders," a societal obsession with materialism, or just a general loss of "civility."[99] That the reduction of fans to props could induce rage, that the *show* of violence might itself be the flip side of a compulsory display of glamour, was rarely considered. In the show-business realm the fans now lived in, rage, even if kept off camera, served to draw attention, to gain recognition, and to express a horror that fame would never be forthcoming.

"I understood the last and most important reason why I fought," the novelist Frederick Exley, tormented son of a small-time football star, wrote in his 1968 "fictional memoir," *A Fan's Notes.* He was speaking of the revelation that came after he provoked a seemingly senseless fistfight with two strangers in the wake of a New York Giants game. "The knowledge caused me to weep very quietly, numbly, caused me to weep because in my heart I knew I had always understood this last and most distressing reason, which rendered the grief I had caused myself and others all for naught. I fought because I understood, and could not bear to understand, that it was my destiny—unlike that of my father, whose fate it was to hear the roar of the crowd—to sit in the stands with most men and acclaim others. It was my fate, my destiny, my end, to be a fan." This was devastating knowledge for a man who, like so many men in the stands, had originally become a fan to be a part of the play. "I came, as incredible as it seems to me now, to believe that I was, in some magical way, an actual instrument of [Giants player Frank Gifford's] success," Exley wrote. Now he understood that modern fame was not to be shared; there was to be no brotherhood of celebrity.[100]

As the fans groped toward this bitter revelation, they began to seek access to the players only so that a shaft or two of the limelight might pass across their brows as well. After a while, the fans could not help but resent the hammerlock the players had on public attention and begin to wonder, if it was all about individuals gaining celebrity on their own, couldn't they, too, be desirable products? Rabid fans increasingly became focused not on helping the players perform but on cultivating their own performances. The show in the stands began to conflict with, even undermine, the drama on the gridiron. In the fourth quarter of a 1989 game against the Denver Broncos, the Dawg Pound fans bombarded the field not only with dog biscuits but with eggs, batteries, and rocks. The in-coming fire was so intense that the game officials actually moved the play to the other end of the field. A couple of weeks later, the Browns announced a ten-point program to "reduce rowdiness," which included banning projectiles, restricting beer sales, and adding video surveillance to the football experience.[101]

The Dawg Pounders originally had come down to the bleachers to "get close" to the players, but having arrived at field level they discovered they were now close to another sort of team, one in a much better position to deliver the national impression they desired: the TV crews. Slowly but surely, their objective changed. Now their goal was to have the cameras turned to the stands. One sign of this fundamental shift appeared on Big Dawg, who donned a Browns jersey emblazoned with the number 98. When bewildered reporters asked which player's number he was wearing, he said, "Mine!"[102] For years, Big Dawg had been dream-ing of how proud he'd be if the Browns won the Super Bowl. Now, he began to yearn for a trip to the Super Bowl himself. "If there ever was a chance to market myself in a big way as a representative of the city," he told me, "it would be at the Super Bowl. That was what I was waiting for." He was thinking, he clarified, not simply of his own gain but of "the exposure Cleveland would get" from his efforts, but the two im-pulses were increasingly difficult to disentangle. There had, of course, been elements of publicity-seeking in the Dawg Pound from the start— why else would Vince Erwin have printed up business cards? For years the callings of team service and self-promotion had dueled in the hearts of the bleacher fans. But by the mid-1990s, celebrity seemed to be tri-umphing.

The press liked to call Big Dawg the "spiritual leader" of the bleachers, but to say that was to badly misunderstand the nature of the Dawg Pound.[103] It had no leader, only increasingly bitter factions squabbling over scraps of media coverage. In the battle for celebrity, it was every Dawg for himself. Any seatmate who drew the eye of the camera was a rival. And because Big Dawg, largely by virtue of his bulk, got the most coverage, his face smack in the middle of so many fan photos in the papers, he became a target of the other Dawgs' wrath. It was Big Dawg whom *Entertainment Tonight* and *Good Morning America* each chose for a segment on crazed fans. It was Big Dawg whose picture appeared in the Cleveland *Plain Dealer*'s promotions extolling its sports coverage. It was Big Dawg whom First National Bank selected to illustrate full-page ads equating depositors with fans ("When you want to bank with the best in the field, you should go with the team at First National Bank of

Ohio . . ."). It was Big Dawg whom the oil company BP America asked to be its "celebrity server" in a fund-raiser for a soup kitchen. And it was Big Dawg who would be surrounded in the bleachers by kids and even a few women with autograph books, all pleading for his signature. "One woman wanted to pay him ten dollars to have her picture taken with him," Big Dawg's wife, Mary, recalled. "With *him*? I was shocked."[104]

The other Dawgs were more jealous than shocked. "A lot of people started making negative comments because I guess they thought I was making all this money off of it, which was not true," Big Dawg said. "That bank ad, they paid me only one hundred dollars and I had to drive down myself to Akron to do the photo. Something like that costs five thousand dollars, I think. They got away with murder. . . . But it was a good way to market myself." It was the "marketing," not the money, that the other Dawg Pounders coveted. On the sports call-in shows, fans denounced Big Dawg as a "publicity hound" and a "media hog." Dawg Pounder Scott Shantery fumed to me, "Who made Big Dawg our spokesman? He always had a cigar in his mouth, just to catch the media's attention. He's so big, how can you miss him?" Vince Erwin, a claimant to the title of first Dawg Pounder with a mask, accused Big Dawg of playing to the media to maximize his airtime: "People booed him because a lot of times during time-outs he'd be barking at an empty field and banging the fence, just because there was a camera out there."

Sometimes Big Dawg's contenders in the bleachers called him "Pig Dawg" and "Fat Dawg." Vince Erwin recalled a more treacherous effort to undermine Big Dawg's status in the pound: "This guy called Beano came up to me and opened his coat and said, 'Here, look what I have for you!' It was Big Dawg's mask. I said, 'Keep that thing away from me!' Big Dawg got the police involved. Two quarters later, they gave it back to him." But that didn't protect him from further offensives. One day, a Dawg Pounder who had downed one too many beers turned on Big Dawg with his fists. "He punched me in the back and then as I turned around, this other guy hit me from the side," Big Dawg remembered. He took off his mask to defend himself and tucked it in his helmet under his seat. When he reached down for it a short while later, it was gone. This time it would not be returned and he'd have to buy a new one.

The fans' depiction of Big Dawg as a media mongrel was disingenuous. They were just as intent on attracting press attention. "After a Browns game," Scott Shantery recalled of his ritual with his pal Ed Kuderna, "we would come home and turn on the TV right away and go to every game news clip to see if we got on. We'd see ourselves about half the time on the home games." They would always wear the same clothes, "like a uniform," Ed Kuderna said, "so when people would see you, they would know who you were." Vince Erwin admitted that the main reason he kept embellishing his getup was to stand out. "Everything became about being seen." In pursuit of "high visibility," he appeared on the BBC three times, on a British television football show called *Blitz,* and in a "no-speaking part" in a 1995 Browns promotional commercial. "It said, 'Here's Bill Belichick and his dogs,' " Erwin recalled, "and then it showed us on our knees and we had to sit up and beg like dogs." Erwin also landed a five-minute spot on *Browns Insiders,* where he was supposed to ask a question of coach Belichick. "Belichick wasn't actually there," he said, "so I guess it was make-believe."

"A lot of people wanted to be on TV, but not us," Bud McElwain told me, as we sat in his brother Joe's cramped house, one of a row of crumbling, tiny millworker homes built so close to the highway that the walls shuddered when a truck rumbled by. A few moments after this declaration, Joe was reeling off a list of their media appearances and playing for me a video of their segment on *The Pepper Johnson Show.* To ensure wider distribution of their images, Joe and Bud McElwain auditioned for a Topps trading-card contest of "extreme fans." The winners were supposed to get their faces printed on a trading card, a tailgate party in their honor, and a day of meeting the player whose card they shared. The McElwains won. "Congratulations!" the letter from the Topps publicist, which they still had, read. "Your support of the Cleveland Browns will finally be rewarded."[105] The McElwains said they never did get their party and the player Carl Banks wasn't available to meet with them. The Topps representative trotted them over to a couple of TV and radio shows, "and then he said, 'Well, I have to catch a plane,' and that was it," Bud recalled. Joe said he "spent about two hundred dollars buying [Topps] cards trying to find out whether I'm on a card." The closest one he found featured a tiny group picture of fans on the bottom of the reverse side of the card; his brother Bud's face was the size of a preemie's thumbnail. Joe's face apparently appeared nowhere. "Because we look similar, I think they only used one of us," Joe said.

The fan who started the whole Dawg Pound phenomenon with his dachshund skull made the move to television more directly: when Tom McMahon wasn't in the bleachers, doffing his shirt in the freezing stadium so the cameras could see the NO. 1 that he had shaved on his chest, he was busy cohosting his own local cable-TV show called *Good Morning Lorain County.* When that petered out, he launched another featuring himself as "Dr. You." Dressed in women's clothes, he invited female viewers to call in for advice about their "boyfriend problems." Like most of the Dawg Pounders, McMahon, a housepainter who struggled to make a small painting business support his family, was trapped in occupational limbo: between the traditional man's job he was trained for and the "feminine" celebrity position he craved. He labored ceaselessly when he was on a job; his wife, a receptionist, remarked at the time that her husband always worked Sundays—except, of course, when the Browns were playing a home game.

In the summer of 1993, he was trying to finish a job on a Sunday when he slipped on a slate roof and fell two and a half stories to his death. The obituary in the *Plain Dealer* was brief. It was followed, a year later, by another small item. At night on a lonely stretch of empty road, Mc-Mahon's devastated wife drove her car headlong into a ditch, flipping the vehicle several times. She was found dead. The accident orphaned their four children.[106] When I asked Dawg Pounders about McMahon, most vaguely recalled hearing something about his death, but none had bothered to find out more. Some confused him with a Dawg Pounder who had died in an industrial accident. Nobody seemed to know what the hardworking painter had done for a living and no one correctly re-membered his name. "McCarthy?" said one, "McCann?" another. "The guy with the dog skull" was the most common identification. They knew him only for his media prop.

The Deadbeat Dad of All Time

"I WISH TO GO ON RECORD AS SAYING that if any school in the country feels the need of a coach any time within the next ten years, they will have to leave Notre Dame and myself out of consideration," Knute Rockne declared in 1924. "Notre Dame is a part of my life, and my one ambition is to spend that life at the school that has made me whatever I am."[107] Less than a year later, he was negotiating for a coaching position with the University of Southern California. The following year, he met secretly with Columbia University and, eager to star as head coach in the nation's biggest media market, signed a deal. It eventually fell apart and, tail between his legs, he returned to Notre Dame, where he con-tinued to claim that his one ambition was to stay with the community that had made him "whatever I am." What he was not, any more than the football chieftains who came after him, was the good father. By the 1990s, the image of the loyal papa at football's helm was an icon long overdue for smashing.

"I'm not about to rape this city as others in my league and others have done," said Art Modell in 1994. "You will never hear me say, 'If I don't get this I'm moving.' You can go to press on that one. I couldn't live with myself if I did that." Less than one year later, Modell would sling the chisel.[108]

On a Sunday afternoon in early November 1995, outraged Dawg Pounders pressed up against the fence separating them from the field, grabbing their crotches, screaming curses, raining down a hail of lethal threats on a man who wasn't there. Some of the men broke off shards of ice big enough to "tear a hole in a person's scalp," *Sports Illustrated* reported, and hurled them onto the field. They fell at the feet of the police and extra security guards called out in anticipation of such an eventuality. "Give us Modell! Bring us Modell!" a mob bellowed. Menacing placards waggled over the Dawg Pound: ROT IN HELL MODELL, GO STRAIGHT TO HELL MODELL. The object of their bloodlust, the seventy-year-old owner, had skipped his first home game in thirty-five years. "Benedict Art," as the fans dubbed him, would not attend another Browns game in Cleveland.

On that terrible Sunday, Big Dawg was, for once, not one of the fans pressed against the fence. He sat glumly in his seat, too shaken to rage. His dog mask, so worn from use that several times Big Dawg's mother had been called in for emergency sewing repairs, was not on his face. Big Dawg hadn't even bothered to take it out of his "Bone Bag." When reporters asked why he wasn't in costume, Big Dawg told them, "You wouldn't wear a dog mask to your brother's funeral, would you?"[109]

Art Modell had signed the deal a week earlier on the private jet of the man who brokered it, multimillionaire financier Alfred Lerner, who had owned 5 percent of the Browns since 1988. Afterward, the men broke out the cigars. Modell had a lot to celebrate. To entice Modell to move to Baltimore, the state of Maryland had promised to build him a brand-new, taxpayer-financed $200 million stadium, complete with 108 luxury boxes and 7,500 club seats, and then let the team inhabit it rent-free. The team would also be allowed to pocket all ticket, concession, parking, and stadium advertising moneys. And Baltimore and the state even allotted up to $75 million in moving expenses. A fancy new training compound, costing $15 million, would also be built free of charge. The cost would be borne by "personal seat licenses," a fat fee that each fan would have to pay simply to earn the "right" to buy a ticket in the stadium.[110]

Maryland was not exactly awash in excess cash. In fact, the state had just reported a $60 million shortfall in its budget for the first quarter of the year. Maryland had lost 2,700 jobs the previous year, its schools were in fiscal crisis, and it had just cut job-training and child-care programs for welfare recipients. Yet it was willing to hand over to Modell about $300 million, more than twice what the state paid annually into its welfare program.[111] Eleven years earlier, Baltimore had lost its own venerable franchise, the Baltimore Colts. That team had packed up and moved to Indianapolis, literally in the middle of the night. By the late eighties, team owners had essentially made the same move as the players before them: they had declared themselves free agents, ready to hop to whichever city offered them the freest ride at the most skybox-studded new stadium. After the NFL tried to stop the Oakland Raiders from moving to Los Angeles in 1982 and lost a $50 million antitrust judgment, the league sat on its hands. In the ensuing years, the Colts bolted, the St. Louis Cardinals jumped to Arizona, the Los Angeles Rams split for St. Louis, the Raiders returned to Oakland, and so on. At the time of Modell's decision, eight more NFL teams were scheming to move to greener Astroturf. The Sunday afternoon the fans hurled ice missiles into the field, the Browns were playing the Houston Oilers, who were on their way to the oil-free environs of Nashville.

"All I want to do is compete," Art Modell plaintively told reporters in a conference-call interview soon after the announcement. Modell said his inability to compete in the new climate had lost him $20 million in the previous two years and the Browns were $60 million in debt.[112] He defined "competing," however, in the same terms as did the kept defense industry: massive government subsidies that made it impossible to do anything but get rich. Modell wasn't alone in this rigged "competition." From the late 1980s to the early 2000s, one estimate projected, as much as $15 billion was likely to be spent on new stadiums, two-thirds of it out of taxpayers' pockets. The Dawg Pound types had been cut out of the loop. The fans of value were the rich and corporate who could afford the luxury boxes and personal seat licenses, the latter costing as much as $5,000 a seat in some cities. Watching a football game in person, even from the carpeted isolation of a skybox, was like buying a car now; it required a down payment.[113] The Depression-era Municipal Stadium, built in 1931, had been designed for the hoi polloi. Modell wanted new digs, especially after Cleveland built a fancy new arena for its baseball and basketball teams. "The politicians *promised* me that they'd build me a new stadium," Modell told me, still sounding aggrieved. "They broke that promise." When city officials stalled, then offered just to renovate the decrepit stadium and spent years debating the financing, Modell became incensed and took his grievance to Baltimore.

The team's money problems probably had more to do with the

Browns' high payroll than with their lodgings, but Modell hadn't exactly looked out for the team's best interests, either. He had talked the city into letting him take over the operation of the stadium and charged his own team rent. Then, strapped for money, he tried to get the Browns' board of directors to buy the stadium operation back from him and assume his loans. Minority investor Robert Gries, Jr., uncovered documents showing that Modell had overvalued parts of the operation in hopes of big profits from the sale. In 1982, Gries sued to halt the sale and won. Modell was stuck with the stadium company, and his debts. Yet he continued to spend as if drawing liquid money from an ever-flowing golden spigot—a $900,000 new field the team didn't really need, $500,000 on a movie that never got made, a publishing foray that lost him more than $1 million.[114]

Modell's defenders suggested that he wasn't moving to Baltimore just for the money; his motives were, ironically, paternal. He wanted his adopted son David to take over the team one day—and his mound of debt, when combined with the intricacies of estate-tax law, theoretically might have compelled his son to sacrifice the team upon Modell's death. The Baltimore deal lifted the financial burden and set the son up for life. Others scoffed at that explanation, pointing out various ways he could have solved the supposed tax problem without selling the team. Whether sincere or not, such fatherly ministrations left the Browns' fans cold. In their view, David Modell, whom they knew only as a cigar-smoking poseur with a much-publicized coke-abuse problem in his youthful past and no allegiance to Cleveland, was an undeserving bene-ficiary.[115] "David's not even his *real* son," many a fan heatedly told me. His "real" sons were them. Shortly after the move, Modell told a Balti-more journalist, "Tell your kids that Papa Art said have a Merry Christ-mas." When word of this paternal philandering got back to Cleveland, *Plain Dealer* sports columnist Bill Livingston's headline spoke for all the city's fans: PAPA ART WALKS OUT ON AN EXTENDED FAMILY. Art Modell, Livingston wrote, "might be the deadbeat dad of all time."[116]

The results of Modell's decision to abandon Cleveland would seem easily reckoned: total win for him, total loss for the fans. But out of the stunning betrayal came an unexpected opportunity to accomplish the mission that had driven the Dawgs to the bleachers in the first place. The fans now had a chance to defend their community. That possibility began to take shape when Cleveland's mayor, Michael White, who him-self was not much of a football fan but understood the Browns' symbolic importance to the city's male populace, delivered a call to arms. "It happened to Oakland and nobody said anything," he told them. "It happened in Los Angeles and nobody said anything. . . . How many cities are going to be threatened this way?" Would the NFL be held accountable for allowing the team's owner "to kick [the] city in the teeth?" Were the men in the stands going to take a stand? "Our community is prepared to fight," he declared. Then the mayor led the fans in a chant that would become their mantra in the months ahead: "No team, no peace. No team, no peace."[117]

Suddenly, the Dawgs found themselves on the field of action, and the government itself was backing them. The city of Cleveland filed suit against the Browns for breach of contract. The court issued a temporary injunction against the move to Baltimore. And the fans deployed for battle. A sign of new kinds of intimacies that might lie ahead surfaced in the Dawg Pound at the home game following the bad-news announcement. In the final seconds of the fourth quarter, as the Browns lost to the Green Bay Packers, Dawg Pounder John Schoditsch hung his head and wept. Big Dawg was standing next to him, pressed against the fence. The two men didn't really know each other, but something prompted Big Dawg to put his arm around the weeping fan and comfort him. "Hang tough, guy," Big Dawg said. Schoditsch broke into sobs and buried his face in Big Dawg's chest. "Let it out," Big Dawg said gently. "I know it hurts. But you gotta hold your head up."[118]

The struggle to keep the Browns had all the hallmarks of an old-fashioned, World War II–style fight: the fans were defending something that everyone agreed was a good cause, and the effort put them on a relatively equal footing with the players, the businessmen in their community, and one another. They had a clear and honorable mission, to rescue their team from the clutches of a clearly defined enemy (or, at least, so they thought). Just as the shipyard workers derived strength and closeness from their Save Our Shipyard campaign, it seemed the Cleveland fans might find a source of old-fashioned masculine rejuvenation in the organization that they now rallied around, Save Our Browns, with its telling double entendre of an acronym, S.O.B.

Duane Salls, a promotions and public-relations consultant who set up the organization's headquarters in his office at the mayor's request, intended it to be "like a military operation," he told me. "We even put up props. We hung up [camouflage] netting. We had our master war plans on the walls — tactics listed with targets. We had big boards with lights. We painted OD [olive drab] boxes just like you'd see in the war room in the movies. It was designed to be organized masses with weapons —

high-tech weapons, phones, faxes, mail, the media. There's probably never been an organized movement like this put on that wasn't a war. And the NFL was our target."

The NFL was due to vote on the team's move to Baltimore on January 17, and the "organized masses"—everyone from Dawg Pounders to former players to local corporate executives to retirees to vagrants—raced against that deadline. Homeless men who wandered into S.O.B. headquarters were put to work manning the phones. An elderly mail brigade helped send 320,000 postcards. Dawg Pounders distributed 12,000 lawn signs. Many traveled by bus caravan to other football games in the region and held boisterous protest rallies. Two hundred Browns fans went to Washington, D.C., to wave picket signs as NFL commissioner Paul Tagliabue passed by them in the hallway on his way to a congressional hearing on franchise hopping.[119] Bernie Kosar, then with the Miami Dolphins, issued an open letter calling on the NFL to honor the fans. "I would love to be part of the movement that would help keep the traditions of professional football alive where it belongs—in Cleveland," he wrote.[120] The executives of the Cleveland-headquartered American Greetings Corporation agreed to send three-foot-high cards to every NFL owner and the commissioner, with the greeting "All Cleveland Browns want for the holidays is their football team in Cleveland." More than forty Mail Boxes Etc. outlets allowed any fan to walk in and send a fax to the NFL for free.

Save Our Browns fighters collected an incredible two and a half million signatures in two weeks on a petition to the NFL. Big Dawg was on one of the four buses that traveled twenty-one hours to Atlanta to place the petition before the league's officials. "Atlanta was the most uplifting fight of the whole thing," he said. They unfurled the petition at the feet of the media, with the signatures taped onto a massive roll donated by a Cleveland paper company. "Then we picked it up with military precision," Salls recalled, "and took it down and took it out the side doors and piled into vans and cars and buses, and picked it up and literally paved the entire huge—huge!—vestibule of the hotel where the NFL was staying." That night, four hundred fans took up a vigil under the hotel windows. They stood silently, the beams from their pen flashlights wavering in starry pinpricks along the dark lawn.

The campaign appealed to the media at every turn. "For the media, we continually produced documents," Salls said. "Every day we had a press release for them." The mass mobilization culminated in "Internet Day." Gary Christopher, a devoted fan and computer wizard, who had just sold a travel agency and was "looking for a job," volunteered his services. Nearly four thousand fans with computers were deployed to send out E-mail alerts in bulk to every institution in the country they could think of that might help—the White House, state legislatures, league officials, NFL sponsors, but primarily the media. "It took ESPN three days to clear their E-mail," Christopher told me jubilantly. "We created a media frenzy. We were helping the newspapers. We were feeding them, keeping them motivated."

But most of the newspapers simply erased the E-mail, and reporters who were targeted, from the *New York Times* to the Duke University newspaper, called to complain angrily about the inundation. What the fans involved in Save Our Browns only slowly came to understand was that the media didn't really want to "help" and weren't really their allies. Individual reporters, particularly from local papers, radio, and TV, might be sympathetic. But the rest of the media were, at best, "motivated" to cover the Save Our Browns campaign as an amusing diversion, part of an entertainment package. In the real war, the war the fans were only half aware they were engaged in, the media saw the world as if through the NFL's eyes.

Big Dawg began to understand this truth only after several futile attempts to have S.O.B.'s plight chronicled by ABC News. ABC, after all, was the network that had built much of its ratings and fortune on football coverage. In Atlanta for the unveiling of the petition, he said, that network's *Good Morning America* backed out of planned live coverage. Big Dawg was beginning to draw his own conclusions. "[ABC News president] Roone Arledge and the NFL are quite tight. Roone Arledge and Art Modell are very tight. Art Modell started *Monday Night Football* right here in Cleveland. Plus he signed their television contract."

In early February, Big Dawg flew to Washington to testify before the House Judiciary Committee on a proposed "Fans' Rights Bill." For the occasion, he wore his brown team jersey, his Dawg collar, white pants with orange and brown stripes, and orange shoes. When it was his turn to speak, he placed his orange-painted dog bone on the witness table. The legislation was cosponsored by two Ohio legislators, and Big Dawg spoke with great intensity on its behalf. "Fans need rights to protect themselves from men who park on runways in Learjets, waiting for secret knocks to sign secret deals," he told them.[121]

The Fans' Rights Bill actually offered protection not to the fans but to league management, who would be shielded from a lawsuit by a team owner if the NFL prevented a move. For the fans it offered only a 180-

day notice of an impending move; like an earlier downsizing bill that required companies to inform their workers ninety days ahead of time of a mass layoff, it provided information, but no redress.[122]

Despite everything the Dawgs did, in the end Save Our Browns, unlike the shipyard's S.O.S. campaign, was not strictly a grassroots effort. Its first meeting included only mayoral officials and business leaders from firms like McDonald's, which offered its outlets as signature-gathering spots because it was a good customer draw, and the locally based pharmaceutical firm Revco, which claimed it was protesting the Browns' move because it conflicted with its own "hometown drugstore" image — yet, three weeks later, announced a planned $1.8 billion merger with Rite Aid (which ultimately did not go through) that would have closed three hundred of its stores, laid off eleven hundred people, and made millions for its top investors.[123] Duane Salls, the prime architect of the "war plan," was a special-events promoter, not a Browns zealot. He saw the fans as colorful window dressing in what was essentially a PR campaign. "We didn't diminish the passion of the Big Dawgs," he told me, picking his words with care. "We just decided we'd be better off to manage that passion. So we brought the Big Dawgs in as part of the team. Big Dawg played well in the media. We told him our plans and he followed." Those "plans," ultimately, were aimed at reaching a face-saving compromise for the mayor and city officials, not a rescue of the team. It turned out that the top dogs at Save Our Browns didn't really see the NFL as S.O.B.s after all. "We wanted to say to the NFL, 'You are not the enemy,'" Salls said to me. "You are not our target."

Two days after Big Dawg's testimony in Congress, the mayor's office announced that it had reached a tentative "peace treaty" with the NFL and was dropping its lawsuit. Its terms read more like concessions. Modell was allowed to take the team to Baltimore; Cleveland would get to "keep" its name, its colors, and its "heritage." The NFL agreed to look around for another franchise for the city. A new stadium would be built, with 8,000 club seats and 108 private suites. The NFL would contribute only a small percentage of the construction costs and, the agreement's fine print revealed, the league would even be reimbursed for those costs by future "personal seat license" fees for season-ticket holders.[124] Modell, for his part, was eager to present the agreement as evidence of his generosity. "I'm the only owner in the history of football to move and leave the colors and the memorabilia and the name behind," he told me. "The Giants didn't do that; the Raiders didn't do that; the Rams didn't do that. I did that for the people of Cleveland. I try to express my loyalty in a different way."

Cleveland, in fact, had taken Baltimore's path out. *Plain Dealer* sports columnist Bud Shaw saw through the euphemisms. "Remember the Save Our Browns campaign?" he wrote. "It somehow became a BMOC campaign. Build a Millionaire Owner a Castle."¹²⁵ A few fans had also caught on to the charade. Shortly after Modell announced his decision, Seth Task, a.k.a. "Rover Cleveland," held a press conference to announce that he was quitting. "I cannot work for Art Modell," he said, removing his giant dog's head with its huge fangs and spiked collar. "I'm a Clevelander and I will always be a Clevelander." He did one final Rover dance step, announced that he was forming a fans'-rights group, then left the stage. By the time he and I talked in his living room, surrounded by stacks of game videotapes, Task had moved from anger to the beginnings of an economic analysis. "People thought they were playing a role because they were faxing the NFL, because they were on every TV station. But they had no power." Task's solution was to create a "fans only" organization he named the American Sports Fan Association, whose mission would be to "demand that NFL owners play fair with their fans." The idea was unorthodox enough to be denounced by Bob Grace, president of the Cleveland chapter of the Browns Backers Club, who told the press, "We can't really see any good coming from it." He later informed me that a boycott was a bad idea because it was "militant." Duane Salls of S.O.B., who deemed the plan "counterproductive," agreed. "They were talking about a 'fan revolution,'" Salls told me, "and we avoided language like that."¹²⁶

"The philosophy was this," Task said. "The NFL has a voice and the money and resources to defend their actions. The players obviously have the money and channels to defend themselves. The owners have all the representation they need. The only people who don't have representation are the people in the seats who *create* the revenue. I can't think of a larger consumer group that doesn't have representation." It was the first time I had heard a Browns fan refer to himself as a consumer rather than an owner of the team. Task embraced a truth that few fans wanted to countenance: in fact, he and his fellow organizers phoned Ralph Nader's office and asked for advice on how to put together a *consumers'* campaign. But by the time we talked, Task wasn't sure what to do next. He stared straight ahead at his blank television screen. "I've always wanted to be able to help people, to help the community I live in." Right now he was working as manager of the Outback Steakhouse, a step up from door-to-door perfume sales, but not exactly what the former Northwestern University student with a double major in anthropology and theater had in mind. "I have a good head on my shoulders," he said. "Maybe I was meant to do something else. I just wish God would tell me what it is."

On March 11, the mayor made official the agreement in a brief noon-hour ceremony in the Red Room in city hall. Big Dawg was one of the honored guests. He wore his anticipatory St. Patrick's Day green sweater, the first time I had seen him in a color other than brown and orange. NFL commissioner Paul Tagliabue made a one-minute teleconference appearance from a Palm Beach resort.[127] While the commissioner's disembodied voice blared out from the speakerphone, rattling on about how the fans "can take great pride" in and look forward to a new team "with a lot of meaning," Big Dawg and a few handpicked fans stood silently to the side, shifting from foot to foot, hands folded in front of their trousers, fig-leaf style. Mayor White then assured the onlookers that "the Browns have been saved" and introduced the project manager for the new stadium construction, Diane Downing, a former state lottery executive in a burgundy Chanel-style suit. She assured them that the new stadium would be "very fan friendly" and "first class."

Big Dawg was allowed the last word at the ceremony. He thanked the mayor and the city council. "I was asked to carry the torch for all the fans," he said. "I told myself I was going to give it my best and I think I gave it my best. . . . The fans were in the forefront." With that, the meeting was adjourned.

In the aftermath of the campaign to save the Browns, I sought out several of the old Dawg Pounders to see what meaning it held for them. I caught up with the McElwains at Joe's house by the highway. He and Bud were seated in the living room, under a giant mounted Cleveland Browns watch, both still attired in their Browns regalia. Joe offered me a drink, in a Browns glass, of course, and chased Mugs the St. Bernard off the remaining chair. Across the tiny room, a catfish with a curiously crooked shape languished in a murky aquarium. Joe and Bud were arguing about what the settlement meant for the fans. "Without the fans, there is no game," Joe was saying.

Bud shook his head. "Not nowadays. They are paying players from TV rights, not from us."

"But you can't put a game on TV without the fans," Joe insisted.

"Sure they can," his brother replied. "They don't care. Look at Houston. They were only getting fifteen thousand, twenty thousand in the stadium."

"If we could just get someone to start another league and have people watch it, we might do away with the NFL," Joe said wistfully.

Joe's wife, Celeste, who had been observing this debate in silence, spoke up. "I don't know how these guys are going to survive without the Browns. He put the wedding off because of the game." She wagged a thumb at Joe. "Football came first. I was second."

"It was a bi-week, where they skip a week of football," Joe said defensively. "That's when we did the wedding and the honeymoon."

Celeste rolled her eyes. "He wouldn't have married if it weren't for that. I mean, he and Bud are sunk into the sport bad. I don't know how they're going to make it. The stadium was their *home*."

Behind her, the catfish limped along the bottom of the tank. Joe saw me staring and explained. "That catfish has a spine defect," he said. "He's slowly dying. The problem is, he's getting too big for his house. That tank doesn't fit him no more, but he's got nowhere to go."

A few days later, I drove down to the Pro Football Hall of Fame in Canton. A light snow fell, and against the slate-gray sky the building loomed, stark and utilitarian. Inside, though, certain adjustments had been made for the new era. FOOTBALL AS YOU'VE NEVER EXPERIENCED IT! screamed huge banners that accosted visitors at every turn. It seemed a curious slogan to embrace. Past black-and-white photos of the Massillon and Canton games with their throngs of cheering millworkers, past blow-up quotations from old greats like Red Grange ("I was just a little guy in a big field"), and past Jim Brown's tattered jersey with its accompanying tribute to him as "a superb craftsman," one entered a realm of gratingly loud electronic pop music, strobe-light flashes, and video games. In "Call the Play Theater," visitors could sit in what looked like cages and push buttons to determine the team's next move. Next door, in the NFL Theater, a film loop played *NFL Rocks: Extreme Football*. The segment under way when I entered the auditorium was entitled "Appetite for Destruction." Music pounded over the speakers, repeating the same lyric over and over again: "I am a glamour boy. I am a glamour boy. I am . . ."

On the way back, I stopped at Wooster to visit Vince "D. Dawg" Erwin. He had bought a house surrounded by cow pastures far out in the countryside. "This is the kick in the teeth I needed to wake up and see what's really going on here," he said as we settled in a living room scattered with kids' toys. The awakening came to him before the end of the season. "I didn't even go to the last game. I chose to go to work instead. I taped it but then I didn't even watch it." Erwin had come to his own conclusion about football. "You take what they did to the retiree benefits at Morton Salt," he said of his own employer. "What is it? 'Well, you worked forty years and here's a kick in the pants.' Yet you've got a CEO who can make one million dollars and a huge bonus and retires with thousands of shares of Morton stock.... It runs parallel with sports. They're doing the *same* thing. It's no longer sports. It's big business. As far as I'm concerned, I think they should take the team, the name and the colors and the rest of it and retire them."

And so Erwin had quit reading the sports page. He'd washed his hands of fan enthusiasms. "By my going to the game, I'm participating." And once he looked at his real relationship to the world of sports, he could think of only one way to protest that seemed meaningful. "I'm boycotting Nike. Maybe it's just my own private boycott. But it's what I'm going to do."

After I talked with Erwin, I drove back into Cleveland, passing the husks of smokestacks over moribund factories and pulling into the city after dark. Just as the highway curved toward a series of old WPA-built monuments by the downtown lakefront and, beyond them, the stadium, two huge billboards rose on either side of the road like blinders clapped on a horse. One advertised the company that had intended to lay off more than a thousand people and merge with Rite Aid until thwarted by federal regulators. REVCO: A FRIEND FOR LIFE, it said. The other featured an ad for the Galleria mall. SHOP WHERE THE BIG NAMES HANG OUT, it invited. Somewhere between these two suspect assurances, it seemed to me, lay the fate of the men of the Dawg Pound. The old work institutions that had promised them brotherhood and masculine dignity in exchange for loyalty had spat them out and the new consumer institutions offered them nothing but a glamour-boy look of "big names" on shirt labels. Given the alternatives limned on these signposts, I could understand why most Dawg Pounders would rather drive blindly straight ahead, toward the darkened stadium or the mirage of a glittery new arena built with fans' money. The stadium had been home. But like the one for Joe McElwain's catfish, it didn't fit anymore and there was nowhere else to go.

Dawg Without a Country

FOR A BRIEF TIME, THE DAWG POUND and the Save Our Browns campaign had turned Big Dawg's image into a marketable commodity, and several merchandising propositions came his way: Big Dawg key rings, a Big Dawg endorsement of a pizza company, a Big Dawg doll. He even got an "agent," the underemployed husband of his wife's boss, who sent him out to "make appearances" at bars and stores, but interest in a man in a dog mask waned fast. Big Dawg spent a bitterly cold Sunday afternoon in December at an autograph table outside a mall without a single taker—"I felt like a buffoon," he said. Finally, he fired his "agent," who was infuriated. "I'm going to get another Dawg from the Dawg Pound," he threatened, pounding on the table.

Still, Big Dawg described his continued marketing aspirations to me one afternoon as we sat in his basement, a dank and drafty space with a perpetual water leak. The cellar was his own personal Hall of Fame, every inch of its walls adorned with Browns memorabilia and Dawg Pound gear. The twins had followed him downstairs and were prancing around the room, coming to light every few minutes on a knee for one of his big bear hugs. What he dreamed of, he told me as his nine-year-olds smothered him with kisses, was "a Big Dawg costume on a mannequin in this basement one day, and these kids are going to be able to look at it and be proud of me. I know they will feel different toward me than I did to my dad." Big Dawg was proposing the patrimony of, literally, an empty suit, and there was a certain hollow ring to his enthusiasm. There was something else that bothered me about his assertion. "Your kids," I suggested to him, "already look at you differently than you did your dad because you show them you love them." He agreed at once. "The girls and Mary are the best things that ever happened to me." Still, he felt driven to mourn the lifelessness of his Big Dawg persona. I wondered why.

Big Dawg had equated the Browns' abandonment with watching "your best friend" die in the hospital. But who was he really mourning? Who was that "friend"? For a time, I suspected "he" was not really the moribund Browns but the long-dead Gerald Thompson, Big Dawg's father. Big Dawg knew he could not reclaim a lost patrimony; his father had failed to lift him into manhood when he was alive and wasn't about to do it from the grave. But the picture Big Dawg had conjured of that empty dog suit hanging on a mannequin gave me another thought. Perhaps the body on the hospital bed was his own. Perhaps he was trying to be an old-fashioned Massillon booster to the boy inside the basset-hound mask, to make of him a man who would be appreciated and respected by other men. Big Dawg was fathering himself.

Three months earlier, the abandoned sons of Cleveland had gathered in their father's house for what they suspected would be the last time. It was December 17, the final home game of the 1995 season. The Browns were playing the Cincinnati Bengals. The final score would be Browns 26, Bengals 10, but in the Dawg Pound no one was celebrating. By the third quarter, game officials had to move the play to the other side of the field for security reasons: some angry Dawg Pounders were lobbing firecrackers.[128] As the game clock wound down, another loud noise began to fill the stadium, a clanging echo that evoked all that rust-belt football had once stood for: the sound of men at work. In the Dawg Pound, men were sawing and hammering and splitting lumber. Only, they weren't building; they were destroying the bleachers. Ed and Scott Shantery joined in with a small hacksaw and sheer force. "We pulled all the bolts off a ten-foot section," Ed recalled, still amazed. "At first it was to take something," Scott said, "to say, 'Hey, I *paid* for something here.'" But at a certain point, the desire to prove ownership gave way to the violent despair of the propertyless. "It was just wanting to destroy," he said, an impulse shared by fellow fans who knocked over Porta Potties and even pulled turnstiles out of the concrete.

Big Dawg didn't join the wrecking party. He sat stone-faced in his seat while the wood splinters flew around him. "The game was close and that kept me from getting emotional, but with twenty seconds left, it got real bad. It got tough to handle." At the very end of the game, a sympathetic player, tackle Tony Jones, "came over and passed me the ball," Big Dawg said. "It was hard to get. I had to knock a few people out of the way so that I got it. I hugged it tight, so no one would take it away from me. I was so relieved when I did catch it, because I knew it was meant for me."

Jones gave Big Dawg a hug and said he would "miss me." Running back Tommy Vardell, standing nearby, did the same. "And then I really got emotional," Big Dawg said, the emotions welling up at the very memory of it. "I just put my head down and cried for about five minutes." Fans filed out around him but still he sat there, his head in his hands. After a while, he was the lone occupant of the Dawg Pound. "At first the police tried to make me leave. I said my knee was shot and they'd have to carry me out. Finally, a couple security guards said it was okay, so I stayed. I leaned against the fence. And Channel Three and the *Plain Dealer* snuck up and took shots of me from behind."

He stayed there for forty minutes. "Then, the head of the grounds crew came up and said, 'John, you ever been on the field?' And I said, 'No.' He said, 'C'mon.'" Big Dawg stepped tentatively onto the mud-covered grass. "One of the grounds crew gave me a peanut bag and told me I could take home some turf. I picked up a clod of dirt from where they had written 'Browns' in orange." Big Dawg still keeps the turf-laden peanut bag, along with the game ball, on his bedroom dresser. "I walked out into the center of the field," he recalled, "and the stands seemed so close. I started thinking how it would be to be playing to a sold-out crowd. To come running out of the dugout on game day with ninety thousand fans cheering—what that must feel like." Some camera-crew men followed him onto the field and a few of them asked if they could kick the game ball that Big Dawg was carrying under his arm. He held the ball for them and, when they were through, he took a shot at it, too. "I ended up kicking the last field goal in Cleveland stadium."

Then he wandered around the gridiron at a loss. At last, some groundskeepers yelled at him to look up at the scoreboard, the enormous, mediagenic ad vehicle that Art Modell had installed. The scoreboard operator had typed out a message in huge electronic letters: "Hey, John, it's time to go home. If you hang around much longer, we'll have to start charging you rent." So Big Dawg picked up the ball and his peanut bag and lumbered toward the exit. "It was close to seven o'clock and it was already dark," he remembered. "It seemed like a long walk back to the car."

5

WHERE AM I
IN THE KINGDOM?

A Christian Quest for Manhood

MICHAEL WORE HIS BATTLE OF NORMANDY T-SHIRT to the Wednesday night meeting of Alternatives to Violence.* For reasons that eluded him—he was too young to have anything but movie memories of World War II—he had flown to France to observe the fiftieth anniversary of D-Day. An impulse of even foggier origins compelled him to carry a photo album of these "memories" to a subsequent meeting of his domestic-violence counseling group, which convened weekly at an office warren moated by burbling artificial streams just off the Long Beach freeway. The men met in a cozy therapist's room upstairs, a frilly setting of floral couches and plush dolls with stitched-on grins, and Michael seemed a bit sheepish as he displayed the photo album with the creamy white cover and lacy embossed script, which seemed a more likely showcase for wedding pictures. Photos of a lone dazed figure blinking in the harsh sunscape of one of the world's bloodiest battlefields seemed to me a peculiar show-and-tell for Alternatives to Violence—at least at the time. But then I had only been attending the group for a short while, and still believed the men were here only to learn how to stop hitting

*Some of the names in this chapter have been changed. Refer to Author's Note, p. 611.

their wives and girlfriends. Maybe that's why they came. Why they stayed, those not mandated to do so, had more to do with D-Day.

The group was populated with men who believed in loyalty and obedience both to the "system," as they typically called it, and the system's authorities—male authorities, from fathers to coaches to corporate managers to the flickering paternal images of 1950s television. "I wanted to be the *good son,*" Jack Schat said. When he married for the first time he told his wife, without a trace of irony, "It'll be just like *Father Knows Best!*" In retrospect, he said, "What really excited me about getting married was not *her* but just being married, doing what I was supposed to do." He wanted to be married to the whole system that defined and supported American manhood, and along with his wife, Jack wed McDonnell Douglas. He became a stress-analysis engineer at the company, a position that involved, as he put it, testing to see if "the structure is strong enough to hold up." The mordant implications of his job title, given his present state of mind, did not escape Jack, whose arch humor was one of the highlights of the Wednesday night group. "In my department," he said, "we answer the phone, 'Stress!'"

Jack's department was spitting men out left and right. Not surprisingly, then, the sense of cold-war mission he had once derived from the idea of defense work now seemed a sham, and most nights he found himself watching the kids while his wife was lifting weights at the gym with a personal trainer. She seemed, like a lot of women, to be in training for a virtuous cause: casting off the fragile-flower image of femininity. Her muscular response seemed like a righteous expression of empowered womanhood, while for him to respond physically to her was just a humiliating admission of defeat.

For virtually all the men in Alternatives to Violence, the struts that were meant to buttress their manhood had given way. But at least in the group they might have one strut left to lean on. This hope explained why the men returned even after they had finished the required nine months of participation; it might even have inspired Michael's T-shirt. The hope was that they might find a place where they would be cared for by other men—even, or especially, by men they didn't know. They sought the close cohesion of an infantry patrol. The men in the group weren't alone in that quest. A nationwide explosion of World War II nostalgia elevated Steven Spielberg's *Saving Private Ryan,* Tom Brokaw's *The Greatest Generation,* and Stephen E. Ambrose's *Citizen Soldiers* to the status of cultural touchstones. For untested baby-boom men, the yearning evoked by the film and best-selling books was less about being part of a battle than about being part of some kind of "structure that holds up," where other men provide support and succor, where, at least in *Saving Private Ryan,* many men would come to the rescue of one man, a man they didn't even know. The heart of such a mission was the meaning of society.

The men in Alternatives to Violence, like men around the country, longed for such backing, such responsibility. They hoped to find it within this small circle of men, but the ground rules of group therapy kept getting in the way. Each participant was expected to "take responsibility" only for himself, to rein in his own anger, to restrain his aggressive tendencies, to see how he was the one "in control." As useful as such principles might have been for individual counseling, they ran counter to the men's need to be embedded in a social matrix. After the group let out, the men would linger in the dark parking lot, talking among themselves, searching for some larger connection. But they were at a loss, and the conversation tended to dribble into exchanges about sports and car troubles. After all, their "bond" wasn't their shared contribution to a society; all they had in common was a violent rage against their isolation, taken out on the bodies of the women they lived with.

One night, Jack told the group that he seemed to be learning how to restrain himself when an aggressive driver cut him off in traffic—a common trigger of rage for these California commuters. "I've been bent out of shape," he said, "but I haven't gone off on anybody." Paul, a twenty-two-year veteran of Hughes Aircraft who had extended his stay in the group, turned to Jack and asked: "You ever figure out who you are mad at? I never figured it out. My wife says to me, 'You are angry *all* the time.' And I am! . . . But I don't know *who* I'm mad at—or *why.*" Jack didn't have an answer. "I guess, a lot of it is me," he said uncertainly. He didn't really feel like he was the one, though. "It's like I'm on remote control." Who held the remote-control device was a mystery to him. Jack and Paul, and men in similar "anger-management" groups that proliferated like highway daisies across the nation in the 1990s, were looking to discover the source of their rage, or at least to relieve it by finding something larger than themselves that they could support and that would support them. But their questions always seemed to come back around to themselves. Many learned to say, "A lot of it is me," and to look no further.

At least some of the men I came to know in the Alternatives to Violence group who felt its inadequacy began to look for alternatives in other gatherings of men. Jack Schat was one. He found himself drawn to a Christian men's movement called Promise Keepers, whose message

captivated hundreds of thousands of men in the mid-1990s. Jack heard
about the organization from some men in his church. He was intrigued
by its vision of founding manhood on spiritual principles; it seemed to
promise a new way for men—no matter what was happening in their
work lives—to reclaim respect, appreciation, and authority at home as
devout husbands and fathers. "What really excited me about it," Jack
said, "was that it wasn't just about controlling my anger." In the course
of the nine months in which I followed the anti-familial-violence group
through one of its cycles, two other men joined Promise Keepers. One
day the Alternatives to Violence counselor, Alyce LaViolette, a bit mystified, told me that her own brother, a highway patrolman in Sacramento,
had attended a Promise Keepers conference. Many of those in local
Promise Keepers groups were also suffering from the post-cold-war restructuring of the economy, and struggling with domestic burdens in
isolated bedroom communities. But with this difference: they hoped to
remove their deteriorating family circumstances from their individual
bell jars and view them in a larger context.

I followed the men's lead. And that's how I found myself journeying
from a counseling office in Long Beach to a living room in Glendora, a
suburb about an hour's drive northeast at the foot of the San Gabriel
mountains, where a handful of Promise Keepers pondered how to remake themselves as spiritual new men.

In the mid-1990s, the men of Promise Keepers had gathered most
famously in football stadiums across the nation. Their weekend-long rallies were directed by born-again evangelist Bill McCartney, a former
football coach from the University of Colorado who had announced in
1994 that he was quitting to devote himself to family and God. The
scene at any stadium looked for all the world like a sports event; the
Promise Keepers "fans" brought their coolers, wore their team hats,
chanted slogans, and even did the wave. But these fans took to the field,
tens of thousands of men amassed on the gridiron as if huddling for their
next play. "This is the first time in my life I've been in a jam-packed
stadium where every single person is cheering for the same team—team
Jesus," a thirty-seven-year-old mall security director attending Promise
Keepers told a reporter.[1] They were seeking to *participate* in this particular game, to earn for themselves laudable manly roles in their families.
They intended to do it by reclaiming what the rally speakers described
as "spiritual responsibility" and "servant leadership" in the home.

The group's promise of virtuous manhood had spawned a nationwide
following almost overnight, culminating in 1997 in a massive convocation
on the Washington Mall, broadcast live on C-SPAN. Promise Keepers

wasn't alone in this enterprise. If anything, its Washington show of numbers had been upstaged by the celebrated "Million Man March" in the
capital in 1995, a "day of atonement" organized by Nation of Islam leader
Louis Farrakhan and attended by hundreds of thousands of black men.
And both conclaves were preceded by a secular "men's movement,"
which had drawn tens of thousands of generally New Age–oriented men
to its weekend drumming sessions and "wild man" retreats in the late
eighties and early nineties. Poet Robert Bly, the men's movement's most
prominent spokesman and author of the best-selling *Iron John,* packed
auditoriums. But Promise Keepers overshadowed all these male gatherings, both in size and in longevity. At the organization's height, and in
spite of the $60 admission ticket, its stadium events were drawing nearly
a million men a year (and 1.1 million in 1996) — and the men returned
home to organize a vast nationwide network of small groups, which continued the organization's quest for "servant leadership," in some cases
for years.

The men who joined Promise Keepers were seeking to build something greater than the sum of their individually distressed lives. Their
occupational betrayal and civic betrayal had been compounded by a powerful sense of domestic betrayal. It was a betrayal that Promise Keepers
was at least trying to address. They hoped that from the ashes of one
male institution, the football stadium that had once promised male communion but was now one big consumer billboard, might rise another,
more traditional and thus more solid one. For what could be more sustaining than a religion that had united and nourished so many men for
two millennia? They were looking to join a grand struggle that would
restore to them not only the love of their wives and children but also
the conviction that they were embarking on a mission, that they had at
last found a purpose that would earn them the appreciation of society,
and that this purpose would be backed by a brotherhood.

Welcome to Testosterone Country!

FROM HUGE STAGES ERECTED BY THE GOALPOSTS and draped with
banners featuring the Promise Keepers emblem — three hands raising a
flagpole, Iwo Jima style — speakers exhorted masses of male listeners to
repent their domestic failings and take back the family helm through
prayer and religious direction. They were to become the masters of their
households' spiritual life, religious authorities who would take charge of
the domestic circle through "submission" and "servitude." To much of
the media and to many feminist groups, such counsel sounded suspi-
ciously like sugar-coated instructions to plant patriarchal boots right

back on wifely necks. It didn't help that Dallas preacher Chuck Swindoll liked to blaze onstage in the company of a tattooed Christian motorcycle gang and lead the crowds with chants of "Power, power, we got the power!" It didn't help that Promise Keepers' speakers were so fond of Saint Paul's famed domestic stricture, "Wives, submit to your husbands" (the same directive that the Southern Baptists would add to their official credo of belief in 1998).[2] It didn't help that the retinue of onstage lecturers hailed uniformly from a religious right that had famously thrown itself with punitive zeal into a decades-long body block of women's progress. And most of all it didn't help that Promise Keepers founder Bill McCartney had proved himself a dedicated foe of women's reproductive rights, not to mention gay liberation. A year before he was urging men to commit themselves to family leadership, he was calling for the criminalization of abortion at prolife rallies and decrying homosexuality as "an abomination against Almighty God."[3] At press conferences during Promise Keepers events, his views on gender roles appeared to be fresh out of a Victorian marriage manual. He was eager to reiterate his theory, before open-mouthed journalists, that "the ladies" were "receptors" who needed to be "brought to splendor" by their men, the "initiators."

It's little wonder, then, that the advice Promise Keepers speaker and preacher Tony Evans gave men on "reclaiming your manhood" would be endlessly quoted by a dubious press:

> The first thing you do is sit down with your wife and say something like this: "Honey, I've made a terrible mistake. I've given you my role. I gave up leading this family, and I forced you to take my place. Now I must reclaim that role." Don't misunderstand what I'm saying here. I'm not suggesting that you *ask* for your role back, I'm urging you to *take it back*.[4]

Evans's words seemed like a smoking gun, incontrovertible evidence that under all the tributes to "servant leadership," Promise Keepers was promoting a stealth campaign of misogyny and macho dominance. Ignored was the rest of Evans's broadside, which focused almost entirely on deploring a "macho" mass culture that told men they were worthless unless they were constantly conquering beautiful babes and single-handedly gunning down bad guys. "Rambo is not only violent, but he's also uncaring," Evans protested.[5] In the same passage, he urged men to reject material values; exhorted them to turn off the TV and talk to their wives; and assured them it was okay to cry. For biblical substantiation, he turned again and again to an Old Testament book that would seem an unlikely choice for a preacher endorsing triumphal male dominance: the book of Job.

As an organization Promise Keepers was, in fact, replete with such contradictions. After Chuck Swindoll barreled onstage in his Harley, speaker Gary Smalley trundled up the ramp on a Big Wheel, clutching a doll with, as he put it, "batteries not included"—a purposeful display of knee-high helplessness. "All of us are like this doll," he said, holding up the molded-plastic girl in pigtails, a pink dress, pink shoes, and barrettes. He confided how his bullying older brother "terrorized me" so much when he was a boy that "when I was twenty-five years old, I couldn't stay in a home alone because I was so afraid." For every "We got the power!" chant, there was an allegory delivered about the solace of relinquishing power, like the one pastor Greg Laurie of Harvest Christian Fellowship told about how unhappy a little bird was until he was returned to a cage, because each man yearns for the "restrictive" bars of God's commandments, "keeping him safe." The same organization that endorsed the submission of wives to husbands also ran first-person articles in its affiliated periodical *New Man* from men who had put their wives' careers first or discovered the challenges of homemaking. In "The Unexpected Choice," Robert V. Zoba, for instance, reported how he had reinterpreted Paul's stricture, "Wives, submit to your husbands," to mean that he should follow his wife to Chicago, where she had landed a prestigious job as an editor at *Christianity Today* and where he, underemployed, "ran chauffeur service for our boys, found the best bang-for-bucks deals at the local grocery store, and learned the difference between delicate and sturdy cycles on the washing machine."[6] Even when it came to the "We got the power" chant, Swindoll revealed to his audience that he had borrowed it from "an old cheer my daughters used to lead in high school."

That the convention stage was more often than not occupied by speakers with alarming antiabortion records and Christian Coalition affiliations was indisputable. But on the field and in the bleachers, the men were not so easily categorized. While speakers thundered for a return to a "biblically sanctioned" patriarchal household and a "traditional" male order, the rank and file sat quietly—polite and attentive, but hardly clamorous. If they were plotting the overthrow of a feminist world, they showed no signs of it. Mostly they seemed intent on being mannerly and tidy. In an era when the sports spectators who were the bleachers' usual clientele left the stadiums littered and vandalized, the Promise Keepers were careful to throw away all their trash. They obediently took notes during the speeches and displayed at all times their Promise Keepers ID bracelets, which looked exactly like the identification bands worn by hospital patients. They stood dutifully and uncomplainingly in endless lines to pick up dreary box lunches, buy PK-branded coffee mugs and caps at the Product Tent, or use the ATM machines. They were willfully docile, as though, if they just obeyed enough, they would at last get their reward.

At a stadium event in Oakland, the longest lines inside the Product Tent were at a booth selling T-shirts with this inspirational biblical message emblazoned across the chest: I AM A WORM. Thus armored, the male shoppers flocked to the Christian Financial Concepts table to thumb through stacks of brochures and books with titles like *Debt-Free Living*, *Your Career in Changing Times*, and *Whatever Happened to the American Dream?* As I wandered around a rally at the Anaheim stadium in southern California, a man called out to me, "Welcome to Testosterone Country!" but his tone was wistful rather than cocky. More typical was the remark of Bill Moore, a Promise Keeper from Beaumont, California, whom I met at the same event. When I approached him and his seatmates for an interview, he told me forlornly, "If you're putting guys like us in your book, you should call it 'Men with Low Testosterone.' "

The men who attended Promise Keepers conferences were not biker outlaws; they were the "good sons." In the stands, Troy Barber, a thirty-two-year-old man from North Dakota who managed a shoe store, told me softly, "Last night, I was crying." Overhearing him, a nearby conferee chimed in with, "I've failed miserably." In the seat behind him, Chris Martinson, a security guard at a private college in St. Paul, Minnesota, said sorrowfully, "We know we aren't effective as men." A plane buzzed the stadium just then, hauling a banner paid for by a local women's group. Its big letters spelled out, PROMISE KEEPERS, LOSERS AND WEEPERS. The men shaded their eyes and followed its arc across the sky in silent bafflement. They didn't necessarily disagree with the assessment. As the plane vanished, a mystified Larry Coleman of Kansas City turned to me. "My wife is the furthest from someone you can dominate." His friend Chris Lopez was confused, too: "Guys out there, we're really lost. We need help."

What kind of help the men were getting from the stadium events was unclear. Bill McCartney's name was rarely invoked in conversations. More than a few men I spoke to got his name wrong—Mc*Carthy* or *Paul* McCartney were the two most common mistakes—and none said he was the reason they came. That McCartney junked a high-paying, flourishing career as a coach to spend more time with his family was unfathomable to them; most of the men in the stadium were there out of fear that their families would junk *them* because they *didn't* have high-paying, flourishing careers. While the coach's press conferences were packed, his customary pep speech at the rally's finale, full of overamped sports clichés ("It doesn't get better than this!"), generally provoked a mass exodus. The men took his ascendancy to the mike as their cue to head for the exits and beat the rush.

Nonetheless, they headed for the parking lots with a flushed enthusiasm. What had they seen that so enraptured them, I wondered at first, but that, it turned out, was the wrong way to frame my inquiry. Because the most commonly cited highlight of the weekend was not something seen. The private huddle, the chance to pray off to the side with a few other men, was what most enlivened them. "You get to cry," one man after another told me of their convention experience, their eyes lighting up at last.

Why did the huddle hold such appeal? And what were the men crying about? If you asked, a Promise Keeper would say he was "repenting," for sins about which he was always vague. He had been "disobedient" and "selfish" and needed "forgiveness." But what was he so remorseful about? What promises hadn't he kept?

The average Promise Keeper was hardly wayward. A Promise Keepers–commissioned survey of men attending stadium events in 1994 found the group of mostly middle-aged men to be dutiful, upright, and eager to comply with social expectations of propriety and judgment. (Sixty-three percent agreed with the statement, "I follow the 'letter' of the law," and 74 percent affirmed "How others perceive my spiritual life is very important to me.")[7] The typical conventiongoer was like the unsung brother in the parable of the Prodigal Son. He had commonly recoiled from the celebrated protest dramas of his baby-boom cohorts. While fellow students were staging sit-ins in the sixties and early seventies, many of the nascent Promise Keepers were joining, if anything at all, "movements" like the Inter-Varsity Christian Fellowship, Campus Ambassadors, and especially the Campus Crusade for Christ.

An organization founded by conservative California evangelist Bill Bright, Campus Crusade for Christ was consciously designed to counter student unrest by coopting it. The group launched "Revolution Now," a proselytizing blitzkrieg in 1967 at the University of California at Berkeley, specifically to assist Bright's close friend and then-governor Ronald Reagan in his efforts to quash collegiate antiwar activism. Campus Crusade targeted college athletes and frat boys, emphasizing "aggressive evangelism" and "brotherhood" (but not sisterhood); by the seventies, its young recruits far outnumbered those of the radical Students for a Democratic Society. While classmates raised fists for a student strike or hailed each other with *V* peace signs, a Campus Crusade recruit would be more likely to sport one of the Jesus movement's "One Way" pendants with a finger pointing heavenward—a logo created partly in response to the antiwar hand gestures of the time.[8]

When Bill Bright became a Promise Keepers speaker and one of its biggest promoters, it seemed a theological quid pro quo: Bill McCartney had been converted in 1974 by a branch of Campus Crusade for Christ called Athletes in Action, relinquishing the institutional devotions of his father's Roman Catholicism for a "tangible, hands-on, heart-to-heart relationship with the person of Jesus Christ," as he would put it later. McCartney was seeking a personalized guardianship where he "surrendered control" and could "actually *feel* his overshadowing presence guiding me and helping me grow." What he and the other Promise Keepers in the making wanted wasn't to break with authority. "I needed to personally surrender my life," McCartney wrote. "What I needed was a *relationship*."[9]

———

"HERE'S WHERE WE HAVE TO START when you start talking about man," Bill McCartney shouted at me, though I was less than a foot away. I had come to talk to him at Promise Keepers headquarters in Denver, a blocklong building that used to house a printing press and truck lobbying association. The ex-coach had gotten down on his knees by my chair with a Bible open to the gospel of Luke in his hand. "What is our purpose?" he asked. He was answering my question about why American men had responded so strongly to Promise Keepers. "The deepest longing of the human spirit *screams* for significance," he said, his pregame, let's-get-'em! delivery turning his face only a shade less purple than his PK-embossed golf shirt. "And the only way you can achieve real significance is to fulfill your *purpose,* okay?"

And what specifically was the purpose Promise Keepers was providing men?

"That they come in touch with how much he loves them. . . . You think of the guy that most closely approximates what it really means to be a loving father, and a loving husband, and he doesn't even scratch the surface when it comes to how much God loves us. See, God the Father loves us so much, with such a passion, with such an intensity, with such a comprehensive caring for us, concern for us, that he doesn't sleep. He never slumbers! He watches over us day and night. And he's always pulling for us, okay? Now—"

I tried to interject a few words into the verbal fusillade, without success. "Now don't stop me!" He waved an arm in the air, as if he were calling a play. "Don't stop me because I'm gonna tell you the whole story. Then you can ask me anything. Okay, so now, picture this: picture somebody being loved like that. He knows every hair on our head, he knows every thought before we think it, he remembers every word before we speak it, okay? He is *intensely* involved in our lives. . . . He loves this guy Jeff, okay? He loves Jeff with this kind of love."

I wasn't sure who Jeff was. The only other man in the room was named Steve—Steve Chavis, the media-relations director. I also didn't quite get how all of this added up to a "purpose" for men. If God was the one sacrificing sleep, working night and day to bring men his love, then wasn't McCartney describing a purpose for *God*?

"He sent his own son!" McCartney belted out enthusiastically when I tried to pin him down on this point.

I tried another tack. How did McCartney see his own "purpose" now?

After several attempts, I finally got this much out of him: "My life can be of some value now because I can help young guys." It seemed a curious remark, coming from a coach who had abandoned a team full of young men to lead an organization whose members were overwhelmingly over the age of thirty. And the young men he left behind, the University of Colorado Buffaloes, had been notoriously in need of guidance.

Under McCartney, the team had made a big splash in *Sports Illustrated*—for its stunning arrest record. The players' criminal activities were so profligate, the magazine reported, that the campus police carried copies of the Buffaloes' roster when they went to investigate a crime. In one three-year stretch, two dozen players were arrested for burglary, sexual assault, or rape. One athlete even turned out to be the community's Duct-Tape Rapist, who had taped shut the mouths and eyes of eight women and assaulted them. The player was charged with four rapes, pled guilty, and was sentenced to twenty-five years.[10]

McCartney was not a beloved coach in the eyes of many of his players, who had to endure his legendary temper tantrums, inflexibility, and religiosity. And some evidently exacted revenge the one way they knew how: they began a Spur Posse–like campaign of sexual conquest against McCartney's teenage daughter, according to an account published in the Denver alternative weekly *Westword*. McCartney fulminated against the *Westword* article as "sacrilege" and claimed that only divine intervention prevented him from killing its author. No disciplinary action was taken on the team, though McCartney could hardly overlook incontrovertible evidence of his daughter's seduction by certain players. She told him that the team's star quarterback and then, four years later, a defensive tackle *both* got her pregnant. McCartney, the chastity champion, had become the grandfather of two illegitimate babies.[11]

As McCartney now continued to testify to me at top volume, media-relations director Steve Chavis squirmed visibly in his chair. A former journalist for a radio station, Chavis no doubt recognized a media disaster in the making. He had been discreetly trying to shepherd McCartney out of the room almost from the moment the ex-coach had dropped to his knees before me. McCartney was feverishly whipping through his Bible once more, searching for an answer to my inquiry into his newfound "purpose." "Isaiah 38:19," he announced at last, an index finger pouncing on the verse. "The *father* to the children shall make known the truth." He looked up at me, triumphant, eyes moistly gleaming. "See, he charged the man with the responsibility of bringing the children up in the Lord, okay?"

In fact, as his wife, Lyndi McCartney, made clear in several commentaries he allowed her to insert in his books and in later comments in the press as well, her husband hadn't been much help bringing up baby. "In a way, being a coach's child is a dream," she wrote in McCartney's first book, *From Ashes to Glory*. "But it was a nightmare as well." The kids hardly saw their father. "Bill never saw the boys play football until they were in high school." Nor did she think much of Bill's husbandly "spiritual leadership" before or after he founded Promise Keepers. Mostly, she reported, he consigned her to a "bottom-shelf existence"; when he was off the field, he preferred bars, where he often drank himself into a stupor. When she miscarried, she couldn't find Bill—he had gone off to "tend bar" at a pub without telling her—and she had to take herself to the hospital. In desperation, Lyndi, who rarely drank, once tried to get his attention by drinking herself into a state of unconsciousness; he didn't even notice. After he launched Promise Keepers, nothing much changed. She described him in a *New York Times* interview as the plumber who was "always out fixing everybody else's plumbing." As Promise Keepers grew, so did Lyndi's distress; in 1993, as both she and her husband recounted in McCartney's memoirs, she came close to a breakdown and considered taking her life. She shut herself away, read "more than a hundred" self-help books, threw up daily for seven months, and ate almost nothing. She lost more than seventy pounds. Bill's observation: "I saw that she was losing weight, and I was proud of her."[12]

I asked McCartney about his wife's account of domestic agony. "I don't sit here as someone you could point to as an example of anything other than a guy who's a sinner saved by grace. But I know something. You know what I know?" I confessed that I didn't. "*He* loves me."

Anyway, McCartney said, reiterating a claim from his books, these days he was working harder to be his wife's "spiritual leader." I asked what that entailed. "It's my responsibility to get things ready," he said, "and to encourage others to let's take some time out now and shut off the television and let's come before the Lord. See, that's *my* responsibility to do that. I don't wait for my wife to do it. I don't. But when I suggest it and she says this isn't a good time, I say, 'Okay, well when do you think would be a good time?' But it's *mandated*. I'm the one. The only way the spiritual work's gonna get done is if the man takes responsibility."

McCartney paused for a breath and, seizing the moment, Steve Chavis jumped to his feet, announced that the coach had "other appointments" that couldn't be missed, and guided him decisively toward the door, leaving me as befuddled as before, if not more so.

And so I gave up on illumination from headquarters. McCartney was not the reason men were flocking to Promise Keepers anyway. If they weren't seeking enlightenment from him, maybe I shouldn't either. If the prayer huddle was the main attraction of Promise Keepers, as its constituents maintained, then neither the organization's executive suites nor the bleachers of Folsom Stadium were the place from which to observe it. And so I turned toward the smaller and stiller domain of a Glendora living room. It would prove a far more revealing listening post.

God Will Save Your Marriage

TIMOTHY ATWATER'S HOUSE HAD BEEN BUILT, like the others on the block, for family living. The kitchen's picture window faced the front yard, a popular postwar innovation to allow housewives to keep an eye on the kids while presiding over their shiny, new, all-electric ranges. Over the years, neighborhood residents had customized their homes with paint, porches, backyard pools. Yet the overall impression was one of numbing sameness. Weeks into my visits, I would still find myself circling the block, uncertain of the house. I finally learned to look for Timothy's particular brand of vacation trailer parked out front. The similarity in home design was meant to induce a feeling of community togetherness, of pioneering families on a shared adventure out west making up a neighborhood as they went along, just as the developers had made up names for their far-flung suburban outposts: Glendora, Monrovia, La Crescenta. Glendora's developer, who fashioned the name from Leadora, his wife's name, billed the town as "a family-oriented community that would maintain a wholesome atmosphere and Christian ideals." Its promoters boasted that its profusion of churches, made even more profuse by a surge of evangelical fervor in the postwar years, and its booming residential subdivisions (for by the 1960s Glendora was the fastest-growing city in southern California) added up to a nester's dream, "a suburbanite's delight."[13] Yet to drive down the long, palm-tree-lined street to the Atwaters' house, a street as long and palm-lined as the streets it paralleled, was to be oppressed by a weight of isolation.

Glendora was the quintessential bedroom community; its Chamber of Commerce opposed the location of any "unsightly" industries within the town limits, though it did welcome Rain Bird Sprinkling Manufacturing Corp., a pioneering maker of that all-important subdivision accoutrement, the lawn sprinkler; they also vanquished liquor stores, pinball arcades, and pool halls, which they found corrupting to family morals (though a movie theater was allowed, run for a time by the McDonalds before they moved on to hamburgers). Throughout World War II and the postwar years, the community's main employer was Aerojet-General in neighboring Azusa, whose rocket-propulsion plant built the Apollo spacecraft's engines. Glendora was said to have taken great communal pride in the moon shot. If so, it was one of the few aspects of the sixties that the town did embrace. The deeply conservative community watched the era's upheavals with rising dread. A *Glendora Press* editorial recommended at the time that "all students who took part in the demonstrations . . . be expelled and further that their names and reason for being dropped from school be sent to all colleges so they would be aware of them if they applied for entrance." Not surprisingly, Glendora's promoters did not advertise the town's connection to one of the era's leading radicals. Mario Savio, leader of the Berkeley Free Speech Movement, who had been raised in Glendora, was arguably the community's most important personage, and the most prodigal of its many sons.[14]

A decor of sentimental samplers and heart-shaped refrigerator magnets inside the Atwaters' home was curiously reminiscent of the counseling room of Alternatives to Violence. The Promise Keepers group sat in a living room adorned with an empty birdcage and ceramic pots sprouting fake ivy. It was an aesthetic I would come to associate with Promise Keepers' households. We sometimes met at the home of Martin Booker, the group's de facto leader, and his living room reminded me of a nursery with its baby-blue coordinated drapes and couches, the latter heaped with an impressive lineup of decorative stuffed animals. Like many of the men in the group, Martin had countered his wife's pastel putsch the only way he knew how, with a steroid-sized home-entertainment system. A "high-end audiophile," as he described himself to me, Martin had installed six giant speakers in the living room to create a "surround-sound effect." He once demonstrated this to us by playing a recording of military jets whistling overhead. The effect was convincing; we all ducked, half expecting bombs to rain on the powder-blue sofas.

I would spend many evenings in the Atwaters' living room, listening as the men told their stories, studied scripture, and closed each meeting with a lengthy prayer circle. But the first meeting I attended, on an October evening in 1995, convened a few miles away at the Bookers'. I arrived early; Martin was percolating the coffee and laying out pastries. He kept glancing out the kitchen window. His wife, Judy, was still at work. A financial manager at an aerospace corporation, she often put in longer hours than her husband. Martin had bounced from one ministry job to another until he finally landed at a nearby evangelical organization, where he directed PR and administration. "Judy balances books worth hundreds of millions of dollars, so I let her pay the bills at home," Martin once ruefully told the group. He liked his job well enough, but he found the constant pressure to promote and proselytize wearing. A moon-faced man with a soup-bowl hairdo who was always waging a battle with his weight, Martin was not cut out for the hard sell. "The thing that's great about Promise Keepers, as opposed to other men's groups," he told me as he got the coffee mugs down from the cupboard, "is that it teaches you to *go home*."

A half hour later, the men arrived and settled in. Martin announced that the topic for the evening would be "success in Christ." He cracked open his worn Bible, New International Version, to chapter 2 of Luke, and around the room the men did likewise. A number of them, I noticed, had attached executive-style leather covers to their Bibles with handles and a zipper, like mini-briefcases. One of the men unlocked his with a key that said JESUS on it. Martin directed us to the last sentence of the chapter: "And Jesus grew in wisdom and stature, and in favor with God and men." He looked around the room. "When we are studying the life of Christ, we're studying all the ways to be a man," he said. "And we make the mistake as men of seeking our stature and success in work and in our bank accounts. We are craving identity. But we are so busy chasing after all these things, we don't see that Jesus is giving us an identity. He is giving us the confidence and security we need."

Jeremy Foote, a tightly strung schoolteacher who often took notes furiously during group discussion, ran a jittery hand through his hair. "It's very difficult to believe you can get security in God," he said. "It's okay when you have a job, but when I don't have a job, boy, I just panic like crazy. I can't get myself to go look, I can't stand up, I can't sit down." A knee bounced nervously, as if by illustration. "Just the *thought* of not having a job . . . and it shouldn't be, right? Because I can believe God will provide, take charge, protect me."

"Millions of men are facing a loss of jobs," Martin said, a comment that elicited a chorus of "mmm-hmms," "and you are going to lose your identity if you rely on your job for it."

Martin wasn't telling many of these men anything they hadn't painfully learned for themselves. Mike Pettigrew had been laid off three times in the last few years, twice from companies where his specialty had been quality control and assurance. Bart Hollister, a field-service engineer who flew to trouble spots for a machine company, had been laid off after twelve years. He was trying to start his own business, "but I'm not very good at it." He preferred the structure of a large institution. Jeremy Foote had lost his full-time job as a math teacher and now pasted together three temporary jobs in three distant high schools that required hours of driving each day. Frank Camilla had been forced into an early retirement buyout at Rockwell's Orange County aerospace plant, after more than twenty years. Dennie Elliott had been laid off four years earlier, after a decade at Rockwell, and hadn't found a job since. In desperation, he was trying to launch a carpet-cleaning service, but so far his only clients had been families of the men in his Promise Keepers group.

"As men, we all need to identify with something that's important," Martin Booker continued. "We drive around and we're surrounded by these billboards that say, 'If you have *this,* you'll be happy,' if you have this car, this trip to Vegas. And it's just a sales job. But if you get your identity from Christ, you don't need any of it, because you are going to get your identity from him. You are going to 'grow in favor' by his doing."

"That's good," Jeremy said, looking up from his note-taking, "because I need to grow."

"And here's the great thing," Martin said. "It's not based on *performance*. You don't have to *do* to earn his acceptance. We're told 'Do the Nike thing,' when we could just be dependent on Him. It's like, I was talking to this guy from Arizona. He lost his job. He was on the verge of losing his marriage. He had a whole wall of self-help books, shelves and shelves of 'em, all about the power of positive thinking and do this and do that by yourself. But once he placed his identity in Jesus, he just threw them all in the trash. He didn't need to *do* anymore. Jesus was in control." Lost job, lost marriage, that was a familiar set of toppling dominoes to these men. The terror of being on the verge of divorce had driven most of them to the group. They were hoping the group would reverse the process; that somehow when the marriage domino was set up again, the other fallen pieces of their lives would pop up, too.

The solution that Promise Keepers offered to this work-marriage dilemma was masterful, in its own way. Once men had cemented their identity to Jesus, so the organization's theory went, they could reclaim a new masculine role in the family, not as breadwinners but as spiritual pathfinders. Promise Keepers proposed that men reimagine themselves as pioneers on the home front, Daniel Boones for Christ, hacking their way through a godless wilderness of broken marriages and homes lacking all spirituality to build a spiritually fortified bunker in which their families could settle for the long haul. The ingenuity of such a solution was that it slipped the traces of traditional male work identity without challenging the underlying structure of the American male paradigm; that paradigm was simply reformulated in religious-battle terms. Men's shared "mission" now became the spiritual salvation of their families; men's "frontier," the domestic front; men's "brotherhood," the Christian fraternity of Promise Keepers; and men's "provider and protector" role, offering not economic but religious sustenance and shielding their wives from the satanic forces lurking behind consumer culture.

This reconfiguration of the male role on a spiritual battlefield helped ease one of the group's greatest collective anxieties, a fear they shared with the Long Beach domestic-violence group: that their wives were really the well-armed ones. Their vision of women as the more powerful combatants was in itself, however, only another way to cloak in metaphor their painful domestic disputes, a way to make them look like so many heroic Davids before feminine Goliaths. "When a guy goes into the military," Mike Pettigrew said one evening, "you can simulate battle training. But when the bullets are flying at you at home . . ." He raised his arms, as if surrendering to an invisible army. War and battle metaphors were never far from the men's lips when they discussed their domestic situations, and they always presented themselves as the ones on the receiving end. "When you're facing one of those World War II fights from your wife" was the way Howard Payson phrased it, or "When the bombs are dropping on you from your family," as Mike Pettigrew put it.

Presented with a real example of their fear that a woman was attacking them, however, they tended to shield their eyes. A year earlier, Frank Camilla's daughter-in-law had been arrested and charged with murder—of her husband, Frank's son. But the group rarely discussed this horrific event or even seemed particularly curious about it. When I first joined the group and heard about the murder, few of the men knew anything beyond the barest details. Frank frequently offered the group updates on pretrial proceedings when it was his turn to talk, but the men tended to mumble polite condolences and nervously change the subject. They didn't know what to do with Frank's story. It was too literal for their purposes, plus his son hadn't won the battle.

The first meeting I attended, the men were still celebrating, or rather recycling, the group's two "success" stories. Both Mike Pettigrew and Howard Payson had been on the brink of marital collapse when they joined. Mike's wife of nine years, Margaret, had moved out and seen a divorce lawyer; Howard's wife of more than twenty years, Libby, had been loudly advertising her imminent departure. Now, Libby had rescinded her threat and the couple had recently renewed their wedding vows. At the same time, Margaret had given up her new apartment and moved back in with Mike.

"What happened to Mike, it's an inspiration," said Jeremy, whose wife was just then trying to get *him* to move out.

Bart agreed. "Mike's story gives me so much hope."

"We got to watch a miracle!" Martin Booker exclaimed.

Mike's "miracle" had unfolded at the group's first stadium event, in the summer of 1993. Nine of them had piled into a seven-seater van and driven twenty hours to Boulder. "The way the guys talk about it," Martin Booker told me, a bit starry-eyed, "it was like *Bury My Heart at Wounded Knee*." I didn't quite get the analogy, but at any rate Mike's was definitely a wounded heart. He had no job and no wife. "When Margaret moved out, I went into crisis mode," he said, but he clung to the slim reed of hope that Margaret would reconsider. After all, she had paid for his admission ticket so he could attend the stadium conference. Mike was broke and she wasn't, and she figured that, since she had to get him something for his birthday, why not a weekend of repentance? Two other men in the group also had their fares paid by their wives.

"At the time," Mike recalled, recounting for the group a story they had heard many times but never tired of reliving, "my wife had rebelled against Christianity. She said the Bible was irrelevant." Worse, she was caught up in the "occult," he said, by which he meant her self-help books with a New Age bent. At the stadium event, "I got very charged up, because I learned how the world had tainted me and steered me wrong. Here I was, forty-one years old, trying to win my wife back by being somebody, being a success at work, all that, when what I should have been doing is praying for her release from bondage. Because that is what it is. My wife was really in bondage. She was in the Satan realm and it was up to me to pray for her return to the spiritual realm."

And so, at the end of the first long day of stadium speeches, Mike Pettigrew and Martin Booker retreated to the van to pray for Margaret. "Martin told me about how Margaret had turned her back on God and she was living deceived by the world that she could make it on her own, that she didn't need God," Mike recalled. "Martin said what we need to do is pray to reclaim her in Jesus' name, to save her. We *attacked* Satan, that bond he had on her, to get him off of her." The two men huddled until two-thirty in the morning. "I confessed to Martin some of my sins, like 'being physical' with Margaret. We wept together." Two nights in a row they huddled and wept. And then the miracle happened. "When I got back to the dorm where we were staying," Mike recalled, "I called my [answering] machine and there were six or seven phone calls from my wife, saying, 'Please call me back! Please call me back!'"

"God flat-out answered Mike's prayers," Martin Booker said.

"That's why I say to guys in the group, just hang in there," Mike said. "Keep at the praying. Because God will save your marriage."

————

"MARTIN TOLD MIKE I HAD A DEMON IN ME," Margaret told me matter-of-factly, over lunch at a leafy patio restaurant in nearby Monrovia. She didn't disagree, though her version of that demon wasn't quite the one the men had in mind. The weekend Mike was praying to reclaim her from Satan's clutches, Margaret was curled up in a chair in her new apartment, reading self-help books and trying to figure out how to break her attachment to a man. Months earlier, at her administrative job, she had met a researcher from overseas; he had been summoned to the company's southern California office for a special project. A romantic fling had ensued. "This man was giving me attention," she said. "He wasn't paying attention to *things*, like Mike always was, but to *me*. And I was eating it up. I started feeling like a human being, like a woman." The romance emboldened her to confront Mike and, finally, to leave him. But on the weekend Mike attended the Promise Keepers convention, her boldness had deserted her. The researcher would soon be returning home and she had to face the fact that he was "just a distraction, a diversion, if you will."

That weekend she sat up half the night consuming whatever inspirational literature was within reach, including a book Mike had loaned her, *The Bondage Breaker*, by Neil T. Anderson, an aerospace engineer–cum–minister who dispensed advice on what to do when "you're trapped" and "you don't know how you ended up in such a mess." A popular tome among Promise Keepers, it instructed readers to "confront the rebel

Prince" and "free" themselves of his thrall by "carrying Jesus' badge of authority."[15] Mike had liked the book's repeated mantra about the "authority" that Jesus conferred on his followers. Margaret, however, fastened upon the idea that she could be "free" of her going-nowhere attachment to the rebel prince from Europe. That Mike had given her the book, that he was spending the weekend trying to be a better husband, that ever since she left him he had been "long-suffering" and "kind," that she was feeling desperately lonely and unable to sleep, all of it drove her to the phone to call Mike.

By the time he returned home, she was already having second thoughts. "I was still feeling emotionally numb to him." She stared at her plate of congealing pasta and sighed. "I wasn't emotional about getting back with him. I didn't have much feeling for Mike at all really." She paused and gave me a meaningful look. "And I didn't, for quite a long while." Margaret's main, and long-standing, grievance with Mike revolved around money. "A husband is supposed to provide a financial future," she was fond of saying. "I had all these expectations, for a house, for financial security. I had a longing for these things, and he wasn't providing them. A husband is supposed to be a *cover* and Mike was not being my *cover*." By *cover*, she meant, quite literally, a roof over her head with a matching mortgage. Their status as long-term renters particularly irked her. Upon his return, Mike promised Margaret that they would buy a house and, at some hardship, they did.

Mike and Margaret had met in a Laundromat in the town of Sierra Madre in the spring of 1982. Margaret was waiting for her laundry to dry and, as Mike recalled, "playing that Beatles' song 'Blackbird'" on her guitar. "Blackbird, fly!" They were married a year and a half later, still in many respects strangers to each other. Margaret's main thought had been "Here at long last is a Christian man with a respectable job." While Mike had indeed made a decent living until the layoffs, he liked to spend his money on antique books and decorative objects. He considered himself a collector, a compulsive and out-of-control one, in Margaret's view. "He developed this obsessive habit of excessive buying. He was just on a buying frenzy. He'd be buying books while I was calling the landlord and saying, 'We have to delay our payment.' *I* was keeping the checkbook and *he* was spending the money." (Mike would finally scrape together the $15,000 down payment on their house by selling his book collection.)

The disputes about money on occasion flared into confrontations that turned violent, particularly on evenings when the cocktail hour stretched well into the night. These occasions were what Mike was referring to when he told Martin he had been "physical" with Margaret. "I'd tell him he can't keep buying these books and he'd lose his temper," Margaret said, "and he'd pick up a shoe or something and throw it at me. And it always hit, because he was a good shot." When I talked to Mike about it later, his response was very much like those of the men in the Long Beach domestic-violence group. "I'd get very frustrated," he said, "and I would blow my fuse a little bit. A few times, I'd do something like, you know, reach out and *SMACK!* . . . but it didn't happen frequently. She became fearful of me, I guess." I guessed so. Mike is a physically imposing figure at six feet and 275 pounds.

One day in June, a year before Mike's Promise Keepers weekend, he and Margaret were taking an after-dinner walk around the neighborhood. It had been a tense evening; as they marched up and down the sidewalk, Margaret told Mike she was disappointed that he wasn't capable of "being close and intimate." Mike exploded. "He has a way of charging towards you like he is going to rip you apart," Margaret recalled. "When I said that, it sparked this temper in him and he started to charge. And when I started to run, that's when he kicked me." He kicked so hard he broke a bone in her hand. She ran home, only to realize he had the house key. "I just sat on the steps behind this giant pedestal," she said, "so he couldn't see me."

The "hand incident," as it was referred to around the Pettigrew household, ushered in a predictable period of repentance. Mike promised to mend his ways and cut back on drinking. But Margaret, who had been through it all before, was unimpressed. "What made it hard all these years was he would be greatly remorseful after. He would realize he'd done something terrible and he would make all these wonderful promises that he never kept. When my hand was broken, I realized, this is a vicious cycle. He'd make up to me as if nothing happened. And nothing might happen again for another six months to a year. But it would always happen."

The broken bone "was the fuel I needed to get motivated." She sought out a counselor and began to think about a future that might not include Mike. She lost some weight and cut her hair short, a style that she liked but that Mike, she knew, would find "mannish." And soon after, she met the researcher. She found it increasingly unbearable to be around Mike, and avoided him by going to bed earlier and earlier every evening. Finally, Margaret said, "I decided to talk to Mike and tell him I wanted out." She picked a day that happened to fall "two weeks after Valentine's Day." Just before he came home from work that Friday evening, she moved systematically through the house, opening every window. "I wanted people to hear me if I had to scream." When he came through the door, she slipped on her shoes, "in case I had to run."

Then she sat him down and in a shaky voice said, "Mike, I've been really afraid of you and I'm afraid of you even now, but I've got to tell you that I've had enough." Then she informed him that she'd been "seeing another person." To her amazement, "instead of being violent, he broke down like a baby." It was a revelatory, strangely liberating moment. "To see his reaction—and I can see it as vividly now as I did then!" she said in a marveling tone. "Knowing I broke a grown man down to tears, it made me realize how *powerful* I am." On the draft of that power, she started sleeping in a separate room, then moved out of the house altogether, enrolled in a broadcasting course, and legally reverted to her maiden name.

As Mike recalled it, he was "a zombie." A few weeks later, he was laid off in a downsizing. He found another job as a quality engineer, but without Margaret, "I was so depressed, Monday and Tuesday, I just couldn't get out of bed. I called in to work the first and second day. And then the third day, I called and they said, 'It would be better if you didn't come in at all.' " All that summer, unemployed, he would drive out to the nearby San Gabriel Mountains and wander for hours, "hiking really aggressively," half hoping for a rock slide, for a broken bone of his own, or worse. Desperate, he phoned Zel Brooks, a marriage counselor he knew from his church, and Zel recommended Promise Keepers.

"I was just very distraught," Mike recalled, "but after a while, I started getting chunks of time where I was feeling optimistic. Part of it was a pride issue. I just decided, I'm going to make myself so attractive to Margaret, get a great job, all that, so she couldn't resist me." He prayed for a job "with specific dollar amounts." But what he found most comforting about Promise Keepers was its message that he didn't have to be a "success" at work to win her back. "The advice I got was to think of my wife like she belongs to God, not to me." Thinking of Margaret as "belonging" to God relieved Mike of some of the burdens of ownership—among them, the terror of being dispossessed by one's own possession. "I saw I was trying to control what wasn't really mine. It was up to God to take care of her, because he owned her, not me."

Even so, when the "miracle" happened and Mike's prayers were "answered," Mike found himself unaccountably in a fury. "I was pissed. Which was weird. It really felt like a threat. Why was I so pissed? It had taken me all this time to get my strength back and not feel vulnerable to her. I was glad and elated that she was back, but I was still mad. Because I kept thinking, 'Is she going to desert me again?' "

Around the time of the first anniversary of the "miracle," I was visiting with the Pettigrews at their new home. We had gone out to dinner and there had been a tense moment when Margaret had parked the car too close to a shrub by the driveway, risking a scrape to the paint job, and Mike had erupted. But there was no damage and he backed off. "Mike and I have been having difficulties," Margaret said through clenched teeth, as she moved past him and into their kitchen with the doggie bags, shooting him a disgusted look. Mike then showed me around the house, a bungalow where most of the rooms run into each other. It didn't seem the ideal spot for a barely reconciled couple in need of space. He showed me the objets d'art he still owned, which he kept in a glass display case. After a while, the tension faded and the three of us settled around the dining-room table to talk. They had recently celebrated their tenth wedding anniversary and Margaret had written a poem to Mike for the occasion. She recited part of it for me now: it was all about how Mike was her "knight in shining armor" and she his "princess." Mike listened closely and with obvious appreciation, the tempest in the driveway for the time being forgotten.

I asked them how their relationship had changed because of Promise Keepers. The organization's injunction that wives "submit" to their husbands received only the barest of lip service. Mike prayed for Margaret and Margaret said she "respected" Mike as her "spiritual umbrella"; other than that, the concessions seemed to be on his side of the ledger. "Mike used to be *way* irresponsible, obsessive-compulsive, about spending on things," Margaret said. "Now, I still balance the checkbook, but it's his responsibility to make sure that I'm taken care of financially, that I'm *covered,* that I have a financial future." Mike also had given up trying to be in charge of home decoration. "See, I wanted to be a decorator, because I love architecture, pottery, all of this." He swept a big hand in the direction of the glass display case. "But I listen to her now." He turned to Margaret. "Do I listen?" he asked in a suddenly plaintive note. She nodded. "Absolutely. Area rugs were unheard of before because Mike didn't like them. And I always wanted a garland for the door, and Mike had always said, 'Not in *my* house!' " Now they had rugs and, I noticed as I left, a garland wreath on the door.

On the long drive home that night I thought about Margaret's poem to Mike, and it occurred to me that "knights" don't financially support their "princesses," but the princesses love and honor them nonetheless— a privilege not extended to many men in suburban bedroom communities. Promise Keepers told men that they could still be valued by their wives without a job, good news indeed in uncertain and changing economic times — if true. Judging by the preoccupation with property in the Pettigrew household, and Margaret's fixation on a "financial future," Promise Keepers' version of knighthood was more fig leaf than armor for Mike Pettigrew. Margaret was clearly willing to play along with the Promise Keepers fiction of male "servant leadership," but what did she get out of the bargain? Like so many of the wives I met in Promise Keepers, she shaped the group's tenets to fit her own needs, and while she might have 1950s-style expectations of support from her husband, she also wanted 1990s-style independence for herself. The more telling aspect of Margaret's poem was her description of herself: she was not Mike's queen, but a princess. And no suitor, no matter how knightly, owns a princess.

"It all comes down to identity," Margaret told me one afternoon when Mike was not around, and it was said with a force and conviction lacking in all her professions to "respect" Mike as her "spiritual umbrella." What she had taken from Mike's copy of *The Bondage Breaker,* in the end, was a sense of her own God-given right to sever traditional bonds of female subordination. "When I was reading *Bondage Breaker,* there were certain feelings I had for this other man that I wanted to break. And then I realized that for me the very best news would be to be set free. The most important thing is freedom, the choice to live the way you choose, and that's what God is offering. And the main thing was, I just had to take it; I had to *take* my freedom. And no one has the right to take that away from me." This was the-truth-will-set-you-free, with a protofeminist spin. Margaret was calling on religious doctrine to justify her refusal to submit to a man, while her husband invoked the same doctrine to elevate, and make manly, what was essentially his submission. Margaret's seemed the more exhilarating revelation to me (and to Margaret and, I suspected, to Mike, too). She was, she told me, more "daring" now in her life. "When I see an opportunity, I take it. I'm not going to let life pass me by." She wasn't sure where it would lead her, but she knew one thing: no longer would she define herself mainly as Mike's wife. "I *know* my identity now," she said. "I *know* there are certain boundaries that Mike cannot cross over. He *cannot* hit me. He *cannot* abuse me. I am my *own* person, separate from him."

She was looking for a second job, despite Mike's objections. She was continuing with school, despite Mike's reservations. And she would resist for several years Mike's importunings to change her last name back to Pettigrew. "I like my name," she said. In a way, she was still single, her own princess . . . and one who might not need a knight after all.

The Marriage Pit

ON THE THIRD DAY OF 1996, the men of the Glendora group were gathered in Timothy Atwater's living room, girding themselves for the new year. They had a new member, Randy, who had been in another Promise Keepers group, "but it dwindled," he reported—an all-too-common problem. In the course of the year, several men whose groups had washed out would turn up at the Atwaters' house, driftwood from Promise Keepers' many flimsy, leaky rafts.

The Glendora group needed the reinforcements. It too suffered from its members' attenuating commitment, despite repeated testimonies to the importance of "men holding other men accountable." One of the group's first no-shows had been its original leader, marriage-and-family counselor Zel Brooks, who was affiliated with the Cornerstone church that many of the men attended. Several had been seeing Zel for private therapy and had joined the Glendora group because he was leading it. After he had bowed out of his promise to be Glendora's "point man," as Promise Keepers calls its small-group leaders, Brooks had assured the men he would still attend. But his attendance had been spotty, and lately he hadn't made it to a group meeting in months. "Maybe we should just go to Zel's house and drag him over here," Jeremy cracked, a trace of bitterness in his tone.

Martin Booker suggested that they go around the room and share their New Year's resolutions to "improve our family life." He had typed out a list of "issues" he wanted to work on in his own life, which he produced for our inspection. They included "more exercise" and "less TV." "I'm going to ask you guys to keep me more accountable," he said.

Timothy Atwater volunteered that he had tried to start the new year right by hauling out the wedding album and "looking at pictures with Nancy over fifteen years of our marriage."

"Did you cry over any of them?" Martin asked. He meant inspirational tears, but that's not what the photos had provoked in Timothy.

"Yeah, I cried," Timothy said, "over a picture of my daughter, where she's first an adolescent, and you can see where she's becoming distant already." Timothy and Nancy's daughter had become a vexing burden for the couple, a troubled and increasingly out-of-control drug abuser who eventually abandoned her children. The grandchildren now lived with them, a crushing blow for Timothy, who had been looking forward to the easing of lifelong financial responsibilities.

"Real quick," Timothy added, apologetic about changing the subject, "I want to share with you guys. One week before Christmas, my boss told me I have to go back on graveyard for a year." For the past thirty years, Timothy had worked in a large corporation at a nonunion machine shop with no seniority system. "I told him I didn't think it was fair because there are others who haven't done graveyard and I have. I tried to tell him that we depend on him to be fair because we don't have anyone to turn to, there's no arbitration in the company. He told me, 'Fair doesn't mean a lot to me. I'm going to do what's best for the company.' So I said, 'Okay, Lord, I'm going to be submissive about this.' I just prayed about it. And then this week, I heard that they were postponing all shift changes and they may go to a seniority system after all."

Martin Booker dubbed it a "miracle" and "evidence of how God works victory in our lives." As it turned out, Martin's declaration was a bit hasty. A few weeks later, a wan Timothy with circles under his eyes would greet me at the door with the news that he had been assigned to the midnight to 7 A.M. shift after all. But at the January 3 session of Glendora's Promise Keepers, Timothy's "victory" was hailed as proof that submission to a spiritual boss was an act of manly assertion. "Prayer is *action*," Jeremy enthused, rapping a pencil on his ever-present clipboard.

Martin Booker asked Jeremy for his plan of action for the coming year. "My New Year's resolution," Jeremy said, "is to get more organized in my prayer life. I'm going to put up a corkboard. . . ."

Jeremy's wife, Glenda, had recently succeeded in her efforts to expel Jeremy from the house, but a week ago, encouraged by Martin Booker and Zel Brooks, who told Jeremy it was his "duty" to stay with his wife, he had moved back in. Glenda was furious and had told off a couple of the group's men when she ran into them the previous Sunday in the parking lot after church. "Uh, Jeremy?" Martin said delicately. "How's Glenda getting used to you being home?"

Jeremy shrugged. "Well, she's almost used to it, I guess. When I moved back, she yelled and screamed. She stayed in her room for two days. I drew up a contract with rules we'd follow. Like I won't go into her room. She tells me she still wants me out of—"

"Well, you've got an obligation to stay with your wife, no matter what anyone tells you," Martin interrupted.

Jeremy stared at his clipboard and said nothing. What he didn't mention, but would tell me later, was that Glenda had called the police. They had asked him to leave. "It was Sunday, so I went to church." He returned that evening, put his pillow on the sofa, and refused to budge.

"Well," Martin Booker said, clearing his throat, "on the New Year, I thought it would be a good idea for us to reaffirm what Promise Keepers is all about. We are going to love and support and pick each other up when we stumble." He passed around the official "Seven Promises of Promise Keepers," and each member read one of them out loud: "a Promise Keeper is committed to pursuing vital relationships with a few other men, understanding that he needs brothers to help him keep his promises"; "a Promise Keeper is committed to practicing spiritual, moral, ethical, and sexual purity"; "a Promise Keeper is committed to building strong marriages and families through love, protection, and biblical values"; and so on.

"Men," Martin said, "I want to commit to these things. And if you see areas in which I'm not accountable, I want you to put your arm around me and say, 'Martin, this is something you've got to work on.'"

"I'm committed to it," Timothy said. "I was reading in Proverbs where God says we need to cry out for discernment. And I thought, I've never really cried out for discernment. God is always willing to go the extra mile for you as long as you are trying to go in the right direction."

Martin Booker asked Timothy to pray for them to set off on the right track this year. We all bowed our heads and Timothy said, "Father, we are hopeless when we try to do everything on our own. We are helpless, Father. This system is ugly we're in the midst of. To know that you really do care about us, Father, is a blessing. Help us to be closer and more intimate with you."

Martin Booker held up a book. The giant red letters on the cover read *Fight Like a Man*. The group would start discussing this book by Gordon Dalbey next week, he said. "It talks about how surrender is the only way for men to become kingdom warriors. It talks about how to battle alongside your wife and prepare for kingdom warfare."

The distinction between battling "alongside" your wife and against her was one Howard Payson said he wanted to work on in the coming year. Howard's resuscitated marriage was the group's other "success" story, but a pulsing vein at his temple hinted at less than total victory. The continuing crisis of a neighbor, he said, had been weighing on his mind. "This guy was a real abuser, screaming at his wife all the time. Everyone on the block could hear. She got tired of it, I guess. He went off fishing at six in the morning and by the time he came home at three in the afternoon, she had rented a U-Haul, loaded up everything in the house, and cleared out. He was just sitting on the doorstep, crying and crying." Finally, Howard Payson and another neighbor went over. They didn't know quite what to say, so Howard just prayed over him and told him about "surrendering." This happened a year ago. The man was still living in the house, a wasted shadowy figure, waiting for his wife's return.

She wasn't likely to knock on the door any time soon: she had launched a new life, gotten involved with another man, and was now pregnant with his child.

The neighbor's ghostly vigil frightened Howard; it was what he feared most in his own home. "A year ago, my wife, Libby, hated me," he said, the blue vein jumping. "It wasn't till God changed my attitude that we fell back in love with each other. But in '96, we are going to be working even harder on our marriage."

———

NEARLY EVERY INCH OF THE COUNTER and wall space in the Payson household is covered with what Libby calls "my antiques." The impression one gets looking around is that the house has been invaded by Hummels, occupied by an army of ceramic Munchkins. Elfin figurines grin from bookcases; teeny critters dance along the mantelpiece; salt and pepper shakers in troll shapes prowl the tabletops. The Paysons had invited me for dinner and we were seated around the family table, surrounded on all sides by this parade of miniatures. Libby, with her apple-cheeked features and diminutive stature, looked a bit like one of her Hummels, drawn to a larger scale. "Every Saturday, I used to go to the antique marts, and I'd see something and I'd just have to have it." She closed her fist suddenly around the neck of a troll pepper mill. "Like that. I'd just go into a buying frenzy. It was a compulsion. I didn't understand it then, I just knew I had to have it . . ." She looked over at her husband, sitting at the head of the table. Howard instinctively put down his fork and crossed his arms over his chest, a lineman preparing for a body blow. She tipped her head in his direction. "He created a monster," she said.

Howard met Libby on a church youth trip to Mexico. "I carried her over a puddle," he recalled wistfully. This one act of chivalry gave way to "years of just being at each other's throats," as Howard put it. They married in a hurry, six months after the puddle jump. Howard was twenty-one, Libby nineteen. "She didn't believe in premarital sex," Howard said. Eager, Howard persuaded her to move the wedding date up. Their pastor was still on vacation, so they just had the substitute minister marry them. "I thought marriage would be this transformation," Libby said. "I thought marriage would be about being catered to." She paused. "I cried every night."

Howard wanted a child "right away," and Libby went along with it, figuring that was "the thing to do" after getting married. Within a year, their daughter Jennifer was born. Domesticity appealed to Howard; he enjoyed looking after his daughter and puttering around the house. The ordinary dailiness of family life comforted him; he had grown up in a broken home, and being with the children—they soon had two daughters—made him feel part of a domestic circle at last. Libby, meanwhile, was doing a slow burn. "All Howard wanted to do was *relax*!" she said, still incensed at the thought of it. "I felt, Why are you just laying there on the couch? Why don't you *do* something?" Howard rose to a middle-management position at his company, but even then his salary barely covered the bills. "I'd see these older couples in church," Libby recounted, "and they had their own homes and nice furniture. Every time I'd go to a ladies' church meeting, I'd think of what I didn't have." She borrowed her grandmother's credit card and refurnished the living room, down to the end tables and lamps. "I thought, If only we had our own house." Finally, she wheedled the down payment out of her father.

"We paid him back," Howard interrupted his wife, his face suddenly red. "Be sure to write that, too."

The house led only to a new cycle of money worries. "Every month, it was, how much did Howard make, how do we pay the bills, how do we pay the taxes?" To defray the house costs, Howard invited his mother to rent out the front room. Needless to say, turning the parlor into mother-in-law quarters did not ease marital tensions. Arguments and screaming bouts became constant. "A few pots and pans got thrown," Howard admitted. One night while she was pregnant, Libby said, Howard came after her, drunk and threatening to hit her. Libby locked herself in the bedroom. "I kept waiting for this miracle man. I kept saying to myself, 'So where's my spiritual leader?'" If he wasn't somebody she could look up to, she asked, then who was *she*? "I'd be screaming and crying, and I would always ask Howard, 'Why do you love me? Do you like me?' Because I had no identity."

In the midst of these pitched battles, Howard became seriously ill twice, the second time with a baseball-size cancerous tumor. Playing Florence Nightingale, Libby admitted with some embarrassment, was not an identity she desired, no matter how much it fit the expected mold of a Christian wife. For a year, Howard staggered from chemotherapy to the office. "I couldn't afford not to work." At home, he retreated behind a wall of silence.

"He wouldn't share his feelings with me," Libby said. "He'd talk to his mother, but not to me." While Howard lost his hair, Libby gained weight, and hated herself. It was the period of their marriage that Howard referred to as "the Great Depression." Libby remembered most clearly the evenings after dinner. "I'd be in front of the TV set in the living room, he'd be in front of the TV in the bedroom."

Libby's one escape was the thrift shops. "If someone had a nutcracker collection, I'd have to have it. Then I'd buy it and then it was, 'Uh, now what?' I just spent and spent. It was the most unwise use of money." I asked what she thought was behind her compulsion to spend and she jerked a thumb at Howard. "*He* let me keep control of the budget." (Throughout dinner, Libby and Howard referred to each other as "he" and "she," as if neither of them were actually in the room.) "He just let me buy and buy and buy." She groaned. "When I think back to what we *could* have had with that money . . ."

Something had to give, and it did, though not in the way either of them had imagined. "I wanted things, so I decided to work," Libby said. She hired a part-time baby-sitter shortly after her daughter Jennifer's birth and took a job first as a secretary, then as an administrator, "because I thought, Well, that pays a little more." When Jennifer turned two, Libby got a job as an administrative aide in a hospital, and two and a half years later, it turned into her first permanent job — and her life changed.

"I did a good job at work, and they liked me for it," she recalled. "They were *praising* me. . . . I had this great fulfillment at work. But not at home."

"What happened," said Howard, crossing his arms again, "was that Libby started to get her identity from work."

Libby nodded. "I used to tell Howard, 'If you don't want to talk to me, I have friends at work who will. Who *like* me.' On the weekends, I'd be just dying to get back to work. I felt more cherished at my job by people I wasn't married to! I felt completed there."

Libby began to inch her way up the office ladder. Soon she was promoted to purchasing and accounting, where the shopper-who-couldn't-stop transformed herself into a meticulous budgeteer. "You know," Libby told me, "before this I had gone to pastoral counseling, I had gone to self-esteem counseling, I had gone to marriage counseling. But it was with work that I started changing. I started losing weight. I started to think about myself differently. I started feeling like I'm worth something." For Libby, as for so many women of her generation, working was uplifting because she was exceeding the bounds of traditional feminine expectation. For her husband, as for most other men, employment was just the expected baseline for traditional manhood. She was distinguishing herself as an individual; he was laboring just to stay on the team.

At home, Libby began to lose interest in adorning the furnishings with gewgaws, much less dusting them. "I started to question, Why do I cook and clean?" Howard observed her transformation with increasing fear.

While he was glad she had curtailed her shopping sprees, he found her attachment to work far more threatening—and rightly so. He saw it, as she did, as her way out. "The man nowadays has to realize, the wife is not going to sit at home and wait," he said to me. "The role of the husband and wife in America has changed so dramatically. Before, everybody's role was defined. Now, women are out in the workforce and there are so many temptations out there. Everything is so worldly now. We've lost a lot of our old identity." Of course, he didn't exactly mean "we." His wife hadn't lost an identity. She had found one that didn't seem to include him.

Howard saw an ad for Promise Keepers on the bulletin board of his church. "I needed to get advice," he told me. The advice he got was, initially, to enroll the two of them in a six-week marriage seminar, in which they studied Promise Keepers speaker Gary Smalley's book, *Hidden Keys to a Loving, Lasting Marriage*. The "hidden keys" turned out to be the revelation that, as Howard put it, "men and women think differently. Women are very emotional and they need to have emotional attention paid to them." Libby said what she learned in the group was, "Men need praise. I realized how, ten thousand times a day, I cut him off at the knees." These weren't bad lessons, just not particularly relevant to the Paysons' crisis. Of course Libby needed "emotional attention"; of course Howard needed "praise"—which, in spite of the seminar's emphasis on men's and women's differences, amounted to the same thing. But what each of them really needed was a purpose to their life, a meaningful engagement in the world, a mission that made them feel, as Libby had phrased it, "I'm worth something." Libby sensed the outlines of such a calling in her work. And Howard sensed that his wife's new mission eliminated his.

In the second week of the seminar, Libby confessed to Howard that she had been having an affair with a man at work but was determined to break it off. Howard, in turn, told her that ten years earlier, while she was pregnant, he had had an affair. "I took the rest of the week off and we just clung to each other," Libby said. "We were so afraid." Libby's subsequent efforts to jettison her work lover turned ugly when he wouldn't leave her alone. She finally filed a complaint with her superiors, which nearly destroyed her career along with his. In the end, both got letters of reprimand.

Soon after graduating from the marriage seminar, Howard and Libby renewed their wedding vows in a small ceremony. "Libby and I stand here tonight proof of God's power and how he can change lives," Howard read from the remarks he'd prepared for the occasion. "Howard is living proof of God's power," Libby read from hers. "He has overcome cancer, smoking, bitterness, and the marriage pit. I have overcome unhealthy eating habits, idle thoughts, compulsive shopping, and the marriage pit!" They exchanged a second set of rings.

Libby told me she now joined her husband in prayer. For several months after their renewed vows, she prayed that she would get a promotion she felt was long overdue and deserved, and she asked Howard to pray for her promotion in his Promise Keepers meetings, too. Every week, the Glendora group ended its session with a prayer circle. Each man submitted his prayer requests and then the man seated to his right would pray for him. From what I'd witnessed, Howard's requests on behalf of Libby's career seemed a bit halfhearted. With head bowed, Howard would pray that whatever God thought best, he would go along with, but "I think Libby needs to break the relationships she has at work for the building of our marriage."

As the saying goes, be careful what you wish for. Howard's prayers were answered. Libby didn't get the promotion, but her employer's snub inspired her to apply to another hospital, where she landed a job with a bigger salary, more authority, and her own staff. "I have a position that's meant for someone with a college education!" Libby, who had not gone to college, told me with much pride. "I aced the interview." (Later, she would go back to school for her bachelor's degree and would find an even better job.)

Howard, regarding her from across the dinner table, said, "Yeah, it helped that no one else applied." She looked up at him sharply. "Only kidding," he added, pasting a smile on his face.

"What's great about it is the bosses are all women," Libby continued. "Before, where I worked, men ran the show. My new boss is great. I'm already implementing changes. Of course, the men working under me are resentful."

"She has a bigger office than I do," Howard said.

If his wife was, as Howard had put it, getting her identity from work, I asked, where did that leave him? "That's what I learned in Promise Keepers. I learned the identity I didn't have I could have in Christ. Jesus Christ *is* my identity."

I wasn't sure how Howard could find his identity by modeling himself after a childless bachelor. Why was the image of Jesus paramount, instead of a seemingly more apt biblical model, like an Old Testament patriarch—Jacob, for instance, fathering the twelve sons who fathered the twelve tribes of Israel—or, for that matter, God the *Father*? Promise Keepers billed its agenda as helping men to become better fathers and husbands. Yet "identity in Jesus" was what Promise Keepers promoted most of all, from the constant chant in the arenas, "We love Jesus! Nothing else matters!" to the repeated declaration that Jesus was "the ultimate Promise Keeper." "You have to start with Jesus," a Promise Keepers representative typically emphasized. "If you don't understand that this movement is about Jesus, all the rest of this talk about keeping our promises is mere gibberish."[16] Finding an "identity in Jesus" clearly appealed more strongly to Howard and his brethren in the Glendora group than any other biblical image of masculinity. But why?

Spiritual Keys to Losing Fat

I MADE MY WAY DOWN THE SCENTED PASTEL AISLES of the Christian bookstore, looking for my next week's assigned reading, Gordon Dalbey's *Fight Like a Man*. It was a little like being trapped in one of those mall boutiques that sell nothing but potpourri and jasmine candles. The "men's" section was consigned to a back shelf, a collection of hardcovers illustrated with profiles of knights on crusades and football players charging down the field. These were hopelessly outnumbered and outflanked by the pink devotional pamphlets and rose-adorned spiritual guides that lined the other shelves, frilly Bible covers and lambs-and-chicks crib ruffles that jammed the cabinets, flower-festooned jewelry and smiley-faced Jesus figurines that blanketed the display cases, out-of-focus portraits of serene homemakers sipping tea and sniffing flowers that covered the walls, and uplifting sugary music that emanated from floral jewel boxes, windup infant mobiles, and music-box-bearing stuffed animals, generating a cacophonous cross talk of treacle.

I found the book. On its cover, the silhouette of a muscle-bound, unclad warrior of classical Greek mien was poised for battle, his sword and shield raised high over blood red letters that heralded his mission: "Redeeming Manhood for Kingdom Warfare." As I stood in line to make my purchase, behind a woman buying a greeting card adorned with a dimpled Kewpie cherub in prayer, I wondered how any man entering this seventh circle of Jesus kitsch could imagine he was embarking on a life of muscular Christianity. The media often likened Promise Keepers to turn-of-the-century campaigns to restore virility to religion, perceiving ex-coach Bill McCartney as the modern incarnation of post-Victorian revivalist preacher Billy Sunday, famed for his sweaty histrionics and testosterone-drenched descriptions of Jesus as "the greatest scrapper that ever lived" and "no dough-faced, lick-spittle proposition." The acts of Bill and Billy, indeed, had their parallels: McCartney as a former coach whose religious testimonials were cluttered with football clichés; Sunday as a former pro baseball player whose onstage contortions before men-only audiences often resembled those of a pitcher about to hurl a fastball from the mound. McCartney asserted that God told him to break his fifteen-year football contract with the University of Colorado; Sunday said God ordered him to bail out of the three-year contract he had just signed with the Phillies. And surely McCartney would have agreed with Sunday's contention that "the manliest man is the man who will ac-knowledge Jesus Christ." Both were looking to rehabilitate the Christian man's reputation from that of "a wishy-washy sissified sort of galoot," as Sunday put it, "that lets everybody make a doormat out of him."[17] But there were distinctions between the movements of the two eras that ran deeper than any surface similarities.

Muscular Christianity emerged at the turn of the century as a protest against an increasingly sentimental strain of Protestantism — and, ulti-mately, against an "emasculated" church's ineffectuality in the face of industrialism's mounting ravages. Billy Sunday's revivalism, restricted in the civic and legislative arena to denunciations of "demon liquor" and its attendant ills (gambling, dancing, and prostitution), was only one and perhaps the most toothless aspect of a populist Christian protest, which found its voice in a series of working-class preachers with monikers like "The Labor Evangelist" and "The Railroad Evangelist."[18] The Men and Religion Forward Movement of the early 1900s, whose call to arms was "The women have had charge of the church work long enough," looked to expand the Christian man's reach beyond repentance, to engage him "in social service and usefulness," by pressing for the improvement of conditions in industry, public education, and government. The move-ment, which engaged more than a million Protestant men in a two-year revival campaign that began in 1911, did not just sermonize; among other "social action" projects, its members built a Labor Temple, cleaned up local jails, and lobbied for improved garbage collection and the inspec-tion of water and milk. Ultimately, though, the movement's leaders re-coiled from mounting a real political challenge to the industrial order; they, too, preferred in the end to fight the safer public "sins" of saloons and brothels.[19]

About the same time, the Social Gospel movement emerged from liberal established churches with a radical critique of capitalism. Its pro-ponents pressed more boldly into the realm of reformist or radical pol-itics, reenvisioning Christian manhood as the willingness to stand up for the "little man" and against the powers of the machine age. The new industrial order, wrote Walter Rauschenbusch, a New York Baptist min-ister and preeminent voice of the Social Gospel, "leaves men stunted, cowed, and shamed in their manhood." The Social Gospelers called for a brotherhood uniting laborer and churchman in a mutual struggle against the new economic inequities. Their vision foregrounded Christ's workingman status, justifying church intervention on the factory floor on the grounds that Jesus was a carpenter who had, as a leading Social Gospel minister put it, "stricken the shackles from the laborer . . . lifted him up . . . and put into his hands the key of a great future." The movement's adherents endorsed a "Social Creed" in 1908, which called for the defense of the workingman against the oppressions "resulting from the swift crises of industrial change." Social Gospelers protested the long hours and high injury rates in factories, called for union representation and retirement benefits and even profit sharing for workers, and demanded the abolition of child labor and sweatshops. Their efforts eventually foundered before the formidable industrial forces arrayed against them.[20]

Just as the Men and Religion Forward Movement had declared its aim "to help find the 3,000,000 men missing from participation in church life" (a reference to the lopsided two-thirds-female membership of American Protestant churches), Promise Keepers sought to bring men back into the activities of the church.[21] But for what purpose? The speeches and literature of its leaders were full of calls to wage war against commercial images of masculinity, the empty promises of sports-car commercials and billboards exalting cowboy smokers, the impossible, degraded virility marketed in movies like *Rambo* and TV shows like *Baywatch*. That seemed like a worthy war. It had occurred to me as I listened to their tales of discord that one theme running beneath the domestic clashes of Mike and Margaret and Howard and Libby, their skirmishes over Mike's book collection and Libby's "buying frenzy" at the "antique marts," was a battle with consumerism and the desires it lets loose.

Yet the organization that rallied its men in arenas surrounded by Bud Light, Marlboro Country, and Sports Channel billboards (and, in the Anaheim stadium, a huge ad for "The Barbra Streisand Lookalike Contest") didn't offer any effective way for its adherents to challenge the market forces these signs represented. Unlike the Men and Religion Forward Movement or the Social Gospel campaign, Promise Keepers made almost no forays into the arenas of civic or social action, except for occasional efforts to pick up litter or paint over graffiti in a local park, generally one-day affairs focused more on cosmetic beautification than community change. The group shrank from all political engagement, including the most conservative and predictable kind; it did not even have an official political position on abortion, for fear of endangering its popularity.[22] In the end, maintaining its own popularity by mass marketing itself and promoting the PK logo were the organization's most evident drives. Promise Keepers amassed in Washington in 1997 not to demand change but to be *seen*. The display of all those bodies before the TV cameras had become an end in itself.

Despite its pitiful calls for its members to turn off their TVs, what Promise Keepers offered its men was but another communion with the marketplace. Every path seemed to lead only to a PK Product Tent or scented bookstore. Promise Keepers–affiliated *New Man* magazine advised its readers, "There's a lot more to being a man than being a breadwinner." But the alternative its editors offered was to be a bread-spender; the "New Man," it turned out, was a shopper. The magazine's cover headlines regularly promised such treats as COOL GADGETS FOR GUYS, SPIRITUAL KEYS TO LOSING FAT, EIGHT SMART VACATIONS.[23]

One afternoon at the Anaheim Stadium, I stood next to an increasingly frenzied PK staff member as she dispatched orders into a walkie-talkie: "Product Tent 1, Product Tent 1, did you get that case of CDs?" "Product Tent 2 has run out of caps! Repeat, we need a delivery of caps to Tent 2, right away!" As I watched the men inside the huge tents, cramming random knickknacks into their official PK plastic tote bags or standing in endless lines to deposit their money in the cash registers operated by tired but chipper female checkers, what I found so striking about this tableau suddenly hit me: the men were all shopping, the women all working.

The muscular Christians a century earlier had tried, no matter how ineffectively in the end, to rebel against what they saw as "feminine" tendencies compromising Victorian Protestantism. In truth, the hearts-and-flowers sermon was only one aspect of a complex transformation in nineteenth-century American Christianity, and such saccharine styles augured less a feminine takeover than the first stirrings of a mass-market national economy. Nonetheless, the muscular Christians were at least reacting against the retailed pieties of a pulpit bent on mass appeal. Promise Keepers, on the other hand, implicitly urged men to surrender to its cosmetic embrace. The Christianity on display in Promise Keepers echoed its constituents' problems rather than pointing toward solutions to them.

Instead of urging men to take a meaningful stance against the humiliations of a consumer culture, Promise Keepers encouraged men, after they fed their shopping appetites at the stadium events, to exercise their consumer "authority" at home. The kind of spiritual direction it advo-

cated men make in the household was on the order of organizing a
Tupperware party; they were told to take charge of the family's worship
acquisition and consumption activities—what religious products to buy,
what Bibles to purchase, what videos and TV shows were acceptable to
watch. Promise Keepers empowered men to be domestic directors of
purchasing and entertainment. They seemed to be challenging not consumerism itself but the more traditional wifely role as head consumer of
the family. Promise Keepers proposed to fight the "feminizing" aspects
of consumer culture by usurping the positions of its female agents. If
men were in charge of shopping, then maybe shopping would no longer
feel "feminine." It was, essentially, a marketing strategy, and a highly
cosmetic one: don't reject the products, just change their colors from
pink to blue.

If the Promise Keepers path only took its followers full circle back
to the ATM and the cap-and-mug concession stand, its participants
didn't seem to mind. They spent staggering amounts on PK-branded
products without complaint; in 1995, merchandise sales were almost double what the organization received in donations. Evangelical Christian
writer Ken Abraham, a regular contributor to *New Man,* expressed head-
scratching amazement at the figures. In his otherwise laudatory chronicle
of the organization, *Who Are the Promise Keepers?,* he observed:

> In 1995, according to PK's audited financial statement, Promise Keep-
> ers took in ... a whopping $14 million from sales of Promise Keepers
> hats, mugs, shirts, and other resource materials. PK books, CDs and
> tapes, and the PK magazine, *New Man,* added $800,000 in royalties to
> Promise Keepers' coffers. To put those figures in perspective, retail
> stores peddling many of the same products as Promise Keepers take in
> annual sales averaging around $750,000. Clearly, the cogs in the PK
> machine are well-greased with greenbacks.[24]

In the Glendora group, discussions often centered on matters that might
have seemed more appropriate to the lifestyle sections of a newspaper:
home decor, fitness equipment, diet products, consumer electronics, the
vicissitudes of the real-estate market. "With the huge insurance settlement Judy and I got," Martin Booker told the group one week, referring
to a check they had received after guests accidentally set their house on
fire, "we've been able to buy some great goodies." Ordinarily, the closing
prayer session was similarly oriented. Martin Booker often prayed to
God for help to "get control of my weight" and "use the treadmill more
often." Jeremy Foote's appeal from week to week was the same: "As you

know, Lord," he said, a bit more irritably as the months went by, "I *need*
help selling that time-share in Palm Springs." One week he even specified
a purchase price in his prayer, and a willingness to discount it by more
than fifteen hundred dollars. Another week, when the discussion topic
was "Do we have a distorted view of God?" Jeremy allowed that, "We
have to trust him for everything and I don't think I do, because I don't
trust him to sell that time-share."

Many of the group's ideas for improving their marriages revolved
around the retail market, too. "It's important to go with Margaret to
decorate the house for the holidays," Mike Pettigrew commented. Dennie said he had pitched in and helped his wife shop for a baby shower
she was hosting, then gussied up the living room with party favors. Getting in on the household's store-bought action also pleased them. "Judy
ordered for Christmas this little house, a snow-covered Disney thing
with a hinge that opens up," Martin Booker told the group around the
holidays. "And when we showed it to Janie [their daughter], she just went
'Awww!' And it was just one of those moments that was special. If I
could be involved in that sort of thing more often, I'd be helping our
family to grow instead of just worrying about the football game on TV."

It wasn't clear to me that unwrapping a Disney toy was much of a
departure from watching a televised football game, but that wasn't what
bothered the men. Their frustration was with their wives' reactions: the
women didn't *want* their "help" in this domain. Margaret was irritated
by her husband's decorative and spending habits. Libby was disgusted
with her husband for wanting to spend more time at home; she saw it
not as devoted but as "lazy." One week in the fall of 1995, Dan Rhodes,
who drifted in and out of the group, reported his wife's chilly response
to a "helpful" proposal of his. Dan owned a spa-and-pools store, but after
it stopped being profitable, he put it on the market and became a pool
repairman. Then he was injured on the job. "While I was out of work
on disability," he told the group, "my wife started making Christmas
ornaments to make money. Now she's branched out into floral arrange-
ments and photo albums. I told her I'm going to retire and help her.
She didn't like that much." Dennie Elliott nodded, wincing. "My cousin
called me last week," he said, "and she was all upset about her husband.
He's not working and she's supporting the family. He's been playing Mr.
Mom, doing the shopping, and she said to me, 'I think he's getting to
like it.' And she didn't care for that at all."

A century ago, Thorstein Veblen famously suggested in *The Theory of
the Leisure Class* that a bourgeois wife's acquisitiveness advertised her
husband's productivity. Her "conspicuous consumption" was a feather in

his cap because it reflected his power on the *producing* end of the market. In the post-Veblen world the men of Promise Keepers lived in, however, their wives' acquisitiveness no longer confirmed their earning power; more often than not, it only signaled a mess of unpaid credit-card bills. The men consumed, in fact, to compensate for their *lack* of producer power. If you couldn't keep your job at an aerospace plant, at least you could buy a recording of military jets and turn up the volume until the windows rattled. Yet the more the Glendora men shopped, the more their emptying bank accounts underscored their lack of productivity. Worst of all, there seemed increasingly to be only one sure path to productivity—to take your aptitude for adornment and sell it on the market. And there the women seemed, at least to the men, to have an edge. Dan's wife, after all, was now marketing the Christmas baubles she had once made free for her family over an 800 line.

An economy driven by display values seemed to the men to be an economy women were inestimably better equipped to navigate. The men's frustrations on that score were widely held. Dan's disappointment reminded me of a complaint voiced repeatedly by Carl, one of the men in the Alternatives to Violence batterers' group. After Carl lost his post at a southern California military base, he had desperately tried to patch together a hodgepodge of service-economy jobs to support his children: as a bouncer in a nightclub, a pastry decorator at a bakery, a freelance cake caterer. "I see how my girlfriend can go anywhere and get good money," he told the group bitterly. "She makes more money than I do. I see it all over the place. I see women buying a house after one year, just for modeling swimsuits. Just for swinging their butts. I'm busting my butt, day in and day out, and where do I get? Nowhere. Sometimes, I wish I were a woman."

Of course, few women actually were making a killing "swinging their butts." Most were busting them, just like the men, and generally for lower wages. That year, women's median wages nationwide were about a third less than men's. In the three decades since the Equal Pay Act had passed in 1965, women had narrowed their pay gap with men by only about ten cents. As much as the men in Promise Keepers and Alternatives to Violence imagined the women in their lives, and women in general, to be the lucky winners of the new ornamental economy, the fact was, most of their working wives and girlfriends were having a hard time making a living; most were still stuck in the low-wage pink ghettos of "women's work," as were more than 60 percent of working women nationwide who slogged away in sales (mostly retail), service (such as waitressing), and administrative support (read, secretarial) jobs. Still, men weren't entirely mistaken when they saw their own disaster reflected in the slowly narrowing pay gap: as much as 60 percent of that "progress," one study found, reflected not an improvement in women's wages but a decline in men's real earnings.[25]

However much a man might envy his wife her Christmas decorating business, it wasn't the kind of work that was going to support a family, or even herself. Libby had a bigger office than her husband, but she didn't take home a bigger paycheck. Margaret dreamed of being an independent "princess," but with her secretary's pay, she still needed another source of income, which may be one reason why she left Mike only after meeting the gainfully employed researcher and returned to Mike when it was clear that they had no future. Of all the Promise Keepers' wives, the only one who could conceivably have sustained herself as a single mother was Martin's wife, Judy, and she had a job in the dicey aerospace industry. The Promise Keepers' wives who had stayed home faced even grimmer prospects if they were to strike out on their own. Nationwide by 1997, 55 percent of single mothers and 61 percent of displaced homemakers were living at or below the poverty line. Single mothers endured a poverty rate three times as high as the national rate, and the poverty rate among displaced homemakers actually rose in the 1990s, even as it fell in the general population.[26]

Nonetheless, the men would have far preferred to go back to a period when "busting my butt" got men somewhere, even if it was only working for a backbreaking factory or a dreary corporation, even if it was just the security of a place to go every day and a necessary job to do there. Dennie Elliott told me he tried to follow the Promise Keepers precepts and "get involved" at home, but it just wasn't how his marriage, or his life, was supposed to work. Mary, who was a full-time homemaker, found Dennie's presence at home trying. "Mary wants to control everything in the house," he said to me. "Even the yard!"

Who Shall Separate Us from the Love of Christ?

SHIPWRECKED IN A SERVICE ECONOMY and held suspect by the wives they once supported, men like Dennie certainly weren't misguided in turning to religion in their search for a purpose. They were seeking an institution to place their faith in, a firm rock to secure their shaky footing, a structure and an order that wouldn't vanish overnight. And so they came, or came anew, to Christianity.

One important aspect of Christianity has always been its power to define the worshipper's relationship with his earthbound world. Among the least abstract of world religions, with a foundational drama of personal, human suffering, Christianity lends itself particularly well to social and domestic application. For centuries, men and women both have seen in the Christ story a way to give meaning and stability to their secular bonds of family, community, and state. But the Jesus with whom the Promise Keepers wanted their followers to identify was not necessarily a Jesus that Christians of every age would have recognized. The popular expression of Jesus has changed as the world has changed. The form of Christianity has proved exceedingly mutable, as has the image of Christ himself, shifting depending on human needs and purposes, desires and fears.

To the cloistered abbots of the high Middle Ages, Jesus was often a nursing (and even sensual) mother whose breasts flowed with the milk of loving-kindness. "Are you not that mother, who, like a hen, collects her chickens under her wings?" Anselm of Canterbury wrote in the twelfth century. "Truly, master, you are a mother." "If you feel the stings of temptation," Bernard of Clairvaux wrote, "suck not so much the wounds as the breasts of the Crucified. He will be your mother, and you will be his son."[27] To many a Victorian bourgeois churchwoman of the mid-nineteenth century, Christ took the form of a gentle, solicitous husband. In the hymns written by nineteenth-century Protestant women, Christ "becomes a very cozy person," as historian Barbara Welter wrote in her 1974 essay "The Feminization of American Religion": "The singer is urged to press against him, to nestle into him, to hold his hand, and so forth. A love letter to Christ was the only kind of love letter a nice woman was allowed to publish, and sublimation was as yet an unused word."[28] Then again, the Jesus of the best-selling book of the mid-1920s, Bruce Barton's *The Man Nobody Knows,* was a successful business and marketing executive who "created an organization that won the world" on the basis of "personal magnetism" and the projection of "amazing self-assurance" and "consuming sincerity." The Jesus of that era was, as adman Barton, among other popularizers of the period, drew him, a "popular dinner guest" with a "hearty laugh" who knew how to make friends and influence people.[29]

All these images were shaped as much by worldly forces as by the religious imagination. For the cloistered abbots, a maternal Christ provided an alternative to the stern and vengeful last-judge God prevailing elsewhere in church doctrine. As Caroline Walker Bynum observed in her study of feminine religious imagery in the Middle Ages, *Jesus as Mother,* the image of a nursing Jesus reflected the monastic leaders' "general ambivalence about authority and about male roles in twelfth-century society."[30] To Victorian churchwomen, the idea of Christ's tenderness compensated for the often emotionally arid life they suffered within their marriages—marriages that, no matter how stifling, the era's prohibitions constrained them from fleeing. To young business strivers of the 1920s, anxious to adapt to a nascent management and marketing bureaucracy in which "personality" already ruled the day, Bruce Barton's depiction of Jesus as an up-and-comer who succeeded with a winning smile served as a comforting self-help manual. Jesus, too, followed a self-marketing plan, Barton assured them, and look where it got him! Like a good adman— Barton himself was a founding executive of the ad agency BBD&O— Jesus set out to snag customer "interest" by making his message "simple and brief" and acting "above all sincere," and that self-promotional strategy led to "the grandest achievement story of all."[31] In these cases, and many others, Christ's image and the form of Christianity conceived around his image helped people to adapt to, reconceive, or even resist expectations society had placed upon them as workers, spouses, or citizens. The men of Promise Keepers had embraced a particular image of Christ; they had chosen it out of a host of other possibilities. But why, and what did it help them negotiate and relieve in their own lives?

Spokesmen for Promise Keepers emphasized that the movement's adherents were focused on becoming more attentive parents and more commanding husbands—these were the roles that supposedly consumed them. And yet, the more time I spent at Promise Keepers events and with the men in Glendora, the more I began to wonder if these were their central concerns after all. The men barely spoke about their children. I never heard a man in the group talk about how he might change the way he raised or related to his kids. In nearly a year of weekly meetings, not one session addressed the question of how to become a better father. Nor did the men seem much invigorated by Promise Keepers' other stated goal: to reinstate marriages along the lines of Ephesians 5:22, "Wives, submit to your husbands." Among the Glendora men, not one had actually shifted the power lines between himself and his wife as a result of Promise Keepers. Nor did they ever talk about putting uncompliant helpmates "in their place"; they seemed more concerned about impressing their wives than oppressing them.

Yet men joined Promise Keepers in droves. And with good reason. I had initially made the mistake, along with the rest of the movement's chroniclers and critics, of focusing on what its leaders were denouncing—feminism, the gay-rights movement, pornography—to explain its wildfire growth. The retributive side of the religious right in general, with its thunderous and noxious fulminations, was hard to ignore; its clamorous insistence drowned out quieter themes. But it slowly dawned on me that instead of looking at what the leaders were railing *against,* I should be considering what the members were searching *for.* And it was then that I began to sense the faintest outlines of another drama, buried in the Sturm und Drang of stadium summonses to "spiritual warfare." What seemed to draw the men most powerfully was a specific aspect of the way Promise Keepers represented Christianity and the way that representation spoke to a difficult and fundamental relationship in their lives that distressed them far more than those with their children or their wives.

I first had an inkling of what that relationship was the week the Glendora group delved into Gordon Dalbey's *Fight Like a Man.* The work of Gordon Dalbey was widely studied by Promise Keepers adherents, and impassioned discussions of his work filled the electronic chat rooms of many Promise Keepers Web sites. It was almost impossible, in fact, to get through a conversation with a Promise Keeper without hearing his name invoked. "Gordon Dalbey rocked my world," one of the Glendora men gushed to me at the first meeting I attended. *Fight Like a Man* was the fourth in a series of books by Dalbey that focused, each more intensely than the last, on one theme: the wounds inflicted on a man by his father.

A minister and counselor who led Christian men's retreats, Dalbey found himself overwhelmed by the desperate need that he witnessed for a father's love.

> In speaking to men's groups of all kinds—at a prestigious university alumni association downtown, an inner-city storefront church, a suburban middle-class church—I have discovered that inside every business suit, every pair of faded overalls, every stay-press sport shirt, lies the wounded heart of a boy longing for his daddy.
>
> The man is hurt—and often, angry. As one burly, flannel-shirted contractor in his forties demanded at question time after a small group sharing at my men's retreat, "I want to know: Are us guys in our group just that off base, or what? I mean, not one of us could name any positive things about our fathers!"[32]

The typical man of the baby-boom generation, to which Dalbey himself belonged, has been singularly afflicted by his "boyhood experience before a fearfully distant, authoritarian father," he wrote. "The first man he loved and needed betrayed him." There was, Dalbey sensed, no escaping such a burden. "Even as an adult, the issue remains: 'Am I a good boy?

Am I doing it right? Do I have a proper, acceptable faith? Do I measure up?—that is, 'Does my father love me?'" As he saw it, these issues were never resolved in childhood because the sons were raised in a time of "epidemic alienation from the father." Instead of being guided by a paternal hand, Dalbey keenly observed, the boys of his generation were offered electronic substitutes by a commercial culture. "Those who once sat in delight learning about themselves from the patriarch and his stories now sit silently before glowing test patterns and canned laughter." These alienated sons had no way of knowing if they were men because their silent or missing fathers had no way of telling them—and that unknowingness "beckons shame."[33]

Dalbey envisioned a spiritual solution to this generational ache for a father, in the figure of Jesus. His image of Christ is of the fortunate son who has come to tell all the abandoned earthbound sons that they do have a loving father after all, in heaven. "Why, indeed, did Jesus call God his 'Father'?" Dalbey ruminated. "He could have said, 'Mother,' 'Brother,' 'Sister,' 'Friend,' 'Higher Power,' 'Life,' or a host of other names. But of all recognizable relationships and concepts on earth, he chose *Father*. Why?" Because, he concluded, Jesus was sent specifically to tell the sons this "good news": "You don't have to be ashamed for not getting what you needed from your earthly father. Your heavenly Father has come to provide it." Jesus' mission is to help each man "discover at last his true Father and destiny as a son." Over and over, Dalbey's books depict Jesus as the generous older brother, the "beloved son" who wants his brothers to be beloved, too, who demonstrates for them by his tears on the cross and by his "radical intimacy" with God that it's all right to be "vulnerable" and "open" with their new Father, that the Father will accept them in a way their secular father never did.[34]

In the final passage of *Fight Like a Man*, Dalbey related a "vision" he had experienced several years earlier. In the vision, he saw "a long line of saddled horses in the foreground of a plain facing a dark horizon tumbling with storm clouds.... Individual men stand beside the horses—broken men, some stooped over, others limping with canes, bandages and splints—and Jesus is helping each mount up." These men are about to embark on a mission, but it's not to conquer territory or crush an enemy. They are setting forth on a journey to find their fathers. Becoming a *son*, Dalbey wrote, is the real male rite of passage. Through Jesus, a man "can face his father-wound, but it no longer defines him, because he's begun to allow the Father God to define him as a true son," Dalbey concluded. "To be a man is to be a son."[35]

In the second week of the new year, the members of the Glendora group assembled in Timothy Atwater's living room to commence their study of *Fight Like a Man*. "Dalbey's new book is about how the secular men's movement has recently awoken to the 'father wound,'" Martin began. Outside a car alarm throbbed in the night; in the back bedroom, Timothy's grandson let out a startled cry, then fell silent. "But while the men's movement identified the problem, it gives no solution. Now, Gordon Dalbey believes there *is* a solution: Jesus." To seek an "identity in Christ," Martin said, wasn't to become *like* Christ so much as to be *fathered* like he was. "Jesus modeled perfectly a life totally dependent on his father. He's saying, 'Everything I'm doing is what my father wanted me to do. Everything is to glorify him. Because my father is a loving daddy.'"

Their group had a clear objective now, Martin told them. Because, as Gordon Dalbey put it, when men gathered "among other men similarly wounded" in an environment that was "safe" and "open," they paved the way for a cure. "Such an emotional sanctuary, like an operating room protected from germs, allows the Great Surgeon to heal his son," Dalbey wrote. That healing, Dalbey added, "can't be done alone. And indeed, God has provided: For becoming a son allows a man to see himself as a brother among other, fellow sons of the Father."[36]

Martin Booker looked around the room at the men, each silent, each holding his opened copy of *Fight Like a Man* like a shield before his heart. Martin put his down and opened his Bible, turning to Romans, chapter 8. "But we ourselves, who have the first fruits of the Spirit," he read in a voice husky with emotion, "groan inwardly as we wait eagerly for our *adoption* as sons, the redemption of our bodies. For in this hope we were saved. . . . Who shall separate us from the love of Christ?" I had never seen Martin as animated as he was that night upon looking into Dalbey and reading of the Father they had all evidently lost and the Man who could replace him. "And *here's* the victory," he told the Glendora men, his voice cracking with feeling. "The only hope we have. We are 'adopted.' We will never be 'separated' from his love." As he closed the Bible, Martin smiled shyly, hopefully. "I think the whole Promise Keepers movement is about this. In a world where fathers are missing, God is intervening. When we get to really know God the Father, then we can be the men we should be. . . . I believe this year could be the best year of our lives."

———

"IT SEEMS OBVIOUS THAT NO GREAT RELIGION has concentrated more on familial symbolism than has Christianity," sociologist Robert Bellah wrote in 1960. "Above all, the father-son relation is symbolically absolutely central." And yet, he remarked, Christian society puts *less* care into the maintenance of father-son ties than any other society on earth. Conversely, father-son symbolism isn't prominent in Chinese Confucianism, "though there is no civilization that has placed greater emphasis on the father-son tie."[37] Paradox, in this case, is also an expression of human necessity; what sons need but cannot find in secular society, they must seek in other realms. But in the religion strung between heavenly father and earthly son, the paternal relationship could prove as complicated as any on earth.

"Only one word has come down to us directly from the lips of Jesus in its original Aramaic: *abba,* 'father,' " scholar and translator Stephen Mitchell wrote in *The Gospel According to Jesus.* One biographical fact stands out among the particulars of Christ's coming of age in Palestine. "The first thing we ought to realize about Jesus' life is that he grew up as an illegitimate child," Mitchell wrote. "If there is one reality that marks what we might call the emotional life of Jesus, as glimpsed through his various sayings, it is the presence of the divine father and the absence of a human father." In the gospel of Matthew, Jesus offered these instructions: "And do not call anyone on earth, 'father,' for you have one Father and he is in heaven."[38]

Forgiveness was Jesus' overriding message. But whether Jesus was instructing men to forgive their earthly fathers or flout them is less clear. His statements on the subject do not exactly add up to a ringing endorsement of filial piety. He expected his disciples to abandon their fathers without hesitation, even when they were desperately needed apprentices in their fathers' trades. Christ's entreaties to snub and even deplore one's earthly father were many: "For I have come to turn 'a man against his father' "; "The father shall be divided against the son, and the son against the father"; "If any man come to me, and hate not his father"—along with the rest of his family—"he cannot be my disciple." He instructed a man seeking permission to bury his dead father before joining his entourage, "Let the dead bury their dead." As Stephen Mitchell concluded, "His teaching about loyalty to parents is uniformly negative, and is so shocking, not only to religious sensibilities but to our ordinary sense of decency, that it is almost never mentioned in church."[39] A number of New Testament scholars have puzzled over Jesus' antagonism toward fathers and his call for the abolition of father-rule. In the society Jesus limned to his followers, religion professor Richard Horsley has written, "there would be no 'fathers' in the local community, especially no 'teachers' as representatives of the traditional established order," only brothers and sisters—and the occasional mother. Biblical studies scholar John Dominic Crossan has likewise observed that Jesus aimed to "tear the hierarchical or patriarchal family in two along the axis of domination and subordination."[40]

On the other hand, Christ's calls to abstain from judgment and revenge, no matter how grievous the domination or cruel the dominators, were legion. His teachings consistently extended the olive branch of forbearance and absolution to all human sinners, and presumably, he intended his precepts to apply to sinning fathers as well. And so, how Christian men perceived the father-son tie has depended very much on the experiences of the men hearing or reading Jesus' teachings. As with the nature of Christ himself, whether they came down on the side of forgiveness or rebelliousness toward fathers involved matters as social and economic as they were spiritual.

Christ's teachings took place in Judean society against a backdrop of roiling and radicalizing hostility toward oppressive religious and temporal authorities, and his predominantly poor followers, yearning to overturn an elite who seized their land and taxed away their future, could draw from his sermons a message of political revolt and dethronement. As Horsley and other scholars have argued, Christ seemed to be limning a world without hierarchy, where the oppression of tax collectors and priests would give way to brotherly communities. In this climate of intense anger, Christ became to some a symbol of resistance to the elders, a rebel who overturned the money changers' tables and inspired sons to desert their fathers even as they labored in the field.[41]

Jesus could, however, also be seen as the model of the good son—the forgiver instead of the flouter, more a projection of the father than a challenge to him. By the end of the fourth century, with the conversion of the Roman Emperor Constantine, Christianity was transformed into an establishment religion directed by the powerful and harnessed to the task of reconciling peasants to the domination of their masters. The official Christian dogma formalized as the Nicene Creed dispensed with an earlier popular belief that Jesus was a human who redeemed mankind through his suffering and so ascended to divinity; now he was decreed to have *descended* from God the Father, of whom he was "of the same essence." He wasn't the rebel black sheep leading an uprising, but a beloved emissary, indistinguishable from his Father. Put in the speculative but nonetheless intriguing psychoanalytic terms of Erich Fromm in *The Dogma of Christ:* "The masses no longer identified with the crucified man in order to dethrone the father in fantasy, but, rather, in order to enjoy his love and grace. The idea that a man became a god was a symbol of aggressive, active, hostile-to-the-father tendencies. The idea that God became a man was transformed into a symbol of the tender, passive tie to the father." Such imagery was, needless to say, also useful to the enforcement of imperial authority under a Christian emperor.[42]

The question of whether Christ counseled sons to struggle against or submit to fathers was not settled in the fourth century. In our own country, we can trace part of its subsequent history, as Calvinists' vision of themselves struggling as "sinners in the hands of an angry God," a harsh elder, unbending and inattentive to their needs, who "does *not* treat man as a father treats his son," gave way to a Victorian depiction of Jesus nurturing his childlike flock while a benign bearded elder beamed down from above.[43] While certainly not the portrait painted from every Protestant pulpit (any more than every Calvinist believed in an unremittingly harsh God), the doting vision of God was one expressed by leading ministers of the day, who described him as the "Indulgent Parent" and "tender father." To become one of his believers, as a Victorian minister put it (using a phrase that Martin Booker invoked to praise Promise Keepers), was to "go home," where you could at last and forever be the cared-for child.[44]

Many Victorian clergymen tailored this often highly sentimentalized message to women, their prime constituents. In their efforts to appeal to women, some moved so far from men's concerns as to fashion a religion focused less on a father-son bond than on a father-*daughter* tie. The preachers were supported in this effort, as Ann Douglas has written, by a raft of popular women's novels which cast passive girlish piety as beatific femininity—most memorably at the start of the Victorian age in Harriet Beecher Stowe's *Uncle Tom's Cabin,* with Little Eva as the virtuous, supine, and expiring daughter.[45] In our own century, especially since World War II, a growing yearning for a renewed emphasis on a father-son tie in Christianity has manifested itself, one that would essentially replicate the paternal tie the Victorian woman had with God. As private and public fathers came to seem increasingly absent, sons longed to attract their attention. Neo-evangelical movements that promised an intimate and fatherly "relationship" with God began to draw large numbers of men in cold-war America—movements like the Navigators (aimed at helping young, returning World War II veterans "adjust" to the dislocations of postwar life), Billy Graham's Youth for Christ, and Bill Bright's Campus Crusade for Christ.[46]

Membership in the nation's mainstream churches began to shrink in the 1960s, the first sustained decline recorded in American history, but the deserters weren't necessarily rejecting the bonds of organized religion; rather, many of them wanted these bonds to be tauter and more personalized, as they were in the evangelical and Pentecostal denominations, where worshippers' numbers were climbing sharply. By 1976, with one quarter to one third of Americans polled saying they were born-again Christians, the Gallup poll proclaimed "the year of the evangelical."[47] In these new religious movements, organizational bonds were typically experienced in emotional and familial terms. "The moment you receive Christ . . . you have been born into His family as a baby," Billy Graham wrote in his 1965 best-seller *World Aflame,* invoking a much-used metaphor. "The most satisfactory way to understand Campus Crusade for Christ is to see it not merely as a movement but rather as an extended *family*," Crusade chronicler Richard Quebedeaux wrote in 1979. For each new convert, the Crusader who brought him into the group "becomes a spiritual 'parent.' "[48] Such movements did not so much challenge institutional authority as respond to its felt absence with the promise of a "relationship" with a personalized authority figure.

The "personal evangelism" programs that these Christian organizations promulgated offered the hope that if their members were as emotional and obediently filial in their worship as the Victorian Little Evas, they would draw the Father's adoring gaze. He would look at them personally: he would seek them out for a relationship that was invariably described in sentimental terms, a cozy and even sugar-spun intimacy of the sort most commonly displayed on the morning talk-show sets of the burgeoning televangelism industry. As a former candy and "fancy food" salesman and proprietor of Bright's California Confections, Bill Bright certainly knew something about corn syrup.[49] He also knew something about the emotional hungers of postwar young men. All other religions were illegitimate, he stressed to his audiences, because they were based on "man's best effort to find God." Christianity, Bright emphasized, was the one way *because* it was all about "God's search for man," his search to restore the sons' legitimacy. The Father had come looking for his sons on earth in the guise of Jesus. (Graham took a similar position: "The most dramatic quest of the centuries is God's loving and patient pursuit of man," Graham wrote, a pursuit he likened to "a compassionate St. Bernard pursuing an imperiled child in the mountains of Switzerland.") And God was looking for a one-to-one involvement. As Bright was fond of telling potential converts, "I am not here to talk to you about religion, but about a personal relationship with God."[50] The predominant trait of the new postwar evangelism was its promise of up-close-and-personal contact with the Lord, a relationship of unwavering affection in which you and all your concerns were his concern, no matter how small, personal, or material. It was a religion in which God actually cared about your time-share.

Yet to say that the millions of postwar men who responded to this message with such intensity were just narcissists fixated on their bad real-estate investments was to explain nothing. If they were looking for fatherly care and guidance from the heavens, then they had good reasons: after all, what aspect of the secular male world could they still trust? The problem of the "absent father" wasn't just about being raised in a home where Dad was missing in action; it was about living in a time when much of the social and economic architecture that the public fathers had been expected to bestow upon their sons seemed to be crumbling, and the rest transforming before their eyes into something unrecognizable. The Bible claimed that "my Father's house has many mansions"; now, it only seemed to have time-shares with strangers. The men who came to Promise Keepers had followed the rules, kept their promises. It was the "fathers" who had broken theirs—the aerospace corporate manager who told them they had to be "processed out" by noon after a decade's loyal service, the machine-shop boss who dumped them on the graveyard shift because he only cared about what was "best for the company," the football coach who screamed at them till his face turned purple no matter how hard they tried to meet his impossible demands . . . and, before them all, the first father, the father who brought them into this world but never armed them to fight in it.

And so the men of Promise Keepers were faced with a question that had confronted so many generations of men before them, a question that would be presented to them in the public arenas of the football stadiums, and that they would try to answer in the "emotional sanctuary" of the small group: whether to seek in Christianity an opportunity to absolve their fathers or to protest the ways in which their fathers had betrayed them.

———

"NOW, THIS PARALYTIC MAN IS KIND OF A SYMBOL of so many of us here this evening that have been paralyzed by sin," Pastor Raul Ries's voice boomed from the speakers at Oakland Coliseum, as the first day of the rally drew to a close. Ries was speaking of the paralyzed young man in the gospel of Mark, who was lowered through a roof on a pallet to be healed by Jesus. The point Ries said he was trying to make was that "sin paralyzes." But the prostrate young man had another, greater symbolic relevance in Ries's speech. "I was paralyzed for almost twenty-four years of my life," he said, "as I had grown up in a home of violence." By violence, he made it clear, he was referring to only one member of his home: "my father, an alcoholic, an abuser, a physical and verbal abuser." As he described the grim figure of his father—who prowled the bars every night looking for a fight, often with his young son in tow; who connected with his son only with the force of his fists; and whose towering rage was his only legacy—the stadium fell silent. The two men on either side of me listened so intently that each appeared to be holding his breath. For many years, Ries told them, his childhood misery gave him a purpose in life as an adult man. "As I began to grow up and as he began to physically abuse me, punch me, my goal was, when I was eighteen years old, to go ahead and *kill my father*." Instead, he said, he joined the marines and went to Vietnam, where his "scapegoat" was the Vietcong and his "release of rage" so maniacal—he even threatened to kill a marine psychiatrist—that he wound up in a lockup VA ward for the insane.

Later, the proxy for his father would become his wife; Ries said he beat her. Finally, his wife packed her bags and announced that she was moving out. "I remember that evening when my wife went to church and I came home and I saw the bags packed, I went through the house and ramshackled the whole house. . . . I took my rifle and I loaded my rifle with rounds and I waited for my wife to come home." It was only, he said, the sight of a preacher testifying on the television set in his living room that stopped him and drove him to his knees. The preacher's words conveyed to Ries a single hope: that maybe there was actually a father who loved him. "Listen, people," he said, his voice choked and rising. "*Men, listen!* This is the most important thing." He was referring to what Jesus said to the paralytic man. "He said this: 'Son, your sins are forgiven you.'"

Not the prodigal son but the prodigal *father* was the theme of many Promise Keepers' speeches, and forgiveness, however difficult, their solution. None I heard offered as stark a vision of that prodigal father as a pastor who addressed the 1994 rally in Anaheim Stadium. "My father gave us away," he said of himself and his siblings. He would see his father only once, when he was four years old. "He held me in my arms and called me 'my baby.' It was the first time in my life I was held and embraced by a *man*. . . . I just knew I had to be with him and embraced by him." For the next twenty-three years of his life, "I went looking for that love." When he became a born-again Christian, he said, "I felt that night like the night my father embraced me. . . . And that morning, I gave my love to Jesus Christ."

If the men in the audience responded intensely to these stories, it wasn't because most of them had fathers who beat them to a pulp or deserted them in infancy. But such stories, in their extremity, distilled an aching sense that plagued many of them: that, in some inchoate but devastating way, their fathers had indeed abandoned them. The 1994 survey of men attending Promise Keepers events asked, "Did you feel that [your] father was largely absent while you were growing up?" A full half said yes.[51] They, too, were disappointed with and embittered toward their fathers, as disappointed as the Prodigal Son's brother, the good son in the parable who had done everything his father had told him to do, yet was left on the sidelines while his father celebrated the return of the self-absorbed boy, the son who had been of no utility to the father's work or land, but got attention seemingly just for pulling a stunt. It was a dynamic that seemed familiar to many Promise Keepers, who had dutifully abided in their public fathers' corporate houses, only to find that their elders' culture had elevated the other son to wealth and fame—the bad boy celebrated only because, like the Prodigal, he has made a dramatic appearance.

At one point during the rally in Boulder's Folsom Stadium, the men in the stands were instructed to break up into groups and talk about their "male mentors." In the group I joined, not a single man could think of one. At the noon break, I went up to the stadium's executive dining room to have lunch with Holly Phillips, the wife of the president of Promise Keepers, whose speech about wives "emasculating" men had inspired a standing ovation. When I told her about my group's difficulty coming up with a man who had mentored them, she wasn't surprised. "This is a movement born out of men who didn't have dads," she said. "This is a time of fatherlessness. And when you are fatherless, who is helping you?"

Holly Phillips had been speaking generally, but, as I learned when I spent a morning with Randy Phillips some months later, she could also have been speaking of her husband's experience. The president of Promise Keepers had the gentle and washed-out vagueness of a Jesus movement adherent, which he was back in the early seventies, when he floated through Hawaii and for a time served as the pastor of a small, straggly evangelical ministry. McCartney hired him, however, not for his religious résumé—the Jesus People's lifestyle was far too flaky for the average Campus Crusader's tastes—but for his skills as a special-events promoter. Phillips had successfully organized several huge events, including the second-largest concert ever held in Hawaii. He had a "knack" and an appetite for organization—"It energized me"—as if it were an antidote to the tumbleweed existence of his drifty youth. When I asked Phillips to tell me about his background, the first thing he said was, "I come from a broken home. My dad abandoned us when I was about six years old." He grasped the arms of his chair as he said it, as if the room might tip and knock him off his perch. "It was a painful time. I haven't seen my dad since I was seven and a half, eight years old." The painful time continued into adulthood. "Within Randy Phillips," he said of himself, "there was a void. God created us to understand and to experience the love of a mother *and* a father. And if it's missing or if it's expressed inappropriately, it certainly creates some voids."

In the next-to-last round of men drafted during the Vietnam War, Randy Phillips spent the summer of 1972 on a base in Fort Ord, California, where he got involved with a Bible-study group led by the evangelical Navigators and became a born-again Christian. "It was there that I heard for the first time the understanding of *why* Jesus died on the cross," he told me. His blurry-soft voice became crisp and pointed in a way I hadn't previously heard. "And it was there that I had the realization that Jesus *personally* died for my sins. And that what that meant was he wanted a *personal* relationship with me. . . . That's what Jesus promises us, a *relationship*."

When I sat and talked with the men in the Glendora group individually about their lives, a broken relationship with a father almost always surfaced as the primary preoccupation underlying all others. Yet, at the same time that each man built an impressive case against his father, he was, I found, as determined to knock it down, to disbelieve his own evidence.

One afternoon, I was visiting Timothy and Nancy Atwater. The house felt less claustrophobic without the group. The blinds were pulled up to admit the sun, and the grandchildren, confined to the bedrooms during Promise Keepers meetings, raced in and out, giddy with play. The table was set for lunch.

"I never had a close relationship with my father," Timothy told me after we had finished saying grace and passed around big platters of cold cuts. "He was a workaholic."

Nancy said, "Timmy's dad taught him how to work hard. But he didn't teach him how to take care of his family in other ways."

As we talked, every conversational by-road seemed to lead back to the main artery of Timothy's misery, his stunted relationship with his father: his father's inexplicable rages, his father's physical threats, his father's kicking him in the back, his father's abuse of his mother, his father's disappearing for days at a time, his father's sending him to live with a blind aunt, a cousin, the grandparents. "I have two vague memories from childhood," Timothy told me. In the first, he and his mother were fleeing his father's violence. "My mom and I got into my dad's paneled paint truck and locked the doors. He was beating on the windows. And my mom started driving, and he jumped on the running board and just kept pounding on the windows, screaming. I can still see his face." The neighbors called the police. "I remember he said to one of the cops, 'Well, I hit my wife, but I don't slap her. I just push her around.'" The other memory is murkier; Timothy was much younger. It was night. Something had frightened him earlier in the evening, and he had trundled down the hall and crawled into his parents' bed. He awoke sometime later, knocked from sleep by a sharp blow. "He was hitting my mother so hard, he was hitting me."

Timothy took a bite of sandwich and concluded, "But it was a pretty good childhood."

Nancy said dubiously, "Look how it's affected you." She turned to me. "It's made him an introvert."

"I had it rough, but I don't remember him beating me senseless. I never had to go to the hospital. He meant well."

"Other than coaching you in baseball," Nancy said, annoyance rising in her voice, "what else did he do?"

Timothy laughed hoarsely. "Yeah, well, when I was in Little League, he actually only came to one game. Then he got obsessed with setting up his own team and that was that. You know, when I was in Cub Scouts, they had a 'father-son dinner,' and some other man had to take me." Timothy caught himself. "But that's just rough spots. Some guys, their fathers just abandoned them, spit in their faces. You ask any six guys in the group about their fathers, at least five of 'em didn't have that relationship with their father. My father was a good man. I don't blame him. He's just a product of the times: the dads get up and go.

"Toward the end of my father's life, we got to see him more," Timothy said. When he and Nancy bought this house, they ran into financial difficulties and Timothy's father agreed to invest in the property, in exchange for taking over the living quarters downstairs. His father was battling cancer. Soon, though, his father claimed that Timothy's kids had stolen his painkillers and he moved out in a fury. "I had to pay back the money he invested in the house. It took quite a few years. But it wasn't ugly."

"Yes, it was!" Frustration darted from Nancy's eyes. "It was very ugly."

"Well, not all of it," Timothy finished lamely. "Before he moved out, I had some fond memories of the two of us playing cards."

Nancy bunched up her napkin and dropped it with a resigned gesture onto her plate. She rose to clear the table, her thoughts sealed away behind pressed lips.

Such conflicting perspectives on the men's fathers often divided the Glendora couples. In the Paysons' household, Libby had come to the conclusion that underlying much of what troubled their marriage was Howard's refusal to face facts about his father.

"I had a lot of resentment because I felt like what my father did was abandonment," Howard said one afternoon as the couple sat talking in their living room. "My father left when I was five. He remarried and had another family. Every Christmas, I'd hope. But he didn't even send a card."

"Howard always wanted approval from men because he didn't have his dad," Libby put in. "I threw his dad up to him more times than I can remember. It was a real bar to our marriage."

"He deprived me of so much," Howard said. "I had a real hatred for my father. It was like a cancer growing inside. It was very hard to forgive him. But I did."

"I always say to him," Libby said of Howard, " 'Did you *really* forgive him?' Because there are still things with Howard that seem so, so"—she hunted around for a word—"Unresolved."

"I forgave him," Howard said resolutely. "But I had to do it on my knees and cry out to the Lord. I had to ask the Lord to take it."

Mike Pettigrew's father, an infantry sergeant and heavy drinker, would "clobber you if you missed a spot washing the car." When Mike was sixteen, his father threw him out of the house for good. Mike's crime was that he had stayed out all night at a party; he hadn't meant to, he said, he had just underestimated his tolerance for liquor and passed out on a friend's couch. "He literally drove me out with a pitchfork," Mike recalled one evening as we talked in the Pettigrews' kitchen, standing by the percolator, waiting for the coffee to brew. "He came in my room with this pitchfork and he said, 'You are moving out. Pack. I'm giving you twenty minutes.' " Mike picked up a kitchen fork and stabbed the air in demonstration. Eventually, his mother found him a motel room in Glendora and a job as a dishwasher in the restaurant where she worked.

A few years passed in this fashion, Mike said. One day, he got a call from his sister, who was sobbing and "near hysterical"; their father had become enraged when she had questioned him on some trivial point and he was now tearing her bedroom from pillar to post. Mike ran over. He yelled at his father to stop, to no avail. Then Mike made the mistake of turning his back and his father lunged for him. The two men struggled across the room and down the hallway, until Mike got in a punch so hard that his father collapsed on the floor. "I remember screaming in my head, 'Stand up, stand up, you fucking fuck! Just stand up!'" His father shouted to his mother to call the police, which she did. The police escorted Mike from the home. "From then on, with my dad and I, it was like the cold war. If I went over to the house, he'd go into the garage and he wouldn't acknowledge I was alive."

But that's all in the past, Mike assured me, suddenly calm. Hospitably he handed me a mug and poured some coffee. "I got the idea to make peace with him at all costs. He loved German wine, so I got this expensive bottle and brought it over to him on Father's Day. He went into the garage and he wouldn't look at me at first. But finally, I got him to shake my hand and then we went to the bar and got skunked together."

His story felt like a Greek tragedy that had just been run through a blender and come out a tearjerker with a tacked-on happy ending: Oedipus 'n' Dad traipse toward the horizon arm-in-arm as drunken pals. Mike, in fact, was determined to see it that way. How else was a son to create a bond with a father he knew so little? He had once been visited by a ghost of that estrangement. "When I was twenty or twenty-one," Mike recalled, "I got a call from my mom and she said, 'Come on over. There's someone here who wants to meet you.'" When Mike arrived, a clean-cut man several years his senior was sitting in the living room. His mother introduced them, as brothers. Unbeknownst to Mike, his father had been married before and this was his first son, whom he had abandoned as a baby. The boy had gone on to the military, but had now come around "to seek his father," as Mike put it. The older half-kin stayed for a couple of weeks. "The sad part was what happened after. He left to hitchhike up the coast. A week later, they found him stabbed and floating in the San Francisco Bay." Mike paused to take a stiff slug of coffee. "They never figured out who did it. There were no clues." He studied the percolator's blank surface, then he said, wonderingly, "It was only the GI dog tags that identified him." It was clear to me that Mike saw the newcomer, in his abandonment, anonymity, and mortality, not so much as a brother but as a double, as himself. The two men's introduction could not help but seal that impression. "Mike," his mother had said, "this is Mike Pettigrew. Mike, this is Mike Pettigrew."

Margaret Pettigrew joined us in the kitchen. Mike snapped out of his reverie and gestured toward a set of tools on the kitchen counter. "Those are my father's," he said cheerily. "He loaned them to me. He's mellowed a lot now. He's a lot kinder."

Margaret placed her hands on her hips. "Maybe, but I think a lot of that has to do with the fact that he's physically *weaker* now."

Mike brushed the remark aside. "Last weekend, my dad and I spent Saturday messing around a flea market. It's assumed that we both forgave each other." Each other? I wondered what Mike had to apologize for? Mike didn't know exactly; it wasn't something he did to his father as much as something he felt toward him—or rather, didn't and couldn't feel. "All I know is, I had to have that forgiveness. It made me more comfortable about loving him." I was reminded of the preacher Raul Ries's words to the crowd in Oakland. "This is the most important thing. He said this: 'Son, your sins are forgiven you.' " But what was their transgression?

It took a lot of sitting and listening in Timothy Atwater's living room before I began to see what these men felt their "sin" to be, what lay at the heart of their anguished repentance at the stadium events, what loomed behind their conviction that, as Mike Pettigrew had maintained, *he* should be asking his father for forgiveness. I had assumed that their grief was about having sinned in all the expected ways: letting down their families, feeling like failures at work, neglecting their children, ignoring or abusing their wives. On one level, those were their sins and they did grieve them. But their deeper agony was over a sin that for them seemed almost unspeakable: a failure of faith. They were the sons who had believed in the rightness of following the fathers; and when their loyalty was betrayed, they found that their faith, too, was sorely tested.

Here then was the crisis, the sin: they had failed Job's trial of loyalty; they had doubted and, sometimes secretly, continued to doubt the "fathers," on earth and even in heaven. The promise they didn't keep was the promise to believe that fathers, even those who didn't or couldn't keep their promises, were still fathers worth believing in; were, in fact, still fathers at all. Their "disobedience" evidently lay in questioning the legitimacy of that lifelong vow of obedience. In giving bitter voice to their sense of betrayal, they were left with a nagging, unnerving feeling of guilt and shame. "I don't know if I can always trust God one hundred percent," Timothy Atwater said, wincing at his own traitorous words, "because sometimes it doesn't seem he's there when I need him. It's like if you walk on a bridge the first time and it breaks, and then they build a concrete bridge and tell you to go ahead and cross it, well, you're going to be reluctant to go." Or as Craig Hastings, a younger group member who didn't mince words, put it: "We assume God hates us." The men sought "identity in Christ," but there was one aspect of Jesus' life from which they recoiled, it being closest to their own. Here, their sin was his. It was Christ's heartrendingly human cry to his Father from the cross. "*Elo'i, Elo'i, la'ma sabach'thani?* My God, my God, why hast thou forsaken me?"[52]

The men of Promise Keepers had been faced with a choice: to flout their fathers or to forgive them. They had chosen, in the end, to try to suppress their doubts. They had chosen forgiveness. But what kind of forgiveness would that be? The choice to forgive contains other choices. On the one hand, there is informed forgiveness, which comes from facing hard truths and making your peace with them. On the other hand, there is the balm of nepenthe, the desire not to pardon the past but to forget it ever happened. Gordon Dalbey's book advised the men of Glendora that through faith in Christ they could begin to see their earthly fathers more "realistically." But that wasn't the part of his message the men fastened on.

"If I give up everything about my father to God," Jeremy Foote said, "that sets me free. You know, I never thought of it before, but that's what 'freedom in Christ' means. I can leave it up to God the Father to free me from hating *my* father and wanting to punish him." Jeremy was suggesting that he wouldn't have to reckon with his own feelings of hatred and retribution; that, too, would become God's job. "It becomes almost like it never happened," he said. Except, of course, that it had.

"I went up till forty years old hating my biological father, who I never knew," Dan Rhodes told the group one evening. "I'd find myself driving down the highway, cussing him out. I gave it up to God at forty and I'm free from it now." What "freed" him? I asked. "Well, maybe I should tell the whole story. All I had was a name on a birth certificate. All I knew about him was he was a private in World War II. I have this friend in the LAPD's missing-persons unit and I gave the name to him. He found him in less than a week." He paused. "In San Dimas [a neighboring town]. So I went to visit him. I knocked on the door. And he came to the door. And I told him, 'I'm your son.' He told me that I was conceived after he left for the war. So he was not my real father. . . . But he told me he wished he was because he'd always wanted to have a son."

The visit "resolved" the situation, Dan said. At least he "knew." Yet nothing had been resolved and nothing was known for sure, as Dan's subsequent remarks suggested. "Today, I was sitting out at this little lunch place, and the *Maury Povich* show was on the TV. It was a show about reuniting fathers and sons. It was all I could do to hold back my—" He struggled to compose himself. "Finally, I had to reach over and change the channel."

In the room, nobody said a word.

"It's like there's something missing," Dan continued. "At Father's Day, I still wonder, Did he care about me?" He paused. "I guess I'm not entirely free of it."

Sitting in that living room in Glendora, listening to the men as they struggled to scourge memory and supplant it with a "loving daddy," I was reminded of another man's anguish, on another evening in another room—the Alternatives to Violence counseling office. Not surprisingly, the men who belonged to the domestic-violence group almost all had hair-raising stories to tell about violent fathers and stepfathers. But none was so impossible to forget, so visceral in its retelling, as Daniel's. His father had disappeared when he was one, and his stepfather had raised—or rather battered—him into maturity. "He beat me up all the time," Daniel said tensely. "Seven years of beatings, and I mean beatings. He hit me in the face and stomach with extension cords, heels, boots, coat hangers." Finally, Daniel "escaped to the army." When he was nineteen, Daniel was summoned home. His mother was dead. His stepfather had shot her with a rifle from two feet away. "He threatened me a lot, that if I ever testified against him in court, I wouldn't live to see another day," Daniel said. He didn't testify. "I was scared to hell with him" was how he put it. His stepfather got eight years; he was out in two and a half. Daniel's failure to testify, whether it would have made much difference in time served or not, was a burden he carried, a personal hell he had been scared into, and at age thirty-three, he was still living in it. "He's on the streets right now," Daniel told the group. "He's roaming about right now. All that's stopped me from killing him is my wife and family." But even if he did fear that he might try to kill his stepfather, he didn't know where his tormentor was. His greater terror was that his stepfather was coming after *him*. "I could go down that stairwell," Daniel said, pointing to the door, "and he could be right there. Boom!" He made the gesture of a gun firing at him. "I have nightmares all the time. I can't hide from him. I could go twelve years, hearing nothing, and then, 'Boom! Happy Birthday!' I need this man off the face of the earth."

That night and many subsequent ones, I would come down the outdoor stairs after an Alternatives to Violence meeting, the artificial streams gurgling pleasantly by the flowering shrubs and pebbled walkway, and I'd imagine I saw the stepfather's shadow there in the hedges, waiting for Daniel. And I'd wonder: If I couldn't forget him—and to me he was only a story—how could his stepson?

That evening in Glendora after Dan Rhodes told his story, Martin Booker led off the closing prayer session. We lowered our heads. "Thank you, Father," he began, "for accepting us into your family as your sons. You are a loving father. You provide for us. You give us what we need."

Jeremy Foote's turn was next. For once he didn't bring up the time-share. "Father, help us," he said. "There are so many things to be afraid of."

———

IF THE PROMISE KEEPERS MEETINGS were to be of any help to these men so in need of support, then it would seem that the key to sustenance lay in the group's potential to foster brotherhood. Jack Schat, who had moved from the Alternatives to Violence counseling sessions to a Promise Keepers group, said to me once: "There's always a barrier between men. The only things you're supposed to do together as guys is work and sports. But Promise Keepers tells us it's okay to share your heart. Because the other men in the group are your brothers. Because we all have the same father now—God. We are all brothers."

In the Glendora group, Jeremy Foote said to the other men one week: "I think God loves us through our brothers. In a sense it makes up for the love we didn't get from our fathers." His example of the bond of brotherhood, though, seemed woven with painfully thin thread. "In '95, I went to the L.A. Promise Keepers conference," he recalled to the group, "and standing next to me was this stranger. He said to me, 'Isn't it right to praise the Lord?' And I wanted to hug him. I felt so warm toward him. I felt so *related* to him. That's the only thing he said to me. But it was just what I was thinking. I need the *brothers* to do that for me."

And did they do that for one another? When I next saw Jack, he had quit one Promise Keepers group and joined another. "The first meeting of the first group, it was all 'How are you?' 'Oh, fine.' 'How's your family?' 'Oh, fine.' 'Oh, I'm fine, fine.' 'Oh, yes, my children are a blessing.' 'Oh yes? Oh, I'm so glad.'" Jack laughed, groaning. "It was like people locked in an elevator and they are all very politely trying to back off from each other. But I thought, Okay, we can make it work. We'll become close-knit. This guy sitting next to me, he'll be calling me at two-thirty in the morning for my help. We'll build a nucleus of brotherhood. We'll be brothers for life." Jack stopped, shook his head. "Well, we never got past 'How do you like your coffee?' Six weeks later, it was still 'How are you?' 'Oh, fine.'" The group began to shrink. Some men would vanish for weeks. "There was always someone missing," Jack recalled. "And a lot of the guys thought we should turn the whole thing into a Sunday school class and just have a few moments to 'share' at the end. I'm not going to share my life with someone for twelve minutes!"

Jack's new group seemed no better. "It's been two and a half months, and it's just gotten to the point where we exchange phone numbers. I want to get to the point where I can pick up the phone and say, I'm worried about my finances, or my relationship, or whatever—the way, quite literally, I'd talk if I had a brother."

The Glendora group was showing signs of the same "How-are-you? Oh-fine" syndrome. As summer began, the group gathered for a backyard swim party. The men brought their wives, who immediately pulled the webbed lawn chairs close, chitchatting away as if this were their group. The men mostly hovered over their wives' chairs or sat quietly at their sides. By the far end of the pool, the youngest of them, Craig Hastings, kept an eye on his splashing toddler son and cast a dubious look at the men across the chlorine-blue water. "This group is too *tame*," he told me. "I want guys who will put the gloves on and get to me. Who will say, 'That's B.S.! Be honest!' Because that's how you become a man, isn't it? Being *honest*?"

Craig would return to this theme on another afternoon, when the two of us were sitting alone talking. "I don't want to blast on Promise Keepers. It's not the institution that's the problem, it's getting that connectedness. And this group, the connectedness is pretty superficial. I kind of ticked Martin off because I'm a brash guy. But he can say some pretty namby-pamby stuff. And it's hard, when we're talking such fluffy stuff, to say 'Quit bullshitting!' Especially because as a Christian, you're not supposed to swear."

He picked up a pen on the table. "This is what I want out of Promise Keepers." He drew what he explained was an artichoke. To each successive layer of leaves, he assigned a label: SUPERFICIAL. CLOSE FRIEND. INTIMATES. In the center, he wrote, HEART. He pointed to the outer layer. "In the group, we are always hanging out here. I have a few guys I know through church and when the women are out, we might rent Clint Eastwood's *The Good, the Bad, and the Ugly* and eat popcorn. We're 'close friends,' but not 'intimates.'" He studied his drawing. "It's like a water-reclamation project. And we have to decide to open up the trapdoor. Because in the heart, that's where trust is established. And we're scared. Even getting to being 'close friends' is scary." If only they could learn to be truly brothers, he said, then maybe they could find the Father. "One thing I wish I could get is a *real* relationship with God. After twelve years [as a born-again Christian] I still don't have that and it hurts. Sometimes I want to grab someone by the shirt collar and say, 'Damn it, why can't I connect? What am I missing? Where am I in the Kingdom?'"

This sense of a lack of progress toward the "heart" was a prime reason why Promise Keepers' appeal began to sag nationally by decade's end. As Bill McCartney's centerpiece message shifted its focus from familial responsibility to racial harmony and then to interfaith unity, Promise Keepers drifted further and further away from the beacon that had attracted these particular men in the first place. As laudable as calls to end denominational strife or racial prejudice might have been, they weren't the reason the men came. (And they had only marginal success in attracting minority men, despite an intense publicity campaign and "scholarship" offers.) The men had seen the glimmerings of an institution where, if they showed their fealty to the Father, the "fathers" might actually keep their promises, too. Hadn't the coach, the emblem of postwar paternity, given up his job to care for them? Didn't all these religious male elders onstage say they were committed to elevating them into masculine maturity? Hadn't the Promise Keepers leadership told them, over and over, that they would be rewarded, that no matter who had betrayed them, they could still find freedom and purpose as men?

And yet, by the close of the nineties, the coach would seemingly replicate inside Promise Keepers the very betrayal that so many of its members had experienced in their everyday lives: in 1998, McCartney laid off his entire paid staff, citing the organization's money problems, financial woes partly of his own making.[53] Bent on drawing ever larger numbers to the stadium events (and ever more expansive media coverage), he had decided to stop charging admission—the equivalent of a magazine publisher offering free subscriptions to artificially inflate circulation figures and bring in more advertisers. Like the top brass who laid off the aerospace engineers at McDonnell Douglas and the team owners who jilted loyal fans, McCartney was a "father" who would not share in the sacrifices of "his" sons: the layoff didn't affect him. He didn't rely on Promise Keepers for his wages, though he did get a $4,000 speaking fee from the organization for every stadium appearance—adding up to $61,833 in 1995 and 1996 combined—plus, the organization paid his health benefits and expenses. McCartney was still enjoying the bounty of his Colorado coaching deal: his fifteen-year contract for $350,000 a year had an escape clause that went into effect after his fifth year (which, it so happened, was when he decided to retire), guaranteeing him about $150,000 a year for the remaining ten years. This golden parachute was supplemented by the ex-coach's book royalties, lucrative speaking fees, and "motivational consulting" deals struck with corporations like Big Sur Water Beds.[54] He had marketed his name, his coachhood, and himself, and so managed to swim quite happily in the consumer economy's deeper waters; it was his followers who were left floundering.

———

JEREMY FOOTE AND I SAT IN DENNY's in Glendora one afternoon in May. He was in a state of suppressed agony. Glenda was once again trying to push him out of the house. They had been in marriage counseling, but she had canceled the last few appointments. She didn't see the point; she didn't want to be married. Martin and Zel kept telling Jeremy not to leave. "They say it's not the right thing to do." Sometimes, he wondered why he was listening to Zel, who hadn't been at a meeting in months, and he wasn't sure about Martin's counsel, either. Anxious lest his words to me be construed as rebellious criticism, Jeremy was quick to add, "But Promise Keepers is a good thing. What's great about it is it introduced this new idea that you can share painful feelings with other men. I never had that before."

And so, his next words came as a shock—because what he said was so clearly painful to him and because he had not shared it with the group. "My father died last month," he said, his voice cratered out, as if he had just received the news. I remembered an earlier conversation with Jeremy, where his description of his father had struck me. "My father would withhold emotion, then explode," he had said then. "He was an *exploding personality*."

For two years, Jeremy hadn't seen his father, who had been on a respirator for the last several months of his life. "I tried to talk to him on the phone," Jeremy said, "but he couldn't speak because of the tube." At the funeral, Jeremy recalled, he stood at the podium and talked about "how my father came to see me at athletic practice and once he went to Denver for a play I was in, though I didn't know it at the time because he didn't tell me." As he described his speech to me, Jeremy's voice wobbled. "I'm glad I spoke. It was an opportunity for me to honor my father."

After the funeral, Jeremy's sister took him aside. She urged him to move out of the house, to ignore the advice of the Promise Keepers men and give Glenda the separation she wanted. He conceded his sister might have a point. "I'm not always sure the group's advice is right. We have a lot of growth to do. A lot of the guys in the group have not even made an impression on me. They don't really say anything." We got the bill and walked out into the sun-struck parking lot. "Promise Keepers is similar to AA in that there's got to be a goal," Jeremy said, still ruminating on the group's failure to "grow" into a brotherhood he could count on. "The men are there for a purpose. You have to have a purpose or men won't come." He stood by his car, fingering the car keys, trying to unlock his thoughts. "Maybe that's what wrong with our group. We've lost our purpose."

The following week, the Glendora group assembled as usual in the Atwaters' home. Frank Camilla, whose daughter-in-law was facing trial for the murder of his son, was back after more than a month's absence, and he started to fill the group in on the latest developments. He was upset. The assistant DA had palmed the case off on an unprepared prosecutor at the last minute. Midsentence, Martin Booker interrupted. "There must be other things doing besides in court." Then one of the men began to talk about a motor-home trip he was planning and the conversation turned to vacation spots.

Martin introduced the evening's lesson from Gordon Dalbey. "What would you do if a fellow in Promise Keepers had porn magazines in his car?" Dalbey had raised this question in Christian men's groups, Martin said, and no one had suggested that the group itself could help. "It shows how difficult it is for men to stand together in our brokenness," Martin said. "The challenge for us is to shape this group into a group that can be honest, and see it as a challenge to reach out to each other and say, 'This is a family member. We're connected.' "

In his seat, Jeremy Foote was squirming. "What if I have a problem with the group? When do I raise the question?"

Craig, the group's younger upstart, prodded. "You should say it."

Jeremy took a breath, then moved the subject back to Frank Camilla. "Okay. When Frank was gone four weeks, no one said, 'How's he doing?' How can we say we care when no one cares? Does anyone care?"

Bart listened with growing exasperation. "But wait a second, Jeremy. If you are so concerned, why didn't you call Frank?"

"I don't have his phone number."

"We gave out a master list," Martin interjected. "To say because we haven't called someone after two weeks we don't care, that is going too far."

"No, I said *do* we care?"

"Jeremy, do you remember how this group was founded?" Martin responded testily. "A lot of people bailed out, but we kept it limping along for a long time."

"I would've called if I had the number," Jeremy said.

The object of all this strife, Frank Camilla, finally spoke up. "It's in the phone book."

The room got quiet. Then Martin said, a bit tentatively: "Frank? We love you."

Frank held up his hands, a no-sweat, please-no-more gesture. "I appreciate it," he mumbled.

"We love you, Frank," a couple of other men dutifully chimed in.

"Even though," Craig couldn't resist adding, "we never call you!"

Everyone laughed, which released the tension from the room. It didn't, however, solve the problem. The following week, the group was already back to its strained politeness. Frank Camilla kept his remarks about the pending court case to a minimum. Jeremy Foote didn't show at all.

A month later, I met Craig for lunch in Pasadena. He wasn't sure whether he would continue attending the meetings. In the quest he had mapped out to me like the layers of an artichoke, the group didn't seem to be leading him any closer to the "heart." "I mean, look at Jesus," he said in a voice full of defeat. "He picked out twelve guys, but you never read about Bartholomew or a lot of the others. Half of those guys are just 'close friends.' Jesus had three buddies, Peter, James, and John, who were 'intimates.' But if he wanted the 'heart,' what did he do?" Craig paused, waiting for my response. When I had none, he answered the question himself. "He left all of them behind, and he talked to God by the tree alone."

EVIL EMPIRES

South Michigan Regional Militia Wolverines, training exercise, 1994.

6

GONE TO SOLDIERS, EVERY ONE

The Vietnam War That No One Dodged

ONE MOMENTOUS ACT IN THE GENERATIONAL DRAMA that followed World War II would cleave, seemingly forever, the prodigal from the good son. A great procession of young men born between the end of the 1930s and the middle of the 1950s, roughly twenty-seven million, would pass through their boyhood and begin to arrive, on the cusp of first maturity, at a national checkpoint.[1] There they were presented with a series of paths on which to continue their journey. Making the choice would be hard, confusing, full of anguish—and once they had chosen, there would be no going back. They would be stuck with that route, and how it defined them, for the rest of their lives.

The choice wasn't entirely theirs to make, though it would be billed that way. Long before the sons decided whether or not to go to war in Vietnam, their World War II fathers had made certain decisions for them. In 1948, Congress enacted a peacetime conscription law and by 1950 put into practice its most notable feature: a deferment for college men who ranked in the top half of their class or scored well on a special aptitude test. The idea, as the Selective Service director Lewis B. Hershey described it at the time, was to use the "club of induction" to "channel" young men in directions that served the national-security state, while giving young men the impression that they were choosing their own paths. Hershey equated this "pressurized guidance" method with "standing in a room which has been made uncomfortably warm. Several doors are open, but they all lead to various forms of recognized, patriotic service to the Nation." Boys deemed smart enough to be prospective engineers, mathematicians, or scientists in the new cold war were directed to the doors leading to corporate America. Their supposedly less promising brothers were shown the door to military service. Those who weren't future missile builders would be future cannon fodder. "As the nuclear age advanced," historian Christian Appy observed in *Working-Class War*, "influential policymakers were increasingly persuaded that the outcome of future wars—whether hot or cold—might be determined not by masses of muddy combat soldiers but by teams of high-powered, white-jacketed scientists and engineers." The same elders who had raised their boys on World War II film fantasies, where men were supposed to prove their ultimate mettle on the battlefield, would endorse a system that regarded soldiers as society's expendable ones.[2]

Within these predetermined channels, the sons were faced with making their own "choices." Of that generation's 27 million draft-age men, about 32 percent wound up serving in the military in the Vietnam era, about 8 percent in Vietnam, about 3 to 6 percent in combat. The majority never served in the military. Of that 15.9 million men who never served, 15.4 million were deferred, exempted, or disqualified; about half a million were apparent draft offenders, nearly nine thousand of them convicted and more than three thousand imprisoned.[3] The generation produced relatively small numbers of either true antiwar "radicals" who took on the system or true-believer combat veterans who couldn't wait to get back into the fray. Most young men fell into a muddled middle group. They had a deferment, but felt uneasy about it; they considered enlisting, then changed their minds; they went into the army, but regretted that they hadn't stayed home and opposed the war; they dabbled at the fringes of an antiwar movement, yet worried that they had skipped the formative event of manhood. Journalist Lawrence Wright expressed typical ambivalence in his 1983 memoir, *In the New World:* "[B]ut now that I stood on the threshold of military service I was flooded with doubt. . . . I found myself suspended between two extreme emotions. On the one hand, I believed my country was wrong, and I thought it was immoral for me to contribute my service. On the other hand, there was a war going on and I might miss it. This was fundamentally at odds with my image of myself as a man."[4] The vast majority of men, like Wright, stayed home and struggled with that image, mostly without resolution. They weren't all of a type, though they would be famously stereotyped as a bunch of pampered narcissists. While the college deferment clearly discriminated against the working class as well as the poor and under-privileged, it also shielded far more than an Ivy League elite. Its umbrella was large and covered millions. One who stood beneath it and grappled mightily with the moral quandary and masculine dilemma of it all was a young man who would grow up to be the idol not of Woodstock Aquar-ians but of Promise Keepers evangelicals.

The Reverend Gordon Dalbey works part of the time in a tiny office among a row of other lookalike offices that march, motel style, the length of the Goleta Professional Building near Santa Barbara, California. The blurry watercolor dreaminess of the beachfront only a few miles to the south might as well be a million miles away; here, all is stippled ceilings and vertical blinds, an antiseptic, could-be-anywhere, waiting-room aesthetic. Dalbey's room, on loan from its official tenant, the staff of the local Vineyard Christian Fellowship, has no desk and is sparsely furnished. A wall-length sliding glass door, when slightly cracked, lets in the dull roar of traffic.

As I sat waiting for Dalbey one August morning, fruitlessly inspecting the surroundings for clues to its occupant, it occurred to me that the barrenness I was gazing upon was the architecture of fatherlessness. The setting was appropriate enough for the Vineyard church. A neocharis-matic fellowship with roots in the Jesus movement, the Vineyard is still, as one of its members observed to me with painful wryness, a "fatherless movement," led for years by the son of an alcoholic who joined Al-Anon at the age of sixty. This prefab shell wasn't exactly the habitat I had imagined for Gordon Dalbey, role model and redeemer for the Glendora men and so many other small Promise Keepers groups. I had pictured a more lived-in edifice, a weathered structure perhaps, suggesting care and continuity—a house that a father might build.

As he would indicate immediately when we met, Dalbey himself felt like an abandoned son, disowned by the Promise Keepers' national lead-ership. "I was very wounded when Promise Keepers rejected me," he said softly, averting his steely-blue eyes. "They rejected me because I talk about healing men. I'm not telling men, Here are the seven stan-dards you've got to measure up to. I was murdered by that. My father was murdered by that. His spirit was destroyed by that."

In 1992, Dalbey had addressed the inaugural Promise Keepers con-vention and had been disturbed by the chastising tone of the other speeches, which just seemed to be replicating the behavior of the cen-sorious fathers. "I met with the senior staff and I told them, 'Hey, you've got to stop just exhorting men to higher standards. You've got to start dealing with the wounds that keep us from maintaining the standards.' " His exhortation, he said, was met by stony stares. "They just looked at me. And I'm sure in their minds they were thinking, This guy is not on the team." As Dalbey sat before the organization's uncomprehending officials, "I realized, Promise Keepers, you know, they are *football players*. That's my *dad*. They are athletes. And they have an athletic approach, that performance-oriented approach. It's my father. And they reject me like my father was unable to accept me and I just projected it onto them. And I finally had to let it go." Dalbey was never again invited to speak at a Promise Keepers conference.

Dalbey has the gaunt look of the habitual jogger, which he is, and a haunted and haunting intensity that comes, one suspects, from a hunger more metaphysical than metabolic. On the surface, he has much in common with the Glendora men. He shares their smoldering sense of paternal betrayal and their urge to get past it. "I want to honor my father," Dalbey told me. "One of the struggles I have in my ministry is that I *do* want to honor my father. Because he gave me so much more than his father ever did. His father would come home from ten hours in a steel mill six days a week, and it wasn't very warm and fuzzy. I've wept for my dad many times. The Lord finally got me to a place of crying out for my father, instead of . . ."

He didn't finish the sentence, possibly because it took so many years for him to arrive at that place. Like the men in Glendora, he grew up with the parable of the prodigal son as his life's trope, but with a critical difference. While each of the Glendora men saw himself as the good older son who stayed home, Gordon Dalbey identified with the younger boy who bolted. In fact, he still thought that way. "I've *never* felt like the older son. I've always been the prodigal." Dalbey views his more obedient cohorts with a certain pity and disapproval—the "yes-men," he calls them in his book *Sons of the Father*.[5] "The rebel is closer to the Kingdom," he told me. "You can't be free to tell your father yes before you tell him no first." When still a young man, he told his father "no," in a manner that made him typical of a significant part of his generation: he refused to go to war.

Dalbey's father, a star football, basketball, and tennis player, joined the navy to serve his country during World War II—and never left. Over the next twenty-two years, he rose from an ensign at the Philadelphia Naval Shipyard to a commander who traversed the globe. He was part of the new military, reorganized along corporate management lines, that emerged from the Second World War. He rose in the ranks primarily as a business manager, an MBA degree acquired early on spelling the difference in his career. Along the way he figured, in both small and significant ways, in many celebrated cold-war moments. He participated in the blockade during the Cuban missile crisis; he helped create U.S.-sponsored navies for Third World countries like Pakistan; he was a supply officer on the aircraft carrier the USS *Randolph,* and so on hand to help retrieve John Glenn from the Atlantic after his historic triple circumnavigation of the globe in 1962. On the occasions when Dalbey senior regaled his son with accounts of his professional life, he singled this out as one of his proudest moments of national service: arranging for an all-American steak dinner for an all-American astronaut.

Gordon was groomed to take his father's place in the masculine firmament of space and technology. The computer, his father told him in 1960, "is going to be the way of the future." An exceptionally bright and precocious student who graduated from his high school as valedictorian at age fifteen, he was sent off to Duke University with a typical paternal expectation of the time—that he would train himself to be a mathematician or an engineer. He chose math. "When I was a sophomore in high school, the Russians put up Sputnik, and a panic swept the country. We've got to produce scientists! And so any male who did well in school, the question was, what science are you going to major in? It wasn't even considered that you would do anything else." But then Dalbey discovered literature—and all around his North Carolina campus, the dawning of the civil-rights movement. Four years later, he boasted a C average in math, a newfound love for the humanities, a conscience awakened to racial injustice, and the overwhelming desire to place as much distance as possible between himself and his father. One day in 1964, he put all his belongings in an old Buick and drove west. On the way, he slept several times in Little League dugouts, as if camping in the ruins of an ancient culture. He was headed toward California and a decade of civil-rights organizing, antiwar activism, willful poverty, and ghetto living.

For two years, Dalbey left the United States altogether, for Peace Corps service in a computer-free Nigerian village. Returning to the San Francisco area in 1968, he protested the Vietnam War, organized against discriminatory housing policies, marched with striking grape workers, and avoided the draft by continuing his education in journalism at Stanford University and then by working as a junior-high-school math teacher in a San Jose barrio. He grew his hair long, moved to East Palo Alto, an impoverished black city south of San Francisco, "dated only black women," and "would never listen to anything but soul music. I tried desperately to be black," he recalled, "because that would get back at my white ancestors, my white fathers." More specifically, he figured it would "cut myself off from my father." Then Dalbey informed his father that he would not under any circumstances serve his country in the Vietnam War. The naval commander disowned his only son. In this way, Gordon Dalbey enlisted in the central masculine crisis of his generation.

———

IN THE SAME YEARS that Dalbey was mounting his rebellion, a young man named Michael Bernhardt was preparing to enter the army. As far back as he could remember watching World War II movies, he could remember wanting to serve. The summers of his boyhood in the backyards of Franklin Square, Long Island, were one long idyll of war play on an imagined European front. Bernhardt has the compact proportions of a jockey, which he once considered becoming, and an intensity that, while not formally religious, is as spiritual in nature as Dalbey's. He is a man trying to figure something out. "We played war *all* the time," he said, half amazed, of his youth on an afternoon when I was visiting his ten-acre horse farm in the north Florida panhandle. "We had leaders and we'd attack things with dirt bombs. We thought war was this big thing where we'd all go in together like D-Day and we would be part of this big army, part of this big coordinated mass of manpower that would *do* something. And then you'd come back and you'd have war stories to tell. It was a transit sort of thing."

Michael Bernhardt didn't get these impressions from adults he knew. "I didn't get a lot of firsthand accounts of the war. What I got was the Hollywood version." The lingering effects of a childhood bout of rheumatic fever had kept his father, Arnold Bernhardt, out of World War II, to the elder Bernhardt's lasting shame. "My father and my 'Uncle' Louie [a close friend of his father's], when World War II broke out, they trooped on down to the enlistment center and they took a physical and my father had a heart murmur. He was 4-F. And Louie had something else, I forget what. Both of these men, they were crushed. And I thought, Hmmm, that must be what it is. You're not supposed to feel real good about it if you're not fit to fight."

Michael Bernhardt's father passed along to his son what he did know about being a man: how to build things, the importance of mastering a skill and of civic responsibility, the belief that masculinity had nothing to do with showboating. His father's measure of manhood was essentially prewar. He ran his own mom-and-pop businesses, near the family home that he had partly constructed with his own hands. He was active in local Republican politics and organized the town civic association with his best friends, two men who always seemed to be on hand for young Michael, too. Bernhardt referred to the trio as as "my three dads." "I remember most fondly when we worked together," Bernhardt said of his actual father. "I learned how to *do* things, how to fix and build. And he would find jobs for me to do in the neighborhood, fixing things, which he'd be unofficially supervising. And his reputation would be riding on the work I did. He taught me things had value."

Michael Bernhardt took away from such lessons a conviction that service based on "taking care," as he put it, was the foundation of manhood. With glorious, Hollywood-style visions of war in mind, he decided that the military was the place to begin. On his own initiative he enrolled not in the Catholic high school that most of his cousins and friends attended, but in Long Island's La Salle Military Academy, a storied all-male, Catholic boarding school run with a strict hand by the Christian Brothers and a cadre of active-duty military men. He had been impressed by young graduates of the school in his hometown. What appealed to him most was that they acted "like grown-ups," a maturity learned not from their peers but from adult men. Unlike the Citadel, where the older cadets ruled, at La Salle "the Brothers were *in charge*," Bernhardt recalled emphatically. "You didn't have bullies, you didn't have upperclassmen running the show. The Brothers knew how to handle things. They always knew what to do." The Brothers continued the moral education he had begun under his father's tutelage: "I learned that there was a path and there was a way to do it, and there was a scorecard, and you had to punch the ticket and make sure you got it punched . . . that there were no easy ways, there were no shortcuts." He also learned that he wanted to become the sort of male leader he perceived the Brothers to be. "I admired those guys so much. I could not believe that anybody could give so much of their lives to a bunch of brats. I mean, let's face it, this school had kids that belonged to Mafia families and Central American dictators like [Nicaraguan dictator Anastasio] Somoza. But the Brothers had total dedication."

At his father's urging, Bernhardt headed off to college at the University of Miami. He was going to major in marine biology. Studying nature appealed to him: "I always wanted to know how everything worked, to see things as part of a bigger system." But his mind was still on a military career. He joined not only army ROTC but a special elite unit at the college run by the Green Berets, known as the Aggressor Company. His roommate Jim Robinson, grateful for the bad knee that saved him from the Vietnam-era draft, was mystified. "Mike was *very* gung ho," he told me. "He was very much focused on wanting to join the army and serve his country and be a military leader. School was of much lesser importance."

In the spring of 1967, in the middle of his sophomore year, Bernhardt dropped out and enlisted in the army. His father, who had dropped out of high school in tenth grade to support his parents and siblings, was disappointed. "But he knew my wanting to serve the country was part of his own doing," Bernhardt recalled. "He knew the values that he had instilled in me." At the time Bernhardt had only the haziest sense of what was going on in Vietnam: "It appeared to be about a small country that was having Communism shoved down its throat, while we were trying, at least *ostensibly,* to give people a chance to do what they wanted to do. Even though I wasn't all that certain what the war was about, I felt I should be taking my chances with other men my age. That if I didn't go, somebody'd have to go in my place, which went against everything I had grown up with."

Michael also had what he called "the Plan": he wanted to be an officer, but he thought he looked too boyish to be commanding. Not only that, he was short—he had quit growing at five feet four. "I needed a few miles if I was going to inspire not just trust but confidence." So the Plan was that he would enlist and train as a ranger and a paratrooper. "I was going to go and do whatever had to be done. I was going to get some stripes on my sleeve and combat experience. And *then,* I was going to get into West Point. I'd have a right to command then."

———

IN THE CRITICAL EVENT FOR YOUNG MEN of their generation, Gordon Dalbey and Michael Bernhardt took different paths—a divergence that would mark them and their brethren in ways the country would never allow them to shake. Vietnam would become a defining event of American masculinity, the bridge that collapsed just as the nation's sons thought they were crossing to manhood. Conventional wisdom holds that this collapse was triggered not by the decisions of the fathers but by the choices the sons made. How the sons approached that bridge— via the induction center or the demonstration line—has become a prevailing measure of a man's worth. The contretemps over President Clinton's Vietnam-era draft record is only the most publicized example of how, for the rest of their lives, a generation of men were to be divided, and perhaps conquered, along these lines.

The divide between the good sons and the prodigal sons of America would still be etched in the popular imagination at century's end, always depicted as a gulf between the patriotic, duty-bound, underappreciated working-class sons of the Silent Majority and the privileged, hippie flouters of authority whose long hair challenged gender conventions and whose disregard for their country undermined the nation's self-image. The boys who went to Vietnam were said to have been "keeping a promise" while those who resisted the war had been "using self-fulfillment" to guide their choices, the latter the words of John P. Wheeler III, the West Point–trained captain whose logistics-information system managed the flow of men and matériel through Vietnam.[6] This dramatic "war" between two kinds of sons loomed large in the country's judgment of a whole generation's—and a nation's—masculinity. In that oft-repeated match, the ring always held only two contestants: the bell-bottomed renegade rocking, taunting, and spitting in the face of the starched good son, who finally snapped and went berserk.

Even in its details, this morality play was suspect. In 1998, the sociologist and Vietnam veteran Jerry Lembcke published the results of his exhaustive research into the singular claim that antiwar protesters had regularly spit on returning vets. The spitters and hecklers, he found, were (with few exceptions) the hawkish veterans of previous wars, men who regarded the young GIs as losers because they hadn't come back victorious. "We won our war, they didn't, and from the looks of them, they couldn't," a VFW member sneered on a videotape filmed during a Vietnam veterans' protest march through Valley Forge in the early 1970s, while his grizzled comrades barraged the marching ex-grunts with slurs and ridicule. In other words, the Vietnam vets were being attacked by their *fathers*.[7] Lembcke's revelation, however, was met with a good deal of disbelief, when it wasn't ignored outright. The showdown between the two sons would remain the controlling myth of the post-Vietnam era.

In fact, between these brothers, determining who was "good" and who was "prodigal" was a far blurrier proposition than the country was willing to consider, nor was it self-evident which of the two types of sons would, in the end, break more deeply with their male elders and the system that those older men had created. After all, vast numbers of returning soldiers turned against the war, sometimes in more radical ways than their stay-at-home antiwar peers.[8] Their fathers had endorsed the masculine paradigm of a common mission, a clear frontier with an identifiable enemy, a shared brotherhood, and a calling to protect a population of women and children. The signs that that paradigm had failed would nowhere be so evident as in the nation's deadly and protracted engagement in Vietnam. The implications of that failure were so devastating that few young men, dutiful or rebellious, and even fewer of their elders, would be prepared to face them.

The "Prodigal" Sons: They Broke My American Heart

AT THE TIME OF THE VIETNAM WAR, a diagnosis of the "rebel" sons' behavior would emerge from conservative quarters and would pass, as the era passed, into mainstream lore: what we were witnessing was no less than patricide. Child psychologist Bruno Bettelheim was the most prolific proponent of this view, proclaiming from the pages of the *New York Times Magazine* and in congressional hearings that the rebel sons were sullen and dangerous boys similar to the German sons of National Socialism, embracing "an ideology that pitted the sons against the fathers." They "remained fixated at the age of the temper tantrum," he told the House Special Subcommittee on Education in 1969. They were boys who imagined the only way "to prove themselves as real men" was to cast their fathers as "deadly enemies" to be overthrown. "All these were the main tenets of academic Hitler Youth, as they are now those of our student left," he declared ominously. "I have no doubt that the ranks of the militants contain some would-be Hitlers and Stalins, hence again their dangerousness."[9] Similarly apocalyptic language emanated from the White House, where Vice President Spiro Agnew denounced the "parricidal mouthings of a few highly publicized malcontents" and blamed permissive parenting. Conservative publications issued a steady stream of declamations against what they called "the Terror," unleashed by bloodthirsty Jacobin boys. A 1969 *National Review* headline summed it up: THE REVOLUTION EATS ITS PARENTS. Pundits in mainstream publications took up the same theme in only slightly muted tones. Typical was a 1970 column in *U.S. News & World Report* that denounced "childish but brutal" radicals under the banner, I AM TIRED OF THE TYRANNY OF SPOILED BRATS.[10]

According to these town criers, a generation of *mother*-coddled sons were banging their spoons on their high chairs, refusing to eat their spinach, and crawling toward the matches to burn their parents' houses down. The sons didn't want to grow up and they didn't want to give up Mom — and they were willing to kill Dad so they could stay mama's boys forever. Unfortunately for such theorists, in studies of antiwar activists that postwar hobgoblin, "permissive parenting," would turn out not to correlate with youthful radicalism. Indulged sons proved no more opposed to the war than the sons of strict parents.[11] Nonetheless, the not-so-subtle implication that the young men opposing the war were feminized Peter Pans clinging to Wendy's skirt was a potent ploy, precisely because it stigmatized them as unmanly. This supposed plague of the "soft male" would be invoked by poet Robert Bly three decades later as a central tenet of his "Iron John" men's movement, attended by so many middle-aged, baby-boom men.[12] Momism had led to radicalism had led to patricide had led to feminization, the argument ran. Interestingly, when it came to this generation's prodigal sons, only mothers were implicated. Fathers had been dropped from the equation, except as unfairly maligned scapegoats.

"All of us hated our fathers," Gordon Dalbey agreed. "It was the season." But what the patricide diagnosis ignored was the source of that so-called "hating." Such fury, as Dalbey could attest, was actually rooted in dashed hopes of fatherly connections, and those hopes hadn't been easy to dash. Not until the very end of the sixties would small numbers of these young men begin to resort to the desperate actions that are now seen as wholly characteristic of the era. At the start, in fact, they hadn't wanted to attack male authorities but to follow them with honor. The liberal establishment in ascendancy with President Kennedy had wooed them with visions of an honorable future and the sons had gladly succumbed. It is no coincidence that a student movement sprang to life not as the war revved up but in 1960, the year of Kennedy's election. What so many student "radicals" of the time recall as their inspirational spark to action was Kennedy's speech at the University of Michigan, unveiling his plan to launch a Peace Corps. Tom Hayden, who covered the address for the college newspaper, hailed it at the time as "a most dramatic and thrilling moment." Author James Miller, former SDS member, recalled how activists were entranced by Kennedy's promise of a "new chivalrous era." Revisiting the New Left's early, earnest appeals to the powerful, Miller would later wonder at the naive assumption that the new leaders "could be cajoled into changing their errant ways, rather as a tolerant, thoughtful father might be moved to respond to the urgent entreaties of an impatient, well-meaning son."[13] But for years that was indeed the ruling assumption. And its adherents would be devastated when it didn't hold up. "Think of the men who now engineer that war," Students for a Democratic Society president Carl Oglesby said at a 1965 anti-Vietnam march on Washington. "They are not moral monsters. They are all honorable men. They are all liberals." The bitterness sprang not from disdain but from violated faith: They "mouthed my liberal values and broke my American heart."[14]

Often young male protesters had their hearts broken twice by these honorable men, in public and in their own homes. While the antiwar movement doubtless drew many hangers-on who were just looking to create a stir or alienate their parents, particularly in its later years, what most typified the original core of activists was their sense of allegiance, expecially to their fathers. Research on committed antiwar male radicals—whether in surveys by Columbia Graduate School of Journalism researchers, canvasses by the Harris poll, or studies by more ambivalent academics like sociologist Seymour Martin Lipset—found that their most distinguishing trait was how much they sought to *identify* with those fathers, whom they generally saw as liberal and ethical. As Lipset wrote, these students "are more idealistic and committed than their parents, but generally in the same direction."[15] Social psychologist Kenneth Keniston, who studied the attitudes and backgrounds of a group of young radicals who led the antiwar effort Vietnam Summer 1967, concluded that the "enduring theme" was "the continuing identification of almost all young radicals with the side of their fathers that is idealistic, effective, and actively principled." To see one's father in such a positive light, the activist son typically maintained what Keniston described as a "split in the image of the father." While he understood his father to be, in many ways, "dominated, humiliated, ineffectual, or unwilling to act on his perceptions of the world," he preferred to focus on an image of his father as idealistic and to see his own role as freeing paternal idealism from its shackled ineffectuality. As they weren't breaking with their fathers' principles but trying to put them into action, they were strikingly unlike members of previous political uprisings. For the sixties male activist, "becoming a radical . . . involves *no fundamental change in core values* [emphasis in original]," Keniston wrote. "The only startling fact is that he takes these values seriously and proposes that American society and the world set about implementing them."[16]

"My father was a very principled man," Gordon Dalbey told me, a man engaged in a socially responsible project: protecting the nation's security. Dalbey still recalled with a glow a day in 1947 when his father took him to work at the naval shipyard in Atlantic City, perched him on a desktop, and put his own officer's cap on the boy's head. Dalbey was three years old. As a young man, Dalbey attempted to follow his father's game plan to the letter; he hoped to win the admiration of a remote and impassive man whom he saw as moral and public minded. Before the Vietnam War heated up, he had, in fact, tried to sign up for Naval ROTC: "I wanted desperately to be like my father, like a boy does." When Dalbey was ruled ineligible because he was color-blind, he was "crushed. I thought, I'll never be like my father. I'll never be a man." When he subsequently joined the Peace Corps, it was in the hope that he would at last be fulfilling what he saw as his father's most principled side—"My father was very service oriented"—and President Kennedy's as well. "Man!" Dalbey recalled of JFK's Peace Corps speech, "when he said, 'Go,' I was ready to go! It was all 'Ask not what your country can do for you,' it was a selflessness, a going outward. My father taught me that."

Dalbey still remembers vividly the literary work that first impelled him to shift his sights from a scientific to a writing career. For an early college paper, he was assigned E. B. White's 1941 essay "Once More to the Lake," an intimate reverie on the mystical connection between fathers and sons. In its closing passage, which Dalbey can still recite from memory, White watches his small son wriggle into wet swim trunks for a postthunderstorm dip and, from the vantage point of his own mounting years, feels his life force pass into the boy, a willing though melancholy changing of the guard. "Languidly, and with no thought of going in, I watched him, his hard little body, skinny and bare, saw him wince slightly as he pulled up around his vitals the small, soggy, icy garment. As he buckled the swollen belt, suddenly my groin felt the chill of death." The story had a profound effect on Dalbey. "I didn't understand that then. I do now, as a father. There's something of me in that boy, a mystery beyond all mysteries. As a father, I am the root, the trunk, upon which my boy is the branch. My history is his history. Who I have been is who he is. My heart is the boy's heart." And that knowledge is "terrifying," he said, his voice dropping to a husky whisper. "Because you have to stop and think, God, did my father ever feel this? And if he did, what short-circuited? *What happened*?"

Dalbey's freshman-year paper on White's essay earned the top grade and turned him toward the humanities, but it did not win him paternal approval. "The most embarrassing thing for me on my first report card from Duke was the A in English," Dalbey recalled. "That I had to explain. *This* is not gonna launch any Sputniks."

His father's continuing silence, and his own need to break it, eventually drove Dalbey to denounce his father. "What came in the sixties," Dalbey said, "really was a spirit of rebellion that comes when children are not permitted their feelings, they're not permitted their voice. Rebellion comes when you can't just say, 'I'm angry at you. You didn't do this for me, and I needed it. You did this, and I'm angry at what you did. You hurt me.'" The fathers were mute for a reason. "Don't forget, the hippies were the sons of the World War II warriors, who did their finest job in protecting us. The war is where they identified their manhood. But the character traits that make you a success in tanks or with a gun don't translate into being a father." For Dalbey, rebelling was a misbegotten attempt at kindling a relationship with a warrior father. "I know women who will say, 'I start a fight with my husband to get him to explode and then we can at least have something to deal with.' I think that's what I was doing with my father, hoping to engage him at some level. And I was not wise enough to realize that it would only drive him further away from me."

The sons found themselves suspended in what Norman Mailer described as "that no-man's-land between the old frontier and the new ranch home," stranded by their fathers. "Society provides no challenge," Berkeley's antiwar leader Mario Savio wrote in 1963, using the very word, "challenge," that had been the centerpiece of JFK's acceptance speech three years earlier. "The 'futures' and 'careers' for which American students now prepare are for the most part intellectual and moral wastelands. This chrome-plated consumers' paradise would have us grow up to be well-behaved children."[17]

What was missing, as the older antiwar activist Peter Marin perceived in a sixties manifesto, "The Open Truth and Fiery Vehemence of Youth," was a legacy that engaged the next generation in the authentic project of building a culture, rather than shopping for one; a paternal connection necessary to "restore to the young a sense of manhood and potency without at the same time destroying the past."[18] The fathers, however, could do little to repair the situation. They, too, were stranded in a shoppers' world; they, too, had been reduced to "well-behaved children" in a "chrome-plated consumers' paradise." So many of them were broken by the very world they had helped to build. Antiwar radical Peter Berg, who barely knew his father but understood him to be both "a politically conscious man" and "a paranoid alcoholic," said despairingly that too often the elders were "wreckage, nothing but wreckage, complete syndromic wreckage." To live in their world as a son was to live in "a linoleum hospital . . . where it's more important to keep the linoleum clean than to keep the people." It felt like "walking . . . on a cellophane surface of the world." Inside this "hospital," he concluded, "there're only certain roles you can play. . . . You can be queer, you can be a character, you can be an entertainer or an artist, you can be an adolescent, you can be a woman—you can't be a man."[19]

The protest movements of the sixties were not, of course, primarily driven by thwarted manhood; they were driven by moral outrage. The many women who thronged to the peace marches were not there because otherwise "you can't be a man"; nor, consciously anyway, were the men. But no matter what reasons brought men to the barricades, a man refusing to go to war could in no case avoid a societal verdict on his masculinity. Those adolescents could either go to war or stay home; but either way, they would be enlisted in a battle for male identity, a battle that would in the end be fought largely on the fathers' terms. The sons who would soon march against the war still hoped and expected that the fathers would deliver something meaningful. Initially, the act of protest was in great measure a leap of faith, a belief against all evidence that if they cried out with enough passion, their remote and "wrecked" fathers might hear them, and might remember that "their heart was the boy's heart."

If they could not get the fathers to fulfill the promise of a masculine passage, the young activists would create a movement in which they might provide transit for themselves. What would be perceived by panicky guardians of the status quo as anarchic, disorderly, self-indulgent, and threatening was, in fact, a fragile and faulty attempt to create a meaningful progression toward manhood, through a system much like the one that had served their fathers, even if that attempt upended many of their fathers' values. The shape and structure of the movement, at least in its early years, could be seen as an effort not so much to break with the masculine paradigm as to jump-start it. The antiwar campaign provided a clear mission: ending an unjust, immoral, and illegal invasion of another nation. The antiwar campaign provided a frontier of a sort, sometimes envisioned in John Wayne cavalry-and-cowboy terms. By resisting the draft, antiwar leader David Harris wrote, he had put himself out in "the badlands, looking for a place from which to hold off the forces."[20] And as time went on, an identifiable enemy came into focus: the American government. Who could have provided a better cast of bad guys than the power holders in Washington by the end of the sixties? "You know, it was patently obvious to any objective point of view that going into Vietnam was wrong," Dalbey remarked to me, "and you had a man in the White House, Richard Nixon, who perfectly epitomized the rigid, insecure paternal figure who would send other men to die and not go himself. It was just perfect, like they handed it to a generation on a platter."

Of course, the setup wasn't perfect at all, as Dalbey and many other young men came to realize. It was disorienting and infuriating to be arrayed against the very male leaders who were supposed to be leading you. Instead of a straightforward reenactment of the old male paradigm in a different context, the activists at the same time scornfully mocked many symbolic aspects of that paradigm: dressing for battle in beads and flowing hair and sticking daisies down National Guard gun barrels. While a hyped-up combat rhetoric sometimes reflected the wistful childhood dreams of World War II, it also was intended as satiric commentary, a bizarre parody of the fathers. John Wayne was copied—and simultaneously scorned as a hollow and dangerous icon. The protesters had arrayed the old male adventure in a new guise, and part of that guise was a heartfelt repudiation of all the injustices the old male adventure seemed to have wrought in their time.

Still, compared with the confused battle lines in Vietnam, the protesters at home were in some odd sense fighting the last conventional war, which was apparent in the preferred epithets they lobbed at the "enemy" in the heat of street battle: "Fascist!" "Nazi!" or, with right arm raised in mock salute, "Sieg Heil!" Even the V-for-victory symbol of World War II, as Tom Engelhardt has pointed out in *The End of Victory Culture,* was returned to action as the movement's peace sign.[21] Unfortunately, the most hostile forces amassed against a young man's journey to masculine authority could not be found in the streets. The faceless authority of corporate bureaucracy, the remote-control methods of a military-industrial economy, the feminization of an onrushing celebrity culture, the malevolence of image-management governance, all these eluded direct confrontation. Indeed, the young activists took to the streets because it was the one place where they felt they *could* make the opposition show its face.

The movement offered, as well, the promise of brotherhood, a bonding on America's streets and a purposeful engagement within the ramshackle apartments, university dormitories, or community-center meeting rooms where the young activists gathered to plan their strategic maneuvers. "Petitions had to be signed, candidates found to run for public office and demonstrations mounted to urge the end of the war," antiwar leader Sam Brown recalled. "Things had to be done. In a way, the very organization of the antiwar movement was ironically similar to that of the military.... And, like the military, those who actively dissented developed a sense of camaraderie that grew from shared risks, values and experiences.... Everything was shared: tactics and strategy, office space and apartments, ideals and hopes."[22] While the movement was hardly martial in respect to order or hierarchy—its "organization" was sprawling, diffuse, and without a controlling, central hub—the fraternal feeling created by a communal effort, a clear objective, and a shared sense of national emergency would have doubtless been familiar to the average World War II GI.

The opening salvo of the New Left's founding declaration, "The Port Huron Statement," spoke at length and with great intensity about a yearning for the bonds of brotherhood:

Human relationships should involve fraternity and honesty. Human interdependence is contemporary fact; human brotherhood must be willed, however, as a condition of future survival and as the most appropriate form of social relations. Personal links between man and man are needed, especially to go beyond the partial and fragmentary bonds of function that bind men only as worker to worker, employer to employee, teacher to student, American to Russian.

Loneliness, estrangement, isolation describe the vast distance between man and man today. These dominant tendencies cannot be overcome by better personnel management, nor by improved gadgets, but only when a love of man overcomes the idolatrous worship of things by man.[23]

Where this left women was nowhere addressed (nor would the language of "man" and "brotherhood" have struck many, male or female, as problematic back then), but the promise of winning women's favor by the offer of male protection seemed self-evident to male activists in the early years of the movement. These men were "putting their bodies on the line," as they were then fond of saying—in the streets or through draft resistance, in jail—while the women of the movement made the coffee, licked the envelopes, and shared their beds. In her memoir of the sixties, *Loose Change,* Sara Davidson recalled the painfully self-conscious determination of her "radical" Berkeley friends to reenact traditional sex roles in an antiwar context:

On Friday, Jeff left home at four in the morning. She helped him smear Vaseline on his face to protect him against tear gas. He put on a jock strap with a metal cup so the pigs couldn't smash his nuts. He wore a football helmet. Susie wore a ruffled dress from Motherhood Maternity. She had a job, her phone number had been given to demonstrators to memorize and call if they got busted, but the phone never rang.[24]

The street fighter and the draft resister, like the frontiersman and the Indian fighter, were making the frontier safe for the female settlers, and it was a job, they imagined, only they could do. That women were "putting their bodies on the line," too, was an inconvenient fact that many of the men preferred to overlook. (The 1967 march on the Pentagon that culminated in the bloody beating of female protesters was only one of the more brutal reminders that the "protection" afforded by young male activists was no match for armed marshals. "A startling disproportion of women were arrested, and were beaten in ugly fashion in the act," Norman Mailer observed in *The Armies of the Night.*) Nonetheless, they preferred to cast their actions in exclusively male terms. "Before, only men could go to war," antiwar activist Mark Gerzon wrote of draft resistance in *A Choice of Heroes*. "Now, only men could go to jail." The slogan "Women Say Yes to Men Who Say No" seemed to signal the achievement of masculine promise. The young men had marched off to "Fight for Peace," they had sacrificed, they had joined in confraternity with other young men, and now they would come home, at last, to the embrace of a woman.[25]

In the end, however, the failure of the movement to make discernible progress in ending the war drove some of its stymied young male adherents into a Hollywood fantasyland of violent display, where the dialogue of shoot-'em-up TV dramas prevailed and where the only clear mission seemed to be advancement to the next serial showdown. Actual violence initiated by demonstrators was not nearly as prevalent as popular mythology would later make it out to be—most antiwar activism was peaceful—but the frustrating sense of getting nowhere did inspire more than a few young men to revert, at least in their fevered imaginations, to a boy's gunplay adventure. For some, it was almost as if they had passed from a boyhood spent watching westerns and war flicks to a young adulthood acting in them. "The final conflict will be between outlaws and criminals," antiwar radical Marvin Garson wrote melodramatically in the *San Francisco Express-Times*, an alternative newspaper, in the winter of 1969. "On one side, millions of Americans turned outlaw by force of circumstance; on the other side, the forces of respectable society at last revealed as Organized Crime." The outcome "will be determined by who has the guns—at the end of course, not at the beginning."[26] In *The War at Home*, a 1981 documentary film about the antiwar movement in Madison, Wisconsin, Ken Mate, a former street rebel and editor of an underground paper, recounted his part in ten days of chaos on campus following the news that four students had been killed by National Guardsmen during antiwar demonstrations at Kent State University. He recalled spotting a policeman leveling his pistol at some target up the street. He and a friend immediately reached for *their* guns: "We both put rounds into the chamber and we just aimed." After a few moments, oblivious to the young men's presence, the cop raised his hand and walked away. The young men reholstered their guns, to await the next dramatic scene. "That cop never knew how lucky he was," Mate pronounced.[27]

It was difficult to create any version of constructive masculinity in such a moment, particularly as the New Left's mission narrowed by necessity to a single-minded focus on stopping the war. "Little to build, much to stop," former SDS president Todd Gitlin would write in his memoir, *The Sixties*. "The sum was an impulse to smash up the [war] machine, to jam the wheels of the juggernaut, and damn the consequences."[28] Yet the burden of the failure to build fell unduly on the sons' shoulders. Their fathers had indeed "built," massively so, but only with the crucial moral and financial backing of their government—from the Civilian Conservation Corps to the GI Bill of Rights. What this government was doing "for" the sons, by contrast, was aggressively infiltrating the antiwar, New Left, and black movements with agents bent on provoking dissension and violent acts. As Theodore Roszak wrote in "Youth and the Great Refusal":

> It is not properly youth's role to bear so great a responsibility for inventing or initiating for their society as a whole. It is too big a job for them to do gracefully. The rise of our youth culture to a position of such prominence is a symptom of grave default on the part of adults. Trapped in a frozen posture of befuddled passivity which has been characteristic of our society since the end of World War II, . . . the mature generations have divested themselves of their adulthood—if the term means anything besides being tall and debt-worried and capable of buying liquor without showing a driver's license.[29]

The young activists who gathered to create Students for a Democratic Society in 1962 in Port Huron, Michigan, at a United Auto Workers hall that had once been a New Deal camp, *had* a vision of a new adult society they wanted to build. It would be a "benevolent community" in which adulthood meant responsibility in a "participatory democracy" and an active commitment to social welfare and human creativity. They understood their fathers' frozen posture to be the result of a system that employed them in meaningless jobs "accepted as a channel to status or plenty, if not a way to pay the bills," as the Port Huron Statement put it, and that reduced each isolated man to "a consuming unit, bombarded by hard-sell, soft-sell lies and semi-true appeals to his basest drives."[30] By the late sixties and early seventies, the achievement of any kind of benevolent community had been long frustrated by a war that the fathers doggedly refused to end. In the chaos of the moment, facing limited and dwindling resources, an overstretched and minimal organizational structure, and the hostility of the government and large segments of the public off campus, movement leaders often fell back on many of the traits of their fathers' world that they had once least admired: a preoccupation with winning, with maintaining control, and with the display of force.

Many of them came to talk, like the war managers they so decried, of "toughness," of "attacking" the Pentagon, of "taking over."[31] The worst offenders tended to be younger male leaders who rose to prominence after 1967; their self-consciously wild-and-restless style only intensified macho inclinations, and gentler male voices, once so eloquently represented by men like founding SDS leaders Paul Potter and Al Haber, became all but inaudible. At the same time, the most high-profile activists seemed to be succumbing to the celebrity culture, with its emphasis on image and media fame. The "heavies," as the movement's leaders came to be called, were increasingly concerned with the courtship of the television cameras and the consolidation of their star power.

The display of aggression, power-play theatrics, a compulsion to perform before the cameras, all of these ran counter to the vision of a "benevolent community" and undermined much of what had been so appealing and strengthening within the movement. A sense of mission and brotherly camaraderie fractured before the competition for dominant status—which, in a rising media culture, was determined by who could claim the national spotlight. More significant for the men's future, though they didn't fathom its portent at the time, the leadership's unbenevolent and self-aggrandizing tendencies were beginning to disturb, and disturb deeply, the movement's women. If few of the male leaders, particularly the younger ones supplanting the old guard, were prepared to examine honestly their drift into celebrity culture, the women who had watched the men onstage were primed for such analyses. Was this the sort of movement they had signed on to help? And what were they doing in the "helping" role anyway? Dissatisfaction with the aggressive showmanship ascendant within the newer male leadership and the underlying values such displays represented led women to fundamentally challenge the men's authority to lead. With that challenge, one support that male activists thought they could rely on, the admiration and affection of women, began to crumble.

"The typical Movement institution consists of one or more men who act as charismatic spokesmen, who speak in the name of the institution and negotiate and represent that body, . . . and the people who do the actual work of the institution, much of the time women," Marge Piercy wrote in 1969 in her classic broadside, "The Grand Coolie Dam," a no-holds-barred analysis of the antiwar movement's degenerating sexual politics at decade's end. "Most prestige in the Movement rests not on having done anything in particular, but in having visibly dominated some gathering or manipulating a certain set of rhetorical counters well in public, or in having played some theatrical role." The men had ascended the pedestal to become what Piercy dubbed "the Professional Revolutionary in the Mirror," the "talkers and actors of dramatic roles who are visible and respected" and did things that "look glamorous" while the women generally labored in the trenches.[32]

As dominance became in the later years a consuming agenda for many of the movement's male leaders, it was increasingly demonstrated over the bodies closest at hand—women's. Some of these antiwar men were counting "points" long before the Spur Posse. As the movement "heated up," Todd Gitlin observed, "its celebrities notched more conquests." One of his compatriots, who was married, "kept a notebook rating his many encounters." Another tried to seduce Gitlin's live-in girlfriend while Gitlin was out of town. And Gitlin himself admitted to "a series of clandestine one-night stands," some "with women who were in the process of leaving comrades of mine."[33] The strategy of "fucking a staff into existence," as Marge Piercy put it, became all too evident in some quarters. "A man can bring a woman into an organization by sleeping with her and remove her by ceasing to do so," she wrote. "A man can purge a woman for no other reason than that he has tired of her, knocked her up, or is after someone else. . . . There are cases of a woman excluded from a group for no other reason than that one of its leaders proved impotent with her. . . . Scalp hunting goes on on both sides of the sexual barrier, but the need to extract a kind of emotional conquest which is sometimes not even sexually consummated, out of woman after woman, seems exclusively the disease of male *machers*."[34]

Even as they protested the raping and killing of women and children at places like My Lai, some New Left men seemed to want to relegate women in their midst to servant status. An "incredible shrinking man" dynamic set in; the less control the men had over events in the streets, the less authority they seemed willing to share with the women close to them. After reaching a high of 26 percent in 1963, the proportion of female leaders in SDS fell to single digits, even though women represented at least a third of the group's general membership. Men controlled the drafting of statements and conference papers; women infrequently spoke at meetings, and when they tried to control the floor, they were sometimes simply hooted down. When Marilyn Salzman Webb rose to speak at an antiwar rally in 1969, men in the audience yelled out, "Take her off the stage and fuck her."[35] The hecklers were never identified; presumably, then, they were not the movement stalwarts. But that they felt free to hurl epithets at sister activists suggests the degree to which conditions had degenerated. Such a spectacle would have been unthinkable when SDS convened in Port Huron. As Sara

Evans observed in *Personal Politics,* her thoughtful study of gender conflict within the movement, in the new climate of "macho stridency and militarist fantasy,"

> even the few delicious moments of temporary "victory," when students sought to show true democracy at work, proved to be theaters for the reassertion of oppressive sex roles, more strongly than ever. When students captured several buildings at Columbia University in the spring of 1968, they turned the housekeeping chores over to women. Rumor has it that in one building women staged a rebellion and refused to do the cooking, but in Fayerweather Hall women cooked for 300, three times a day, in a kitchen the size of a telephone booth. Later that summer Mark Rudd, the most prominent leader of the Columbia uprising, advised his girlfriend that she could go to "chicklib" class while he was busy with other things.[36]

The women finally organized a single session on the woman question at an SDS conference, and Casey Hayden and Mary King drafted a gently prodding memo, "Sex and Caste," which politely asked, "Perhaps we can start to talk with each other more openly than in the past." The document was hardly a call to arms. "Objectively," they wrote, "the chances seem nil that we could start a movement based on anything as distant to general American thought as a sex-caste system."[37] Objectively, they couldn't have been more wrong. By the end of the decade, the New Left women famously revolted, storming out to join a movement that would have a far more profound and permanent effect on American society than the one they had just left.

Some of the men would fight back, often lamely with snipes on and off the convention floor or childish mockery, such as the cartoon in *New Left Notes* of a girl libber in a polka-dotted minidress with her panties showing.[38] But these juvenile responses betrayed a certain understanding that women had already captured the high ground. For the men, feminism was more than just a threat to their pride or "power," what little they had or imagined they had. The shame went beyond the fact that the women refused to do the dishes, stood up to the men, or even dumped them, though these experiences were mortifying and, for some, shattering. The deeper humiliation was that the women, unlike the men, were on a building mission. Not only had the men failed to construct a benevolent community, but now it looked like the women might do it without them. Women had effectively hijacked their mission. And the men sensed they had no one to blame but themselves. As Todd Gitlin observed:

> The tough-talking men of steel, committed to their revolutionary mirage, were losing their grip on reality. Which is one explanation for why the independent women's movement spread as fast and as furiously as it did. Sisterhood was powerful partly because movement brotherhood was not. The women's groups reacted against movement machismo—*and also copied it* [his emphasis] with their own version of revolutionary apocalypse—but either way, feminist rage thrived on the sense that the men ostensibly running the show (giving the speeches, calling the demonstrations, editing the papers) were vulnerable. The heavies, beneath the prevailing bluster, were losing their troops.[39]

Most young male activists, of course, weren't "heavies"; they had no troops to lose. More typically, they dabbled on the fringes of the movement, attending local or campus antiwar rallies, maybe trekking to a protest march in Washington. Mostly, they struggled in private with their consciences and their confusions about the war and their relationship to it. In their lives, the draft was a looming presence that cast its shadow on all their deliberations and, at the same time, strangely focused them. What it meant to be a man seemed now to ride entirely on the decisions they made about deferment, resistance, or enlistment. A rite of passage is supposed to induct the young into adulthood, but the draft ordeal proved a portal to nowhere.

At summer's end in 1970, Gordon Dalbey turned twenty-six, relieving him of the threat of induction. "I was free of the draft for the first time in my adult life. I was free to say to myself, 'What do you want to do, Gordon?' And I had no idea. No idea." Evading the draft had defined and framed his experience, and now the threat had vanished overnight, seemingly leaving no more of a trace than a bad dream. "I could see no central concern in my life at that time, no compelling cause or focus." After several months' deliberation, he hauled out his sleeping bag, typewriter, and guitar, packed them in his Volkswagen Bug, and set out for Santa Fe, a place he knew nothing about other than it sounded like the properly craggy southwestern backdrop for a male "adventure," to "make something happen," alone. The dream of a caring communion of brothers had given way to the myth of the cowboy. "The American male character who's held up as a hero always manages by himself," he said. "He's always a loner. All that he needs, he carries with him. He doesn't need anybody else." He had the notion that he would become a writer, vaguely recalling other rugged authors who had supposedly launched their careers this way.

Dalbey crossed the Sierras and reached Death Valley the first night. It was October and cold sleeping out. He arrived in Flagstaff "in a stiff, seven-thousand-foot-high wind," intending to build a fire and cook his dinner, Jack London style, but the bitter gale drove him into the one free public space he could find, a nearby college campus. He sat in the student-union lounge for hours, dully attentive to a flickering television set. "Finally, they came and locked all the doors and I had to leave." He parked his car just off the highway to Phoenix and, before bedding down in the backseat, stared out into the "high and chilly plateau of Flagstaff," the dark chasm of the land and his life. He began to cry. "I knew it was all over." The next morning, he turned back toward San Francisco.

He had headed toward Santa Fe in pursuit, he said, of "this heroic manly model of the guy who has no roots and who flies, he flies away when it's time to go. The Flying Boy." But on that night he saw himself "naked and impotent, as if I were a baby again." He felt "suddenly not valiantly alone, but painfully lonely. . . . I missed people. I needed people. I'd never allowed myself to feel that way before. . . . It felt like defeat. And, in a way, it was." He knew of only one circle of people who had managed to create the sort of tightly knit community that the Port Huron Statement authors had dreamed of. So he drove toward a place in San Francisco where he would feel welcomed, connected, and maybe even useful: a commune where he knew a woman and her friends. "I went back to a woman," he said. "When I felt lost, I wanted to go back to where it's safe, and I didn't have any experience of safety among men."

A few years earlier, Dalbey had almost taken the highway to Arizona on a very different errand. In between the Peace Corps and the teaching deferments, he had impulsively applied to the army and lined up a commission to missile-launch training school in Fort Huachuca, Arizona. He was still deeply opposed to the war, so why the out-of-the-blue enlistment fervor? "You don't get to be a *man* unless you go to war," Dalbey said to me without irony, a fifty-three-year-old adult channeling the thoughts of a nineteen-year-old boy. Before he signed the army contract, a woman in the peace movement took him aside and talked him out of it. "She very graciously helped me see that this was not best for my spirit," he recalled. She told him, "You're *more* of a man if you don't do it." He bought her argument, returned to teaching, and eventually went to Harvard Divinity School, emerging as a minister with the liberal

United Church of Christ. On another level, though, her argument never convinced him.

In the end, most of the young men on the fringes of the antiwar movement stayed relatively close to the map their culture had handed them, overlaying it like a transparency on the terrain of the antiwar effort. When it failed to deliver them to their destination, many of them concluded not that the map had failed them but that they had failed themselves. Maybe protesting the war just wasn't as good as "putting their bodies on the line" in a combat zone. Maybe sharing a struggle with other protesters wasn't the same as a brotherhood forged under life-and-death conditions. Maybe fighting the establishment fathers wasn't as transforming as fighting in an actual war. The problem, as many came to see it, wasn't that the antiwar campaign had been cast as a war, but that it hadn't been war *enough*.

Seated in a folding chair in his generic office space, Gordon Dalbey contemplated the rigorous choices of his young manhood—and doubted them. "I opposed the Vietnam War, I oppose *war* itself," he said with slow bafflement. He stared down at his open palms, as if trying to read the faint tracings of a lifeline whose meaning eluded him. "And yet," he said, "all my life I had longed for a war that I could be a part of."

The "Good" Sons: Lost Before We Got There

ON THE MORNING of March 16, 1968, Michael Bernhardt rose before dawn, having spent the night, as usual, in a hole in the ground, a bunker dug out and lined with sandbags topped with wooden pallets and a tarp to keep out the rain. He assembled in uneasy silence with the 105 other men in Charlie Company, several tons of weaponry and ammo heaped around them on the base camp's airstrip, their necks craning toward the horizon and the angry hornet's buzz of nine helicopters descending. They were on their way to combat, eleven kilometers through dense brush to a village in Quang Ngai province near the coast, a mere fifteen minutes by chopper. Bernhardt's company had been in Vietnam three months; today, from the sound of the briefing, they were finally going to get the war they had come to fight, the sort of World War II–style battle they had dreamed about. The night before, their captain had briefed them: A whole battalion of Vietcong would be amassed when they arrived, a crack unit of as many as 280 soldiers. The GIs would be outnumbered two to one and should anticipate "a hell of a good fight." The enemy would be in uniform and "this would be our chance to get even with them and to go in and face them," the captain said. Women and children would all have gone to the market by 7 A.M. No civilians would be present on the battlefield. After American aircraft and artillery softened up the terrain, the grunts would leap from the helicopters, storm the enemy positions, and destroy their bunkers.[40] It sounded like a little D-Day.

At about 7:30 A.M., Bernhardt was among the first of the men to drop out of the helicopters. The enemy, wherever they were, were silent. "I heard no firing," Bernhardt said. The men were ordered to move out and sweep the area. As Bernhardt's platoon set off, the company commander, a captain, ordered him to stay back for a while with the command post, which had been set up in a bombed-out building. They had found a GI ammo box and the commander wanted Bernhardt, who was carrying the rope they used to test potentially explosive objects, to make sure it wasn't booby-trapped. Bernhardt tied the long rope around the box and yanked a few times to see if it would explode. It didn't. Finally he gave up and popped the lid. Inside were some medical supplies and a Sony transistor radio.

While Bernhardt was investigating the first-aid kit, he began to hear gunfire in the distance and the two radios by the captain's side came crackling to life. "I could hear some of the conversation and I could tell the captain wasn't hearing what he wanted," Bernhardt recalled. "From his tone of voice, I could tell who he was talking to." It was that "disgusted, what-kind-of-an-idiot-are-you tone of voice" that the captain reserved for the head of the First Platoon, "Lieutenant Shithead," as the commander most often called him. Suddenly, the lieutenant's voice cut out; it appeared his radio had gone dead. Bernhardt glanced over at the captain, who was showing no signs of leaving the command post to investigate. "I suggested I go out there with a radio," Bernhardt recalled. "He said no." Bernhardt found it strange. The captain "always wanted to know what was going on." The commander lounged with his back against a dike, next to an older man with no insignia, who Bernhardt suspected was the CIA "spook" who had provided the day's intelligence. As Bernhardt listened to the gunfire in the already oppressive heat, a sudden chilling awareness came over him. He could only hear the sound of guns firing into the village. No one was shooting back.

Bernhardt slipped out to make his way back to the platoon. Shortly thereafter, the captain rose to his feet and gave the signal to the rest of the men in the command post to move forward. They passed under a lush tangle of banana leaves, through whispering stands of bamboo — and onto a battlefield for which no John Wayne war film had prepared them. The first casualty they spotted on the trail was an infant, his intestines unraveling from a gunshot wound. In the hamlet, old women slumped

leadership. We didn't need Vietnam to create a My Lai. We had social problems *here* that created that."

A similar opinion had been reached by the Army War College. In 1970, it conducted an exhaustive study of leadership in the officer corps. The results were so damning that General William C. Westmoreland, commander of the American troops in Vietnam, who had ordered the study in the first place, immediately classified it and permitted only generals to review its contents.[46] At decade's end, however, a Pentagon intelligence analyst and a retired army officer turned academic conducted their own independent study and reached a similar verdict: the problems in Vietnam had begun, they suggested, in the post–World War II years, when the army remodeled itself after the management style of an ascending corporate technocracy, turning its officer corps into a few "corporate executives" and many "middle-tier managers" (officers in combat units) who were rewarded for massaging statistics and cost-benefit ratios but not for inspiring in young men the sort of loyal and brotherly ties that are the lifeblood of successful combat. As Richard A. Gabriel and Paul L. Savage, the authors of the study, wrote in a book based on their research, *Crisis in Command:*

> The pathologies so clearly present within the officer corps during the conflict were the logical culmination of a series of forces which had been set in motion almost twenty years before the United States ever became enmeshed in the second Indochina war. . . . By the time increasing numbers of the American officer corps took the field in Vietnam in 1964, the American military structure had already become permeated by a set of values, practices, and policies that forced considerations of career advancement to figure more heavily in the behavior of individual officers than the traditional ethics associated with military life. . . .The army had begun to develop and adopt a new ethical code rooted in the entrepreneurial model of the modern business corporation. . . . That these new ethics would ultimately encourage [the officer] to consider *his* career to be of the highest personal and professional importance should have surprised no one.[47]

The army's wholesale shift from the ethic of leadership to the ideal of systems management (expressed so well by General Westmoreland's declaration that "good management is good leadership") had its origins in the years when the United States poured its ever-expanding military budget into the coffers of defense contractors, whose way of doing business soon spread back to the military. "Throughout the fifties, more and more of the internal control practices of the business corporation were adopted by the Army," Gabriel and Savage wrote. "With the appointment of [Ford Motor Company executive] Robert S. McNamara as Secretary of Defense in 1961, the identification of the two structures was nearly complete."[48] In other words, the explanation for the breakdown in army discipline lay, in part, not in the dank terrain of Vietnam but in the dry, statistically rationalizing realms of managements like McDonnell Douglas. Long before that company's DC-3 became Vietnam's notorious "Puff the Magic Dragon" — for its fire-breathing and pyrotechnic combination of magnesium flares and rapid-fire machine guns that spat out a precise six thousand bullets per minute — McDonnell Douglas and its fellow defense contractors dropped over the military a managerial grid that would go a long way toward destroying the traditional social relations of soldiers.[49]

Behind the ascendancy of the aerospace companies loomed the bomb. After the leveling of Tokyo by B-29s and of Hiroshima and Nagasaki by atomic bombs brought Japan's surrender, it seemed evident that nuclear weapons carried by bombers and missiles would be the wave of the warring future. Whichever branch of the service won the struggle to control nuclear weapons would win the budget battle of the postwar era. Not surprisingly, the air force triumphed. As government money flooded into aerospace companies, the postwar army hustled to get in on the action with a new "air cavalry" division; its strategists envisioned "airmobile" land warfare, atomic battlefields to which its foot soldiers would be ferried by helicopter.[50] In the army as in the air force, a new organizational ethic fell in line along aerospace-management principles: "victories" tabulated on computers, raw data produced by interchangeable field workers and processed by systems analysts. The new organization men of the military "laid emphasis on the army as a corporate structure, as a business conglomerate, to be promoted and expanded in much the same way as General Motors or IBM," senior army officer Cecil B. Currey wrote under the pen name Cincinnatus in *Self-Destruction*, his withering study of the Vietnam-era army.[51] Long before McNamara created the Office of Systems Analysis to ensure a more cost-effective war, the army was adopting the principles of business management. To Colonel David H. Hackworth, the most decorated soldier of his era and author of a scathing indictment of the army's engagement in Vietnam, the "increasingly impersonal, almost corporate" nature of what was hailed in the 1950s as the New Look army was first evidenced by a seemingly minor development, the introduction of name tags. "To me, their advent was a sure sign that U.S. army leadership was on a downward slide. Napoleon was said to have been able to recall fifty thousand of his soldiers by name; in the New Army, a CO didn't even have to learn five."[52]

A 1971 Army War College survey of its officers and enlisted men found a prevailing pattern of the "ambitious, transitory commander — marginally skilled in the complexities of his duties — too busy to talk with or listen to his subordinates, and determined to submit acceptably optimistic reports which reflect faultless completion of a variety of tasks at the expense of the sweat and frustration of his subordinates." The enlisted men grasped the point: their superiors, they reported, couldn't care less about them. They weren't supposed to care; that was no longer their job, observed James William Gibson in *The Perfect War,* an incisive examination of the connection between the military's policies in Vietnam and the peacetime technocracy that preceded them. Given the new corporate management model of organization, he wrote, the social relationships "within the military disappear and all that remain are technological-production systems and ways of managing them."[53]

Under the corporate army's new "up or out" policy, most officers deemed the price of caring too costly. Like the middle-management ranks at McDonnell Douglas, the officer corps bloated during those years. Post–World War II, the percentage of army men who were officers more than doubled, and inflation did not bring quality. These officers shared with the McDonnell Douglas "engineers" a largely bureaucratic and decorative function. "The officers of World War II had a different culture, which focused on the substance of their *work* rather than on the institutional definition and status of their *jobs,* as in Vietnam [emphases in original]," Dr. Jonathan Shay wrote in *Achilles in Vietnam.* Each officer's status had to rise or he would be forced out, and the prime way to rise in the prevailing managerial ethos was to make no waves and keep one's record "clean." A bad performance review could derail a career. If there was a problem in the unit, it was better to ignore it or, if need be, cover it up.[54] The result was, as the original War College study put it, "disloyalty to subordinates." Even the Vietnam-era generals were in rare agreement that corporate-style careerism was creating a crisis in army ranks. In a survey conducted by a fellow retired general, aptly entitled *The War Managers,* nearly 90 percent called careerism a problem in Vietnam; nearly 40 percent "a serious problem." In conditions such as prevailed in Vietnam, wrote another army officer conducting his own study in the 1970s, the GIs would come to perceive their leaders' demands as "illegitimate."[55]

The traditional primary infantry combat units — the company, the platoon, the squad—are essentially all-male families, each ideally a circle of brothers melded together by a commanding father figure who cares about their welfare and shares the risks and sacrifices of battle. As much affection as the brothers hold for each other, it's the father-officer who binds them all together. When Gabriel and Savage looked for the sources of the loss of cohesion in combat groups in Vietnam, they found that such frequently blamed problems as the antiwar protests at home, the poor education of the recruits, racial tensions, or a "permissive society" were either of marginal significance or irrelevant. Time and again, the overriding factor in whether a unit underwent brotherly bonding or social disintegration proved to be the ability of the officer to father his men; and a "middle-tier manager" obsessed with career advancement through the manipulation of short-term statistics was not a man likely to father.[56] Especially when, in the context of the Vietnam War, those short-term statistics became "kill ratios" and "body counts."

The problem wasn't simply "bad leadership" in the war theater, as some military strategists still like to argue. "If only we'd called up the Reserves," they lament, as if better-educated captains could ever have redeemed the moral bankruptcies that sustained America's intervention in Vietnam. Even if an emergency airlift of fatherly officers had provided better battlefield guidance, it could not have rescued a battle misguided from the start. Good national leaders, good fathers, wouldn't have deployed their sons to such a war in the first place.

Once deployed by a numbers-infatuated Pentagon, the sons found themselves betrayed all over again by a field-grade version of the same corporate-management ethic. The new army manager didn't share with his men the risks required to generate the data he needed to advance. In an effort to rotate more of its officers through Vietnam to get their "ticket punched," the Pentagon gave them half the tour of duty of the troops, so each only logged six months in combat. Higher up the ladder, the senior managers took even fewer risks. Despite JFK's promise that his generation's leadership would share the sacrifice, fewer than five hundred of them died in Vietnam, most from accidents or illness, not combat wounds.[57] The consequences of that unshared burden fell on the sons. "The American Army since World War II has experienced a progressive reduction of primary-group cohesion until the Vietnam War, when, it may be argued, it almost ceased to exist at all," concluded Gabriel and Savage.[58]

Michael Bernhardt's experience of unit disintegration began the day he reported to Hawaii's Schofield Barracks for duty with Charlie Company. Until then, he had assumed that most American boys were raised the way he was and had learned, as he had from his father, that "being a man is about responsibility, it's about taking care of people." His military experience had actually started out promisingly enough. He had excelled in basic training, earning the second-highest rifle score in the entire training battalion; he burned through advanced infantry training with similarly high marks, then aced a special leadership course at Fort McClellan in Alabama.[59] He turned down Officers Candidate School. "I was thinking I'd be too young-looking an officer. Who would take me seriously?" Instead, he went to paratrooper school in Fort Benning, Georgia. "It was the best. *The best*. We were all together in a class. Everybody had a sense of belonging and pride."

On a late-summer afternoon thirty years after his Vietnam experience, Michael Bernhardt sat in a coffee shop near his home in Quincy, Florida, and described for me the moment when "the Plan" started to go to pieces. His hair was thinning, his face lined, but his memories of that time seemed unfaded; years of pondering had kept the details sharp. Talking with Bernhardt had the disembodied feel of time travel; the middle-aged body sat in a LaQuinta Inn diner in 1998, while his voice seemed to teleport from 1968.

Bernhardt had arrived at Schofield Barracks to train as one of the first group of "long-range reconnaissance patrol" soldiers, or LRRPS (which the soldiers pronounced "lurps"), the ghostlike men who would slip behind enemy lines to collect intelligence. They were an elite; Bernhardt was one of only seven men selected to train to become the first lurps. His early months in Hawaii were spent rappelling, sliding across great ravines, and doing "daring underwater stuff." "I had so much confidence in this group of men," he recalled. "The emphasis was on teamwork. We were not the Rambos. We were the guys they sent to *rescue* the Rambos when they got in trouble."

Then, two weeks before the 11th Brigade was to leave for Vietnam, new orders came down: the lurps were to be disbanded. The army needed bodies to replenish the ranks of the infantry, depleted by so much death. "We thought, 'What are we now, *numbers*?' " Bernhardt said. "Before, we were something irreplaceable, a tradition being built."

Bernhardt and three other lurps were reassigned to Charlie Company. "And when we saw what we had been put into . . ." Bernhardt drew a sharp breath. "I was nowhere near prepared for what I was seeing. It was like I was in another army." It was not that Charlie Company was so unusual. Bernhardt's earlier experience with the lurps had been the exception. Charlie Company was, if anything, a bit above average. The unit had won a company-of-the-month award and was regarded as the best in the battalion. It wasn't overburdened by sullen draftees; most of the men were volunteers. A later study found that 87 percent of the company's noncommissioned officers had graduated from high school and 70 percent of the other ranks also held high-school diplomas, figures somewhat higher than those for the average company in Vietnam.[60]

What troubled Bernhardt and his fellow lurps was more subtle than levels of mental or physical prowess. "It was clear to us that something was wrong from the moment we brought our stuff up to the barracks— from the way the barracks looked, and the way they addressed their superiors." The barracks' disheveled state called to mind a fraternity more than a military facility. No duty roster was posted, so there were no rotating obligations; no one seemed responsible for anything. "There was no accountability," Bernhardt recalled. "If there was a formation and you missed it, there was no follow-up. Orders were grudgingly carried out, or not. They didn't seem to have much respect for their elders." Which was, in Bernhardt's opinion, close to the heart of the problem. The young men in the company, as he saw it, weren't simply disobedient rabble-rousers who enjoyed bucking orders. Rather, they were boys looking for direction from elders who offered none. They were aspiring dutiful sons in a world without fathers. In this regard, the army was shaping up to be a continuation of, not a respite from, what most of them had known growing up.

Looking back, Bernhardt can only remember one other man who spoke fondly of his father, or spoke of a father at all. Most of them behaved like orphans who had joined the army looking for protection. "There were a lot of these types of guys who seemed to have no father or to have lost respect for their father as a role model and were out there looking to adopt one who was tougher, who was violent, who was the kind who whacks women." Of all these seekers, none struck Bernhardt as more unfathered than William Calley, which was, plainly, a double problem for the unit: he was, after all, a platoon leader. He was supposed to father them. "Before it all happened, when I first met Calley in Hawaii, it was almost as if he was learning certain social skills as he went along," Bernhardt recalled. "Yet he was twenty years old. He was still learning how to fit in, how to find his place in the pecking order, how it all works. He just didn't seem to know. All he had was the [lieutenant's] bars. There was something about him that made me sure he didn't have a father figure when he grew up. It was as if there was a piece missing in him." Bernhardt's view of Calley was widely shared by the men in the company. "He was always trying to be the big man," platoonmate Rennard Doines told journalist Seymour Hersh. As Charles

Hall, a machine gunner, remembered him, "Calley also reminded me of a kid, a kid trying to play war." Calley's favorite expression, his men recalled, was "I'm the boss," repeated ad nauseam precisely because he had such little confidence in his own words.[61]

Calley revealed little of his story at the time that the crimes at My Lai were exposed, and, except for an as-told-to 1971 autobiography, he has maintained a steadfast silence since, turning away all interlocutors who show up from time to time at his jewelry store, inherited from *his wife's* father, in Columbus, Georgia. Calley was no more loquacious with me, cutting off all conversation after ten minutes. "Most people totally obeyed orders and did as they were told" was all he wanted to say about My Lai. At the time of the My Lai investigation, he did say that he came from "an emotionally cold family, one that had never been close." He complained to psychiatrists who examined him as part of the inquiry that his father "drank too much" and an older sister was the only family member he could talk to. Calley's father was a navy veteran who made a comfortable middle-class living as a salesman of heavy-construction equipment; the family had a big home in Miami and a summer retreat in North Carolina. Just before Calley joined the army, however, his mother was dying of cancer and his father's business went bankrupt. After his father sold their Miami home, Calley headed west, eventually for California. He left no forwarding address and wrote no letters home. "[My father] didn't *really* listen . . . to me," Calley protested in his autobiography. Certainly, something about his boyhood was disturbing enough to give him a stomach ulcer by the time he was nineteen.[62]

There was little in Calley's background that suggested potential leadership. He had failed seventh grade for cheating, bombed out of a military academy, and dropped out of Palm Beach Junior College after racking up four Fs. He had originally been rejected for military service because of his ulcer and because he was tone deaf. Later, when it looked like he was about to be drafted—the need for bodies had prompted the army to reclassify him as eligible—he enlisted and was recommended for Officers Candidate School, from which he graduated in the bottom fourth of the class.[63]

Second Lieutenant Calley found himself on both ends of the army's new management system. When he looked down, he saw only unpredictable young men whose actions could destroy his clean paper record. When he looked up, he saw no one who was concerned about his welfare. It was later said that he was driven by dewy-eyed adoration of Captain Ernest Medina, his company commander; that he was a "boyish" (the favorite press adjective for him) and diminutive (5'3") acolyte, so eager to impress the gruff captain that he took literally an order to wipe out every living thing. "If you can imagine a hard-nosed father who cared nothing about his son and a son who would do everything he could to get his father's approval, that was basically the situation between Medina and Calley," Greg Olsen, a former GI in the unit, told me. Calley's attorneys naturally made much of the image of their client as just an overly zealous good son. "If [Captain Medina] had ordered Bill [Calley] to lead the platoon up a mountain and jump off it," defense lawyer George W. Latimer said approvingly, "he would do it."[64] Thirty years later, Calley was still sticking to that position, if a little less avidly. "Basically, Medina had a handle on it all and appeared to know what he was doing, while the rest of us were inept," he told me, "so there basically is the basis for admiration." But some men in his company saw another side to Calley. Bernhardt was one of them. "Everyone said Calley worshipped Medina, but that wasn't the whole story. He was getting this infantry thing out of the way and he intended to come out with a sparkling recommendation. He *was* always trying to please Medina, but only because that was the only way he could advance himself. What he was after was a good performance rating."

Whatever Calley was looking for, the troops in Charlie Company needed a dedicated commander badly and so were heavily invested in the legend of Captain Medina as the good father. They were, after all, anxious to get through their year in the field and get back home in one piece. Fred Widmer, a radio operator, described Medina as "the kind of officer that you see in war movies; the men would follow him anywhere." Another GI told journalists that it was "like [Medina] was some kind of hen taking care of her brood, if you know what I mean." A couple of months into Charlie Company's hitch in Vietnam, Medina was leading the troops through the countryside of Quang Ngai when they walked into a minefield and began triggering explosions. Men panicked and ran, setting off more mines. Three men died and twelve were horribly mutilated. Some of the men blamed a sergeant for marching them into the disaster and credited Medina with leading the survivors out of the field. He would later receive the Silver Star for his "courage, professional actions and unselfish concern for his men." What Medina's champions chose to ignore was the fact that he probably shouldn't have sent his men into the area at all: the mines, most likely "friendly," were marked on the map.[65] On this and all other matters involving his notorious tour in Vietnam, Medina remains publicly silent to this day. "That was some thirty years ago," he said to me when I called him at his home in Marinette, Wisconsin. "I have nothing to say."

As much as the troops tried to fashion Medina into an old-fashioned leader, there was something off about the portrait they painted, and they knew it. Fred Widmer expressed it as an uneasiness about the curious familiarity between the captain and the troops, as if they were all on the same plane: "Medina's failing, the failing of the whole company, was that we were too close together. You are not supposed to be." Witnesses recalled in Michael Bilton and Kevin Sim's *Four Hours in My Lai* that when the company turned violent in Vietnam, long before My Lai, Medina was in the thick of it, encouraging his men by beating up prisoners himself. When a beating of a civilian turned to homicide, as it did for a village woman only two days before My Lai, the captain was said to have turned a blind eye on the offenders and helped conceal it with fictional stories. His was evidently not a mature or moral adult presence. Much of the time, as the men would later tell journalists, Medina appeared to be "one of the boys."[66] Yet if they were following Medina and he wasn't the commanding father, who was he?

Bernhardt was one who put another name to him. "People talked about how tough Medina was," Bernhardt commented as he sat over his untouched breakfast in the motel coffee shop. "Then others would say he was one of the boys. I'd say his style of leadership was more that of a gang leader. Which explains why he wanted it both ways, to be our buddies and our boss. He wasn't tied to protocol. He wasn't tied to a chain of command. He was a gang leader, running his own war."

The rogue captain unaccountable to a higher command was no anomaly in Vietnam, nor was a street-gang mentality. "In the Vietnam War, combat troops became psychologically isolated and socially anomic with respect to traditional military values," Gabriel and Savage observed in *Crisis in Command*. "In this specific sense, they differed little from a mob."[67] In a war where most anyone above a captain's rank was far from the ground action, and in a corporate army where the higher ranks were dedicated to a hear-no-evil, see-no-evil path of personal career advancement, Captain Medinas proliferated. He distinguished himself only by the degree of the control and the charisma with which he compelled his younger troops to follow his lead. Medina, the army inquiry report later noted, "was looked upon with awe and, in some instances, almost fear." He looked the part: bursting with muscles, he was physically intimidating, "swarthy and powerfully built," as he was described at the time. Before the company even left Hawaii, the men were calling him "Mad Dog," a moniker more suited to a young street gangster than a thirty-year-old commanding officer. In his autobiography, Calley said enthusiastically: "A man would have to commission close to a half million officers before he had someone equal to Captain Medina. A real leader: I think if Medina had gotten drunk and screwed every girl in Hawaii, the troops would have too."[68]

The members of Charlie Company each found their place in the new order of the gang. "There were a few men in the company," Bernhardt said, "who—I can't imagine what they are doing now—they were just sadists, they just wanted to sexually molest and kill for the hell of it. Then there were guys like Calley who did it for the numbers. And then there were men who did it just to be a part of it, to belong. It was all the same reasons gang members do what they do: hate, fear, a need for acceptance.... Military leaders hold themselves responsible for what people do. Gang leaders don't—except to rob a store or to get from point A to B without being blown up. And Medina was good at that. But whatever the people did in the company, good or bad, and it was mostly bad, he wanted it taken care of internally—no reporting, no court-martial, no military justice."

That street gangs fill a void created by the absence of fathers is a familiar story. But it is only half an explanation, pointing a finger at individual male elders while ignoring the reasons for their absence. In the environments where street gangs flourish, the fathers have been decommissioned by a catastrophic collapse whose origins are social, not personal. In a world without utility, there is no role for the father. Where there is nothing for him to master and so nothing for him to hand on, he becomes at best a glorified baby-sitter, or, in the case of war, a bodyguard. Stateside, gang members need only look around at the boarded-up businesses and crumbling civic infrastructure in their neighborhoods to know that their fathers were not about to find them a responsible place in the community. In Vietnam, the soldiers of Charlie Company who peered past the army agitprop could see a reality hard to ignore, a whole organization in incipient collapse, incapable of providing guidance or clear purpose, and so, empty of real fathers.

Despite his later insistence that he was just dutifully abiding by the all-American system he believed in, Calley in his as-told-to autobiography coauthored by John Sack revealed how deeply he understood that the system was a fraud. "Of the infantry's mission here, we didn't get to part one," Calley said. "Everything in today's society is 'How many thousands?' 'How many millions?' 'How many billions?' And everything was in Vietnam: was numbers, and I had to furnish them. So television could say, 'We killed another thousand today,' and Americans say, 'Our country's great.' The body count—damn." Calley also saw that Vietnam was no frontier struggle: "We were men in a pond pushing away the

water: destroying things, and as fast as we pushed it away it rushed in."
He saw that there was no clear enemy: "I wondered, *Now where in the
goddamn hell are the VC here? Or aren't there any?*" He saw that there was
no brotherhood, only a keen sense of isolation: "I was there in a vacuum:
in a jar. . . . I got so I stayed away from [the troops]. . . . I couldn't talk
to the soldiers under me." He saw there were no women and children
seeking his protection: "I'm here to help these people, and they couldn't
care less. . . . Show me that someone wanted us: one example only! I
didn't see any." Calley's one reinvigorating experience came when he was
briefly attached to a civic-aid unit where he built wells. "I felt alive now,
as I never had in America. I felt helpful, even if I couldn't build an SST,
a spaceship, or something spectacular."[69]

In his autobiography, Calley described an epiphany he experienced
while on a rest leave, shacked up with "Yvonne," a Vietnamese prostitute. At first he fantasized about bringing her to America. "I'd love to
have swept her to Miami, my family's home. See the shows and tell her,
'You're free now. We'll go to the Castaways, the Carillon, the Boom-
boom Room, the Fontainebleau." Then it dawned on him: "I was there
in a Vietnamese teahouse and I was thinking, *Gee, I'm great. I'm American:
I got a flushing toilet and an electric light that I can switch on.* . . . I was
sitting there and I suddenly saw, *She's speaking to me in English.*" He realized that here was a woman who knew more than he did, who supported her family and had a connection to her society he could only
dream of. "Ask anyone back in Miami what he would use a million dollars
for. He may say 'A yacht,' he won't say, 'To take care of my mother and
father.' Yvonne will, or Yvonne will say, 'To keep learning things.' . . .
So who is smarter than who? Or who needs who? I bet, if I asked her
to Miami she would tell me, 'I like my village, thank you. I don't like
the Fontainebleau. I don't really want the American Dream.' "[70]

His revelation, however, was immediately suppressed. "*I don't want to
think about it.* Jesus. I would be some officer if I let myself think, *I can't
help the Vietnamese people.* I was on leave, anyway, and I didn't want to
be depressed. I didn't want to go into heavy philosophy. I escaped it: I
had a [Jack] Daniel's, hot towels, etcetera, and I conked. . . . I didn't
think of Yvonne again."[71]

Calley looked into the same abyss as so many of his fellow GIs in
Vietnam. How could he not? Everywhere he turned, only one group
seemed able to claim a genuine mission, a brotherhood, and the support
of women—and that group was the Vietcong. As Vietnam scholar Marilyn Young wrote of the findings of an American study of more than
two hundred Vietcong prisoners who were interrogated, "The enemy was

sustained by a sense of mission, by the trust of the rank and file in the leadership, by the relationship of the soldiers to the villagers, and by the 'nonexpectation of defeat.' "[72]

To gaze into that chasm of doubt too long was to risk madness, to lose one's bearing entirely and wander through a terrifying wilderness without limits. So Calley looked away, as did most of the men of Charlie Company. If the average grunt couldn't create a real mission himself, something obviously beyond his grasp, he could at least come up with a private definition of the enemy that his unit might privately accept, and then he could have an "enemy" to kill. If the enemy became everyone who was not in the gang, as would be true for Charlie Company in the weeks leading up to and culminating in My Lai, then killing the enemy could in itself become the mission.

They had roamed around Quang Ngai province for months without seeing or engaging with troops from the other side in any traditional sense. They had taken casualties from invisible or inanimate opponents: booby traps, land mines, hidden snipers. "We did a lot of walking in the jungle, but never once did we have a confrontation with a mass enemy that we could see," former GI Greg Olsen told me. Their experience wasn't unusual; in the Americal Division to which they belonged, more than 90 percent of casualties that year were inflicted by booby traps and land mines.[73] "At last it had dawned on me," Calley wrote, *these people, they're all the VC.*" This was to be Calley's anti-epiphany. "I realize, there are Americans who say, 'How do you really know it?' Well, I was there. I made decisions. I needed answers, and I didn't have a more logical one." For Calley and for the many men in Vietnam who shot at fleeing women, lassoed old farmers from helicopters, or executed cows and pigs as if they were part of some secret high command, the killing of civilians was not simply a primal rampage in an out-of-control realm; it was also an attempt to reimpose an expected framework, no matter how hideous the fit. The Americans had been promised a certain rite-of-passage drama in which they would emerge the good victors, modern Indian fighters who could tote up their authority in numbers. If the Vietnamese were uncooperative players in this drama, then men like Calley would force them to stick to the script, make their bodies count. The men would have their mission, one way or another. "My duty in our whole area was to find, to close with, and to destroy the VC," Calley said. "I had now found the VC. Everyone there was VC. The old men, the children—the *babies* were all VC or would be VC in about three years. And inside of VC women, I guess there were a thousand little VC now."[74] No wonder by the time they got to My Lai, Calley and his troops could misconstrue a briefing promising a recognizable enemy to mean shoot anything that moves.

The architects of the American Century had drummed it in that manhood was all about the score—on Little League fields, in pro football stadiums, on television's Old West frontier, in the space race. You could not score without an opponent, and so, finding and "closing" with the enemy mattered more than building or cultivating or protecting. When National Security Adviser Walt Rostow (who coined the phrase "the New Frontier" for JFK) was asked to pinpoint the origins of American involvement in Vietnam in the 1974 documentary film *Hearts and Minds*, he responded, "The problem began in its present phase after the launching of Sputnik."[75] What he meant by "the problem," of course, was the threat of a Communist enemy. But the real problem was trying to fashion a meaningful masculine drama out of the "threat" of a tiny beeping satellite or a small, impoverished Southeast Asian nation's struggle for self-determination. It was impossible because these were not meaningful threats or even meaningful potential conquests. And so, in the end, the American sons in Vietnam were left with nothing but the imperative to score—as were their corporate fathers, who had invented the concept of the body count. For My Lai, those fathers would log an official body count of 128. It would be one of the few times the body count was *de*flated; the massacre took the lives of as many as four hundred civilians, and perhaps more.[76]

In Vietnam, the "contest" would become a controlling metaphor. Every company, battalion, division had its versions. The army's 25th Infantry Division's "Best of the Pack" contest was typical, with 100 "points" for each enemy kill and the reward a few days' liberty pass. On that day in My Lai, several members of Charlie Company held a contest, to see who could score the most dead civilians.[77] This was nothing new. As Bernhardt observed, in a war whose daily "contest" was enacted in free-fire zones and whose results were measured by body counts, "not only will an unfortunate civilian be killed or injured in the course of all of this, but it didn't *matter*. The use of body counts meant that they could also be counted as a score." In every encounter with a Vietnamese, he said, you could decide whether "the person is a threat to the security of yourself and your unit, or not a threat. The person is a threat and you decide to kill the person and that's a correct action. . . . Or the person is not a threat, and you can kill the person. The trouble is, the outcome *looks* the same as the correct action. It doesn't look any different, and it's not scored any differently. And you need the score. The individual soldier needs the score, the commanding officer needs the score, the battalion commander and the division commanders need the score. So what else is going to happen?"

That "looks" matter was another lesson the American Century's sons absorbed early. As boys, they had imagined themselves in the shoes of Hollywood warriors. As soldiers, they found themselves cast as the stunt-men brought in to do the action shots, while audiences somewhere presumably watched and applauded. It was hardly surprising that many of the grunts in Vietnam spoke of their experiences as "unreal" or "like a movie"—though no movie they had ever seen—and spoke of everything beyond that country as "the world," as if they had passed into another dimension. Seymour Hersh described a GI who struck a pose that morning in My Lai, "firing his weapons from the hip, cowboy-movie style." Other men that day assumed crouching and kneeling positions fit for TV combat. One soldier jumped on a water buffalo and rode it "like a rodeo bronco rider" while stabbing it over and over. Calley would explain to himself the postmassacre letdown he experienced in cinematic terms: "To be at D-Day or Iwo Jima, to do that shooting and TV shit, and to stop, is a similar thing, I'm sure."[78]

Few would puncture such willful illusions, certainly not Captain Medina. Within a month of the company's arrival "in country," according to an officer's sworn statement, Medina had ordered his men to shoot unarmed fishermen, and they became Charlie Company's first bodies counted. Nor was the illusion punctured by the rest of the Americal Division, which had already made a name for itself for brutality, rape, pillage, and the murder of civilians. A couple of months into Charlie Company's tour in Vietnam, its troops were torturing "suspects," cutting off their ears, dropping lit cigarettes down their pants, gang-raping young girls, lynching old men. And the less likely the prisoner's status as the enemy, it often seemed, the more vicious the torment.[79]

And yet, as in combat units across Vietnam, more than a few men held out. They looked into the same abyss and chose to keep looking. Michael Bernhardt was one of them. He would prove an essential figure in the public exposure of the My Lai massacre, the first soldier to talk to Seymour Hersh, the investigative journalist who broke the story. His prominence did not surprise Michael Terry, a fellow lurp who was also transferred into Charlie Company. Terry ran into Bernhardt in the mess tent after the massacre and remembers him as "appalled and very upset." "It made perfect sense," Terry, now a cement contractor in Orem, Utah, told me, "because he was a guy who had a strong set of values. Mike wasn't going to do what he thought was wrong no matter who ordered him to." Or as Michael Bilton, the British journalist who coauthored

Four Hours in My Lai, the meticulously researched 1992 account of the massacre, put it to me, "Michael Bernhardt is a guy who knows where he's going—his compass doesn't really waver from true north." Bernhardt still isn't sure why he acted as he did. Maybe, he speculated, it was his outsider status. "I only joined the company a week before they left Hawaii. I didn't train with them." Maybe it was his initial and continuing disgust with Calley. "I could see he had no control," Bernhardt recalled, "and he was mean. And it wasn't just because he was short; *I'm* short, too." Maybe because he saw the company as "messed up" from the start, he was less prone to blame anything that went wrong on any available Vietnamese. Or maybe it was because he still felt anchored back home, tethered to the world of "my three dads."

Whatever the reasons, Bernhardt found himself alone in the company, as if existing in what he called a "parallel universe." "Kafka should've gotten ahold of this," he said wryly. "Imagine a virus loose in the world that distorts reality, and the entire world is stricken. Somehow you have an immunity, but everyone else is delusional. So they think *you* are the crazy one. And after a while, *you* think you're crazy, too." He never, however, was crazy enough to believe that the invisible-enemy problem could be solved by murdering civilians. "Not knowing who the enemy was became the major driving force, maybe *the* driving force. Not knowing the enemy became the justification for a certain mythology about Vietnam." One piece of the myth was "the Vietnamese kid wanting candy with a Claymore [mine] clapped to his chest," which prevailed in the company even though it had never happened to any of the company's members and even though they had never heard a substantiated report of it happening to anyone else. "[The children] didn't have wireless devices," Bernhardt said. "Which isn't to say that I trusted them. But I didn't treat them as the enemy either. You take precautions. It was a matter of limits." The company also "followed the mythology of the 'friendly' villagers who lured us into a trap." Again, the company had never actually had such an experience.

Bernhardt had gone to Vietnam to become a seasoned adult leader who inspired trust and confidence. Now he could only trust and rely on himself, on the grown-up who still resided in his head, the only grownup around. As the violence spun out, he tried to rein in the men, knowing it was a fool's errand and yet burdened by his failure. "I was trying to play the role of company conscience," he said, his voice scorched in shame, "but I was not doing a good job." Well before My Lai, Bernhardt had several go-rounds with the gang's "bullies." When one of them began to beat a villager, Bernhardt stepped in, knocked the man's rifle aside, and "grabbed him by the collar." He found they backed off relatively quickly. "They were typical bullies, who are actually cowards, terrible cowards. Just being there after a while was enough. It wasn't that they were afraid of me—I don't think I look that dangerous, now or then. It was almost like Mom looking over your shoulder, I guess.... You could see a pattern and what was coming next. If it looked like they were ready to shoot somebody, I could go ahead and give 'em a nudge. Or I'd lie to 'em and say, 'Brown! Buchanon wants you over on the other side! Go now!' Or I'd just stand in front of a person so they couldn't shoot without shooting through me." The incessant killing of livestock infuriated him. "I'd say, 'Okay, so you think these people could be VC. But the *animals*?!' "

And then there was Calley. Soon after the company arrived at the base camp near My Lai, the platoon was out on patrol. As they passed a village, Calley spotted civilians running around. "He said, 'If they don't stop when you tell 'em to stop, shoot 'em, waste 'em,' " Bernhardt recalled. "I said, 'What for? They may not know what we're saying. This is a very delicate language—we might be telling them to run instead of stop.' Then we got into an argument, and he told me to shut up." On a subsequent patrol, Bernhardt said, Calley ordered him to shoot at a woman with a basket on her shoulder hastening away. Bernhardt made a perfunctory show of pursuing her, shouting "Stop!" in Vietnamese, but did not shoot. Shoot her, Calley ordered again. "I said, 'Well, suppose I miss?' He said, 'You see to it that you don't.' " Bernhardt shot from sixty yards away and missed. "He knows that I can shoot. He said, 'You did that on purpose!' I said, 'Well, I guess I'm not as good as I'm cracked up to be.' " Calley fumed, but he "avoided giving orders that he knew would be refused.... So it eventually came that he left me alone." But Calley did not leave Vietnamese villagers alone. One day, as witnesses recounted, Calley oversaw an "interrogation" of an old farmer who was beaten and then shoved in a well. He clung to the sides by his hands. A GI tried to push him down with his rifle stock, but still the old man hung on—until Calley pulled out his M-16 and shot him dead.[80]

Calley also apparently liked playing at heroics. Repeatedly, he endangered his platoon for a chance to star as the "big man." Eventually, his act proved lethal. After calling in a massive artillery support when his platoon came under small-arms and mortar fire, a disoriented Calley marched his men into the open, where his radio operator was immediately blown to bits. Calley would then claim a fabricated body count of six Vietcong soldiers in his after-action report.[81]

"Maybe if I had killed Calley..." Bernhardt said to me, brooding on a past that was, for him, far more present than the people milling around the restaurant table. "Maybe it might have been different then." Was that something he contemplated in the field? "There were times," he said slowly. "There were times when I had such serious trepidations about what was going to happen with this man who could do anything . . ." One morning, as Bernhardt remembered it, they came across a series of tunnels. As the designated "tunnel rat" because of his small size, he crawled in. "I was down inside of this deep dark tunnel complex, and I spent a lot of time down there. And when I crawled out, I was probably about a hundred yards away from where they all were, at the rim of the village." Bernhardt glanced over at the other soldiers and then scanned the perimeter, and what he said he saw was something that Calley adamantly denies. "It's an absolute lie," Calley said to me. But Bernhardt remembers it as if it were yesterday. "There's Calley, and he's standing there with his drawers down to his ankles, and he's got a naked Vietnamese woman kneeling in front of him. . . . He had a .45 in his hand. I mean, he was out in the open." Bernhardt stood there, still covered in tunnel mud, a black rage running through him. He remembered thinking, "This guy has gone as far as you can go, he's sunk as far as—" Or, more frightening, maybe he hadn't. "Someday," Bernhardt recalled thinking to himself then, not yet able to put words to the unimaginable, "he's going to do something as—as ridiculous as you can get. . . . I've got to kill this man. I've *got* to kill this guy." But he didn't. "I still had very strong inhibitions." Bernhardt stopped there in his telling of the tale, and his hands flew up to his eyes as if shielding them from a harsh light. "God, I wish I had."

———

IN THE EYEWITNESS ACCOUNTS of the horror that was My Lai, a number of men recalled a peculiar vision: a tall senior officer descending from a helicopter, clipboard in hand.[82] If he did in fact exist, he was never identified. The only "authorities" to intercede that day were a twenty-five-year-old helicopter pilot, Hugh Thompson, Jr., accompanied by his crew chief, Glenn Andreotta, and door gunner, Lawrence Colburn, who was only eighteen. Spotting the heaps of slaughtered civilians below, Thompson landed his helicopter and, after ordering Colburn to hold some of Charlie Company's troops at bay with his machine gun, rushed a handful of surviving villagers onto a gunship. As Thompson and his crew were leaving, they took a final pass over the ditch filled with bodies. Andreotta saw something moving. They landed and the crew chief fished out from the gruesome swill a blood-slicked three-year-old, still alive. On the way to the hospital, Thompson wept.[83]

As is now well known, no senior officers, tall or otherwise, descended to stop the events at My Lai while they were occurring or to remedy them afterward. While the top brass in Charlie Company's division knew of the grisly affair within twenty-four hours, they took no action except to cover it up. The brigade log was altered to conceal the truth and the division commander issued a "hero-gram" for the so-called My Lai mission, a memo that read like the management document it was: "The quick response and professionalism displayed during this action has again enhanced the Brigade's image in the eyes of higher commands." Medina was even put up for an award, a recommendation that was ultimately rejected. (Senior officers in Vietnam were often given awards for murky or imaginary acts. As casualties fell in the war's concluding years, awards for courageous acts mysteriously skyrocketed; more than half of the general officers in Vietnam would come home decorated for their "bravery.") General Westmoreland himself added his congratulations to the mounting paper stack of praise, commending Charlie Company "for outstanding action."[84]

Yet many senior officers *had* been present at the massacre. They were floating safely above the bloodbath in clean, hierarchical lines: Lieutenant Colonel Frank A. Barker at one thousand feet, Colonel Oran K. Henderson at fifteen hundred feet, Major General Samuel W. Koster at two thousand. Later Henderson and Koster claimed they saw nothing (Barker died in a helicopter crash before he could be questioned), even though two dozen combat pilots and crewmen at similar heights did.[85] The officer with his clipboard was most likely a hallucination, but what he represented was quite real. He was the management phantom that Richard Matheson, aerospace worker turned author of *The Shrinking Man,* had described in his 1952 short story, "Brother to the Machine": one of the "invisible men" in "the control ship," who was "looking down to see that work was done properly." Those GIs who understood the true nature of the invisible men understood, too, that the airborne superiors were not the fathers, nor were the grunts in the field the beloved sons. "When it came to you one day that this was so," as Matheson wrote, "you saw there was no reason to go on with it."[86]

And when that revelation came to the young men in Vietnam, they saw no reason either. By the late sixties and early seventies, whole platoons and even companies began to mutiny. In 1968, GI units refused to fight on 68 occasions in seven combat divisions of the army alone. In 1970, 109 soldiers of the glamorous First Air Cavalry Division laid down their arms. Army court-martials for acts of willful disobedience rose to

382 a year by 1970. By 1971, 84 of every 1,000 U.S. soldiers were "absent without leave," and the ranks of deserters had doubled in four years to 89,000. And then there was that more stationary method of escape, retreat into a drug-drenched haze. According to a 1971 survey conducted by the Human Resources Research Organization, as many as a third of the GIs in Vietnam had used easy-to-purchase "hard" narcotics like heroin by the closing years of the war.[87]

The GIs also conceived of a more direct way to resist their managers in the field: "fraggings," attempts to murder a commanding officer with an explosive device, most classically a fragmentation grenade rolled under a tent flap. Soldiers placed bounties on officers' heads; the highest was probably the $10,000 reward raised in 1969 by the men of the 101st Airborne (Airmobile) Division to assassinate their commander for ordering them to attack Hamburger Hill. The army reported more than 600 fraggings from 1969 to 1971, causing 82 deaths and 651 injuries. By 1972, a major general investigating military assassinations in the army would put the count at 1,016. No doubt, both were conservative figures. The Judge Advocate General Corps estimated that only 10 percent of fraggers were arrested and tried.[88]

The way that vast numbers of GIs came to see it, the invisible men in the control ships had left the troops to die on the ground while they buzzed back for hot showers, martinis, and movies in their air-conditioned suites at base camp. "We felt abandoned," Bernhardt said, using a verb commonly invoked by Vietnam vets. "We felt abandoned," he amended, pointing skyward, "by all the men *up there.*" Long before GIs began deserting, their superiors were missing in action. It was the *fathers* who were the truly prodigal ones. Major General Samuel W. Koster, the Americal Division commander who hovered above the My Lai massacre at two thousand feet, returned to his luxurious digs, where steak and lobster were often served on engraved china.[89] Meanwhile, the men in the field faced another night of "ambushes." Often, in fact, they were meant to be the ambushable "bait," put there to attract enemy fire so that the air force could swoop down and claim a fat body count. Many times, body-count-hungry commanders wouldn't even warn grunts of enemy troops in the area. "Story after story from infantry soldiers," sociologist William Gibson has written, "concerns commanders who knew large enemy formations were in a given area, but did not tell their subordinates because they did not want them to be cautious." Bernhardt was bitterly familiar with such procedures. "They called it 'target acquisition.'" The grunts weren't acquiring and they weren't ambushing; they were waiting to be acquired and ambushed. They were the alluring objects set out to produce desire in the enemy. As one GI vet would later say, cutting to the nub of it: "We were the system's women."[90]

Michael Bernhardt had a name for the invisible men in the control ships: "the eye in the sky." They watched, they ogled, but they did not participate. "They were up there, way above where you could get killed, and they stayed there." Except when they descended to engage in an "action" that would give them the necessary badges and medals for advancement. Every few months, Bernhardt witnessed the same charade. He described a typical encounter. "A few months into it, the first sergeant and executive officer were flown in by chopper with resupply and dropped within the night perimeter, and they went out and let a few rounds go, so the commanding officer could say they'd come under fire. And then the first sergeant and the executive officer were flown back. And that's how they got their CIBs [Combat Infantry Badges]." The failure of senior officers to share the risks galled Charlie Company's troops. One day, the battalion commander, Lieutenant Colonel Edwin Beers, paid a brief visit. As he was getting ready to take off, he was overheard on the radio, "saying he had to get back to base because his beer was getting cold," Bernhardt recalled. "And that was something that rippled through the whole bunch, and it kind of was the punctuation, I guess, for their attitude toward us, for what we knew they thought." And so "it didn't surprise anybody," he said, when one of the soldiers decided to give the colonel "a good scare." As his chopper lifted off, Beers suddenly came under fire. The GIs could see him frantically spinning around trying to locate the source of the bullets. "We were all about ready to fall down laughing, because we knew the place was secure. There wasn't a chance that there was VC anywhere."

Most of the time, though, Charlie Company was on its own, with no senior officers for the men to place in their gunsights. The men on the ground well understood that even if they gunned down every officer who flew overhead (and the soldier who shot at Beers had, Bernhardt noted, actually missed on purpose), they would still be the targets. And not just of the "enemy" in the bush. The monitoring men in the sky knew how to silence dissent. In the weeks following My Lai, no one would be more aware of that than Michael Bernhardt. In a gang, any one of the brothers who challenges gang rule is in danger, because if you are not a member you are, by definition, an enemy. When Bernhardt held his rifle to the ground throughout the four hours of shooting in My Lai and cried out, "This is wrong!" he mounted that challenge—and became that enemy.

DAYS LATER, when Charlie Company returned to base camp, Michael Bernhardt was summoned to the command-post bunker. He found Captain Medina seated with one of his platoon sergeants and "a few select people in his little group. . . . I think they knew the way my mind worked," Bernhardt said. The captain knew better than to issue him a distasteful order directly. "Medina didn't threaten me. He just said that nothing would be accomplished by taking the route of writing my congressman. That it wouldn't 'help the mission.' " Bernhardt listened, keeping his own counsel. "I didn't say much of anything. I didn't say yes or no to him. I just said I would do what I thought was right." More than eight months of his combat tour stretched ahead. "It wasn't beyond the imagination that someone in the company would just decide to eliminate me as a problem. I mean, we were all armed to the teeth."

The brigade commander, Colonel Oran Henderson, had popped over for a show of investigating the My Lai "incident," an officer investigating his own command to produce a memo that he would never officially file.[91] Nonetheless, the GIs who had murdered at My Lai were uneasy. "They knew I was regarded as the one most likely to spill the beans. I had to watch my back from then on," Bernhardt said.

As Michael Bilton and Kevin Sim chronicled in *Four Hours in My Lai,* the GIs also turned on their junior officers with a vengeance. They heaped insults on their lieutenants, typically insinuations about their manhood. "What are you doing tonight at ten o'clock?" a GI of Charlie Company sneeringly asked an officer, as a replacement soldier who had just joined the company witnessed. "You come by my bunk anytime, and I'll be ready for a blow job." Lieutenant Calley, who was still seeking good grades by volunteering his platoon for dangerous duty, became the particular object of the troops' wrath. His platoon placed a bounty on his head.[92] When Charlie Company member Greg Olsen was reassigned to a military-police unit, he told me, "I remember stumbling across this incident in the [military police] blotter that had happened after My Lai, where some guys beat up their [superior] officer. And guess who it was? Calley."

About three months after My Lai, Medina got a new combat-free posting; Calley received a civic-affairs job, and eventually a promotion from second to first lieutenant. The grunts of Charlie Company stayed behind, banished to the jungle for record-long stretches. For nearly three months, they barely saw a village, much less a base camp. "They tried to bury us out there," Fred Widmer later recalled bitterly to Bilton and Sim.[93]

"After My Lai," Bernhardt said, "this company was treated like shit.

I think they were hoping every damned one of us would die." If the brass had a hit list, Bernhardt's name probably topped it. Day after day on patrol, Bernhardt was assigned to the most life-threatening positions, slots that generally got rotated. "I was in the front or on the flank all the time. I don't remember being inside the column once. I *never* brought up the rear." Night after night, Bernhardt was placed on ambush. If it wasn't his squad's turn, Bernhardt was simply moved to the unit whose turn it was. "I'll never know, but it did give the appearance of putting me in greater danger."

In the final months of its tour, Charlie Company moved to a base in Duc Pho. One platoon at a time would be sent into the bush, giving the remaining men a chance to dry their clothes and prevent the terrible infections that thrived in the damp. One man recalled that he did not get that chance: Michael Bernhardt. "Every time, I'd be reassigned to the platoon that was going out," he remembered. For weeks on end, Bernhardt waded up to his hips in water. "Jungle rot," a skin disease that essentially rots away the flesh, crept up his feet and legs. Soon, he could barely walk. As the jungle rot was setting in, he was suffering a nightmarish case of dysentery. His weight dropped to 105 pounds. His skin hung off his arms like empty bags, the result of severe dehydration. Nothing the medics tried seemed to have any effect. They asked the commanding officer to send Bernhardt back to the camp infirmary. The captain, Medina's replacement, said he'd try to get clearance from the command, but the base turned down his request.

The date he was scheduled to return home was fast approaching and Bernhardt figured if he could maintain himself to within a few weeks of the date, he would survive. Combat soldiers in Vietnam were typically withdrawn from the field several weeks before their tour officially ended. But in Bernhardt's case, there was no sign of relief. "Then the question became, was I getting out at all?" When he was two or three days away from his return date, a medical helicopter arrived to pick up an injured soldier. A sympathetic medic drew Bernhardt aside. "He told me, 'When that dust-off chopper comes, you get on it.'" He did. "I picked up the wounded guy and I kind of rolled in with him." As the helicopter ascended, Bernhardt was overwhelmed with grief—and shame for leaving the others behind.

At the hospital in Chu Lai, the doctor took one look at Bernhardt's feet—only days away from requiring amputation—and fired off a vitriolic letter to his patient's command. The orderlies moved Bernhardt to a cot, elevating his purple balloon feet on a makeshift sling. Barely a day after Bernhardt's arrival, a GI appeared at his bedside eager to hear his story.

Ron Ridenhour had been a lurp-in-training with him back in Hawaii. A draftee, he became a door gunner on an observation helicopter. He had seen his fair share of atrocities. He once saw troops try to skin a Vietnamese alive. But genocide on a grand scale, he had imagined, was the province of the air war.

One night at a base camp, however, Ridenhour bumped into an acquaintance from Hawaii. They settled into an empty tent with some beers to get caught up. After a few minutes, the GI began to brag, "Hey, man, did you hear what we did at Pinkville?" That was the name the soldiers gave, after its color coding on the map, to the area encompassing My Lai. "Oh, man, we massacred this whole village . . . three or four hundred I guess, at least. A lot, everybody we could find. We didn't leave anybody alive, at least we didn't intend to." Ridenhour would recall later a flooding sensation that he recognized as guilt. "Just simply having the knowledge, I felt, made me complicit, unless I acted on it." He began to make discreet inquiries. He dug up the official, sanitized report of the day's events in My Lai, and sought out other members of Charlie Company to nail down what had really happened. He found several men who were as happy as the first to tell him all about the massacre, but no one was willing to confirm it publicly. After all, they had been a part of it. "I needed somebody that I could count on," Ridenhour wrote later, "and I knew of such a man. His name was Michael Bernhardt." By a fortunate coincidence, Ridenhour happened to be in Chu Lai when Bernhardt was admitted to the base camp's hospital.[94]

Now, Ridenhour stood by his fellow former lurp's bedside and, for a while, talked of other things, biding his time. Finally, Ridenhour came out with it. When he finished, Bernhardt stared up from his pillow, as if from the mucky bottom of a well. "Yeah," he said, it was all true. Well, Ridenhour recalled asking him, what did he intend to do about it? Bernhardt stared back from his private tunnel. "I have a plan," he said at last. And it bore no relation to "the Plan" with which he had enlisted in the army. "When I get back stateside, I'm going to make a list of the chain of command. Then I'm going to take 'em out, one at a time." Bernhardt said he figured he'd use a rifle; he might as well put his marksmanship skills to good use for a change. "Now, I have to say that I believe he was serious," Ridenhour wrote years later. "We were serious people."[95]

"You have to understand, I had lost it," Bernhardt told me, examining that moment at a thirty-year remove. "I was a little nuts. And I had trouble grappling with the idea that I was still alive, and that I was going to go home. I didn't quite believe it. Out there, somewhere, they were going to get you. The plane would crash or some such crap." So was this assassination plot just "babbling," as he had put it, the product of delirium? Bernhardt pondered the question from a long way off. "I don't know if I was serious or not," he said, his not-there eyes locked into their own private vision. "No," he said at last, "I *was* serious. I think if I had remained in that state of mind, I *would* have carried it out." He laughed ruefully and his eyes snapped back into the present. "And then I would've been this sad footnote of history: the guy who went berserk."

On that day, though, Ridenhour told him, "Well, you won't get out for a while"—Bernhardt still had time left to serve in the States—"so why don't we try my plan?" His plan was to launch an investigation. "How?" Bernhardt said. "I don't know," Ridenhour replied, "but somehow. And if I do, will you tell the truth?" Bernhardt said, "If you tell the truth, I'll tell the truth." And Ridenhour said, "Okay."[96]

———

BACK HOME, conservative pundits accused the protester sons of wanting to slay their fathers. But in the end, it was the good sons in Vietnam, some of them anyway, who came closer to contemplating patricide. Whether they were serious or not about putting these thoughts into action—and the hundreds of officers fragged suggests that some were—was less important than the revelation itself. The fathers had brought Bernhardt and his brethren down a path that led directly *away* from adult manhood and then abandoned them there. The generative power that was the province of grown men engaged in society had been denied them, and they knew it. "It completely castrated the whole picture of America," as Ridenhour would put it later, speaking of the shame of My Lai, which was also a personal shame, the shame of masculinity lost. "As far as I was concerned," Ridenhour wrote, "it was a reflection on me."[97]

The outrage Bernhardt felt about My Lai was about his own truncated masculine growth, as well as the victimization of so many innocents. "I should have felt more about the My Lai tragedy," Bernhardt said in his usual unblinking way. He had learned to examine himself in a hard and unforgiving light; he viewed it as his only hope. "I should have felt more about the victims. But to be honest, what I really felt was that the whole command, from Calley all the way up to the battalion, had screwed *me* up. I had had this *plan*. If they had maintained some kind of order, I could've gone home and felt like a big fat hero. I did what I was supposed to do and they didn't. I couldn't be proud of what I did. I knew it had turned to shit."

And yet, Bernhardt did not remain in an assassin's "state of mind." When he returned to the United States, he found he still wanted to believe, like Ridenhour, that if the facts were disclosed, the fathers *would* take responsibility. In that, Bernhardt and Ridenhour and many of those returning from Vietnam were, at least at this stage in their evolution, much like their prodigal antiwar brothers: still clinging to a hope that they could ultimately keep the faith with their fathers by holding them accountable. In 1967, a new group of men, the Vietnam Veterans Against the War, was founded on this premise. Almost a decade after SDS had congregated in Michigan to draft the Port Huron Statement, these vets gathered in the same state to participate in the VVAW's "Winter Soldier Investigation," an anguished inquiry into the true sources of the war's atrocities. "We intend to indict those really responsible for My Lai, for Vietnam, for attempted genocide," said a veteran from Charlie Company's parent unit, the Americal Division, in delivering the conference's opening statement.[98] The vets were determined to make their elders adhere to the promises they had made.

That was Bernhardt's hope on the day he flew home. "I was still going to try to find my way through it. I still was thinking that somehow I might be able to follow my original plan." He reported to Fort Dix as a drill sergeant, where he volunteered to take "the worst, the problem boys." His recruit platoons were consistently ranked the best on the base. All the while, in the back of his mind, he was preparing for the call he knew would come one day, if Ron Ridenhour was successful. Shortly after his return to the States, Bernhardt paid a visit to his childhood home, to prepare his father for that call, too.

His father was stunned and aggrieved on his son's behalf. "My father's concern, the focus of it, was me. He was disgusted because they'd taken something away from me." The larger implications of My Lai, however, were too unfathomable or frightening for his father to countenance. "He just thought, Well, there are some bad people out there. It was like, yes, there's a criminal element out there." Bernhardt's father still saw Vietnam in the framework of World War II. "He just never faced it. I told him, 'We lost. It's over.' He said, 'It's not really over.' I said, 'Yes, it is. It really is.' And that was really unthinkable, that this was not going to be a war where you get 'em to sign a surrender on the USS *Missouri*."

Yet, in the months that followed Bernhardt's return, the greatest tension between father and son was over not Vietnam per se, but over the son's decision to speak publicly on My Lai. "He believed that dissent and opposition to the government were uncalled for. He never doubted authority and its responsibility. He felt there were always channels for getting things done." This was what Bernhardt had believed, too. "Up until Vietnam, it never occurred to me that I'd be opposed to the authorities in the army, not in a million years. It was the *last* thing I expected." Bernhardt and his father had long, agonizing arguments over his plan to air the truth about My Lai. "He wondered if I had defected to the other side. There was a lot of confusion, a lot of strain." His father was also distressed that by speaking out, Bernhardt would be calling attention to himself, a posture that violated his conception of what constituted manhood. "He didn't believe a guy should be in the spotlight. It made him very uneasy." But "we didn't fall apart," Bernhardt added. "It never came to 'This is the end.' Our relationship was strained as far as it could go, but he was still there. I always knew he was my biggest fan."

Ron Ridenhour's exhaustive campaign to launch a public investigation—letters to the army, letters to thirty congressmen and senators, appeals to an overwhelmingly uninterested press—finally prompted Arizona congressman Morris Udall to request a government inquiry.[99] Soon after, Bernhardt got a call from Udall's office. He wasn't much happier about the spotlight than his father—"I knew I was probably shooting down my career in the army"—but he felt compelled. "You know what I really, really wanted?" he said. "To have the entire picture come out, and that it be accurate. Because I thought, If the army just knew, they would see to it that it never happened again. The army wasn't all bad, it was just the corps leadership that was pretty stinking at the time. And it didn't have to be that way. They could still turn this around. I wanted the army to take it and run with it—and leave me alone."

But the army's leaders weren't going to hold themselves accountable and Bernhardt wasn't going to be left alone. Emerging from a daylong debriefing with army investigators, Bernhardt found a mass of reporters and camera crews waiting for him on the steps. The army had called a press conference and put him in front of the microphones, with no time to prepare or order his thoughts. "I didn't know what to say." The media, however, knew what they wanted him to say: they wanted names. "They were interested in individuals, and I was reluctant to give out names, because I don't think that's important. Of course, it was important to the media. But I don't give a damn about that. I don't believe in making guys overnight celebrities for being mass murderers." And he felt queasy about singling out individuals; it seemed to him that My Lai was about something far too large and systemic to pin on particular men.

One of the names the army seemed most interested in purging from its rolls was Bernhardt's. When the news broke, the army yanked him from his post as drill sergeant and assigned him to administrative tasks where he could be supervised, as if *he* were the suspect. He was not

asked to reenlist when his term ended, even though retaining drill sergeants was a critical priority in the army. Instead, along with his "authorization for separation" came a document for him to sign saying he
would say no more about anything he saw in Vietnam. His battalion
commander told him the higher-ups wanted him to sign it. He refused.

With the spotlight came a raft of threatening phone calls and letters,
vicious correspondence that poured in for weeks "by the bushel." Some
wrote saying they hoped he would die, others wrote offering to help him
on his way. Bernhardt tried to shrug it off. "So, some guy's telling me
he's going to kill me. Who cares? It was all silliness." Along with the
venom and the death threats, though, came a few messages that helped
him keep his balance. "I got a letter from one of the Brothers," he
recalled, one of the priests from La Salle Military Academy. Bernhardt
grinned at the memory. "Even though I could be kind of a problem at
times at school, he said he always knew that I was all right."

Bernhardt testified for hours on end before the army panel investigating My Lai, only to be called back again and asked all the same questions. The second time, one of the panel's senior officers, Colonel J.
Ross Franklin, was seething. When Bernhardt described how a woman
carrying baskets was shot when she tried to flee, Franklin lit into him.
"Well," Franklin fumed, "can you think of a better way to stop people
that are running than doing that? . . . The only point I want to make to
you is if you are going to make damning accusations like this, and these
very general statements, you had better have something to back it up.
You're still wearing the uniform and you're portraying people that wear
the uniform as really animals. . . . In the future when you are called before
any kind of an official body, and also in your conversations, what you
saw you saw, and what you heard you heard. You don't want to confuse
the two, Sergeant Bernhardt."[100] Bernhardt, who didn't think he had
been confusing anything, began to feel dizzy, almost "delirious," he recalled. "I kept spinning in the chair. I'd try to stop and I just couldn't."
He began to wonder if he had been drugged, knowing that he was "being
paranoid," yet knowing, too, that he was beginning to believe "anything
was possible." And anything was: as White House files in the National
Archives would later reveal, President Nixon had ordered a secret investigation of My Lai whistle-blower Ron Ridenhour, surveillance of My
Lai investigative journalist Seymour Hersh, and a "dirty tricks" campaign
to discredit My Lai witnesses.[101]

Later, Bernhardt learned the source of Colonel Franklin's sudden fury.
Between Bernhardt's first and second appearances before the panel, the
colonel himself had come under investigation for failing to report the

torture-murder of at least five Vietnamese prisoners at the hands of men under his command.[102] "I could see him watching that star fly away," Bernhardt said. "He was never going to be a general. And there he was, he had all the trappings, all the gongs—he had the CIB, he had silver wings, he had four or five rows of ribbons. He'd done all the school. He'd done the warfare college. He'd done it all, but he was just not going to get it now, and he could see it. And he was pissed at me."

In spite of all efforts to quash the story, it looked for a brief moment like the horrible crimes committed at My Lai would, perversely, have the salutary effect that Bernhardt had imagined—that faced with the enormity of the atrocities and their documented nature, Americans would not be capable of looking away. The nation's citizens would have to reckon with the direction in which their country had been heading, and make a change. We "could still turn this around," as Bernhardt had put it. Indeed, many readers were shocked and sickened. Letters poured in to such press guardians of the postwar status quo as Henry Luce's *Life*, the family magazine that had nonetheless run the most incontrovertible evidence of My Lai's evil: a combat photographer's documentation that day of the heaped bleeding corpses and other scenes of horror. And while some letter writers expressed only a desire to cover their eyes, others seemed to be making connections that ranged far beyond the particulars of what happened in a village they'd never heard of. "We have a thousand Mylais every day right here in America," wrote Jule Lohn, a fifty-three-year-old Chicago businessman, in *Life*'s letter column. "I am talking about the brutalization of individuals in the everyday life of urban communities. . . . Yet our society goes on its frenetic way with hardly a second thought to what is happening. We are accepting killing. . . . It can grow into a way of life. I am absolutely agonized by this kind of window-shade response." U.S. Senator Mark Hatfield wrote, "We as a people are also on trial." And Mrs. Robert Barron of New York penned, "As I weep for them, I feel like shouting and screaming for *someone* to say STOP!!"[103]

Months of investigations, twenty thousand pages of testimony, and five hundred supporting documents later, the army panel concluded that the My Lai massacre had been covered up "at every level within the Americal Division." And yet only a handful of officers were charged, only four court-martialed, and all but Lieutenant Calley acquitted. Calley was found guilty of the premeditated murder of twenty-two Vietnamese civilians and sentenced to a life of hard labor. Three days later, Nixon had Calley released from the stockade and allowed him to serve his sentence under "house arrest" in his own apartment. Then the army secretary cut

Calley's sentence in half, and finally paroled him. All told, Calley spent four and a half months behind bars.[104] While he was serving his truncated jail time, his father lay dying in a trailer park in Hialeah, Florida. "I want to help my boy, but I just don't know what to do," the senior Calley querulously told the press. Calley made one visit to see him. Soon after, his father died, and the army granted Calley permission to attend the funeral. He declined the offer, evidently preferring house arrest.[105]

"Instead of changing the system, the army just drew a big circle around Charlie Company," Bernhardt said. "I had hoped the army would come out of this with a sense of purpose, knowing why and what we are doing. That a change in culture would begin where we started rewarding officers who acted out of responsibility instead of careerism. But they studied this particular group of soldiers like they lived in a vacuum. They never found out the *why* part. The army just distanced itself from the whole thing and concentrated on looking good." As did most of the rest of the country. After a brief flurry of outrage, large percentages of the American public came to agree that My Lai was an anomaly, maybe even a fabrication. (In one survey, 49 percent of respondents deemed the story false.)[106] Calley was anointed a crucified victim. Polls found 80 percent of Americans opposed to Calley's guilty verdict. Military and political elders were vocal: American Legion and Veterans of Foreign Wars groups organized pro-Calley rallies and raised money for his defense; legislators tried to pass bills urging clemency for him; governors had state flags lowered to half mast in his honor. A recording of "The Battle Hymn of Lt. Calley," a tuneful homage to a Christ-like lieutenant, sold more than two hundred thousand copies in three weeks. Women inundated him with mash letters and locks of hair. He received four marriage proposals. Mobs of fans thrust autographs books at him. An admirer loaned him a white Mercedes.[107]

Calley had become, almost despite himself, a man of the new age: a celebrity killer. The rising young star kept careful track of his ratings. As Wayne Greenhaw, an *Alabama Journal* reporter, one of the few to spend time with Calley in this period, noted, he obsessively monitored every news program and newspaper. "Every afternoon at news time he found a television to see where he was being played," Greenhaw observed. "If the networks dropped his case for a day, he'd be disappointed."[108] Once he vanished from the TV set, Calley seemed to understand, he would vanish for good.

Captain Medina was the last officer to be acquitted. His trial would be Michael Bernhardt's most bitter pill. Bernhardt was the prosecution's star witness and greatest threat to the defense team, led by the glamorous F. Lee Bailey. Another key prosecution witness had already disqualified himself by conversing with one of Medina's lawyers after consuming four quarts of wine the night before his scheduled testimony.[109] Bernhardt, however, was no drunk; their approach with him would have to be subtler. The night before Bernhardt was scheduled to testify, Captain Mark Kadish, the army attorney on the defense team, came by his hotel room and engaged him in a seemingly benign and abstract bull session. "We talked about many things," Bernhardt recalled. "We talked about lying and telling the truth, integrity, religion. We got to philosophy, what we thought was right and why we thought it was right. It was all about the order of things. We went for hours. . . . And I fell into his trap." Kadish, he said, had asked "if I would lie to preserve a principle of justice I truly believed in, and I said, 'There are levels of things. If I was in Germany under the Nazis and I had Jews in my attic, I'd lie on any Bible to say there weren't, and I wouldn't have a bad conscience about it.' It was about very, very hypothetical stuff, way out of the courtroom. It got to the far reaches of what was important."

The next morning, Bernhardt mounted the witness stand. Wasn't it true, F. Lee Bailey demanded, that Bernhardt had told a defense lawyer, "I could lie or conceal the truth for a principle of justice"? Hadn't he said, "What I *think* [the truth] is is what is important" and "I could tell an untruth to preserve not a person but a principle—namely justice"? Every time Bernhardt attempted to explain himself, Bailey cut him off. A short recess was called. After the break, the army's *prosecution* attorney rose and said, "We wish to withdraw the witness."[110] Or, as Bernhardt said later: "The prosecutor rolled over and played dead. We weren't *supposed* to win." And thus ended all of Bernhardt's efforts to hold the army accountable for the My Lai massacre.

———

AFTER MICHAEL BERNHARDT LEFT the army, he found himself sinking into another quagmire, the collapsing American economy of the 1970s. He moved to Florida and found work on a land surveyor's crew, then at a sign shop that made billboards for Sheraton and Kmart. He lived in a twenty-two-foot travel trailer, which he parked in a vacationers' lot in Tarpon Springs, on the Gulf of Mexico, and commuted to work on a motorcycle, keeping to himself, avoiding any real emotional involvements, brooding. "I could put Vietnam behind me," he told me. "It was more what was going on *here*. When I was little, it looked to me like after you came back from war, if you just had a good job, then you could expect to own a home and start a family. That was a man's life to me. It turned out there was another war to fight here. And again we were at a disadvantage. You couldn't find the enemy here, you couldn't find it there. If I could've just put my *hands* around it, but I couldn't. I couldn't."

Many days, Bernhardt just got on his motorcycle and sped aimlessly up and down Florida's highways, an uneasy rider. "I thought maybe I should just give up on it, just let things *happen*. Because the odds were probably just as good that way of finding whatever it is you've got to find. Finding your way through the world was just a matter of chance anyhow, so what the hell." One day, he was out just "riding around on my motorcycle." What happened next remains a mystery to him. All Bernhardt knew was that the next morning he came to on the kitchen floor of his trailer "with my motorcycle on my head, and the screen door smashed up." He lay there contemplating the thin aluminum walls and the jumbled rat's nest his life had become. "I looked around and I said, This is no way to live." He extricated himself from the motorcycle and went down to the beach to take a long swim in the Gulf. First as he swam, and then in the days and months that followed, he began to consider his life from a radically new vantage point. It occurred to him that the problem wasn't the authorities themselves, nor even the betrayal of the promise they had made to their "sons": maybe the promise itself wasn't worth keeping. Maybe the rite of passage offered to his generation had been bogus from the start—not because it wasn't fulfilled, but because it wasn't worth fulfilling. Bernhardt wondered: if it were true that he shouldn't have bought into his elders' man-making mission in the first place, then forcing the fathers to make good on the mission was pointless. Bernhardt would have to find his own way, with his own conscience, without the aid of a male establishment. For Bernhardt, it was a frightening prospect.

"For years, I had been asking myself, Did I do all the right stuff? And I had thought that you just added it all up and you could say, This is my manliness score. Everything was supposed to be for points. You get points for going through the service, and bonus points for extra military stuff, and points for a job and a marriage and kids. But it didn't add up. There were all these people walking around with a high score who weren't much of a man in my estimation." He swam in the Gulf and drifted with the current of his thoughts. "I thought to myself, Let's forget all that other stuff. What do you really want to do?" A possibility awakened in him—that he might construct his manhood on other grounds, and in terms that didn't require the standard male checklist or checkpoints. What if, instead of dutifully adhering to the Plan, he tried to, as he put it, "define my manhood by being true to *my* promise, by doing what I care about and being what I say I am?" That was when his life began to change.

———

ALL THROUGH THE LATE summer of 1998, thunderstorms drenched the Florida panhandle. But on the August morning when I drove from Tallahassee to the rural outback to visit Michael Bernhardt and his wife, Dale, the rains had stopped and the sky was clear. His surroundings bore witness to his transformation. After his long-ago revelation in the Gulf, he went back to school, earning a degree in biology; subsequently he worked his way up to his current job as a food-safety administrator with the Florida agriculture department. "I went back to animals," he said. "It made me feel like maybe there was some sense to it all." People took years longer. He met Dale in a karate class. She was studying to be an operating-room nurse and would later become something of an expert at treating gunshot wounds. Her first love was animals, too. They married late and decided against having children. They were going to look after animals instead. The couple bought ten acres outside of Quincy, a "town" that was barely populated. The land they had purchased was overgrown, lush, and fertile, a landscape not unlike the lowlands of Vietnam.

I found Michael Bernhardt that morning in front of their modest brick farmhouse overlooking the pecan orchard, brushing Classy, one of his three horses, and examining a wound that had recently healed on her hind leg. "She hurt her leg badly on the barbed wire," Bernhardt explained, scowling at the scar. The previous owner had run barbed wire around the yard to mark the property. After he discovered the injury, Bernhardt had ripped all the wire down; he had had enough of cordoned perimeters, anyway.

As we stood talking, the back screen door flew open and Dale came out, dressed casually in shorts and T-shirt, accompanied by the latest of their adopted "children," a part–German shepherd named Smoky whom they had found wandering on the lonely stretch of road by their house. "People come out here and dump their pets when they don't want them anymore," Dale said, disgusted. The Bernhardts currently had a census of six stray dogs and seven cats, including two half-bobcats called Nala and Bob. "We're trying to get a humane society started here," Bernhardt said. Dale sighed. Except for a couple of neighbors who also rescue strays, she lamented, "Right now, we *are* the humane society."

We went inside, where dogs greeted us in ecstatic bounds and with a cacophony of yelps as if Bernhardt had just come back from a long journey. We sat at the kitchen table, drank coffee, and talked, while

Annie, an albino mongrel with forlorn eyes, got up on her hind legs and wrapped her front paws around Bernhardt's waist, like she was clinging to a lifeline. "She's deaf," Bernhardt explained, soothing and patting her. She always hung on to him like this; she relied on his ears for protection. Behind Bernhardt, I noticed, hanging on the walls were many medals and ribbons. They weren't military regalia, however. They all honored Bernhardt's horses.

Toward evening, Michael Bernhardt and I wandered outside to exercise the dogs, who ran in giddy circles on the now darkening lawn, under the shadows of spreading trees freighted with pecans, apples, and pears. In the rich soil, shrubs grew as big as trees; redtop and loquat towered above us, as if we were lilliputians in a giant's garden. Even the dragonflies seemed oversized. "I wish my father could've seen this place." Bernhardt sighed heavily. His father had died twenty-one years before. "He would've loved it. He loved horses, like me." Following the dogs, Bernhardt and I roamed into the big field in front of the house. He pointed to the tree line in the distance, where coyotes and southern red wolves prowl in the thick woods. The southern reds are considered extinct, he said, but they aren't protected because they have interbred with coyotes and so aren't purebreeds. "The hunters pretend like they can't tell the difference and shoot 'em," he said, his mouth pulling down into a frown. To the hunters, he observed, anything that moves is the enemy. He gazed out at the luxuriant acres for a while without speaking and watched the dogs play.

"In Vietnam," he said finally, "we threw more ordnance than in World War II. The tonnage per day was staggering. And you looked at the countryside, we defoliated it—we bomb-saturated it—we napalmed it. We practically killed all the livestock."

Was that why he went back to animals? I asked.

He looked out at the lowering sun and shaded his eyes. "I'm not religious, but I think sometimes there is a reason for everything. It makes me feel good if I do something to make life better for the animals in particular. They are as helpless as the people were in Vietnam. The people in Vietnam were actually more helpless. Yet they seem to get along like my bush wolves out there, as long as we don't mess it up. And it makes me feel like maybe by caring for the animals, you can try to reestablish the thing that was lost over there." By "lost," he referred not to the death toll or the war itself, but to the death of values. "In Charlie Company, cowardice and courage was all turned around. If you showed any sign of caring, it was seen as a sign of weakness. If you were the least bit concerned about the civilians, you were considered pathetic, definitely not a man." But from such a loss, recovery was possible. "If you can define your manhood in terms of caring," he said, "then maybe we can come back from this."

These days, Bernhardt said, he found himself bothering less and less about categorizing what it meant to be a man. "I'm not sure there is anything where you can say, *That's* what it means to be a man. All these years I was trying to be all these stereotypes. And what was the use? It's a variable thing. You can't *score* it. I'm beginning to think now of not even defining it anymore. I'm beginning to think now just in terms of people."

———

MICHAEL BERNHARDT HAD TO WITNESS a massacre in a village thousands of miles away, had to go up against a military he loved, had to live through years of cover-up and opprobrium and betrayal, a several-decades-long, grueling path, all to get to the point where he could simply begin to imagine a life without predetermined masculine expectations. It says something about how deeply entrenched those expectations are that it took a horrific and protracted ordeal to dislodge them. For many men of Bernhardt's generation who did not confront directly the agonizing dilemmas the war posed in their young lives, there would be no such prolonged ordeal—and no such liberation. They continued to measure their lives by a masculine yardstick imposed on them, and they continued to feel, each time they took that measurement, that they had come up short.

Gordon Dalbey wouldn't be the only one who caught himself yearning for combat. A number of chest-beating articles began to flow forth in the years after the war's end, often penned by men who had avoided the Vietnam-era draft with a deferment and now felt guilty about it. That was just the public expression. More common were the private confessions to friends or lovers; few of us who have had relationships with such men haven't heard one. "I don't think I'll ever have what they have," Christopher Buckley wrote of Vietnam veterans he knew, in an article in *Esquire* called "Viet Guilt," "the aura of *I have been weighed on the scales and have not been found wanting* [his emphasis], and my sense at this point is that I will always feel the lack of it and will try to compensate for it, sometimes in good, other times in ludicrous ways." He would also, he said, always feel embarrassed in the presence of a soldier or a war memorial. "It's guilt at not having participated," he wrote. "At not having done anything. I blew up neither physics labs in Ann Arbor nor Vietcong installations." That neither act was effective or worthy was irrelevant to

Buckley in his judgment of his own "incomplete" masculinity. "Now I know I should have gone," he concluded, "if only to bear witness."¹¹¹

One of the most famous of these public self-castigations, "What Did You Do in the Class War, Daddy?," was penned by journalist James Fallows in the *Washington Monthly* in October 1975. After drawing a low lottery number in his final year as a Harvard undergraduate, Fallows starved himself down to 120 pounds to obtain a physical-fitness deferment. The stamp of UNQUALIFIED on his draft folder marked "the beginning of the sense of shame which remains with me to this day," he wrote. He had saved his hide, he berated himself now, while the working-class "Chelsea boys" who had passed through the induction center the same day were shipped off. He had abandoned his brothers. The better part of valor, he believed now, would have been to go to jail like the draft resisters, the "few noble heroes of the movement," or to go to war, in the hopes that privileged college boys filling up the prisons or dying overseas would have brought matters to a head faster. "By keeping ourselves away from both frying pan and fire we were prolonging the war and consigning the Chelsea boys to danger and death."¹¹²

Journalistic male peers who paid lavish tribute to Fallows's article— "brave" and "courageous" were the most common adjectives employed— were still trying to fit their muddled youthful experience into a traditional male mold, to figure out a way in which they would come out of all this confusion feeling like recognized warriors. "Were the real prisoners of war the young Americans who never left home?" *Esquire* asked. Could a man who refused to go to war "also suffer post-traumatic stress"? was the question raised in an "About Men" column in the *New York Times Magazine*. These male writers seemed to be trying to convince themselves that missing the war could be as "wounding" as having been shot at on the battlefield or going to jail.¹¹³

These men weren't wrong to feel pain, anger, and a sense that they were incomplete. By the terms of their country's definition of masculinity, they had been "left out." As therapist Edward Tick, the author of the "About Men" column who had avoided the war thanks to a college deferment and a high lottery number, acknowledged: "Not one of us feels whole. All our choices—service in Vietnam, service at home, freedom from service altogether—failed to provide the rite of passage that every man needs. I want to feel my own strength, worth and wholeness, and I want to belong to my country and my generation."¹¹⁴ What they truly missed, however, was the opportunity that disastrous war might have provided for a deeper confrontation with their country's definition of masculinity itself. While there were some murmurings at the time about the restrictive and destructive aspects of American manhood, no challenge to it was ever more than skin—or rather, hair-length—deep. What discussion there was mostly came out of the nascent women's movement, and even there, analysis frequently degenerated into speculation that maleness was destructive in and of itself, a matter of testosterone unbound. Such reductionist biological arguments served the women's cause in the short term by casting men as the "enemy" from whom women must be liberated, but it was hardly a line of thought likely to inspire men to challenge their own circumstances.

Even in their disillusionment, the postwar sons clung to a romanticized, cinematic vision of their World War II–forged fathers and felt guilty that they hadn't lived up to their example. Much of the silence of their vet fathers, which the sons assigned to "stoicism," was in its own way just a refusal to confront the horrors of their war in the context of a society celebrating their triumphant acts, and a reluctance to face the paralysis that beset them in the ensuing cold war and consumer-culture juggernaut. Perhaps what the fathers' silence also hid was a private sense that it hadn't, in fact, been enough to serve one's country as a foot soldier if, when you returned, you didn't claim your full place as an adult *maker* of society. Out of the variety of the fathers' experience, society only deeded the sons the example of World War II—and only the victorious side of it, thereby setting a trap that some of the World War II fathers undoubtedly recognized. Perhaps that recognition was part of the reason why they wouldn't talk about "their" war, while the culture talked of nothing else. The individual private fathers understood what the culture didn't: to have the gun without the plough, to be a soldier without a society, was just to be a hunter with blood on your hands and the ghastly, indelible knowledge of your ability to kill.

If the sons hadn't managed the crossing to manhood, well then neither, in truth, had many of the fathers. They had camped, barracks style, in their strip-development houses, but had little relationship with the communities they occupied. They reported to corporate headquarters each day like soldiers, but made little dent in the bureaucracies. They still lived in something like a militarized setting where decisions were made for and handed down to them. That was fine as "a transit sort of thing" (as Bernhardt had described wartime service). But in the postwar years it became a permanent state, an arrested state, and so a generation was suspended in the foyer of manhood forever. It was a spell that could have been broken, if the sons had just dared to name it. But that was a lot to ask of young men who were, if anything, more invested than their elders in a media-inflamed heroic vision of their fathers' battlefield exploits. Nor were they allowed a forum in which to begin to raise such questions.

The sons might mount a private challenge to the masculine formula, as Michael Bernhardt did on his horse farm in the Florida outback, but they couldn't challenge it publicly, as those soldiers who returned to oppose the war found out. Like many of those veterans, John Kerry hoped his opposition would lead to the creation of "a New Soldier" with a new path to masculinity. As he told the Senate Foreign Relations Committee in 1971, he and his fellow Vietnam Veterans Against the War wanted most of all "to undertake one last mission": "to search out and destroy the last vestige of this barbaric war, to pacify our own hearts, to conquer the hate and the fear that have driven this country these last ten years and more, so when thirty years from now our brothers go down the street without a leg, without an arm, or a face, and small boys ask why, we will be able to say 'Vietnam' and not mean a desert, not a filthy obscene memory, but mean instead the place where America finally turned and where soldiers like us helped it in the turning."[115] But instead of turning around, America turned away, stranding its potential New Soldiers and their quest for a new masculinity in hostile territory.

And so the men who opposed the Vietnam War and the men who fought it both passed the place where they might have staged a meaningful confrontation, the place where they might have started to question the very map they had in their hands. They were angry at their fathers for failing to supply an enemy they could defeat with honor. They were angry because they didn't get to win as their fathers had. But, generally speaking, it did not occur to them to be angry at the terms by which "winning" had been defined, to challenge the core tenets of superpower masculinity. Why did a man have to "win"—and what were the costs of that expectation in a time when winning was no longer meaningful? Wasn't there another way to serve society, to feel truly useful, to be loved by your brothers and appreciated by the women in your life? Why couldn't they let go of the idea of a "New Frontier" that President Kennedy had promised but never produced?

These questions were painful and hard to face, much less answer honestly. But a few of the good sons had dared to raise them. "He saw [Kennedy] before him, his overwhelming sincerity," Robert Roth wrote in his 1973 novel *Sand in the Wind*, a fictionalized account of his Vietnam tour of duty. "Again he wanted to believe, was willing to sacrifice everything to the myth. . . . He felt he understood why the radicals could deride things Kennedy had done and everything he represented, yet still squirm to avoid the mention of his name. They too had believed."[116] Likewise, Vietnam veteran and author Tim O'Brien turned a brutally honest eye on his own choice *not* to flee the draft and saw how he had been led not by a manly call to wartime valor but by a fear of derision from his winning-obsessed society. In *The Things They Carried,* O'Brien described a fictionalized version of himself who sat in a boat on a boundary river in northern Minnesota, contemplating flight to Canada and imagining a seething mob of people on the shore—his parents, his girlfriends, the Chamber of Commerce, the Joint Chiefs of Staff, Gary Cooper—all screaming at him "[l]ike some weird sporting event: everybody screaming from the sidelines, rooting me on—a loud stadium roar. . . . Traitor! they yelled. Turncoat! Pussy!" He "couldn't endure the mockery, or the disgrace, or the patriotic ridicule." And so, he concluded: "I was a coward. I went to war."[117]

The Vietnam-era generation of men would be divided, and would divide itself, between the good and the prodigal, between the ones who went to war and the ones who didn't, between the ones who dutifully submitted to their elders' agenda and the ones who opposed it. But the fissure was more superficial than most of them imagined. The prodigal sons began their "rebellion" to defend what they thought *was* the elders' agenda, and many of the good sons ended their "submission" with an unprecedented revolt against that agenda.[118] Both the dutiful and the rebel son wanted the same thing in the end: to go home and be recognized by the fathers. Neither got the homecoming he had wanted. The real dividing line would be between the vast majority of men still determined to "win" and a handful who recognized that their manhood lay in coming to terms honestly and agonizingly with loss. The men who dared to face the full implications of that found themselves in terrifyingly uncharted territory, no matter how "good" or "prodigal" was the path on which they had originally set out. If anything, it was the good son, the one who went to Vietnam, who found himself deepest in this wilderness—and, if he was very brave, was able to make his way into the unknown without the old trail markers to guide him.

A man didn't have to go to Vietnam to confront the jungle. Reverend Gordon Dalbey was one "prodigal" who sought a new route to manhood not based on either saluting or shaking his fist at Dad. "God brought me to my knees," Dalbey told me, "to where I could see: killing your father doesn't make you a man. It makes you a killer." But he also understood that to free himself from the restrictions of received manhood, to find his own path, he would need the strength of a father's love to support him. In 1979, he believed he had found it.

"I tried all the pop psychologies. I did primal scream therapy. For fifteen dollars an hour, they let me scream in the basement, and I beat pillows and smashed things to get my anger out. I even tried some spooky occult stuff, pendulums and all that, that's supposed to open you up to the supernatural." Nothing worked. In 1979, Dalbey had a born-again conversion experience and began to see God in direct and personal terms. At the time, Dalbey was the pastor of a mainstream church near Los Angeles. After his conversion, his laying on of hands and talk of "demons" appalled his more restrained congregants, who forced his resignation. "Within a month after I resigned as pastor," he recalled, his wife of ten years asked for a divorce. Everything Dalbey had worked toward was in tatters; "I had a neat little liberal Harvard package and it was just blasted, everything fell apart." Yet he wasn't regretful, because now, he believed, he had a father, and so could start again.

"It was like I had a father I could talk to, who talked to me, who did things, who was powerful, who saved me," Dalbey told me. "It's like a whole new world opened up to me." His conversion freed him, he said, "to trust God, to trust his definition of manhood. I guess it just sort of took away all definitions, so I could beg God, 'You've got to put a new definition in me, because I don't trust mine anymore.' And he did."

The new masculine definition Dalbey said his Father showed him was "the power to heal," particularly other men who felt as lost as he did. His new masculine role was to be of service in a "spiritual battle" that he could pursue through his writing and counseling. His new enemy, of course, was the evil embodied by Satan. In this way, "I *am* a commander of men," Dalbey said to me, thinking of his commanding military father. "In one sense, I'm a supply officer like my father was in the navy, who provides men with the materials, so to speak, to draw close to the Father. But the 'material' is my heart." Whether this was really a new blueprint of manhood or just a retooled version of his father's was hard for me to know. Dalbey was still relying on the tropes of battles and frontiers and enemies, yet my impression was that his masculine path was still very much a work in progress. If he hadn't abandoned the old, worn course yet, it wasn't for lack of trying.

Dalbey remarried in 1990, and in caring for his preschool-age son he was finding a deepening and durable source of manhood. Whether the embrace of a father found in heaven would allow Dalbey to "draw close" to his own earthbound father was another question entirely. And it was here, it seemed to me, that Dalbey was most stuck, most anguished. As a boy, Dalbey recalled, he and his father had shared one activity only. "My dad took me to church when I was a boy," he said, just the two of them, without the women. "It was the man thing to do." It was a familial masculine tradition. Dalbey's father, in his youth, had gone to church accompanied solely by *his* father. In light of that, Dalbey hoped that religion might reunite him with his father, might begin to thaw all those silent, icebound years.

A few weeks after our conversation in the Goleta Professional Building, I received a note from Gordon Dalbey. He had returned to North Carolina to speak at a church near his childhood home and had invited his father, who had never seen him deliver a talk before. Dalbey had even arranged for a driver to chauffeur him to the church. But his father declined, with a thin excuse about how "it's wrong to 'put people out' like that." Only after the event's organizers intervened and requested his presence did the father relent. "Naturally, it hurts," Dalbey wrote to me, "but I realize the hurt I feel is not only mine. . . . The discipline for me is just to cry it out to Jesus . . . in order that 'all may go well with you in the land you are about to occupy' (Exodus 20:12). That's the only way I can ensure my son will escape the vicious generational cycle."

I hoped, for Dalbey's and his son's sakes, that he could escape the cycle. And I feared, for him as for so many men like him, that the odds were stacked against any man who tried to make the break alone. Perhaps, in the end, Michael Bernhardt was managing to navigate that treacherous terrain where so many others failed because his father's commitment to a caretaking masculine ethic had *not* been ruptured by World War II. In any event, he was able to see what few others noticed: that the enemy was finally neither the father nor the son; that there was, in fact, no "enemy"—only the dangerous prescriptions of manhood into which they all, fathers as well as sons, had been drafted.

7

THE CREATURE
IN THE MIRROR

The Fantasy Cavalry
to the Rescue

ONLY FIVE YEARS AFTER THE FALL of Saigon, presidential candidate
Ronald Reagan declared in a campaign speech, "For too long, we have
lived with the 'Vietnam Syndrome.'" [1] His words and his subsequent election were advertisements that the war memory had been canceled, to be
replaced with a feel-good celluloid alternative. "It is time that we recognized that ours was, in truth, a noble cause. A small country, newly
free from colonial rule, sought our help in establishing self-rule and
the means of self-defense against a totalitarian neighbor bent on conquest. . . . We dishonor the memory of fifty thousand young Americans
who died in that cause when we give way to feelings of guilt as if we
were doing something shameful."[1]

Vietnam had often seemed like a movie while it was happening—"war
as performance," as historian Marilyn Young has called it.[2] Its body
counts were media-managed by the Pentagon, its audience glued to the
nightly news, its ultimate disaster often attributed to a hostile press
corps. Finally, years after it was over, Americans received the cinematic
resolution that the actual war had denied them. Instead of honoring the
dead by grappling with the war's true lessons, Americans chose to apply
the balm of movie magic. If war overseas was already long lost, a battle
continued over what sort of damage it had wreaked on American mas-

culinity, the violence done to men's sense of mission, confidence, even virtue. The nation sought a fantasy to redeem its manhood, and it would find no better ringmaster than the great fabulist himself, Ronald Reagan.

Reagan's combat conjurings predated Vietnam. He remembered vividly and recounted unashamedly battle scenes from World War II, even though he had never left the environs of Hollywood during the war years. Declared ineligible for combat, he spent the war narrating flyboy training films and appearing in a few of them like *Rear Gunner* and *For God and Country*. Later, he recalled how his "service" (in the Army Air Corps First Motion Picture Unit in Hollywood) had ripped him from home and hearth. "By the time I got out of the Army Air Corps," mused the man whose battlefield grime had all been applied by makeup artists, "all I wanted to do—in common with several million other veterans—was to rest up awhile, make love to my wife, and come up refreshed to a better job in an ideal world."[3]

For the rest of his life, he imagined scenes from the war he never fought as if they were his own. Such sentimental memories—the gunner dying in the arms of his pilot as his B-17 crashed, the black sailor on KP duty who integrated the navy by manning a machine gun at Pearl Harbor—were all screenplay memories. He horrified many when, in a 1983 meeting with Israeli Prime Minister Yitzhak Shamir, he suggested that he had actually photographed the liberation of Nazi death camps as a member of the Signal Corps, and even kept a copy of the film. More startling than his made-up personal experiences was his unshakable belief in them. No matter how often critics pointed up the speciousness of his wartime claims, how often they located the source of his anecdotes in one long-forgotten war movie or another, he remained unfazed, serenely confident of his own borrowed recollections. He still believed in them because he had acted them out or witnessed them himself—as a spectator in a movie theater. "Because films were real to Reagan, he remembered them with the clarity of actual experience," Lou Cannon wrote in *President Reagan: The Role of a Lifetime*. As Reagan himself once remarked, "Maybe I had seen too many war movies, the heroics of which I sometimes confused with real life."[4] Long before Arnold Schwarzenegger's character in *Last Action Hero* slipped off and on the screen, Reagan was effortlessly passing between real and cinematic dream states.

More than a fanciful retelling of military history, Reagan's was a full-blown remake of postwar *masculine* history. He believed in the promise made to the era's young men: submit to the new corporate-management and national-security powers, fight the enemies they designate on the frontiers they choose, and they will make a man of you. He had good reason to; it had paid off in his case, in subsidized fortune and fame. Reagan had begun his career ashamed of his Willy Loman of a father, a floundering, boozing shoe salesman who had nothing to pass on but a frenetic, hopeless itinerancy, and he fretted famously in his autobiography *Where's the Rest of Me?* that a Hollywood career was as much a threat to an actor's manhood as the train that had amputated his character's legs in the film *King's Row*. "If he is only an actor, I feel, he is much like I was in *King's Row*, only half a man—no matter how great his talents." Yet he reported that in the end he found "the rest of me"—as a company man in postwar business culture.[5]

In Hollywood, as the Screen Actors Guild's president, he informed for the FBI to cleanse the guild's ranks of Communists, and he carried out studio directives that diluted actors' rights and consolidated corporate power in the industry. Where his corporate handlers saw Reds, he saw Reds. "The Communist plan for Hollywood was remarkably simple," he declared assuredly in 1965. "It was merely to take over the motion picture business. Not only for its profit . . . but also for a grand worldwide propaganda base. . . . It would have been a magnificent coup for our enemies." At the behest of his employer, the defense and entertainment conglomerate General Electric, he tirelessly traveled the businessmen's luncheon circuit warning of the Communist threat, "the most dangerous enemy ever known to man."[6]

In return, in contrast to Willy Loman and the flannel-suited functionaries of postwar corporate culture, attention *was* paid to him. Reagan's new fathers rewarded him with a GE-wired house; they finagled an ornate and murky real-estate deal that turned him a 3,000 percent profit and made him a millionaire; and they financed and orchestrated the public-relations campaign that leveraged the wholly green "politician" into the California governor's house.[7] The postwar deal had worked like a dream for Reagan; submission and verbal shadow-boxing at celluloid enemies had led to celebrity and political showmanship that felt, at least to him, like the other half of his manhood. As political scientist Michael Rogin wrote, "Reagan has realized the dream of the American male, to be taken care of in the name of independence, to be supported while playing the man in charge." He was a man *because* he played one on-screen, on all the screens of his projected life. And when his movie career waned, General Electric saved him by appointing him host of *General Electric Theater*, its number-one-rated TV show on CBS. "This television show came riding along," Reagan recalled. "The cavalry to the rescue."[8]

At the time of his presidency Reagan seemed like the ultimate throwback to an old-fashioned manhood, splitting logs on his ranch, espousing small-town virtues, displaying a stoical and self-deprecating humor that might have come straight out of an Ernie Pyle dispatch. But, more accurately, he was a man ahead of his time. As early as the 1930s, as a sportscaster delivering "live" play-by-play of baseball games he re-created (or on occasion, fabricated) from telegraph wires, he had shown himself to be comfortable with virtual worlds, with the power of the media to create realities as well as celebrities. The rise of Reagan was the ultimate repudiation of Ernie Pyle's masculine vision. Pyle saw a war being won by grunts who weren't glamorized. Reagan was the "airman" who had experienced nothing but the wartime glamour of on-screen battle—and won. To the end of his public life, he remained a man happy to invoke movies as public prescriptions. "Boy!" as President Reagan enthused to the American public in 1985 as the thirty-nine TWA hostages held in Beirut were being released. "After seeing *Rambo* last night, I know what to do the next time this happens." In another age, in the voice of another man, such a remark might have seemed merely whimsical, but in an age when fantasy, history, and celebrity were increasingly confounded, and at a time when the nation desperately needed to come to terms with the reality of its Vietnam experience, those remarks took on a darker cast. "[W]hat happens," Garry Wills wrote in *Reagan's America*, "if, when we look into our historical rearview mirror, all we can see is a movie?"[9] Reagan had found the missing half of his manhood in the celluloid images he conjured in that mirror. But what would other men find there?

———

IN THE LATE SIXTIES, as Michael Bernhardt was leaving the University of Miami, a young man who would come to exemplify the Vietnam-era military in the public mind enrolled. He was as confused about the war as anybody. He had spent the last two years in a college in Switzerland, the only place that would admit him because his high-school grades were so poor, and he had been partial, when not starring on the college football team he had founded, to delivering broadsides against the antiwar movement. "In English class, we had a choice to write a paper, pro or con Vietnam," he would recall, "and I wrote totally pro. The whole thing was written against the detractors and the pacifists, the conscientious objectors. I really went to town on those people. I portrayed them as not people speaking out for the freedoms of all people in the world but cowards afraid to go. They were hiding behind this rhetoric. In truth, they were yellow." By the time he arrived at the University of Miami, though, he was feeling less certain. "When I first heard about Vietnam in college, it hadn't really been played out on the airwaves, and

I thought, 'Oh, this'll be a simple war. It'll be over in no time at all.' And it was very romantic, the fact that it was the Far East, and we were so superior, and they're writing songs about it ["The Song of the Green Berets"], and John Wayne was endorsing it [in his Vietnam-based film *The Green Berets*], and it looked easy compared with World War II, this looked like literally a scrimmage." He laughed ruefully. "I really didn't know what I was talking about."

In this young man's senior year at Miami, with the draft looming, his thinking changed "very much. That's when I did everything in the world to stay out of it." When he was summoned to the army recruitment center in 1968 for a draft physical, "I made like I couldn't hear too well." The army rejected him, he said, but not for deafness (though years later he realized his hearing was in fact impaired). "The truth is, after doing all this psychological testing, they made me 1H, which is 'only to be called in the event of a national emergency.' What does that mean, like when you run out of people? A national emergency! Only take him if they're coming over the fuckin' walls of Atlantic City! When they hit Malibu, give him a gun! I asked, 'What is this about "you're psychological?"' And they said, 'You have the kind of temperament that you would shoot your commander in the back rather than take a bad order.' And that's the truth, I would."

The truth is, in fact, murkier: The designation 1H generally meant that you had drawn a lottery number so high you were unlikely to be called, except in the case of a national emergency; the young man's lottery number the following year was 327.[10] The man seemed to remember two encounters with recruitment officers, and perhaps with the passage of time, he had conflated the two memories, highlighting the story of the psychologically unstable boy. In any event, his way of recollecting his handling of the draft departed notably from the self-flattering revisionism employed by such saber-rattling Clinton haters as talk-radio personality Rush Limbaugh or Vice President Dan Quayle, one of whom reportedly used a benign cyst, the other family connections in the National Guard, to get out of active duty, and each of whom later claimed that they had made no effort to avoid the military.[11] By contrast, in casting himself as a troubled renegade, this man was evidently being *harder* on himself retrospectively. But then, he had a certain theatrical bent—he had been a drama major in college—and a perception of himself as an angry lone-wolf hero, the sort of solo leading man who, for the sake of his own principles, would indeed shoot his commander. He had played Biff in a college production of *Death of a Salesman,* and it was a role he had found deeply satisfying: the dark son who smashed his father's delusions. Something in the part, he felt, though he couldn't quite say why, expressed his deepest self.

His objection to military service wasn't ideological. He had grown up enamored of the armed forces; as a teenager, he had tried to enlist in the navy when he was sixteen. Nor did his opposition rest on moral grounds. "I wasn't completely opposed to the war—I didn't know enough about it," he explained. "But by 1969, I realized it was absurd because there was no way you could *win*. Once they [halted] the bombing, I knew they didn't want to win. It's like a boxer tying his best hand behind his back. . . . That's when I really became angry. There's no chance we're ever going to win! . . . Because they wouldn't *let* them win." (He wasn't alone in that view. By 1979, a Harris poll reported that 73 percent of Americans believed the nation's political leaders "wouldn't let [the soldiers] win" in Vietnam.)[12] So the young man looked for another arena in which to stage his victory drama. He spent the war years of his youth trying to launch a career in film. After many false starts and rebuffs in Hollywood, he finally achieved success, fame, and riches in 1976 with the story of a come-from-behind boxer whose musical mantra of pugilistic victory would be invoked at the 1996 Republican National Convention as presidential nominee Bob Dole's fight song. But the pinnacle of the actor's career as a well-muscled lone underdog would come not with *Rocky* but in 1982, when Sylvester Stallone appeared on-screen as Rambo in *First Blood*, the very personification of a come-from-behind nation.

It is commonly accepted that the *Rambo* trilogy transformed the lost war in Vietnam into a triumphal confirmation of American virtue. But it would be more accurate to say that the film series reclaimed the virtue of the solitary American man. The government technocrats, whom *Rambo* called the "stinking bureaucrats" back in Washington, remain sullied in this revisionist history, while the lone grunt emerged as a warrior-saint. A lost army would be pulled one by one from the quagmire of the war and reimagined as a cast of individual good men because potentially each of them could have been a winner if only he had had a fair shake, or at the very least a superhuman body and the superior weaponry to go with it. Winning—that first principle of manhood in the American Century—would be reaffirmed and encapsulated in a famous exchange in *Rambo: First Blood Part II*. "Sir, do we get to win this time?" Rambo demands of his commanding officer, Colonel Sam Trautman, who has ordered the hero back to Vietnam. "This time," Trautman assures him, "it's up to you." This is reassuring news because John J.

Rambo, we are quickly informed, is an all-American supergrunt—a former POW with enough ribbons, citations, and medals to rate him as the most decorated soldier in world history. "Lemme just say that Rambo is the best combat vet I've ever seen," Trautman gushes. "A pure fighting machine, with only a desire to win a war that someone else lost. And if winning means he'll have to die, he'll die. No fear, no regrets."

Conventional perceptions and clichés about the *Rambo* series are drawn almost entirely from the second of the three films, which scored by far the highest returns at the box office; if any movie was a "winner," it was this one. Its cartoon mythology gave its male fans what they wanted: complete victory, generated by a clear mission on a straightforward frontier, filled to the brim with identifiable enemies. Rambo's redemption in the film was total. Sprung from hard labor in a federal pen by his devoted superior Colonel Trautman, he is sent on a specific mission: to find the remaining American prisoners of war in Vietnam. He locates their POW camp, but the government bureaucrats who never really wanted him to rescue the imprisoned troops double-cross him and strand him in the jungle. Nonetheless, he fights on, against clearly uniformed Vietnamese soldiers who man their fortifications and bloodthirsty Soviets ("damn Russian bastards") who for unexplained reasons are patrolling the Southeast Asian jungle in the 1980s. These enemies inflict electric shock and other sadistic psychosexual torments on the erotically bared torso of Rambo—atrocities that, in reality, were the preferred war crimes of the *South* Vietnamese interrogators we sponsored and our own intelligence agents in such programs as Operation Phoenix.[13] Our hero, by contrast, is principled, long-suffering, respectful to a Vietnamese woman, and harms no innocent civilians. In the end, of course, Rambo breaks free of his tormentors, single-handedly rescues the POWs, and, bathed in the admiring gaze of Colonel Trautman, heads into the Vietnamese backcountry, with his *second* Congressional Medal of Honor waiting in the wings.

The myth of the "forgotten" POW-MIAs became the war's new mission: as early as 1972, as Jonathan Schell has written, "many people were persuaded that the United States was fighting in Vietnam in order to get its prisoners back." By 1991, 69 percent of people responding to a *Wall Street Journal*/NBC News poll maintained that American POWs still remained in Southeast Asia. In fact, as American studies scholar H. Bruce Franklin has written in *M.I.A. or Mythmaking in America*, his careful dissection of the POW-MIA legend, about half of the 2,273 American servicemen who were said to be "unaccounted for" at war's end were actually known at the time to have been killed in action; and

81 percent of the remaining half were airmen lost over the sea or in remote or mountainous terrain. By 1973, all but fifty-three men had been accounted for; by 1976 that number fell to about a dozen; and after exhaustive study, the Defense Department concluded that *no* POWs or MIAs remained, except for one air force captain whose name was kept on the list as a "symbolic gesture" only—he had died in the mid-1960s. Yet the mythical captive serviceman would become a potent political tool, used by Nixon first to prolong the war and then to refuse reconstructive aid promised under the 1973 Paris Peace Agreement, and used by succeeding presidents to block Vietnam's admission to the United Nations and to prevent normalized relations between the two countries. Reagan declared the search for remaining prisoners of war "the highest national priority," and elevated that search to the highest fevered consciousness in the national imagination. In 1982, the POW-MIA banner became the only flag other than the Stars and Stripes to fly over the White House, and it soon waved over public buildings nationwide, with its motto, emblazoned below the bowed head of a solemn POW, announcing its intentions to the world: "You are not forgotten."[14]

The roots of the POW myth were distinctly domestic. The POW became a stand-in for all the ways the postwar sons had been deserted by their "commanding officers," left imprisoned in the anteroom to manhood. For many of the men who responded so dramatically to the Rambo myth, those "stinking bureaucrats" may have brought to mind not wartime officialdom but all the anonymous post–World War II fathers—public and private—who had abandoned them on the fields of masculinity and showed no signs of coming to the rescue. The second Rambo film derives its power from the wishful pretense of the abandoned son—that he doesn't need the father after all, that he can heal himself. Rambo, a former prisoner of war, imprisoned a second time by his own country, drops like Superman from the skies to emancipate his brethren, and so himself. Even without a grown-up search party, in fantasy at least, deliverance can be achieved. Or can it? In the end, Rambo has to bring his achievement back to his father Trautman to appreciate it.

By *Rambo III*, the son would be rescuing the father. In that 1988 film, the hero emerges from virtual sainthood—having moved to a monastery in Thailand—to pluck his mentor Trautman from the Russians' grasp in Afghanistan. This new setting relieved the film's makers of any need to take into account the Vietnam War's pesky details: now the Americans could defend "freedom fighters" with a clear conscience and the Russians, who were by then fighting a Vietnam-like war in Afghanistan, could be the invaders. As Colonel Trautman tells his Russian captor: "We already had our Vietnam. Now you're going to have yours!"

The nature of the relationship between the supervictimized hero and the supervicious enemy that went international in the second and third *Rambo*s had been established in *First Blood,* where the enemy was domestic and the battle intramural. That film was set in the rugged Pacific Northwest, when Rambo was a mildly scruffy vet newly returned from Vietnam, bumming his way through the backwater town of "Hope: Gateway to Holidayland." He incurs the wrath of the town's piggishly redneck sheriff, Will Teasle, whose deputies' taunts trigger a flashback to Rambo's experience as a prisoner of war of the Vietnamese. A panicked Rambo lashes out and soon has to take on a whole posse of bloodthirsty deputies, a pack of snarling Doberman pinschers, and eventually the National Guard. Presiding over this massive onslaught is the sheriff, who wants "to kill him so bad I could taste him." Told Rambo is a "war hero," Teasle vows, "I'm gonna get that son of a bitch, and I'm gonna pin that Congressional Medal of Honor to his liver." In the wilderness of a rain-drenched North American jungle, armed only with a huge serrated knife, Rambo eludes them all using Vietcong-style guerrilla tactics. He whittles Third World weaponry—lethal tree spikes—and stops only to suture his own wounds or hunt for his supper. Finally, the American supergrunt and the American superenemy, Rambo and Teasle, have their showdown *mano a mano,* in the trashed ruins of the town police station. Rambo prevails, but is stopped from delivering a fatal bullet by the intercession of the only man he can trust, Colonel Trautman. With his trench coat draped tenderly over Rambo's shoulders, the colonel escorts the "war hero" to a safe surrender.

Rambo's is the ur-story of the late-twentieth-century American action hero, and the films that featured him were carefully tailored to avoid any reckoning not only with the Vietnam War but with a domestic crisis of masculinity. That was why millions of male moviegoers, most of whom were too young to have watched the Vietnam War on the evening news, leaped to their feet in theaters across the country to cheer. Rambo told them there was no need for a reckoning; there was no crisis. And yet, the evolution of *First Blood* from novel to final film suggests an unreckoned-with past involving the figure at the tormented heart of that unreckoned-with crisis, the familiar father.

Just before *First Blood* was released, the filmmakers arranged for David Morrell, the author of the novel of the same name, and his family to see a screening for the first time. "Orion [the film's distributor] had arranged to show the picture only to us on an afternoon in one of these theaters in Iowa City," the novelist recalled. "So, at two o'clock in the afternoon in this very big empty theater, we saw the movie. It was very strange." But not half as strange as the story Morrell saw on-screen. "We were pretty overwhelmed. I walked out of the theater into the sunlight and I was in a daze, because I didn't know what I'd seen. It was a different animal. [Teasle] had been reduced to nothing. It was a one-sided story. Instead of Teasle and the kid sort of being equal and playing off each other, it had become the kid's story."

Morrell's original tale had little to do with any now familiar formula of superheroes and superthugs. In fact, it contained no enemy at all. The filmmakers had to appoint one. And the one they chose was telling. Though in the movie Rambo refers briefly to "all those maggots at the airport, protesting me, spittin', callin' me a baby-killer," the antiwar radicals were not the film's designated nemesis. And though the hero should have hated the military brass who were, after all, to blame for his best friend's Agent Orange–induced death and his own horrific tour of duty in Vietnam, they, too, were given a pass. Curiously, the filmmakers chose as Rambo's archenemy the character in the novel who had the greatest affinity for him, who was his spiritual kin.

In the book *First Blood,* police chief Wilfred Teasle is a Korean War vet, a marine master sergeant with a Distinguished Service Cross (second only to a Congressional Medal of Honor), who finds himself magnetically and mysteriously drawn to Rambo upon first meeting. The book's Captain Trautman, on the other hand, is not even Rambo's former commanding officer. He is one of the invisible war managers, a man whom Rambo has never met.

Why did the movie version erase the sheriff's connection to Rambo? And why with each sequel was Colonel Trautman fashioned into an ever more benevolent and fatherly protector? The film was not the John Wayne World War II film that Sylvester Stallone and his generation had been raised on; it was not about the simple antagonism between a hero and a foreign enemy. Just as the POW myth wasn't primarily about the Vietnamese, neither was the Rambo saga. *First Blood* and its sequels chronicled a domestic war. That was what put Rambo so squarely in the center of Reagan-era reconstructions of the war. And that is what brought young male audiences to their feet. The reconstituting of American masculinity after Vietnam was a shadow drama between sons and their fathers.

Would Teasle or Trautman become Rambo's father? And what kind of father would that be? The answer went through as many revisions as the movie's screenplay went through rewrites, as David Morrell and the playwright David Rabe and ultimately Sylvester Stallone himself struggled with the text and with their own private and difficult patrimony. Each level of the Rambo story, it turned out, held another level within it, like Russian nesting dolls. But as book followed inspiration, as script followed book, as more scripts followed that first one, and as movie followed movie, the nature of the necessary father would remain *the* abiding issue for everybody involved in the project.

Now I Have Shed My First Blood

DAVID MORRELL AND HIS WIFE, Donna, moved to the high desert of Santa Fe in 1992 because they wanted someplace arid and empty, someplace stripped of associations. The house they chose had the same quality—scrubbed terra-cotta floors, whitewashed walls, big hollow rooms that echo, but not with memories. The yard was ringed by junipers, piñons, and prickly cactus. On the day I came to visit, a stack of war histories lay on the coffee table, including the latest biography of Robert McNamara, but Morrell, who had recently been asked to draft a treatment for a prospective *Rambo IV,* was mentally far from Vietnam. He was intent on showing me the fruits of his latest preoccupation, a rare-photo collection. His purchases had been few and selective; great care had been lavished in mounting and framing black-and-white prints by Ansel Adams, Edward Steichen, Alfred Stieglitz, and Berenice Abbott. I appreciated the clarified beauty of the images, but they conveyed a piercing loneliness that troubled me. It was only later, as I was driving back through the endless, mountainous dry land, the vast and unrelieved red-rock vista, that I realized what had saddened me: the photos were all landscapes, empty of people.

In 1987, the Morrells' only son, Matthew, died after a prolonged battle with a rare form of bone cancer. He was only fifteen. A few years later, the couple traded the family home in Iowa City for the thin air of a New Mexico plateau. Their life is now segmented like the Roman calendar—before Matthew's death and after—and it is obvious in spending time with them that most if not all of their psychological resources have been expended in weathering this terrible crossing. Donna Morrell seems to manage by mothering whoever is at hand and erecting a security fence of chitchat, belied by a fate-stunned gaze and the tendency for her small talk to stray into large matters. When we went into the den to retrieve one of Morrell's books, Donna took my arm, pointed at an urn on a shelf, and said, "That's Matthew; we like to keep him close at hand." Her husband has a different survival strategy, one that has helped him to work out private demons much of his life. David Morrell has turned his anguish into fiction. A prolific author of dark psychological thrillers, he directed his more recent heroes toward a new mission. "After Matt died," he told me, "the search for the father turned into the search for the son." The search for the father had produced the larger library, eight books from the 1970s to the late 1980s. It was, indeed, the search that drove Morrell to try writing fiction — and eventually to *First Blood*.

David Morrell never knew his own father. "I grew up haunted by the loss of a father and bitter at seeing other boys who had fathers." George Morrell, a British RAF bombardier who met Morrell's mother while teaching at a nearby air force school in Canada, was shot down over France in 1943, the same year David was born. At least, that was the story Morrell was raised to believe. When he was nearly four, his mother, an upholstery seamstress in a factory, sent him to a Catholic orphanage, "because she couldn't afford to work and take care of me." He cannot recall how long he stayed in the orphanage, only that he ran away several times and was always returned. "I do remember being taken there — vividly. My mother said we were going for a ride to the country and when we got there, she said, 'We're going to go play now,' and she put me on a swing. A nun was pushing me, and after a while I said, 'Wait, where's my mother?' and I saw her getting into a car. The nun stopped me. I remember crying, and that's all."

Morrell remembers the orphanage as a nightmare. "On Sunday, we'd all be lined up and we'd have a treat on occasion. A nun would come along with a box of red, white, and blue popcorn, and we'd each get a kernel." He was finally released by the return of his mother — or in any case a woman who said she was his mother. "When she picked me up, I didn't know for sure it was her. I didn't remember her face." He came home to an apartment over a bar in a seedy neighborhood in Kitchener-Waterloo, Ontario. His mother had remarried, a bartender, "a man she shouldn't have married. She thought I needed a father figure," Morrell said, "but he had no interest in children. I needed the attention and he wasn't willing to give it, and the more of a fuss I made to get it, the more I alienated him. He barely spoke to me. If we said three words to each other a day, it was a lot." By early adolescence, Morrell had attached himself to a local gang for the sustenance it could ill provide. The thwarted struggle for paternal recognition persisted into adulthood. Already a writer, he came home one night and his stepfather retreated, as he often did, behind a Burpee seed catalog. The endless silence, as Morrell recalled it, was finally broken when the brochure was lowered and his stepfather, pointing to the pages of beefsteak tomatoes and gladiolas, announced: "This is real. The stuff you do is fake."

As a boy, Morrell had learned to retreat, too. "I spent my youth in the movies," he said. The local theater charged fifteen cents. "I'd go to the bus stop and beg the money, claiming I'd lost my bus money." He gravitated toward westerns, rescue thrillers, and sci-fi flicks where invading aliens were repelled. Audie Murphy, the former war hero, was a consuming fascination in his cowboy roles, but the one genre he shrank from was the war movie: "I mean, they just terrified me." The World War II movie, to be precise. "I developed a morbid fear about war." Even watching the news on television, "I was certain that in the middle of the weather report somebody would come on and say, 'Listen, we've got to stop all this because we have got some real trouble. War has been declared!'" All he could see was the vision of his unknown father, a flaming meteor crashing toward earth.

It wasn't until he was twenty-three and a graduate student at Penn State that he was given cause to doubt that image. After several beers, his mother on a visit let slip a strange remark. "She was talking about something or other, and then she said, 'Oh, that reminds me of something George wrote after he was shot down.'" Morrell stared at her. "What did you say?" he asked hoarsely. "Oh, yes," she replied, "he was in the underground. He died in the hospital." Morrell could get little more from her. "So," he said to me, "my father died twice. Or did he die at all? Did he exist?" Morrell asked his mother for photographs or any mementos she had of his father's life. "She claimed to have burned everything. She had no records on him. She had no birth certificate on me." All that she could produce was a medal. "He was a ghost," Morrell said.

In the course of his young manhood, he sought out three proxy father figures, all of them writers. The first he selected when he was about seventeen, from the credits of a television show. "What turned it all around for me was *Route 66*. I saw the first couple episodes and it changed my life." A well-crafted weekly drama that ran from 1960 to 1964, *Route 66* was the quintessential road trip for boys. Every week, two young buddies, Buz and Tod, sped down the highway, turned randomly onto a byroad, and entered what was generally a harrowing adventure. They were both orphans. Buz had raised himself on the streets of New York City's Hell's Kitchen; while Tod was the son of a tycoon who had died bankrupt, leaving him nothing but his two-seater convertible Corvette. "And I saw in these two characters me," Morrell said, "though I didn't know it at the time."

Saturated with psychological dread and the threat of small-town violence, *Route 66* was a sort of postwar *Adventures of Huckleberry Finn*, with the asphalt highway as the Mississippi River navigated by the two orphans on their Simonized raft, and Buz as the scrappy Huck who defends Tod, a gentle Jim in whiteface. The most violent figures in the series are the town fathers the boys often encounter when they stray from the ribbon of highway. It falls to the boys, time and again, to break the spell of these patriarchal brutes. In 1963, the storyline would be updated for the times. When the actor who played Buz fell ill and had to be replaced, a new character was introduced. Linc Case is a U.S. Ranger returning from a stint as an "adviser" in Vietnam, an escapee from a Vietnamese prison camp who feels orphaned by a cold father who nevertheless wants to parade Linc through town as a war hero. Linc bitterly reminds his mother that as a boy he never wanted a mirror in his room, because it would remind him that he'd never been mirrored in his father's eyes: "I wasn't there."

But it was the original Buz and his fatherless nightmare with whom the young David Morrell most identified. In a 1961 installment called "The Mud Nest," Buz tracks his ancestry to a bleak dead end—a mother who is not, it turns out, his mother, who has allowed her own infant son to die because she hated the child's father so much. "I used to have this terrible dream about an airplane that flew over the place I lived," an anguished Buz confides to the strange woman, and it was a dream straight out of the skull of David Morrell. "It always fell. It used to come down along with the sounds of screaming angels. . . . It always crashed in the middle of my garden where my mother was planting flowers. . . . After the crash, the garden always burst into flame and the roses burned down like fuses, real fast, right down to the ground. And my mother, she burned down, too, just like the roses, till everything around me was ashes. Except me."

Dialogue like this gave the teenage Morrell the idea that writing might be a way to conjure a literary career out of the ashes of a paternal inheritance lost in a fiery plane crash. He copied down the name of *Route 66*'s story writer, Stirling Silliphant, and then "handwrote a letter to him, saying, 'I want to be you.'" Morrell didn't dare hope for a reply. But a week later, a letter appeared in his mailbox that, much to young Morrell's amazement, began, "I'm terribly sorry it took me so long to get back to you . . ." Silliphant's advice was brief. "He told me, 'If you want to be a writer, you've got to write and write and write,'" Morrell recalled. "So I took him at his word and set out to be a writer." Along the way Morrell sent Silliphant—an eminent television and screenwriter whose credits would later include the Academy Award–winning film about racial intolerance *In the Heat of the Night*—updates on his progress, including ultimately a copy of his first novel, *First Blood*. "Stirling called me!" Morrell said, still after all these years full of stunned gratitude over the attentions of this older man, "and he said, 'This is a good book. And the fact that you wrote it because of me, I'm just overwhelmed. I'm just purring like a kitten.' " As was Morrell. Later, Morrell flew to Los Angeles to spend a blissful week with Silliphant in Beverly Hills. When Morrell's novel *Brotherhood of the Rose* was published, the screenwriter promoted it to the networks and served as executive producer on the eventual NBC miniseries.

In 1966, Morrell came to Penn State to study under Hemingway scholar Philip Young, whose work he had worshipped from afar. He talked his way into a job as Young's graduate assistant. Young, too, took the fatherless tutee under his wing, even allowing Morrell to use his home to write while he was away one summer. At Penn State, Morrell also "met the third man most responsible for who I am," Philip Klass, a science-fiction writer with the nom de plume of William Tenn. Klass taught a creative-writing class on campus, and Morrell corralled the reluctant teacher. "I asked him to teach me one-on-one," Morrell recalled. "I bothered him and bothered him until he finally said, 'Okay, write a short story a week, and then we'll see.' " Morrell's efforts did not receive a warm reception. "He said to me, 'This is the worst stuff! What are you *doing*?' What I was doing was writing bad Hemingway." Klass then gave him some precious advice. "He said, 'I don't know a lot about you, but I think one of the primary emotions in your world is *fear*. You're afraid of a lot of things, but you don't know what it is you're afraid of.' " Klass told him to pursue that fear " 'as if it's a ferret inside you, because it's going to hide, it's going to dart, it's going to do everything that it can not to identify itself to you. But you have to keep trying to identify it, and as you do and as you get closer, you will find yourself.' "

For months, Morrell sat and wrote abstractly about fear. "I wrote about the fear of heights and the fear of drowning and on and on. I did exactly what he didn't want." Then, one oppressively humid August day, seated at his typewriter in his mentor's empty house, he drifted into a heat-exhausted reverie. "I found myself going down a path through a thick wilderness, the branches all draping down. And I heard a noise behind me, a footstep. Then nothing. Then I heard the step again. And again, but now it was ahead of me. I had this terrible sense someone was in the forest who was meaning to do me great injury. I was turning in a circle looking for the threat. And at that moment, I became conscious that I was still at the typewriter. The ferret had identified itself." The half hallucination became a short story about a target shooter, "The Plinker," his first piece of work to win enthusiastic praise from Philip Klass. "I didn't choose to write thrillers," Morrell told me, "but that's what I was led to, because I was afraid. I'd been living with fear for so long that it had become my major preoccupation. I felt threatened by the anonymous 'they,' I felt threatened by the people I imagined had killed my father, I felt threatened by whatever had taken my father away. I felt betrayed because I didn't have a father. But now whose fault was that? Global forces. I could not control what was being done to me. But I could control how I react. That's my theme: How do you survive? That's ultimately what my books are about."

In thriller after thriller, Morrell's orphaned heroes grapple with their fear by becoming elite, guerrilla-style soldiers in a murky military-intelligence underworld, lone warriors trained by secret government agents who present themselves as surrogate fathers, only to be revealed as the enemy instead. Their identities are always elusive, always at the heart of the hero's journey. The protagonist is invariably plucked from orphaned status and sent off on what the fake father claims is a moral mission, only to discover that the mission is corrupt, the proxy father a predator, and the hero the prey. With the private father dead or vanished, the public "fathers" exploit the boy's vulnerability in the glorified name of national service. The hero's charter is to expose their deceit, while making peace with the impenetrable mystery of the private father's disappearance. It's Morrell's *Route 66*.

David Morrell was certainly trying to follow his sci-fi mentor's advice to face what frightened him on paper, and the fear he had uncovered was real enough. Yet the heroes he filtered his fear through were largely made up out of pulp fantasy; they were early action heroes. In a way, he had resorted to the very "abstract" writing his teacher had advised him against. He wasn't drawing from his own experience—he had neither fought in Vietnam nor resisted it in any way; and he hadn't been, like John Le Carré, a member of the intelligence "community," or earlier, like Dashiell Hammett, a private eye. He based his novels' fantasies of "war" and of the shadow world of intelligence on other fictions—mystery novels, movies, television—and so, while putting real fears in hidden form on the page, he may also have avoided them.

Even so, despite his thriller backdrops and all the governmental and military intrigue, Morrell's heroes are out to rescue not the world but their own unfathered selves through the discovery of the true story of their lost fathers, no matter how terrible or disappointing. While Morrell's heroes fight representatives of human evil and injustice along the way, in the form of rogue intelligence officers or right-wing paramilitary groups, theirs is not really a political engagement. The quest for paternal love remains the central drama. In *Blood Oath,* the hero, Houston, goes to France to find the grave of his father, who supposedly died in World War II, and finds himself up against mysterious killers. But the real "mystery" that he must resolve doesn't involve them. "My father's at the center," he says. "Dear God, what kind of person was he?"[15]

Morrell's orphaned and betrayed warriors belong to a distinctly modern cultural flood of seemingly fatherless cops, hired guns, and soldiers on the loose; his heroes are cousins to Clint Eastwood's Dirty Harry, Mel Gibson's Martin Riggs in *Lethal Weapon,* and the fatherless men in Ross Macdonald's postwar mystery novels. While they bear a passing resemblance to their Depression-era forerunners, the lone detectives of noir fiction and film, these new avengers are, in fact, a radically different breed. Raymond Chandler's Philip Marlowe fought a corrupt and venal society; his postwar heirs fight the theft of their private patrimony. In their world, there is very little in the way of civic infrastructure; their landscape is more like an open sea, in which shadowy men who may be good or evil float by, unmoored to any recognizable social geography.

Such new heroes speak to a generation of men raised with both the heightened expectations of a father-knows-best culture that promised too much and the anguish of having fathers physically and psychologically lost to World War II and its aftermath. Morrell, contemplating the displacement of Depression-era noir heroes by postwar solo warriors, observed to me, "Maybe the difference is, after World War I, there were no massive family changes. But with World War II, something big happened to the fathers. It seemed like the fathers abdicated or vanished or something." That suspicion is widely shared among his male cohorts and is reflected not only in film and literature but in certain changes in psychological theory. As social psychologist Joseph Pleck observed in *The Making of Masculinities,* in the wake of World War II the vanishing father soon displaced the authoritarian father as the central male "problem."

> In many senses, the father's absence as a large-scale social problem had been created by World War II. The war had, of course, directly taken fathers away from their children (for many, permanently), and the earliest studies [of male sex-role identity] concern these wartime separations. But more indirectly, the changes in male-female relations resulting from war had led to a spurt of postwar divorces, creating more absent fathers. The war also greatly stimulated the migration of rural

dwellers, particularly blacks, to cities, where many factors led to the breakdown of their traditional two-parent family structure.... The effects of paternal absence on sons quickly became one of the most frequently studied topics in the sex-role field. The contrast with the earlier period is striking. In the psychological theories of Freud and Jung, the father is the towering figure in the psychological development of the child. In the 1950s and 1960s, he became a dominating figure, not by his presence, but by his absence.[16]

In trying to understand the mystery of his father's absence, David Morrell turned to the autobiography of a childhood hero: the celebrated World War II soldier Audie Murphy. Unlike Morrell's father, Murphy had returned from the war, to acclaim, the Congressional Medal of Honor, and Hollywood glamour. Yet he had left an essential piece of himself behind, never to be recovered. "He stood back from himself so much" was Morrell's comment on Murphy's autobiography, *To Hell and Back,* which he had read and reread with an intensity for which he couldn't precisely account. "I was two pages past the action that he won the Congressional [Medal of Honor] for before I realized what he had just told me, because he said it so flatly." The flat delivery wasn't just modesty. World War II's most decorated soldier returned to a lifelong private battle with violent despair that ended in 1971, as the Vietnam War convulsed the nation, when he died in a plane crash over Virginia. "Here was a man," Morrell said, "who goes to war and wins the Congressional Medal of Honor, and comes home to play cowboys in all these movies, yet he was in this agony, sleeping with a gun under his pillow, nightmares every night, his home life a wreck. The plane crash was a violence at the end of his life that was almost a closing of the circle." In Murphy's tormented, unresolved life, Morrell sensed the roots of his own fearful incompleteness.

Murphy wrote *To Hell and Back* in the present tense, as if the experience had untethered him from history's time line forever. "Now I have shed my first blood," began a typical passage, "I feel no qualms; no pride; no remorse. There is only a weary indifference that will follow me throughout the war." Postwar periodicals like *Life* turned his freckle-faced Tom Sawyer boyishness into a symbol of "the American GI who endured combat and returned home unscathed by it all." But he was scathed, irreparably. He carried the bloody knowledge of his own capacity to kill. He was haunted by what he had *made* happen: his personal body count, much trumpeted by the postwar press, of 240 Germans. He wrote that he had "shed the idea that human life is sacred." Finding himself in the ruins of the Riviera on the day of Germany's surrender, Murphy recalled his mood among the revelers. "In the streets, crowded with merrymakers, I feel only a vague irritation," he wrote. "There is VE-Day without, but no peace within. Like a horror film run backwards, images of the war flicker through my brain. . . . It is as though a fire had roared through this human house, leaving only the charred hulk of something that once was green. Within a couple of hours, I have had enough. I return to my room. But I cannot sleep. My mind still whirls. When I was a child, I was told that men were branded by war. Has the brand been put on me? Have the years of blood and ruin stripped me of all decency? Of all belief?" From henceforth, he wrote, he would lay claim to only one belief: "I believe in the force of a hand grenade, the power of artillery, the accuracy of a Garand. I believe in hitting before you get hit."[17] He knew this was a predator's faith, and he hated himself for it.

While the Hollywood publicity mill and a starstruck media endlessly recounted the details of the heroic moment that won Murphy the Congressional Medal of Honor—his one-man stand against German soldiers from atop a smoldering tank destroyer—another wartime memory burned in the hero's mind. In battle against the Germans in Montélimar, France, Murphy had moved from house to house, searching for snipers. As he stood in the dimly lit interior of an abandoned home, "the door of a room creaks open. Suddenly I find myself faced by a terrible looking creature with a tommy gun. His face is black; his eyes are red and glaring. I give him a burst and see the flash of his own gun, which is followed by the sound of shattering glass." It is only then that he understands: "The horrible being that I shot at was the reflection of my own smoke-blackened self in a mirror."[18]

It was a moment he would revisit in peacetime. One night in the late 1940s, the insomniac actor rose from his troubled marital bed, grabbed his pistol, and shot the bedroom mirror into shards. He spent the next three decades attacking shadow selves—waving guns at terrified actors on movie sets, pursuing street thugs, beating senseless a girlfriend's dog trainer, and pummeling countless men who committed some often imaginary slight. He unofficially attached himself to the Los Angeles Police Department as a "crime fighter" and, with an honorary deputy sheriff's badge from the Dallas and Tucson police departments, stalked dope dealers or punched out young men idling on the city streets. As one of Murphy's closest friends concluded, "Audie was a one-man Army." The media called him "the most decorated soldier"; he called himself an "executioner." The director Don Siegel, whose credits included *Invasion of the Body Snatchers,* was one of the few Hollywood filmmakers to recognize

Murphy's essence: in 1970, Siegel tried to cast Murphy in his latest film, *Dirty Harry*. "We started to talk and I suddenly realized, my God, I'm looking for a killer and here's the killer of all time."[19]

Audie Murphy might have had a chance at reconciling with his killer self if he had returned to a nation interested in an honest reconciliation. But the country he came home to wanted a poster soldier with a sunny smile; it turned a blind eye to the moral darkness etched upon the faces of its traumatized troops. Instead of a reckoning, social guardians and media spokesmen spoke cheerily of postwar "adjustment"—a return to "normalcy," to be achieved by consumers who could purchase domestic bliss. "They took army dogs and rehabilitated them for civilian life," Murphy remarked bitterly, more than a decade after his return. "But they turned soldiers into civilians immediately and let 'em sink or swim."[20] The triumphant nation presumed that because he and his fellow GIs were the victors, they were the virtuous; somehow winning had cleansed them and their countrymen, absolved them of the need for contrition.

Winning, however, had cleansed and absolved American men, and America, of nothing, as the son of one World War II veteran astutely observed more than five decades later. The Reverend Gordon Dalbey recalled to me a story from the Talmud's Mishnah, in which the Israelites had crushed their enemies, laid claim to their land, and begun to celebrate their conquest. Furious, God sent an angel to upbraid them for their failure to grieve the deaths of their enemies, and to pass on his message: "Don't you know these are my children also?" In the celebratory aftermath of World War II, Dalbey saw the outlines of the same parable. "Repenting means literally to turn around, and unless you own up to your own sin, you don't get that transforming power. That's why the victor has it tougher, because he can be seduced into thinking he doesn't have to repent. That's what happened with our fathers. There was no repentance for the sins of World War II." And no transformation—a failure that would have grievous implications for the next generation of men. Postwar culture denied its returning soldiers the opportunity to grapple publicly with their horrific secret burden (not to mention the more public horrific burden of the war's atomic-bomb finale), thereby denying them a moral knowledge to pass down to the sons. All they could instruct their sons to do was to rerun the moment of victory, as Audie Murphy did, time and again, in his innumerable shoot-'em-up star turns on-screen.

Murphy himself perceived the dangers of handing down such a hollow lesson. The "nasty business" of war, he said, was "not the sort of job that a man should get a medal for. I'll tell you what bothers me. What if my sons try to live up to my image? What if people expect it of them?"[21] Some of his nation's "sons" indeed did try to, including Lieutenant William Calley, who told his biographer, "We thought, *We will go to Vietnam and be Audie Murphys. Kick in the door, run in the hooch, give it a good burst* — kill. And get a big kill ratio in Vietnam. Get a big kill count."[22]

During the war, Audie Murphy began to doubt the convenient conceptions of victors and enemies. In his autobiography, he described the disturbing ambivalence that washed over him upon observing a captured German prison-camp guard. "There is something pathetically human about his odd, hobbled walk. What it is I do not know. Perhaps it is the knowledge that we carry in our hearts that nobody ultimately wins. Somewhere we all go down. Force used tyrannically is our common enemy. Why align ourselves with it in whatever shape or fashion?"[23] But his nation had little interest in exploring such thoughts, particularly out of the mouth of their preeminent war hero. Murphy had nowhere to take his revelation, and so he shelved it and went hunting for enemies on his nation's city streets. Take away the honorary deputy's star and there was little to separate his postwar mentality from that of an L.A. gangsta's.

The nation's failure to support penitence would be repeated after the Vietnam War. As Peter Marin wrote in "Living in Moral Pain," "posttraumatic stress disorder" was in many respects but a euphemism for the torment Vietnam vets experienced in returning to a country that would not let them repent, and would not repent itself.

> No one who speaks to many distressed vets can doubt that their involvement in the excessive violence of Vietnam is a fundamental source of their inner turmoil, and that it expresses not just psychological stress but moral pain. It is here that our collective wisdom fails the vets.... We seem as a society to have few useful ways to approach moral pain or guilt, it remains for us a form of neurosis or a pathological symptom, something to escape rather than something to learn from, a disease rather than—as it may well be for the vets—an appropriate if painful response to the past.

The key to addressing moral pain was understanding that it was not just the individual vet's burden, that shame should not be "treated" but shared. "For in making the guilt his alone, or in making it sound as if it were his alone," Marin wrote, the Vietnam veteran was deprived "of precisely the kind of community and good company that make it possible for people to see themselves clearly."[24]

———

DAVID MORRELL HAD a standard story he often told in the 1980s about why he wrote his 1972 novel *First Blood*. Morrell maintained he got the idea for the novel while watching the war on TV.

> The program was *The CBS Evening News,* and on that sultry August evening, Walter Cronkite contrasted two stories whose friction flashed like lightning through my mind.
>
> The first story showed a firefight in Vietnam. Sweaty American soldiers crouched in the jungle, shooting bursts from M-16s to repel an enemy attack. Incoming bullets kicked up dirt and shredded leaves. Medics scrambled to assist the wounded. An officer barked coordinates into a two-way radio, demanding air support. The fatigue, determination, and fear on the faces of the soldiers were dismayingly vivid.
>
> The second story showed a different sort of battle. That steamy summer, the inner cities of America had erupted into violence. In nightmarish images, National Guardsmen clutched M-16s and stalked along the rubble of burning streets, dodging rocks, wary of snipers among devastated vehicles and gutted buildings.
>
> Each news story, distressing enough on its own, became doubly so when paired with the other. It occurred to me that, if I'd turned down the sound, if I hadn't heard each story's reporter explain what I was watching, I might have thought that both film clips were two aspects of one horror. A fire fight outside Saigon, a riot within it. A riot within an American city, a fire fight outside it. Vietnam and America.
>
> What if? I thought. Those magic words are the seed of all fiction. What if I wrote a book in which the Vietnam War literally came home to America?[25]

Morrell recited the same story for me in the slightly dulled tone of someone recycling a stock answer. Actually, those news clips had made only a glancing impression on him; he couldn't even date them. "Was it the riots at the '68 convention," he mused out loud, "or was it the Watts riot?" (Watts was three years earlier and sparked by racial discrimination, not the Vietnam War.) He shrugged. He couldn't remember because a half hour spent before a TV set was not what drove him to the novel. When Morrell sat down to write about the postwar anguish of a much-decorated Vietnam vet, he turned to another war and another hero, a

hero whose real-life torment had long preoccupied him. "The real inspiration was Audie Murphy," Morrell said to me. "When I was writing
First Blood, I *always* thought of Audie Murphy. The point of *First Blood*
is the point of Audie Murphy's life."

While *First Blood* is not classic literature, what is remarkable about
the novel, as opposed to the film, is that it *does* in its way attempt to
address the question of the returning vet's "moral pain"—specifically,
the need for that pain to be shared with male elders back home. While
the movie Rambo is an innocent and a victim, in the book, as David
Morrell has observed, Rambo was "haunted by nightmares about what
he had done in the war."[26]

Like Audie Murphy, the unreconstructed killer of the book prowls
the domestic front, stalking his shadow self, shooting at men whose
violence represents his mirror image. "Six months ago when he finished
convalescing in the hospital," Rambo says of himself in the alienated
third person of *First Blood,* "he had been unable to keep hold of himself.
In a bar in Philadelphia some guy had kept pushing ahead of him to see
the go-go girl take off her pants, and he had broken the guy's nose for
him. A month later, in Pittsburgh, he had slit the throat of a big Negro
who pulled a knife on him when he was sleeping one night by a lake in
a park. The Negro had brought a friend who tried to run, and Rambo
had hunted him all through the park until he finally caught him trying
to start his convertible."[27] This was no high-minded warrior who fired
only when fired upon. While the film Rambo does not himself draw first
blood and kills no more than five people, the book Rambo kills hundreds. This Rambo is looking for a fight, and a fight to the death. He
returns again and again after police chief Teasle drives him to the county
line and tells him not to come back—even after Teasle has treated him,
unlike the sheriff in the film, with some civility. "This cop is friendlier
than the rest were," Rambo says to himself. "More reasonable. Why bug
him? . . . Or do you want the trouble that's coming? You're hungry for
some action, is that it? So you can show your stuff?"[28] And he does show
his stuff in all its sanguinary horror, slashing and splattering and dis-
emboweling innumerable people over the next three hundred pages. He
is, in fact, the embodiment of what America set loose in Vietnam returned home to extract a price in blood.

Yet the desire for human destruction is not all that draws Rambo.
He is pulled, too, by a face that could be his own but isn't. The opening
pages of the novel find Rambo seated at a coffee-shop counter, gazing
into a mirror when Teasle's image appears in the frame. They are each
transfixed. When Teasle first drives Rambo to the edge of town, drops

him off, and is pulling away, he is unable to take his eyes off the young stranger's image, receding in his rearview mirror.[29] They recognize in each other a connection that transcends hunter and prey, that may even offer both of them a way out of the cycle of killing. They are stalking each other, but they are also seeking a patrimony neither received.

Teasle's mother died in childbirth and his father, we are told, died when he was thirteen in a hunting accident, leaving him an orphan. He was raised by his father's best friend, a hunter who owned "the best trained pack of hounds in the county" and who handled him like one of them, forever correcting and scolding and yanking his short leash, but never treating him like a true son.[30] Even as an adult, Teasle still trembles, cowed and emasculated, in his foster father's presence.

When Rambo arrives in town, Teasle is in a tailspin. His wife has packed up and moved to California and is demanding a divorce. They are irreconcilable on one important matter: Teasle wants a child and she doesn't.[31] With the appearance of Rambo, Teasle's paternal yearnings find a strange and frightening match. For this reason, Morrell told me, he "made Teasle old enough to be Rambo's father." Teasle feels a growing kinship with "the kid," as he calls Rambo. He understands the way in which a monstrous desire to reenact the dark moment of "first blood" and a desperate need for love battle in Rambo without cease.

Rambo's biography echoes Teasle's: his mother died when he was young and he was separated from his father, not by death but by his father's violence. "The most important scene to me in *First Blood*," Morrell said to me, "is when it is revealed that Rambo's father beat him." Like so many of Morrell's stories, the key to the narrative lies in a half-buried boyhood memory of paternal betrayal: in this instance, a haunted recollection of how Rambo's father in a boozy, murderous rage "tried to kill him with a knife, and how he ran from the house that night with a bow and arrow that he shot at the old man, nearly killing him."[32]

Teasle's father and foster father and Rambo's father all represent hunters unredeemed by husbandry, and their bloody legacies become the spiritual bond that yokes Teasle and Rambo to each other and eventually locks them in a grisly but oddly empathetic combat. They are not enemies but an older man and younger man who suspect that the key to their redemption lies in each other. Teasle quite literally channels Rambo's psychological and physical agonies, intuits his every movement through the wilderness. "You can't believe the pain in his chest," Teasle moans to the state police, who are mystified by their superior's diagnosis: how could Teasle know when Rambo is nowhere in sight?[33] As the showdown looms, Teasle pleads with the other officers to leave him and

Rambo alone. " 'I shot him and all at once I didn't hate him anymore,' " he says of Rambo in a kind of rapture. " 'I just was sorry. . . . It wouldn't have made a difference if he shot me or not. I still would have been sorry. You have to promise to let me be there at the end. I owe it to him. I have to be with him at the end.' "[34]

Morrell took great pains to dismantle the hero-enemy dynamic and to present Rambo and Teasle instead as father-and-son secret sharers. "I structured the novel," he wrote, "so that a scene from Rambo's perspective would be followed by one from Teasle's. . . . That tactic, I hoped, would make the reader identify with each character and at the same time feel ambivalent about them. Who was the hero, who the villain, or were *both* men heroes, *both* men villains?"[35] Morrell said he wanted readers to "not know who to cheer for." He evidently succeeded: the book's reviews were divided in identifying the hero as either Rambo or Teasle.

The closest character to a "villain" in the book is Captain Sam Trautman (the film promoted him to colonel), who represents the national betrayal that afflicts both Teasle and Rambo. "I gave him that name," Morrell told me, "because to me he was an allegorical version of Uncle Sam. The mechanism that had created [Rambo] destroyed him." He chose "Trautman" because it suggested to him a coldly professional fisherman, "an angler, who lures them in with his bait." The Trautman of the novel is the technocrat on high; he introduces himself to Teasle as the man who "trained the men who trained" Rambo. Rambo recalls Trautman bitterly from his training days as the man who was "never in sight," a martial Wizard of Oz issuing orders from behind a curtain; "the persistent voice over the camp's loudspeaker," Rambo calls him, "the voice that never failed to signal hardship."[36] Trautman personifies the new military of kill ratios, technological values, and image management, a system that views grunts like Rambo and Teasle as mere inputs in a computer tape and denies them their moral needs. When Trautman shows up in the town to "help," he seems most interested in determining how many men Rambo has killed; his first concern is the body count. Teasle is horrified. He uneasily contemplates Trautman's chilly and machinelike demeanor, "his uniform molded perfectly to his body, not a fold or a wrinkle," his skin "the color of lead," and his thin face and sharp chin reminding him of a ferret—the same one, perhaps, that Morrell's old professor once identified with fear itself.[37]

In the end, Trautman's system prevails. It's the war manager, not the sheriff, who delivers the mortal shot to Rambo with steely efficiency, from a sanitary distance, an expert disabling an obsolete piece of weaponry. "I took the top of his head off with this shotgun," he reports coolly to Teasle, who lies dying from a bullet from Rambo's gun, a bullet that Rambo, unlike Trautman, instantly regrets delivering. Teasle, though, dies at peace. As he lies bleeding, he tries to make himself focus on his wife, his home, the life he led to that point, but all he can think of is Rambo. "He thought about the kid," one of the last lines of the book relates, "and flooded with love for him."[38]

What Morrell expresses in his novels is the idea that an estranged father and son can connect only by reckoning with their shame and pain, only by coming to terms with the terrible loss that comes with violence. "The final confrontation between Rambo and Teasle," Morrell wrote later, "would show that in this microcosmic version of the Vietnam War and American attitudes about it, escalating force results in disaster. Nobody wins."[39] For him, the understanding that "nobody wins" is the potential foundation on which a father and son might create a new and more trusting bond. In such a new filial relationship, the father's legacy to the son would be his own reconciliation with his moral pain; the trail he blazed for the next generation would be the path of penitence that led them both out of the moral wilderness.

Years earlier, Morrell had sat at his typewriter and imagined an enemy stalking him in a forest. His search for that enemy, whose footsteps seemed to be both behind and before him, took him in a circle, but it wasn't in vain. His enemy, after all, was at the center of that circle, inside himself. What he feared was all that he carried around unreckoned with, all the moral shame denied under the precepts of an American Century manhood that defines masculine victory as masculine virtue. This is the discovery that comes to Teasle at the end of his pursuit of Rambo—that he is actually hunting himself, his own shame and moral sorrow. And this was the revelation that drove Vietnam veterans to testify at the "Winter Soldier" investigation—against themselves. "I have helped in torturing prisoners," Sergeant Murphy Lloyd of the 173rd Airborne Brigade, a typical self-witness, said into the microphone. His confession, along with so many others, was offered up not to titillate a domestic audience with gory details but to engage that audience in a mutual grappling with a mutual burden. "Whatever it was that was in these men, that allowed them to do the things they did, is in all of us," Master Sergeant Don Duncan of the Special Forces said in the closing remarks of the hearing. He beseeched everyone in the room to "carry away the realization of what you have done, and I have done, and why we did it. And I want us all to do something with that."[40]

In the American Century framework, however, fathers and sons were supposed to connect over victory, not loss; and so the Winter Soldier investigation was largely ignored and quickly forgotten. Many of the grunts might have been ready to reckon with their moral crimes, but their country was not. There was to be no shared contrition, and no ground laid for a new foundation between fathers and sons. The video-taped testimony of the Vietnam Veterans Against the War would ulti-mately be replaced by documentaries like *Vietnam: The Soldiers' Story,* a 1998 six-part television series in which veterans would be invited to speak mostly of how they suffered.[41] The message of *First Blood* would be re-placed in a similar fashion as it made its way from the page to the screen. Teasle's epiphany would be buried in the movie, and the plot reconfig-ured to portray a world where martyred sons are redeemed by all-powerful fathers, a world where, in the end, victory is assured in the kingdom. While it now seems a foregone conclusion that the film of *First Blood* would turn out as it did, there would be some hairpin turns on the road from novel to movie.

I Will Be Your Father

ONE OF THE EARLY WRITERS contracted to draft the *First Blood* script was playwright David Rabe. He was the only one engaged in the decade-long process of writing and rewriting the script who actually was a Viet-nam veteran, and his efforts took the tale into some dark territory even Morrell's book had skirted.

In 1973, a year after the book's publication, Warner Bros. optioned the movie rights, already the second studio to do so. (As there were serial scripts, writers, directors, actors, and producers involved in the *Rambo* films, so a string of movie companies—Columbia Pictures, War-ner Bros., Cinema Group—came and went before Carolco, a company newly formed by producers Andy Vajna and Mario Kassar, finally pro-duced the first of the films in 1982.) Warner Bros. offered the part to actor Al Pacino, and shortly thereafter Pacino called David Rabe to see if he would write the script. Rabe recalled the conversation: "*Jaws* was out and Pacino described to me that the guy should be like the shark—a mindless, driven, single-minded thing that is not available to any plea once it got loose." He gave an eye-rolling laugh. "Actually, it appealed to me. It seemed apt. In the sense that, if the guy is going to embody war, then, that's what war is."

The driven, mindless nature of war, the false glorification of combat as a meaningful transformational experience, was a subject that Rabe had explored with ruthless honesty on the stage. Pacino had, in fact, just starred in the Theater Company of Boston's production of *The Basic*

Training of Pavlo Hummel, the first of Rabe's searing trilogy of Vietnam plays and the one most directly expressive of this theme. The so-called "training" of the green, eager-beaver Pavlo in boot camp and as a medic in Vietnam proves no education at all. Combat training makes him neither older nor wiser, only dead, after a rear-echelon superior who doesn't want to share a prostitute with him lobs a grenade at the young man's feet. Even in death, Pavlo's corpse idiotically repeats from his coffin the empty Jody cadence that a beribboned ranking soldier barks out at him. As Rabe wrote later in an author's note, he is afflicted with "a true, real, and complete inability to grasp the implications of what he does. . . . Pavlo is in fact lost. . . . It is Pavlo's body that changes. His physical efficiency, even his mental efficiency increases, but real insight never comes."[42]

To his eye, Rabe said to me, the novel *First Blood* seemed "a little on the romantic side" in this regard, and "false in the synthetic way that things are balanced out." The book was romantic because it assumed that the fathers who created the war felt responsible for their young men, that they desired contrition, that they sought an honest reconciliation with their sons as much as their sons sought it with them. Appealing as these notions were, Rabe saw little evidence of them in the real-world behavior of the men who sent their sons to war. Rabe had grown up in Dubuque, Iowa, in a world where the postwar version of masculinity was everywhere reinforced. Manhood was attained by total submission to authority; that was the model reinforced by all the male authorities in his life—his father, who gave up a high-school teaching post he loved for a better-paying but unfulfilling job in a meatpacking plant; his football coach, whose every call he was expected to follow to the letter; the priests at his local Catholic church and later at his Catholic college, who harshly silenced his youthful questioning of the strictures they taught.

It seemed to him that America's fathers, private and public, had far more interest in shoring up the crumbling walls of their authority than in working their way toward an authentic reckoning with the lies they had told themselves or their sons. "In the Midwest, and in the Catholic church, and on the team, adults were right because they were the adults. And if you felt something against them, then you were wrong," David Rabe told me one afternoon as we sat in the chill emptiness of a hotel suite in Beverly Hills, where he was stationed for the week while cautiously witnessing the transformation of *Hurlyburly,* one of his plays, into a movie. Rabe has the brooding aspect of a Rodin figure and the features to go with it, a jagged geometry of planes and angles. It is easy to see him as a football player (he played high-school and college football and dreamed of turning pro) and heir to a meatpacker. He hunched forward on a floral couch as he spoke in halting fashion, contemplating the reflective surface of the coffee table as if looking down a well.

"The way I grew up thinking about coaches and authority figures and captains," Rabe said, "there was this *faith* that got expressed in these figures." Rabe called it being in "that team state of mind." It was a state not confined to football. "That idea of belonging to an institution or a team, having your team goals supplant or amplify your own goals, validate them, that was through everything. You had to be loyal, take care of your buddies, endure and be reasonably stoic in the face of pain. You had to be tough and willing to take a beating, and give one. And find your slot in the pack." Looking back now, he said, he could see how that whole team notion of manhood was already, by the 1950s, a collection of attributes with no clear application. "The whole idea of manhood was beginning to seem like an artifice of itself. It wasn't like the Gold Rush or the Civil War where there was something to be done and you really had to do it." By the Vietnam era, it had degenerated into "a fiction, a ghost," and yet "although the war already appeared to be in question, it seemed absurd to question them," Rabe said of his elders. "The entire structure has to be questioned if you are going to question them. And I certainly wasn't going to do that. It was very hard to see a way out."

Rabe didn't question the authorities during his basic training in 1965 at Fort Gordon, in Georgia, or during his year with a hospital-support unit in Long Binh. When he arrived, the area had just been "cleared" by the 1st Division, and onto the scorched, emptied land, Rabe's unit hastily erected a massive snarl of Quonset huts, barracks, bunkers, and PXs— a snarl that produced, down the road, an instant industry of bars and whorehouses. "It became this megalopolis, this huge, huge place where there was everything but a McDonald's," he recalled. "It was hard to see how anybody was going to benefit from it. There was this strange treatment of the Vietnamese. The average GI was not there in any way to help them or understand what was going on."

Rabe's confidence in various authorities had been teetering before he arrived in Vietnam; he had already lost confidence in the priests at college and had resolved to leave the church. Yet he refrained from questioning the Pentagon's mission throughout his tour of duty. "Now whether that was to protect myself or what, I don't know. But I still had this basic faith in it . . . until I came home." The delayed response made sense; the inklings of what troubled him in Vietnam were writ large on the landscape to which he returned. "It didn't take long after I got back. My experience was very much like that sequence in the movie *Heaven and Earth,* where the Vietnamese woman who comes to America goes into her first supermarket and she is overwhelmed by the huge piles of food, the colors. It just almost makes you sick, watching this *abundance.* It's frightening. And you realize, there is *nothing.* It's fake. We're over there for nothing. Nobody here cares. The country was not threatened in any real way. It was a fiction." Rabe paused and studied the shiny tabletop. "The best way I can put it is, there was nothing at stake."

Rabe was beginning to see the Vietnam War as only one lie in a larger construction of falsehoods. "There was this whole architecture in my mind of hierarchies, of authorities, and it ran from the Catholic Church to the military through the senators. It was very hard to figure it all out, because it was all mirrors and support systems that don't seem to be artificial or in collusion but they were. There was this whole manipulation of reality going on, this thing called the 'Communist threat.' And that was something I believed in one hundred percent." Rabe's willingness to believe was rooted in the romance Hollywood had wrapped around World War II. Who could doubt the virtue or legitimacy of the fathers who were that war's undisputed heroes? "World War II was this big rich fantasy life to me," Rabe recalled. "My father wasn't in World War II, but I had an uncle who was in the Battle of the Bulge. And my mother's cousin was a marine captain or lieutenant. I remember once reading a book and coming across this guy's name, in Iwo Jima, and it was this amazing experience. It felt *mythical,* like you were somehow connected to it *personally.* You see the war films and then you see your uncle in a book and it's like they get mixed up in your head." Rabe began to see Vietnam as more the end of a national breakdown than its beginning; he discerned the obscure route that led back from Vietnam to the misconceptions of World War II — to be exact, to those glittery movies and silent male relatives all jumbled up in his mind.

In the painful years that followed his Vietnam tour, Rabe grappled with his waning faith in the reliability of such figures. "Losing faith in the authorities, that's the rest of my life," he said. "It didn't happen overnight. It's all one flow of collapse — my disillusionment with the church, Vietnam. . . . You can get rid of the objects of faith, but it's very hard to get rid of the impulse." Among the authorities Rabe questioned was his father. "We had this strange sort of relationship that was objectively fine and yet something was wrong. I'm only coming to see that now. Now that I am myself a father, I can see in myself that sense of not being effective in the world and the way that can make you behave to your children. My father was very frustrated by his life. He was very smart but I don't know how really connected to reality he was." His father had sacrificed a teacher's role in a real community for the recommended postwar role of a breadwinner with only a tenuous connection to civic life. The Dubuque Packing Company was one of the biggest employers in the area, and Rabe's father submitted himself to its blood-soaked floors so that his family could shop for the choicest cuts of meat in a gleaming supermarket. His son was never exactly sure what his father did at work, and understood only that his authority at home was never to be challenged. "I used to feel if I didn't obey him or accept an ideal or a gesture of his, that what I felt wasn't valid. I was very much in his thrall. The one thing that was to me a benefit of the army was it actually gave me the credentials in my heart to not have to have his approval, or his stamp. I could kind of go my own way.

"Vietnam changed my relationship with my father in subtle and subterranean ways." Rabe noticed that his father, who had only talked about his life during the Great Depression in a very romanticized way, was suddenly eager to impress his veteran son with grisly tales of "how he had worked in Chicago, where he had some strange job where he had to go around and collect dead people who had starved in the street." Rabe's father wasn't offering up this memory as an opportunity for father-son bonding. "It came out in a very competitive way." The war didn't bring them together; it only brought to the surface all the repressed resentments of his father's frustrated life. "My father was very much a reactionary guy, a staunch union man, a believer in the authorities. After I came back, I'd sit still through his tirades." Some of the tirades were about the war, others about the cultural challenges advanced by his son's generation. "I didn't try to change his mind. I didn't let him tell me too much about what he thought. We never really worked anything out."

It seemed to Rabe that the fathers, by their silences and absences, by their blindnesses and the submissions they condoned, had deceived the sons into believing they were on their side. They had all been fooled by the faux-tender screen fathers with whom the sons had spent more time than with their real ones. "Who . . . was . . . my . . . father?" the illegitimate son Pavlo demands of his mother in Rabe's play, and the ensuing conversation seems to echo the crisis in David Morrell's life that inspired *First Blood:*

PAVLO: Where is he?
MRS. HUMMEL: You know that.
PAVLO: No, I want you to tell me.

MRS. HUMMEL: I've already told you.

PAVLO: No, where is he now? What did he look like?

. . .

MRS. HUMMEL: No, you had many fathers, many men, movie men, filmdom's greats—all of them, those grand old men of yesteryear, they were your father. The Fighting Seventy-sixth, do you remember, oh, I remember, little Jimmy, what a tough little mite he was, and how he leaped upon the grenade, did you see, my God what a glory, what a glorious thing with his little tin hat.

PAVLO: My real father!

MRS. HUMMEL: He was like them, the ones I showed you in movies, I pointed them out.

. . .

PAVLO: What was his name? I don't know what it was.

MRS. HUMMEL: Is it my fault you've forgotten?[43]

Hidden behind the glorious celluloid fighting men and the perfect TV dads like Ozzie Nelson, the real fathers were anything but grand old men. They had, Rabe saw, often been reduced by their own submission in a consumer culture to a dangerous befuddlement. In Rabe's second Vietnam play, *Sticks and Bones*, a Vietnam vet named David, blinded in the war, returns home to his uncomprehending, ever-chipper parents, Ozzie and Harriet. Ozzie responds to his son's brokenness by trying to fix the TV so that he can watch the game. "There's a picture but no sound," he complains to his wife. "I'm gonna call the repairman." His wife tells him, "No, no. The TV repairman won't help, you silly. . . . There's something wrong with David."[44]

Of course, there's really something wrong with Ozzie, a fact that his son's crisis forces momentarily to consciousness. "It's like stepping into a hole, the way I feel each morning when I awaken, I see the day and the sun and I'm looking upward into the sky with a sense of looking down," Ozzie confesses. "A sense of hovering over a great pit into which I am about to fall. The sky. Foolishness and deceit, you say, and I know you're right; a trick of feeling inside me being played against me seeking to diminish me and increase itself until it is larger than me filling me and who will I be then? It. That feeling of being nothing." By the end of his soliloquy, though, Ozzie has talked himself back onto the surface of his prepackaged suburban life. He produces a thick packet of paper, hundreds of pages, on which he has inscribed an inventory of everything he's ever purchased and its price. He distributes them on chairs, a stack for each family member. "Here's my portfolio summarized. My mortgage. Life insurance! Now the idea is that you each carry a number of these at all times. Two or three copies, at all times, and you are to pass them out at the slightest provocation. Let people know who I am, what I've done."[45]

The price of the father's return to consumer complacency is the son's life. The son's blinding in Vietnam has forced the father, briefly, to see. The son can't lead the father out of the wilderness any more than the father can guide the son. David tells Ozzie: "In time I'll show you some things. You'll see them. I will be your father." But as Rabe observed, "David is trying to take Ozzie into madness." The shared reconciliation that Morrell imagined is, in Rabe's bleaker vision, only a shared insanity. Ozzie so violently does not want the madness that his son calls "seeing" that he is willing to restore his own blindness by murdering his son. To this end, the family gathers in the living room at the close of the play to assist David in slashing his own wrists. "You'll feel better," Ozzie assures his son.[46]

That the fathers would rather see the sons dead than see into the deadness of their own culture or question the terms of their version of manhood is a recurrent theme in Rabe's Vietnam plays. As a corporal in *The Basic Training of Pavlo Hummel* recounts, "My ole daddy—the last day he saw me—he tole me good—'Don't you ever run on nobody, Boy, or if you do I hope there's somebody there got sense enough to shoot you down. Or if I hear you got away, I'll kill you myself.' "[47] Those lines, Rabe said, were inspired by a real-life young corporal with shrapnel in his eye, who was checked into the army hospital in Long Binh while Rabe was on duty. "He was in that team state of mind and he was going on and on about what he and his buddies did, which was hold some hill or whatever. He was so proud, and yet there was something haunting, you could feel it as he talked. He kept saying, 'We didn't run, we didn't run, and my dad would've been so proud of me. Because my dad said, If you ever run and I find out about it, I'll shoot you myself.' He was proud as he was telling me, but there was this other thing beginning to be in his mind, some question about what the hell that meant." What it meant was a father and son bound only by their madness, and it was this horrific revelation that Rabe intended to hammer home in *First Blood*.

"When they came to me to do the script, I thought, Well, this could be a great opportunity to do almost an action version of *Sticks and Bones*. In *Sticks and Bones*, this guy comes home and goes through phases before he realizes the only way that they're going to understand is to become participants and get a firsthand taste of it. So what he's really doing is attempting to rub their faces in the gore of it, and say, 'Isn't this fun!

Aren't we having a good time!' Of course, in that he miscalculates. He fails to understand that they are far more dangerous than he is."

In Rabe's version of *First Blood*, Rambo makes the same fatal error. He returns to an America that celebrates and denies its own violence. In the opening scene of Rabe's draft, Rambo is depicted hiking past a drive-in. "Crudely painted on its wall," Rabe's directions state, "are huge figures of Wayne and Eastwood mowing 'em down and Hell's Angels brawling." Rambo pauses before a home-appliance shop, and, as Rabe describes it, "in the window, Brod Crawford is shooting someone on one of the TV sets. Bob Stack is machine-gunning someone on the other." Rambo crosses the street, dodging a jeep with a dead deer across the hood and a couple of hunters toting rifles, and comes up against a gun-and-tackle shop, its window overflowing with rifles, shotguns, pistols, and revolvers. Before this bounty stand two men greedily eyeing the merchandise, with children in their arms.[48]

As in the novel, Rambo tangles with police chief Teasle, who escorts him two times to the edge of town and warns him never to return. But Rabe's Rambo represents a grisly repressed knowledge about America gained in a war that he intends to bring home and force the town's fathers to face. "They are going to see me," he says. "In the fires. In the children, crying. They are going to see me." He is insanity itself, a primitive bearing snakes and covering cave walls with violent stick drawings. "In my script," Rabe said, "the pattern of betrayal and its incredible force launches Rambo into this death vector and once it goes far enough, that's where you go. Nobody brings you back." But the town fathers don't want to receive Rambo's message, and in their refusal they are, like the domestic father in *Sticks and Bones*, stronger and more dangerous.

Rambo thinks he's stalking Teasle and his posse. "I been lookin' for you, Teasle," he says. "Don't you know I been lookin' for you?" But Rabe's Teasle is not interested in developing a spiritual connection with Rambo. He's into repression—he whacks his deputies like dogs. He wants to see Rambo and the consciousness he signifies crushed for good. Teasle is both the blinded private father and the eager-for-a-body-count military father. For this reason, Rabe had no need for Trautman and was considering reducing him to a minor character or scrapping him altogether.[49]

The blood for Rambo's killings is on Teasle's hands, too. "You wanted me to do everything I did," Rambo sneers at Teasle. When Teasle snarls back, "I saw you on the street, I wanted your guts in my hands," Rambo replies calmly, "I know that. That's what we are, Teasle. The both of us. Only I'm better than you." By "better," he makes it bitterly clear, he means only that he beat the fathers at their own game by laying claim to a higher body count. "We counted the bodies, man; we killed 'em and counted 'em. It made us the best there ever was."[50]

Rambo proceeds to demonstrate this principle on the bodies of the townspeople. He stops everyone he meets on the street and demands their name. When they say it, he kills them. This goes on throughout the night, as Rambo slaughters without cease and finally sets fire to the town. In the morning, Rambo marches, unarmed, through the ruins to Teasle's office door. "I want to report the count, sir," he tells Teasle. "The bodies. I want you to know how we did. Eighty-seven. Eighty-seven. Bobby, Billy. That's what we got. Helen, Janie—" At which point Teasle shoots him. Rambo jerks backward and grunts, "Yes, sir!" Again Teasle shoots him, and again Rambo grunts, "Yes, sir!" and again, "Yes, sir!" The image freezes, the script's final shot.[51]

Rabe's *First Blood* was a return to My Lai on domestic soil and Rambo was Lieutenant Calley come home to roost, while Teasle was Captain Medina, the gangster-father who eggs his "son" on to murder, but takes no responsibility for the consequences. He walks away scot-free. But as it turned out, the entertainment industry didn't want to "see," any more than did the fictional Teasle, or Ozzie in *Sticks and Bones.* Hollywood was constructing films to bury My Lai, not revisit it; to make American men "feel better," not worse. Rabe was still working on the script when he got a phone call, instructing him to send the filmmakers what he had written so far. Rabe assembled the incomplete script, appended a few pages outlining the ending he envisioned, and popped it in the mail. He returned to his typewriter, but before he had even finished the first draft, he got the second phone call, telling him not to bother. They would no longer be requiring his services. "They didn't really give a reason," Rabe said. "They just said it 'wouldn't work.'" Which was true enough, from the studio's perspective. Hollywood, after all, was working to hammer shut the door on what Vietnam might actually reveal about American manhood.

Adam's Supplication to His Creator

FOR THE NEXT HALF DOZEN YEARS, the script for *First Blood* passed through many hands and many incarnations. At least eighteen versions of the script were ordered up by more than nine directors as it moved from Columbia Pictures to Warner Bros. to Carolco. Crack directors were called in—Richard Brooks, John Frankenheimer, Sydney Pollack, Martin Ritt—and seemingly every leading man was tapped for the part—Paul Newman, Al Pacino, Steve McQueen, Robert De Niro, Clint Eastwood, John Travolta, Nick Nolte, Brad Davis, Michael Douglas. Meanwhile, Rambo's story kept mutating: at one point he was a jester, at another, a patient overly attached to his female psychiatrist.[52]

A similar problem had beset filmmakers two decades earlier, when they tried to make a sequel to *To Hell and Back* about Audie Murphy's homecoming years. As with *First Blood,* Hollywood couldn't, or rather wouldn't, tell the real story—about a Murphy who was a human wreck, a self-styled "executioner" who rampaged through the streets seeking enemies, a belligerent husband and negligent father, a gun hoarder who could only keep himself in check by channeling his rage into the more socially acceptable outlets of shooting ducks, rabbits, and squirrels and "crime fighting." So the filmmakers invented fictions, each more risible than the next. In a 1956 script, *The Way Back,* never produced, Audie Murphy was "cured" of his "war nerves" by therapeutically reliving his most harrowing combat experiences. In a revised version, Audie found serenity after going to a ranch with his wife and sons and clapping eyes on a newborn colt; in a third version, after saving a buddy from alcoholism.[53] In the end, the filmmakers gave up and Murphy went back to westerns.

The makers of *First Blood* would run through a similar process, with one exception: a film was finally produced. Ronald Reagan was galloping out of the West and into the White House when the latest screenwriter on the job, Michael Kozoll, got a phone call from the latest coproducer, Andy Vajna. "Vajna told me, 'We have to clear out a lot of that crap and make it cleaner,'" Kozoll recalled with wry bemusement. "It was said in that tone of tough film distributor talking to crappy writer: 'Look, can you come clean the leaves out of my pool?'" But Kozoll understood what Vajna meant. "He meant, Make it a western." Kozoll declined. "I'm totally antiwar," he told me, "antimilitary." And the last war Kozoll wanted to glorify was Vietnam, which had horrified him. A "hippie potter" in San Francisco, he had opposed the war from the start and, disgusted with his nation's adventurism, had moved for a time to Europe.

Kozoll's 1980 script, though substantially tamped down from Rabe's, still veered too close to the truth for any studio's comfort. "You have to understand," Kozoll said, "that this movie was done in an atmosphere where Warner Bros. said to us, 'Absolutely nobody wants to see a movie about the Vietnam War!'" Kozoll finally washed his hands of the project and put it out of his mind. "I don't even like war movies, anyway. When *Rambo* came out, I never even saw it." He would not think of the screenplay again until Halloween of 1985, the year that *Rambo: First Blood Part II* was released. Kozoll lived on a street in Santa Monica that was always inundated with trick-or-treaters. He opened his door that night to a sea of identically dressed monsters. "At first I thought they were pirates," he said. "Then I realized, they were Rambos. They were *all* Rambos. Thousands of little Rambos."

In the end, the layers of falsehoods slathered on *First Blood* by the endless rewrites would have crushed what vitality remained in the story if it hadn't been for the arrival of an unintentional revivalist: Sylvester Stallone. He seemed an unlikely spokesman for a Vietnam film. His interest in and knowledge of the war was minimal, yet he breathed life back into the story. He envisioned the drama "like the Frankenstein monster and the creator," a creator who "understood what he made" and "felt guilty" for it. In a deeply personal way, it turned out that he understood something about Frankenstein's creation: the monster was on a rampage for a reason; he was seeking love from his creator. "My heart yearned to be known and loved," Frankenstein's monster relates in Mary Shelley's classic tale. "I was alone. I remembered Adam's supplication to his Creator. But where was mine? He had abandoned me, and in the bitterness of my heart I cursed him." Mary Shelley conjured the famous tale out of her own orphaned experience; her mother, the founding feminist Mary Wollstonecraft, had died eleven days after giving birth to her, and her father, William Godwin, had been a distracted presence, stricken with his own loss and debt-ridden.[54] Out of his own experience, Stallone would perform a similar conjuring.

In the Vietnam War, Stallone saw the outlines of a disturbed family life. "It was like a bad marriage," he told me, "and America was the battered wife who didn't know how to get out, didn't know how to leave with dignity." America would seem more properly cast as the batterer, but maybe Stallone wasn't talking about a literal Vietnam so much as one viewed through the shattered lens of his own boyhood. Like Rabe, like Michael Bernhardt, Stallone seemed intuitively to understand that the sons were betrayed at home long before they shipped out for Southeast Asia. What Stallone did with that understanding, though, is something else again. Rabe was prepared to break with the fathers to tell the truth. Stallone, for all his disappointment and anger, still harbored hopes for some kind of paternal recognition. He was, like Audie Murphy, the dark son who wanted to play the good one. As much as Stallone identified with Biff (in 1998, he could recite his lines from *Death of a Salesman* as if his last performance had been three days, not thirty years, earlier), he was still auditioning for the part of Happy, the son who only wanted to be welcomed home. In that, Stallone expressed the unarticulated yearnings of so many American sons. He would become their spokesman and exactly the sort of leading man the filmmakers needed if they were ever to make credible an otherwise dishonest script.

All conversations with Sylvester Stallone led, sooner or later, generally sooner, to life with father. In his mind, Stallone was still fighting a war that supposedly ended more than three decades earlier. At fifty-two, he was still trying to kick the post–Frank Stallone syndrome. "Everything with him was a competition, a challenge," Stallone said about his father one evening as he sat brooding over a barely touched drink at the bar of the Four Seasons Hotel in New York City. My meetings with Stallone were always in such predictably first-class surroundings, yet his demeanor was that of the vagabond boy who had sneaked into the palace and could be tossed out at a moment's notice. He had found his way into the kingdom, but it was not his inheritance. "My father always had a challenge going. So if it's cold, and you say, 'I need a coat,' he'd say, 'Cold! It's nothing!' So now he's gotta prove it. So now he has to throw his shirt off. . . . When I was about thirteen years old, he bought a few hundred-dollar horses, and it just became one long, ridiculous challenge. He became incredibly combative on horseback. He played polo like an immortal warrior, take no prisoners." As Frank's ex-wife, Jackie Stallone, remarked, polo appealed to him not because it was fun but because it was competition that was violent. "It's the only way you can hit someone on the head and get away with it," she said. "Whatever it was," his son continued, "he had to win, he had to prevail at all costs. . . . There was never any explanation about *how* to do anything, just this challenge that he could do it, whatever it was, better than me."

Stallone's father was the son of working-class Italian immigrants who measured manhood by artisan skill and physical labor. Frank had other aspirations, more in keeping with the rising entertainment age. "I tried to be a singer," he told me. "I could've been very good, but I had stage fright." When Jackie Stallone met her future husband, she recalled, he was working with a relative who was a cobbler in the Bronx. Jackie was a chorus girl with Billy Rose's revue. After a brief courtship, they were married in 1945; Jackie was already pregnant with Sylvester. She gave birth in a charity ward and then returned with her newborn to their Hell's Kitchen apartment. By the end of the decade, though, the Stallones had moved to suburban Maryland, and Frank Stallone found himself running a beauty salon that his wife had helped start and proving his manhood in ways wholly unrelated to his work. His challenge to his son went far beyond chest-baring. "Winning" was everything, and winning ultimately was about force. Stallone recalled his boyhood in Vietnam terms: "It was just a day-to-day attrition."

Jackie Stallone recalled that her former husband's competitive violence was on display much of the time in angry street encounters and even on the job. But her firstborn son suffered the brunt of it; she recalled that he was beaten on the slightest pretext. "He'd step on Sylvester, jump right on him, in the middle of his stomach. It's a wonder this kid's still alive." Competition, she said, always seemed to be the trigger for her ex-husband's rage, a competition that prevailed long after the son had left home. When Stallone became famous, she recalled that Frank complained to her that "*he* should be getting the Oscar, that it was *his* talent. Sylvester 'inherited' it from him, and by rights [the Oscar] belonged to him; Sylvester didn't deserve it. I cannot imagine a father being jealous of his son being successful, can you? But he was." Whether he was violent, competitive, or jealous, Frank Stallone will now not say. "I'd rather not get into it," he told me, deflecting further inquiry. "No, I'd rather not say. I have nothing much to say. Whatever [Jackie] said, you can take with a grain of salt . . . something that's conjured in her own mind." He had a bit more to say about his treatment of his son in 1990, in an interview in *Vanity Fair:* "I guess you could say I was rough with him, yeah. But I didn't beat him three times a day."⁵⁵

It felt like a competition to the son, and the young Stallone responded in kind, emulating rather than eschewing his father's example. "I'd take horses out on a moonless night and ride through unmowed fields and jump barbed-wire fences, at *night*. That's insane. I mean, why? And then I'd take that horse and plunge it off a ten-foot ledge into water and try to stay on its back. All this crap you see in movies. And for what?" Yet Stallone kept trying to leap the barbed-wire hurdles and win his father's favor. "I remember, there was this Catholic retreat for children I went to. And the priest was talking about hellfire and damnation and how our souls would be burned into perpetuity if we defied the scriptures. And he goes, 'Just to give you an example of how hot hell will be . . .' and he took this very large candle and he said, 'If anyone here would stick their finger or hand over this flame for five seconds, it would cause irreparable damage. You'd be scarred for life.' So I went up and volunteered. I was about nine or ten. And I stuck my hand over the flame. And I went, 'One . . . two . . . three . . .' It was excruciating. At four, he snatched the candle away. And it never made any sense why I, among these five hundred people there, would volunteer, except I had something to prove. Even though my father wasn't there, his life lessons were always there. And it was always about pain."

Pain was both to be endured and inflicted. "He'd come home with his teeth in his hands, and then he'd just sew it up," Stallone recalled.

"He'd bust his skull, and stitch it *himself*. My father's like a real-life Rambo." At home, Jackie Stallone said, Frank inflicted the pain and they endured it—like the Christmas morning in 1957 when he threw her under the tree and nearly strangled her. He was angry, she recalled, because she bought him a belt that cost only three dollars. "But what else do you give a man when he gives you an allowance of three dollars a week?" she asked me querulously, as if still defending herself from his accusations. Her most vivid memory was of an incident when Sylvester was only six years old. She was in the backyard with some friends, hosting a barbecue. Suddenly, her son appeared, "leaning over the rail looking at me, 'Mommy, Mommy!' Blood was pouring out of his face. He was beaten to a pulp." Sylvester's father had reprimanded him, as Jackie recalled, with a horse's whip. "What could he have done that bad?" She met my eye, then looked away. "And what do you do?" she said, meaning herself. "You live with it. I should have taken these two kids and left years before. . . . But every time you open your mouth, he'd say, 'I'm taking these kids and shipping 'em to Sicily and you'll never see 'em.' Which is true; he would. So you were stuck, waiting for a miracle to get rid of him."

It was in this period that the young Stallone became enamored of an orphaned hero who managed to transform himself alone into the ultimate flyboy: Superman. "I must've known something was wrong when—I was eight years old—I made a Superman's outfit and wore it under my clothing to class—and truly believed, *truly* believed," Stallone recalled. "It was a barber's cape, and I had a Rit-dyed T-shirt with an 'S' kind of drawn on haphazardly with those yellow wax crayons. And I told my friend Jimmy Colen, I said do you know who I really am. And he said, 'Yeah, you're Sylvester, Binky [a hated childhood nickname].' I said, 'No, no, no! Look!'" And Stallone showed him the concealed costume. "And he went out and told everyone in class. And this teacher made me come out and stand in front of the entire student body, take my clothes off to show the class. I was humiliated. And I ran outside, and there was this giant storm drain that ran for half a mile, so I ran into this giant storm drain, and by the time I got to the other end, I was fine. And I tried to fly home."

The young Stallone would try to fly another time. He dove off the roof of the family home, headfirst into the concrete mixer that Frank Stallone had been using to construct that essential accoutrement of sub-urbia, the backyard barbecue pit and patio, and broke his collarbone. "I lived on the roof," Stallone told me. "I used to go up on the roof so much that there was literally a path. I had literally worn out the tar paper." On the roof, he could imagine himself shooting through the stratosphere, the nation's youngest astronaut. "I went up there because the roof was a spaceship. It was an amazing place. You ever just walk on a slanted roof? It's so uncluttered, and so angular, and so beautiful. And you are the only force up there. Everything else is mechanical or dead. You're alive. And you just sit up there, the house, the people, straddled between each leg, riding it like some tar-paper beast. I used to sit right on the peak of my house, the very very peak. Every night. That was my domain." From there, he prayed for unearthly strength. "I would always wish that all of a sudden, a star would explode in front of me and now I'd have this power of fifty men and just go around and do incredibly great things for humanity." Once the space race began, he scanned the heavens from his perch, for signs of satellites or rockets. "I was always thinking about the dog," he said of Laika, the canine who went into space aboard Sputnik 2 in November 1957. "It was a black-and-white dog, a mutt, I'll never forget it. A floppy-eared thing. And I couldn't stop thinking about what must have happened to him. Because he was sent way up there and then he came crashing down to earth." Laika, in fact, died before the fireball plunge, suffocating when the satellite's oxygen equipment failed.[56]

Stallone fed his superhero fantasies with endless trips to the movies. "I aligned myself with *Spartacus* and *The Vikings*," epic vehicles for the bodily torments and heroics of the young Kirk Douglas. "He was the focal point of my young hero worship," Stallone recalled of Douglas. "He was like my father figure." He mimicked Douglas's muscular gait, his shirtless poses. "Every picture I have as a child, I'm flexing. Every one. This skinny malnourished body, but there I am, shirt off, flexing." If he could just make his body powerful enough, he imagined, not only would he be able to endure in the contests with his father, he might soar above them. That fantasy would later attract him to the boxing ring. "It's being able to take it," he said of boxing's lure. "That you can take the anger because you have this fuel, to go, to make yourself airborne."

Jackie Stallone finally fled with the children, eventually to another state and a new marriage as rocky in its own way as the last. But by then it was 1958 and Sylvester was nearly twelve. She had two reasons for waiting so long, reasons as old as domestic violence itself: fear and lack of money. Every time she made moves toward leaving, Frank threatened her, she said. He beat her, she recounted, choked her till she blacked out, threw her out of a moving car, and once stood her before the fireplace mantel and "just fired rounds, just kept shooting all around me." After she had moved out of the house but was still living in Silver Spring,

Maryland, he'd come over, she said, and "shoot the door locks off." Finally, after her father died and left her some money, she put her two sons in military school and fled to Philadelphia.

A custody squabble ensued, and Sylvester wound up returning to his father (lured, Jackie remembers, by the promise of a gift horse). But a week or two later, an unhappy Sylvester hitchhiked back to his mother's house. He would run away many times, once as far as Florida, along the way "sleeping in abandoned churches and perverts' cars," he recalled. He eventually resided with his mother, who sent her son to one school after another, including a boarding school for troubled boys when he was sixteen. Finally he was packed off to the American College in Switzerland, an ocean between him and his painful boyhood.

Stallone could never, though, travel far enough to free himself from the familial combat. He came to understand that only in 1991, on a polo field in Palm Beach. "My father wanted to play on the number one polo field, where Prince Charles plays. He told me to set up the game. So I set up the game, at great expense. We go down there.... We're on opposite teams. And we're right next to one another, playing opposite. All of a sudden I'm speared in the back by a horse, knocked to the ground. The horse just misses stepping on my chest cavity. I'm laying there. And I look up. And it's my father who speared me. And he's looking down. And like, 'You okay, son?' The next play, I rammed him so hard I took the ball one hundred and fifty yards and scored. It was almost like bad moviemaking! After the game, I said, 'You almost killed me. You could've crippled me. You coulda broke my spine. You hit me in the back with an eleven-hundred-pound horse!' He said, 'It's a fuckin' accident, whadya crying about?'" The father's near trampling of the son was captured on film by a camera crew from *Entertainment Tonight*. "When the bell rang at the end, I never got on a horse again. I was finished. I sold the ranch, forty horses, everything.... When I saw that guy on that charger, on that horse, with that mallet, looking down at me, I said, This is fucking perfect. You know what, this has really brought into crystal focus exactly what he's always thought of me. What I *am*. I'm not his son. I'm an opponent."

Stallone was never going to win the recognition he craved from his father, because to do so meant his father had to lose. And so he turned to other realms where good fathers might be found—or, if not found, constructed. He birthed his new fathers on film. For the orphaned Rocky, Stallone created the grizzled Mickey, a round-the-clock devoted coach. And when he joined the set of *First Blood,* he was determined to find a father for the orphaned Rambo, too, even if it meant turning the script inside out. Stallone's fatherlessness and that of his moviegoing fans found its perfect metaphor—the abandoned POW who, at long last, would be rescued.

"After I got involved," the film's director, Ted Kotcheff, told me, "we worked on several scripts for months, but I'll tell you, the person who made the biggest difference was Sylvester Stallone." Kotcheff cited three fundamental changes Stallone made. "Stallone said to me, 'This guy shoots like he's in a shooting gallery, and it's going to alienate the audience. What if he puts 'em out of action instead of killing 'em?'" The second change was to transform Rambo from a foul-mouthed ranter into a stoical silent type. The last, and most important, was the ending. The script called for Trautman to walk in "like Dr. Frankenstein," Kotcheff said, intending but unable to bring himself to blow away his creation. So Rambo was to reach for Trautman's gun and commit suicide. "When we were shooting," Kotcheff recalled, "Stallone came up to me and said, 'Ted, after what we put this character through, you think they are going to hate us because we killed him in the end? I don't want to come back in six months and redo this.' So we shot an alternate ending." While it would seem to negate the film's Frankenstein message, Kotcheff went along with it, figuring "there's nothing wrong with doing it and having it in our back pocket," in case the distributor insisted on a new ending.

The alternate finale was shot and set aside. The test screenings, though, were disastrous. "The audiences roared with anger and frustration that he was killed at the end," Kotcheff recalled. The moviegoers booed furiously and yelled, "Who decided to kill Rambo?" Kotcheff began to get nervous. "The audience practically wanted to lynch me! People said, 'Where's the director!' I ran out of the theater!" When the director reviewed the audience evaluation cards later, the response was overwhelming: "Every card, in big letters, 'Great picture but *horrible ending!!!*'" In response, the alternate ending was hastily set in place. With that, from first shot to last, Stallone's Rambo was no longer a monster who had to be decommissioned. In the opening sequence, a gentle Rambo is introduced in close-up, gazing tenderly at some children playing. This humble soul is now in town to find his war buddy, a black fellow Green Beret named Delmar. There is nothing threatening about Rambo—although he's supposed to be a vagrant, his army jacket looks fresh and clean, and his far-above-the-shoulders haircut recently styled. As he lopes down the road, he antagonizes no one and is polite when Sheriff Teasle approaches; it is Teasle who picks a fight, a theme that prevails throughout. "It's not my fault," Rambo cries out after a sadistic deputy who's been trying to shoot him falls from the police helicopter.

"I don't want any more hurt. . . . I didn't do anything." He fires only in self-defense, and when he has a chance to cut Teasle's throat, refrains, urging Teasle to "let it go, let it go." The horrific knowledge gained in war of his capacity to kill has been expunged from his memory. "They drew first blood, not me," he says virtuously of the deputies. Rambo had become Rocky, the good son. Now all he needed was a good father.

Stallone said he remade Trautman into "a father figure," because Rambo "needed someone who was his voice and would explain how difficult things had been for him." His Trautman "loved John Rambo because he went far beyond his expectations." Stallone's final change was to turn the chilly colonel into a proud papa, who calls Rambo "Johnny" and rhapsodizes about his "very special" boy. No longer the rear-echelon war manager, "I was there with you," he tells Rambo, "knee deep in all that blood and guts. I covered your ass more than once. Seems like bailing you out of trouble's getting to be a lifetime job for me."

There was to be a personal bonus in this choice. Kirk Douglas was slated to play Trautman. "I was thrilled, absolutely thrilled," Stallone recalled. "My hero, my role model!" The only problem was, Kirk Douglas hated the script he had read, and before he would agree to play the part, obtained what he thought were assurances from the director that the script would be altered. But when Douglas arrived on location, he found that none of the revisions had been made. "I was flabbergasted," Douglas wrote in his autobiography, *The Ragman's Son*. The "bone of contention" was one change in particular that he had demanded. "I thought that it would be better, dramatically, if my character realizes what a Frankenstein monster, amoral killer, and menace to society he has created, and KILLS STALLONE. If they'd listened to me, there would have been no *Rambo*s. They would have lost a billion dollars, but it would have been *right*."[57] As Stallone said, his voice still edged with disappointment, Douglas wanted his character to kill Rambo without compunction. The Rambo that Douglas had in mind, Stallone recalled, "was a lot less developed, less sympathetic, and absolutely disposable." He was the unwanted son. Douglas was replaced by the more accommodating Richard Crenna.

But fashioning a good father was only the first, and easier, of Stallone's tasks. Before he could reunite with the good father, he had to vanquish the one who did not think he was "very special," who liked to triumph over the son in every contest. And so the sheriff, who had sprung from David Morrell's typewriter as Rambo's secret sharer, was transformed into his deepest enemy. And this time, the son got to win. In the final scene, Rambo shoots Teasle through the skylight at police headquarters, and the sheriff, crashing through the roof, lands at Rambo's feet. Now, in the reverse of Stallone's final experience on the polo field, it is the bad father who finds himself lying on his back, looking up at the unapologetic and triumphal son.

"When the sheriff sees this Vietnam vet, it proves to be a windfall for him because now the best of one war gets a chance to go against the best of another war," Stallone told me. "So Rambo gave him a new lease on his life's competitiveness. But in the end, he didn't prevail. He got shot down when he didn't have to, because he had to *compete*." Stallone's own desire to shoot down the sheriff far exceeded the bounds of method acting. "At the end," Stallone said of the days before the showdown with Teasle was filmed, "it was terrible, all these emotions were building in me. I wanted him so bad I was actually *salivating*." Stallone's words were a curious echo of Teasle's scripted line: "I wanted to kill him so bad I could taste him."

The new, empathetic, ever-supportive, never-competitive father is enlisted to legitimize the son's choice of enemies; Trautman sides with Rambo against the old father-cum-killer. In Stallone's rewritten script, Trautman expresses nothing but contempt for Teasle, a dolt from "Jerkwater, USA," who can't begin to fathom the war-forged spiritual bond between Rambo and him. "What the hell," Trautman says to Teasle, "you're a civilian. You can go home to your wife and your house and your little flower garden. You're under no pressure to figure all this out." It would seem that all the loose ends have been tied up. The bad son has become good; the good father has recognized his worthiness and honored his passage into manhood; and the bad father has been defeated and expelled. Except that the ghost in the machine can never really be expelled. Paternal betrayal had been at the root of *First Blood*'s genesis a decade earlier, and no number of revisions and recastings could fully purge it. In spite of everything, the father's deception still haunts the film in phantom traces, remnants of dialogue, and plot turns that even the most skillful of rewrite men failed to exorcise.

As much as Stallone tried to make Trautman the devoted dad, in the end the transformation was not complete. "He trusts me," Trautman tells Teasle. "See, I'm the closest thing to family that he has left." But Trautman uses that trust to lure Rambo into surrender, and what will surely be a life sentence in prison. Trautman's at a loss when Teasle demands to know what he would have done in the sheriff's position, "Wrap your arms around him, give him a sloppy kiss, or would you have blown his brains out?" After silently considering the question, he says, "I couldn't answer that till I met him face-to-face."

In the final scene, Trautman does have that face-to-face encounter, and, on closer inspection, it is a deeply ambivalent one. Yes, Rambo breaks down weeping in his arms. Yes, Trautman drapes his coat over the poor kid's bare shoulders. But what really happens? Convulsed on the floor "in a fetal position," as Stallone put it, Rambo pours his heart out to Trautman for a long time before the colonel hesitantly steps nearer. Even then, it is Rambo who must reach up, seize Trautman's hand, and pull him down to his side; it is Rambo who must force his head onto Traut- man's shoulder. If the colonel finally puts a hand on his charge's back, it is a visibly reluctant half embrace. "In a sense they're really not that close," Stallone observed to me, regretfully. "It's wishful thinking under combat stress." Trautman pats his back, "but it's almost out of embarrassment. . . . He doesn't really commiserate with me. I feel there's no remorse." Maybe a paternal wound could not be healed, Stallone was beginning to think. "The father-son bond is the foundation on which you have to build the rest of your life. And once that foundation is flawed, everything may stay upright, but it's shaky. It's never going to be right."

It was this painful knowledge that caused Stallone to weep uncon- trollably in the final scene. "It's the closest I've ever gotten to looking at the dark side," he said. "That final scene of *First Blood*, I was really gone . . . all these jumbled thoughts were trying to come out. It was weird. I don't know where that came from." Only, he did know: "My childhood." As he sat bunched up on the floor, sobbing and pleading for an explanation from the stiff figure of Trautman, another visage rose before Stallone: his father's.

———

FOR THE SECOND FILM, the filmmakers started from scratch; there would be no author's buried narrative to extirpate. The order of book and film were reversed; this time, a few months before the film was released, David Morrell was enlisted to write the novelization. At first, he refused. "They sent me the script and it literally was 'Rambo shoots this, Rambo shoots that,'" Morrell recalled. He was disturbed by what seemed to him a glorification of "violence without consequences." The story he had birthed had become "a version of all those terrible World War II films that I hated and was terrified by as a kid." When an acquaintance asked him what the sequel was about, Morrell said, "It's about a million gallons of gasoline going up!" The producers from Carolco kept pressing him to change his mind. "This was a problem for them because they had counted on the book for promotion," Morrell recalled, and under the terms of his contract with the studio, only he could write it. Finally, Carolco sent Morrell a five-minute clip of the film's final firefight. "They had definitely torqued up the level tremendously. Just from a visceral point of view, it was amazing. And I realized, This is going to be a big movie." And so he came around, his rationale being that he might at least make the violence "more complex" and the message less hubristic on the page. He made Rambo a student of Zen and ended the novel with a slight jab at Ronald Reagan and his Vietnam-like adventure in Nicaragua.[58] "I had to do it in three weeks," he recalled, at a twenty-page-a-day clip. He had "mixed emotions," he said, but he told himself the book would be worth writing because "I wanted to add characterizations that weren't in the film."

Morrell's readers, though, bought the second book mostly to reexperience the second movie, and for this reason alone it far outsold its predecessor, just as the second movie, with its unequivocal triumphalism, far outstripped the first's box-office returns. *Rambo: First Blood Part II,* the book, was on the *New York Times* best-seller list for six weeks, selling about one million copies. Morrell had certainly passed the studio test as a good son, willing to adapt a product that ran against the essence of his own creation. Now, the story had no father-son struggle. "Trautman's character was almost benign," Morrell said, and war just an opportunity for pyrotechnic special effects. "I saw my book as an antiwar novel," he said, then sighed with resignation. "Maybe I delude myself."

If the faint remnants of a bad father might still be seen in the bloodless Pentagon bureaucrat who abandons Rambo in the jungle, by the third film, there would be nothing but interchangeable foreign devils, and the good father. The father problem had finally been eliminated. And Morrell would write that novelization, too.

In Stallone's life, though, erasure was not so easy. He and his father still circled each other in the domestic boxing ring. "He's in Palm Beach, only an hour away from me," Stallone said, "so he just drops in—still wearing my old clothes, my Beatles boots . . . and my Rocky buckle." The display of the Rocky buckle was not meant as an endorsement of his son's achievement. "Do you think he *liked* Rocky?" Stallone asked rhetorically. "He goes, 'Well, I coulda fought better, I coulda played the part better' . . . and right down the fucking line." Indeed, Frank Stallone told me he had shopped around his *own* script for *Rocky VI* in Hollywood against his son's wishes, and actually sold it to a producer, figuring that they could get another actor to replace his son.

One evening, after Stallone had returned from a fifteen-hour shooting day on his latest film, we sat talking in his Four Seasons suite. I had been reading Gerald Early's exquisite meditations on prizefighting in *The Culture of Bruising,* and I had Xeroxed a passage to show Stallone. There, Early described Jake La Motta's terrible truth-telling encounter with his father, a man who had made a lifelong career of beating his wife and children. La Motta, long past his prime and desperately poor, went to his father's house to plead for four hundred dollars to help pay for the birth of his child. His father eyed him with contempt, then handed him a ten-dollar check. La Motta recalled the moment in his second auto-biography, *Raging Bull II,* which Early quoted: " 'Is this all I'm worth,' [Jake] asked, his eyes glued to the check. ' . . . You dragged the family from one slum to another, and pimped me off to fight every kid in the neighborhood. Did ya forget all those nickels and dimes I made you? And this is your answer—a lousy ten bucks. How heartless can ya be? . . . What do ya want from me—another championship? I'm an old man, too, now. I come to you begging for help, and you give me a kick in the ass like I was still eight years old. Why did you always hate me, Pop? All those beatings, and for what?"[59]

When Stallone finished reading the passage, he dropped the page and crossed the room to his golf bag. He selected a club and wordlessly began swinging it hard over and over against the plush carpet, hard enough to make the drapes tremble. Does La Motta's father ring a bell? I finally asked. Stallone just kept practicing his shot. "If I didn't have money, you know," he finally said, the club whistling metronomically to his words, "if I was desperate, here's a man who would say, 'Here you go, I'll pour you out a couple glasses of vodka and you be on your way.' That's about it. He would revel in it. But it's . . ." He paused, the club poised in midair. He was no longer addressing me. "I don't know. I just take a real hard look at that and I want to just lash out and physically destroy it. I really do. It's like, Why are you on this earth? What is your legacy? That I hate you? That you forced me to withdraw into a world of such obvious fantasy? And I will for the rest of my life see you in every obstacle that tries to—like if it's a difficult game of golf, it's like it's your fault, *you.* It's like, I'll try hard to beat him, because I hear *you* laughing. I hear you mocking. It's everything. A guy bumps into you in an elevator, and you get angry. I know what it is, it's *him* that's bumped me, even though he's not there. . . . I look back and it was all set up from the beginning. It was all a setup. I look at the boy in those pictures, flexing his muscles at six, that boy in that Superman outfit made out of a barber's cape and swim trunks, and I see a direct line to Rambo."

A couple of years later, Stallone would tell me that he had finally put the struggle with his father behind him. He had sold some land he owned in Maryland on which his father had been living. And with that connec-tion severed, he felt he had "purged" his family demons. I hoped that was true, but I knew the odds were daunting. You only escape in the movies.

8

BURNING DOWN THE HOUSE

The Fire Last Time in Waco, Texas

OFFSCREEN AND ON THE POLITICAL STAGE, the male electorate was having as hard a time reconstructing the public father as Sylvester Stallone had deconstructing his private one. If Ronald Reagan was the fantasy elder come to lead the sons in triumphal battle against the Evil Empire, when the credits rolled and the sons awoke from that stardusted dream, most felt farther away from the promised land of adult manhood—less triumphal, less powerful, less confident of making a living or providing for a family or contributing productively to society. And no new elder statesman, celluloid or otherwise, loomed on the horizon. Distracted by the ever more voracious demands of image management and campaign finance, the newest presidential candidates seemed less like commanding figures and more like the dependents of spin doctors and big donors.

No wonder the following political decade would be driven by the phenomenon of what the media came to call "the Angry White Male." Reagan had been more than a patriarch, or rather, less—for in his public as well as his private life, he was at best an absent parent. He had played both ends of the male drama. He was everyone's favorite septuagenarian and, as the perennial Gipper, everyone's favorite fresh-faced boy, thereby distracting his constituents from the crisis at the core, the need for a guiding father. In the 1990s, there was no one in American politics with that chameleonlike ability. The final presidential race of the millennium would be fought between a sonless father figure and a fatherless son.

Other conservatives tried to don the Reagan mantle, right down to its combat-movie derivation. Pat Buchanan, the former Nixon speech-writer and pugnacious right-wing cohost of CNN's *Crossfire,* campaigned in the Reagan mode not as a politician but as a virtuous "Braveheart"—his favorite celluloid warrior. Like Reagan, he had sat out the central combat of his era stateside.[1] But he felt no compunction about rallying his supporters—those he called the "Peasants with Pitchforks"—with martial imagery. "Mount up, everybody, and ride to the sound of the guns!" he cried all the way to the 1996 Republican National Convention in San Diego, which proved a debacle for true-believer Angry White Males.[2] Buchanan, their chosen Braveheart, who without significant financial support had held his own in a surprising number of primaries, was betrayed, his "prolife" agenda virtually aborted and his presence banned from the convention podium—and eventually he betrayed his own, throwing his weight behind the very party "elite" against whom he had continually inveighed during the primary season. The Buchanan delegates were ordered, for the sake of "party unity," to change their votes on the first ballot to support the party's choice, Bob Dole.

Michael Bayham, a Buchanan delegate from Louisiana who had spent his entire savings to get to San Diego, assured me that his delegation was not going to succumb to such intimidation. They were going to protest with their feet. "There are at least twelve of us who are going to walk," he said as we stood in the Louisiana section of the convention hall, surrounded by increasingly forceful Dole handlers. In the end, though, only Bayham walked—with me as his sole follower, carrying his camera. (He'd wanted a shot of the dramatic exodus.) "Yeah, it was kind of like the invasion of Normandy," he said. "They got all the boats lined up, and they were ready to attack, and then I'm the only grunt who jumped out and stormed the beach." GOP apparatchiks applied the most pressure to Buchanan's twenty-one delegates from Michigan, his largest contingent. In the end, all but five switched to Dole. "I'd be the man in front of the tank at Tiananmen Square if I thought it would do any good," Michigan Buchananite Mike Flory told me forlornly as he changed his ballot. "But I have no choice. . . . We have no voice. We are outside the castle with no way to cross the moat."

Some months later, Flory called me with an update: all five holdouts against GOP pressure had lost their posts in the state party organization.

"They were all silenced so quickly. It was really a huge bloodbath. They were willing to go down with the ship and that's exactly what happened." That wasn't the only fallout he found troubling. In the wake of political disillusionment, he noticed, his brethren had begun heading off in strange and disturbing directions. "There's a huge amount of paranoia coming out now with some of these guys," Flory said of his fellow travelers. "Black helicopters, New World Order, get-your-guns militia stuff. I mean, yes, I think government could be doing things that aren't right, but for crying out loud, I don't think the government has implanted a microchip in my ass!" It wasn't just the government that the untended flock seemed to fear. When Flory tried to organize a "Conservative Summit" that year, he discovered that the conservatives were seething with paranoia about one another. "The Christian Coalition didn't trust the Michigan Conservative Union and the Michigan Conservative Union didn't trust the Liberty Caucus and on and on." With the quest for the father stymied, the quest for the enemy had turned frantic and fevered, its aimless searchlights ranging everywhere in the darkness.

In the final decade of the twentieth century, thousands of men would take up arms against metastasizing and morphing enemies. Suspicion pulled their gun sights in a thousand directions: toward the "jackbooted thugs" of the federal Bureau of Alcohol, Tobacco and Firearms, bankers conniving in a "New World Order conspiracy" hatched by the Federal Reserve, the Freemasons, and the Bavarian Illuminati, gang-bangers secretly deputized by the UN, Rhodes scholars mobilized by the Rothschilds and the British crown to restore America as an English colony, a techno-geek plot to end the world via a year-2000 computer glitch, or even a total population surveillance scheme embedded in the Universal Product Code bars stamped on grocery items.[3] The more the Angry White Males looked, the more blurred the enemy's face became. Yet a pattern emerged, if not of the enemy's behavior, then of their own. The specifics of combat conjured by America's new self-described "patriots" bore an uncanny resemblance to those on an actual battlefield on which American men had fought and lost: Vietnam. The men who joined the militia, Patriot, and survivalist "communities" in the nineties imagined black helicopters in the skies, tanks rolling over rural grassfields, innocent women and children mowed down by automatic fire. Like Rambo, they had essentially defected to the insurgent side. They were trying to restage the Vietnam War, this time casting themselves as the virtuous Vietcong guerrillas. They were determined to be the good guys, even if it killed them. Which was one of the reasons why, of all the domestic skirmishes the Patriots dreamed of fighting, none would entrance and transfix them like the war they imagined themselves waging in Waco, Texas.

An American My Lai

ON THE MORNING OF APRIL 19, 1998, a group of men gathered in a grassy field outside of Waco, as they had for five years running, many dressed in paramilitary gear, field pants, and combat boots. Beyond them lay the ruins: hunks of concrete foundation and reinforced steel, the mangled remains of two torched buses, several twisted motorcycles lying on their sides as if just abandoned by their drivers, and the empty shell of an Olympic-size swimming pool. The first spring growth of morning glories wreathed the wreckage, speckling the ground in pink and white. Hand-painted along the cement edges of the pool's foundation were direction markers, with arrows pointing visitors to the most requested sites: CNN VIDEO, 2 MILES, FBI VIDEO, 1/10 MILE, and OTHER MEDIA VIDEO, 2 1/2 MILES. A sign proclaimed HISTORY'S MOST PHOTOGRAPHED MASSACRE. Less photographed were the neat rows of crape myrtle seedlings planted by the survivors, in memory of the nearly eighty family members who died during the siege. Earlier, the men had followed the arrows and stopped at all the places where the famous videos had been shot, like penitents making the stations of the cross. Now they trudged back through the dew-drenched crabgrass in their combat boots, to a spot by the parking lot where media vans were circled, camera crews unloading equipment and taking sound checks.

A flatbed truck bearing a Macy's Thanksgiving Day Parade–size Liberty Bell had already been maneuvered into position. Folding chairs were placed in rows before the front stoop of a "museum," a hastily erected clapboard shack in which the remains of charred toys and scraps of burned cloth were on display, like so many modern-day pieces of the True Cross. The museum's porch became the ceremony's dais. "We have a common bond with those who died here," Jack DeVault, a retired air force colonel and author of the self-published screed *The Waco White-wash,* told the assembled men. "They really were sacrificed for us. There are prisoners still being held, political prisoners." Behind his sunglasses, William Haines, representing the Michigan Militia's "legislative arm," the Third Continental Congress, mounted the podium to pronounce in a tear-choked quaver: "It was a whole nation that died here. . . . I know that someday they're going to come after me. My only hope is that I can show as much courage as the smallest child did." Jesse Enloe, the president of the "Provisional Government of the Republic of Texas," called for a "common-law grand jury panel" to bring police-state thugs to justice. On the sidelines, a thin young man in sunglasses and a T-shirt depicting Lee Harvey Oswald tapped me on the shoulder. He had seen me taking notes and, hoping I was a television reporter, wanted me to feature in my story his towering sign listing "criminals" he believed should be indicted, a litany that ran from the FBI's PR spokesman to President Clinton. "These guys should all be in prison, solitary confinement, next to John Gotti," the twenty-one-year-old, whose name was Scott Horton, declared. I never heard his reasons; another young man raced up just then to alert him to the arrival of a TV camera crew. "I gotta go get on the media," said Horton, excusing himself. "I want to be on CNN. I want to be on national news."

The event they all came to commemorate happened five years earlier, when a fifty-one-day federal siege of a communal complex housing a small, armed Christian sect called the Branch Davidians ended in a fiery blaze that killed seventy-four residents, including twenty-one children. The standoff had begun in late February 1993, when seventy-six well-armed agents of the Bureau of Alcohol, Tobacco and Firearms arrived by land and by air in the early morning, in a rumbling convoy eighty vehicles long overflown by Blackhawk helicopters. The agents' mission, which would seem to have required substantially less firepower, was to deliver search and arrest warrants to the group's leader, David Koresh, whom the ATF suspected of possessing unregistered weapons and illegally converting some AR-15 semiautomatic rifles into machine guns.

Moments after the troop carriers pulled up on the front yard, bullets instead of a warrant were delivered in what the ATF later termed a "dynamic entry." Each side would claim that the other fired the first shot, and the truth may never be ascertained. What is known, though, is that within minutes, the Branch Davidians dialed 911, begging the police to ward off the attack from their own government. The help never came, and six Branch Davidians and four ATF agents were killed before a cease-fire was finally declared at noon. Koresh, who was wounded, and most of his followers then refused to leave the building; the FBI arrived, and for the next month and a half federal agents encamped on the property brought in ever more high-tech weaponry and military equipment while devising plans to drive the Davidians into surrender. The final plan was executed on the morning of April 19, as federal agents in M-60 tanks and Bradley fighting vehicles rammed the wood-frame building, punching huge holes in it, and then firing round after round of a powerful form of tear gas, CS, through every aperture. By noon, the house was in flames. Fire trucks that responded were held back by federal agents blocking the road. Most of the bodies of the Davidian women and children were found huddled in a concrete storage area near the kitchen, where they had gone to flee the tear gas.[4]

The federal government maintained that the Davidians set the fire themselves as part of a Jonestown-style mass suicide pact. Quietly, a handful of fire and weaponry experts wondered if the ramming and gas-firing assault might have unintentionally created the conditions for the firestorm. (Methylene chloride, a chemical agent in CS, is flammable. Safety literature from Dow Chemical Corp., which makes the agent, warns that it "forms flammable vapor-air mixtures"; the army's manuals say that it's unsafe to use inside; and the 1993 Chemical Weapons Treaty prohibits its use even in wartime.)[5] Far more vociferously, thousands of "Patriots" held that an oppressive federal government bent on destroying the slightest signs of independent thought and dissent had willfully ig-nited the Davidian complex, massacring a whole community of innocent citizens. In other words, where the feds saw a self-incinerating cult, the Patriots saw My Lai and Ben Tre. That view was expressed by many such men, but none so succinctly as Staley "Mad Mac" McGuyre of Houston, Texas, who asserted in an E-mail he sent to the Waco93 Web site several years after the fire: "It takes a government to raze a village."[6]

By reversing the polarity of My Lai, the Patriots were relieved of any culpability. The federal agents who committed atrocities no longer rep-resented them. "They don't call 'em civil servants anymore," William Haines of the Third Continental Congress stressed in his memorial speech. "Servants and masters are turned around." The Patriots were the enslaved, prisoners of war in their own occupied nation, and the federal agents the imperialist aggressors. Bill Buford, an ATF agent, acknowl-edged the dynamic before a congressional subcommittee investigating Waco. "This is very similar to how I felt when I came home from Viet-nam," he said. "They made us feel that we were the enemy."[7]

Waco provided a My Lai in which any American man who wasn't an ATF or FBI agent could feel like he was *not* the oppressor—and the appeal of that drew hundreds each week to the bloodstained site. But it may not have been the most powerful draw. The extreme anxiety and emotional intensity with which so many of these men responded to Waco suggests that the siege was something other than simply a com-forting symbol of American manhood cleansed of its Southeast Asian stain. Waco afflicted as much as it comforted. The men could not shake its image from their minds. "The events at Waco changed my life," wrote Carlos Balarezo, who described himself as a "34 year old college educated male," in response to a posted inquiry of mine about Waco on the Internet. His words were echoed in a virtual deluge of responses that for months turned me into a sorcerer's apprentice bailing a never-ending cascade of vitriol and victimhood out of my electronic mailbox. A thirty-eight-year-old defense laboratory researcher typically wrote to me that with Waco "my identity . . . history, safety, a sense of capability to address the trials of life . . . all these things came crashing down for me. . . . The sense of anguish I experienced was thunderous."

What exactly was producing such anguish was hazy to these men. Even in conversation, the Patriots spoke in abstractions about what had collapsed for them so thunderously at Waco. Nelson Clayton, a forty-one-year-old aerospace engineer who responded to my Internet query, told me when we talked, "The establishment made lots and lots of promises to me in the past three decades, and now they are not only not keeping their promises, they are threatening me." How Nelson Clayton, a law-abiding suburban town-house dweller with an aerospace job supported by federal funds, was being threatened by the government mystified even him. The most he could come up with was that he owned some guns, and the ATF might conceivably try to break into his home to confiscate them. "Okay, it's unlikely," he told me, "but there is that very small chance it could happen." It hardly seemed like the kind of thing to keep one up nights. Yet this fear gripped him. Lately he had taken to compiling a book-length compendium of federal agent sneak attacks by helicopter and other means on private citizens. "The National Park Service SWAT team got a military Blackhawk helicopter and stormed this hunting camp because they heard someone was messing with a buried Indian bone," he recounted, "and they hog-tied everyone on the grounds, including the fourteen-year-old girlfriends."

If the black helicopters represented a fantastic reprise of Vietnam, there was another war the militia men were refighting, a more intimate combat involving girlfriends, wives, and families. The battle that consumed them was quite literally a war at home. What these men were looking to reverse was not the loss of the fathers but the loss of a family to protect, a loss felt by many men, whether they had served in Vietnam or not. The men drawn to Waco weren't just fighting My Lai; they were fighting Jane Fonda, at home, in the United States. They were fighting a world transformed by the women's movement.

The images that transfixed the Patriots were of the Davidian complex as a home and the Davidians as a family—a home and a family destroyed despite everything a helpless patriarch could do. "I've been out to this place a number of times," Mike McNulty, a featured speaker at the memorial service, told the gathering in emotional testimony. "And the kind of thing that I experience when I come here is probably strongest when none of you are here, with all due respect. But when it's quiet and the wind blows, I hear the sounds of fading battle, the horrific sounds of battle passing away into the wind. I hear the sounds of breaking hearts of mothers and fathers, the sounds of fear in children's voices." To these children, he said, pointing at the assembled men, "You have a responsibility." This "responsibility," as a family protector, was precisely the one the men feared they had lost, and that they hoped to regain at Waco.

To populate their morality play, the Patriots needed a cast of women and children screaming for help—trapped in a burning house, tied to the proverbial train tracks. A cast of desperadoes was naturally essential to place the women and children in jeopardy and in need of rescue. In this drama, the "jackbooted thugs" of the ATF weren't just the enemy. They were the *necessary* enemy. To that degree they were collaborators. Without the enemy, how were the Patriots going to prove themselves useful to the women and children? Such an enemy restored to them an old domestic role, as guardians of families. The immolated communal home was symbolic to these men on two levels: as a bitter reminder of their own domestic predicaments and as a fantasized redemption. The old roles for men in the home had gone up in smoke, but from the flames of Waco, the Patriots dreamed of a dramatic reinstitution of domestic responsibility. As William Haines of the Third Continental Congress said at the memorial service, when the federal agents "willfully endangered the children," they "galvanized" his brethren. "We have a purpose."

For this drama to work, the enemy had to be a predatory male figure victimizing a vulnerable female population. But lurking behind him was a more subversive enemy, far closer to the lives of these men and far more threatening. The men preferred to imagine themselves battling G-men in Third Reich regalia—"Federal agents wearing Nazi bucket helmets and black storm trooper uniforms" was how executive vice president Wayne LaPierre put it famously in his "jackbooted thugs" letter to his fellow members of the National Rifle Association.[8] But that advertised conflict, so heroic, so traditionally male, concealed a deeper, less flattering battle in which they were also embroiled—against women who didn't want their protection. The Patriots, like other men who would not rally to a militia banner but who could sympathize with such sentiments, were angry at women for not wanting to be "protected" anymore. The enemies they singled out for the greatest opprobrium were women who were most prominently showcased by the culture as independent, self-sufficient, and unintimidated by men. In militia circles, no one was more reviled, resented, or feared than a high-profile trio who might as well have been called the Three Witches of Waco: gun-control advocate Sarah Brady, Attorney General Janet Reno, and Hillary Clinton. These were women who, as the Patriots saw it, refused to take direction from any earthly male. "Reno's master is Satan," William Haines fumed that April morning. The Patriots preferred to present themselves as so many Sam Adamses and Tom Paines, rebelling against an oppressive government of "elitist kings," but their mouths gave them away. No matter how often they started in on black helicopters, they ended up raging against a certain kind of woman. On their unofficial war map, it seemed, all paths led to feminism.

Coolidge Gerder and L. H. Miller, fellow militia members of the Republic of Texas, stood in the dusty parking lot, scuffing their boots on the gravel and talking of government conspiracies. Miller, an ironworker until a fall on the job disabled him, sported a Liberty Bell tattoo on one arm. "The United States government from the top dog on down is to blame," he maintained. "This government has been moving to a one-world government for years. But Clinton brought it further." He turned to me. "I've got something in my car you should see. It's about how everybody Clinton associated with has been killed—169 people." Coolidge Gerder, a tax accountant, interjected, "Do you know who Clinton is? The bastard son of Winthrop Rockefeller." L. H. Miller nodded. "I knew that," he said. "But it's really Clinton's wife who's the treacherous one. Her and Janet Reno."

Once the conversation had turned to these women, there was no hope of diverting it. "Who gives Clinton's wife the authority to get on the plane and give away money everywhere she goes?" Miller said, suddenly shouting. "She gave away a million dollars to each first lady she visited in Africa to get educated, to get *computers*," Gerder declared. "She and her kind are taking money out of Social Security." Miller, nodding furiously, put in, "They are paying for *abortion* with Social Security." And so it went.

Gerder: "It's women's liberation. They are all screaming for the government to take care of 'em. So men start stepping back. Men are belittled, shrunk to nothing."

Miller: "They've downgraded us."

Gerder: "Men have been relegated down to nothing, nothing but a pawn."

Miller: "When I was an ironworker, there were some women up there, thirty feet in the air. Women shouldn't be up that high. They're gonna get you killed. They need to stay where they are placed."

Miller turned to me again. "They're all lesbians, you know, Reno, Clinton's wife, all of 'em." Gerder chimed in: "Reno was a *man* in Florida, before she got *changed*." When I started to laugh, Gerder took offense. "I'm serious," he said. How had he ascertained this "fact"? I inquired politely. "How do I know?" he repeated, at top volume. "Because I *know* things."

My conversation with the two Republic of Texas militiamen had turned ludicrous and psychosexual, as such conversations so often did. A favorite story of the militiamen involved Hillary Clinton and a strap-on phallus, a fantasy that obviously revealed more about the tellers than the told-upon. The same fears of the changeling woman on top surfaced in many conversations I had the morning of the memorial service. Talk about gun control immediately segued into diatribes against Sarah Brady; her crusade to stanch the spread of weapons—like the one that had so tragically crippled her husband, former press secretary Jim Brady, in the 1981 assassination attempt on President Reagan—was perceived as a plot by a woman who "has to have all the control" and who "wants to take men's authority away." To hear them talk, it was her assertive nature that had put her husband into a wheelchair—and might put them there next. Scott Horton, the young man with the indictment placard (which included, naturally, Janet Reno and Hillary Clinton), seamlessly transitioned from government oppression to feminist oppression. "Our republic's on its knees," he told me. "Our throat is about to be slit. We're about to be a one-world order. Radical feminism gave the government all this power. They pushed this whole let-the-state-raise-your-kids. They pushed this wear-a-man-tailored-suit-and-take-over-the-company-cubicles. They really *pushed* it."

I was only a minute into a conversation with William Haines, the Third Continental Congress's representative and a former air-traffic controller, when he announced, "Basically, the white male is the most discriminated-against minority, the largest minority in the country." Haines was, he assured me, speaking from personal experience. "It basically was the feminist movement who destroyed my marriage," he said bitterly. "Because my wife went to college in the sixties. She is so twisted now she can't trust a man, especially a husband. She could not trust me, no matter what. Always she acted as if I beat her regularly. Just the way she would talk about me, like, 'The slime! He's doing this, he's doing that!' I gave her everything we had, the house, all the furniture, paid all the credit cards. But it was never good enough. She resented being taken care of."

Listening to the Patriots fume against the putative furies of feminism,

I felt like I had slipped through the looking glass and was viewing from within a problem that feminists had first identified from the other side. The "protection racket," as feminists had dubbed it some decades earlier, worked to keep women in their place by requiring them to turn to men for protection—from other men. Women's fears, produced by one set of "bad" men, drove them timorously into the arms of another set of "good" men. Chivalry was just the flip side of male violence. The two forces complemented each other, reducing women to eternal dependents, allowing men to play eternal caretakers.

What I hadn't understood, until Waco, was how the protection racket entrapped men, too. The Patriots, who were still seeking to play their parts as the "good" men, were its victims as well, because they couldn't conceive of a useful life outside of it. They believed they had to have "bad" men to go up against to prove themselves worthy human shields. For these men, then, the search for the enemy was the search for someone who could keep the protection racket going. As much as the male paradigm demanded a clear mission, an enemy, and a frontier, it also required dependents—woman and children to fight the mission *for*, to rescue from the enemy, and to homestead with on a conquered (but still insecure) frontier.

It was the beauty of the protection racket that it could be employed by every side. The Patriots' enemies—the ATF agents—had invoked a similar premise when they raided the Branch Davidian household. By their lights, they were on a "hostage rescue" operation, freeing terrorized women and children from the clutches of David Koresh, whom they depicted as a sinister, mind-controlling child molester. The image of the defiled girl was essential to give their actions meaning. "Koresh was sexually abusing children as young as ten," ATF agent James Moore asserted, crediting "former cult members," in his assessment of the agency's actions at Waco. "One girl was fourteen when she gave birth to a Koresh son." While such allegations were "irrelevant to ATF's official mission," he conceded, they were nonetheless crucial because they "eliminated any possibility that Koresh was a misguided technical violator of federal laws. This suspect was 'a bad guy.'"[9] Koresh did have multiple marriages, an aspect of his religious beliefs. But whether he had, in fact, molested girls—the testimony of one young woman was contradicted by other survivors, and a Texas Department of Human Services inquiry found no compelling evidence—the fact remains that the ATF, hardly the appropriate agency to be investigating molestation, was not rescuing hostages.[10] There were no hostages. The women hadn't been kidnapped; they were at home, and voluntarily remaining there. If the women inside felt terrorized by anyone, it was by the ATF and FBI, who had ringed the house with frightening weaponry. This is the problem with the protection racket: the "savior" is so often the real oppressor. "These men came in here and they started firing on us," said Lorraine Sylvia, a Davidian whose outrage was captured on a home video made inside the house during the siege. "The bullets came through the walls and people were killed, people were injured and—this is America?"[11]

If David Koresh was the bad man whom the ATF agents had to defeat, he played the reverse role for the Patriots. The militiamen reduced Koresh to another kind of caricatured profile—as the American pioneer patriarch, a frontier father and husband (in this case, of many wives), standing vigil at the farmhouse door, shotgun in hand, protecting his family from Indian attack. Koresh himself encouraged such depictions. "You gonna argue with me, you come argue with me," he declared in video footage intended for FBI and public consumption. "You come pointing guns in the direction of *my* wives and *my* kids, damn it, I'll meet you at the door anytime." It was his favorite theme. (" 'This is for the little children . . . ,' " he sang during another videotaped declaration, asserting, "For the children's sake, you know, you might have to bear a gun one day.") He symbolized, and represented himself as, the old domestic deal, where papa is in command and his dependents cheerfully obey and submit. "You know, our children know how to respect," Koresh told the FBI in still another video he produced during the siege, in which he sat on the floor, nursing a bullet wound in his side, surrounded by towheaded kids and their quiet young mothers. "They know how to be mindful, they know how to do right, because they see it here."[12]

The Patriots who made the yearly pilgrimage to Waco imagined themselves picking up Koresh's gun, filling his empty shoes. It was their turn now to guard the burned husk of Waco "for the children's sake." If they patrolled the grounds, maybe women and children everywhere would once more assume their "rightful" places. Their guardianship, however, was not always welcomed. Even the most courteous of the Davidian women were quietly dubious about the attentions of the militiamen. As the Patriots bustled about in preparation for the memorial service, Sheila Martin stood at a watchful distance. Her husband, Wayne, a Harvard Law School graduate and former law librarian at the University of North Carolina, was the Davidian who had placed the initial call to 911 on that terrible day of the ATF raid; he later died in the fire, along with four of the Martins' seven children. Ever since, Sheila had muddled by on her own, raising and supporting her surviving children, who on this day played nearby, practicing gymnastic moves on the museum's porch railing. I asked her why she thought these men were so preoccupied with Waco. She smiled wanly. "These men are the ones with the guns," she said. "They go to the gun shows. They are more apt to believe the government is doing these bad things they have to fight. I think a lot of them believed the government was doing these things *before* Waco. Then when Waco happened, well . . ." She raised her arms and let them fall with a resigned shrug. "They say it's in the spirit of man to *protect*."

The Waco women didn't see the militiamen as their protectors, however; nor did their children. In fact, the youngest Davidian survivors seemed to have difficulty distinguishing militiamen from federal agents. "A lot of the militiamen came in camouflage in 1995," Clive Doyle, a Davidian and the unofficial spokesman of the survivors association, told me. "And I asked them not to wear camouflage again because it scared the children." Sheila Martin's son Daniel took one look at the uniformed men and fled. Doyle found him down by the trees, weeping. "I asked him why he was crying, and he said, 'Why are these men who killed my daddy here?'" As Doyle told this story, he stared down at his hands, scarred from the fire, then looked away. "That kind of tore me up. And why were they dressing like that?" he continued, a bewildered expression on his face. "Matter of fact, why were the *government* guys dressing like that?" It would seem pointless to wear camouflage gear in the sparse exposed flatlands of Waco. Yet throughout the siege, Doyle pointed out, "everybody was in camouflage, even the *doctors* in the hospital tent miles away! Even the *coroner,* a doctor and a *civilian,* was in camouflage during his press conference."

From whichever side men approached the Waco battlefield, they were suited up to participate in the oldest American male myth, the original protection racket—the captivity narrative. In that formative genre, conceived in precolonial days and enshrined in American literature, a basic script pertains: a young woman is "captured" by raiding Indians who attempt to strip her of her whiteness. The pioneersman's mission is to search out and rescue her before she "goes native," which is to say, before she has sex with an Indian. Applying the captivity narrative to real life always had its problems. The first book devoted to a captivity story, Mary Rowlandson's 1682 account of her own capture, also subtly chronicled the ways in which "captivity" freed the author from subordinate wifely status and concluded with an embrace of her shared humanity with the Indians. Also troublesome were the women who *did* go native and declined to return to the "civilized" colonial world.[13] Certainly, by the close of the twentieth century, the narrative was painfully threadbare as a workable masculine drama. Few women, even the most conservative, were interested in exchanging independence for protection.

Men who were determined to keep the fantasy going had to range far to find a viable pretext, which may be one explanation for the remarkably consistent correlation between militia membership and antiabortion zealotry. Both "movements" are about protection—and the silent fetus, unlike the unpredictable modern woman, is one captive who can't reject a protection offer. No wonder that fetuses in antiabortion literature are most often depicted as little girls. That convention was in evidence at the Waco memorial service, where a huge blow-up photograph towered over the proceedings, the largest emblem on display: a picture of a fetus, with a caption entreating us to save "her" life. But even rescuing the captive fetus has its problems. The fetus's captor, after all, is a woman. Even here, then, the men found themselves back in battle with their true nemesis: the independent woman.

As the Patriots blamed feminists for "downgrading" masculine roles, they overlooked the real force that was feminizing their lives. Bedeviling them—just as it bedeviled the cadets of the Citadel or the boys of the Spur Posse—was a rising culture in which femininity (rather than feminism) seemed to be ever more celebrated. "I gotta get on the media," the young Waco-ite Scott Horton had declared, yet all he could do was wave his handmade sign and pray that a camera lens might turn his way. From the vantage point of the Patriots, women seemed to have gone from holding none of the cards to holding all of them. Not only had women moved into some of the old male job categories, even scaling thirty-foot-high scaffolds, but they appeared to have the natural advantage in the new image industries of media and entertainment. It hardly mattered that women had made only tiny inroads into the construction industry and other well-paying "male" job categories, and were more likely to feel oppressed than elevated by image culture; to men who saw themselves as contestants in a zero-sum game, the conclusion seemed self-evident: if they were the losers, women had to be the winners.

No matter what the Angry White Males did, they always seemed to lose out. In their efforts to become their own Bravehearts they would be betrayed, just as Braveheart was, by the entrenched establishment of their time. Waco, like *Braveheart,* would become a movie. The figure at the heart of that conversion to film, and ultimately at the mercy of that same establishment, happened to be attending the 1998 memorial service: Mike McNulty, the speaker who testified to hearing "the sounds of fear in children's voices," was the originator of a celebrated new film,

Waco: The Rules of Engagement, a documentary that had played to packed houses across the country and generated extensive media coverage. "There he goes, *the big producer!*" some envious fellow Patriots called out, not entirely in good humor, as he passed by, a slightly rumpled, roly-poly figure in an Eddie Bauer khaki travel vest, plaid shirt, and bill cap. They shouted as if across a great divide. Several men pursued him with their personal camcorders, hoping for an interview with the man who had forded the treacherous channel from marginal protest to celebrity and popularized their tragedy. His film had even been nominated for an Academy Award.

McNulty, however, was not convinced that his passage was the grand success his peers imagined. He had weathered the crossing only to find the destination a surprisingly unnerving and questionable one. Which was one of the reasons he was not basking in the glow of fame that morning. "The problem with the modern age is too many idiots have got their hands on the technology," he told me irritably, surveying the field of men with camcorders. "Most of the people here are not journalists. They are rank amateurs. They think they can get access if they have a camera on their shoulders." That's what he thought once, too. Now he was not so sure.

This Wild, Bucking Thing

ONCE, BACK WHEN MIKE MCNULTY LIVED in southern California, somebody banged on his door at one in the morning, and, so Mike McNulty said, he was glad he had his gun, even though it just turned out to be a motorist needing gasoline. This was typical of the stories McNulty told about how crucial his guns had been to him. The tales left me wondering, but he was convinced that it was necessary to arm himself—even though he now lived in Fort Collins, a low-crime city north of Denver.

"The reason I got a permit in Colorado was because of threats because of the film. It's a big responsibility." Several "shadowy" people with Washington connections suggested "I better watch my step," he said. "That's the way it's done. It's not going to be a federal agent who comes after me. It's going to be a local gang-banger hired on to take care of business. So I watch my step. I have a lot of back doors."

However embattled by enemies, shadowy or real, McNulty's home was definitely well fortified. The onetime Buchanan supporter evidently subscribed to the candidate's "lock and load" philosophy. On a winter's afternoon several months before *Waco: Rules of Engagement* was nominated for an Academy Award, Mike McNulty had ushered me into the inner sanctum of his personal arsenal. The arsenal filled half the family "crafts room" in his basement; the other half was occupied by his wife's sewing kits, knitting yarn, Christmas decorations, and Easter-egg paint sets. On McNulty's side of an invisible Maginot line, a locked safe stood sentinel beside what looked like a home workshop. "I make my own [ammunition]," he explained, pointing out the various devices on his worktable for the process: the reloading press, powder scale, powder "trickler," and something called a "vibratory cleaner." He demonstrated how he carefully brushed the primer, measured out his powder to "within one-tenth of a grain," funneled it into the case, and slid in the bullet. The resulting ammo was the largest I'd ever seen. "They are big dudes," he conceded of the three-inch rounds.

Unlocking the safe and several cabinet drawers, McNulty brought forth some other substantial accessories: a Tanto knife ("You can penetrate car doors with one strike"), a custom-made saber ("made by the same guy who made the sword Conan the Barbarian used—it'd cut through your whole waist"), a Nighthawk micro-light that strapped to a finger and flashed an eerie amber color ("so it doesn't mess with your night vision"), an ammo vest, a rehydration unit, a two-way radio, and so on. "These are all things you'd need if you had invaders come into your home," he told me. "I'd be in a position to defend against intruders." He kept the radio's twin in the bedroom, "so if I get caught, I can communicate with my wife." He explained, "I never look at it as trying to kill them. I'm trying to stop them."

The last piece of weaponry to come out of McNulty's safe was a seeming Howitzer, a monster shotgun, which, along with a rifle and his .40-caliber pistol, was all that remained of a once-large collection. It certainly seemed sufficient to me—a military-style semiautomatic twelve-gauge with a three-inch chamber and an extended magazine that could pack nine of his "big dude" rounds. "It's not made for bird hunting," McNulty remarked gratuitously. The imposing weapon sported a "combat sling," which was a good thing, because I could barely lift it. "That's why women should never be in combat," McNulty averred. "You have to have that upper-body strength." That didn't dissuade him, however, from proposing that we drive out to the Larimer County firing range so he could teach me how to shoot it.

The drive to the range was long, and by the time we arrived, it was nearly dark and bitterly cold. We got our ear-protector headsets and hustled over to our designated shooting booth. The range was about to close, I noted with a certain relief, and we were the last shooters for the day. McNulty hurriedly pulled his weapon out of its case and pressed it into my hands. I lifted the Rambo-style shotgun to my shoulder and aimed, more or less, in the direction of the target. Whether I hit it or not—and I didn't—was impossible for me to say right off. The fiery flash and recoil gave me a momentary concussion, almost as if I had hit myself in the head. I had been unprepared for the power and force of such a cannon. After two rounds, I had had more than enough.

McNulty then converted the gun to semiautomatic and pounded out a rapid series of shots before the announcement came over the loudspeakers that it was time to leave. "Now, see, what I was doing by getting us there at the last minute and hurrying you," McNulty explained to me on the drive back, "was creating a tactical experience. And you didn't react well. When someone breaks into your home, you have to be ready to react. You have to be ready, after the first and second shot, to shoot again if necessary. Because if you don't, you give the intruder the opening he needs to blast you and your family into a million pieces."

I said that what had disturbed me was not the time pressure but the terrible violence of the gun itself. But that, McNulty told me, was the whole appeal—not the violence, but that it was a violence "that could be controlled. A twelve-gauge full-bore shotgun going off is such a horrendously violent instantaneous event. It has a mind of its own. In order to physically control what's going on takes a certain amount of self-control. It's this wild, bucking thing that you can control. It's an explosion, but it's a *controlled* explosion." As we drove down the long hill, bouncing around in his Aerostar van with 150,000 miles on the odometer, I thought of a remark a male friend had made to me once—that being a man isn't about dominating, but about *not being dominated*. It struck me now that to handle the violence such a gun gives out, to be knocked half unconscious by its explosive force and survive, followed the same principle. By then, I knew something about the many explosions that had occurred in Mike McNulty's life, and I understood that none of these were explosions McNulty could hope to control. I didn't want to fire the shotgun again. But then I didn't feel as if for some years now an invisible army had been firing at me.

Mike McNulty's odyssey, from laid-off fire-insurance agent to Oscar aspirant, held lessons for every American man, regardless of his place on the political spectrum. The lessons were more pointed, though, coming from a man traveling on the margins. As McNulty himself had put it: "If you want to see what's happening in the stream called our society, go to the edges and look at what's happening there, and then you begin to have an understanding—if you know how a stream works—of what's going on in the middle." Anyway, McNulty seemed to be both on the edge and in the mainstream. He defied easy stereotypes of "militiamen" (a term he eschewed) storming against multicultural America from their redneck mountain redoubts; his middle-class family included his adopted eleven-year-old daughter, who is half African-American, and his two half-Hispanic adopted sons from his wife's previous marriage. McNulty's story in many ways followed the classic arc of postwar male experience. He was a son of a World War II marine veteran and aerospace engineer. He had anticipated a masculine transit through military service, company loyalty, and a suburban marriage. What he found, instead, was the Vietnam War, corporate downsizing, and a marital crack-up. "Every promise that's been made to me has been broken," he said.

Before the McNultys moved to Fort Collins in 1994, they had become accustomed to a comfortable life in suburban southern California. They were supported by McNulty's often six-figure annual income, thanks to the big commissions he accrued as an aggressive commercial-insurance agent, an independent broker affiliated with the corporate behemoth Nationwide Insurance. His specialty was fire and liability. Nationwide had courted the McNultys with a family-friendly pitch, and after Mike took the job, the company sent a series of letters to his wife, Julie, to let her know how much Nationwide "cared" about the whole family, wishing the kids happy birthday, and thanking Julie for being "a good wife." The approach especially appealed to Julie, a Mormon who at that point believed strongly in a wife's helpmate role. Mike, who was raised Catholic but converted to Mormonism when they married, was also pleased; what he found most gratifying was how the company helped him "to live up to my family responsibilities."

Mike loved the job. "The harder I worked, the more rewards I got," he recalled. "In '88, I sold more commercial insurance than any other agent nationwide, out of fifteen thousand agents. And I felt like I was making a contribution, safeguarding people's property, rescuing people. And I was good at it. My talent was fire protection. It was my specialty; other agents came to me to learn how to do it." Then, in 1991, McNulty recalled, the Columbus, Ohio–based Nationwide began raising rates to astronomic levels and refusing to renew policies in California. As a result, McNulty lost two-thirds of his income that year and had to declare bankruptcy. It soon became clear to him and fellow agents that Nationwide had decided the money it had poured into its westward expansion could be more profitably invested elsewhere. "It turned out the employees were only used to make the company a nest egg so it could go gamble in the stock market" was how McNulty characterized it. At the end of 1993, the company abruptly jettisoned all its California agents and left the state.[14] McNulty then struggled to make it on his own in an unsupportive business climate. "The day of the small independent agent is over," McNulty observed. "The agent used to design the product for the customers. Now they've all become sales reps, untrained and unlicensed, and the company controls the product." McNulty found himself out of work for the first time in decades; he lost his business and had to sell the family house. It was in these years that a part-time interest in guns became a full-time vocation, as McNulty became increasingly outraged by what he saw as orchestrated government efforts to disarm citizens. At the helm of a gun-rights group he had organized called COPS (California Organization for Public Safety), he lobbied against the state's assault-weapons ban and backed a lawsuit to force the Los Angeles Police Department to issue concealed-weapons permits. Soon even these became secondary concerns to an all-consuming preoccupation with Waco, and the making of a film about it.

McNulty would wind up spending twenty-eight months and $400,000 of his savings, along with $7,000 in grants from the NRA and the Gun Owners of America, to research a documentary about the federal government's role in the fiery deaths at Waco. He had gotten his hands on a government surveillance film taken from the air during the siege; he believed it showed federal agents shooting at the Branch Davidians from behind their building, an area the media never got to see. He shopped the evidence he had collected to every network and news program he could think of, hoping they would make it the basis for a story, without a single taker. Finally, he approached Dan Gifford, a former CNN business reporter who had moved to Los Angeles to pursue a career in acting and movie producing. McNulty said he had met Gifford through the concealed-weapons permit lawsuit; Gifford was one of the plaintiffs. In his pre-CNN days during the eighties, Gifford had made millions as a security-and-commodities broker in Texas, and he was looking to spend some of that money to launch a Hollywood career. So far, he had only gotten bit parts in a few films, often playing a reporter or banker, and had yet to produce a movie. Waco looked to him like an attention grabber. Gifford got out his checkbook. Eventually he would sink more than $1 million into the film.

McNulty had already found a director, William Gazecki, who had won an Emmy for sound mixing on the TV show *St. Elsewhere.* For ten months, McNulty and Gazecki traveled together, attending the Waco hearings on Capitol Hill and hopscotching around the country. Gazecki trailed after McNulty with a camera as the ex–fire insurance salesman interviewed fire investigators, firearms experts, law-enforcement officers,

medical examiners, and religious scholars. They returned again and again
to Waco to gather more evidence. "I liked McNulty," Gazecki said as
we sat talking one day in a deli by the Santa Monica beach where the
director, a nature lover and sometime supporter of environmental
groups, liked to spend his free moments. "He's this cherub of a man,
gregarious, passionate. And he *loved* being an investigator, carrying
around all these big files in his car." On the long road trips, the two men
sometimes had "heated talks" as McNulty's speculations ran up against
Gazecki's more pragmatic nature. "You know, he had all his theories and
feelings and blah, blah, blah," Gazecki recalled with a grin. "He had this
soapbox under his arm and he'd put it on the ground and climb on top
of it. And I'd say, 'Michael, I don't care what you think. Can you prove
it?' "

The resulting film painted a thoroughly condemnatory picture of federal culpability at Waco, interspliced with grisly, lingering shots on
charred corpses, set to a mesmerizing, moody New Age soundtrack.
Piecing together excerpts from FBI negotiation tapes with David Koresh, home videos taken by the Davidians, footage from the congressional hearings, and interviews with local law-enforcement officers,
independent investigators, scholars, and scientists, the documentary built
inexorably toward the conclusion that on April 19, while FBI tanks
rammed the building, FBI agents also shot into the Davidians' home
with machine guns, sparking a firestorm. The FBI denied the allegations,
but the filmmakers had what they believed was literally a smoking gun:
the heat-sensitive surveillance tape taken that day from the air by the
FBI. Made with special "night vision" technology, the tape showed spo-
radic flashes of heat, and the filmmakers found a former supervisor at
the Defense Department's night-vision lab who was ready to testify that
these flashes were likely to be hot spurts of gunfire.

That evidence was not as ironclad as it appeared, however. After the
film was released, the Justice Department produced its own experts who
said the flashes were just sunlight reflections. If the heat flashes were
from gunfire, federal officials argued, then where were the agents holding
the guns? The heat from their bodies, like the heat from the gun muzzles,
should have created an image. Meanwhile, the *Washington Post* asked
twelve infrared experts to review the tape; only four believed the light
bursts could possibly be gunfire.[15] Regardless of the flashes, the film was
a chilling document, depicting government paramilitary thuggery during
the siege and highly irregular and disturbing practices by the FBI afterward—in particular, the way the federal agents withheld forensic evidence from the local authorities, handpicked what evidence should be

kept or tossed, and bulldozed the property before it could be independently analyzed.[16] *Waco* was unveiled at the Sundance Film Festival in January 1997, and it subsequently received respectful, mostly laudatory reviews from critics across the political spectrum and won the International Documentary Association's feature award. When I flew to Denver to meet McNulty in early December of 1997, I expected to find the first-time filmmaker celebrating his wholesale triumph.

"RIGHT NOW I'M GOING THROUGH THIS BUSINESS with my wife of 'You didn't fulfill your commitments to me and I'm leaving,'" McNulty told me as soon as he picked me up at the Denver airport. "She doesn't like what I'm doing. She doesn't like the subject matter. She doesn't like the people I'm dealing with. The past four to five years dealing with Waco, true colors have come to the surface. Things like loyalty, moral support." What it boiled down to, he maintained, was that his wife, Julie, wanted him to provide a "white-picket-fence life." McNulty's substitute, a protectionist crusade on behalf of the Davidians and their burned-down home, did not impress her in the least. She wanted their three-thousand-square-foot house in Corona, California, back. But McNulty couldn't even afford his guns; he'd pawned all but the shotgun, rifle, and a pistol that he carried with him at all times. The McNulty family was now clipping coupons and fending off bill collectors from their smaller rental in snowy Fort Collins. Their economies were many. He hadn't even repaired the driver's-side seat belt in his van; the clasp had given way and he had to loop it around the passenger's belt when he drove.

Nevertheless, Mike wanted to do a second film on Waco, and a third on the Oklahoma City bombing, which he theorized was the result of a government undercover operation gone wrong. So far, the only money his ongoing antigovernment investigations had yielded was consulting fees for advising attorneys handling the Waco and Oklahoma City bombing litigation. During the sentencing phase of Timothy McVeigh's trial, the defense team hired McNulty to compile everything the convicted bomber had read and seen about Waco, mitigating evidence the attorneys hoped might stave off the death penalty. (While McNulty believed McVeigh was guilty and should be imprisoned, he opposed his execution because "McVeigh was not the brains of the operation.") The judge, however, never allowed the lawyers to use the material. Not surprisingly, none of these pursuits pleased his wife; nor did she care for his other "job," hosting a weekly conservative radio show, broadcast on the survivalist-inclined American Freedom Network out of nearby Johnstown, Colorado. The station had burned down a week before my visit, no great loss as far as his wife was concerned—it was not even a paying gig. In the last few months, McNulty said, Julie had begun talking about getting a job, finding an apartment, and filing for divorce. "She's discovering herself," McNulty told me, without relish. "It's her time to become, I guess, liberated, not dependent on me."

After an hour's drive, we reached the new and smaller McNulty home. He unlooped the jury-rigged seat belts and we jumped out, both of us slipping on the icy driveway. His holster with the pistol shook loose and hit the ground with a noisy clatter. I prayed the handgun didn't have a hair trigger. Indoors, the house was empty; Julie was out grocery shopping. McNulty gave me the grand tour of his office, with its "Waco museum," a cabinet countertop that displayed the yield of his on-site foragings: a gas-mask filter, an AK-47 bullet, a ruptured rifle-shell casing, an orange "body flag" used to mark the location of corpses, a couple of grenade casings, a patch from a sandbag, a piece of dental work, and a three-by-five index card with a recipe for no-bake cookies scribbled in a child's hand. On the wall was a Viking knife replica under glass, a simulacrum of Napoleon's sword on a plaque, and a map captioned THE FILM INDUSTRY'S VIEW OF AMERICA. The East Coast was marked LETTERMAN, the West Coast HOLLYWOOD, and the rest of the nation INFLIGHT MOVIE. On a shelf that held bills and outgoing mail, McNulty had stacked his business cards, stamped INVESTIGATIVE REPORTER. Actually, McNulty told me, he preferred to describe himself as "an American colonial pamphleteer," and his organization COPS as "the moral equivalent of a committee of correspondence," established after reading the early American revolutionaries "and looking at how they dealt with the government of King George and seeing how I felt dealing with the government of King Bill." The Waco film was "my Thomas Paine pamphlet," he said, adding meaningfully, "I just hope I don't have to follow in his footsteps." While he was talking, my eye wandered to a stack of outgoing mail piled next to his business cards, including several stamped and sealed return envelopes to various sweepstakes, made out in Julie's hand.

McNulty showed me his "$3 Hillary bill" with "Madame President" stamped on it, which got him on the subject of the Clinton administration, a topic on which he could hold forth indefinitely. "Clinton saw to it that the ATF's budget was increased and their personnel numbers were increased. In some circles, they are known as Clinton's Praetorian Guard. They'll do exactly what he wants them to do. . . . A couple years back there was an air force jet, an executive-type jet, it crashed with four significant air force generals aboard. There's a newspaper called *The*

Resister that is written by a number of Special Forces operators, [which had] this story about this jet crash of generals that said basically these boys were on their way to Washington, D.C., to pull off a coup d'état. They were going to arrest Bill Clinton as the commander in chief and subject him to military court-martial for some of the crap that he's pulled, and they were discovered when the aircraft took off. And it was a similar circumstance that occurred with Mr. [Ron] Brown [the late commerce secretary] in his aircraft in Bosnia. Mr. Brown was getting ready to spill the beans about Mr. Clinton's funny-money games, and that was the motive for making sure Mr. Brown's aircraft took the hit. . . .

"Why would the president of the United States sign an executive order that exempted certain military units from federal whistle-blower protection? And these certain military units comprised the United States Navy divers that did the diving on TWA 800. What do you think they saw down there when they were gathering all of that evidence off the bottom of the sea floor? I've got a copy of the executive order; a friend of mine, a chief of staff of a prominent western senator's office, dug it out for me. What is that about except that he didn't want these people to have any protection or cover if they stepped forward and started saying things about what they saw during the course of their evidence-gathering at the bottom of the ocean. If I had to guess, they saw evidence of a missile strike on the aircraft, not necessarily a high-explosive warhead. There's another kind of missile that's used by the navy, it's a high-velocity penetrator that goes so fast that when it strikes a body like an aircraft, the impact shock causes the disintegration of the airplane. It was part of the development for SDI."

My head was beginning to spin. I pointed out that SDI, the "Star Wars" initiative, was Reagan's creation, not Clinton's. But McNulty was undeterred. If I was looking for the real enemy behind the enemy, Reagan wasn't the problem. It was Hillary. "Hillary is a very strong-willed human being. I think she's literally and figuratively the power behind the throne. I don't think Bill is competent enough to pull off some of the things that have been written about. Hillary's a very smart woman— also very dangerous. Usurpers are always dangerous, because ultimately they have to exercise evil in order to achieve their ends." Efforts to get off the topic were unavailing. "When it comes to who called the final shots, figuratively and literally, on April the nineteenth," he continued, "I have got clear information, although I can't prove it all, that [Clinton's former associate attorney general] Webb Hubbell was on the telephone that day getting directions from Vince Foster. Now, I believe Mr. Foster was receiving his directions from Hillary. And *she* was the one who was calling the shots at the White House. Can I prove it? Not convincingly, but that's my theory. The reason Billy wasn't aware of what was going on in detail is because Gary Aldrich [an FBI agent who wrote *Unlimited Access,* a dubious, rabidly anti-Clinton tome about his days on White House detail] told me that Hillary was in charge of domestic policy. When Hillary made her famous stand on *60 Minutes,* standing by her man in the light of the Gennifer Flowers thing, a deal was cut. And the deal was if Hillary stood by her man and helped get him elected, she would be given complete control over domestic matters. And that's why on Inauguration Day, there was a big knock-down-drag-out yelling match in the White House between Hillary and Al Gore, because Hillary wanted the vice president's office."

I became accustomed to such monologues over my four-day visit; at any rate, I could rely on the incessantly ringing phone for respite. The callers were generally McNulty's "sources," returning his many phone calls; he was nothing if not persistent. In the late afternoon on one day of my visit, and much to McNulty's delight, the anti-Clintonian Georgia congressman Bob Barr phoned in the middle of one of these soliloquys. "The real Bob Barr!" he said happily, or "Bob," as McNulty addressed him. (Barr's office later confirmed that, indeed, McNulty often speaks with the congressman.) McNulty told Barr about a phone conversation he had with an aide to another congressman who might be stalling further investigations of Waco. "If you'd like to have the documentation, including a tape recording of my conversation, let me know." Then McNulty told the congressman he was getting ready to do a second film on Waco, explaining, "I happen to be in possession of some evidence," supposedly sinister, of a top secret military presence in Waco. Barr said he was on a cell phone and would call him back on a "secure" line.

On the first evening, though, the disquisition on the all-powerful Hillary was interrupted not by the phone but by a key scratching in a lock. The front door opened and slammed shut. Julie was home. She gave a warm hello to me, a curt nod to her husband, and headed for the kitchen. Mike trod gingerly behind her. He hovered silently while she began to unpack the groceries. The man who had been talking a blue streak about going toe-to-toe with the "usurpers in Washington" was struck respectfully mute. Over Julie's shoulder, a framed sampler adorned the wall. FAMILIES ARE FOREVER, it read.

"You want me to make dinner?" Mike finally asked hopefully. She handed him a package of Hormel chili and Mike hastened to pull out the pots and pans from the pantry and started dicing onions. "You like the chili on your potato, right?" he inquired solicitously of his wife. She nodded, and I sensed a discreet thawing in the kitchen's frozen tundra.

"It's the only time he cooks," Julie couldn't help needling, but she said it with a small smile.

"No it isn't!" Mike shot back, hurt. Unable to resist a return jab, he quickly pointed out to me that she hadn't bothered to look at his film once during all the months he was shaping it.

"I didn't see it till Sundance because I wanted to see it complete." Julie turned to me. "When Mike gets involved in something, he jumps in with two feet and the focus is on nothing else. At first I thought, He'll get over it. And three years later, he's still at it."

McNulty tried for some levity. "It's my Waco affliction," he said cheerfully. "Waco-itis. It becomes obsessive for a lot of us, a grand obsession."

Julie shot him a dark look, then turned back to me. "Because he's so obsessed with what he's doing, he's ignoring the family he's supposed to be supporting. He's ignoring his responsibilities."

"I'm focused," McNulty protested.

"Well, there's supposed to be another focus—working in the insurance industry, supporting your family."

"Well, that insurance job went away." He chopped at the onion ever more aggressively.

"Well, I also talked to the secretary in his office," Julie said to me, unrelenting. "The one who was doing all his work while he was doing Waco."

"That's not true!" McNulty sputtered.

"We *lost* our house," Julie bored in.

"That was the insurance business!"

"We'd have struggled but not gone under."

"Look at all the guys I know in insurance who went under.... All of my friends who were independent agents, all but one, were wiped out. Yeah, we could've staved off the inevitable for a little longer, but I chose to make a transition, and the transition was from insurance to what I feel will be a good career in filmmaking."

Julie, however, was not interested in transitioning to filmmaking. "I like *stability*," she said. "Look, my dad was a postman. He went to work every day and he got home at three o'clock every day."

"But insurance got to the point where it was just a struggle," he said, more for my benefit than Julie's. "Not only was I not making money, I wasn't having fun. I liked it when you could show people that the insurance could protect them. Or giving a widow a small consolation for the loss of her husband. But it became so competitive. . . . A lot of what you were being asked to do was immoral or illegal. A lot of people in financial difficulty are looking to *burn* their way to success. I have to feel like I'm making a *contribution*."

Julie clattered the plates on the table and said nothing. Supper was consumed hurriedly, a glacial crevasse expanding between them. It was with some relief that Mike and I piled back in the wheezing Aerostar van to make the long drive to Boulder to view a screening of *Waco* at the University of Colorado. It was not a victorious curtain call so much as a covert operation. McNulty hadn't been invited, and he wouldn't be the one introducing the film or answering questions afterward. Those honors had fallen to the film's executive producer and financier, Dan Gifford.

On the ride, a gloomy McNulty returned to the question of making a contribution. "One night, I was down in the [Mormon] temple, and I was thinking, Why does God make heroes? It's bothered me for some time. And I realized, God makes a hero so he can be of greater service to his fellow man and woman. That's the good kind of fame, not just being famous. Most of the founding fathers died penniless, but those kind of men were heroes because they contributed something to society."

McNulty grew up enraptured by JFK's call to manly service. His father had spent four years in the Pacific during World War II, a marine at Guadalcanal, Tarawa, and Iwo Jima. Aside from these names, Mike knew very little about what his father did. "You could never get my father to tell any war stories. All I knew is he had a Japanese rifle from a Japanese he killed." In any event, his father's postwar career convinced McNulty that service was something to be exercised not on the ground but in the air. His father's aerospace work took the family to Edwards Air Force Base for several years, where young Mike even got to meet the supersonic-flight pioneer Chuck Yeager. "My dad worked on airplanes, and I loved airplanes," McNulty said. One night in 1957 (when he was eleven) "I'd been in bed and my father came and got me and said, 'C'mon! Let's go see the satellite!' We lived in the high desert and the skies were very clear. I remember it was cool outside. I remember standing out in the front yard with my dad. And we were looking and looking. And finally we found it, this light moving across the sky. At first, I was a little disappointed, like 'So?' But then he explained to me what it took to get it up there, and how it had never happened before, and how it was going to change everything."

McNulty's father had then gone to work for Hughes Aerospace on largely classified defense projects for many years. As he was growing up, all the son would know about the father's work was that it involved infrared technology, similar evidently to that used to track the alleged FBI machine-gun fire at Waco. "I never really learned anything from my father. I definitely never learned what it meant to be a man." Still, the general notion of his father on the cutting edge of military technology and science enthralled the young McNulty. He was intending such a career for himself when he enlisted in the navy in 1964. "My plan was to learn electronics technology, nuclear stuff." A year later, though, he was sent to Vietnam aboard aircraft carrier USS *Bon Homme Richard*—fresh from the Long Beach Naval Shipyard, its air-conditioning foundations newly installed by Ike Burr.

In a way, McNulty's military service would be his introduction to a media culture. Which is to say, his primary job was to operate the closed-circuit television system aboard ship and videotape and photograph aircraft launches and recoveries. "I didn't see a lot of combat," he said. But he saw enough over the course of three tours of duty to make him question America's involvement; he joined the Vietnam Veterans Against the War after his final tour. "It just seemed more and more senseless . . . a kind of unthinking, mindless bullshit that was a constant daily fare." Then there were the "constant accidents because you were just always working at these very high speeds." By the late sixties, their frequent twenty-four-hour shifts, assigned for reasons no one could fathom, left exhausted crews vulnerable to fatal mistakes. One day, a weary air-crew man and friend of McNulty's walked directly into his own propeller just below McNulty's filming platform. "A good portion of him got splattered up all over the windows of my platform. And I got a call from my commanding officer to go down and take the medical-examination photos of the corpse. I told him I didn't want to do it, but he insisted. So I went down and took the pictures of what was left of him. I came back and threw the camera and the film at the commanding officer," an act of insubordination for which he was nearly court-martialed.

The most spectacular horror that McNulty witnessed occurred in the Gulf of Tonkin on July 29, 1967, when a fire engulfed the USS *Forrestal,* another aircraft carrier close to his own, killing 134 men. The disaster, one of the worst in recent naval history, was triggered by the accidental launch of a Zuni rocket on deck, which hit a parked plane with future POW and U.S. senator John McCain in the pilot seat. An inquiry by the navy's Judge Advocate General's office a few months later concluded that it was likely that an inadequately trained crew had prematurely connected the rocket-launch wiring in violation of safety regulations. (Ordinarily the wiring should not be connected until a plane is ready to be catapulted off the deck.) No disciplinary action, however, was taken.[17] But as McNulty recalled it, the accident was a product of the contest-crazed mentality that had gripped the fleet. He said the USS *Forrestal* and the USS *Oriskany*, which were positioned at the time nearby his carrier, were having a race to see which one could launch their entire air wing the fastest, not an unusual practice. "It got to the point to where a lot of drinks were bought by the losers for the winners when we went back into port," he said. He recalled crew members on the USS *Forrestal* telling him later that they had decided "to get an edge" on the competition by wiring the rockets ahead of time, before the planes were positioned on the catapult. Whatever the cause, the launched rocket ripped through a plane's fuel tank, sending the flight deck up in flames and detonating a stack of shipboard bombs.[18] McNulty's crewmates helped put out the fire while McNulty videotaped the disaster. The moment he recalled most vividly was of "this one kid who hauled butt from the stern of the flight deck all the way to the island structure. He came through that door and collapsed against the wall, and at that point we all noticed that his left foot was missing above the ankle, and blood was just pumping out on the deck. And he looked down and said, 'I'm dead,' eyes closed, that was it."

"What drives me in Waco?" McNulty asked himself as the van churned through the oceanic darkness of the wide-open Colorado landscape. "The sons of bitches lied to us again. They lied to us about Vietnam. They in essence have done the same thing as in Vietnam. Tell me Waco wasn't My Lai all over again."

We pulled off the highway and into a small business park where McNulty's friend and "business manager," Chris Parrett, was waiting. Parrett, a computer program expert and self-styled "American Patriot," on occasion helped fellow Patriots self-publish their work. His current product, with a camouflage-print cover, was James Wesley Rawles's *Triple Ought: A Novel of the Millennial Crash and the Second Civil War*, in which an embattled band of survivalists shoot their way to freedom in an outpost in Idaho. "So, you ready to tell Gifford where to get off?" Parrett asked affably as he climbed into the back of the van. "So what are you going to ask him?" Parrett wanted to know. "We should come up with some questions."

Thinking of his executive producer, McNulty rolled his eyes. "How about, 'Gee, Dan, like how many interviews did you do for this film?'"

McNulty suggested. " 'Gee, Dan, who went all around the country to make this film? Was it you? Or Amy?' " Amy was Amy Sommer Gifford, Dan's wife and the vice president of the couple's production company, SomFord Entertainment. McNulty turned to me. "Now Gifford acts like he owns the whole thing.... Do I see Gifford as another King George? Sure."

McNulty pulled into a parking lot at the University of Colorado. Hands shoved in pockets, caps pulled down to shield their faces, McNulty and Parrett slunk into the back row of the auditorium and slid low into their seats. The film had already begun. Afterward, Gifford was introduced as "executive producer and senior producer." McNulty sat bolt upright. *"Senior producer!"* he whispered indignantly. "That's a new one." As Gifford answered audience questions, McNulty stewed and sniped sotto voce. When Gifford mentioned how they had the infrared tape for ten months before they noticed the gunfire, McNulty muttered, "No, *eighteen* months." (Nor, he noted, did *they* spot the gunfire; it was an investigator advising the Davidians' legal counsel who pointed it out to McNulty.) When Gifford talked about ATF agents killing a Davidian who was returning to the building, McNulty sputtered, "That's not true. He's spinning yarns he picked up from the fringe. I sent him a memo refuting that." When Gifford told the audience, "I don't care for guns myself," McNulty groaned and shook his head. In this whole presentation, Gifford never mentioned McNulty. Mike McNulty had been disappeared from his own film. McNulty elbowed Chris and me. "Let's leave. I'm sick of hearing this."

On the way to the car, McNulty seethed. "I loved how he says, *'We learned,' 'We found.'* Oh, and 'I don't care for guns myself.' He has guns, too. He carries a gun. We celebrated his birthday one year at his house and I bought him an antique powder horn to go with his antique guns."

"He wants to play the liberal Hollywood guy. He comes across as a very polished Hollywood person," Chris Parrett said, in what he intended as a compliment to McNulty. "You come across as GI Joe, in the trenches."

"That's what bothers me about Dan," McNulty said, unmollified. "He's very suave. I'm surprised he didn't have his ascot on."

Parrett wondered why the video of *Waco* wasn't on sale in the lobby, an idle comment that instantly triggered McNulty's suspicion radar. "It's what isn't there that's telling," he said ominously. "It's the omissions. It certainly leaves open the possibility that Dan is part of a third-party agenda. He's a pawn." Of what? I inquired. McNulty shrugged. "Dan seems to have an agenda other than the success of the film. Why are there only three prints? Why is there no advertising? Why is there very little promotion? There's this continuing pattern where he shows a minimal effort while at the same time making sure the film's not going anywhere." Was he suggesting, as some Patriots had been rumor-mongering on the Internet, that Gifford was an FBI mole? McNulty would only say, "Who knows? But there's a continuing pattern."

Showdown on the Hollywood Frontier

I HAD SEEN *Waco: The Rules of Engagement* four months before my Colorado visit, at a Los Angeles screening in the Simon Wiesenthal Center's Museum of Tolerance, a human-rights institution dedicated to the prevention of another Holocaust. On this particular evening, though, the theater looked like a scene from a Waco reunion, especially its back rows, where men in T-shirts emblazoned with gun-rights slogans hissed and booed every time a hated "Clintonite" appeared on the screen. The attorney general was greeted with the bellowed mantra "Butcher Reno!"

Other than heavy-handed editing of congressional hearings that put right-wing Republicans like Bob Barr in the best light and liberal Democrats like Charles Schumer in the worst, it was hard to locate *Waco's* politics on first viewing. The filmmakers appeared, in fact, to be positioning *Waco* as a liberal product. The venue choice of the Museum of Tolerance was one indicator, as was the movie's rollout at Robert Redford's Sundance festival, its selection as the lead film at the Human Rights Watch International Film Festival, and several ACLU-sponsored screenings. The press kit distributed by the Giffords' production company portrayed the documentary as a project inspired and created by the counterculture: "In the tradition of those in the '60s who exposed government lying during the Vietnam War and Watergate eras," the press release began, "we have exposed massive government lies."[19]

After the screening, Dan and Amy Sommer Gifford had mounted the stage to field questions. Amy told the audience that Dan was just a hard-working investigative reporter with no axe to grind who had unearthed some compelling evidence, and how she, a Wellesley graduate, believed this was a "civil rights" film with a simple message: "You don't have the right to shoot people just because they look weird." This was their typical posture to the media, even in conservative outlets. When Gifford appeared, for instance, on *The Ron Hunter Show,* a New Orleans talk-radio program with right-leaning political sympathies, the host inquired genially, "Are you a right-wing, wild-eyed, radical, conservative fanatic constitutionalist?" Gifford chuckled. "Well, I guess I'm in Hollywood, so I'd have to be a wild-eyed radical Democrat liberal, I suppose." After a break for a gun store ad, the host returned to the question of politics. "Dan, do I understand you correctly? Basically, you would not consider yourself conservative?" Gifford answered by pointing out that he had been a correspondent for network news programs, as if that résumé eliminated any possibility of conservative sentiments.

A member of the Museum of Tolerance audience asked what had happened to the director, who was absent from the stage. The Giffords mumbled something about "creative differences" and hastily called for another question. Asked where the seed money came from for the film, the Giffords changed the subject. Asked for their affiliations, Dan emphasized that he was a former CNN and *McNeil-Lehrer NewsHour* reporter who once wrote for the *Village Voice*, and Amy said she was a former producer at *Maury Povich*, adding, with a toss of her Shirley Temple mop of blond curls, that she was just a gal trying to make it in Hollywood. The name Mike McNulty did not pass their lips.

————

"I JUST GOT BACK from an audition," Dan Gifford said in his booming television announcer's voice as he ushered me into the wood-paneled office of his high-ceilinged Tudor brick manse in Brentwood, California, a few weeks after the screening. "It was for a TV show, *The Magnificent Seven*." He picked up a dagger-size envelope cutter from his desk and twirled it. "No gunslinging, though," he said, sounding disappointed. "The role was for a banker."

Looking around his office, I could see why he had been hoping for the gunslinger's part. The walls were covered with old muskets, flintlock rifles, swords, and knives. A miniature covered wagon perched on Gifford's desk. A "jackelope" (a jackrabbit head with glued-on antlers, to weed out greenhorns) loomed overhead. And everywhere hung sepia photographs of gunfighters and Indians. Portraits of Pancho Villa and Geronimo were just two of the Wild West icons on display; most of the pictures were of Gifford's ancestors. "That's my grandfather on my father's side, Montana Jack, used to work the ranches up in Montana," he said, pointing to one. "He exchanged shots with Pancho Villa when he came across the border." Another ancestor, a great-uncle and Texas Ranger named Lee Korn, Gifford noted, "was awarded a couple of pistols for killing more Indians than anybody else and used to run around with scalps in the saddle. That's not very politically correct, but . . ." He sank in his red-leather desk chair and sighed. "My family has always been on the frontier fighting Indians, which is not a popular thing to say now. . . . I'm the first of my family not to live on the frontier."

We retired to the den, a baronial room with a rancho-size fireplace and one of the family dogs sprawled in front of it as if resting from the hunt. A mounted steer skull presided from one wall. Gifford soon had an impressive bonfire crackling in the hearth and settled on the couch, where he continued to bemoan the right-wing conspiracy theorists who called radio stations and tried to attach themselves to his film. He said he tried to keep his distance from "the fatigue wearers from flyover land." Hollywood and the media, he noted, "do look down their noses at these people," and the last thing he wanted was to get classed as a "right-wing wacko." Nonetheless, as the evening wore on, Gifford's monologues ranged deeply into wacko territory.

The government might have been "testing classified weapons" on the Davidians, he speculated. He couldn't disclose his sources, but "that stuff that was being fired back there, maybe it wasn't a firearm as we know it." He alluded darkly to "microwave energies. It cooks your insides, causes people to have bowel movements, hemorrhages." From there, Gifford moved on to rumors he had heard about government "thought control," like a claim forwarded by a Church of Scientology magazine that government documents "show that the Jonestown mass suicide was really a cover-up by the CIA to hide its mind-control experiments." If I wanted to investigate federal shenanigans at Waco further, he said, he had found "very, very accurate" information on the government's clandestine operations in *Soldier of Fortune* magazine and the John Birch Society's newsletter. He noted in particular a *Soldier of Fortune* report that claimed the White House didn't want David Koresh taken alive. "This starts to sound like Vietnam," Gifford said.

Being the repository of all this top secret information had made him a target, he suspected. "Either they figure I'm stupid or it is sending a Sicilian message, so to speak." Ever since he began working on the Waco film, he said, "I've had a lot of people in bookstores, total strangers, come up to me, and they'll steer a conversation into politics . . . and it will usually end with 'Can I have your phone number?' " He pointed out two cases where women in stores had approached him to chat. Then there was the time a year and a half ago when he was in Washington, D.C., waiting for a cab to go to the airport and "these two guys came up and started a conversation with me." He got suspicious when they offered him a ride. "Their haircut sort of looked too short, and their shoes were a little too shiny," he said. "You been around enough military-type people, you spot 'em very quickly."

Amy came in then to tell Dan he had a phone call: their lawyer. Gifford and I repaired again to his office, where for the next half hour he fussed and fumed into the phone. "Aw, Jesus!" he declared. Finally, he dropped the receiver in its cradle and his head into his hands. What seemed to be the trouble? I inquired. Gifford looked up from behind his desktop covered wagon and explained that the trouble concerned a man whom he and Amy had "hired" to assist in the research for the film. This man was "selling all his bootlegs [video copies of *Waco*]," Gifford said. "He tried to screen the film in Colorado without our permission." The Giffords had gone to court to get a temporary restraining order to stop the video sales, but there seemed to be no controlling this man. Mike McNulty was his name. "It's typical little-guy stuff," Gifford said. "He has nothing else to be doing except chasing down Waco and Oklahoma City and being a big guy in his Patriot community." He picked up the dagger envelope opener and slapped it against his palm absentmindedly, thinking. "If you want to talk to men in crisis," he said, pleased to pass me along, "you should talk to Mike McNulty."

THE FILM'S DIRECTOR William Gazecki would describe for me how *Waco: The Rules of Engagement* had gone from a crusade of the heart to a contested political bauble. After a year of filming, he and Mike McNulty had returned to southern California, and Gazecki had retired to the editing room for months, preparing the film for its Sundance debut. Until then, Gazecki recalled, Dan Gifford had virtually no involvement with the film, other than to finance its production. Then Dan discovered that he had spent far more money on the project than he had intended and everything changed. "Dan went ape," Gazecki recalled, "frenetic, totally off the edge. He came down to my studio and went ballistic. He said, 'This is gonna be over in three weeks.' I said, 'Listen, pal, you don't own me.' It went downhill from there." A couple of weeks before Sundance, Gifford decided to become a hands-on executive producer. "Dan handed out this seventy-five-page script for the middle part of the film and says, 'Do it my way, or you're fired. Cut it this way, or else.'" Gazecki said Gifford wanted to insert "gun-rights stuff"; Gifford said he wanted a less "emotional" film. The recut film was delivered literally hours before the screening at Sundance. Afterward, Gazecki and Gifford exchanged bitter words in the parking lot. The next morning, Gazecki announced that he was leaving; the Giffords could promote the film on their own. The couple was furious. "Amy turned into a hysterical pogo stick, screaming and yelling and slamming doors."

They were upset, the Giffords explained to me later, because they had been counting on Gazecki to do the lion's share of the film's early promotion. That was because he was the one with the liberal credentials. "Because of the cultural war," Dan told me, only Gazecki was "socially acceptable to the Hollywood crowd. You must come from the left if you are going to have any validity." The Giffords had mapped out a "three-part marketing strategy," on the advice of their Washington, D.C., PR consultant, Bob Preiss of Forum Associates. "I thought the first place to go was the arts community, and so I was hoping that William [Gazecki] would be the lead spokesman for that," Preiss told me. "He's fairly apolitical. He doesn't care about Second Amendment gun rights. Then I figured the news people would catch on, and I figured Dan would be the key spokesman as a former *McNeil-Lehrer*, CNN, et cetera. And then finally, Michael McNulty could sell it to the gun-show crowd." Preiss paused for a small, dry laugh. "Obviously, that strategy fell apart."

Without Gazecki to provide liberal cover, the Giffords became even more intent on keeping McNulty on a short leash, starting at Sundance. They tried to discourage him from attending at all by refusing to cover his expenses or comp him a ticket, but McNulty paid his own way. When he appeared at the press conference after the screening, McNulty recalled, Amy slipped behind him and another crew member and hissed, "Keep your fucking mouth shut," before he had even ventured to say a word. When I asked Amy about the incident later, she readily confirmed it, word for word, and explained why such hardball tactics were necessary. "I'm sitting there seeing dollar signs in my eyes. I saw our sales going bye-bye." What seemed to bother Dan and her most, though, was not McNulty's unpopular politics but his less than chic appearance. Dan complained that McNulty was not "presentable." Amy said he was "boorish" and "has a potbelly." They were trying to appeal to "the PIBs [people in black], the Hollywood people," she said, and at the Sundance screening, she worried, the *Waco* contingent's attire had "way too much color" to fit in. "I wanted a deal.... We were there to sell the fucker." McNulty had to be kept under wraps, Amy said—using language that would seem to undermine her remarks at the Museum of Tolerance—for one simple reason: to the PIB eye, he "looks weird."

"It's all Dan-spin" was McNulty's response. "It's times like this that I wish I had the money to take it from him, to do it myself." That was not likely to happen. In fact, the Giffords had filed suit to stop him from selling or showing the video and were now refusing to release any of his portion of the proceeds until he signed a new contract, which would give him 50 percent of the profits (generally negligible on a documentary) and give them full ownership. McNulty was right that the Giffords had failed to distribute *Waco* widely. But it wasn't because Dan had a "third-party agenda" or was an FBI mole. No distributor would have taken the commission until all major parties involved in the production of the film signed a contract; otherwise, the distributor would be opening itself up to lawsuits. And McNulty wouldn't sign. He held that the original letter of agreement—which he had drafted, and he and Amy Sommer Gifford had signed—made him the owner; the Giffords argued that, because the movie had grown in length and changed in form, the agreement no longer pertained. Charges went back and forth for about five months before a court settlement was finally reached, denying McNulty ownership of the film he had conceived.

"I didn't have the money to fight it," McNulty said. Eventually, he gave up entirely, settled with the Giffords, and signed the new contract. Under the terms of this agreement, he couldn't so much as give an interview to the media without getting the Giffords' permission. "I feel like I'm standing outside the Branch Davidian compound and trying to plead with them not to come in and burn down the whole thing," he said to me. "I'm standing between the FBI offensive—the Giffords— and the Branch Davidians, symbolized by the film itself." Then again, McNulty had his moments where he preferred to imagine himself on the offensive, charging the Gifford moat and all it signified. "I get so upset with all this. I have fantasies sometimes," he said jokingly, "that I dress up like Rambo and go over there and ram a vehicle through the gate of his damn mansion." But it was only a fantasy, he said. He was no terrorist. His Aerostar was no Bradley.

You could see where the Giffords' hauteur might gall him. "When I first met Michael," Amy told me as we lunched in December 1997 at the Book Soup Bistro, next door to the Giffords' offices on Sunset Boulevard, "he was an unattractive geek who would be perfect for the job. You want to sit him by a phone and he could take care of details. If the FBI can hire Mormons to be honest and hardworking, why the hell can't I?" He was one of those "guys in flyover land," Dan said, who "wear off-the-rack suits," Amy added. McNulty was supposed to "sell home videos to his community," Dan said, but then he "went off the reservation." Amy noted that *her* "community" was affluent Manhattan and Hollywood. "I grew up in a culture where people like McNulty not only were pond scum, they didn't exist, because they were gun toting."

"I don't particularly like guns," Dan Gifford offered. I asked him if he owned any. "Why is that of interest?" he asked, suddenly wary. After much hedging, he conceded that he did own guns, but "wouldn't call them a collection." He declined to identify them. "Do I like guns? No. Are they a necessity if we have another riot? Yes." Do you have a concealed-weapons permit? I asked. More hedging. Suddenly, he reared back, pulled out of his wallet a laminated card, and slapped it on the table. It was the permit. "As a reporter, I've had a lot of threats" was his explanation for carrying a concealed weapon. I told him that Mc-Nulty had said Dan carried a Glock strapped around his midsection. So are you carrying it now? I asked. Dan glowered at me across the salad remains. "What do you think?" he finally said. Yes? I ventured. He nodded solemnly. "Do you want a cappuccino?" Amy interjected.

Dan Gifford and Mike McNulty were more alike than either would have wanted to admit—both, in their way, on the fringes, riven with suspicions. Yet far more than any jackbooted, Nazi-helmeted, paramilitary thugs, the Giffords represented what Mike McNulty was up against because, as they said, they could handle the Hollywood side. McNulty and Gifford were "gun nuts" in an era when the gun in America had been transformed into but another symbol of an ornamental masculinity. McNulty made his ammo by hand and he shot it. But while he stockpiled homemade shells to defend himself against his perceived enemies, he became more vulnerable to his real ones. In a world where disowning gun ownership could be a promotional tool and the real enemy couldn't be shot, the gun was a vastly symbolic item, a reality that only Dan Gifford, of the two of them, seemed to comprehend. While, as McNulty had claimed, Gifford "had guns, too," for the journalist-cum-actor-cum-producer, they were something to buy and collect, like the cars in his three-car garage or the horns of an animal he hadn't hunted that were mounted over the fireplace. Even when concealed, they were a conceit. McNulty's disaster was in not realizing that the emblematic tool of the frontiersman was now an affectation.

———

BEFORE MY VISIT to Fort Collins ended, McNulty and I drove up to Johnstown to view the remains of another fire scene: the radio station that had been broadcasting McNulty's talk show. It had burned to the ground the week before, even though it was across the street from the town's fire station. The conflagration had merited a small wire-service story that, much to McNulty's irritation, noted the station's so-called militia-inclined broadcasts and said arson was suspected.[20]

McNulty inspected the building with the eye of a former fire-insurance agent. "Look at the curve of the door," he said. "It's kicked in but the flashplate's intact." He contemplated the possibilities. "There's a certain number of people who are unhappy with this station. The neo-Nazis are mad because Don [the station's owner] wouldn't let them come in and spew. We've taken pokes at the government. There's the Waco film. In fact, just that I do a show here could open us up for attack. . . . But then again, it could just as easily be vandals looking for stuff to pawn." (The Colorado Bureau of Investigation, in fact, would conclude that the offender was a hot plate left plugged in in a back room.) McNulty and I made one last circuit of the building so he could collect mementos, but there wasn't much to recover. In all the rubble, the one intact object remaining, strangely untouched by the blaze, was a computer monitor.

The morning before my flight home, I went out to breakfast with Mike and Julie McNulty. The tension between them had lifted noticeably. Mike nudged me. "You see, my wife's put her wedding ring back on? We've kissed and made up." How long their détente would hold was anyone's guess. It had been sorely tested that very morning. Julie had woken to the sight of a page-one story in the Fort Collins newspaper listing local residents carrying concealed weapons. Her husband was named.

"I might sue for invasion of privacy," he fumed. "The paper has this attitude of, people shouldn't own guns, so we are gonna expose you. Bunch of busybodies pulling your pants down."

Julie cleared her throat. "Fort Collins is the safest town for its size in Colorado, and it was on a list as one of the safest in the country a few years ago. I have a hard time with the guns. I don't like them. I don't feel the *need* for them here. I never even lock the doors."

"There's been numerous occasions when my guns saved our bacon," Mike said.

"True," Julie shot back acidly, "the pawn shops love 'em."

"You were glad for that gun in L.A. when the doorbell rang at 1 A.M.," Mike said.

Julie shrugged. "Did you tell Susan about the kidnapping?" she asked. When Mike shook his head, she looked at him with disbelief. "All this time you've been talking, you *never* told her about *that*?" Mike said nothing.

So Julie told the story. After she left her first husband and moved in with Mike, she said, her ex-husband wouldn't pay child support and began showing up drunk or high to pick up the kids. When he threatened to spirit away the children, Julie went to court and pleaded for custody protection. Instead, the judge granted her ex-husband permission to take the children on a two-week vacation, from which he and the children, then nine months and two years old, did not return. She finally got a call from her ex-husband's father, informing her that the children were in Mexico and she would never see them again. "Mike began searching," Julie said. "Palm Springs, Chino. He staked out their old house. We followed rumors, followed the paper trail they left of bad checks and credit cards. The police weren't doing anything." Finally, after six months of searching, Julie's parents and the local Mormon church administrators hired a private investigator. "Thirty days and twenty-one thousand dollars later, they found them in Texas," she said. The children were in temporary foster care, the ex-husband in police custody, arrested on a California warrant. (The charges would later be dropped.) The McNultys flew down in a terrible thunderstorm and reclaimed the children.

Julie gripped her cocoa mug. "That's the worst thing that's ever happened to me. Anything that's happened since, it's no big deal." I could understand why Mike hadn't shared this story with me. In the dream-world of "jackbooted" federal agents and knife-wielding "gang-bangers," a man with a gun could be triumphant. In the reality of domestic life, an ex-husband could take the kids to Disneyland and vanish, and all the guns in the world couldn't bring them back, or truly equip Mike McNulty to protect his family.

"Guns are important to Mike," Julie said. She had done a lot of thinking about why. For a while, she thought it was "about his father," then about his experience in the Vietnam War. ("I don't know all of what he went through in Vietnam, and I know it still bothers him.") Finally, she came upon a more satisfying explanation, far closer to home. "Over the years, I've come to understand that with the gun, it gives Mike a feeling of *responsibility*. I really think he feels this, even though he hasn't thought about it. He has more responsibility to *act* responsible because he has this gun."

"I *have* thought about it," Mike said. "It does make me more responsible." I was glad I would be leaving the couple on a point of agreement. But I also felt sorry, and suspected Julie did, too, that so much of what remained of familial responsibility for this particular husband had settled onto the purely symbolic ability to handle a gun. It wasn't his fault that a hoped-for skilled career had dead-ended off the coast of Vietnam. It wasn't his fault that an insurance company pulled out of California for business reasons. As McNulty had said, "I have to feel like I'm making a contribution." But like so many husbands, he was at a loss to say what contributory service he could provide any longer. In an image culture, all he could think to do was offer a caricature of a patriarchal image that may have come to him largely from old movies in the first place. The guns were the props in what was essentially a performance of masculinity. For McNulty and many other men, the Second Amendment amounted to a "Defense of Marriage" Act. But unless they could conjure up an endless array of black helicopters, ATF agents, or for that matter invasive extraterrestrials, the guns in their lives were nothing but vestigial totems.

The modern-day Patriots' obsession with the Second Amendment's right to bear arms is a sentimental throwback, a paean to the protection racket. As such it was more pretension than protection. Frontier tools had become suburban baubles; the guns adopted by their Angry White Male owners as evidence of male essentialness turned out to be precisely the opposite: mantelpiece ephemera. And this is why when it comes to a showdown between the Dan Giffords and the Mike McNultys of this world, the Dans will invariably win. He, at least, understood that the whole gun-rights drama is for show. The Second Amendment is not really about survival on the plains anymore or, for that matter, in the city. It's not about protecting women and children from marauders or from FBI agents trying to burn down the family homestead. It's about having something to feature on the walls of your fancy house. If Dan Gifford wore his Glock to lunch at the Book Soup Bistro, it was not because he thought he was going to need it.

Many months later, Mike McNulty called me up and, almost in passing, dropped a bombshell. Grand-jury testimony in the Branch Davidians' litigation had surfaced in which one of the Davidians had testified that they *did*, in fact, spill gasoline in the chapel and had planned to light it, because they believed it was God's will to ignite a fiery conflagration. This seemed to directly undermine the film's main indictment of the FBI. McNulty said he had questioned Clive Doyle, the spokesman for the surviving Davidians, about this latest development. "I asked, 'Have you told me everything you know about a fire in the chapel?' Clive said, 'No.'" Then McNulty asked, "Will you tell me everything you know about a fire in the chapel?" And Doyle, after a painful pause, said, "No." Wasn't that a pretty big problem in making the case that the feds had set the fire? I asked. McNulty was quick to respond. Even if the fire was set in the chapel, he said, the FBI still could have set the fires that broke out first in the Davidians' gymnasium and dining-room area. "It's interesting stuff, but not conclusive," he said, a bit breezily.

A Thief in the Night

WHEN *Waco: The Rules of Engagement* was announced as a finalist in the Academy Awards' feature documentary category, the film's official owners were thrilled. They had only one problem. On the off chance the movie won, the Giffords didn't want McNulty up there accepting an Oscar. While Dan Gifford readily acknowledged that his own role had been largely financial and "hands off" until he stepped in at the last minute to reedit the film for Sundance, he was adamant about keeping McNulty out of the spotlight. "I certainly don't want him onstage; I don't want him anywhere near a microphone," Dan Gifford told me. "What he does not grasp is that he cannot be the star of his show." When asked why not, he added emphatically, "He's not part of the film community. He is not politically acceptable here." McNulty's politics weren't all that was unacceptable. "I've told him over and over again, and so has Amy, shave the beard, lose weight, learn how to speak in sentences that do not clue people that you are a Mormon or a conservative," Gifford said. "It doesn't matter what comes out of your mouth, people see that image."

The Academy Award rules require that all those with a producer's or director's credit on a film must sign the official forms for Oscar nominees. Only one person can officially speak to accept the award and no more than two statuettes are billeted per film, so the parties must also agree ahead of time on who's going to speak and who's going to claim the trophies. And so began another round of Giffords v. McNulty. McNulty listed himself and Gazecki as the recipients, while Gifford appeared at the Academy Awards office and filed a new form, listing himself as the sole producer. Gifford refused to sign McNulty's form; McNulty refused to sign Gifford's. "The award's being given for the one who did the work," McNulty said. "I feel like I've caught the thief in the middle of the night in my home and I'm doing my best to prevent him from stealing what is mine, not his." Attorneys were called and skirmishes continued for more than a month, with both sides knowing that unless someone relented by the deadline, the film would be eliminated entirely from consideration.

In the end, McNulty assented to a "compromise" brokered by Gazecki. If they won, the two names announced would be Gifford's and Gazecki's. "Basically, it's one of those compromises that sticks in your throat," McNulty said, "but there's nothing you can do." At least Gazecki had consented to allow McNulty to co-parent his Oscar: six months' custody each, and they would each get their own screw-on-nameplates, McNulty told me.

While they all waited for Academy Awards day, the Giffords launched their next project—a safe, "sappy love story," as Dan Gifford described it to me. McNulty, too, was coming to the understanding that railing against supposed government conspiracies was not the way to launch a Hollywood career—not, at least, unless it was via an action-hero film. "I'm in the middle of chalking a script," he told me. He described the plot: The hero, a cop ("like me, a Mormon"), investigates a "Waco-like scenario," in which it turns out the government has bombed several federal buildings and blamed the acts on militiamen, in order to divert the public's attention from presidential crimes and provide an excuse for a declaration of martial law. The conspiracy is masterminded by a nefarious former CIA operative who worked with the Special Forces in Vietnam, and was previously behind not only the disaster at Waco but the atrocities at My Lai, which the hero investigated as a lieutenant in the military police. The hero's wife "is killed by the government," McNulty said, "and he works with a young gal who develops into a love interest." (Later he would rewrite the story so the wife lives, and the estranged hero and spouse reunite in the end.) The hero rescues the girl, gets the goods on the president, and hastens to Washington "to start impeachment proceedings." (McNulty was prophetic in one regard: he invented the plot nearly a year before Clinton's impeachment.) He had entitled his script *Executive Order* and hired an underemployed friend and sometime screenwriter in Colorado to draft a treatment. "It's going to be something on the order of a three- or four-million-dollar budget unless we can get Harrison Ford or Clint Eastwood," McNulty told me. He had encountered only one sticky point so far: the screenwriter had turned in a lengthy treatment and was now demanding that he be cut in as co-owner of the film.

The McNultys flew to Los Angeles on the day of the Academy Awards. Mike had scraped together enough money to buy Julie a Zelda evening gown; the New York designer let them have the dress at wholesale for publicity's sake. A Fort Collins men's store loaned Mike his Pierre Cardin outfit, which he described to me as "a contemporary tux with the preacher collar, no bow tie, and a big onyx stud." Whether he won or not, McNulty said, he was looking forward to making the rounds of the celebrity parties and "rubbing shoulders with the big boys."

Waco: The Rules of Engagement did not win an Oscar that night. And Mike McNulty did not attend any parties. When Robert De Niro mounted the stage to read the nominees for the long documentary category, he described *Waco* as a film made by "Dan Gifford and William Gazecki." Because McNulty's name was not on the official Academy form, only Gifford and Gazecki got on the invite lists to the Governor's Ball and some of the other glamorous postceremony festivities. "I stopped by and talked to Roger Ebert because he was out front," McNulty told me, "to thank him for the good review he'd given the film. . . . And he gave me his condolences about not winning, and that was that; he was busy." The ceremony itself was a disappointment, too, so stage-managed for television that it didn't seem "real" to him. "It's so busy being a show, you can't enjoy the moment," he said. On the way out, as on the way in, he watched the third-string wanna-bes "out of favor with the paparazzi" who were practically hurling themselves before the cameras. "You could hear 'em scheming how to get their faces on TV," he said. He found himself transfixed, "just watching all these people like little children, clamoring for attention. That's what feeds the machine, the attention. . . . I'm not sure who drives the beast, but it is a beast."

By the time the McNultys got out of the Shrine Auditorium lot, it was late, and they still had a long drive ahead of them. Most restaurants were closed, and the couple wound up dining at Carrow's. The fluorescent glare and canned Muzak of a chain eatery wasn't exactly how McNulty had anticipated capping off a night at the Oscars. But that didn't bother him half as much as the other disappointment. Julie didn't seem to care about his nomination.

"There hasn't been a congratulation or anything" from her, he said. In the car after the ceremony, he asked her why she had been so silent, and she insisted that she had complimented him when he first got the news. Whether she had or not, he knew in his heart that being up for an Oscar wasn't what would save their marriage. Soon after they returned home, Julie left for two weeks in Montana, to spend time with her grown daughter and to think. Mike didn't know what was going to happen next. He hoped he could win her back, but he wasn't sure he knew a way any longer. The "white-picket-fence life" that the postman's daughter yearned for no longer existed—not for Mike McNulty, anyway. It had been replaced by "the beast," a beast that Mike McNulty couldn't slay with a semiautomatic shotgun.

Whether McNulty was trying to fulfill his obligations at home, fight the feds in Waco, or stake a new claim in Hollywood, the gunslinger's image had proved of little utility. In fighting his way into the new ornamental culture, McNulty had discovered that his arsenal was, if anything, weighing him down disastrously. Of all the people involved in the Waco film, as Amy Sommer Gifford observed, she was the one who got the most face time in the media, even though she had done the least work, for one reason only: "I'm the best looking."

HOOD
ORNAMENTS

Details magazine fashion layout from 1992, entitled
"The Bad and the Beautiful:
Everything Is a Movie. Stage Your Own Scene."

9

MAN IN A CAN

Moon Walkers, Ghetto Stars, and
Cross-Dressers in a Gilded Age

BY CENTURY'S END, the dictates of a consumer and media culture had trapped both men and women in a world in which top billing mattered more than building, in which representation trumped production, in which appearances were what counted. This was good for no one, of either sex, but at least "femininity" fit more easily into the new ethic—the sort of femininity that was a continuation of the supposedly feminine "vanity" to which women had once been relegated. Whether this was the only role women wanted or not—and, as the success of the women's movement made abundantly clear, most didn't—it was still, for women, a familiar role, with familiar rules and perks as well as debits. Women could take consolation in the assurance that, no matter how demeaning their objectification, it at least would not threaten their sexual identity. Society might hold a vain woman in contempt but would never question her femininity; rather, the very fact that she gazed into the mirror confirmed her womanliness. But what would it mean to be a man in this new realm? Narcissus was not celebrated for his virility. Was there a route to manhood through the looking glass? What could masculinity possibly mean in a display culture?

In 1965, Leslie Fiedler had mused in an essay, "The New Mutants," about what looked to be the start of "a radical metamorphosis of the

Western male. . . . All around us, young males are beginning to retrieve for themselves the cavalier role once piously and class-consciously surrendered to women: *that of being beautiful and being loved.*" To become "new men," Fiedler remarked, "these children of the future seem to feel" they must become "more female than male."[1] Fiedler had in mind a crop of male writers, particularly Beats like Allen Ginsberg or William Burroughs and their young followers. But the signs of a masculine "metamorphosis" in progress were hardly limited to literary bohemia. At about the same time as Fiedler and fellow social critics were casting a nervous eye at Greenwich Village and North Beach poets and writers, a massively financed government project was under way that appeared to be elevating the same sort of "new men," and unlike the Beats, they had the White House, Congress, the Pentagon, *Life* magazine, and virtually all of Middle America behind them. Perhaps no group of men has ever been so on display yet so valued, so ogled yet so championed for their brawn, than the handful of pilots anointed by a nation to navigate the stars. They were held up as virile new scouts blazing a trail into the ultimate unknown region, and for a while it looked like they might actually succeed in finding a route through the looking glass.

The astronaut served as an emblem in many matters preoccupying cold-war America: beating the Russians, demonstrating national mastery, wedding technology to progress, proving the power of man over machine. But paramount among his symbolic roles, he was to be a masculine avatar for a strange and distinctly new realm on earth. The man toddling across the lunar surface, sheathed in an impenetrable jumpsuit and visored with a helmet that looked for all the world like a TV screen, was a first-draft response to disturbing questions about manhood in an ornamental age. The astronauts were billed as reincarnations of Daniel Boone, setting out across a new wilderness to inhabit virgin lands. But their manifest destiny, it seems, was to travel in media space and open up a new entertainment age. They weren't the first media-destined icons of the western frontier; Sitting Bull and Wild Bill Hickok had performed their last acts as sideshow attractions. But the astronauts heralded a time when the sideshow would as never before supplant the main event.

I. On the Dark Side of the Moon

IN THE SUMMER OF 1969, Apollo 11 settled into the Pacific Ocean under its deployed chutes and was picked up by an aircraft carrier. Three men, Neil Armstrong, Buzz Aldrin, and Michael Collins, were plucked from the capsule, ferried by helicopter to the USS *Hornet*, and put into quarantine. Several weeks later, they were released from their aluminum-and-glass-walled isolation chamber—a retrofitted mobile home—into a larger fishbowl, which NASA billed as "Operation Giant Step." The first moon walkers were swept up in a largely televised, round-the-clock circuit of ticker-tape parades, trophy-claiming ceremonies, and grip-and-grin appearances. They did twenty-three countries in forty-five days, and even then, the tour didn't end. A year and a half later, the second man to tread on the moon, Buzz Aldrin, found himself still airborne—as a passenger, not a pilot—as the Apollo 11 astronauts shuttled endlessly from one media event to another. And with every passing day, he slipped deeper into depression. He was at a loss to explain it. Long ago, he recalled, he had read a science-fiction novel about astronauts who returned from the moon insane, and it had "given me nightmares as a youngster."[2] But the one thing he was sure of was when his anguish had begun: not the night he stepped on the moon, but the hazy morning of splashdown, when the helicopter dropped him onto the aircraft carrier and he saw those rows of camera lenses, like ship cannons, all aimed in his direction. "It would take a couple of years for it to become clear to me," he wrote later, "but that day on the USS *Hornet* was actually the start of the trip to the unknown. I had known what to expect on the unknown moon more than I did on the familiar earth."[3]

On January 14, 1971, Aldrin left NASA. He wasn't the first to have "sunk in a morass of despair," as he described his state. "As the traveling and speaking wore on," Aldrin recalled, "Neil [Armstrong] became more and more withdrawn."[4] By the end of the tour, Armstrong would turn and run from the microphones, lenses, and sound booms, too: he called a final press conference in 1971 to announce that he was quitting NASA for a job as a space-engineering professor at the University of Cincinnati (and eventually for a farm in Lebanon, Ohio), and was not going to be granting any more interviews—a vow he kept with almost no exceptions in the years to follow. A year earlier the third Apollo 11 astronaut, Mike Collins, had submitted his resignation. He went briefly to the public-affairs office of the State Department before becoming director of the Smithsonian Institution's new National Air and Space Museum, as if committing himself (and the old kind of manhood that he and the other astronauts thought they represented) to an archive for safekeeping. The first moon walkers were to prove unexceptional in their flight from space flight. By 1979, ten of the twelve men who walked on the moon had aborted their astronaut careers.[5]

The ghost of celebrity had haunted the manned space program from the start. The pilots who first volunteered for space in 1959 labored under the misconception that they were continuing the missions they had carried out in the skies over Europe, Japan, or Korea. The Mercury astronauts were required to be military test pilots. "The Mercury capsule is a job for a pilot, not a berth for a passenger," a NASA official declared to the press as the first seven astronauts were unveiled.[6] They were the new flyboys, the nation's finest. They were the essence of the century that Henry Luce had envisioned, the century of winningness, dominance, and control. These would be the stratospheric jockeys who would conquer the ultimate skies for "the free world."

Henry Luce's personal skywriter, *Life,* and a *Life*-derived book, *We Seven,* wasted no time in making it official: "Here is a modern adventure of truly Homeric magnitude, told for the first time in full by the heroes who achieved it . . . the first of a new and heroic breed of men who have the enormous responsibility of serving as symbols of the nation's future." This new breed was typified by the sort of man for whom "competition comes naturally," who would not let another man "beat him at anything," who "would have to be . . . physically strong, of course. For space flight would be strenuous work; it would expose them to greater stresses than most pilots had ever encountered, even in combat."[7] The Mercury Seven were "the cream of the crop." On John Glenn, the first man to orbit the earth, the media focused its most intense flame of adoration: he represented "the hero a whole nation had waited for"; he had "dramatized before the eyes of the whole nation the noblest qualities of the human spirit"; he had given us "a revival of the hero image," "man's finest hour," and "probably the most universal expression of the spiritual feeling of mankind that we have witnessed in our time."[8]

The Mercury Seven's knighting occurred at a press conference on April 9, 1959, in which NASA revealed their names and faces. They had yet to venture into space. They had yet to do much of anything other than allow the media to take their pictures. Not much was known about them beyond their average age (34.4), religious affiliations (all Protestant), marital status (all married with children), hobbies (fishing and hunting), and average weight and height (164 pounds and 5'10"). They were asked how many of them felt "confident" that they would prevail in space and return to earth victoriously unscathed, and *Life* freeze-framed in panoramic glory the moment that all seven raised their hands in response. John Glenn, the Mercury astronaut who best understood the demands of the new age and how to play them, held up both hands. They were heroes not, like Charles Lindbergh, the first man to fly across the Atlantic, because they had done something, but because they were confident they *would*. *Life*'s headline summed it up: SPACE VOYAGERS RARIN' TO ORBIT.[9]

"To orbit" might not previously have served as quite so active a verb, but it now evoked Wild West visions of cowboys taming buckin' broncos. That such a portrait contained certain absurd implications occurred to only a few people in those years, like movie director Stanley Kubrick, who ended his classic 1964 parody, *Dr. Strangelove,* with the cowboy-hatted Slim Pickens straddling a falling nuclear bomb, yippee-yi-yay-ing his way to oblivion. For the rest of the culture's guardians, Mercury astronaut Scott Carpenter offered a typically acceptable explanation of why he volunteered: "Here was a chance to serve the country in a noble cause and to pioneer on a grand scale."[10]

NASA's house organ, *Life,* which had immediately bought up exclusive rights to the personal stories of the astronauts *and their wives,* hammered home the pioneering myth in every issue: these were men who would steer their spaceships as surely as their forebears had held the reins of teams of horses on the Overland Trail. You flew the Mercury capsule just like you drove a car, astronaut Alan Shepard assured the American public. "No two models drive exactly the same way." With his capsule, for instance, "we got to know that there was just a little difference in the feeling of the control stick here from what we'd experienced before in the trainers." What Shepard failed to mention was that there was no "steering."[11] His "control stick" would have about as much effect on the course of his journey as the plastic controls on a Fisher-Price Queen Busy Bee.

The astronauts were not actually self-delusional. They were painfully aware of how little control they had. "Spam in a can" was the derisive term for the Mercury program at Edwards Air Force Base. "We found all the jokes real funny," Deke Slayton said caustically in a 1994 documentary, referring to cracks equating the Mercury astronauts with Ham and the other monkeys who had preceded them into space. " 'Time to feed the chimp!' . . . 'Shepard, Grissom, and Glenn: the link between monkey and man!' We hadn't signed on to fly standby while Bonzo pushed the outer edge of the envelope."[12] The Mercury Seven suspected that neither they nor Bonzo was pushing the outer edge of anything. Deke Slayton expressed his qualms this way: "From what I heard, I had the impression that this was just a matter of tying a man onto one end of a missile and flinging him out there. I rather doubted that they cared whether they had a trained pilot in there or just any human body."[13]

In spite of their press pronouncements, NASA officials were clear on the concept: they were looking for passengers, not pilots. That was why the selection process occurred at a medical and mental-health clinic, not on an airstrip. That was why the astronaut's chief trainer was a psychologist. That was why NASA's selection committee originally wanted to pick twelve men, not seven; the panel was sure a good number would drop out when they discovered how passive their role would be. President Eisenhower had narrowed the pool of astronaut candidates to military test pilots simply as a time-saving convenience; their records were already on file and NASA wouldn't have to waste months on security clearances. The only real requirement was that the men be no taller than 5'11", small enough to fit in the capsule. "They were virile," Norman Mailer wrote in his 1969 book about the first lunar landing, *Of a Fire on the Moon,* "but they were done to, they were done to like no healthy man alive."[14] Houston, not the capsule's joystick (or "hand controller," as it was called), was the site of Mission Control. The Spam did not drive its own can.

The Mercury capsule's automation was so total that, according to a military conference on "astronaut training," the astronaut "does not need to turn a hand"; he "has been added to the system as a redundant component."[15] The "training" was mostly in psychological adjustment, to condition men for cramped-quarters captivity. They were prepped for surrender—to the rocket thrusters, to the g-forces, to weightlessness, to the shepherd's hook lowered from a helicopter that would collar them on splashdown.

The dissonance between their public profile and their private knowledge irked the Mercury Seven, who occasionally pitched a minor fit. As befitting the rebellions of an essentially kept and pampered population, theirs were halfhearted and largely defensive "revolts." If they really wanted to fly, all the astronauts had to do was quit. But they were like young women wed to rich old men, discontented with their dependency but reluctant to give up the mansion. Or rather, as they preferred to put it, they were boys bridling at maternal smothering. "On future space flights," John Glenn asserted, "some of the apron strings will have to be cut." But by the late sixties, astronauts were still viewing themselves in diminutive terms; they called their windowless one-room office "Boys Town."[16]

"As astronauts, we believe they should leave the flying to us," the Mercury Seven's Deke Slayton harumphed in an unusual (albeit entirely mild and innocuous) public outburst against NASA in *Life* in the fall of 1963. "We've come a long way since those early days when seven of us signed on," Slayton went on to assure *Life*'s readers. "The biggest change is that the Astronaut has become a full-fledged pilot both in theory and in practice." Slayton described how the astronauts had taken charge. They had elected him "chief," and insisted that from that time onward they would have some say-so in the design of the capsules. "Both Gemini and Apollo are designed with man as a vital part of the controls," he insisted. "In Gemini, in fact, he will take full control of his spacecraft and actually fire up powerful thrusters to kick his vehicle from one orbit to another."[17]

Whether pressing some buttons to shift orbit really ranked as "full control" was a subject Slayton skirted. He also passed over the only reason men were given some "control": to save their own necks in case of disaster. An unmanned spaceflight would have obviated this problem and been, as many scientists then maintained, more scientifically useful and cost effective. As Eugene Shoemaker, NASA's principal investigator of field geology on the moon shot, said, "The same job could have been done with unmanned systems at one third the cost three or four years ago."[18]

The astronauts were arguing that men were needed in space to take care of the men in space—a sort of self-referential protection racket. John Glenn held forth most expansively on this subject following his return from the dicey flight of Friendship 7. Glenn proclaimed his minimal participation to be a turning point in the whole space program, one that returned the principle of male utility to its rightful place.[19] But even his proclamation betrayed misgivings; he spoke largely in the negative.

> I also tried to point out that it was not just an adventure we'd been on, that we hadn't just gone up for a ride to prove that Americans could tame rockets and fling test pilots around the earth a few times. If that were the only purpose, it would be a little like saddling up a bunch of knights and telling them to ride off into the dusk with their swords without giving them a mission.[20]

Whatever the mission, it was important that the men feel in control of it, or at least in control of themselves. They collectively insisted that NASA substitute the term "the spacecraft" for "capsule" and bridled against the assignment of a general as their "chaperon." It would become "Chief" Deke Slayton's mission to stage such semantic showdowns and enforce whatever euphemisms were necessary to salvage the astronauts' self-esteem. He proudly announced that under his reign, every astronaut would be in charge of his own personal fitness program.[21]

The astronauts did, in fact, have one genuine pitched battle with the spaceship builders. It was over a window, and struck at the heart of their predicament as astronauts and as men. The first Mercury capsule had only two tiny side portholes, such as might be suitable for a *passenger*. "The main thing that bothered us was that for some reason the engineers had decided not to provide us with a window so we could look out and see the view," Wally Schirra recalled. "It seems that some engineers just don't think the way a pilot does. . . . We all felt that a pilot ought to have a clear visual reference to his surroundings, no matter what kind of a craft he's flying. Otherwise, he would have trouble keeping his bearings and maneuvering with real efficiency."[22] But the real pilots were having no trouble keeping their bearings; the computer technicians seated in front of their monitors at Mission Control could see just fine, thank you. Besides, a window was an added danger; it might crack under pressure, thus imperiling the other "mission," getting the astronauts back in one piece. But the Mercury Seven kept up a chorus of complaint. "We were persistent," Schirra recalled, "and we finally got our way. The engineers built us a window."[23]

Their triumph was illusory, because their trouble wasn't the lack of a view. *They* were the view. In a sense, the whole capsule, the whole space program was a window. If the astronauts couldn't see out, the entire world was looking in. The astronauts had a mission after all, and it was to be watched. "The Mercury Seven were the biggest celebrities around," Deke Slayton observed. "And we knew it. NASA needed us. . . . We were carrying the image of the whole space program on our shoulders." From the very first manned space shot, televised in its entirety, to the "inspirational" Christmas reading of Genesis on Apollo 8, to the moon flights in which up-close-and-personal command performances from inside the capsule were many and mandatory, the astronauts were on parade, plastic smiles on pasty faces as they uttered scripted inanities and tried to keep the home-movie cameras they were required to operate from floating out of their grip in the weightless compartment. They grinned and waved morning, noon, and night, homecoming queens on a space-age float.

Wally Schirra, who had felt so strongly about the need for a window, led the revolt against that other "window." During the Apollo 7 flight, he refused to do Saturday morning TV. When Mission Control instructed the crew that they had no choice—they were the scheduled entertainment for this hour on earth—the astronauts committed what may have been the most insubordinate act of the entire space program: they popped the lens cap onto the camera. As Deke Slayton put it later, "The first war in space! And the Russians weren't even involved!"[24] The crew eventually relented, with Schirra indulging only in a discreetly sarcastic opening line: "Hello, all you fine people out there in televisionland. This is Captain Wally, high atop everything. . . ."[25]

This was a war neither Schirra nor his fellow spacemen to follow could win. Upon disembarking onto luna firma, one of Apollo 11's first tasks, before even unfurling the flag, was setting up a TV camera. On later trips, as the astronauts bounced across the strange new world in their moon buggies, one of the cameras strapped to the dash was always tuned in, fixed on the only "stars" that televisionland wanted to see, the spacemen. They had submitted themselves to the indignities of endless and unnecessary medical probings in the astronaut clinic—sperm counts, prostate prods, enemas and more enemas; "*Up yours!* seemed to be the motto of the Lovelace Clinic," Tom Wolfe succinctly observed in *The Right Stuff*. They had suffered through mind-numbing hours of floating "weightless" in a swimming pool, baked in a hothouse chamber, been hurled around in a centrifuge with thermometers in their rectums (*"Up yours!"*). They had endured the humiliations of being shot out of a rocket with their bodies strapped down and their every heartbeat monitored. They had put up with it all because they had been led to believe that in the end, they would still be pioneers in one important regard—bearing witness. But instead, they were witnessed. The astronauts had gone off to be new frontiersmen, but they had come back as space-age equivalents of pinup girls.[26]

It was an irony that might have struck Buzz Aldrin as he sat for weeks in the quarantine lab, killing time until the NASA authorities decided that the first moon walkers were "decontaminated" enough to be sprung. To occupy them, NASA showed movies: one starred Raquel Welch "as a man-eating Spanish revolutionary," Aldrin recalled, and another featured "three sex-starved women [who] imprison a virile young man in their attic and proceed to wear him out."[27] No doubt the films were intended to provide the same service as government-issued pictures of Betty Grable displaying her bottom on GI footlockers during World War II. But to the astronauts, the glamour girls on parade were uncomfortably close to their own footage, with one embarrassing difference— the women were at least in an active mode. The astronauts identified more with the masculine prey being devoured. They were, after all, "in their gilded cages," as former astronaut Brian O'Leary recalled bitterly, "pawing away at glass barriers through which TV lights and thankful wives and reporters will glare."[28]

In 1969, the year of the moon shot, Berkley Books issued a new edition of Richard Matheson's *The Shrinking Man:* the cover portrayed the miniature man stumbling alone across a great pocked and barren expanse that could only be called a moonscape; overhead, hanging like an intergalactic eyeball, a Cyclopean satellite with its quivering multitude of antennae, was the clear champion of this showdown: the huge, black spider, suspended from her vast World Wide Web, was *looking down at him*.[29]

———

AT ONE STOP on the Operation Giant Step tour following Apollo 11's splashdown, Buzz Aldrin was nearly crushed by a hysterical mob of fans; at another, after the jeep escorting the astronauts broke down leaving the airport, "people were crawling all over us," Aldrin recalled. "I was overcome by nausea and dizziness."[30] For a year and a half, Aldrin was almost constantly before the camera lens, "a blur of airports, antiseptic hotel rooms, hands to shake, autographs to sign, speeches, banquets— no one of them especially different from any other. . . . It had no beginning, middle, or end. . . . At no time did I feel I had any control over what I was doing or being asked to do, and this made me very uneasy."[31]

By 1971, Aldrin was ingesting antidepressants prescribed by NASA doctors, but even the drugs couldn't ease the heart-pounding terrors that rose at every stop, with the inevitable probing and prodding of his emotional boundaries, the chat-show faux intimacies, the humiliating queries, above all the question he loathed most, the question that "was anathema to me": how did it "feel" on the moon? He had gone to the moon armored and swaddled and face-shielded because he was intent on "proving man's usefulness in space"; now he was only being asked to demonstrate his ability to emote.[32] At a media appearance a year into the circuit, the how-did-it-feel question came one time too many. Aldrin stammered, his throat went dry, and the room swirled, almost as if the feminizing implications of the query had reduced America's new hero to the status of a Victorian lady in need of smelling salts. Overcome by dizziness, his hands shaking uncontrollably as he signed autographs, Aldrin finally ran from the room; "in the privacy of an alley near the auditorium," he recalled, "I choked back my emotions and quietly wept." His wife, Joan, tried her best to offer comfort and steered him to the nearest bar.[33]

As time passed, Aldrin's symptoms only worsened. Soon, he found he could barely get out of bed, where he lay "off and on for a week." When he did rouse himself, he made it only as far as the television set, in front of which he collapsed, as if in surrender to the unacknowledged beast, the enemy the astronauts hadn't even known they were battling. Aldrin's armor now would become an involuntary physical retreat: his fingers began going numb, his neck was painfully tense, and ultimately he found he often could not finish a sentence. "I could see no hope, no possibility of controlling anything," he said. Frantic, but terrified of asking for help that might appear on his military medical record, he held off for months. Finally, in the fall of 1971, verging on total collapse, he sought out psychiatric help. By October, a doctor at UCLA ordered him immediately flown to San Antonio and checked into the air force base hospital there for intensive treatment, therapy, and Thioridazine.[34]

By the time Aldrin arrived at the hospital, he had already made a decision that would pave the way for his cure—he announced his resignation from the astronaut program. Through the blur of his mental breakdown, he had been able to see one fact clearly: he had become a prop. He knew there would be no more space frontiers for him to explore. "Catching up with the rapid changes in technology was all but impossible and what was the point of trying? By now it was obvious we would never fly in space again and could never return to any sort of routine life at NASA." No one at NASA apologized for this detour because, as he was beginning to understand, it *wasn't* a detour. "It was never actually stated by anyone, but ... [w]e had, in effect, a duty to perform, a duty for both our government and NASA. We were to become public relations men for space exploration."[35]

NASA needed the pleasing faces, the frenzy of celebrity, to seduce the government, the media, and the public into accepting the huge expense of the aerospace program. The astronauts might be called "flight commanders" or "pilots" of the capsule or that ungainly lunar module that looked more like a washing machine, but as historian Michael L. Smith pointed out in his insightful essay "Selling the Moon," the astronaut's "functional role in the flight was not unlike that of a rather elaborate hood ornament."[36] As Tom Wolfe observed, it had come down to who "*looked* the most like a hot pilot. It was not only a popularity contest, it was a *cosmetic* popularity contest."[37] Such a contest could have only one winner, and the tiara went to John Glenn. He wasn't selected for his piloting skills, and his hadn't been the most challenging flight. Nor was he elected by his peers, who resented his moist-eyed God-America-and-apple-pie manner. But the media adored him. He was the first to orbit and, most important of all, he looked the best on camera. He won the charm war. Glenn's flight inspired what was then an astonishing $2 million worth of radio and TV coverage—"a second by second account that blanketed the nation's television screens," as an impressed *New York Times* remarked at the time.[38]

"He had touched an emotion as fundamental and as deeply buried as the memory of long-ago Fourths of July and the uncomplicated passion of a schoolroom Pledge of Allegiance," declared the ever-reverential *Life*. With his "freckled" face, "a smile as wide as the Mississippi," and his "unabashed, star-spangled sincerity," the magazine continued, Glenn "evoked the pride of nation of a far more innocent age" in his speech before Congress.[39] By personifying an unsullied Norman Rockwell vision of America, Glenn was actually bearing the banner of America forward into the media age. He was a hero because he played one on TV. "He projected himself as the humble instrument of a mighty cause," *Newsweek* enthused; so did the National Academy of Television Arts and Sciences, which awarded him an Emmy for "outstanding TV achievement during the past season."[40]

John Glenn seemed instinctively to come up with the right sound bites, before the term was in common parlance. "I still get a real hard-to-define feeling down inside when the flag goes by" and "I feel we should all live our lives as if this were the last day" were typical Glennisms.[41] All it took was a slurpy smile from the preflight hospital bed, a mawkish word or two from the flight sofa, a slow wave from the hearse-like parade limo, and the media locked in for another lump-in-the-throat moment. "That was what the sight of John Glenn did to Americans at that time," Tom Wolfe wrote. "It primed them for the tears. And those tears ran like a river all over America." Everybody teared up in his presence: cynical congressmen, flinty New York cops, even that toughest of old codgers, the president's father, Joe Kennedy. Glenn won the Mercury Seven contest by conquering the camera. He won because, like the moon, he reflected light. As Glenn himself said happily and without complaint, "I was sort of a figurehead."[42]

Of the Mercury Seven, only one would be remembered. There could only be one figurehead, only one focal point on the screen, only one face in the mirror. Such were the rules of the rising image culture. And the space program, an event that was so wholly experienced via television that some wondered in print whether the entire moon shot was a hoax, was shaping up to be a national demonstration project for that new culture. If NASA didn't hold the media's eye, Congress might pull the plug. It was a ratings game, and to win it the agency needed a superstar celebrity. At the start of the space program, the astronauts had thought of themselves as football players, all on the same team facing off against the All-Star Soviets. But after a while, the nature of this masculine showdown became clear: the enemy was one another. They were gladiators in a celebrity forum.

Buzz Aldrin's breakdown was all the more poignant for this irony: his happiness was ruined by his celebrity, but he wasn't even given top billing. The determination that made Neil Armstrong first down the ladder onto the moon and Buzz Aldrin second was as arbitrary as the bureaucratic rotational assignments that put the two men on the moon in the first place. What mattered was that Armstrong got there first and so delivered the crucial sound bite. "From a technical standpoint," Aldrin wrote later, "the great achievement was making the first lunar landing, and two of us would be doing that." But *Life* saluted the liftoff to the moon with the face of only one astronaut on the cover: Neil Armstrong. When the U.S. Post Office issued its commemorative moon-walk stamp, only Neil made the cut.[43]

The space program had replaced traditional male utility of a sort Aldrin had expected with an unexpected ornamentalism. And then he had been arbitrarily cast as a second-rate ornament, stuck back in a box like a holiday bauble after Christmas to gather dust in the cellar. He had suffered fame's trauma without ever winning manhood's newest sweepstakes. "It caused me to feel rather useless," he recalled with painful understatement.[44]

He had at least one important consolation: After trailblazing the frontier of ornament, he had turned away from it. In the battle to enlist men into a celebrity role, he had the distinction of being an early and prominent conscientious objector.

———

ON A JULY MORNING IN 1996, Buzz Aldrin found himself crisscrossing the vast media flats of Los Angeles in a chauffeured town car. Nearly three decades had passed since he landed on the moon, and a mini–Giant Step tour was again under way. He had written a science-fiction book about space travel, *Encounter with Tiber,* with coauthor John Barnes, and he was on the road to promote it.[45] It wasn't exactly easy. Early in the day, he had stopped at television station KTLA, and the questions had concerned the same two subjects he encountered everywhere, the blockbuster summer movie *Independence Day* and the horrific cleanup of TWA Flight 800, which had exploded a week earlier off the Long Island shore, killing 230 people. When he described the futuristic spaceship in his novel, with the aid of a tiny plastic model "Starbooster" he had brought along as a prop, the bright-eyed morning-news anchor wanted to know, "Did you see *Independence Day*? Did it look anything like that?" After a brief chat about "space tourism," the segment concluded with the announcer predicting, "Disney's going to be the first one to have a hotel up there!" Things had been little different at the Museum of Flying, the backdrop for a two-minute interview with Turner Entertainment. The museum had no spacecraft exhibits, and the Turner correspondent got off the subject of *Independence Day* only to discuss *The Cape*, a new syndicated TV drama about the lives and loves of fictional astronauts.

In the car afterward, as he searched for a bottle of glue to reattach the wings of his damaged spaceship model and the driver chattered on about how much his son had loved *Independence Day*, Aldrin seemed morose, and I assumed he was suffering the same disaffection with celebrity that had crippled his public life so many years before. But I was wrong. "I have a lot of admiration for people in the image-making business," he said. He didn't really object to the interviewers' preoccupation with pop culture; after all, he had signed up to be a "technical adviser" on that new TV show, *The Cape,* and he had produced his own video called *The Apollo Dream,* featuring "the eight most exciting minutes" of the Apollo 11 mission set to music. "Ever since the beginning of the movie business, there has been this pedestal and it just seems to be getting to be a greater and greater thing," he said. If he didn't hoist himself onto that pedestal, he seemed to fear, his pioneering moon walk would be forgotten. Already, most of Apollo 11's paraphernalia had been thrown away, he pointed out, and the lunar flight had barely been acknowledged in national history commemorations. "Americans just want the new product: What's the new TV show? What's the new movie-of-the-week? What's the buzz?" So, Buzz Aldrin had determined, that's what he would give them. With the millennium approaching, he had decided that the century wasn't going to close with his moment before the cameras forgotten. He was intent on staging another televised splashdown.

A half hour later, we pulled up in front of the Planet Hollywood in Beverly Hills. Inside the restaurant rock music was blasting at brain-scrambling levels. We ascended leopard-carpeted stairs to the Planet Hollywood Pool Room. "Is this the sort of thing you expected on your book tour?" I shouted into Aldrin's ear.

"Planet Hollywood fits with our marketing strategy," he shouted back, "and with theirs." He jerked a thumb in the direction of the restaurant chain's publicists who were leading us upstairs. "Space and astronautics promotes live action and entertainment, and vice versa." In fact, by the end of the book tour, he informed me, he intended to visit *twenty* Planet Hollywoods.

A crisis awaited in the Pool Room: Aldrin's publisher had failed to deliver books for him to sign during his visit to the restaurant. Aldrin was ready to lose his cool. "Is there a conspiracy or something against making this book a best-seller?" he fumed.

Mike Roth, the national promotions director for Planet Hollywood, a rangy and enthusiastic Tony Robbins type, assured the astronaut that the restaurant would make the event worthwhile. "We'll give out auto-graphed vouchers and we'll get our video crew out there, and people will feel they got something for it. We'll make people feel special here be-cause that's what we do." Aldrin nodded and took a moment to calm down. His eyes scanned the walls covered in glam shots, every one of a movie star. Suddenly, the door flew open and a woman in a leopard-print wraparound dress and matching sunglasses bustled in, with a dapper older gentleman in tow. The gentleman was Dick Guttman, a Beverly Hills publicist. The woman was Lois Aldrin, Buzz's third and current wife.

"Listen, Buzz, Dick thinks this TWA thing is just *wonderful*," Lois said. The tragedy, apparently, had offered up an opportunity: it so hap-pened that in Houston, Buzz Aldrin had signed a copy of his novel for Shannon Lychner, a girl who had died in the crash along with her mother and sister, and the publicist thought it would be a good idea for Aldrin to place a call to the grieving father—and alert the media. "We *must* get you on the phone with that poor, poor man," Lois said.

A call from an astronaut, Dick Guttman said grandly, "would give this man some surcease from his pain."

"Buzz, it's so wonderful," Lois said. "It's just the nicest thing in the world. It will make a nice inspirational—" She paused. "Tears just come down my eyes. . . . We've tried to call him a dozen times but he's been busy."

"I got his mobile phone," Guttman put in.

"Oh, that's perfect!" Lois exclaimed. "Buzz, you *are* going to call him today. . . . It would be extremely foolish not to do." She seemed to sense a certain reluctance because after a while she prodded him. "C'mon, Rocket Man."

"Yeah," Aldrin allowed doubtfully. He said he guessed it was "a win-win situation, all the way around."

The promotions director Roth bounded over just then. "It's un-be-liev-able timing!" he gushed. "Don Johnson just walked in. For his party!" Aldrin gave a pained smile. No matter how cheerfully Mr. Promotion might recast it, we were about to have a midair celebrity collision.

Aldrin was led downstairs to the restaurant and positioned in front of a microphone. The astronaut stood in the midst of the lunch din, gazing out at the celebrity-hungry tourist mob: giggly girls craning their necks for a glimpse of Don Johnson, grim-faced families on meal break en route from Disneyland to Universal Studios' Citywalk, squirming chil-dren scarfing mounds of french fries, surly teenagers staring dubiously, or was it uncomprehendingly, at the unfamiliar man who had mounted the stage. The room was adorned with movie-star costumes and accessories past and present, mostly present. Behind Aldrin were larger-than-life cutouts of Arnold Schwarzenegger, Eddie Murphy, Demi Moore, Michael Keaton in Batman gear, and Sylvester Stallone in full Rambo regalia. On display were guns said to be shot by Clint Eastwood and Stallone's warm-up boxer's robe from *Rocky*, under glass. A cardboard mock-up of the *Star Wars* mother ship dangled from the ceiling. What could Aldrin say to make himself recognizable to this crowd? Apparently, all that came to mind was an animated action figure in *Toy Story*.

"I am Buzz Lightyear," he said at last. The audience appraised him in a brief sullen silence, then the babble of mealtime conversation started up once more.

Mike Roth, the promotions director, came to the rescue. "Speaking of travel," Roth said into the microphone, though no one was, "what were you *feeling* as you were orbiting the moon right before you landed?"

"We just couldn't wait until the opportunity came to begin the descent . . ." was the only part of Aldrin's answer that was audible from where I sat.

Roth turned to the audience, that sea of slow-moving jaws and ever-roving eyes. "How many people here would like to go into space?" he asked. No hands went up. He turned back to Aldrin. "Buzz Lightyear, was that inspired by Buzz Aldrin?"

"Yes," Aldrin said. "We had a lot of fun talking to Tim Allen, whose voice was Buzz Lightyear. And if you haven't seen the Disney-Pixar production of *Toy Story*, I'm telling you, it's not just for children. It's for people of all ages. And I'm happy to say we are working together with its creators to see if there aren't parts of *Tiber*, especially the parts about aliens coming here, that wouldn't be very well done by computer animation."

A few tables away, two young men snickered and one of them burst out, "Buzz *off* !"

Aldrin was led off the stage and to the autograph table. The line there was not exactly long, but at least there was a line. "I guess I like astronauts," nine-year-old Branden Van Damme told me as he waited his turn, "but I don't want to be an astronaut." His eight-year-old friend Miles Millen didn't either. His ambition, he told me, was "to make a lot of theme parks. I'd get to test all the rides." The only astronaut he could think of, he said solemnly, was that schoolteacher who died in the *Challenger* explosion.

Two autograph collectors brought up the end of the line. "We came here for Don Johnson," James Reese, who was thirty, explained. "If you go to Hard Rock Cafe, you're bound to see more people," Bob Wood, thirty-eight, added. Aldrin's signature was no great catch for his collection. "Neil Armstrong, he's the real guy. That's a name I'll remember for the rest of my life."

As Aldrin returned to his banquette to finish a barely touched lunch, he realized his model spacecraft was missing. Waiters were dispatched to the Pool Room to search for the missing prop but returned empty-handed. While Aldrin brooded, his wife, Lois, talked on a cell phone with the Beverly Hills publicist, arranging her husband's telephonic encounter with Joe Lychner, the man who had lost his two daughters and wife in the TWA crash. I tried to distract Aldrin from the missing-model crisis with a discussion about his new visibility, but it provided no salve. Whatever subject I broached, Aldrin returned to Neil Armstrong, his infernal firstness and his failure either to capitalize on his celebrity or to share it with his moon-walking "brothers." "Being in the shadow of someone who's not even in public," Aldrin said, "it's very, well . . ."

A squeal went up at the surrounding tables. I looked around and saw all eyes fixed on our banquette. Had the Planet Hollywood denizens suddenly developed astronaut worship? No, they were staring slightly above Aldrin's head. He turned to find hovering there the gleaming tanned visage of Don Johnson. "Hey!" Johnson said brightly, and stuck out his hand. Aldrin mumbled a hello and met his grasp. That was all. A few seconds later, Johnson was sauntering away, and he took the human klieg lights with him.

Lois prodded her husband. It was time to make that phone call. She led the way out of the restaurant and into the waiting car. While the driver double-parked in front of the publicist's office, Buzz ran inside. About five minutes later, he was back, not eager to relive the conversation. "He talked about how much it meant to his daughter," he said. "I guess it did some good."

On the forty-minute ride to Glendale and Aldrin's last appearance, the astronaut spent most of his time arguing over the cell phone with his publisher's publicists. "If anybody has promoted a book more than I have, I'd like to know who it is. And then to have a pissant thirty thousand copies . . ." They had cancelled his appearance at the Planet Hollywood in Costa Mesa, and he demanded to know the reasons. I gazed out the window and found myself worrying about that missing miniature spacecraft, lost forever in celebrity-franchised space.

At the *Ray Briem* talk-radio show, Aldrin's segment was introduced by a tape of Neil Armstrong saying, "That was one small step for a man . . ." followed by the host saying, "The most famous words I guess ever spoken!" A listener called in to ask about the theory that the moon shot was a hoax produced and shot in a television studio. Aldrin gritted his teeth, and after a few more calls about space aliens, the host wrapped things up. "Thanks for keeping the spotlight on space exploration, because we need it," he told Aldrin, and then, as if to console a moon walker after a long hard day, he added, "We really do."

Even if Aldrin had succeeded in entering celebrity orbit, how would his earthbound countrymen have followed? They had no way of participating in such a drama except from their sofas. Some male spectators would begin to suspect that they, too, had landed on a lunar surface of sorts, where masculine productive powers had been rendered useless, where the important things were not made but filmed, where control was exerted from afar. As the century drew to a close, it could feel that way whether you were a laid-off craftsman with a busted-up union or a part-time employee working two jobs to get by, a football fan watching your relocated team in a sports bar or a family spiritual "leader" watching celebrity preachers hold forth on the big screen of a football stadium, a young man selling space-shoe-style Nikes amid towering Michael Jordan cardboard cutouts at a sporting-goods outlet or a night clerk surrounded by action-hero posters at a video store. Even men within the triumphal media were not spared; male correspondents watched their profession reconfigure itself around entertainment journalism and doubted their own utility. "I'm out of some pretty important loops now, status-wise," veteran *New York Times* political correspondent R. W. Apple, Jr., wrote in 1998, "because I know little about television and less about movies." The rise of celebrity media, he suspected, had led to his profession's demotion. "Journalists' loss of standing must have something to do with the fact that they have emerged from relative anonymity, reporting less and talking more, part of an ever-growing mountain of commentary resting on an ever-shrinking base of fact."[46]

As I traveled through this new landscape of masculinity, I was struck by how many men I encountered had the feeling that something or someone had stripped them of their usefulness and stranded them on a new decorative planet. The masculine drama of the Mercury astronauts would be played out endlessly and everywhere in the decades that followed the lunar landing, even on an artificial lake behind a strawberry farm between Rosemead and the City of Industry, California.

II. Monster in a Cage

COMPETITORS IN THE North American Model Boat Association only assemble intermittently to race their remote-controlled miniature vessels at the Rosemead lake, but every weekend, the powerboaters can be found testing their craft, perched along a raised concrete platform on the shore, their distant boats zooming in tight, frantic circles, emitting a buzzing drone like a hundred angry hornets. With very few exceptions, the boaters are male, and they are adults. Most of them wear fishermen's thigh-high rubber boots, which are of unclear usage, since little wading is required. When one of these yard-long vessels conks out midlake, the men generally recover it via a rowboat or from the shore using a long fishing reel attached to a tennis ball with a hook. On the ledge, each pilot plays mission controller, intently steering his wee speedster around the oval course of five buoys with a handheld Airtronics console. The remote-control device, with its buttons to determine direction and fuel, is metallic black and the precise shape and size of a revolver. The men tend to refer to it as "my gun." Armed with these lethal-looking Equalizers, the powerboaters stand cheek to jowl along the rail and stare hard across the water.

Their chaotic armadas contest in miniature the grand battle within modern masculinity—some of the men come for the love of hand-building well-crafted machines, some for the thrill of winning. This division coincides roughly with the two classes of motorboat on the Rosemead lake—old gas outboards and new nitrous-powered inboards—and the personalities of those who prefer one or the other. "The gas guys and the nitrous guys don't get along," one of the men, Kerwin Scott, told me. Scott is a gas guy. He had come out this particular morning in the summer of 1997 to test his "cracker box," a diminutive flat-bottomed outboard racer he had built from scratch. "When I first got into this, I thought I was doing it for the speed, the power of it." But he was discovering that it was the mechanics of making the boat work, "the challenge of figuring it out," that most appealed to him. "Any fool can pull a trigger," he said. What he was after was mastery, the kind that takes knowledge and time.

Kerwin Scott was then thirty-six years old, a man with a muscular build who worked at a grocery store in inner-city Los Angeles. It was good that he was content with the more humble version of his sport. His modest paychecks mostly went to support his family and his mother, whose rent and mounting hospital bills he largely underwrote. He was used to making a little go a long way. "I've never wanted to ask anyone for money," he told me as he stood on the edge of the lake after the practice runs, feeding the ducks. Scott had brought some sandwiches and a huge bag of popcorn—the sandwiches for us, the popcorn mostly went to the birds. A crowd of ravenous mallards honked and scrabbled for position as we talked. "As a kid, I'd wash windows, cut grass, anything rather than ask for money. If I don't work, I feel guilty." As I would learn in my time with him, the value and meaning of work was a prevailing preoccupation. "I don't understand how certain people can not work, yet they think if they wave a gun around, then it's 'I'm a man! I'm a man!' Anyone can go like *this*," he said, pantomiming the pulling of a trigger. "My nine-year-old son can shoot someone. That doesn't make you a man. It makes you an idiot."

By "certain people," Scott was not referring to the men pulling the triggers of their Airtronics "guns." His struggle with ornamental, winner-take-all masculinity was not something confined to the gyrations of boats on a pond: it was a theme running through his life, an essential part of the crisis of his family since his childhood. It was the failure of his own younger brothers to work and help out in the support of their mother that baffled and distressed him. He flung another fistful of popcorn toward the squawking open beaks at his feet. "Growing up, we were all really tight. Now the family is split. They're on one side. And I'm on the other side by myself." He was alone in at least one other regard: he wasn't a celebrity. A job in a grocery store offered little the media might find glamorous. His brothers, on the other hand, were notorious stars, nationally, even internationally known for their escapades in the L.A. gang wars.

The Scotts had grown up in the sixties in a middle-class neighborhood of comfortable homes with front-yard gardens in the Crenshaw district of Los Angeles. Their parents, Ernest and Birdie Scott, had moved to California from Houston, Texas, in the late fifties, lured by the Golden State's promise of jobs for all. Ernest worked long hours for decent wages as a forklift operator at a unionized warehouse in Boyle Heights, in east Los Angeles. The Scotts rented a two-bedroom house and raised four children: one daughter, Kendis, and three sons—Kerwin, the eldest, followed by Kody and Kershaun. (Birdie also had two children from a previous relationship, Kim and Kevin, who remained for a time in Houston with their grandparents when the couple moved to California.)

Ernest Scott thought of himself as the family's prime breadwinner and discouraged his wife from working. Nevertheless, Birdie Scott, a transplanted Texan with a dramatic flair and aspirations to be a disc jockey, enrolled in broadcasting school and worked at a series of nightclubs that sometimes drew an entertainment crowd. She reconnected with an old friend of hers from Houston, who was living in Los Angeles and married to the legendary Ray Charles. Eventually, Birdie persuaded Ray Charles to be the godfather of her second son, Kody. Birdie felt her newborn would need a godfather, although she didn't tell Kody the reason why until he was seventeen years old. His real father, she then informed him, was a man she had met while hobnobbing with celebrities who had frequented Ray Charles's home: Dick Bass, former running back for the L.A. Rams. Bass never acknowledged Kody, much less supported him. When I called him at his office at the Chamber of Commerce of Norwalk, California, Bass told me: "I don't know if I'm the father or not. That's something that's in the past. I've gone on with my life." Birdie's husband, however, suspected soon enough that Kody was not his biological son. The couple were already mired in an unhappy marriage, and the presence of an illegitimate son evidently did not help matters. The children recalled blistering arguments and raised fists, both their father's and their mother's.

In 1970, the Scotts separated. Birdie found herself working two bartending jobs, then three, and in 1972, she moved the family to a less promising locale, South Central, where, as each of her sons put it in identical words, "everything changed." By "everything," the brothers referred to the social climate, which in South Central was dominated by the area's notorious agonies of crime, drugs, gangs, and violence. But to define the change narrowly, as particular to South Central, was to miss the larger blow that had befallen the Scotts: it was as if the family had been cleaved in two by the ax of American culture. Younger brothers Kody and Kershaun wound up on one side of this new continental divide; Kerwin found himself on the other, "by myself."

The young men whose lives unfolded on the bereft streets of South Central Los Angeles in the final decades of the century were born too late to remember much about the moon landing. Nor would it have moved them if they had watched it; a white man in a white suit claiming a white moon was hardly the stuff of young black men's dreams, particularly young black men struggling to get by (though Kody Scott did recall that one of his valued childhood toys was a plastic Moonwagon). In South Central in these years, the oxygen of opportunity was thin, and young men's options for purposeful engagement were sparse: the landscape offered no work in the community other than in a handful of convenience stores, fast-food franchises, and gas stations—and no way out, either. That hadn't always been the case. In the early 1950s, South Central had been a working-class community where many men from the Long Beach Naval Shipyard and the industrial belt of steel and auto and tire plants had raised families in homes they owned. Now, the only ladders of ascension dangled before young men were athletic star, music-video star, and movie star, and only a very few would get to climb them.

The rest were marooned when the tiny lunar module of celebrities retro-rocketed out of South Central to begin the impossibly long trip to Hollywood, a few miles away.

Kody Scott, the brother who was "known," began his climb into that module in 1993. An overnight celebrity, he was sought after by TV journalists, movie producers, and talent agents after he published his prison memoir, *Monster: The Autobiography of an L.A. Gang Member*, in the wake of the Los Angeles riots. Its cover photo of the pumped-up, bare-chested author clutching a semiautomatic Mac-10 turned Kody Scott into what he rightly called a "ghetto star"; the best-selling book sold about 100,000 copies in hardcover, 150,000 in paperback. Long before he ascended to the media firmament, though, he was just a kid on the corner with a sharp mind and a gift for drawing, which his mother encouraged. He filled artist's sketch pads and fantasized about a career as an illustrator. His more immediate problem, however, was how to deal with menacing older kids on the block, who had welcomed the Scotts' Christmastime arrival in the neighborhood by destroying Kody's new bicycle. As the brothers got older, the neighborhood thugs became more threatening. Kody, in particular, felt vulnerable. He was robbed of his lunch money and beaten up repeatedly, "not because I decided to defend my dime or my honor, but because my assailant simply whacked me. Early on I saw and felt both sides of the game being played where I lived," he wrote. "There was no gray area, no middle ground. You banged or held strong association with the gang, or else you were a victim, period."[47] Kody Scott sought gang protection.

When he was eleven, Kody began to "put in work" with the Eight-Tray Gangsters, a set of the infamous Crips who dominated his neighborhood. Putting in work meant raining violence and retribution on his set's "enemies," who eventually became mostly other Crips in a rival set, the Rollin' Sixties. "This was my 'rite of passage' to manhood," Kody Scott wrote later of his gang service, and he took it seriously, seeking to distinguish his passage with a particularly brutal brand of violence. "Revenge was my every thought. Only when I had put work in could I feel good that day; otherwise I couldn't sleep. . . . And I was a hard worker." In 1977, a thirteen-year-old Kody stomped on a robbery victim for twenty minutes, then abandoned the comatose man in an alley. For this "work," he earned the moniker "Monster," borrowed from the word the police on the beat that day used to describe the sort of person who would commit such an atrocity. On New Year's Eve, 1980, sixteen-year-old Kody was ambushed by the side of the neighborhood Western Surplus store by three young men who emptied a six-shooter into his stomach, back, and limbs at point-blank range. The Eight-Tray homeboy who was with Kody at the scene turned and fled before the first shot was even fired. Hospitalized for two weeks, Kody miraculously survived.[48]

Growing up, Kody's younger brother, Kershaun, could generally be found at the library a mile from his house, hungrily working his way through the bookshelves. From an early age, Kershaun was the family reader and writer; his mother, Birdie, told her son she figured he was headed for a literary career, and Kershaun hoped so, too. "I used to go to this library on Sixty-fourth and Vermont," he told me. "It was open five days a week, Tuesday through Saturday, and I spent a lot of time in that library between the ages of nine and fourteen. All my brothers, with the exception of me, were bodybuilders. I'd be going off to the library and every day we went through this 'Why don't you get your skinny ass over here and come lift weights?' And I'd say, 'Why don't you go to the library and lift some books?'" City budget cuts eventually shut down the library, but even before the closures, Kershaun had relinquished his allegiance to books and followed his older brother Kody into the Eight-Tray Gangsters. By the time Kody was shot, Kershaun had already "put in work," and had claimed the gang moniker of his choosing, "Li'l Monster."

Kershaun grew up close to Kody; the two brothers were only eighteen months apart in age and shared a room. That fraternal closeness became a stand-in for paternal care after their father moved out of the house and, as the years passed, dwindled as a presence in their lives. The abandonment was a terrible, unexpected blow to Kershaun. "I was his favorite," he recalled. "Our relationship growing up was fantastic." Kershaun's favored-son status contrasted starkly with that of Kody, whose very existence was a perpetual reminder to Ernest Scott of his wife's reputed dalliance with a football star. The sons recall that when Ernest Scott struck out at his children, which he did increasingly as tensions mounted in the house, he saved his most punishing blows for Kody. Kershaun, on the other hand, said he was never hit. In the first few years after the divorce, the imbalance continued: when Ernest Scott came to pick up his sons for a weekend of movies and restaurants, he often left Kody behind. Then, in about 1975, the paternal visits ended. "He just stopped being our father," Kershaun said. His father was still in Los Angeles — Kershaun would sometimes try pedaling his bicycle over to his apartment in hopes of seeing him — but he seemed lost to another world. One Christmas, he promised to come by bearing gifts for his sons, but he never even showed.

On New Year's Day in 1981, with Kody clinging to life in the hospital, his body strung like a Christmas tree with IVs and breathing tubes and sensors, his brother Kershaun prepared a mission of retribution; as Li'l Monster, the duty fell to him. For the mission, he needed guns, and he knew where he could get one. "For as long as I can remember, my father carried a .38 on top of the dash of his blue Pinto, on the dash in a brown paper bag." The father's omnipresent Saturday night special was one of the prevailing mysteries of Kershaun's youth. "I wonder what it was that made my father so afraid that he always carried that gun. Always, always. He always had that gun." Only one time did Kershaun see his father actually fire the weapon. It was soon after the divorce and seven-year-old Kershaun was spending the weekend at his father's apartment in the Wilshire District, near downtown Los Angeles. "Something must've scared him, because he spent the whole night on the sofa in the living room with his gun in his hand." Ernest Scott finally fell asleep, but a nightmare rocketed him to his feet, "and pow, pow, pow, he shot the gun off at the ceiling."

On that New Year's Day in 1981, however, as Kershaun Scott paid a visit to his father's apartment, he was less concerned with the reasons for his father's armament than the extent of the stockpile. On this score, Kershaun would not be disappointed. His father also had a twelve-gauge shotgun and a twenty-gauge pump. "He gave me the shotguns and fifty dollars and he told me to bring the guns back when I was done. There wasn't much conversation. The whole visit took ten minutes." Did Ernest Scott try to stop his favorite son from committing murder? "All he said was, 'Be careful,'" Kershaun replied, his hands balling up with anger at the memory. "I think it was because in his heart, he realized he had ceased being my father, and he had no rights." Kershaun left with the guns, though not necessarily with what he was really looking for. "Driving home, I decided I would never give the guns back. It was just this feeling of 'Well, to hell with him.'" In fact, he would not see his father again until the elder Scott was on his deathbed, thirteen years later, comatose from a head injury. "He was basically a skeleton," Kershaun recalled in a shaky voice, "waiting for the power to be turned off." Kershaun sat by the convalescent-home hospital bed and told the motionless body "all the things I always wanted to tell him, how hurt and angry I was that he couldn't be a father in my life." Then it fell to Kershaun and his brother Kerwin to make the decision to take him off the respirator.

The night after Kershaun picked up the guns from his father, he drove around the Rollin' Sixties neighborhood with a few other Eight-Tray buddies, randomly firing at young men they spied on the street. Or, as Kershaun put it later for the cameras, in the melodramatic terms that make gang stories such a media staple: "Once the sun went down, the mission was in action. . . . We started on our journey into enemy territory."[49] The boy whom Kershaun eventually murdered was fourteen or fifteen, his own age. Kershaun didn't even know him; he was just a figure spotted moving swiftly in the dark. As he passed, Kershaun leaned out the car window and "gave him both barrels of the twelve-gauge shotgun that was not sawed off." The force of the explosion obliterated the boy's entire midsection. The murdered boy "wasn't necessarily the person who actually pulled the trigger on my brother," Kershaun said later to a film crew. He had no connection with the assault on Kody, at least none that would have been known to Kershaun, "but he was affiliated with that neighborhood, and that's just like getting the triggerman himself."[50]

Avenging the attack on his brother landed Kershaun in Juvenile Hall for five and a half years. In all that time, his father never paid him a visit. He was able to see his brother, who was in and out of jail. Some members of Kershaun's gang set showed up, too, and back in the neighborhood, he was granted new respect for having risen to the challenge, proving himself a gunslinger and surrendering his freedom out of devotion to his brother. He had earned the right to the "Li'l Monster" label and claimed local-hero fame. As Kody wrote later of his brother's "taking the call to colors": "I was Li'l Bro's hero, the closest thing he had to total invincibility. Everything I did, he did. And now, with my being wounded, he knew that there was someone out there that was stronger, more determined than me. The vast weight of this fell heavy on his shoulders and it became incumbent upon him to destroy that person and 'save the world'—our set."[51]

By then, Kody Scott had elevated himself to the status of Original Gangster, or O.G., which he regarded as the equivalent of General, and he saw his brother as a rising junior officer. "Each set actually functions like the different divisions of, say, the U.S. Army," he wrote. "Protecting" the set and "defending" a brother's honor were part of a comforting fiction that made the Scott brothers and fellow gang members feel like they were caught up in an old-fashioned, war-forged masculine operation based on valor, loyalty, care for each other, and courage under fire. "Combat was starting to take its toll on me," Kody Scott wrote. "But still my dedication, my patriotism, was strong." The language he used was wholly martial: the Eight-Tray members were "combatants," "elite shooters," "troops steeled in the ways of urban guerrilla warfare." Being in South Central was like being "'in country'—in the war zone," and Normandie Avenue "can be compared to the Ho Chi Minh Trail." When his set unleashed an attack on a rival set, it was "launching a final offensive on the [Rollin'] Sixties—our own little Tet offensive." The "well-seasoned veterans" in his set "could be compared to Long-Range Reconnaissance Patrol Soldiers in Vietnam. There was nothing else for us but war, total war."[52]

Despite Kody Scott's martial rhetoric (and despite the Los Angeles Police Department's fondness, especially at budget time, for portraying the gangs as highly organized conspiracies), L.A. gangs were distinctly *un*military in structure, with loose hierarchies and an organization based on amorphous and changing notions like "respect" more than on specific functions.[53] But if one had to use war as a metaphor for the gang strife in South Central, the American experience in Vietnam was at least an apt point of comparison. The meaninglessness of turf gained, the pointless and horrific body counts, the arbitrariness of how one defined the "enemy," the toll on the young and innocent, the meaninglessness of "winning," all of these were hallmarks of both "wars," as Kody Scott understood quite keenly. "Sets began to predict the winners," he wrote, "a virtually impossible deed as our war, like most gang wars, was not fought for territory or any specific goal other than the destruction of individuals, of human beings. The idea was to drop enough bodies, cause enough terror and suffering so that they'd come to their senses and realize that we were the wrong set to fuck with."[54] The point of gang violence wasn't the one the "combatants" imagined, as Kody Scott hinted at when he suggested that the whole idea was to produce not real gains but just the *image* of terror. In South Central, it was truly a produced-for-television war.

The night that Kershaun succeeded in killing one young man and wounding four more, his passage into manhood was not yet assured. One confirming proof yet remained. "I can remember hitting the corner and looking back and seeing all five people stretched out, and I knew the job had been well done," Kershaun recounted in the documentary film *Eight-Tray Gangster: The Making of a Crip.* It was well done because his opponents had not only been felled but were *visible*—"at which point I went over to my girlfriend's house, sat back, and watched the eleven o'clock news."[55] To be a man under the new rules of showmanship required having the fruits of one's destructive acts ogled by an audience. Violence was not about defense or even aggression per se but about glamour, albeit a gory glamour, which helped explain why it didn't really matter whether Kershaun Scott killed the real triggerman or not. In celebrity culture's approximation of revenge, a good visual, not a precise target or purpose, is the thing.

Like the astronauts, the "combatants" in South Central were contestants under new rules of ornamental masculinity. The martial rhetoric, the stockpiling of weaponry, the display of violence, all were part of a nitrous-fueled drama that had as much to do with "winning" under the image terms of the new culture as it did with proving valor under any traditional warrior code. As Kody Scott himself would realize later, the war he had been engaged in throughout his coming-of-age years was, above all, a ratings war, a campaign to attain what he came to call "neighborhood celebrity."[56]

"MY FATHER'S GENERATION was the last responsible generation," said Sanyika Shakur (now Kody Scott's legally adopted name) as he welcomed me in August 1997 to his girlfriend's two-bedroom house in the San Fernando Valley. He had just moved in, having been released from jail three days earlier, after a year's sentence for a parole violation—his second such since the publication of what was supposed to be his transformational autobiography.

Newly out of prison, Shakur was unnerved by wide-open spaces. He led the way to the smallest room in the house, a back bedroom that his girlfriend, Felicia Morris, had converted to an office. Morris waved goodbye from the living room; a radio disc jockey and songwriter, she was on her way to work. Behind the office was the garage, where Felicia's guard dog, a Rottweiler named Kody, barked ceaselessly. "When I first moved to South Central," Shakur continued, "there were industrial ties still. Men still owned their homes, supported their families. But then something happened. It turned to a neighborhood of renters. I started seeing an increase of men in the streets. It was like the economy in this country had reached its apex, and we black men had outlived our usefulness."

As a young man, he had still hoped that he could demonstrate a workmanlike "usefulness" within his gang set. "You put in work and you feel needed in a gang. People would call on me because they needed me. You feel useful, and you're useful in your capacity as a *man*. You know, 'Don't send me no boys. Send me a man!'" But he was beginning to see his former life in a different light. What he once perceived as "work" now seemed more like PR. "What the work was," he said, "was anything you did in *promotion* for the gang." He found it amusing how the media viewed gangs as clannish and occult. "We're *not* a secret society. Our whole thing is writing on walls, tattoos on necks, *maintaining visibility*. Getting media coverage is the shit! If the media knows about you, damn, that's the top. We don't recognize *ourselves* unless we're recognized on the news.

"There's a lot of talk about loyalty and mission and all with the gang, and that's part of it," he said. "But my initial attraction to these guys I saw who were in gang life was that these dudes were ghetto stars. And I wanted to be a ghetto star." He set out, as any PR man would do, to get his brand name out. "I considered it advertising, being on the campaign trail. Bangin' is very much like promoting for the Republican or Democratic party. What you do is, you have your name ringing on the wire, on several levels. You do it by promoting." The publicity effort took many forms. "You write your name all over. You had to always have your marker and your gloves because you are on the campaign trail. When you shoot somebody, you say your name, loud. And I wouldn't hide my face. You leave people alive, knowing that the word will get out on who did it. You go to parties and you shoot in the air and say your name. Or you go to parties and you shout-whisper your name in girls' ears, tell 'em what a bad ass you are, or tell 'em, 'Tell so-and-so, he can't kill me.' You'd primarily use females because they had the gossip thing down. They are very important because if they are impressed, they spread the word." He'd gauge the progress of his fame by how speedily a rumor he started about himself spread. "You'd know your celebrity by the return rate, how fast it would get back to you. The return rate is what you look for."

Kody Scott's image-enhancement strategies were not homegrown. "I got all these ideas from watching movies and watching television. I was really just out there acting from what I saw on TV." And he wasn't referring to *Superfly* or *Shaft*. "Growing up, I didn't see one blaxploitation movie. Not one." His inspiration came from shows like *Mission: Impossible* and *Rat Patrol* and films like *The Godfather*. "I would study the guys in those movies," he recalled, "how they moved, how they stood, the way they dressed, that whole winning way of dressing. Their tactics became my tactics. I went from watching *Rat Patrol* to being in it." His prime model was Arthur Penn's 1967 movie *Bonnie and Clyde*. "I watched how in *Bonnie and Clyde* they'd walk in and say their whole names. They were getting their reps. I took that and applied it to my situation." Cinematic gangsterism was his objective, and it didn't seem like much of a reach. "It's like there's a thin line in this country now between criminality and celebrity. Someone has to be the star of the hood. Someone has to do the advertising for the hood. And it's like agencies that pick a good-looking guy model. So it became, 'Monster Kody! Let's push him out there!'" He grinned as he said this, an aw-shucks, winsome smile that was, doubtless, part of his "campaign."

Kody Scott and his brother Kershaun took their campaign into the world beyond South Central's streets in 1991, when a (female) fashion model-cum-journalist, Léon Bing, wrote *Do or Die,* a book about the Los Angeles gang wars that devoted a chapter to the brothers.[57] It put their names in play, mostly Kody's, actually, for one simple reason: his picture graced the cover. He looked like the bad guy in an action blockbuster, with his movie-star shades and a Mac-10 assault pistol clutched to his muscle-bulging bare chest. Kershaun was supposed to pose with his brother, but at the last minute he couldn't make it to the photographer's studio. As Buzz Aldrin had learned on the moon, on such happenstance does celebrity turn. Both brothers found the photo inauthentic. The photographer, Howard Rosenberg, asked Kody to take his shirt off and pump up with some weights he had on hand. "It was not menacing enough," Rosenberg told me. "It was just a way of giving a little more edge to it." But as Kershaun observed, "My brother always wore khakis and a button-down Pendleton shirt when he was out on a mission, and he did *not* take his shirt off." Posing with a gun wasn't Kody's idea, either. The weapon wasn't even his; it was on loan from a Blood who had been interviewed for Léon Bing's book. "Kind of disproves the theory that Bloods and Crips hate each other so much!" Kershaun noted archly.

Misleading or not, the photo attracted the eye of the media, and whenever reporters wanted an L.A. gangster quote, they invariably phoned Léon Bing to get in touch with Kody Scott. The cover picture drew a few Hollywood nibbles as well. When William Broyles, Jr., a Vietnam vet and former editor of *Newsweek* turned screenwriter, wanted to research his pilot script for a prospective ABC television series about life in South Central, he called up Léon Bing and she took him to meet Kody Scott in jail. The two men exchanged war stories, as Broyles recalled, and the writer sensed that they were bonding over their shared "military" backgrounds. "Going through South Central for Kody was in some ways like me going through Vietnam," Broyles, a former marine, told me later. "It was a combat scene." In fact, both men's battle experience was limited: by Broyles's account in his memoir, *Brothers in Arms,* he didn't see all that much combat on his Vietnam tour of duty, half of which he spent in relative comfort, living "with the generals and colonels in permanent houses built on top of Freedom Hill," where they dined on steak and lobster and played Ping-Pong in the evenings. ("My biggest challenge was trying to beat the division surgeon, a Navy captain with a deceptively soft backhand that sliced right off the table," he wrote of his Freedom Hill stint.)[58] And while Scott's early teen years, by his book's description, sound like they were spent in nonstop shoot-'em-ups, his street-warrior days were quickly cut short by jail; since turning sixteen, he has rarely been outside a penitentiary for more than a few months at a time. Nonetheless, Broyles felt, "If Kody was alive in Napoleonic times, he'd be a general. . . . If he'd been in my unit [in Vietnam], I would've been thrilled to have him there." Broyles mailed his brother-in-arms a copy of *The Warriors*, J. Glenn Gray's classic 1959 account of his World War II experience; the book's famous analysis of war as a source of male bonding and community seemed pertinent to Scott's situation.[59] If Broyles and Scott shared a connection, however, it was more likely to be found in the study the screenwriter had made of another group of males: the astronauts. Broyles cowrote the screenplay for the Tom Hanks vehicle *Apollo 13*. In any event, the network turned down the TV drama about life in South Central, and it looked as if Kody Scott's tiny media flame would be snuffed out as quickly as it had ignited. The 1992 Los Angeles riots rectified that.

In some respects, the riots were themselves a media event, staged with significant production assistance from the Los Angeles Police Department. With news that the jury had acquitted the police officers charged with the brutal beating of black motorist Rodney King, the Los Angeles Police Department knew it might be facing an uprising in South Central. First a group of Eight-Tray Gangsters decided to protest the verdict by stealing armfuls of forty-ounce bottles of malt liquor from a package store a few blocks from the corner of Florence and Normandie. Then, at that famous corner, young men began hurling rocks and bottles. Police officers swooped down, arresting one of the young men and hauling him over a gate and onto the ground, an act that inflamed onlookers. The LAPD notified the media of a police action in progress, then promptly pulled out of the area. The police department's mind-boggling decision to withdraw all law-enforcement officers for the next several hours, combined with the massing of helicopter-borne camera crews above the corner of Florence and Normandie, literally set the stage for the riots. "Once the police pulled out, that was it," recalled Kershaun Scott, who was there that day with his fellow Eight-Tray Gangsters. "Because then the media was there, broadcasting the scene live with no cops in view. And so everyone else saw it and thought it was a green light to riot." In one telling early confrontation, captured on film, a young man charged a news photographer and tried to commandeer his camera, while spectators cheered. (It was Kershaun Scott who attempted to intervene to escort him to his car.) For sets like the Eight-Tray Gangsters, it was a day for "maintaining visibility," a once-in-a-lifetime opportunity to get their names out.[60]

Kody Scott missed out on the grand media event. When South Central exploded, he was once again behind bars. As it happened, his incarceration proved to be only a temporary setback. In the aftermath of the riots, members of the media, entertainment, and publishing industries swarmed around South Central, searching for its most visible representatives. With "Monster" in prison, "Li'l Monster" inherited the mantle. Television and print reporters clamored for his time; his phone rang nonstop with interview requests. He was invited to give speeches, and soon he had a lecture agent. He fielded a number of movie offers, including one from rap star Ice Cube. A one-hour documentary was made of his life, *Eight-Tray Gangster: The Making of a Crip*, directed by Thomas Wright, the original screenwriter for the quintessential gunfight-and-drug-dealing black action flick, *New Jack City*. (That film's script had undergone its own market-driven violence inflation: by the final cut, a screenplay that had originally called for only two deaths — each with ramifications — was, much to Wright's distress, a wall-to-wall meaningless bloodbath.)

When Ted Koppel showed up to do a special *Nightline* on the riots — his "next Tiananmen," as the ABC News anchor would later describe it in his book on the program's history — he made a beeline for Kershaun Scott.[61] All told, Kershaun appeared on *Nightline* four times. "I was honored to be on *Nightline*," Kershaun told me. He reveled in the sudden recognition, but in a subtly different fashion than his brother. Kershaun saw the camera as an opportunity to take the knowledge he had gathered in all the years of reading and put it to use. "Ted was blown away because he expected to get this gang member who was all 'uh, cuz, this' and 'uh, bro, that,' and instead he got a guy who was very aware of our history." Kershaun turned the tables by, for instance, confronting Rebuild L.A. director and former Major League Baseball commissioner Peter Ueberroth on the need for inner-city jobs.[62]

Soon enough, however, the klieg lights were packed up in the TV vans and driven off. But upstate in the solitary-confinement wing of Pelican Bay State Prison, Kody Scott was about to make the biggest postriot splash of all. He had started writing a book on his gang experiences with a prison-issue pencil and sending the installments to his media contact, Bill Broyles. The former journalist, in turn, had his secretary type out Kody's manuscript and forwarded a partial draft to his own agent and to the editor of *Esquire*, who published an excerpt. Word of Scott's tell-all gangster confessional quickly made the rounds of a publishing industry eager for a piece of the marketable L.A.-riots drama. Kody Scott had gone on the campaign trail again. While Broyles was under the impression that he had the only copy of the prison manuscript,

Kody had also sent the draft to Kershaun and asked him to get director and author Thomas Wright to plug the book to *his* publisher, too. Wright sent the manuscript to Avon Books, which Federal Expressed a contract to Kody in prison. A bidding war soon ensued, with each side frantic for victory. Declining an initial offer of a $25,000 advance from Atlantic Monthly Press, Kody Scott argued, reasonably enough, that he should at least get the $75,000 that the first-time author Léon Bing had received for *her* gang book. By the time he had finished campaigning, Kody Scott had landed a $150,000 advance, with the promise of additional payments to come of as much as $100,000.

The winning publisher, Atlantic Monthly Press, was eager to get the book out in time for the first-year anniversary of the riots, and Kody Scott was pressed to make quick work of it. He said he was also told to drop his concentration on the history and development of gang life and just focus the book on himself. "I said I wanted this to be a book about gangs, not an autobiography," Kody recalled telling the president and publisher of Atlantic, Morgan Entrekin. "And Morgan said, 'Well, I'm not interested in gangs. I'm interested in you.' " Entrekin recalled that he had advised Kody to cut sections toward the end of the book, where "he had started to become more politicized and more into Marxist and Marxist-derived thoughts. I argued with him that I didn't think it was appropriate." But the original manuscript, Entrekin said, already was mostly a personal narrative.

For the cover, Atlantic Monthly Press went back to photographer Howard Rosenberg for a shot from his *Do or Die* portfolio. They settled on another shirtless, gun-clutching pose. Rick Pracher, the art director at the publishing house, later explained to the *Los Angeles Times* why he selected that particular picture: "There's a slight head tilt, which gives him a fuck-you attitude. I found it much more menacing." The picture was in color, but Pracher converted it to black-and-white for "that rough-hewn edge—raw, more gritty."[63] Or, as Kody told me later, more candidly: "It was some sexual shit. Here's this black dude with his shirt off, with his gun extended like a phallic symbol. Yeah, it was menacing; it was menacingly *sexual*." He was being packaged and marketed as a sex object. "And the reason I know that," he told me, "is when the book came out, I got inundated with letters—thirty to forty a day—and ninety per cent of them were love letters."

Kody Scott wanted to call the book *Can't Stop, Won't Stop,* a gang slogan he had tattooed on his chest. But his publisher had other ideas. "They came up with *Monster,* not me," Kody said. "Morgan [Entrekin] flew out and said, 'Here's your cover!' And pride overrode logic." What

Entrekin had unveiled in the prison visitors' room was a mock-up of a cover with the elongated letters in "Monster" stripped across Kody Scott's body like jail-cell bars. At the time, Kody acted like "he loved the jacket," Morgan Entrekin told me. He even requested "extra copies so he could put them up in his cell." But as time passed, Kody began to feel queasy about the implications of the cover. "It was 'Monster in a Cage,'" Kody Scott said now with a grimace. "It was this whole celebrity thing of 'Let's take this whole gang thing and let's take it down to one person.' And I begin to wonder, Did they think they had found the one guy who could elucidate it all from having survived it? Or did they just take this guy and use him for the moolah in an exploitative relationship? Was I their guide? Or was I the talking gorilla?"

If the publisher was after "moolah," that goal was certainly achieved. Only a day after Atlantic won the bidding war, the book's foreign rights went for exorbitant sums in a feeding frenzy at the Frankfurt Book Fair.[64] The press was similarly ravenous, although more to look at Kody than to hear him. *Vibe,* the hip-hop magazine, was the only mainstream publication to offer him a writing assignment. The broadcast media salivated to get him on their sets. Prison officials turned most of them away, but *60 Minutes,* the most-watched television news program, was soon setting up its cameras in the visitors' room to produce an episode on his life and times—entitled, in a quaint effort at gang-hip, "Monsta." "Over the years, no gang has received more attention than the Crips and no gangster has become more notorious than Kody Scott," narrator and host Steve Kroft intoned. "For nearly two decades, the tattooed, bullet-scarred veteran of L.A.'s gang wars robbed, mugged, and murdered his way to the top ranks of the gang underworld, earning the name 'Monster Kody' for his distinctive brand of brutality." The preamble ended on an *Entertaintment Tonight* note, with the observation that this "handsome" and "bright" new author had a book contract worth "a quarter of a million dollars" and "now Hollywood mogul Michael Ovitz's agency is peddling the movie rights."

When Steve Kroft asked Kody Scott about his response to a good review in the *New York Times,* Scott said: "I kinda jumped around the cell a bit. It's the first time I've ever been recognized by a civilian for something other than aggression, naked aggression." But he was on *60 Minutes* in recognition of the sort of "naked aggression" displayed on the book cover, the sort that made him, in Steve Kroft's account, "a full-fledged ghetto star." And that was why Kroft asked the media's favorite gang question, the oft-repeated question that would begin to eat away at Kody Scott the way the how-do-you-feel query had driven Buzz Aldrin half out of his mind. "Do you have any idea," Steve Kroft asked, "how many people you've killed?" Scott, already annoyed by the media's eagerness for graphic body counts, retorted: "No, no, I don't know, no! I wonder how many people Oliver North killed? Or Norman Schwarzkopf. He's a hero, isn't he?"

One moment in the interview revealed another side of Kody Scott. "You don't have most of the usual excuses," Kroft said disapprovingly. "You didn't grow up in the projects, you had a very strong mother, your biological father is—"

"Absent!" Scott interrupted. "Absent! Missing in action—"

"—an NFL football player," Kroft continued, as if Dick Bass's celebrity made up for his absence.

But, Kody Scott said, "While my father was on the football field . . . I was in the street, you know what I mean? . . . And Dick never came."

"Do you resent that?" Kroft asked.

"To a great extent. No doubt about it. I *hate* him. Because I think about what I could've been. I can't dig that, runnin' out on your kids, you know. The father thing, that's just heavy to me now, that's just heavy to me."[65]

As he spoke, Kody's head ducked in and out of the shot. It was soon apparent what he was doing. His hands were chained and he was trying to rub his face on his shirt—to wipe away the tears. It was the one unposed, unpracticed moment of the interview and, according to Kody, it almost wasn't aired. After the taping, he recalled, "Steve Kroft wanted to cut it out. He kept telling me, 'We can cut that out.' He didn't want people to think that I was not who they perceived me to be."

"I may have told him don't worry about it," Steve Kroft said, and explained that he was probably just protecting Kody's feelings. "I may have asked him if he was upset, but I don't think I'd promise not to use it. There are ways you can cut something like that so he wouldn't be quite so teary. It *was* very teary."

Anguish over paternal abandonment was an ever-present phantom in my conversations about manhood and media recognition with both Kody and Kershaun. "I am the product of a man who wasn't there," Sanyika Shakur—Kody—told me more than once, with a bitterness absent from his commentary on his most mortal gang enemies. "My father never passed any knowledge to me." In early 1999, Shakur spoke to the man he believed to be his father for the first time in his life. Shortly thereafter, Shakur returned to prison. Four months later, I learned of the call from Dick Bass. "He just called to give me an update," the retired running back told me of his only conversation with his possible son. "He was working on some project, I don't remember what it was, maybe a TV script. He asked me if he could call me 'Dad,' because he said he'd never been able to call anyone 'Dad.' I said okay." Then, Bass recalled, "I said, 'Maybe we can get together.' But we never did."

But even if Dick Bass had been around all those vital years, what sort of knowledge could he have deeded a son? Bass wasn't likely to pass on to Kody the ability to become an NFL football player. That isn't the sort of "skill" one can generally teach; as in all celebrity vocations, every man is on his own. Ironically, that was the lesson Kody learned even in Bass's absence, though his quest for stand-alone celebrity followed a more violent path, to gang-banging notoriety. The mystery was how to explain the different path of the third Scott brother, Kerwin.

———

ON THAT FIRST DAY of rioting in 1992, while Kershaun Scott was running around with his gang set on the corner of Florence and Normandie and Kody Scott was sitting in jail transcribing his goriest recollections of gang life, Kerwin Scott was reporting for another day of work. All around him, buildings were being looted, trashed, going up in smoke. But the 32nd Street Market grocery store was untouched, as was its sister branch in Long Beach, where three black ministers, self-appointed sentries, stood guard outside throughout the riots. Their presence was comforting, though probably unnecessary. The Market's owner, Morrie Notrica, had a long-established reputation as a dedicated community supporter. He had been in business when the Watts riot had erupted in 1965, and his store had been spared then, too. While the major supermarket chains had, one by one, bailed out of Watts and South Central, the 32nd Street Market had steadily opened new branches in the area to fill the gap. Over the years, Morrie Notrica had won dozens of community-service awards for his quiet efforts at civic responsibility.

Those responsibilities extended to a young man who had come to work at the Market when he was sixteen years old and decided to stay. After a few years, as he trained at Morrie Notrica's side and began to master the grocery business, Kerwin Scott got in the habit of calling the grocer "Dad." That Notrica was half Greek-American and Kerwin Scott African-American seemed irrelevant, just as it would have been at the Long Beach Naval Shipyard, where black shipfitting "fathers" showed the ropes to their young white apprentices, and Hispanic welder "dads" revealed the secrets of the trade to their Filipino novices.

"He was the only adult man in my life who was honest," Kerwin Scott said. "Most adults in my life have been full of shit. Everything Morrie said he would do, he did. Morrie saved my life." Before Morrie offered him the job, "my life was going like this," Kerwin said, drawing an imaginary spiraling-down circle in the air. He had quit going to school regularly and had several scrapes with the law. He had shoplifted, held up a Taco Bell for lunch money, and dabbled in gang life, once joining a group of other wanna-be young gangsters on a leather-jacket-stealing spree in school. (The Crips' de rigueur uniform that year was a leather jacket.) Midway through the heist, a hall monitor yelled, "Stop!" No one did but Kerwin, and he was promptly arrested and had to spend a night in Juvenile Hall. "It was the worst night of my life," he recalled with a shudder. "Whatever I did, there was no way I was going to go back to *that*."

After the Juvenile Hall episode, Kerwin Scott's mother decided what her son needed was an occupation. She marched him down to the one man she thought might help, Morrie Notrica, and told the grocer her son required a job. "Morrie asked me, 'What do you do for money?'" Kerwin Scott recalled. "I said, 'I shoot dice. I rob people.'" As they were standing around talking, a cashier started yelling that a shopper had made off with some unpaid merchandise. Kerwin jumped up and raced after the shoplifter, nabbing him in the parking lot. Morrie Notrica decided that Kerwin Scott had potential.

"He'd worry me to death, talking to me about what I was going to do with my life," Kerwin Scott recalled. Morrie bugged him to stay in school. Something about the way he said it, no-nonsense but engaged, appealed to the young Scott. "He was always giving me the third degree, but it was only because he cared." One evening, he heard about a police action some distance from his house and bicycled over to investigate. Morrie Notrica, who happened to be driving home from work, saw Kerwin transfixed by the blue lights and a body bag on the ground. The next day, Notrica pulled him aside and told him he didn't need to be hanging around crime scenes. He shifted Kerwin to a later shift, to keep his evenings occupied. Eventually, Kerwin began working full-time, punching out at close to midnight.

When Kerwin Scott graduated from high school, Morrie Notrica loaned him money to buy a car. When Kerwin Scott got married, Morrie Notrica took the place of the father at the wedding. When Kerwin Scott wanted to take his bride on a honeymoon, Morrie Notrica surprised them with plane tickets to Jamaica. These were acts of paternal affection, and the fatherless Kerwin recognized them as such by calling Morrie "Dad." But Kerwin also turned to Morrie for another kind of paternal inheritance. "To me, Morrie was like a college," he said. "I *learned* from him." Kerwin valued being a son, but what he wanted to *learn* was how to be a man—an adult, responsible, independent man.

Most mornings, Morrie Notrica can be found directing traffic inside a bustling refrigerated warehouse in the well-named City of Commerce. The stretch of road from the Los Angeles freeway exit to the 32nd Street Market's loading bay belongs to another time and place in the world of men. The day I drove it, the sky was an appropriate shade of industrial gray. I was one of the few motorists behind the wheel of a car; trucks and the unburdened cabs of trucks lumbered by in either direction. The roadway was lined with matter-of-fact signs: COMMERCE TRUCK STOP, TRUCK PARTS, TOOL SHACK. I passed a nylon-coating shop, a refrigeration-repair center, an industrial-medical clinic, and an old-fashioned barber shop with a red, white, and blue pole. I didn't see a single franchise.

To get to Notrica's bay required threading through a vast parking lot jammed with refrigerated trucks, each with its leviathan doors flung open and backed up to a leviathan unloading dock. The sprawling compound belongs to Certified Grocers, a cooperative venture; Notrica was one of its six hundred members statewide. I spotted him, seated at a cluttered desk just inside the bay, a distracted, graying figure arguing on the phone. "Medium yellow bananas, six dollars?" he barked incredulously into the phone. "C'mon, we're feeding poor people here, remember? Besides, it's Mother's Day."

The activity in the warehouse was deafening and the temperature ice-cold. After a few more shouted exchanges, Morrie Notrica led the way upstairs to a quiet office. It wasn't a place he used often, he said, apologizing for its spartan furnishings. He sat me down and, while he went in search of coffee, I surveyed the impressive array of local community awards, plaques, and citations—for supporting the schools, involvement in a guns-for-food program, the advancement of racial harmony, and so on—gathering dust in this back room. A framed certificate noted his election as chairman of the Mexican-American Grocers Association, the organization's first non-Hispanic leader.

Notrica returned with two brimming Styrofoam cups, dropped into a chair, and, without further ceremony, said, "So, how can I help you?" He had a no-frills quality that reminded me a bit of Ike Burr's abrupt manner at the shipyard. He was here to work. I related what Kerwin Scott had told me about him and especially that he thought of him as "Dad." Notrica shrugged, a what's-to-explain sort of shrug. "The kid's always been honest with me, I've always been honest with him," he said.

End of story. I tried again: What made him hire Kerwin Scott in the first place? "I kinda understood the kid," he said with the same isn't-it-obvious expression. "He had a tendency to go over the line, but you know, like any kid. He didn't have a father. The kid just needed guidance like any other kid." What did he think of Kerwin Scott calling him "Dad"? Notrica said it made sense to him; after all, "I treat him like a son. I've always tried to be in his corner. Sometimes you need someone to talk to."

Where Notrica turned loquacious was on the subject of their work relationship. He gave me chapter and verse on Kerwin Scott's job history at the Market, culminating in his elevation to the post of receiver. "Now the receiver's the most important thing to be in the store," Notrica said, "because if the count isn't right, we lose big. The guy's gotta be sharp to do it. I wouldn't put just anybody there. Thousands of dollars in merchandise roll through there. You've got to watch the count of everything and you've got to be thinking about safety. Kerwin's the best. He watches everything, and he takes no crap off anyone. He has integrity. And all you get in this life is honor and integrity."

Morrie Notrica had lived in the neighborhood since birth. His father, a Greek immigrant, opened the first store on Thirty-second Street in 1953 and brought his son into the business in 1959. "My father taught me, you work Saturdays, you work Sundays. My father's biggest thrill was to go to work. He worked until two weeks before he died." Notrica's definition of work was not just about getting the right price on bananas, though; for him, work was tied to community service: the right price for bananas for his neighborhood. While we were talking, an urgent phone call was forwarded upstairs and he took it with his customary bark. "I'm getting calls about that black gorilla on top of the Denny's. What I'm hearing is get that goddamn gorilla off of there before you have a community up in arms." He hung up with a groan. "I mean, *Denny's*," he muttered to himself, "didn't they just get sued, for God's sake?"

The last independent grocer was trying to define his manhood through community service while living in a franchising world. He might win a few skirmishes over roof decor, but in the end the Denny's of South Central were likely to prevail. Morrie Notrica couldn't bestow on Kerwin Scott what shipyard "fathers" like Ike Burr had bequeathed to their apprentice-sons. Kerwin could not lay claim to an apprentice's full masculine inheritance. The problem wasn't just the pay, though his grocery-store income was no union wage. The nature of work itself had changed. Morrie and Kerwin had established a useful semblance of father-son, constructive utility, and it had saved Kerwin's life. But, iron-ically enough for an employer, in the new service economy Morrie could best fill the shoes of a private father, rewarding the graduate with a car, playing the proud pop at the wedding, showing up with honeymoon plane tickets, and to a young man whose father had failed on all these fronts, that was no small thing. But Morrie couldn't fulfill the ultimate role of the public father, couldn't give his protégé a craft in a chain-store world, couldn't give him skills to fashion an occupational life indepen-dent of "Dad's" goodwill.

Kerwin chafed at these limits. He moved up to the San Francisco Bay Area in 1987 to strike out on his own and wound up in a Food Farm in the Silicon Valley suburbs, with a boss who was hostile. "He harassed me every day," Kerwin recalled. "I was so stressed, I didn't sleep at night." Finally, he gave up and returned to Los Angeles and to the Mar-ket. Morrie Notrica provided a refuge; he clearly cared for "the kid," but his was a "college" from which Kerwin could not graduate. "I'm thinking of leaving again, going to find work in Oregon," Kerwin told me. Maybe there he could establish himself as his own man. Kerwin knew it was probably unlikely, but he kept hoping to discover some passage through the consumer economy that would lead to a useful manhood, grounded in work and care.

"I'm not looking for recognition," Kerwin said to me. "I don't feel because I work every day I should be on *Oprah*. I don't feel invisible. I'm very visible—at work." Whether this was enough was another ques-tion. The culture of notoriety that his brothers belonged to kept intrud-ing. After *Monster* was published, Morrie Notrica was honored for his community service to young people at a regional sales organization in Long Beach, and Assemblywoman Juanita McDonald presented him with a citation. Notrica brought Kerwin Scott to the ceremony and called him up to the podium for public recognition. But Kerwin's achievement was eclipsed when it was announced that his brother Kody had written a best-seller and copies of the book were displayed.

———

MONSTER KODY HIMSELF wouldn't be doing many book signings. In Sep-tember 1995, he was paroled, his first time out of prison since *Monster* was published. He was supposedly a new man, with the new name of Sanyika Shakur and a new line of work—he had a contract with Propa-ganda Films to consult on a screenplay based on his book. Five months later, the police pulled him over while he was driving near his home. They found a gram of marijuana in his car. A week afterward, parole officers arrived at his home to search for narcotics and administer a drug test. Shakur ran out the back door. For the next three months, he was a fugitive.[66]

One of the people to hear from him in that time was screenwriter and filmmaker Tom Wright, who had made the documentary about Kershaun. "It was the most bizarre juxtaposition," Wright recalled. "He was calling because he wanted me to help him surrender—he was afraid otherwise he'd wind up getting killed by the cops—but at the same time he was calling me to get advice about how to write his screenplay!" Shakur peppered Wright with professional questions: Should he sketch out scenes on index cards? Was it a good idea to use a lot of voice-overs? Did you write the dialogue before or after the plot outline? Wright encouraged him to talk about the screenplay, figuring it would at least keep him on the phone, while at the same time trying to get him to surrender to the police. "I kept saying, 'Kody, man, you've got bigger problems than that!'" But looking back now, Wright saw that the on-the-run script consultation made a certain perverse sense. "It was very sad, but in an odd sort of way, it was his salvation—because he cared enough about maintaining his own image to stick around. All he had was this vision of himself and, thankfully, it did not include his demise."

A few days after that conversation, the police finally arrested Sanyika Shakur. They found him on a front porch in South Central, seated before a line of about ten people bearing pens and paper. He was signing autographs.[67]

On a Saturday morning a year and a half later, Sanyika Shakur, again on parole, was sitting in his girlfriend's living room, wringing his hands and looking nervously at the time. The clock's hands were moving much too fast. Soon he would have to leave for the audition. He had agreed to try out for a part in *The Bouncer*, a feature film about "the toughest bouncer in Los Angeles," according to the advertisements of Bulletproof Productions. The film's screenwriter and director, Stuart Goldman, had invited him to the casting call, which was just down the road at House of Champions, a martial-arts and kickboxing studio. "What are you so worried about?" Felicia Morris's mother asked, looking at the kneading hands. "You're already a ghetto star. Now you're going to be a movie star." Shakur stared at the floor morosely. "I don't know," he said. "Movie star, that's a whole other realm."

We drove over to the audition, Shakur clutching a copy of the casting call flyer. "Think You're a BADASS?" it said in huge letters. "Let's Find Out . . ." When we pulled into the parking lot at House of Champions, scores of beefy men were lined up out the door and around the corner.

Shakur surveyed the crowd and visibly cringed. "Oh man, look at these guys." He gazed out at the sea of bulging biceps. "This is just what I was worried about. I haven't been working out enough. I'm too small."

As it happened, Shakur's build was of no matter. The casting call was only a gimmick to generate media attention that, in turn, might generate financing for the film. "I tried to set up a publicity stunt," Stuart Goldman told me. "I was going to stage fisticuffs and then have a pal of mine who's an undercover cop arrest someone. But the owner of House of Champions wouldn't go for it." Goldman was disappointed, but he still had one card left to play: Monster Kody. "I'm thinking I could use him for the publicity." Goldman already had some ex-gangsters on display: on the judging panel that day were two former "high-ranking gang members," he informed me. "I'm just one of these guys who likes hanging around with tough guys. It's a man thing. Men want to be acceptable to gangsters." That impulse had already netted him interest from Mickey Rourke, the movie actor whom the Spur Posse boys had imagined was so intrigued with them. "Mickey Rourke's hung out with Tupac [Shakur]," Goldman said. "When I called him about the film, he said he wasn't really interested, but when he heard about Kody Scott, he got all excited. When I said I actually met him, he was fawning over me. He said if ever there was a project, this is it. He compared Kody to Billy the Kid, a real gunslinger."

The son of a chilly movie-music composer whom he likened to the unreachable father in the film *Five Easy Pieces*, Goldman had rebelled against his classical music background, first by going on the road as a steel-guitar player with various country performers, including Dolly Parton and Linda Ronstadt, and later by writing rock music reviews for the *Los Angeles Times*. He then wrote a sex-advice column for *Hustler*, impersonating a female counselor, and another for the alternative *Los Angeles Reader*, which he soon tailored into a regular screed against "political correctness." "I was just trying to get as much attention as I could," he said. He did: After he got an offer to write a column for the other alternative paper, the *LA Weekly*, the entire staff of that publication signed a petition to block the hire on the grounds that his writing was racist, sexist, and homophobic. The petition inspired Goldman to pen what even he characterized as a "vicious" broadside in the *Reader* against his critics, which in turn inspired the *Los Angeles Times* to fire him. He moved on to screenwriting.

At the House of Champions, so many men had showed up that Goldman gave up on even the pretense of an audition, instructing everyone just to turn in their résumés. Monster Kody exhaled a great sigh of relief.

As he was getting ready to leave, Goldman hurried over: "We should really work together. Your book is so amazing. We could work together on a script." They agreed to get lunch.

A week later, my phone rang and it was Sanyika Shakur. "Stu is pissin' me off left and right," he said. The movie negotiations had broken down; either Goldman had offered a loan or Shakur had requested one, but in either event no money had been forthcoming and the film deal was a dead letter. "I'm so depressed, I feel like going out and robbing something," Shakur told me.

Goldman groaned when I called him. "It was my fault really. I said to Kody, if we do this, you could write part of it. And he said to me, 'I'd want nothing more than to write with you. You could *teach* me.' I should have cut it off there." When Goldman called back to say he couldn't raise the funds for the film, he said, Shakur offered to sell him the movie rights "for an incredibly low amount—fifteen hundred dollars," then asked for a loan of about the same amount; Goldman said he didn't do personal loans and the conversation degenerated from there. "It's too bad. I was looking forward to having him pal around with me. I was going to wait a few days and have him take me to the 'hood."

As the week progressed, Sanyika Shakur's mood continued to decline. He called me again to report the latest deal that had fallen through, the promise of a whole episode of *Geraldo*. The producers had finally decided that the gang thing was a bit old and canceled his appearance. Maybe it was just as well, Shakur said. "I mean, was this producer inviting me on because he admired me, or just so I could be attacked?" It was a familiar trap and he said he didn't want to be known as a killer anymore. "What is that? To become a man you have to be a man killer? It's a negation of a negation. It's my whole psychosis of being a man."

Still, if this was the end of media recognition, even if it was just for being a man who killed men, what did he do now? "I keep thinking of robbery," he said, for the second time that week. "I don't know, it's weird. It's like I've got the Stockholm syndrome." What did he mean? I asked. "I don't know, but it's like, in prison, at least the guards are paying attention, you know what I'm saying?"

A week later, Sanyika Shakur missed a required weekly drug test and so violated his parole. The violation came with a mandatory three-month sentence. Monster Kody was back in jail.

Some weeks into his reincarceration, I arrived for visitors' hours at the Los Angeles County Jail and ran into Felicia Morris in the waiting room, which wasn't surprising; she was a loyal and regular visitor. She had a pile of paperwork on her lap; she used the long wait to catch up on her job. Finally, the guards announced, "Rudy Scott!" Felicia sighed at the mangling of his name. "The guards do that all the time," she told me. It was their way of letting the inmate's girlfriend, and the inmate, know that they weren't impressed by Monster Kody's notoriety. In a cubicle on the other side of the Plexiglas, Shakur was waiting. "What can I say?" he said to me, chagrined. "This is like my norm. This is where I get my writing done." He did have a question he was eager to ask me, though. "Did you see me on ESPN?" I hated to tell him I hadn't; I knew he'd be disappointed.

Afterward, Felicia and I walked through the dank parking garage adjacent to the jail, its many potholes overflowing with oily water. We stood by our cars and she broke down in tears. "I just hate to see him in chains" was all she could choke out. At the other end of the lot, a scuffle erupted. We looked up to see police officers throwing a skinny young man against the hood of a car. He lay still as they searched him. Two of the young man's buddies stood skittishly at a distance, hands at their sides, powerless to help.

———

KERSHAUN SCOTT ABANDONED the field in a different way. He retreated first to an anonymous suburb and a classroom at California State University in Long Beach, where he got straight As. But he still felt unnervingly exposed, and eventually he moved with his new wife, their daughter, and his wife's two children from a previous relationship to the desert town of Ridgecrest, 150 miles away. He was looking to escape the grinding poverty of South Central, the perpetual crises of his brother, the appeals of his former gang friends to get back into the action, and the police who seemed to dog his steps. But he was also fleeing the media. "After *Nightline*, every day I was doing an interview," he told me as he drew the blinds against the merciless sun. Children's toys littered the floor, where his two-year-old daughter sat twisting the legs off miniature action figures. A large photograph of Kershaun's old Eight-Tray Gangsters set, throwing gang signs, hung in the center of the living-room wall like an extended family portrait. "After a while," Kershaun said of the media onslaught, "the pressure got to me. I just wanted to go somewhere and just be Kershaun, not be everyone's Li'l Monster."

What troubled him was not so much the media's approach as his response. "The questions I was being asked—I started to ask, Are these the right questions? And what gives me the authority to answer these questions? You know, a lot of people got exposure after the '92 rebellion, but it didn't lead to anything. It didn't change anything. It started really bothering me. I began second-guessing myself." One of the first things he started questioning was his attire. "At first I went dressed as a gang-banger, with the hat turned backwards and the pants sagging. Now, I haven't dressed that way since 1981." Then there was the pose. "I wanted to come across as hard as possible." But when he watched the tapes later on, he became disturbed by what he saw. He had thought he could shake people's assumptions by wearing clothes that contrasted sharply with his articulate delivery, but instead it only seemed to reinforce their preju-dices. And why did he want to project that image anyway? When a gang truce between the two major gangs in Los Angeles, the Crips and the Bloods, was largely dismissed by the media, he wondered if part of the reason was the do-or-die killer poses he and so many others had been projecting.

So he put away the gang gear and stopped acting so hard-core before the camera. The change didn't seem to register; interviewers were still asking The Question. "The last time I was on *Nightline,* Ted [Koppel] called me a thug," Kershaun said with a wince. (He was referring most likely to a remark Koppel made to him and another young man during a retrospective on the L.A. riots that aired in October of 1992: "You're a couple of—let me put it gently—a couple of ex-gangsters, or are you still gangsters?")[68] "I don't hold it against him," Kershaun said. "I know he was taking a lot of flak from the network for all that gang coverage and he didn't have a choice. But still . . ." Kershaun went over to a closet full of videotapes, pulled out a tape of his appearance on a TV news program in Los Angeles, *Midday Sunday,* and popped it in the VCR. The show, billed as the first time a Crip and a Blood had ever appeared together "in peace" on a news program, was something of a historic event by media lights, but the host, Tony Valdez, seemed intent not on peace-making but on knocking down two gunslingers as social menaces. After detailing the bloody body count of this "war" in South Central, Valdez turned on them: "I'm sure that there are people who are watching this this morning who think that that's barbaric, savage. How can you justify it?" The two guests sat speechless before his tongue-lashing. "It's in-credible! . . . Where are your morals?" Valdez closed by asking whether either of them would still pull a gun on a rival gang member. "Would you do it today?" he demanded. From his living room in the desert, Kershaun offered the reply he wished he had delivered: "Well, Tony, it *would* be good for ratings, right?"

Kershaun couldn't imagine any way out of the role into which he had been cast—and had cast himself—short of total withdrawal. He saw how his brother Kody shuttled in and out of jail, in and out of the media eye, and he wanted nothing to do with this crime drama anymore. "I can't understand for the life of me what he finds so interesting about being in jail," Kershaun said. After so many years of following worshipfully in Kody's path, he was coming to grips with some painful truths: his brother never was in a position to teach him, and underneath his fraternal devotion, he felt betrayed. Just about every time he had been arrested, Kershaun observed, it had involved a caper Kody had instigated. "Don't get me wrong," he said carefully, not wanting to be misunderstood. "I'm thrilled my brother wrote that book *and* that it was a major success. Because it was the one moment in his life when he could say he had succeeded. A book, you have it for life. A book is *knowledge*." What bothered him was not his brother's authorship or the fame it had brought him, but the false image on which the fame was founded. "He wrote this book and people everywhere read it and looked to him as someone who's been through the rough waters and succeeded. But in fact, it's quite the opposite. Because he's back in jail. He doesn't walk the walk. He's just let me down on too many things."

In the months to follow, Kershaun would find a part-time, minimum-wage position at a Blimpie down the street, but even in his desert town, where rents are rock bottom, the salary hardly covered the basics. He began working on the side on a book of his own, about the politics behind the riots and his own personal struggle to change his life. He was planning to call it *Crossroads*. His wife, Vanessa, would go through a difficult pregnancy that required her to stay in bed for months while Kershaun took care of her and the children and bicycled to his job at the fast-food outlet and back. For the time being, that was enough. One day, in Vanessa's ninth month of pregnancy, Kody called. "I need you to come down here, man," Kershaun recalled him saying. "I need your help." Vanessa wept and pleaded with Kershaun not to go. "The only thing that prevented me was I didn't have a car," Kershaun said. Which was a good thing. Because if he had, as it turned out, he would have been away when Vanessa went into labor.

"He was my hero, my father figure, my role model, all that," Kershaun said. "I admired him, I admired what he was doing. I made that choice." What he was trying to understand now was why he made that choice. "I could've admired Kerwin for getting up at five-thirty in the morning and biking four to five miles [to the Market] when it was cold outside and for not missing a day of work. I could've admired that." And these days, he did. "I used to think being a man is to be straight with your gun and to have sex with as many women as possible," he told me. "Now

I'd say it's to take care of your family and make sure they are safe and have a roof over their heads. What makes a man is owning up to your responsibilities."

Moving to the desert was, of course, an extreme and shaky remedy for Kershaun. It wasn't likely to be far enough away to flee the world that he was so much a part of, as the framed picture of his gang in the living room indicated—or to escape the culture of celebrity. Even in the desert, after all, the TV's in the living room, the phone's ringing, and your toddler is pulling the legs off action figures.

FOR SO MANY YOUNG MEN of Kershaun's generation, the deserts to which escape was possible seemed few and far between, and the great display magnet exerted its irresistible pull. Even older brother Kerwin hadn't been immune. He was still trying to graduate from Morrie's college, but when he looked around, what was there to break into except celebrity? One afternoon, while we were sitting at Chin Chin, a popular restaurant on the Sunset Strip to which Kerwin was partial, he told me the story of his attempt to stake a claim in a celebrity world, a tale punctuated by interruptions from a curious waitress. "You *must* be someone famous," she said to Kerwin for what felt like the fifth time. "You're being interviewed." He smiled and let her think so. He knew the other reason she thought he was famous; he had an extraordinarily muscular build. "People are always asking me if I'm so-and-so from the NFL."

In fact, his physique came from a foray some years back into the world of bodybuilding. It had started out as a kick. He liked lifting weights and discovered he was good at it. What appealed to him, at first anyway, was weight lifting as an extension and expression of the strength required to do his job; it seemed like an honoring of his work life. "I know this sounds crazy, but I enjoyed working up a sweat. It was the sweat part I loved, because it feels like you are *working*." He started training seriously at Gold's Gym, and then began entering bodybuilding competitions. After a while, it became an all-consuming endeavor. He lived alone—he wasn't married then—and soon all his unoccupied hours were taken up with lifting weights. "I'd work my full-time job and then I'd spend five hours training. I practically lived in the gym." Sometimes he'd come home from the gym, climb into bed, then—convinced he hadn't worked out enough—get up and go back to the gym. All that mattered in bodybuilding was winning. "I'd be mad at myself because I could've done more, I'd be furious. If I trained hard, there was always someone training harder. There's no such thing as being equal. You have to be better." In 1992, he won the Orange County Muscle Classic and the Iron Man. In recognition of his victory, he was invited to host four days of *Muscle and Fitness,* an ESPN show.

For a time, Kerwin began to think that he might become a professional bodybuilder. "I was taking steroids like mad. I could bench four hundred and fifty pounds like it was nothing." In model-boating terms, he was definitely one of the "nitrous guys." But the steroids frightened him. "They altered my personality. I was mean." His meanness was inflamed by the reactions he got whenever he left the gym. "Everybody thinks you're stupid, a joke. Everybody stares at you, everybody wants to touch you. I was a freak. It hurt my feelings." The bigger he got, the more he felt like the Incredible Shrinking Man.

Needing more money to cover the costs of what turned out to be a pricey vocation, Kerwin Scott accepted an invitation to be a bouncer at a nightclub called California Dreams. "When you're a bodybuilder, everybody wants you to be their bouncer." One evening, the club owner declared it "Exotic Night" and commissioned him to pour shots in an exotic outfit: a collar, bow tie, and cuffs but no shirt, and a pair of shorts. He was an instant hit—"I got tips just for that!"—and was promoted to the club's "California Heat" stage show, an all-male exotic dancing revue. "It was a lot of fun at first," he said, and it paid about $200 a night. He made his own costumes, dressing, and then undressing, as a fireman, a cop, a Top Gun fighter pilot. But the evenings soon soured. "The ladies would be yelling, 'We want Kerwin! We want Kerwin!' And they'd all be trying to put their hands on me. And I might not be in the mood to be touched, but I couldn't say no because I was taking money from them." Sometimes, he was so mobbed by women he needed a bouncer to help him off the stage.

"I felt degraded," he said, and his analysis of his degradation was one any female stripper would find familiar. "Everybody wants to have sex with you, but only because they want to see what you look like in bed. I'd meet women and all they'd want to do is talk about my body. They were that way with all the male dancers. The thing was, there was no one I could *not* go out with, but they'd go out with *any* of us." He found himself coming home in tears. "I was as depressed as I've ever been in my life. I was the loneliest I've ever been. I was making all this money, but it was like I lived in this empty space. My heart just had a hole in it."

One night, two years into the exotic revue, another nightclub owner invited him to dance for a while in her Palm Springs club. Kerwin accepted the invitation, though he had misgivings when he learned the club's name: the Cell Block. When he arrived, he discovered that the interior was set up like a prison and Kerwin was to be the dancing inmate. A few nights into this gig, he was in the middle of his dance number when a woman raced out on the stage. "She pulled me down by my bow tie and ran her nails across my chest and drew blood. She said, 'I love to scratch. I'm a scratcher.' I quit right on the spot. I didn't even change. I left with just what I had on."

We finished our meal at Chin Chin and the check arrived. Kerwin Scott scooped it up at once. "I'm paying," he insisted. For all the nights of exotic dancing, Kerwin Scott was still an old-fashioned man. "Coming to see me race next weekend?" he wanted to know. He was launching his battered old cracker box in the regionals on the Rosemead lake, traditional gas-powered outboards only. I said I would. There was something about those clunky old boats that appealed. If it wasn't quite the same as watching an overhaul at the shipyard, powerboating had its comforting utilitarian aspects nonetheless. At least the boats, not the men, were on display.

The waitress swung by one last time with the change. "Now are you famous or not?" she demanded of Kerwin Scott. He flashed a wide-angle smile. "*What?*" he said in mock horror. "You mean you *haven't* seen me on TV?" She scurried off, blushing, and he slapped a hand to his forehead. "I can't believe I lied to her," he said. "But actually, I didn't. I mean, I was on *Muscle and Fitness,* right? So I guess I am somebody."

III. What Sort of Man Reads *Details*?

"IMAGE" HAS LONG BEEN American society's weapon of choice against a few ostracized groups—black men and gay men in particular—whom it has saddled with cartoon-strip stereotypes. In turn, those groups in various ways have used the imagery of denigration to fight back, sometimes in coded and covert ways, sometimes in a conscious effort to turn a cultural straitjacket into political armament.

For black men, a historic strategy for breaking the hammerlock of judgment was to take up society's ugly depictions and wield them in ironic, inflated, often ludicrous ways. Turn-of-the-century black performers took the blackface minstrel show, a white creation, and its stereotypes of subservience and stupidity, and held those images at bay through further burlesque exaggeration. When Billy Kersands did his version of the "grinnin' darky" act with billiard balls stuffed in his cheeks, he turned shuck-'n'-jive into a subtly satirical reflection of white fantasies and fears. "Black men, like white men," historian Nathan Huggins wrote in *Harlem Renaissance,* "could use the theatrical grotesques as ways of marking distance between themselves and their horror." The comic could even, Huggins observed, use grotesquery to elevate himself above his denigrators, "because his perspective allows him to judge himself and his people and because his pose places him above even those who had disdain for him to begin with." The blackface minstrel made of his blackface image a one-way fun-house mirror that shielded him while reflecting back to white gapers only their own inner paranoias, magnified to ridiculous proportions.[69]

Similarly, black men often protected themselves from stereotypes of "threatening black manhood" by wrapping themselves in them; if the culture wanted to cast them as marauders and rapists, then black men might use a display of super-glowering hostility to comment on, inoculate themselves against, or deflect that verdict. To that end, Black Panthers marched armed through the halls of the California Assembly, and their "minister of defense" Huey Newton posed for a photo brandishing a rifle while sitting on a rattan throne.[70] In the same way, a ghetto kid may flash a gang sign at a journalist. In either case, there was power—even if only the power to scare the bejesus out of whites using whites' own preconceptions. By donning the masks whites offered them, blacks also created a little private space within which black identity might exist relatively unmolested. Trying to defuse white fears by assuming an exaggerated "respectability" often proved less satisfying, as Robert Williams, president of the Monroe, North Carolina, chapter of the NAACP, discovered. In the early sixties, a months-long picket that he led of a whites-only swimming pool yielded only further humiliation and death threats—until the day he appeared before a threatening white mob with an Italian carbine in his hands. In his book, *Negroes with Guns,* Williams recalled how the mere sight of the weapon instantly reduced his tormentors to infantile hysterics, one older white man "screaming and crying like a baby" until finally "somebody led him away through the crowd." As Malcolm X would later note (and famously put to his own political uses), "An image of black men learning anything suggesting self-defense seemed to terrify the white man."[71]

The society that Williams and Malcolm X inhabited in the sixties could still be confronted because it still knew how to be offended. But how much would any pose, however hostile, however threatening, however mocking, protect against a voracious display culture capable of seizing upon any pose and marketing it? What security would a brandished weapon offer once an image industry recognized the sales potential of black-male hostility and turned it into a visually exciting show of "gangster" violence that could be retailed as style to suburban white teens? The gun then became but another glittery object drawing media attention and Hollywood interest. What got you arrested on the street was glamorous on-screen.

In the postwar years, a similar strategy of minstrel exaggeration was deployed by gay men against the stereotype of the sissy. One group in particular tried to disassemble the culture of denigration in which they were portrayed as mincing and pitiable femmes by arming themselves with the raiments of drag and its companion code of camp. To take socially sanctified "women's wear" and flaunt it on a male body was to send up society's most sternly guarded definitions of masculinity and femininity. The female impersonator challenged the prevailing culture and its gender imagery by making outlandish and oversized fun of it, by blurring visual definitions of sexuality, by pulling the curtain back to reveal that behind the glamour was just a bunch of underwire foundations and greasepaint. "The whole point of Camp is to dethrone the serious," Susan Sontag wrote in her famous 1964 essay "Notes on 'Camp'" (which was largely reticent on camp's gay progenitors). "The effect of the drag system," anthropologist Esther Newton wrote in her field study Mother Camp, "is to wrench the sex roles loose from that which supposedly determines them, that is, genital sex." A San Francisco architectural illustrator by day, drag queen by night, who went by the name of "Jersey," put it more colloquially. His objective, he said, was "to be able to laugh at myself and the roles we're constantly doing, and to get other people to laugh at it and to loosen their feelings. Jiggle some nuts loose, I guess."[72]

Camp's use of artifice, of stereotyped imagery in the service of mockery to expose society's manipulations, was "the lie that tells the truth" (as an encyclopedia of camp aptly defined it), "the heroism of people not called upon to be heroes." Drag displays once largely sequestered in the world of the gay demimonde might have seemed an unlikely vehicle for social change, just as camp's withdrawal into witticism seemed an unlikely path to political engagement. Sontag maintained in her influential essay, "It goes without saying that the Camp sensibility is disengaged, depoliticized—or at least apolitical."[73]

But it didn't go without saying, not after June 28, 1969, anyway. On that date, at one in the morning, the New York City police made a more or less routine raid on the Stonewall Inn, a popular gay bar in Greenwich Village. Typically, these raids were staged dramas—the bar owners paid off the cops, the cops tipped off the owners, and the customers slipped out the back as the raid began. Such bars were among the very few "public" gathering spots for gay men, albeit hidden and only quasi-legal, and so their denizens were motivated to play by the rules.[74] But that night at the Stonewall Inn, the police arrived without prior notice—and found themselves facing a fierce counterattack from evicted bar customers and younger homeless queens squatting in a park across the street. As some of the police barricaded themselves in the bar, the crowd lobbed bottles and bricks and hurled a trash can through the bar's plate-glass window, soon to be followed by a spray of lighter fluid and lit matches. A parking meter was uprooted and deployed as a battering ram against the front door. The riot had its standouts: among the first and the fiercest of the combatants were the drag queens. By some accounts, it was a drag queen named Tammy Novak who sparked the melee when a policeman shoved her—and she shoved right back. Transvestites who had already been arrested and loaded into the police van armed themselves with that most lethal of feminine attire, the stiletto pump. A nyloned, high-heeled leg shot out of the back of the paddy wagon and sent a cop flying backwards. "One queen mashed an officer with her heel," Martin Duberman recounted in his authoritative account, *Stonewall,* "knocked him down, grabbed his handcuff keys, freed herself, and passed the keys to another queen behind her." When the police department's elite riot-control unit (created to contain anti–Vietnam War protesters) arrived in football-style wedge formation, it was greeted by its inverse image: a Rockettes kick line. As the female impersonators cancanned before the startled cops, they sang:

> We are the Stonewall girls
> We wear our hair in curls
> We wear no underwear
> We show our pubic hair . . .
> We wear our dungarees
> Above our nelly knees!

The riot that lasted on and off for several nights, along with other protests, sparked the gay-liberation movement into its greatest renaissance since the Mattachine Society mobilized in the 1950s.[75]

"I just had had enough," Sylvia (Ray) Rivera told me. Rivera came to be called "the Rosa Parks of the gay-liberation movement." When the police raided that evening, Rivera was inside drinking with friends and mourning the burial of singer Judy Garland earlier that day. "I had on full-face makeup and a nice blouse," she (the preferred pronoun by Rivera and some other drag queens) recalled. "I was basically in drag except I wasn't wearing a bra or false tits." Rivera was one of the few drag queens allowed in Stonewall in such attire; despite its false billing later as a "drag bar," in those years of hidden and repressed gayness, Stonewall

barely tolerated female impersonators, a step up from the outright hostility emanating from most gay male bars of that era.[76] Transvestites were
considered déclassé and embarrassingly effeminate. Along with the more
violent insults of the street and especially of the police, who had beaten
Rivera more than once because she wore a dress, that attitude summed
up why Rivera "had had enough." When the police hustled them out of
the bar that night, Rivera stood at the edge of the crowd for a while,
watching as fellow street queens hurled loose change, then bottles, at
the cops. Someone handed her a "Molotov cocktail," she said, and she
hurled it. A rage welled up inside and she charged into the crowd breaking windows, helping overturn cars. "What I felt was relief, because I
knew our movement had come to life. I remember screaming in Spanish," said Rivera, who is of Puerto Rican descent, " 'The revolution is
here! The revolution is here!' "

Seemingly overnight, an entire gay generation burst into political consciousness. "Stonewall's lessons were less about sex and more about
politics," journalist Charles Kaiser observed in *The Gay Metropolis.*[77]
Cross-dressing and the witty contemptuousness with which female impersonators sashayed across a stage could, it turned out, be more than
personal nose-thumbing at a judgmental world; they could be part of
transforming that world. The political content underlying the private
performance of drag would soon become explicit in the street theater of
Radical Drag, or "gender fucking," which drew from both gay liberation
and feminism to challenge sanctioned sex roles. Within a year of Stonewall, "Gay Power" and "coming out" were the rallying cries of thousands,
the Gay Liberation Front had mobilized, and gay-rights organizations
had sprung up across the nation. Stonewall's first anniversary was marked
in New York by a march of more than ten thousand activists to a Gay-In
in Central Park.[78]

Transvestites had helped catalyze a revolution. They had taken sex,
the currency of ornamental culture, and found a way to exchange it for
the coin of politics. Later popular accounts, while often characterizing
drag queens as the movement's initial shock troops, credited them with
little more than being first on the scene, clearing the way for the "real"
gay liberation led by more mainstream groups. But to relegate them to
such a role was to miss their deeper defiance. Gay-rights activist and
scholar Martin Duberman, who chronicled the riots in *Stonewall* and who
used to be a regular at that bar, observed to me that drag queens were
heroic challengers not merely in street demonstrations but in their daily
confrontations with a culture that violently sought to contain them. "The
fierce determination of Sylvia Rivera to be herself wherever she went

was a landmark challenge to our most guarded concepts of gender, to the whole binary idea of gender," he said. The display of drag proved a powerfully disruptive tool on many fronts, not just along the gay-straight divide. Rivera had reported to her draft board during the Vietnam War in full regalia, because she "had no intention of going to war against a country that we had no business being against." (The draft board was so eager to see her leave that they even assented to her demand to be driven home in style, free of charge.)

In the years after Stonewall, Rivera could be found at the many gay-liberation demonstrations in New York City. She was even jailed for scaling the front of City Hall in spiked heels to reach an open window and gain admission to a closed City Council session on a gay-rights bill. But very quickly Rivera and other drag-queen activists learned that they were not really welcome in a movement increasingly concerned with its public image. "They paraded Sylvia to every event if it was a demonstration that required an arrest," commented Bebe Scarpi, the only drag queen in those years to sit on the board of the National Gay Task Force. "But when it came time to go before the cameras, no one managed to call Sylvia. There was a very strong feeling in the gay movement in the early seventies that a drag queen destroyed the male image. These guys saw it as an insult to their masculinity." To Scarpi, the "visibility" of drag queens was the key to their destabilizing political power: "You *saw* us," she told me. "We never had the luxury of hiding, but that's also what gave us our strength." And ultimately what got them excluded from the movement. "First they used us for our visibility," Scarpi said bitterly. "Then they used us for our determination. Then they had no use for us, so they pushed us out so they could get acceptance." She herself eventually quit the National Gay Task Force, tired "of being used as their token transvestite."

Hostility from both gay men and women became shockingly palpable to Sylvia Rivera at a 1973 Gay Pride Day celebration. As a start, her name had been stricken from the list of speakers, on the grounds that the festivities were supposed to be free of "political" statements. When Rivera tried to make her way to the stage, observers there recalled, she was shoved, kicked, and booed, by both men and women. "My own brothers and sisters beat me," Rivera remembered, her voice still edged in hurt. A videotape of the event partially recorded the dustup, along with voices from the audience screaming "Shut the fuck up!" during her speech—which was a screed against the audience for not acknowledging the sacrifices made by drag queens, many of whom had been jailed, beaten, and raped, and for failing to help those who were still in jail.

Afterward, the cross-dressed editor of *DRAG* magazine, wearing a tiara and gown, approached the microphone, her voice shaking with outrage. "You go to bars because of what drag queens did for you," she said, referring to a change in the city code, which she had successfully advocated, legalizing New York's gay bars. "We gave you your pride. . . . [Drag queens] are oiling the doors for you people to come out of the closet, but I'm not going to oil the doors with my tears any longer. Gay liberation, screw you!" With that, she hurled her tiara into the crowd. The organizers quickly hustled Bette Midler onstage, who burst into song: "You got to have friends . . ."[79] Two days later, Sylvia Rivera tried to slit her wrists. "I was really pissed at the world and at the movement."

In the end, however, Stonewall's drag-queen legacy would fall prey to a force—ornamental culture—far more effacing than the old misogynies and censorious puritanisms, a force that could leach cross-dressing of all political content. Under its spotlight, "acceptance" itself would gain a new meaning. Within a matter of years, seedy Stonewalls would give way to glossy Studio 54s and, by the 1980s, Limelights, and the often mobster-paid bodyguards who once repelled homophobic thugs would be replaced by handsome doormen manning velvet ropes, guarding a club's glitterati image from crowds of wanna-bes and wanna-sees. Being seen, not shielded, became the point; a buffed younger clientele who came of age in the late 1970s and early 1980s in the commercial gay club scene jockeyed for the chance to display themselves, alone, on one of the pedestals that rose from many a new dance floor. A few of the younger men still swathed themselves in outlandish, gender-bending costumery—though typically for attention, not political effect. Most dressed not to challenge rigid sex roles but to fit commercially approved styles of seduction, a conventionally "masculine" uniform of polo shirts and khakis endorsed by Calvin Klein or Ralph Lauren, not Candy Darling or Holly Woodlawn. "Though few activists seemed aware of it, the gay movement in important ways was moving in the same direction as mainstream sexual culture," John D'Emilio and Estelle Freedman observed in *Intimate Matters,* their history of American sexuality. "And, the commercialism that came to characterize the gay male subculture of the 1970s was not different in kind from the consumerist values that had already made sex a marketable commodity."[80]

The first victim of this image-conscious era was drag itself. By the mid-seventies, some quarters of gay male culture were taking up a new, aggressively macho pose that, as several alarmed gay commentators noted at the time, notably lacked the self-consciously mocking attitude of camp. In a 1977 article in *Gaysweek,* Jack Nichols cast a troubled eye over the leather bars springing up across the country—"decorated with ropes, skulls, masks, chains, crowbars, hardhats, and even swastikas"— and asked: "Is this influx of S&M fashions really pioneering a new breed of sexual liberation and awareness as the dominant/submissive S&Mers insist? Or is this dominance/submission trip partly a revival for same-sex lovers of elements at the base of old-fashioned male/female roles?" In the 1980 essay "Where Have All the Sissies Gone?" gay writer and literature professor Seymour Kleinberg uneasily remarked upon the "relentless pursuit of masculinity" he was witnessing in the sea of young gay men making the scene sporting their identical sculpted torsos, crew cuts, tank tops, and leather jackets. They were the emblematic opposites of the drag queens, who "imitated women because they understood that they were victims in sisterhood of the same masculine ideas about sexuality." For the new cookie-cutter models of macho, on the other hand, "manliness is the only real virtue; other values are contemptible." The new gay he-men were "eroticizing the very values of straight society that have tyrannized their own lives."[81]

At least the butch pose of the muscle-bound "marine" might still contain some individual wit, a touch of drag. By the nineties, however, as Daniel Harris has written in *The Rise and Fall of Gay Culture,* an astute diagnosis of the commercialization of gay life, a gay-rights slogan could well have been "MasterCharging our way to liberation." Shopping had been redefined as a form of activism, and questioning the right of entertainment companies and advertising agencies to play cultural gatekeepers and gender definers was distinctly out of style. Maybe nowhere was this more evident than in the realm of gay media. There, formerly "underground" periodicals were morphing into *Vanity Fair* read-alikes at an astounding clip.[82] In the magazine world as in the club world, the revolt against culturally dictated masculinity had been triumphant just long enough to acquiesce in its own demise.

WHEREVER THE AMERICAN MAN TURNED in the nineties, he seemed to be facing a display case. Worse, he seemed to be in one. Ornamental culture could assume many forms, but at its core was a virulent voyeurism, and as Kerwin Scott would discover, as the Spur Posse always knew, sex was its gold standard. In the nightclubs of Palm Springs, in the exotic-dancing ads at the back of "alternative" weeklies, in the come-hither layouts for Nike and Calvin Klein in *Vanity Fair,* in the billboards hovering over Times Square and Sunset Boulevard, its display was the standard by which so much else was measured.

"Men are the sex objects now!" Sam Shahid declared cheerfully, greeting me at his advertising agency in downtown Manhattan, its ledges adorned with glossy testaments to that judgment. The adman was nested amid a heap of photos, slides, and tear sheets of barely clad male models. The former creative director of Calvin Klein's in-house advertising agency, Shahid had helped shape the trend-setting Obsession for Men ads, and later similarly themed male-idolatry images for Banana Republic, Versace, Perry Ellis, and Abercrombie & Fitch (where he once used the son and grandson of John Wayne as his come-hither models).[83] "Pecs are the new breasts now!" he said. He was nothing short of giddy about the dethronement of the female body as the prevailing idol of consumption. "Men have become *bigger* sex objects than women! They are the sex gods now! They have replaced women!" The problem with women, in his view, was that they no longer wanted to be sex objects. "Women think it's sexy to be behind a desk; that's the secret of Ann Taylor's success," he exclaimed, referring to Ann Taylor's muted professional wear. "Women got too politically correct. Women say, 'Don't use me.' Well, men say, 'Use me!' "

Shahid dated the male invasion of the ornamental garden to President Kennedy's election. "Kennedy started it," he said, recalling with awe the day he first saw shots of the president at poolside. "John Kennedy walked around without his shirt on, and overnight, it became acceptable. Men could be adored." In the shorter term, he gave full credit to Calvin Klein, for whom he had crafted ads from 1981 to 1991. Shahid pulled out some past Calvin Klein campaigns to show me the process by which he had helped to elevate men into sex-object heaven. It began, he told me, when he was still an underling at the company's in-house agency, assisting in the development of the legendary Calvin Klein men's underwear ad, featuring a pole vaulter's bronzed and barely clad body. The photo provoked a great stir when its five-story billboard version was unveiled in Times Square in 1983. "That was shot from below, looking up," Shahid mused, "so it made him very majestic, bigger than God." He flipped open another portfolio to show me the next step, a Calvin Klein ad suggestive of a ménage à quatre: "It was three guys and her. So she was just about the men." Then it was on to a Calvin Klein 1991 multipage "rock concert" ad campaign. He pointed to the final shot of a bereft-looking female model by herself, while the male "superstar rock star," as Shahid put it, was being lavished with adoration. "It's about what women have become and what men are now. Look at her," he said with indignation. "She's tough. She's in control."

A few blocks from Sam Shahid's agency was the headquarters of a magazine whose ad pages were filled with his handiwork. As I visited the downtown Manhattan loft space of *Details* magazine in the summer of 1997, I would be reminded of how handily a pose of protest could become a stance of compliance. The loft's aesthetic was more IBM than bohemian, with its tiny warrens of cubicles bookended with closed offices. Not that the decor mattered; the magazine would soon be relocating to the uptown, gleaming, new headquarters of its parent company, Condé Nast, the publisher of *Vanity Fair, Vogue, HG,* and *Gourmet*. That would be but the next in a series of abrupt changes at the magazine for the "stylish" and "cool" young man, whose circulation had risen fivefold by the mid-1990s to nearly half a million readers. *Details'* openly gay editor, Joe Dolce, had been forced out in a particularly crude fashion by his supposedly close friend and mentor, Condé Nast editorial director (and former *Details* editor) James Truman, who had been secretly interviewing prospective new editors for months. When Dolce found out and tracked down Truman at a vacation hideaway in Brazil, his boss confirmed the betrayal in a two-minute phone conversation. Dolce quit before Truman could fire him. "I felt like my balls had been cut off," Dolce told me.

Condé Nast's emasculation of Dolce was, in fact, part of a larger corporate strategy to attach hetero *cojones* to the magazine. The company higher-ups had decided that the way to further increase *Details'* circulation was to hire an editor who could "heterosexualize" the magazine (as a number of Condé Nast executives phrased it). Michael Caruso, a former *Vanity Fair* editor who had recently tried to launch a sports magazine, seemed like their man. Soon after he was hired, he assembled the staff at a Manhattan sports bar to watch the NBA playoffs.

On the day I first visited *Details'* office, the newly ensconced Caruso was studying sleek modeling shots for his first, hetero-ized issue. "Here's the model I want to use for the suits layout," Derick Procope, his new fashion director, told him while fanning out eight-by-ten glossy photographs on the new editor in chief's desk. Caruso looked them over and wrinkled his nose. "I'm worried this guy looks a little too pretty. You know, jailbaity." Procope assured the editor he needn't fret. "We can make him look masculine." Procope unfurled magazine tear sheets of two athletically attired black men. Caruso nodded: "Now these guys look *masculine*." Procope, a black British fashion editor whom Caruso had hired away from *Vibe* magazine, already had a feel for what his new employer wanted. The two men had just returned from Italian Fashion Week in Milan, where, en route to one of the runway shows, Caruso had turned to him and said, "Derick, we've got to find a place to watch the Tyson fight!" And the two men had retired to the American Sports Bar.

The week I visited, in the summer of 1997, Caruso had been on the job less than a month; the only adornment on his office walls, purely functional, was a large bulletin board, on which he had tacked up titles for upcoming features: "Demo Derby," "TV Babes," "Burning Man," and something called "Slash." He had renamed the magazine's service section "Peak Performance," and titled his first issue's fashion layout "Power Play." This week, he had been preoccupied with calling the agents and sneaker representatives of celebrity sports players, in hopes that a professional athlete would agree to be featured on the cover. But it was hard going. "You call to get sports people in the magazine," Caruso told me, "and the reaction you get is, 'Oh, isn't that a gay magazine?'" He sighed. "If you have *any* gay content, you're perceived as a gay magazine." Sexual orientation aside, most sports agents viewed a half-million circulation as still not "big enough" to merit their attention. In lieu of a sweaty basketball player, Caruso had settled on a cover photo of Vince Vaughn, star of the movie *Swingers,* who conveyed, as the editor put it, "the kind of confident, easy masculinity" the magazine needed to portray. He held up a shot of Vaughn lounging in Armani slacks and Prada loafers, glanced up with a suddenly rueful expression, and said, "Men want to look at what looks confident." He paused, then added, "At a time when we really aren't."

Caruso's hetero-macho "swashbuckler" attitude (as the *New York Post* dubbed it at the time) may have been more of an accommodation to Condé Nast's demands than a reflection of his real self.[84] His sports journalism had hardly been an expression of traditional macho. When he edited the sports pages of New York's *Village Voice,* he had assigned stories on such subjects as "the culture of trapping in Mississippi," camel racing in Australia, and "geriatric swimming in Seattle." To blame the "de-gaying" of *Details,* as some staff members bitterly called it, on the new editor—or even on the new policy directives issued from Condé Nast—was to ignore the original betrayal of the magazine's mission. That had happened seven years earlier when Condé Nast took over what had been an independent, campy downtown publication about nightlife and fashion with a large gay male following and turned it into a corporate "men's magazine."

The original *Details* emerged in 1982 from the downtown Manhattan club scene. A black-and-white periodical on newsprint with grainy photos and a homemade feel, its motto was "Our doorman is your mailman."

If much of New York's club scene, following the lead of the uptown Studio 54, had already capitulated to commercial conventionality, the new magazine's sensibility was still largely bohemian. The magazine's creators made regular connections between gay liberation and feminism, between upending gender assumptions, however idiosyncratically, and expanding the personal freedoms of men and women. As its founding editor, Annie Flanders, told me, "It was our own private revolution." A feminist-minded "old hippie" and an unofficial earth mother to a largely gay artistic circle, she had previously been the style editor of the alternative paper the *SoHo Weekly News,* where she had cultivated a relaxed, overtly gay style in men's fashion. "I was very tuned in to the gay world early on," she told me. "My brother was gay, and because I started out in the fashion business, my closest friends were gay." Flanders was also tuned in, intimately and tragically, to the ravages of homophobia. Her brother had waged an agonizing lifelong battle with self-hatred and depression over his sexuality, inflamed in no small measure by their homophobic "superjock" father, who once told his daughter, "A homosexual is the lowest thing on earth, and people like you who don't think so are the second worst." Flanders and her brother were always close, and for years she tried to salve his pain. In 1977, he committed suicide. In the aftermath of his death, their father was afflicted with unrelenting insomnia and suffered a massive heart attack on the tennis court a year later, dying at the age of sixty-five. It seemed to Flanders that a gay-hating culture had killed them both.

While Annie Flanders edited the magazine, its persona belonged to Stephen Saban, a gay writer whose wry and gently teasing column on the downtown Manhattan club scene rapidly became the magazine's beating heart. The mainstream press dubbed him "the Boswell of the Night" and "a 1980s Noël Coward."[85] But his dispatches read more like letters to friends. ("I must apologize that I was thoroughly unpleasant to everyone," he confided in a typical column, "having awakened late with a brand-new cold and cough.")[86] His devoted readers were rarely at the clubs; they were young gay men in the hinterlands, painfully familiar with the sort of anguish that Flanders's brother had endured. Saban himself grew up in the stifling confines of 1950s Florida and Georgia before fleeing at eighteen to art school in Philadelphia. "Most of the fans of my column were small-town kids who felt like outcasts," he told me, "and the column gave them hope that they could move to New York City and not be pariahs." Saban soon took to running photographs of outrageous New York drag queens like the Lady Bunny, Hapi Phace, and the International Chrysis with his columns, because their images seemed to sustain his readers. "The idea that when you come to New York, you could win a trophy at the [drag] balls for being gay, for *realness,* that was this beacon of light, that you could burst out of the constraints imposed on you and that would be okay. So many gay people are unhappy, and part of the idea of *Details* was that it was possible to be gay and happy." Saban was deluged with mail, and while much of it was from young gay men, his correspondents were both men and women, gay and straight, from across the country, seeking a way out of their isolation. Many wrote desperate to join the magazine's staff; one avid fan from Baton Rouge even packed his bags and showed up at the office, ready to be put to work.

That fan was welcomed, as were virtually all unannounced visitors. The early *Details* staff had an open-door policy, an extension of their open-door editorial philosophy, which intended, as Flanders put it, to create "a place where we could have the freedom to have our opinions." The magazine was the equivalent of a pre-Stonewall bar, a safe if confined social space where people could be themselves. "There was an atmosphere of freedom and generosity," Saban said. "It was a very kind and good place to work, and that came out in the pages of the magazine." Mitchell Fox recalled with baffled bemusement the scene that greeted him when he was installed as publisher in 1989: "The door of the building was always open and prostitutes and street people would come in." He didn't know quite what to make of it. "It was like this community of people."

After the magazine got its first investor in the winter of 1983, Flanders, Saban, and about five other writers who had come to *Details* from the old *SoHo Weekly News* met and agreed to some principles that they hoped would foster a democratic and inclusive ethic: they would all receive the same salary (up until then they had volunteered their services, but now they agreed they would all get $25,000 a year), have a financial stake in the company, encourage everyone from the messenger on up to write if they desired, and keep ad rates low so struggling independent designers could afford to advertise. The staff also welcomed to their pages illustrators and photographers whose avant-garde or simply homoerotic work could not find more mainstream outlets. It was to be a forum for the full-throated, unapologetic political voices of gay performers like rock musician Boy George, who, in a piece by Saban, sounded off on the homophobic religious right. ("I happen to have had sex with men and Jerry Falwell hasn't, so for him to tell me it's abnormal . . .")[87]

The magazine got much of its support from downtown club owners, who advertised in *Details* and made their membership lists available to the magazine's circulation department. In return, *Details* "covered" after-hours club life, but in such an eccentric, irreverent, and random manner that it couldn't exactly be called a quid pro quo. The columns responded to clubland the way drag queen Jersey responded to American puritan-ism: they aimed to "jiggle some nuts loose." While Saban's subjects weren't overtly political, he aimed to splash a little eccentric limelight on the inhabitants of an unsung underworld and, by vicarious extension, on his isolated readers in Dubuque.

Relaxed and spoofish attitudes toward sex roles were evident through-out the magazine. In fashion spreads featuring risible bearded Russian cossacks in knickers kick-stepping beside a boom box in the park, or a banker in a gigantic ten-gallon hat trying to eat a hamburger with chop-sticks, the magazine insisted on a lighthearted frivolity in men's fashion. The intent was to remind men that it was okay "to have fun with your clothes," that fashion was just "one of life's rewards with literally no hangover."[88] Fashion features weren't necessarily consumer plugs—they sometimes spotlighted clothes that came from flea markets or were homemade—and in any case favored small and struggling local designers. Some of the magazine's writers used clothes to dissect the decade's social ills: a March 1983 commentary observed that new "totalitarian" styles reflected a rage generated by "the ultimate consumer society" in which a few could buy private planes and the rest felt, "Well, if I can't have it all, I'll look like a Nazi."[89] A deconstructive and humorous approach was applied to displays of traditional femininity: on the fashion pages, women modeled chain-mail gowns, towering beehives, and fish headdresses; the editorial pages featured an account of a "Trapped in the Body of a White Girl" performance project, in which a female artist had turned Farrah Fawcett doll heads and hair dryers into six-foot-high "sci fi Wongo women."[90]

The staff understood that the freedoms of women and men, straight or gay, went hand in hand. The insight that homophobia's roots can be found in misogyny—that "effeminate" men might not be so hated if the feminine was more respected—was an early and important discovery of the gay-liberation movement, one often set aside in the years to come. In a magazine devoted to nightlife and design, that conviction was mostly tacitly expressed. But in the latter years of the 1980s, with the coming of AIDS, *Details* made its politics overt. "We were one of the first [fashion] magazines to be open about AIDS, supportive and really concerned in every way," Annie Flanders recalled. Concern about AIDS inspired a more general political outspokenness on gay issues. By the end of the decade, *Details* was running stories decrying the threatened censorship of AIDS-related art shows by the National Endowment for the Arts and calling for an end to discriminatory and homophobic sodomy laws. The language of such articles was explicitly activist, often ending with a direct plea to the reader to take a stand. "Get angry, get active."[91]

"Right before the end of 1989," Flanders recalled, "we had a very important editorial meeting. I remember that I said, 'I have serious concerns about the world. The nineties is going to be a whole different time, and we really have to think about the issues we want to get involved with.' The parties were over." She laughed painfully as she recalled her words. Because one of the parties that was indeed over was theirs. A sympathetic early investor and former owner of the British *Tatler,* Gary Bogard, had assumed the role of publisher after Flanders decided she shouldn't both edit and publish the magazine — "my first disastrous mistake." By 1986, Bogard had lost vast sums in the Texas oil and real-estate bust and, to retire his debts, he sold the magazine to a venture capitalist, who in 1988 resold it to Advance Publications, the corporate parent of Condé Nast. S. I. Newhouse, Jr., the company's chairman, told Flanders and the press that the company "would be crazy to change *Details*" and he had no intention to make "any changes in the editorial product."[92] But two years later, with publishers and media pundits declaring the nineties "the decade of the male," Newhouse announced that he was turning *Details* into a "men's magazine." Flanders and almost the entire staff were fired. Only Saban and one other staff member were spared. Newhouse, Saban was informed, liked his style. Whether the new boss cared for his subject matter was another issue. It soon became apparent that for *Details* subscribers, entering "the decade of the male" would mean dropping political self-assertion for sartorial self-marketing. *Details* seemed to be heading toward a gay sensibility cleansed of political utility.[93]

Details wasn't the only magazine in pursuit of the credit-card-waving male reader. A sudden burst of men's consumer magazines had hit the stands or were promising to soon, among them *Men's Health, Men's Life, M Inc., Smart, Healthy Man,* and *Men.* Condé Nast was already pouring money into its other fashion-conscious men's magazine, the ad-fat *GQ.* And the once lone standard bearer of men's magazines, *Esquire,* was frantically remodeling itself to compete, its era of elegant fiction and scathing political and cultural criticism long forgotten. "Men are hot," *GQ* editor Arthur Cooper enthused.[94]

To remake *Details,* Newhouse appointed as editor in chief a thirty-two-year-old British journalist, James Truman, then in Newhouse's stable at *Vogue*. Truman, a writer for British publications on pop music, had landed his *Vogue* job by dazzling editor Anna Wintour with his taste in apparel. When they first met at a party, Wintour had swooned over Truman's "tight black-and-white houndstooth-check Armani," as she breathlessly told *Los Angeles Times* reporter Geraldine Baum. Wintour gave Truman his first assignment at *Vogue:* to write about how he dressed.[95] Now, his assignment at *Details* would be to convince young male readers that his story could be theirs, too; that dressing could get them where they wanted to go. The new slogan he chose for the retooled magazine was "Style Matters."

I had been waiting almost an hour when James Truman finally arrived, fashionably late, for a fashionably late dinner with me at a fashionable downtown restaurant where Kurt Vonnegut and other luminaries mingled loudly and the noise was deafening. When I suggested we repair to a quieter side room so I could actually hear what he was saying, Truman gave me a pained look, as if I'd proposed that the captain of the high-school cheerleading team sit in the cafeteria with the unpopular pimply girls. "That's . . . not *done*," he said, and he meant it. We stayed in the cool people's zone.

Truman said that he had revamped *Details* with a primary mission in mind: teaching its young male readers "how to dress as an expression of their individuality rather than as a set of rules on how to fit in." This sounded like a variation on the drag-queen ethic, though coming out of the mouth of a man who couldn't bear even to be seen in the "wrong" room, I wondered at his definition of individuality. By the clothes and even the makeup a man chose to wear, Truman said, he could declare himself a "freedom fighter." He saw cross-dressing rock stars that way, as "transvestite freedom fighters," he said, borrowing a phrase from a *Details* article penned by actor Nicholas Cage. It was one of the qualities Truman appreciated about his favorite band, Depeche Mode, whose lead songwriter Martin Gore blurred the gender line by wearing eyeliner and shiny lederhosen onstage—"he looked like a huge queen." Depeche Mode's songs—processed dance music with banal lyrics about sex gone right or wrong—could hardly qualify as "freedom-fighting" anthems; indeed, the old *Details* had dismissed the British band's music as "depressingly slight" and, in Thatcherite England, appallingly apolitical.[96] But Truman contended that a style-consciousness in a band could be "revolutionary" in itself, and that such a style could create a "community" of young men capable of defining their own masculinity.

This notion had coalesced in Truman's mind just before he took over *Details,* at a Depeche Mode concert in the Rose Bowl in Pasadena in

1989. "It was sold out and I had lost my backstage pass, so I had to stand outside," he recalled, and as he stood outside watching "all these people, incredibly stylish in each and every individual way, I suddenly became aware that there was suddenly no unifying definition of masculinity in America, and here was this group of people that had been pulled together, sixty thousand strong, and that they did have some things in common, one of which was some sophistication of the style cells in the brain, which at a fundamental level is what *Details* is about. I saw that something new was being born in America. I felt that all these young guys—I was just aware of the guys that night; I didn't notice the girls— had come together to worship this group absolutely sincere about the pain of being a man. It was quite a revelation to me." This revelation led him to believe that the new *Details* could be "about the anxieties and nervousness about what a man's place is now." Or rather, about how to relieve those anxieties by offering "sensitive" and "confused" young men an individual and a collective identity through style. "It was about seeing everything through the prism of style."

The "style" offered up by the new *Details* in Condé Nast's first issues was impossible to discern: the layouts were a cacophony of jarring, haphazard images and blocky siren-red and orange print prickly with exclamation points, against headache-producing yellow backgrounds. The first issue's gallery of photos, which Truman selected and posted on his office walls, included the scorched shaved head of a Death Row inmate after his seven-minute-long electrocution, a pile of garbage at the base of Mount Everest, and a woman's disembodied legs propped up on the front seat of a convertible, her undies dangling below her knees.[97]

"The original idea was that it would be this scabrous, toilety tabloid," Roger Trilling, an editor at large and Truman friend, recalled. "It was supposed to be rude and in-your-face." Its obnoxious, teenage-boy aggressiveness was also meant to ease readers' worries that style might not be a very masculine concern. "What's tricky in a men's magazine," said Bill Mullen, creative director for many years and a formative influence on the magazine's look under Condé Nast, "is you don't want to objectify men because your readers don't want to objectify men." The magazine struggled to mitigate that problem early on by a relentless emphasis on style as a force of energy that could demonstrate virility and be deployed to get a man a kind of power. That the rebel clotheshorse could achieve manly status through dress was the magazine's constant drumbeat in the early 1990s: "fashion respects the outlaw," wearing leather was acquiring "stealth, speed, mastery," and "Remember, 'dress' is an active verb."[98] Men were supposedly wearing active wear for an active reason. "We were saying clothes serve a *purpose*," recalled *Details'* West Coast editor David Keeps—albeit a purpose that remained murky.

For a time, *Details* codified its vision of the style-made man under the rubric "samurai" masculinity, and anointed yowling rock "poet" Henry Rollins as its exemplar. On its January 1994 cover, *Details* declared Rollins "Man of the Year" for forging a "new artistic identity," which they deemed a fusion of, among other things, "the anarcho-savagery of Iggy Pop," "the horrified observations of Coppola's Colonel Kurtz," and "a little bit of Hollywood ingenuity." Mainly, Rollins seemed to have fashioned his "samurai" rep via the modeling of faux-Beat clothes, cultivating a vaguely alienated, man-alone persona, and talking a lot about his weight-lifting regimen. ("The Iron is the great reference point, the all-knowing perspective giver. Always there like a beacon in the pitch black.") "I believe that the definition of definition is reinvention," Rollins informed *Details'* readers. "To not be like your parents."[99] Especially if you couldn't, as *Details* indicated in an editorial statement: "If you're not able to jet off to Jamaica this weekend, dress like you're already there."[100] What this "new artistic identity" offered was a promise, familiar to any young comic book reader: if you put on this cape and strike this pose, at least people may think you can fly.

The message that, as *Details* photo director Greg Pond put it, "you did not have to live up to your father's example, you could invent your own," was assumedly comforting to a young male readership—and to a young male staff—many of whom doubted they could live up to their fathers, and wondered what that meant for their manhood. At a staff retreat in Saratoga, James Truman floated the question, "When did you know you'd become a man?" The most common answer, staff members in attendance told me, was a stymied silence, followed by some variation on, "I don't know if I am a man yet." When I asked Truman what he made of that response, he said, "What I read into that pause was that they weren't sure if their fathers had *recognized* them as men." Which would explain what Truman recalled as the second-most-common answer: "When my father died."

The new men on staff, like the new readers the magazine was trying to attract, belonged to the baby boom's downwardly mobile tail end or the even more economically diminished "baby bust" generation. The thirty-three-year-old Greg Pond observed that his father, a print and broadcast journalist, was able to support a family and pay for "an Upper West Side apartment and a car and a country home" by the time he turned thirty. "And that's impossible for me." This was the story for most of the staff members I met. Senior features editor Tim Moss, who was thirty, told me, "My father was married his junior year in college, he became a lawyer, he had the house and the swimming pool and the car and three kids by the time he was twenty-six." The staff tried to design *Details* to ease this sense of male deprivation. "Lifestyle of the not very rich and interestingly dressed," West Coast editor David Keeps archly called it. "What these images in the magazine speak about," Greg Pond said, gesturing to his favorite tear sheets of glossy lone young men on motorbikes or idling on deserted street corners, "is that maybe this life you have isn't that bad. It gives you the idea you don't have to do what your father did."

Except that men like Greg Pond and Tim Moss, and so many of their male peers, often privately regretted being deprived of their fathers' lives. In a nation where the benchmark for adult masculinity had been not measuring up to your father but *surpassing* him, *Details* seemed to be offering young men a thin gruel of consolation. "It seems inconceivable to me to have the life my father had," Pond said, his voice etched with regret, "but my ego would also love to be able to do that. . . . We really genuinely as Americans are *not* interested in men who don't make a lot of money. When I didn't make money, I was really amazed by the number of women who never, ever would have anything to do with me. . . . I'd love the idea that I could support my girlfriend. I'd love to take a month off like my father and go to the country. In seven years, I haven't taken a day off." I asked Pond how he personally expressed his "individuality through style." He shrugged. "I love to wear suits. I'd wear a suit on the weekend. What I'd really love to wear is a white linen suit, but I don't have the nerve." Why not? I asked. He gave me a gimme-a-break look. "That's something you wear, you know, when you're on your vacation in the country home."

If drag queens had used "style" to challenge an oppressive society, *Details* was using it to reassure men that they needn't challenge society just because it had put their expectations on the economic and social skids, that wearing the trappings of a life denied them could be satisfaction enough. Moreover, *Details* suggested that its readers use the drag ethic not to question oppressive sex roles but to succumb to a role as oppressive as the gender yoke: that of consumer. The original *Details* had employed a gay sensibility to mock, play with, or dismiss socially or corporately endorsed styles. But certain style-conscious corporations and their allied ad agencies soon realized that such a sensibility, stripped of its political content, could be a Trojan horse. From its belly might come the images that would turn a nation of young men into colonies of slavish male shoppers.

When S. I. Newhouse bet on the nineties as "the decade of the male," he likely had his eye less on gender struggles than on sales trends: 1990, the year of *Details'* relaunch, was also the year that men's clothing sales began to boom. The trend would continue into the nineties, driven heavily by the "collection" business of such designers as Calvin Klein, Ralph Lauren, and Tommy Hilfiger; between 1989 and 1996, the sales of men's apparel rose 21 percent to record highs, even as women's clothing sales fell 10 percent.[101] Women might be abandoning the field, but Condé Nast and its advertisers hoped to recoup any lost profits on the other side of the gender divide. As Condé Nast's original mission statement for *Details* declared, in huge, screaming letters, "There are 13,469,000 MEN under 35 with household incomes over $35,000 obsessed with essential *Details*... coats, cars, compact discs, vacations, videos, sneakers, spirits, sunscreens, beer, barbells, bikes and belts.... Young, well-educated, gainfully employed and out to spend disposable dollars on themselves, *Details* men means business."[102]

Within a year, even Truman's edgy "in-your-face" attitude had given way to the needs of the marketplace. Which is to say, advertisers preferred an environment leached of even the faux kinds of "freedom fighting." A few major Condé Nast clients pulled or threatened to pull their accounts after *Details* ran the photo of the electrocuted inmate's burned head. Nine months after the relaunch, glossy celebrities ruled the cover, there were almost no violent photos inside, and an endless array of editorial layouts shamelessly shilled for advertisers' products: one feature was nothing but close-ups of advertisers' athletic shoes, a sneaker per full page, presented like religious icons.[103] Condé Nast had "heterosexualized" a gay-friendly magazine by removing the content usually thought of as masculine—active engagement in political and cultural matters—and replacing it with the conformism, passivity, and consumerist mirror-gazing traditionally held to be feminine. But the implications of a gender reversal weren't what troubled *Details* readers, who seemed ashamed mostly of their earning capacity. After all, in spite of Condé Nast's hyperbolic pitch, the magazine's readers actually earned a median income of $27,000 a year.[104] They could hardly afford the designer duds featured in the magazine. As one letter writer remarked snidely about a feature story on the "average" man's wardrobe: "After taking inventory of my closet, I made a list of all the items I didn't have and found that I would need to spend at least $3,216 to achieve the 'average male wardrobe.'"[105]

The subversion of individual expression by commercial interest was neither a particularly surprising nor a new phenomenon. But *Details'* betrayal went far deeper, for there was a subtler, more personal promise the magazine had made to its young readers. All its talk of "style" really promised was a better way for the new man to compete in the new *sexual* marketplace. If its readers couldn't prove their manhood in traditional ways—pursuing an honored craft, making a decent living, supporting a family—then, so its pages suggested, maybe they could derive a sense of masculine confidence from the exertion of sex appeal. The power of sexual attractiveness, passively displayed, might even serve as a foundation for manliness. This was the subtext behind just about every fashion layout and was occasionally expressed overtly in articles as well. The new "boss man," a May 1992 article cheerfully proclaimed, was the guy with "the playboy career" (resort bartender, ski instructor, personal trainer, and croupier were among the options listed), jobs "high on glamour and pheromones," for men "who would rather think about getting laid than getting laid off"—and all you had to do was "look good, have fun, and foster the illusion of great expertise and congeniality."[106] There was only one post-drag sticky point to finesse: how to be a seductress without being a beauty queen. "I realize, of course, that it sounds narcissistic and selfish for a guy to wait around for women to approach him," Blake Nelson wrote a tad defensively in a December 1993 article about how men could adopt a style of "quiet craftiness and repose" to lure women passively. "Sure I think about how I look. That's going to determine which women might be interested in talking to me. But does that make me self-absorbed and vain? No, that makes me smart."[107] Convincing men that they weren't just replicating the lady fair was going to take some doing, and the editors knew it. "If the man attracts the woman and the woman initiates the sexual interest," *Details* editor Roger Trilling said to me, "then the problem is, how can the man be the man? That's one of the central issues *Details* dealt with."

In its July 1992 issue, *Details* laid out a solution to this gender dilemma. The magazine's cover presented the embodiment of what the editors deemed the ideal new man: Anthony Kiedis, lead singer of the rock band the Red Hot Chili Peppers. On the cover, Kiedis stood in a pinwheel-like pose, arms akimbo, legs spread wide. He wore a shirt that featured a huge pair of winking, come-hither eyes. And popping up between his straddled legs, right where his crotch should have been, were the pouting lips and plunging cleavage of Lady Miss Kier, the singer for Deee-Lite. It was not so much that he had conquered her body (after all, she wasn't even looking at him); instead, he had replaced her. Her sex appeal had been subsumed into his own; her face had become his genitals. Inside, between shots of Kiedis smoldering seductively into the camera, baseball cap turned back, shirt off, legs spread wide again, the rock musician described how his "semi-maniacal womanizer for a father"—the "playboy kingpin" of the Sunset Strip's Rainbow Bar & Grill with an ever-changing "congregation of nymphlike maidens"—had taught him to attract women like flies and thereby built "my not necessarily warranted sense of self-confidence."[108]

"We loved Anthony," the magazine's then–creative director Bill Mullen recalled. They discussed him ad nauseam in admiring terms. As a rock star, Kiedis was "in the position of being pursued by women but he wasn't feminized by it," Trilling said, in explaining why the young musician had become the magazine's beau ideal. Kiedis got to be manly, he added, without being "predatory" in the traditional male ways. Kiedis himself seemed more ambivalent about his pioneering new-man role: "My disadvantage now is that women I think are right for me are generally put off by my not entirely deserved status as a rock 'n' roll slut," he complained in Details.[109] Nonetheless, the magazine's male editors were in awe. As Maura Sheehy, a former Details staff writer and one of the rare women on the senior staff, put it with exasperation, "They loved that whole Kiedis thing where he and the other guys in the band are performing naked with socks on their dicks. Where it's all about showing his body but because it's so raw it seems to be very masculine." If Kiedis was relying on "feminine" charms, no one would question his manhood as long as he kept that dick front and center. Like Details itself, Kiedis was legitimizing "fantasies we had that weren't considered legitimate," Bill Mullen said, "where you sing in a hairbrush in front of the bathroom mirror." It was an aspiration that Mullen, the son of an army general, fulfilled in his own way when he adopted at Details what his fellow staffers described appreciatively as a sort of rocker mystique (minus the actual playing of music), manifested by wearing black clothes, arriving at the fashion shows sometimes with an entourage in a rented stretch limo, and having emphatic views about what was "cool" and what wasn't. Rock stars who are truly cool, Mullen said, "are our heroes. . . . That's the standard for my generation of men."

A number of Details editors were riveted by speculation that made the rounds of the office that Kiedis's "playboy kingpin" father could have been a pimp; though no one ever related to me any evidence that he was, they seemed to find the possibility intriguing and glamorous. Later, the significance of this would dawn on me. Kiedis's manipulation of women was evidently his paternal inheritance—his "self-confidence" as a ladies' man, he wrote, was "instilled in me by my father."[110] He had learned from his father how to cash in on sexuality, using his own sexual allure in a way that did not detract from his masculine status. As Trilling wrote in a memo to Truman: "If Anthony Kiedis is some kind of resonant role model, it's because for better or worse he's managed to share and continue something his father taught him." Trilling proposed that the pimp might be a model for a new kind of manhood that the magazine could explore. "A pimp is a master of romance," he wrote. "He may not love his girls, but they most certainly love him. Why else would they give him their money? Coercion? Ridiculous. You can always buy cheap protection. However sado-maso, the bond between pimp and girl is romantic and therefore fascinating."[111]

Kiedis appealed for the same reason that James Truman deemed the 1983 film *Risky Business* (starring Tom Cruise as a suburban boy–cum–pimp) to be, as he never tired of telling the magazine's staff, one of "the two most important movies" of modern American cinema (the other being another Tom Cruise vehicle, *Top Gun*). "It's about a boy who wants to get laid and the only way he can get laid is by going to a hooker, and that proves to be such a success that he decides to open a business selling hookers to his friends," Truman said to me, bringing up his fascination with that movie within the first fifteen minutes of our dinner conversation. "He turns his father's house into a brothel." But more important to Truman, the boy becomes the ruling sex icon, and the women's sexual power falls away. "Tom Cruise was the biggest sex object in that film," Truman said, sounding as if this were a moment of conquest for all men, "whereas *she* [the main hooker played by Rebecca DeMornay] was just the whorehouse tramp. The body you remember in that film was Tom Cruise's." Which is why, Truman noted, Cruise's character ultimately is the one who "triumphed."

This drama of triumph was replayed in the pages of *Details*, where fashion layouts featured strippers cast as the trashy wallpaper and male models as the true spectacle to behold. "The Bad and the Beautiful," a twelve-page fashion spread in the March 1992 issue, summed up the new priorities precisely. "Everything is a movie," the text stated. "Stage your own scene." In page after page, the scene set was of "bad" women dressed as fifties B-movie sluts, gazing worshipfully at "beautiful" men whose crotches were the focus of virtually every shot. Who was supposed to be object and who the subject was made plain enough in the opening shot, where female paparazzi aimed their cameras at a lone stud languishing against a car, his leather-clad legs spread for a fuller view.[112] At least these women were active. As time went on, *Details* became increasingly enamored of the female model made up to look like a battered old mannequin. Mark Healy, a *Details* editor, recalled that after a while, the shots of ruined and discarded women began to disturb him:

"I said, could we stop showing women as these broken creatures in seedy hotel rooms?"

Elevating the male sex star above the dancing girls became the veiled point of the magazine's most memorable feature: a regular column by Anka Radakovich, ostensibly about her sexploits with various men, in which the male viewer got to play Peeping Tom. But like DeMornay in *Risky Business,* Anka's persona in the column increasingly slipped into the comic-strip girl in heat, leering at the ornamentally superior men. Truman would've called that model "the whorehouse tramp," but that wasn't exactly the columnist's original intention. "I wanted to write about male behavior," Radakovich told me. "I find the behavior of men when they are sexually aroused funny." While "there was definitely a voyeuristic aspect to it," she said, "I wanted to do more of a participatory journalism." The participatory soon gave way to pure voyeurism, as the column became not so much an account of men and women's sexual interactions as a fixed spotlight on the stand-alone male sexual performer, like the former Chippendales dancer turned prostitute who regaled Anka and a friend with accounts of his moneymaking style. In a typical column, entitled "Voyeurvision," Anka bought a camcorder; after a self-inspection that ended in self-loathing (she recounted being revolted by the sight of her own unattractive body parts on film), she turned the lens on the naked guys in the next apartment and ultimately on a man she lured home, who willingly performed before the camera. Anka's column reached its logical endpoint in the June 1995 issue, when she dressed up as an unattractive, "sleazy" man and, after prowling stripper bars, capped the evening with a foray into a gay sex club to gape at the men in action.[113] What stuck in her mind later, she told me, was how "ugly" she had been made to look by the stylists who remade her as a man. "I looked so sleazy that I couldn't even get a cab home afterwards."

How Anka felt about her role at the magazine was murky. If she came off to her critics as a through-the-keyhole panter, then their double standard was to blame, she said. "I'm always having my morality questioned by the media. If a man is writing about sex he's a hero, but if a woman is writing about sex she's a whore." Playing her part as the female pornographer had become her bread and butter—the basis for two book deals and a movie deal about her life as a sex columnist. Privately, though, a *Details* editor recalled how she had complained that she "had been turned into a blow-up doll," and that a slathering Peeping Tomgirl "was not who she was." But in *Details,* women were relegated to the role men were fleeing: the ogling "sleazy" onlooker. The sex columnist had to be female—the senior men on the staff were clear on that point from the start. The voyeur was losing status in the new culture. There was no entitlement behind his gaze anymore; he was just a crummy consumer, and so it was reasonable to cede the position to a woman, while male readers were exhorted to emulate the "masculine" figure of the rock 'n' roll sex object who was gazed upon.

The *Risky Business* fantasy was replicated after a fashion at the magazine itself. James Truman was said to be fond of jaunts to lap-dancing clubs and cheesy topless bars. (He sent the magazine's best writer, Chris Heath, to write a feature on one of his favorite topless clubs, a gaudy Dallas flesh palace run by an ex–oil trader, where many of the women sported silicone implants.)[114] One year, Truman capped the staff Christmas party with a trek to the Baby Doll Lounge, a low-rent New York strip club. One of the few staff women in attendance, Maura Sheehy, recalled looking around in bafflement at the seedy surroundings: "There wasn't a whole lot to watch because it was all so low-budge'—with this one little runway the size of a desk, and the girls were not exactly the cream of the crop." But the fascination with such environs wasn't simply about old-fashioned leering: the *Details* men were there not so much to look as to be looked at. "It was almost like they thought they were on a stage set," Sheehy recalled of her fellow staffers parading around the Baby Doll Lounge, "like *they* were the ones on display—here we are in our nice clothes, looking superior. It always felt like that at *Details,* with every guy strutting around in his black clothes, making such an effort to be the cool, on-display man."

Among the male staff at *Details,* sex had become a weapon in a new kind of power play, one in which men were trying to reclaim ground they feared they were losing to women in an ornamental age. "The guys were the ones who always seemed to be shoving their sex in your face," another woman who worked at the magazine observed. "It wasn't that they really wanted to have sex with you or with anyone. They just wanted everyone to look at them." Some of the men on staff confirmed that view. "To me, what was distinctive about *Details* was its sexuality," John Homans, a former features editor, told me. "But it wasn't a magazine where everybody was fucking each other. They were constantly *performing* in this sexual way because they felt they had to. It felt forced and there was something unreal about it."

In the old *Details,* loosening up men's roles was connected to expanding women's options; gay liberation and feminism were two sides of the same coin. Stories in the new *Details,* however, tended to take a chilly view of feminism. "The ultimate problem with serious feminists—and we hate to make blanket statements—but the problem is, *they don't like guys that much,*" declared an August 1993 article by Blake Nelson. Remember, he advised, feminists believe that "you are expendable."[115] Women's freedom was now judged to be the flip side of men's uselessness. It was as if the *Details* editors believed that women's advancement in the workplace had left men with no place to go but the sexual stage, and that on this stage, women were not only competitors but, humiliatingly enough, arbiters of what constituted a manly performance. Women seemed to be in control wherever they looked. "Feminism has been crippling to my whole generation of men," Roger Trilling said, not so much by taking jobs but by making things "more morally and psychologically difficult for men." James Truman complained to me that he felt feminism had gone far beyond its original charter of "success in the workplace" for women. "Perhaps its ultimate victory is that it has come to *dominate* the culture," he said. "It doesn't seem to have made anyone very happy, though."

Eventually, the male staff even filmed their own version of *Risky Business,* a short starring Anthony Kiedis that opened (as a staff member described it to me) with the camera gazing at Kiedis passed out on a couch, his chest naked. He wakes up, and looks down to see a young woman—a *Details* fashion assistant at the time—lying on the floor asleep. He reaches down and removes her shirt, not to ogle her but to model it on himself, as if stealing the power of the sleeping beauty. Then the rock star leaves the apartment and gets picked up by rock musician Debbie Harry, playing the "idolmaker," who along with another woman dresses Kiedis in various clothes, gives him a makeover, and gets his hair done. He proceeds to a club where he performs, stripping down to his Calvin Klein underwear before he is chased down the street by a pack of admiring drag queens. It was a cinematic moment the Spur Posse would have envied, particularly since the *Details* men had the money at their disposal to do the film up right: the price tag, which staffers recall as being as much as six figures, was charged to the magazine's photography budget; a subsequent issue featured an eight-page layout of still photographs taken from the movie. "She said she'd make him a rock 'n' roll star," the layout's banner read. "He didn't know the price he'd have to pay."[116]

The reinvented *Details* had borrowed from the gay sensibility of the original magazine to make straight men feel commanding in a display culture. Truman said he had also made a point of hiring several "out" gay men and, in 1995, as Condé Nast editorial director, promoted gay staffer Joe Dolce to be editor in chief. But this show of gay-friendliness proved only skin deep. It was okay to be gay as long as that meant good taste in clothes, but the transgressive aspects of gay culture, no matter how subtly expressed, were not welcome.

Stephen Saban's campy style put him inevitably on the outs. "James basically castrated me," he said. Right after the Condé Nast takeover, Truman discontinued his column and redirected him toward what Saban called "masculine adventures," seemingly taking pleasure in dispatching the writer to places and events that made him feel uncomfortable. Saban's first assignment for the new magazine was to hang out with lumberjacks.[117] Inside the magazine's offices, he said, "I was basically excluded." His assistant was fired without his knowledge, Saban recalled; then Truman suggested that without an assistant he no longer really needed an office and could work from home — and his distinctive, intimate style disappeared under a hail of rewrites. "I wasn't allowed to be who I had been." Two years into the magazine's new era, Saban was demoted from associate editor to contributing editor, paid only by the story and with no benefits. A year later, Truman phoned Saban and, offering no reason, fired him. "We've come to the end of the road" was all he said, as Saban remembered. Later, Joe Dolce brought him back for a while as a contributor, but the damage had been done. Shamed and paralyzed by doubts about his writing ability, Saban spent years nearly unable to compose an article, ran out of money, and for a time had no place of his own to live. "I was broken," he said.

Details' editors also stripped out of its pages everything that wasn't commercial. Readers were no longer welcomed into a "community of people"; they were ushered into a shopping mall. This neutered gay sensibility, however, was evidently not as successful as its originators had hoped in making straight men feel like kings of an ornamental realm. In its calculated effort to draw "consumers," the magazine unwittingly fell into the miasma of the male dilemma. Trying to be ornamental without being acquiescent, trying to invent a dominant male grounded only in display, left the magazine floundering, stranded between two worlds.

Details' circulation stalled at the half-million mark — a respectable enough figure, but not in the Condé Nast "family," where the million-plus circulations of glossy women's magazines yielded huge advertising accounts. The company wanted to see *Details* increase its circulation by a hundred thousand readers as soon as possible. Truman responded by declaring the downtown scene, and implicitly his own previous pronouncements, "dead," and proclaiming work as the new way to be a *Details* rebel. "It's much sexier to be the next Bill Gates than the next band with a hot independent album," he announced.[118] But the subsequent careers issue, "Opportunity Rocks!," which spotlighted such "working" men as a floor supervisor at a Las Vegas casino and the *X-Files* actor David Duchovny (the issue's cover boy), was a dud.[119] Condé Nast then resorted to older and cruder formulas. After Dolce resigned, what was left of the gay sensibility was expunged. Instructions came down from company headquarters to "macho-up" the magazine.

Condé Nast had bought the old *Details* because the magazine's gay fashion sense seemed like an ideal vehicle, once the gay aspect was muted, for selling ornamentality to a much larger population of straight men. What the company didn't understand was that the old pre–Condé Nast *Details* had been grounded in a communal, not commercial, gayness. In that way, oddly enough, the original *Details* was closer to the old *Esquire* than to *Cosmo*. The traditional formula for men's magazines had been based on male utility: whether the *Popular Mechanics* version of building furniture in a home workshop or the *Esquire* version of critiquing and shaping civic life. Beyond showing men how to rebuild furnaces or how to size up a political trend, those magazines were utilitarian because they connected male readers to a larger public system. The editors of those magazines, and of the original *Details,* intuitively understood what the shapers of the new *Details* did not: that male utility is not only about finding work and being appreciated by women; it's about finding one's place in a societal structure.

Within the pages of the older men's magazines, the male reader found a place that conferred on him a sense of authority, based on knowledge and a feeling of control. He was in the know because the magazine showed him how the world worked, whether under the hood of his car or in the halls of Congress. He was in control because the magazine created an environment where the male gaze determined *what* and *who* were looked at. Male readers of the early *Esquire* inspected the Varga girl, and part of her appeal (lamentably) was that she didn't inspect them back. Her passive accessibility gave her male admirers the illusion of being in the driver's seat. The Varga girl was retired by the sixties, but *Esquire*'s stable of male writers in the magazine's heyday reinforced that one-way male gaze more effectively by their commanding and often withering inspections of prominent personages and social movements, presidential candidacies, Vietnam War atrocities, and antiwar campaigns. Norman Mailer and Tom Wolfe, Garry Wills and Terry Southern, Michael Herr, Gay Talese, and Gore Vidal pinned their subjects with knife-sharp scrutiny. With aggressively confrontational prose (which could at times be embarrassingly macho, not to mention sexist), *Esquire*'s writers were intent on challenging the culture, not just reflecting it, in articles in which it was always clear who was author, who was object. *Esquire* editor Harold Hayes observed that the "writer kings" he oversaw at the magazine saw themselves as central to events in that era: "freedom-riding down South, slogging through the Mekong Delta, marching on the Pentagon, backtracking Kansas killers, running from cops in Chicago and so on—keeping witness in the truest sense."[120] The cumulative effect was to place a frame around the public world that allowed male readers to feel that they, too, were bearing witness simply by reading the magazine; that they, too, were the critics, and not the critiqued.

Even then, though, the male-controlled, male-framed vantage point of men's magazines was already beginning to crumble. *Esquire*'s naughty twin, *Playboy,* had undermined it in ways that were as profound and permanent as they were discreet and deceptive at the time. The Varga-like voyeurism of *Playboy* seemed to be like *Esquire*'s, only more so—the centerfolds granted male readers photographic X-ray vision. But sandwiched in between the Playmates came the Playboy Philosophy, a vision of manhood that was enhanced not by knowing but by shopping.[121] *Playboy*'s ideal new man defined his masculinity only superficially by looking at women: he was to judge himself as much or more by having possessions worth looking at. You were a playboy because you displayed a roomful of playthings, not just the girls but the hi-fis, the latest jazz LPs, the Playboy cocktail set ("emblazoned in 22K gold . . . a must for the complete playboy," the magazine enthused), the Playboy Ski Sweater ("You'll appreciate the calculated comfort, special styling and smart good looks"), the New Playboy Shirt ("For those who desire the best in casual wear").[122] Just as the Bunnies displayed their cottontails, Hugh Hefner wanna-bes were expected to sport their silk pajamas. WHAT SORT OF MAN READS PLAYBOY? inquired the famous banner on the magazine's long-running promotional ads, accompanied by the answer: shots of suave hipsters in their decked-out bachelor pads, admiring their own ties, record collections, and all the accoutrements of an upwardly mobile, swingin'-single lifestyle. The *Playboy* reader, the ads advised, was the sort of man who "considers the right attire essential," who wants commodities "that will set him apart," and who "reflects taste in tune with his proven ability to acquire all the components of good living."[123] At its inception, *Playboy* was hailed by many liberal-minded male journalists as a courageous battering ram against American Puritanism, a perception that Hugh Hefner assiduously reinforced in his many media appearances decrying "our ferocious antisexuality, our dark antieroticism in America."[124] But the magazine proved to be less the advance guard of a sexual revolution than of a consumerist *Anschluss.*

Details and its genre ultimately picked up where *Playboy* left off, offering the same devil's bargain to its male readers: we'll help you pretend you're dressing to dominate, while we pretend that you're not being dominated while shopping for stereo equipment and "active wear." But the directives on shopping increasingly drowned out all other messages, and the pretense wore thin. Buried doubts gnawed and grew. The magazines told men that they could win women's approval by wearing the right clothes, striking the right pose, but making such a claim gave the lie to an older promise—that men would control the public gaze of inspection, that men would decide who and what got looked at.

The more abject the commercial surrender, the more sexual saber rattling was required to obscure it. One new men's magazine forcibly shifted the gaze back to women's bodies, and instantly became a hit. With plunging-cleavage covers and a leering attitude, *Maxim* was one of the early "lad" magazines, pioneered in England, to conquer American newsstands in the late 1990s; in a little more than a year, its circulation leaped from 175,000 to 950,000.[125] *Maxim* looked like a return to *Esquire*'s old Varga pinup approach, with men doing all the looking. The magazine had, in fact, managed to take one aspect of the old formula and inflate it to burlesque proportions. *Maxim* was *Esquire*'s degenerate distillation, all Varga and no Norman Mailer, a magazine to help its readers get in touch with their "inner swine," as *Maxim* editor Mark Golin (formerly deputy editor of *Cosmopolitan* magazine) gleefully put it.[126] ANY WOMAN ANY TIME, the banner headline on the March 1999 issue typically proclaimed. 8 PICK-UP TRICKS THAT NEVER FAIL (WE BAR-TESTED 'EM!). *Maxim* pretended to defeat the female gaze by outwitting it. The idea that women were something to be "tricked"—snookered, scammed, and bagged—prevailed in the magazine's pages: how to dupe your date into thinking you have a big career ("When your *real* job doesn't qualify, it's time to lie"), how to take advantage of the holiday-melancholic lonely girl, how to snake another guy's woman ("A no-fail plan for commandeering someone else's girlfriend").[127] *Maxim* helped its lads to imagine they were hunters once more, their prey the opposite sex. As a last blast of anachronistic masculinity, it was simpering and sneaky, but *Maxim* flew off the stands, and panicking men's magazines tried to follow suit with a bumper crop of cleavage.

At the floundering *Esquire*, which had already undergone several makeovers in the 1990s, the latest editor in chief, David Granger, devoted much of the February 1999 issue to what the cover announced as THE TRIUMPH OF CLEAVAGE CULTURE (with such stories as BREASTS, REASSESSED, A FEW WORDS ABOUT HER BREASTS, and A FEW WORDS ABOUT MY BREASTS), and filled issue after issue with interviews with supermodels and sniggering, swaggering accounts of penile conquest. At *GQ,* a similar panic button was hit—the babe-du-jour supermodel Heidi Klum was slapped on the January 1999 cover with the headline RHYMES WITH BOOM-BOOM.[128] At *Details,* a similar transformation was already under way. One afternoon in the summer of 1997, a month into the new regime of editor Michael Caruso, I watched while he and his art director, Robert Newman, designed an upcoming cover story. Before them was a sketch of the cover, an all-female assemblage of television stars in lingerie, entitled TV SLUMBER PARTY TONIGHT. Unless he could recruit sports stars or the occasional rocker, Caruso told me, covers for the foreseeable future would be returned to the female domain. The cover boy's day was done. Newman was pondering the composition. "Are they all going to be lying on the bed?" he asked Caruso. "Well, some can kneel," Caruso replied. "The bed should be huge."

The gaze, it seemed, had at last reverted to its traditional vector, the male eye viewing the female body. The advertising pages might still tell men they had to shop and dress and mousse to attract feminine approval, but the rest of the magazine now offered to avenge this humiliation. But women, whether dominant or submissive, oglers or ogled, were only stand-ins. The invasive, prying gaze that so unsettled men didn't really emanate from female eyes. It came from ornamental culture itself, from corporations and advertisers and publicists with their one-way mirrors and tabulations of you and your purchases. The male crotch could be replaced by the female breast on *Details'* cover, but no matter how many lingerie-clad babes knelt before the cameras, no matter how huge the bed, the corporate leer persisted. The cleavage shots were fig leaves, camouflage to hide from male readers their own fears of their own naked passivity in the face of display culture, their own prone positions as the objects of corporate desire. Ironically, the only real antidote to that passivity might have been political action and community involvement, precisely the elements of the old journalism that Condé Nast had stripped from *Details.* Whether the ostensible objects of desire in the new *Details* or *Esquire* or *GQ* were breasts or pecs, a male reader couldn't help but suspect as he leafed through his newest issue that he was not the hunter but the hunted, run to ground by the radar of reader surveys, demographic subscriber studies, and focus groups.

The magazine's staffers were as cheated as their readers. "I wanted to be that old *Esquire* style of literary journalist," Michael Caruso recalled morosely one morning shortly after he was named editor, as we sat in the SoHo Grand Hotel, a trendy establishment nearby. (The lobby was designed, for reasons best known to the architect, to look like a penitentiary—"prison chic," as Caruso put it. "All that's missing are the guards.") "It seemed like they had figured out a way for a man of letters to be a man of action," Caruso said of *Esquire*. "I grew up with this idea that journalism was this great adversarial system, and I could be this crusading journalist who saved the community." He gazed around at the designer prison mesh in the lobby. "This new boomlet of men's magazines, you can't feel manly about them." And it wasn't just the men's magazines; the whole world of journalism had reconfigured as a marketing vehicle for corporate-generated entertainment and celebrity. "There are a bunch of emasculating things about it," he continued. "There's just a lack of gravitas, a complete lack of importance. You can't write critically. And if you do, the risks are huge, even for small things. If you say a movie star took coke, even if he told you about it, you risk the wrath of PMK [the agency of Pat Kingsley, the preeminent Hollywood publicist]. So you have to make nice about someone you shouldn't even be writing about in the first place, and all because you fear you'll provoke a powerful person who is probably a female publicist."

Ultimately, however, it was the wrath of his male bosses that Caruso had to fear the most. Though circulation had jumped from 475,000 to 600,000 in his year-and-a-half tenure, a spectacular rise in magazine terms, Condé Nast's brass decided that he wasn't moving fast enough in the direction they wanted to go, remaking *Details* as a "lad" magazine. Like Joe Dolce before him, Caruso learned about his imminent career demise from media gossip. He phoned the executive suites to find out what the rumors meant, and was summoned to a meeting, where James Truman and Condé Nast president Steven Florio fired him. When he pressed for a reason, Caruso recalled, all Truman would say was, "I found the last couple issues heavy-handed," a view Caruso had hitherto not heard. The real reason became clear when the new editor of *Details* was announced: Mark Golin, the editor in chief of *Maxim*.

Details would still exist in name, though its essence had become the opposite of its original intent. The magazine's invasion of the "feminine" ornamental sphere had failed. But what if men actually stormed the battlements of display in person and found their way onto the stage of sexual performance? How gratifying might that be? Across the continent from Condé Nast headquarters, in a small corner of the San Fernando Valley, some men were finding out.

10

WAITING FOR WOOD

A Death on the New Frontier

FOR A GENERATION OF MEN who had to pursue their masculine destinies in a Planet Hollywood world, the journey often seemed almost an extension of that old TV series *Route 66*. Like that show's protagonists, they, too, often felt like orphans turning endlessly off some open road, pulling into unfamiliar towns, looking for fathers they could not find.

So many of the men I met as I began this book were still trying to find their manhood by finding their fathers. Shipyard workers sought their mentors in the craft shops; Gordon Dalbey and his Promise Keepers brethren reimagined their fathers in celestial form; David Morrell and Sylvester Stallone hoped to remake theirs on the printed page and the movie screen. They still wanted to believe in a patrimony, not of money but of know-how, the sort of secret knowledge that a father mastered and taught his son, the sort of knowledge that a son would know he had learned by the approving glint in his father's eye. By the attentive paternal gaze, they understood, they could measure their movement toward adult male society. But as this book—and the 1990s, and the male dilemma—progressed, the search for the father itself began to be abandoned. Many men seemed to lose sight of the first object of their search. Their journeys had run off the map. All that was left was the road, which, like the actual Route 66, seemed to end, literally for some, metaphorically for many more, in Hollywood.

Men who forsook their paternal quest had their reasons. Wherever they traveled, wherever they turned, all they could see was the blankness of a fatherless landscape. The paternal eye of society appeared to have vanished. What replaced it was a disembodied corporate onlooker that contemplated them in a wholly different manner. Historically, the paternal gaze had encouraged or judged, upbraided or approved, within a social context. As senior participants in a society, the fathers were assumed to know things that their sons needed to learn. But in an entertainment culture where youth was given an edge over age, in a technological culture where kids knew more about the newest gizmos than their elders, in a consumer culture where what was "needed" was the ability to buy, not produce, the father's eye was no longer a beacon; the experience and knowledge that a son might seek was no longer reflected there.

The sons, though, felt themselves to be under a new kind of inspection, a scrutiny that emanated from the lens of the camera. Most of them, of course, weren't literally the object of that gaze, but in late-twentieth-century America it was impossible to live without feeling either the heat of that spotlight or the chill of its neglect. That gaze, unlike the father's, *only* looked. It celebrated without comprehending. It had no knowledge to impart, couldn't teach or guide. This was not the eye of experience. All a man saw reflected there was a stand-alone, larger-than-life version of himself that was the image of masculinity in a display marketplace. The only way to amount to anything in this new world, it seemed, was to attract that unblinking eye, to make it swivel, however momentarily, in your direction. What seemed to matter most now was mastering the art of self-presentation, fathering your own image, reproducing a self that could be launched into a mediated existence. With manhood measured in such terms, the quest for the father no longer appeared so relevant to the quest for masculinity. Even if you found the father, what could he tell you? It was even odds that he knew less than you did.

By the mid-1990s, the media was full of quizzical and grumpy commentary about the proliferation of "permanent adolescent" men snickering and farting and mooning in an endless stream of movies, talk shows, sitcoms, and cartoons. "When did we become a nation of 12-year-olds?" culture writer Michiko Kakutani lamented in the *New York Times Magazine*—and as her examples, from *Beavis & Butt-head* to Howard Stern to

Jerry Seinfeld to Dennis Rodman, made clear, she meant a nation of twelve-year-old *men*. "The unspoken premise of much of American pop culture today," National Public Radio commentator Steven Stark wrote in an article in the *Atlantic Monthly*, "is that a large group of men would like nothing better than to go back to their junior high school locker rooms and stay there." But were men really retreating into a longed-for boyhood idyll, or were they advancing toward the only sort of masculinity that the culture now recognized? As successful manhood increasingly got measured by how much you were viewed, many men sought to draw the gaze in ways that didn't leave them feeling "emasculated," that made them feel they had captured the spotlight rather than succumbed to it. As Kakutani noted, when a market-research firm polled teenage boys on their aspirations, they rated "being funny as the personality trait they value most and being athletic as their most prized skill."[1] These young men understood that the wisecracking stand-up comedian and the muscle-bound sports star were the most watched and thus most highly valued male objects of our time.

The other attention-grabber obviously available to men in an ornamental culture was sexuality—an aggressive, ever-ready, action-packed display of it. Sexual performance was the quintessential response to commercial scrutiny, to the leer of the camera lens. The controlling angle of vision belonged to the corporate Peeping Toms. Not surprisingly, then, X-rated imagery soon migrated into mainstream culture. By 1999, the *New York Times* was pondering the rise of what it called "pornography chic": "the appropriation of the conventions of pornography—its stock heroes, its low-budget lighting and motel-room sets—by the mainstream entertainment industry, the fashion and fine-art worlds and Main Street itself." The article maintained that porn appealed because it was the outpost of the "perpetual renegade," a way to thumb one's nose at societal taboos.[2] That was undoubtedly one of its appeals, but quasi-pornographic display also provided a way to perform to the reigning culture's specifications, to be not a rebel but a courtier in a new mirrored palace.

The quest on which so many sons embarked by century's end was a search for how to be a man in a fatherless landscape. In that quest, they had to pass through a desolate geography monitored by a roving marketing eye, a journey that played in their psyches like a perpetual road movie. In its extremity, the search of the sons would take a few of them west on the Ventura Freeway, all the way to the Van Nuys Boulevard exit.

A Woodsman in a Microwave World

IF YOU TRAVEL UP VAN NUYS BOULEVARD to the 4500 block, you can meditate, like Ebenezer Scrooge, on the hollow murmurings and frenzied forebodings that are the ghosts of American commerce, past and future. This particular business strip belongs to the San Fernando Valley suburbs of Los Angeles, which means it could be anywhere. The east side of the street displays the flattened state of things to come: a blocklong minimall parking lot lined with consumer franchises—a Blockbuster Music store, a Baskin-Robbins, a Humphrey Yogart outlet, a General Cinema two-plex next to large signs announcing, coming soon, a General Cinema "Multi Theater Complex" offering A UNIQUE MOVIE GOING EXPERIENCE with FIVE MORE SCREENS, BIGGER AND BETTER. Across the street, on the west side, is the past, and crumpled newspapers and discarded Baskin-Robbins cups skitter up and down its crud-caked sidewalks. At the boarded-up entrances to former hardware stores and shoe-repair shops, where tradesmen's tools once clattered, clouds of gnats hover, making loitering unpleasant. The small independent businesses have abandoned the field. On the day I first passed through here in the winter of 1995, even a thrift store bore a FOR LEASE sign.

Only one veteran remains open for business, tucked away on a second floor, up a well-worn set of stairs. Behind an unmarked door lies a room the size and shabby complexion of a one-man private detective agency from another era; dust-covered vertical blinds quiver in the stale air circulated by a floor fan. A frayed gray-blue carpet with a permanent crease down the middle is held down by two chipped desks, each with an over-flowing ashtray and a five-line phone, which blinks and rings ceaselessly from nine to six. The company sign with its blue globe logo has presided over the street for most of the firm's nineteen years, an exemplar of discreet advertisement from a more decorous time: FIGURE PHOTOGRA-PHY FILMS. WANTED: FIGURE MODELS FOR IMMEDIATE PLACEMENT. 986-4316. SUITE 203. The ad belongs to the World Modeling Talent Agency, central casting for the nation's pornographic film, video, and magazine industries.

The agency has survived, despite the old-fashioned propriety of its sign, by accommodating the forces unleashed across Van Nuys Boule-vard. In a world where desire is packaged in videocassettes and marketed in malls, where self-worth is quantified by exposure, World Modeling has become the last-chance opportunity for a generation desperately seeking "immediate placement." It is a backstage door to the current

American dream and an emergency escape hatch for some who find themselves capsizing in a reconfiguring American economy. Which is why, by the last decade of the century, World Modeling would become a mecca beckoning not just women but men. More men, in fact, than women; more men than this industry of feminine display could even begin to absorb.

Every two or three months, the hopeful troop here for "talent call," a day when prospective "new talent" can market themselves to porn filmmakers and photographers, and old talent can refresh their connections. Talent call is by invitation only; otherwise, World Modeling would have to rent out the Hollywood Bowl to process the hordes of hopeful performers who phone here daily. On this particular day in February 1995, fifteen minutes after the agency's doors opened, the stairs, the hallways, the main room, and an adjacent balcony were already dense with bodies. In this sea of fishnet and spandex and Nautilus-assisted torsos, the hopefuls darted about like nervous but directionless schools of fish seeking sustenance. There was an overpowering smell of tanning oil and cheap cologne, and, above it all, a ceaseless din, the sound of forced laughter, as from strangers trapped at a cocktail party—in this case, without the cocktails.

In the dead center of this restless throng, one job applicant stood motionless, his slacks neatly pressed, his shirtsleeves rolled back to display ever-flexed biceps. He was a thirty-ish young-old man with a tanning-salon bronze, a buzz cut, and a smile gamely plastered on his face. He cracked his knuckles methodically as his searchlight eyes roved the crowd for a welcoming face—he found none—and scanned the framed glossy photos of moneymaking stars on the agency's walls, none of whom were male.

"This is my first time," the aspirant, who identified himself as Damon Rose, told me. He had been trying to get the agency's attention for two years now, he said. He did not, on the face of it, seem the type to be pursuing a career in porn. The son of a conservative San Diego orthopedic surgeon, he possessed, at the age of thirty-one, a sociology degree from the University of California at San Diego, an enrollment certificate from the executive M.B.A. program at Pepperdine University, and a recently expired real-estate license to practice in the state of California. "All my education is for naught," Rose said. It had landed him a job as marketing director for a surfboard retailer, which yielded him an income insufficient to meet his student-loan payments. The selling of his own physique, on the other hand, had proved more remunerative; his résumé included, so far, basic training as a Chippendales dancer, three years in which he ran his own "male-exotic-dance service for women," and, most recently, a modeling assignment for a phone-sex ad. He posed naked underwater, cradling a telephone receiver.

"I was born to do this," he said repeatedly, rehearsing his enthusiasm in preparation for the audition he hoped to land in one of the agency's two tiny back rooms, where production-company executives had set up camp for the afternoon. After several failed attempts at "making contacts" in the main room, Damon Rose joined the crowd outside one of the closed doors in the back. But he was passed over again and again as the door flew open, a voice boomed, "New girl, please!" and another spangled woman elbowed by him. A despairing Rose turned to the closest actress, who was shellacked in hair spray and leaning against the wall. "You want to give me some pointers?" he appealed. She looked him over grudgingly, as if she were doing him a favor to lift her eyelids. "Just get it hard," she said. Then she turned on her heel and vanished.

The other men in the hallway kept their distance. Stag films may once have served as the male-bonding glue of bachelor parties, but today, at least in the occupational end of modern porn, male performers face each other with Darwinian teeth bared, aware of their endangered status. "Actresses have the power," Alec Metro, one of the men in line, ruefully noted of the X-rated industry. He had sold mattresses previously, he said without irony, and before that worked as a firefighter, an occupation he claimed to have lost to the forces of affirmative action. "No one said it, but it's known they are looking for more minorities and women," he said bitterly of the all-white fire department in his hometown, which, he asserted, had rejected his application when he had tried to transfer from the San Jose Fire Department. But if he hoped to escape "reverse discrimination," he was already divining that porn might not be the ideal career choice. Female performers can often dictate which male actors they will and will not work with. "*They* refer *us*," Metro said. "*They* make more money than *us*." Porn, at least porn produced for a heterosexual audience, is one of the few contemporary occupations where the pay gap operates in women's favor; the average actress makes 50 to 100 percent more money than her male counterpart. But then, she is the object of desire; he merely her appendage, the object of the object.

By now, the door to the back room had opened and slammed shut in Damon Rose's face five times. He wouldn't let it happen again, he vowed. When the next new girl was ushered in, Rose slipped in right behind, riding her sequined coattails.

Inside, the porn production scouts sat on a foam-spitting couch and folding chairs. They barely glanced up as Damon Rose made his pitch. Maybe it was his voice, straining to please, that dampened their interest. Or maybe it was his look. Jack Stephen, of Cinderella Productions, muttered to me behind his hand: "We get these beautiful buffed guys, but they can't *do* it. They're just fluff. These new guys come apart like a bad suit."

Damon Rose was speaking to them earnestly: "I've only done one thing through Ron Vogel—for phone sex—but otherwise I'm a virgin. But I'm—" The producer Mitch Spinelli interrupted, "Thank you, Damon," eyes craning over his shoulder for the next prospect. The porn producer and actor Steve Drake called out, "New girl, please!"

Damon Rose slunk out shamefaced, flung back into the masses in the main room, where I spotted him busy converting hurt to aggression. He had sneaked up behind an actress and grabbed her breasts. She shook him off, then turned to appraise his pectorals. "Your boobs are bigger than mine," she said. He laughed uncertainly, then wandered off, his face sunk in despair.

In the hallway by the stairs, Tyffany Million, one of a small but growing number of female porn stars who have stepped into the role of producer, scrutinized the new talent. She was unimpressed. "I won't use a guy who's brand-new," she said. "Their performance is too unpredictable." Million was joined by the ponytailed Nick East, a proven performer. "This is a lot different than my talent call," he told her. "There were only two to three guys. Now, there's guys everywhere."

East speculated that the increase was due to all the "publicity" from soft-core adult cable channels, from Spice to Playboy to Showtime, whose *Red Shoe Diaries* was one of its highest-rated programs. "So many guys see it and say, 'Hey, I could be a *star*.'" He rolled his eyes. "Guys are coming in with different ideas of what it means to be the guy in porn." East sketched out for me what he regarded as the three evolutionary stages of the modern porn man. "The first batch," he said, referring to the male initiates of the seventies, "came in wanting to be real actors. The second batch"—and here he pointed to himself as a representative—"came in to be lazy and have a great easy job. But the third batch came in to make a name for themselves."

The first batch, actors like John Leslie, Paul Thomas, and Eric Edwards, had been legitimate theatrical actors on and off Broadway—Paul Thomas was in the original Broadway productions of *Hair* and *Jesus Christ Superstar*. That generation wound up in porn films partly to make a living and partly out of a vaguely political urge to rebel, or at least revel in the freedom of the sexual revolution. This was the heady Golden Age of porn feature films invoked by such surprise mainstream successes as *Behind the Green Door* and *Deep Throat*. The second generation, drawn by a mid-eighties boom in video porn, saw X-rated performance as a low-rent version of that era's Wall Street ethic, just a quick and undercapitalized way to "make a lot of money," as East said. But this third generation was another story. This was their chance at televised notoriety, their bid for celebrity as famous phalluses, Natural-Born Drillers. It was their way of crossing Van Nuys Boulevard.

"The first and second batch of guys made it because they didn't care," East said, an allusion to their lack of performance anxiety; they didn't care because the whole experience was a goof or a quick buck. "But the third batch . . ." East stopped and, frowning, looked away, leaving the unfinished sentence hanging in the air. Tyffany Million briskly changed the subject. She knew what he was thinking, what a lot of the male performers had been thinking recently: that the third generation cared too much and that caring was dangerous.

In the agency's main room, barely visible on a low side table tucked behind a stack of porn magazines and a shedding ficus plant, sat a large snifter glass. It contained not brandy but dollar bills. A handmade label taped to it said FOR CAL. It was a collection plate of sorts for one of the generation of actors who "cared too much." Cal Jammer had succeeded where Damon Rose could only aspire. And two weeks before, he had committed suicide, at the age of thirty-four.

———

SOMEWHERE BETWEEN the 12th Annual Adult Video News Awards ceremony in January 1995, which coincided with the Winter Consumer Electronics Show in Las Vegas, and an afternoon spent with Bill Margold, self-appointed "daddy" to many porn actors, a month later, I began to get a glimmer of the landscape the new young men of modern porn were struggling to traverse: a treacherous terrain that had more to do with work than sex, more to do with gender identity than genital excitement. It was also a terrain more relevant to the larger working male population than most men would care to contemplate, just as the death of Cal Jammer had less to do with pornography than with the franchise economy on Van Nuys Boulevard and the great celebrity-making machine created in the Hollywood studios.

Though its organizers are loath to admit it, the Consumer Electronics Show, the product presentation of the electronics industry, also hosts the annual exhibition of porn—a rare public opportunity to survey the fruits of porn's huge but hidden market, an estimated $4.2 billion annual business whose product accounts for more than a quarter of all rentals and sales at the average video store.[3] On a rain-drenched Saturday, sodden but determined pilgrims from the Consumer Electronics Show trooped to the porn exhibition at the Sahara Hotel, in numbers so vast that by midafternoon the hotel's security guards had to bar access to the hall. Those who made it inside jostled past novelty booths advertising "Pin the Macho on the Man" games and "Growing Pecker" blow-up dildos to line up before autograph booths featuring porn starlets. While the lines for Kirsty Waay, Lexus Locklear, and even for some unknown actresses snaked around the corner, the male actors had to work the crowd to drum up signature requests. Only one man had a line, but he was a man known for a member that didn't work: John Wayne Bobbitt was here to promote his recently released sex video.

That evening, the talent reconvened in a ballroom at Bally's Hotel for the awards ceremony. The older men, casual in rumpled jackets, treated the awards as the ludicrous honors that they were—"Best Anal-Themed Feature!" "Best Specialty Tape: Spanking!"—and headed for the bar. The younger ones, with their gelled hair and their designer shirts partly unbuttoned to display waxed chests, sipped mineral water and discussed their "five-year game plan," "career moves," and the possibility of merchandising items like boxer shorts with their names on them. Sean Michaels, a porn actor and director who was one of the first to market such designer underpants, ascended the stage in a tux to be inducted into the Adult Video News Hall of Fame, and asked his mother to stand and be recognized for "giving me strength." Then, nodding regally to what he called "my constituency," he moved slow as a wedding barge through the crowd of onlookers, trailing cologne.

The young men's how-I-got-here stories were of a piece. They had all bailed out of sinking occupational worlds that used to confer upon working men a measure of dignity and a masculine mantle but now offer only uncertainty. Steven St. Croix (who, like every porn actor, adopted a name to go with his new persona) went to vocational school to be a mason, but all the job openings he found involved busing tables or washing dishes. Stripping, then porn acting, gave him a livelihood, and "recognition." Julian St. Jox was an Army Airborne Ranger, but once he entered civilian life he found that his job as a bartender wouldn't pay the rent. "Porn pays the bills," he said. Vince Voyeur, twenty-nine, worked for four years as a forklift mechanic, one of the men who "built things," he said, before realizing that such men belong to a rapidly receding past.

"WHO KNOWS WHO BUILDS THINGS? Who cares?" Bill Margold said to me as we sat in his cat-hair-strewn apartment a month later. Margold, who was fifty-two, joined the porn industry in 1969, and moved from scriptwriter to performer to unofficial papa of distressed porn stars. He invited despondent actors here to hug one of the scores of teddy bears he had collected for this purpose. As we spoke, a perpetually yowling tomcat called Pogo competed for his owner's attentions, storming from chair to chair, his switching tail knocking porn glossies and adult magazines to the floor. It used to be, Margold said between fruitless efforts to shush the cat, that you proved your manhood by building things. "That was the artisan mentality. That doesn't exist anymore. We live in a microwave-oven mentality. Before you even think about it, it's already there on the table. It's all too fast now. There's no time to even watch it be created." In a microwave-ready culture, building is "not proving anything." The "new Paul Bunyan," Margold said, was the man who displayed his big ax. "Better to wield the ax than create from what the ax has cut, because that's the center of attention." Young men flocked to porn, he said, to become that new "woodsman," the industry's term for a reliable male performer—the lumberjack whose penis was his hatchet.

Of course, the porn industry has its old-fashioned artisans, he assured me. Cal Jammer, in fact, had been one, an electrician, set designer, and general handyman as well as a performer. Margold had met Cal Jammer on the set of *Aussie Exchange Girls,* and he recalled Cal's eager, almost desperate need to please. "Basically he was a sheepdog that didn't know when to stop licking your hand." Margold jerked his head in the direction of the caterwauling Pogo. "It's like this cat, essentially, only this cat is not as good-natured." At that, the cat made a lunge for Margold's chest, and the exasperated porn daddy hurled Pogo into the kitchen. Returning to his chair, Margold turned pensive and glum. He stared silently into a far corner of the room, where the evening shadows were stealing across a row of teddy bears.

"I lament that I wasn't there for Cal," he said finally. The night after Cal's death, Margold got two calls from anguished performers, one at two and the other at three in the morning, wanting to know why Cal did it and if they should do it, too. Margold had set up a hot line the year before, after the suicide of the female porn star Savannah. Porn actresses' committing suicide was a concept the industry veterans understood; they'd seen it before. But for a male actor to despair, to exit the stage so violently—what did it mean? When did *they* begin to care so much? And why, in the winter and spring of 1995, did the men of porn care so much about Cal Jammer, a man whom most of them found irritatingly clingy and had known only casually, but whose name now provoked teary diatribes, fists slammed into walls?

Cal Jammer—or Randy Potes, as he was called until he entered the business in 1987—was one of five boys of a navy veteran turned physics professor and a mother who worked at the General Motors plant in Van Nuys. When he was still young, his parents divorced and his father retreated from their lives. More recently, the GM plant had closed and his mother had gone back to community college for "retraining." The brothers all had trouble finding work; the most successful became a school janitor. Cal's strength and dexterity lent themselves to skilled labor and athletics. He worked on construction crews, installed solar panels, and, when he wasn't working, surfed and Jet Skied. In the late eighties, he got work building sets for a porn-photo studio, began modeling there, and soon thereafter became obsessed with finding his place before the camera. He could see that what counted was not building the stage but appearing on it.

Cal's journey from the Santa Clarita Valley, where he grew up, to the San Fernando Valley was a short one, but his other journey—from building sets to posing on them, from being a golden boy on California's surfing coast to being a man marketing himself as the very image of a California surfer—was epic. The riptide of celebrity culture, whether it surged over pornography or professional sports, aerospace corporations or magazine offices, seemed to be reversing an ancient force field, and the "male gaze" felt its strength ebbing before the rising power of the woman on display. In truth, that gaze had never given men more than a fleeting sense of power, just as being gazed upon still gave women only an illusory power. But these were fine distinctions to men like Cal Jammer. For them, it was plain that the "feminine" ornamental occupations they had disparaged had become employment oases. It was like consigning the Indians to the barren desert, only to discover oil on the reservation.

Porn might seem to be the one "profession" on which the ascendancy of ornamental culture would have little effect. Wasn't it already a realm of total display? But like everything else, modern porn has a history, and it is a chronicle of formative changes, induced by the same celebrity forces operating everywhere else. Even within the X-rated hothouse, the new cultural dictates were taking their toll.

As Nick East had sensed, the 1970s generation of male porn performers subscribed to a very different ethic. "We were all experimenting back then," Eric Edwards, a porn actor from the Golden Age, said. "It was a fun time, an experiment, like taking LSD." One doesn't want to overstate the insurgent attributes of that porn era: the dissent, if you could call it that, didn't much register on the larger political stage, and the experimentation often amounted to little more than exploitation, especially when applied to women. As Linda Lovelace, the "star" of *Deep Throat,* made clear in her autobiography, *Ordeal,* she was not having a "fun time."[4] Nonetheless, the actors themselves weren't in it for the ratings — or the money, which was minimal. What some porn performers did get out of the experience was a sense of belonging to and participating in a tightly woven society; they were players in an X-rated version of a repertory company.

In these years, porn transformed itself from short, silent "loops" of film shot hastily in back rooms to full-length features with a "narrative" and a full cast. In porn director Harold Lime's trend-setting films of the late 1970s, *Desires Within Young Girls* and *The Ecstasy Girls,* however crude they were by Hollywood standards, men and women jump in and out of the sack but also have relationships, a range of interactions, and plot complications. (*The Ecstasy Girls* even sends up a Jerry Falwell–style patriarchal religious figure named Edgar Church.) The filming took place over weeks or even months, not days, and there was time for spontaneity and improvisation in the bedroom scenes. "It was much more leisurely," longtime porn star Nina Hartley recalled to me, "and it was more of a camp where you hung out, had camaraderie." It wasn't wall-to-wall sex, and most critically for the male performers, evaluating the performance of the *man* in the sack was not the point. Quite a few of the films of that era didn't even bother with the now de rigueur "money shot": the close-up of the ejaculating penis. In straight porn, at least, the male actors weren't exactly on display. Rarely dolled up, they were slovenly stand-ins for male viewers. In these early films, the male actors generally appeared oblivious to the camera; they weren't meant to be an attraction, much less the main attraction, only the most privileged witness, the voyeur with the best seat in the house.

In the eighties, the VCR put the seedy porn theater out of business, while turning porn itself into a mass-marketed product and unleashing a merger-and-acquisition binge in the industry, a binge similar to that convulsing the mainstream entertainment business in the same decade. The "video revolution," as it was known in the porn world, "changed everything," Ira Levine, a longtime porn screenwriter and director, told me. "It began the advent of consumer porn, user-friendly porn that people could take home and pop into their VCRs. . . . Up until then, the numbers had always been very small, and the profits were measured in thirty thousand dollars, fifty thousand dollars. Now we're talking about CD-ROMs and hotels and satellites and cable. This is what has produced the corporate culture of porn as it now exists."

At these big new porn corporations, the executives were more likely to act and dress as if they were managing Sony, not Sin City Video. The distributors now wore Ralph Lauren suits, drove BMWs, and, as Levine put it, "work in nice little offices full of golf trophies." At VCA Pictures, one of these blandly named behemoths, president Russ Hampshire ushered me into his pristine corner office, which had a boardroom table, presidential desk, and not a sign or scent of porn anywhere. He did, however, have on display a framed collection of photos of himself and his son attending the World Cup. He was wearing a United Chamber of Commerce Golf Classic shirt, and he wanted to talk not about sex but about corporate perks. "We probably have better benefits than most companies," he told me, ticking off the medical and dental policies before taking me on a tour of the recently refurbished production plant. When we reached the "slave room," a reference not to captive actors but to the two thousand machines running off dupes of master videos, Hampshire asked me to wait outside for a moment while he made sure that no unseemly visions danced on the monitors. "I don't want to embarrass you," he said with Procter & Gamble earnestness. I assured him that was unlikely, seeing as how I'd already attended several porn shoots, but he was as adamant as a Lutheran minister. "I do it as a common courtesy," he said. When I reviewed my notes later, I realized that in the entire conversation, he had uttered not a single sexual word.

Bill Margold told me he feared that the industry was falling prey to "the feminization of Hollywood." "I defy you to name one really rugged masculine hero in Hollywood," he fumed at me on another afternoon. "Eastwood's too old now. Brad Pitt, who probably could be a contender, is just too damn pretty. What is this rush to trying to be female? These men have no flaws because they're being designed almost as if they're women. Where have all the men gone?" And he saw it happening in his world, too. "Even this business is losing its masculine fiber. We're being absorbed into the mainstream, which terrifies me." The X-rated shelves were overrun now with what Margold disgustedly called "coffee-table porn"—prettified, MTV-style adult videos produced for the "couples market" or big-budget designer erotica featuring faux-aristocratic ladies cavorting and contorting under chandeliers, X-rated versions of Victoria's Secret ads.

With the rise of the corporate powers in porn came an economic polarization no different than the one in the broader economy. In the left-behind end of the porn world, a slew of low-rent producers began churning out rock-bottom-cheap videos featuring harsh sex for a more despairing, downwardly mobile market. Porn director Ron Sullivan, a.k.a.

Henri Pachard, one of the market's bottom-feeding architects, called it "the hard-core, in-the-toilet type of up-against-the-wall bookstore product." The basement version of porn is all visuals, no narrative, and favors a brute sort of "masculine" display, where the man wields his penis like a whip and where sex tends to end in the "pop face"—an angry version of the money shot, where the man splatters the woman's face. That shot was so common in the low end of the market that some of the cameramen I met referred to it in shorthand: "Get a pop face 'n' go." Some low-end porn is, in fact, just a pastiche of money shots without any context, an endless reel of exploding geysers—"the triumph of the dick," as porn screenwriter Ira Levine sarcastically put it.

The advent of cheap video production introduced a wedge that now threatens to break the porn world in two. "There's going to be two ends of the business," porn actor turned director Buck Adams said. "It'll be those who are doing 'The Project' and those who are doing the garbage. And there won't be any middle ground. And that's when I think this situation might get even more scary." While the corporate porn makers were raking in breathtaking profits, the low end was morphing into "the flesh eaters," Adams said. "One half of the industry is eating itself, eating each other's legs off." He waved his arms in frantic praying-mantis motions. "More, more sex, sex, sex, sex! And sell it for a dollar ninety-eight and sell ten bazillion copies of it, and make six cents a tape and we are going to make fifty dollars at the end of the month!" What scared him most was the effect on the male talent. "There's getting to be a real wide gap in the performers. Either you're bitchin', got everything, and you are in, or you're just missing one piece so you're out."

The modern male porn actor confronted an impossible career obstacle course. He could try to make it as a money-shot man, a "pop face 'n' go" guy of hydraulic regularity, known for his heroic capacity to come on a dime. A money-shot man, or "Mr. Wood," as Buck Adams called him, wouldn't be paid much in the nether reaches of porn, where he'd do most of his work, but he could take pride in the fact that it was his masculine prowess on display, pumping away like a well-oiled machine. The money-shot men considered themselves the last workingmen of America. They were like "blue-collar people, welders," another porn actor turned director, Paul Thomas, told me. They were defending traditional manhood by showing that the one irrefutable proof of genetic maleness was up and running. "We're the last bastion of masculinity," Bill Margold, a proponent of the in-the-toilet variety of porn, insisted. "The one thing a woman cannot do is ejaculate in the face of her partner. We have that power."

But if a male performer really wanted to rise, if he wanted to become a "star" in what Buck Adams called "The Project," instead of one of the welders in "the garbage," wielding the punisher simply wasn't enough. Big-budget porn demanded of its male actors not just sexual performance but cosmetic adornment. The men who rose to the top were those men who could compete with the women in their own realm, not ejaculate in their faces.

The 1992 adult film *Chameleons,* directed by former porn star John Leslie, presented a futuristic male nightmare of where such a "feminization" of porn might lead. The leading lady's vampiric effort to occupy her lover's body first saps his energies, sending him to bed with the vapors, then threatens to kill him outright. "It's either me or you," she tells him, "and I have to survive." In their final struggle, the male lover saves himself, but only by transforming himself into a woman.

Fear of that metamorphic dislocation underlay the heat with which many male porn stars discussed the Cal Jammer story: they attributed his death to the violence of the gender battle he had been swept up in; that is, they blamed his wife. After a yearlong affair with Cameo, a fledgling porn actress, Cal had married a stripper named Jill Kelly. She launched a porn career of her own just after the couple separated in late 1994 — and, according to the men of porn, crushed her husband in the process. "She destroyed him," one of the men told me. "She might as well have put the gun to his head," another said. This was a convenient fiction that quickly became the industry men's party line. But, as a grieving Jill Kelly observed to me later, the men who put forth this line had "no idea" what had passed between her and Cal, nor could they fathom the depths of her own devastation. The only fact that anyone could state for sure was that on January 25, 1995, Cal Jammer stood on the sidewalk outside Jill Kelly's home, held a gun to his right temple, and pulled the trigger.

———

DEEP IN THE SAN FERNANDO VALLEY is an area where the strip malls and condo communities drop away to reveal a prairie of electronic plants and business-park tiltups, all metallic and windowless and low to the ground. One such warehouse contained Trac Tech, the only professional soundstage in the porn industry. The photographer Ron Vogel had opened it a few years ago, to serve the expanding needs of upmarket porn production. Cal Jammer had been modeling for about a year when Vogel, aware of his experience in construction, appointed him the studio's master builder. For Cal, the assignment was a calling. To provide the industry with its own state-of-the-art soundstage became his all-consuming vocation. "The epitome of all that epic drama," Vogel recalled to me, "was the ceiling." For ten days, Cal lay on his back on a scissor lift, twenty-six feet in the air, stapling special sound-enhancing insulation to the five-thousand-square-foot ceiling. The project required more than twenty-five thousand staples. "It was a superhuman effort," Vogel said, "Cal Jammer's Sistine Chapel."

Two days after Jammer's death, I visited Trac Tech to observe the shooting of an upscale production. *Cyberella,* a porno version of "*Barbarella* in outer space," as crew member Raven Touchstone described it, involved a female cyber-agent who travels through history fighting evil and "saves the world." The production company was industry titan VCA, and the corporation's healthy balance sheet was evident in the lavish backdrops and the substantial crew, including assistant and technical directors, multiple cameramen and technicians, a stylist, and a caterer.

This afternoon, the crew was shooting a scene in which a "Who's Sexier?" contest is broadcast into cyber-space. The scene's main attraction was Sunset Thomas, VCA's current hot commodity, a young woman whose prime selling point—though none of the corporate suits would admit it—was her teenage appearance. That feature was amplified this day by her hairstyle—bangs and two bobbed ponytails, à la Cindy Brady—and a cheerleader's outfit. She was playing Susie Flatbush, a contestant in the competition. The long-standing and ubiquitous male actor Ron Jeremy was to play the contest's master of ceremonies. Cast as the competition's judge was Zack Adams, who in real life was Sunset's husband and "manager." Behind the cameras, members of the crew were muttering ominously. Husbands, as one of the technical-crew members informed me, rarely functioned well with their wives on camera.

A porn shoot is an intricately delineated ecology. Directors, while still more or less on top, have increasingly been challenged by the rise of the "contract" and "box-cover girls," of whom Sunset Thomas is one. With the advent of video, the box, not its contents, generally sells the product, which means that the box-cover girl can sometimes trump her supposed bosses. The big porn companies court this woman's favor by offering her a generous contract (by porn standards) in return for "exclusivity." While the number of highly paid box-cover girls is small, their presence seems vast and domineering to male actors, who speak resentfully of the women's rising fees and prima-donna airs. The contract girls at Vivid, another industry giant, are perceived as the most indulged; I'd heard them referred to as the "Vivid Queens." "In the porno chain of command," actor Jonathan Morgan said to me bitterly one evening over drinks, the contract girl "can choose who she wants to fuck, where she wants to fuck, the script that she wants to fuck in, what day they are going to fuck."

Unlike the top female performers of the 1970s, such as Georgina Spelvin (*The Devil in Miss Jones*) and Marilyn Chambers (*Behind the Green Door*), who actually styled themselves as actresses and sexual adventurers, the contract girls are undressed-for-success career women, making a calculated professional move that will get them into and out of the porn film industry as quickly as possible and inflate their long-term salaries as exotic dancers. "They are purely mercenary," porn star Nina Hartley, who belonged to the earlier era, said of those she contemptuously called "postfeminist princesses"; she viewed them as hypocrites who got financial independence by playing to retro male fantasies. "They are very traditional. They are not sexual revolutionaries." With the explosive growth of table- and lap-dancing stripper clubs, large numbers of dancers have realized that they can quadruple their income simply by appearing on a few porn box covers. They then become "feature dancers" who return to the circuit to make as much as $10,000 a week. This kind of windfall is not available to men, with the exception of a few gay porn stars.

Under the directors and the contract girls is the reliable "male talent," fewer than thirty regulars whom the industry can count on for on-call erections. On the *Cyberella* set, Ron Jeremy was holding down that position, as he had in more than one thousand movies, an industry record. Unlike the younger men of the business, who seemed to be constantly at the gym or the cosmetic surgeon's office, the middle-aged Ron Jeremy was hirsute and flabby, an unapologetic glutton who could care less about his gut. He was known as "The Hedgehog" in the industry. He lived, it seemed, to gross people out. One of his proudest stunts is auto-fellatio. (A few weeks after the shoot, he invited me to his apartment to watch a videotape of a *Beavis & Butt-head* segment in which they sniggered endlessly about Jeremy's paunch. "Isn't this great?" Jeremy crowed, as he sat on the floor before his wide-screen TV, devouring an entire platter of bagels, lox, and cream cheese, which was supposed to be brunch for three. "I don't care what they say about me," Jeremy said cheerfully, as he snaked his tongue along the empty bottom of the deli cream-cheese container, "as long as they spell my name right.")

Male actors are generally paid by "the scene," as it is decorously called. No ejaculation, no paycheck — though some of the more sympathetic filmmakers offer a kill fee. The pressure is too much for most male performers. As much as the Bill Margolds might wish to portray porn acting as the last arena of the traditional male work ethic, getting it up isn't the kind of work in which industry guarantees rewards. Quite the contrary, by choosing an erection as the proof of male utility, the male performer has hung his usefulness, as porn actor Jonathan Morgan observed, on "the one muscle on our body we can't flex." The beautiful woman in a porn film applies her glamour from a bottle and she's ready; the man must wait for an erection to happen, an agony known in the business as "waiting for wood."

Ranked just beneath the upper tier of male "talent" is a seething, ever-changing mass of B-girls or "fill-in girls," many of whom either stumble onto the set hollow-eyed and strung out or don't bother to stumble in at all. They are endured as the necessary bane of porn's existence, and disparaged behind their backs—or eventually fired. Below the B-girls, way below, are the new male wanna-bes, who, if they don't perform, are immediately sent packing. Finally, at the very bottom, the lowest of the low, are the "suitcase pimps." These are the husbands and boyfriends who claim to be "managers" or "marketing directors" for their eminently more marketable mates. Increasingly, they insist not only on a cut of their women's wages but a spot in the camera lights as well.

Off on a side track is the far less hierarchical and more jaundiced society of the technical crew: camera operators, assistant directors, box-cover photographers, and the various production assistants known as "crew hogs." Some are young film-school graduates who discover upon graduation that they can go to Warner Bros. and carry coffee or report to 4-Play Video and start as a senior editor. On the set, their moods range from affectlessness to acid sarcasm, both a protective pose and a reasonable response to the fact that watching sex performed for a camera quickly becomes dreary.

On the VCA set this afternoon, nerves were already strained. Ron Jeremy had vanished, just as his scene was at hand. Probably went to stuff his face, growled the crew hogs. Hours passed. Around 4 P.M., just as the crew had given up and had started to set up the brass bed for the following scene, Jeremy resurfaced. He jumped into his costume—a cheap, shiny tux, gold lamé cummerbund, pointy shoes, and gigantic sequined glasses—and bounded onstage to pronounce the start of "The Battle of the Cheerleader and the Nurse." "Strip!" he bellowed with the broad gestures of a circus clown. As the nurse and cheerleader climbed out of their respective costumes and clambered on Zack the judge, the director called out, over and over, "Lots of soft, guys," a reminder that while *Cyberella* would be released as a hard-core video, the needs of the thriving cable and hotel business must be kept in mind. The version recut for TV would have to be entirely "soft," which meant, among other things, no erect penises and no semen.

With the "dialogue" scene, such as it was, completed, the crew hogs hauled in the bed for the main event. Zack Adams stood to one side, psyching himself up for the money shot. "Nobody says that *we* do all the work," he said to me—a common male actors' lament. "The industry is very tough for men. The slightest thing you do wrong, you don't work." Zack said he got into the business after bringing Sunset out to Los Angeles to do modeling, then B-movies, and, when none of that panned out, porn. Zack had a degree in business management from the University of Maryland, and had been, he said, a business consultant for ten years, mostly to clothing retailers. "Marketing is my speciality. Now I market Sunset" and six other women in the industry. While he acted in porn films, too, his and Sunset's marketability—and their wages—were miles apart. She could make more than $4,000 a day on a shoot; he was lucky to make $300 a scene. Zack first entered the business, he admitted, on the back of Sunset. "It's very hard to break in if you don't come in through a girl." And hard to stay in without a woman's support. "Ninety percent of the work I get is from women. They pick the men they are going to work with, especially the contract girls. They have a lot of authority." It used to be the man got a job to win the girl; now he must win over the girl to get the job.

Zack said he rarely had trouble getting wood, that he'd had only three bad days out of 170 performances. But the possibility of a failed money shot was a constant anxiety that could be triggered by the slightest challenge to one's manhood. This afternoon, someone had already planted the seed of self-doubt. "See, this is how they put pressure on you," Zack told me. "They said to me, 'It depends on how well you do on this scene whether we use you on Saturday.'" A production technician overhearing Zack's complaint slapped a hand to his head. After Zack was summoned to the set, the technician turned to me with a pained sigh. "This is not good," he predicted. "We're going to have wood problems."

Sure enough, half an hour later, Zack was still struggling at half mast and the crew members were becoming increasingly impatient. They had made little progress in moving through the paces of "The Formula," which requires a set number of sexual positions. In this case, the batting order announced by the director was: "Cowgirl [with Girl #1], Cowgirl [with Girl #2], Doggie, Doggie, Missionary."

"Okay, we'll shoot the soft," the frustrated director said. "Back up on your action a little bit," he told Sunset. "Pick it up on you ripping his shirt." More time passed, and still no wood. In the next room, the technical director and various crew members sat around the monitor, stifling yawns and picking at the remnants of the catered repast. A Vivid contract girl who was waiting for her boyfriend on the crew to finish checked her watch for the tenth time and scowled: they were supposed to be catching a "regular" movie. At last, the technical director threw down his headset, stood up, and shouted toward the set: "Guys, take a break." The crew doused the hot lights and left Zack alone with Sunset, who did her best to "fluff" him back into readiness. The technical director sank into his chair and groaned. "This is not going anywhere. It's a fucking Slinky."

A sleeping production assistant woke up and wandered down from upstairs. "What's going on?" he asked.

"We're waiting for wood," a crew member said wearily. They all gazed hopelessly at the monitor, where all that remained on Sunset's person was a dangling pair of spiked slippers. "Well, this dispels the myth that high heels give men an erection," a member observed.

The scene started up again, with Zack grasping the base of his penis to force engorgement. "Ah, the famous pinch technique," the technical director mumbled to himself. "I created 'The Grip,'" Ron Jeremy announced proudly to no one in particular. At last, after a lengthy masturbatory effort on Zack's part, the money shot was delivered. By the monitor, the pooped crew members fell back in their chairs with a collective release of breath. Sunset scooted to the edge of the bed and reached for a towel. Zack grabbed his clothes and raced upstairs without speaking to anyone.

"We'll use [Sunset] again," the assistant director told me, "but we probably won't use him . . . except as a voyeur." That is, a nonsex role, which will pay little to nothing.

Nobody Worked Like I Worked

"OF THE MAJOR STUDS in the history of this business, there are only a handful of names," Bill Margold told me one afternoon as we sat in his darkened one-room office next door to World Modeling; he kept the lights off to effect "the feeling of the womb" for the "porn kids" who might come here seeking counsel. Of the studs currently working, he said, T. T. Boy was "the only one that really qualifies in today's genre as the superwoodsman. T.T. is the perfect example of the video stud, because as video becomes more and more prolific, the quantity overtakes the quality, and T.T. is capable of just knocking them out, one after another after another after another. It's as if he's in the ring with a series of sparring partners and goes though thirty of them in a day and none of them has a face and that's what makes T.T. special. . . . It's high noon, gunslinging time, and T.T. is still walking and they're all lying dead in the street."

A couple of weeks after the *Cyberella* shoot, veteran porn filmmaker Ron Sullivan was shooting footage for "one of my down and nasties" for Caballero Home Video in his down-at-the-heels studio in the Valley. In the eighties, Sullivan shot "graphic, no-prisoners" porn films in New York City for many companies. When Caballero fell on hard times and was sold, its new owner hired Sullivan to rebuild it, which he set out to do by targeting the low end of the market. He joined the overpopulated world of shoestring West Coast operators who generate "one-day wonders" (so called because they are often shot in a single day) that serve an audience craving an endless display of facial cum shots, pounding anal sex, and gang bangs (culminating in Fantastic Pictures' *The World's Biggest Gangbang*, which involved 150 men).

If the Vivid Queen was the crown jewel of upscale "pretty porn," then T. T. Boy was the poster boy of this downmarket variety. "T.T. reflects exactly what that sort of porno is about," Caballero's senior video editor, Bud Swope, said, "where you screw the hell out of the woman and come all over her face. He throws girls around. He pile-drives till they protest . . . He's just aggression." In an interview in the April 1995 issue of *Hustler Erotic Video Guide*, T. T. Boy had this to say: "I was a shy little kid when I started, and now I'm just a guy who wants to fuck the shit out of all these girls. Just fuck 'em to death." He then proceeded to deliver the following message to all those women in the business "with big egos": "You don't want to work with me. I'll beat your boyfriends up and spit in your faces. That's what I think of you bitches, and then I'll kick you in the head."[5]

T. T. Boy arrived the morning of the Caballero shoot without his script. Not that it mattered. As he rightly pointed out to Ron Sullivan, in a Brooklyn mouth-full-of-marbles street voice (although he was raised in California), "Hey, I can remember two fuckin' lines." Despite his nail-'em-to-the-wall billing, his callow looks and self-conscious manner conveyed more of that "shy little kid." He swung a few mock punches in the direction of the production assistant. The move seemed more stagy than aggressive. Maybe it was the fact that, midswing, he was looking over his shoulder to see himself on the monitor.

"Hey, don't hurt your hands," Sullivan shouted, playing along. "Remember when you showed up that time with a bandage on your face because you got in a fight. You mook!" He gave T. T. Boy an affectionate plug on the shoulder himself—a regular Lee J. Cobb jousting with the young Brando in *On the Waterfront*. Then Sullivan handed his star a script and sat him in an armchair on the set. T. T. Boy rehearsed, reading out loud, over and over, one of his two lines: "Perfect. My own wife wants to watch me commit a perfect act of infidelity sodomizing her best friend's asshole." But soon his eyes strayed back to the monitor, and he put down the script and watched himself make various toothy grins and grimaces to the camera. He seemed transfixed by the image. Two attractive women in lingerie were stretched out on a bed a few inches from his chair, but they might as well have been in another universe. Finally, Sullivan came over and turned the monitor away.

This was a one-cameraman operation. A queen-size bed was pushed up against a facade of bedroom walls with a fake window overlooking a painted landscape. A comforter had been thrown over a sheetless mattress. The cameraman, the once-legendary porn actor Eric Edwards, scrounged among plastic dishware and congealed Danish—what passed for smorgasbord on the lower-rent sets—assembling a cup of coffee. When Edwards had retired from porn acting a few years before, he had attained the distinction of being the business's only "four-decader." A working stage actor who had attended New York's American Academy of Dramatic Arts in the late sixties on an ABC-TV fellowship, Edwards performed for years in summer stock and touring theater productions before he became a full-time porn actor in the late seventies. He recalled it as an era when a porn shoot involved rehearsals and dinner parties, when whole days would go by where they were shooting just dialogue and no sex, when he sometimes made $1,000 a day and had his hand and footprints immortalized in concrete on the sidewalk outside the Pussycat Theater in West Hollywood as klieg lights swarmed the night sky. "Those were the glory days when you felt like a human being," Edwards said, gazing into his Styrofoam cup. Now the actors "don't know enough to not look into the camera."

"Okay, T.T., we're going straight to sex," Sullivan said. "We're going to full hard-core. No cable. Never hide it. Keep it nasty all the way." T. T. Boy tried to catch my eye, and I realized that, in the absence of the monitor, I was to be his audience. The sex itself seemed of little interest to him; the thrill was being seen. He ground away on the actress, Christina West, with the monotony of a jackhammer, his mind fixed on some invisible distant point, his hips moving as if to a metronome.

After a while, the grinding turned to pounding, the bed and the facade of the bedroom walls and the picture frames and the lamps all rattling in time. I was beginning to feel like an observer on the set of *Earthquake*. A large painting over the bed thumped against the wall, threatening to crash down on the performers' heads. Several times, Sullivan entreated T. T. Boy to lighten up. "Now be careful," Sullivan said. "This woman's got to work for a while." West herself asked for a short break, to apply makeup to her legs, which were bruised. After she had been gone five minutes, Sullivan began to worry. "We've got wood here!" he called after her. At last she returned and T. T. Boy climbed back on as if there had been no interruption.

After several clockwork transitions and an endless anal scene, Sullivan, satisfied, said, "Okay, bring it home anytime." And T. T. Boy, as if hearing the voice of Mission Control, coolly withdrew, waited for the camera to wheel into ideal position, then brought it on home.

"Okay, T.T., we're going to do the second scene back to back," Sullivan said, looking over at his lone male performer to see how much time he needed to refuel. T.T., who was now shoveling Wheat Chex into his mouth from a family-sized box, looked inert, as if he had done nothing but watch television for the last half hour. Which, in a sense, he had. "I'll be ready in five minutes," he said. I recalled a remark that the former porn actor Cid Morrison had made to me about T. T. Boy: "Basically, the guy is a life-support system for a penis."

Christina West returned from the dressing room in a robe and settled on the couch, a meditations book in her hands. She had a distant, dream-state air about her, as if she were trying to will her mind into a feather, floating far above the present scene. This was her third time with T.T.; the first was when another actress couldn't handle him and West agreed to step in. "I asked him for that moment of gentleness and he gave me that. He does have an attitude, but it's not his personality. It's what the industry built him up to be."

In the other room, T. T. Boy continued to crunch on cereal. "Women are scared of me," he said, between mouthfuls. "They take off." He didn't say more because by then five minutes had passed and it was time for Round Two. T. T. Boy was, as always, ready.

———

LIKE AN UPDATED VERSION of the Woody Allen childhood scene under the Coney Island roller coaster, the apartment complex where T. T. Boy lived was situated almost directly beneath the exit ramp to the Ventura Freeway. The building was a convenient block from World Modeling, just past a NO OUTLET sign at the end of a dead-end street. There are a million complexes like his in southern California—cracking aggregate-concrete steps with flimsy railings, motel-style units built over a parking garage guarded by malevolently grinning metal teeth, a permanent NOW RENTING banner coated in highway dust. The furnishings in T. T.

Boy's one-bedroom apartment looked like they were bought in an afternoon, which they were. Over the TV he had mounted a factory-made tomahawk and a bow and arrow, rare decorative touches. Next to the VCR lay a video of Mike Tyson's "Greatest Hits." The day I visited, a dinner setting for four—plates, bowls, place mats—was arranged on the dining-room table. I asked T.T. if he was expecting guests. He looked at his shoes and mumbled that he had placed the dishes out there some time ago, he wasn't sure why. "I just thought it looked homey."

One afternoon we headed out to a nearby restaurant designed to look like a rain forest, complete with piped-in jungle roars, and for the next several hours T. T. Boy spoke almost entirely of having been dumped by Amy, his girlfriend of two years. "I watched over her. I took care of her better than her mother." Amy said later that during their relationship he had become violent and choked her several times. She even obtained a restraining order against him. "I didn't hit her," T. T. Boy told me, "but I pushed her around."

In any case, T. T. Boy explained their breakup this way: "She went off with Hollywood people." One of the painful truths of this business is the double standard imposed on the personal lives of the performers: it is chic for a man outside the industry to date a woman who has been involved in porn (witness Charlie Sheen's public romance with Ginger Lynn), but for a woman on the outside to date a male porn actor is slumming.[6]

The couple split up for good soon after a friend landed Amy a job as a massage therapist on a Hollywood set. T.T. vowed to move out of the X-rated world and "sold everything to get out of the business, to make her happy." He even sold his BMW, enrolled in acting school, and accompanied Amy to the set one day to seek a position with the stunt coordinator. The visit yielded no employment, but T.T. was recognized by the crew—by "all those hypocrites" who "watch these movies but think you're a piece of shit," as he put it. The next day, Amy called him from the set, crying. The crew members were shunning her now, she told him; they thought she was trash by association. Not long after, she broke up with him.

While the villains in T. T. Boy's stories about his life's disappointments were generally women—girlfriends, girlfriends' mothers, girlfriends of his girlfriends, porn starlets—the figure who first and forever broke his heart was a man. After his mother's death in a car wreck when T.T. was four, he and his younger brother were brought up, on and off, by their father, who owned mining and heavy-equipment operations and worked his sons like company mules. It was one story that T. T. Boy was reluctant to tell. I gleaned the harshest details not from him but from his brother. The father had put the two boys to work mining azurite and malachite when they were very young. By age eight, T.T. was breaking and carrying rocks all summer long under the stone-hard sun over Baker, a tiny California desert town near the Nevada line. During his grammar-school years, he was often in the mines toting one-hundred-pound gunnysacks. By junior high, he was repairing and driving his father's heavy equipment, sometimes until two in the morning. When T.T. resisted, his brother told me, their father often beat him. The father withdrew T.T. from high school so he could work full time, fourteen to sixteen hours a day, on tasks like scouring the insides of cement tanks, where the temperature reached as high as 150 degrees and the chemicals burned his skin. "You'd climb inside with all these limestones that could eat your body up, just scraping contaminated stuff." He made a gesture to demonstrate, and it looked eerily like a jack-off gesture. "When you'd come out, it was weird. It would be like you were freezing. Outside, it would be one hundred and ten degrees and it would be cold.

"Nobody worked like I worked," T.T. told me in a voice half proud, half numb. "I was like a robot. He programmed me like a machine." At least, though, he thought it was leading to something. "My goal then was to work hard, take over my dad's business." His other goal, to be a boxer—"my one dream"—was thwarted by his father. In school, T.T. was a spectacular wrestler, too strong, in fact, for his weight size. ("I weighed ninety-eight pounds and I'd bench-press two-twenty.") But his father pulled him out of wrestling, then out of boxing and Tae Kwon Do training because, in T.T.'s view, "I was getting good." He laughed hoarsely. "Maybe he was afraid I'd beat him up."

Eventually, his father would unintentionally thwart T.T.'s other goal. The father's expensive solo vacations and private planes pushed the company into bankruptcy, and his sons into limbo. T.T.'s brother recalled how their father had impressed upon them that their only chance for a decent living was his business. "My dad told me that we needed him for the future of our lives. He told me, 'If you don't work for me, you work for McDonald's. You'll never be able to find a job.'" It was T.T.'s uncle, a bus-company worker in Los Angeles, who helped find T.T. a job in porn.

In spite of a childhood of indentured servitude on a patrimonial plantation he never inherited, T. T. Boy insisted on paying tribute to his father as a "man of power." His denunciations he reserved for the "powerful" and "evil" women of porn, whom he perceived as threatening his livelihood. "The thing that irritates me is that the girl has so much power. Lots and lots of times, the girls say, 'Oh, T.T., he's so rough.' I say, 'How am I supposed to know? Just ask me.' Instead, she'll tell the other girl who hasn't worked with me. I'm losing all kinds of work because of girls like that."

In the weeks following Cal Jammer's suicide, T. T. Boy's broadsides against "girls like that" invariably segued into diatribes against Jammer's wife. "I see lots of parallels," he said, between his and Cal's experiences with the women in their lives. "He quit because she couldn't handle it anymore. He quit for her. Then she broke it up and she got back in the business." What T. T. Boy preferred not to get into was his (and other male actors') petty cruelties to Cal on the set, where they often ridiculed his lackluster performances. While the male porn actors liked to see themselves as old-fashioned workingmen, the brotherhood of blue-collar work sites did not pertain. One man's failure was another man's chance, and the men in the wings often helped failure along with derisive comments or boasts about sleeping with the male actor's girlfriend. Cal Jammer, in particular, had proved himself vulnerable to such psychological harassment. Buck Adams recalled how the male chorus was forever sneering at him on the set: "It was all, 'whisper, whisper, ha, ha,' pointing fingers, and for someone like Cal, it became a very humiliating experience." T. T. Boy acknowledged that he was "a little mean" to Cal, but he maintained that the real culprit was Cal's wife, whom he anointed "the wicked bitch." If he had been in Cal's shoes, he said, he would have dealt with Jill differently. T. T. Boy gave me a hard stare to underscore the point. Cal "wasn't very violent," he said. "In my case, I might be too far gone and"—he paused—"be trouble."

I wasn't sure whether this, too, was for effect, another mock punch, another flourish for the ever-present camera in T. T. Boy's head, or whether his father's violence was the inheritance that he did receive. Then again, maybe it was just the loud clamorings of a young man alone, trying to beat back the tundra silence of an apartment where the table was always set for a family of four, and no one was coming home.

Behind You All the Way

"THE EXPLOITATION OF THE MALE" in the adult business, porn star Nina Hartley told me, "is very distinct, in that he must cut off his dick from his heart." This wasn't as true in the days when the porn world was more of a community that sustained a certain collegiality and longer-term relationships. "Now, it's much more assembly-line nature." And those who can't shut their hearts and minds off, she said, get chewed up in the gears. Cal Jammer "had a heart to break," and it was still connected to his penis.

Cal did not have T. T. Boy's metronomic abilities. Much to his frustration, he often found his erections held hostage to his feelings. But he also didn't want the pile-driver reputation. He wanted to be, or at least thought he wanted to be, more of a box-cover boy. And, to a certain extent, he succeeded; it was rare for a male actor to make it onto the box, and Cal had more box appearances than most. He even headlined in a video takeoff of *Batman,* which was to be his big break. However, the video, wretched even by porn standards, was recalled soon after its release over a copyright-infringement dispute.

Cal compensated for his lack of cocksmanship by marketing himself around the industry as a carefree, windjammin' California boy. He sank substantial sums into the development of his aura: the most expensive sports gear, Jet Skis, speedboat, sports car, the fanciest fluorescent surfer duds, gym and tanning-salon memberships. Porn actor Cid Morrison recalled Cal buying two-hundred-dollar sunglasses one day, just "because he thought they gave him 'a different look.'" The surfer-boy image buoyed his career to some extent, but it did not reflect a more personal quest, one that drove him to buy a condo at the earliest opportunity and furnish it as befitted not a beach-bum bachelor but a fifties nesting couple. He assembled all the trappings of middle-American family life as advertised in family magazines: the camping gear, the barbecue pit, the volleyball net. "He really wanted to be a father, a husband," said Katina Knapp, Vogel's office manager, who served as Cal's maternal confidante for many years. "He never mentioned his father, but he was very into family."

Soon after he began acting in porn, Cal found a ready-made family and persuaded them, for a time, to move into his domestic bower. He met Cameo, a single mother, on her first porn shoot; the video was *Behind You All the Way.* Cameo, who had just divorced and moved to Los Angeles from Colorado, needed a home for herself and her five-year-old son. Cal, as she recalled, was eager to play the gentleman and protector, opening doors, taking her arm. When her ex-husband stalled in sending her son to Los Angeles, Cal gallantly flew to Colorado to act as a bodyguard while she retrieved her child.

There were, however, some less appealing aspects to his traditional family-man performance. "He was very strict about the way I kept the house," Cameo told me. "It had to be absolutely spotless." He also didn't want her to return to college. In fact, he didn't really want her to work at all, but he desperately needed her income to help pay his mortgage and utility bills, so he let that part of the *Father Knows Best* picture slide for a while. Cameo wasn't sure where Cal had acquired such notions of traditional family life. He rarely spoke of his own family, except to express a yearning for or bitterness about his father. In fact, one of the few times she saw Cal angry was over an incident involving his father. "His father sent him a ring for his birthday, and he got really mad about the ring and threw it across the room." Cameo, bewildered, tried to calm him down, but he was inconsolable. "It was turquoise. And he said, 'If my father knew me better he wouldn't have bought me a turquoise ring. It just goes to show you my father doesn't know me.'"

Cameo's own vision of family life was more informed by feminism than fifties television. "Everything was always *his* and I just said, How can I marry someone and have an equal relationship with somebody where everything is his?" While she first found his desire to shield her from porn employment "really sweet," after a while, she began to suspect it was only a "double standard—and I'm going nowhere. I didn't move two thousand miles away from home to be a servant." Eventually, without his knowledge, she signed a contract with Arrow Film and Video, requesting a two-thousand-dollar advance so she could put down a deposit on her own apartment. "I finally just had to go behind his back. [Otherwise,] I would have always constantly been under his thumb and there in that apartment to clean it forever." When Cal heard about Cameo's contract with Arrow, he stormed onto her set. He found her in the makeup chair and "threw a big stink." Then he charged into the parking lot and let the air out of her tires.

In the wake of their breakup, Cal began to have more problems "breaking down on the set"—the male talent's euphemism for a lost erection. His insecurity was not exactly diminished by the relentless jeering from other male actors, who needled him about momentary softness, tormented him with speculations about his girlfriend's infidelities, or simply made fun of his latest hairdo. No matter how much the taunting tore at him, Katina Knapp recalled, "he kept it all inside. He always tried to be cheerful." From time to time, the situation would become too much and Cal would go back to building sets. But set design provided little in the way of money or recognition, and soon he would be badgering directors for another shot, until one day someone would need a stunt dick and there he'd be, ready to get back into the game. This on-again, off-again dance continued for several years, the apprehension that caused him to flee the stage being the same that caused him to return. "Cal's whole perspective was fear of male performance anxiety," Cid Morrison said. "That was his life force."

———

"NOW REMEMBER WHAT I TOLD YOU," Nick East said as he greeted me at the door of his apartment in 1995, a one-room guest cottage in North Hollywood which you entered from an oil-stained back alley cluttered with trash cans. "This apartment is not a reflection of who I am." He dropped onto a couch and reached for the remote control, desultorily flipping channels on a giant TV screen, his only possession of any significance. East once shared an apartment with Cal Jammer, at a point when Cal was between women, but he said he was still too upset about the death to talk about that time, and became angry when I pressed it. What he wanted to talk about was lost manhood. "I'll tell you one thing," he said. "The definition of a man is gone." In Nick East's history of gender relations, the golden age was the forties and fifties, when, "if a man said something, women took him at his word and acted accordingly." The man had a job that lasted and a wage that went farther than a weekly run to the A & P. At the center of Nick East's dream of a Happy Valley past was a father who would take care of them all. "Back when my dad was able to support three children and a wife who didn't work and buy a house when he was twenty-three . . ." was how a typical Nick East sentence began. What made that possible? I asked. "Because the workforce was not flooded with females," he said, suddenly angry. "The government tricked our women into working and women became men."

Nick East's father was an electrician, a dedicated union man. Nick grew up in the Midwest, the youngest of three children. He tried to follow the work formula of his father's generation: directly out of high school he joined the navy, then quickly got married and left the navy for family-wage employment. But the jobs he found in civilian life could barely support him, much less his wife. He sold cars, then copiers. "That's all I did," he said. "I sold things." His wife moved back in with her mother in California and found a job at a dental-products firm. Nick went looking for a factory job, figuring, based on his father's experience, that it would pay better. But the manufacturing world that he ran up against no longer manufactured a middle class. He worked in an aluminum plant that was hiring only nonunion labor; his job was to "ream out" siphon tubes, seven days a week, twelve hours a day. "I make more now," he noted.

He drove to California to reclaim his wife, but she wasn't interested in being reclaimed. He moved to Ohio, where his mother and stepfather lived, but couldn't find steady work. Finally, he held his nose and took a job at Burger King. "Eight hours of 'Would you like fries with that?'" The night after his first day on the job, he had a nightmare: "They had locked me in a Burger King and made me work there." The next morning, the image of Burger King incarceration still vivid in his imagination, he found himself immobilized by panic before the franchise doors. "So, I returned my uniform at the drive-through window." Soon after, he moved to California and auditioned at World Modeling.

"That was 1991—four years!" Nick East said. In today's market, that rated as a job with longevity. "The business saved my life. It gave me something to go on with."

As Nick surfed through the channels, he hit the Playboy program; glancing over, I jolted in my seat. "Hey, that's you!" He shrugged. "What movie is it?" I asked. He didn't know; he'd made too many to keep track. "I'm always on TV." His voice held no enthusiasm. "I'm on every day of the week." He stared blankly at the image of his thrusting hips.

"I know I'm nothing. Though most of the world has seen my face, I'm nothing because I didn't *do* anything." But one day he would do something to make himself "worthy" of real public recognition; and he would know that day had arrived "when I'm on the talk shows—the next O. J. Simpson, not that I'm going to kill somebody, but the next media sensation—when all the *Hard Copy* shows, when the world is going to pay attention."

If he was on TV every day of the week and still thought of himself as "nothing," I asked, then what must Cal Jammer, who was a mere spear carrier by comparison, have thought of himself? But Nick was not interested in exploring the connections between celebrity culture and male despair. As far as he was concerned, there was only one force behind his former roommate's suicide: his wife. "Cal's death, it was over a woman," he said flatly. The relevant facts, as he saw it, were these: Cal's wife "asks him to get out of the business. He got out. She wanted a divorce. She got into the business. . . . As someone told me, Cal said, 'This is for you, babe,' and shot himself in the head." At the funeral, Nick said, "I didn't pay last respects because I would have had to walk by *her*." He leaned back on the couch and closed his eyes for a moment. "She tortured him, which is the way that the sexes have changed."

Nick reached in back of the couch and, much to my surprise, pulled out a Bible. He had been reading it lately, he said, because he was looking for "direction," thinking about quitting the business, and working on a memoir "about the way home." He wanted to read me his favorite

passages and so turned to John, chapter 14. " 'I will not leave you desolate,' " he read, his face catching the light of his own image still flickering on the Playboy channel. " 'I will come to you.' " He paused, then
turned to chapter 10. "This is the most intense part of the Bible. 'My
Father, who has given them to me, is greater than all, and no man is
able to snatch them out of the Father's hand. I and the Father are one.' "

I borrowed his memoir-in-progress to read that night. It turned out
to be less an account of a life than a mystical wish fulfillment fantasy,
in which a "guardian angel" materializes one day as Nick is driving cross-
country and promises to be his divine guide through life. The angel first
appears to a grateful Nick East in the clothes and guise of his own father.

In the Land of the Flesh Eaters

PORN ACTOR TONY MONTANA and his shih tzu pup Luli were languishing
by a slime-covered fountain in front of a crumbling mansion in Pasadena,
a few weeks after Cal's death. Tony was waiting for his next scene and
filling me in on what he would have liked to say at Cal's funeral if only
the minister had let him. "Nobody knew that he was dying inside. Nobody knew anything." As his voice began to wobble, he scrabbled in his
bag for his sunglasses. "I don't know what happened," he said, blinking
back tears, "because to tell you the truth Cal Jammer was the most
positive person I ever met in my life. The first time I met him, I go,
'Who the hell are you?' and he goes, 'Cal Jammer, dude! Number one
surfer!' "

The movie Montana was shooting was "sort of *Scarface* with Italians,"
set in Chicago during Prohibition and Montana was Frank LaBianca,
owner of the "baddest" nightclub. "I have the most beautiful women,"
he said. "I have a wife, or well, I guess wife or possession, you could call
it. Her name is Victoria, played by Dallas."

A young man emerged from the mansion just then and Tony gestured
frantically and yelled: "Hey! Dallas's husband!" Dallas's husband, who
went by the name Austin McCloud, joined us at the fountain. Tony told
him, "Not yesterday but the day before, I had the best sex scene I've
had in a long time, and I had it with Dallas." He waited for a reply.
McCloud said nothing.

"I'm serious!" Montana said.

McCloud told me that Dallas kissed only him; it was one of the rules
they had agreed on in their marriage. "And I have to choose all the guys,
actually."

"Why, thank you," Montana said. "I didn't know that."

"Well," McCloud said, "she comes out with a list that she wants to work with, and then—"

"So am I ranking number one on that list?"

Austin McCloud was one of a small group of male "managers" in the business who, for one reason or another, have chosen to relinquish the charade of themselves as costars. Such men no longer labor under illusions of cinematic glory; still, they cling to their own set of fictions.

I visited Austin and his porn-star wife, Dallas, at their house in the Valley, a two-story tract home at the stub end of a suburban street. It was what I had come to think of as a porn star's home: large rooms that echo from the emptiness, walls without pictures, marble-veneer fireplaces without logs. The furniture was sparse, usually an oversized white sectional couch, no bookshelves, and a giant television set suitable for a sports bar. The home of Dallas and Austin more or less fit this description, with one variation: there were children's toys and from upstairs came the tinkling giggles of small voices. "They're watching *The Lion King*," Dallas said with a smile. She was dressed in sweats and wore no makeup, and looked like she preferred it that way. She settled on the couch, resting her head on Austin's shoulder.

"We met in McDonald's," he told me. "My car kept cutting off going through the drive-through." Dallas was nineteen, and was working at a McDonald's in Nashville to save money for college. She had "a 3.987 grade point average." Austin, twenty, the son of an architect, was selling car phones. "I drove up to the second window and I saw Dallas standing there and I thought, That's the girl I'm going to marry." Several months later, in the summer of 1988, she was pregnant, and in August they married.

That Christmas, Austin enlisted in the air force as an air-traffic controller. The couple was uninsured and, he said, "we were scared we couldn't afford the kid." As it was, Dallas said, "we were paying doctor bills with cash." The air force sent Austin to Rapid City, South Dakota, where Dallas worked as a waitress at a restaurant and a secretary at a retirement home, and both of them sold real estate on the side. But even supplemented, air force wages proved insufficient to support their growing family—they now had two children—and soon they were back in Nashville, where Austin drove trucks and tried to launch a transportation service for indigent handicapped patients. But when the state switched to a managed-care program, Austin said, he couldn't get reimbursed for his Medicaid patients, and within six months, he had to file for bankruptcy. At one point they wound up living in a twelve-by-twenty-foot room with no electricity or plumbing. Then Dallas got laid off from her job as a store manager in a downsizing. That's when she began waitressing at Déjà Vu, a stripper bar.

One thing led to another, which is to say that Dallas realized she could make between $600 and $800 a night dancing without her clothes. They bought a house. Dallas went to the grocery store, giddy with $100 bills in her purse. Austin found an agent in Florida who advised the couple to move to California and make some porn films. With a few box covers, the agent said, Dallas could clear $2,500 a night as a feature dancer. They sold everything and reported to World Modeling the morning after they arrived. By the evening, Dallas had her first job, a video that Ron Jeremy was directing. She worked seven days a week for a full month.

In the first scene that first night, Austin was allowed to play her lover. "We wanted to say that we would just work with each other," Austin recalled, but "you're going to lose about seventy-five percent of work if you say you're the only guy that will work with her." Male viewers don't want to see the same man with "their" girl. So instead Austin appointed himself Dallas's manager.

According to the McClouds, Dallas's fan club now had about one hundred thousand members, at a $25 membership fee. Dallas had several 900 lines, a mail-order catalog hawking clothing, and custom-made videos that ranged in price from $300 to $5,000. And now the talk shows were calling. The meaning of a hundred-thousand-member fan club became real to them, Austin recalled, when they attended their first Consumer Electronics Show and a hundred photographers mobbed them in the lobby. "I was surprised that they knew who we were," Austin said. "That's when we figured out we had a name." Of course, "we" didn't have a name. "They were all yelling for Dallas."

Sometimes this knowledge became difficult for Austin to bear. "I went through a month feeling I was not needed. I mean, I do a lot of work. I know for a fact that I do more work than she does, but the fact is that they are not paying me."

Dallas touched his shoulder. "It's hard for Austin, from a man's point of view."

Austin nodded toward his wife: "If she really stuck to her guns, she could do it all on her own. If she got tough, she wouldn't need me."

In the porn community that season, all conversational roads seemed to lead to Cal Jammer, and this discussion was no different. "You know," Austin volunteered, "Cal called the night he killed himself." That night, however, Austin was upset himself, having "lost it" and blown up on the set and then having had a fight with Dallas—and he wouldn't take the call. So Dallas had talked to Cal. "He was just mumbling on about lots of weird stuff," she recalled. "He was like, 'Well, how do the two of you handle it, because me and my wife, I don't know what to do.'"

Dallas recalled that Cal "would always talk for [his wife]. Like, *We're* gonna be doing a scene,' *We're* gonna do this.' It was always a *we*." Austin said that Cal told everyone that his wife "got into the business just to make him jealous." But Austin didn't think so. "The reality of it is she got into the business and decided she didn't need Cal."

CAL JAMMER MET HIS WIFE, Jill Kelly, about two years after his breakup with Cameo. The porn star turned producer Tyffany Million introduced them. Cal had briefly dated Million a few years earlier. At the time, she had just emerged from an abusive relationship and she had a baby. He mistook that, she said, for her needing to be saved. "What he didn't realize," she said, "was I was *strong*." She went out with him a few times, but his intense possessiveness disturbed her. "The *first* date he was talking to me like I was already his wife. It was 'You're not going to date other guys.'"

At twenty-nine, Tyffany Million was an example of a new kind of woman in porn, one who was moving behind the camera. A few years before, she had launched Immaculate Video Conceptions, and the videos she created asserted a feminist point of view in a playful rather than hectoring way. Unlike the self-conscious fastidiousness of the porn that had previously been designed for a female audience, which tended toward a cloying Hallmark-card view of sex, Million's work managed to break down the girls-like-romance, guys-like-grinding division that so much of standard-issue pornography enforced. "I want to see hard-core fucking, but I also want to see passion," Million said. "'Romance' doesn't have to be all soft and mushy. You can have both romance and hard sex." Her challenge to the gender divide had already met with resistance: cable operators refused to air her video *Jailhouse Cock,* a slapstick parody in which an all-female staff of prison guards have their way with the male inmates and one another. In spite of its goofy and obviously good-natured role reversals, the cable programmers "didn't like the fact that it showed men at women's mercy."

In the winter of 1993, Tyffany Million brought her friend Jill Kelly to the Consumer Electronics Show in Las Vegas. They knew each other from dancing at the Mitchell Brothers' O'Farrell Theater in San Francisco, and Tyffany had told Jill how she could triple her dancing salary by making a few porn videos. "Tyffany was going to be my guide," Jill

Kelly recalled. "I just wanted to do girl-girl scenes" because it seemed safer, less humiliating somehow, a preference shared by many female performers. "Most girls would rather do girl-girls because it's less mucky," porn star Sara-Jane Hamilton told me, and "you don't have to sit on their lap for an hour before and tell them how great they are. With a girl, you can just chat in makeup."

The first night, Cal Jammer spotted Jill Kelly at the bar at Bally's and promptly took the adjacent stool. At twenty-one, Jill had the long lines of a dancer. She gave Cal a second look, too. "He was beautiful," she said. He invited her to a party in one of the suites. They sat in a corner and Cal snapped open his briefcase to show her his "book," a photo album of his glossies from video appearances. "He always carried it around with him." They talked until the sun came up, or rather, Cal did: "He said he wanted to start directing his own movies. He talked about getting out of it and moving into directing and producing." He poured his heart out to her. And Jill, who had danced in front of men for five years and knew "what men are like," felt touched by the neediness she sensed, the vulnerability. "The feeling was, 'God, he is so sweet. He's the sweetest guy in the world.'"

The following day, he escorted her around with an excess of courtliness, pulling out her chair with a flourish, paying for dinner, asking permission to hold her hand. Jill was working at the time at the T & A Club in Upland, California, contemplating her next move. The first night back, Cal invited her to his house and talked about how *he* should be her guide into the business instead of Tyffany, how much he could "help" her. She said she'd think about it. About a week later, she became seriously ill with a viral infection. Cal came charging to the rescue, ferrying her to doctors and paying the doctors' bills. A month later, on Valentine's Day, they were married in the Little Brown Church in Canyon Country. The preacher, whom neither of them knew, called Cal "Larry" throughout the ceremony.

A couple of weeks after the marriage, Cal announced that he didn't want her to go into the business after all. "'I love you too much—I don't want you with those guys,'" she recalled him telling her. "I said, 'Okay. Oh, he must really love me.'" Cal wanted very much to be the provider. "He wanted to work at a legitimate studio like CBS and get in the union and get benefits. He wanted to have a normal job. And he wanted me to stay at home and have kids and go to church on Sundays." But even if Jill wanted to stay home, which she didn't, her wages still paid most of Cal Jammer's bills. From her dancing income, Jill bought the groceries and paid the utilities, the insurance, and half his mortgage. After he died, she discovered that he was five months behind in the mortgage payments; the bank was about to foreclose.

In Jill's account of their marriage, the only aspect of the "normal" American family life her husband seemed to have mastered—other than leading the prayers over dinner, a nightly ritual he insisted upon—was accumulating things. As with some of the men in the Glendora Promise Keepers, his consumer appetites soon spun out of control. "He kept buying and buying and buying," Jill said, even later, when they were deeply in debt. "We'd go to the mall. You know how usually it's the woman who goes crazy? Well, in Cal's case, it was him."

At the same time, Cal's porn career was being plagued by the old "wood problems"; at home, he could talk of nothing else. "Cal felt like he wasn't a *man*" because he couldn't perform, Jill said. "He dwelled on it too much. He cared about it too much." He was devastated when the trade publication *Adult Video News* took a few digs—"Oh, Cal Jammer, same dead seed" was the gist of it, as Jill recalled. He became obsessed with his performance, treating himself with ginseng and herbs, instituting a rule at home that there be no sex twelve hours before a shoot, "so he'd have his strength up." And after a while, he looked for other people to blame. "He'd come home every day pissed off because so-and-so wouldn't hire him, pissed off because 'this bitch' wouldn't work with him, pissed off because she wanted him to wear a rubber. He was so unhappy."

At the following year's Consumer Electronics Show, Cal and Jill shared a hotel room with Tyffany Million and her new husband. Tyffany was disturbed by Cal's "constant picking on [Jill]. . . . It was, 'You're getting a little fat. This doesn't look right on you. This is too tight.' Finally, I let him have it. 'Cal, lay off her!' He said, 'Well, my wife can be a bitch.' He'd always say 'my wife.' I said, 'She has a *name*. She's not your property.'" Soon after, Jill discovered that Cal had been cheating on her, and left him, but then reconciled. Cal told her he was going to leave the business "for her." Jill replied, "Don't quit it for me, quit it for yourself," aware of how such an unasked-for "sacrifice" might some day be thrown back in her face.

Once out of the business, however, Cal fell into a deep gloom; weeks went by when all he would do was play video games and drive around aimlessly in his truck. To make up for the lost income, Jill started dancing double shifts, seven days a week, at Venus Faire. His criticisms of her turned ugly. On a Colorado rafting trip with friends in the summer of 1994, he suddenly began screaming, calling her "a fucking bitch." On the drive home, he continued to yell and, after she kicked the dash of his truck, snapping one of the plastic air vents, he grabbed her and, Jill said, "started socking" her. She fought back, but the next day she was the one with bruises.

A month after the rafting trip, they were camping with another couple on the coast and he lit into her again, saying how much he "hated" her and how he had got out of the business for her and now his career was ruined. She finally said, "Fine then, I'll leave." In September 1994, she moved out. "I told him I was going into the business, and I was going on where I left off with my life." He replied, Jill recalled, that "this was *his* business, that I had no right invading his business, that I had my dancing to fall back on." She asked him, "Are you going to support me?"

The day she moved out, Cal lined up a scene in a porn film. A short while later, he had his wedding band resized to a smaller width; while performing on porn sets, he wore it as a pinkie ring.

————

"CAL COULD BUILD ANYTHING. Cal's the one who did this whole living room." Buck Adams turned and swept his hand across a vast empty expanse of white carpet and marble veneer. It was another porn house, down to the white couches, but on a grand scale, on the top of a hill overlooking the San Fernando Valley. Most of the rooms were empty and some of the construction appeared unfinished, as if the contractor had abandoned the project three-quarters of the way through.

Buck Adams took me through the house, showing me Cal's handiwork. "Cal was a very responsible guy in a lot of ways," Adams said. "He was very normal. He had this very big view of how things should actually work. You know, you work hard every day and in the end you will be rewarded. . . . But he was finding that just isn't true nowadays. It gets you a lousy stinking little paycheck, and that's that. That's where it ends."

Buck Adams had the exaggerated gestures and oversized voice of a country Texan, which he was, though one suspected that his home-on-the-range act had been pumped up considerably since his arrival in Los Angeles. A boxer turned porn actor, he retained the bantam strut of a man forever preparing to enter the ring. His sister, the porn star Amber Lynn, pulled him into the business after neither boxing nor working as a bouncer seemed to be leading him anywhere. "For the first three to four years in the business, I was 'Mr. Wood,' " Buck Adams said, flexing a biceps. "No talk. Just a cowboy."

Several years ago, Adams started directing videos, bigger-budget numbers with car and helicopter chases; he invented a new genre, "action porn." By his own admission, he liked to "blow things up," on camera anyway, and his signature film formula became the car wreck followed by the wrecking of the sheets. But he was working on a very different kind of film now. It was the story of the porn star Savannah's suicide; she shot herself soon after an auto accident that scarred her face. "I don't even show the car wreck, which would've been a natural. I mean, I *lived* to do things like that." At some point in the last few months, he had lost his appetite for cinematic explosions. He had almost lost his appetite for the business altogether. Cal's death had left him shaken, sobered. On this morning, he looked pale and drawn, the ride-'em-cowboy persona barely limping along. If he was more haunted than most by Cal's suicide, he had his reasons. He was the last to speak to Cal, moments before his death.

"The big problem with this business," Buck Adams said, seated cross-legged on the floor of his living room, adrift in the open sea of shag, "is there's less and less story." On the low end of the market, where the "flesh eaters" prowled, all that was left was a random and hastily assembled flow of images. "My God, they can make a video in one day for about four grand. Sometimes they even try to shoot two movies in one day for seven or eight grand. It's absolutely incredible. People are just rolling through like cattle. Say nine words and fuck the whole piece together. They shoot it on a home-movie camera with two idiotic lights like somebody would work on your car with. And they actually release them, like this 'movie.' . . . It's heresy." With the story line gone, he said, "looks is all there is to it. It's making the actors feel isolated to the visual aspect." Of course, the "story" had always been threadbare, even in porn's Golden Age. Still, that thin veneer of narrative had provided an emotional fig leaf; without it, the performers felt painfully exposed. "For the actors, it's really tough. They've taken away your one big justification for who and what you are: your work. And a whole bunch of things fall with that."

One of the first things to fall was the male actors' pay, which had plunged even in the high end of the market. With the exception of a very few stars, the paychecks of even relatively well known porn actors had dropped from $800 to $600 to $200 a scene. Cal Jammer, in the last months of his life, was making less than $200 a scene. One of his last paychecks was for $100. "Pretty soon," Buck Adams said, "you're going to have to *pay* to be in a porno movie." Even more painful was the psychological fall. "The actors that are in the high end are afraid of dropping out and having to deal with the flesh eaters." That was Cal's fear, Adams had concluded. "That's what was going on with Cal, that loss of fame." And in the days since Cal's death, Adams said he'd come to understand how that fear operated on him, too. "I just realized I'm a 'have' who's panicking because I'm scared I might be a 'have-not.' A couple days ago, I just realized it. And, oh God, is that why Cal killed himself?"

Buck Adams sat at home now and thought back over the previous few months to the times Cal had asked him what he could do to establish himself as one of the "famous" porn men. He considered Cal's frantic need to be "number one," his mounting agitation in the face of minor setbacks, how he had even suddenly challenged Buck to a fight. And he saw how Cal felt endangered, saw his grip slipping, saw himself dangling above the pit of flesh eaters. He thought about how they had all "screwed with Cal" for his wood problems. "All of sudden, it really started to bug Cal. And I think that's pretty much what made him nutty, trying to find all these reasons. First it was this and then it was that." And after a while, Adams said, Cal settled on a reason: Jill Kelly.

"Right at the end, sometime in the last three to four days, I noticed it start to happen. He all of a sudden started to fixate all of the problems he had on, 'Oh, that's why all this is happening, my wife's leaving me.'" Adams had argued with Cal that such scapegoating was unfair and "stupid," but Cal remained firm in his conviction. Jill was starting to get work in the business, and Cal saw in the launch of her career the crash of his own. Buck Adams feared he might have inadvertently contributed to this impression. For his video *Snow Bunnies in Tahoe,* to be shot in Big Bear, he had hired both Cal and Jill. Cal was excited about shooting on location and getting a chance to ski. But at the last minute, Buck decided not to use Cal after all; it was a bit part and Buck was trying to cut costs.

Two days before his death, Cal phoned Buck Adams: "Buck, I've got to come by right now!" Cal arrived, in a state. "Please," he said, "you've got to talk to me about this and keep it very quiet."

Buck agreed. ("I'm always waiting to hear some fantastic story," he told me. "You never know, it may be my next movie.")

So he waited, expectantly. And Cal said, "I've got to kill my wife." He had it all "figured out: She is evil. She is purposely trying to screw me up." Buck tried to talk some sense into him. But Cal plowed on. "It's getting to be where it's her or me, Buck."

Buck told him, "C'mon, Cal, you want to be 'Porn Star on Trial for Murder! Blah, blah, blah, buried his old lady in the backyard!' . . . And I kind of got him to the point where he was laughing about it, like 'Oh yeah, I guess I am going crazy.'"

Then Buck Adams sent him home.

ON A SATURDAY FOUR DAYS before Cal's death, Jill left on a two-day trip to San Francisco, and from the moment she got off the plane her pager beeped incessantly, flashing Cal's number. When she called him back that night, he was teary at first, then vengeful. When she asked if he was "threatening" her, first he said yes, then he said no, he was just going to kill himself. She pleaded with him not to think that way. Then, Jill recalled, "he said he had a gun." She put her hands to her face at the memory, her shoulders heaving. "But I didn't believe him."

The next day, Cal Jammer shot his last video, *Adult Affairs*. It starred Nina Hartley as a conniving tabloid journalist who, as the video's producer and director, Mike Johansson, described it to me later, "hires boy toys to play with." Cal played her husband. He had a brief scene in which he seeks solace with another woman, then is caught in the act by his wife. "He had some wood problems," Johansson said. Cal kept apologizing for his slowness — it had taken twenty minutes "to get wood" — and told the producer that it was just because he was "having problems with Jill" and hadn't slept the night before and that " 'The last few ones were solid, real solid. No problem. No problem.' " But Johansson barely listened; he'd heard it all before. "Cal's heyday was done. He was known more often for having wood problems than not. He was not the constant woodsman anymore."

On Wednesday afternoon, Cal showed up at Ron Vogel's photography studio around four-thirty. "I'd asked him many times to finish up some sets," said Vogel, who was mystified by Cal's sudden sloth. "Working was his main goal," Vogel said, "just working, the love of working, using his creativity and energy to work. That was what was important to him." So Vogel was even more taken aback when Cal walked in that afternoon, "kind of briskly walked up to me and said, 'I don't feel good. I'm not going to work tonight.' " Vogel was on the phone. Before he could get off, Cal walked out the door.

Cal's next stop was World Modeling. He sat in a chair opposite the agency's founder, Jim South. "He was a little teary eyed," South recalled. "I knew that something was wrong, but I never assumed, because he never said anything." South asked if he was okay. Cal looked at him and said, "I'm losing work because of her." Then he got up and left.

Cal's last stop was Trac Tech. He made a point of talking to everyone on the set. No one could figure out why he was there. "It was strange," Tyffany Million recalled, "because usually he was there because he had a reason to be there." Usually he was there because there was work to be done. Then he got in his car and started driving to Jill's house. On the way, he picked up the car phone and dialed her number.

Cal told her he was on his way over. She said she was about to leave and suggested he not come. He said, "If you don't wait for me, then you'll find me dead on your doorstep." In a panic, she called a porn actor and friend, Chuck Martino, and Martino called Buck Adams. While the two men were talking, Buck Adams's line clicked, signaling another call. He put Martino on hold and picked up the other line. It was Cal. He was about a block down the street from Jill's, Buck later realized. "Why don't you tell me why I shouldn't do anything to my old lady," he said to Buck. "What I'm thinking is to go hurt her, and then hurt myself." Recounting the conversation, Buck halted and gave me a sharp look. "I mean, he wouldn't say 'kill,' wouldn't say 'kill' or 'suicide.' So that's why I didn't think it was that kind of a situation." He was silent for a moment, then went on with his story. "And I said, 'I want to tell you something flat out front, Cal!'—because I always tried to be real stiff and stern with Cal. And these are the words I will always regret saying, because Buck tried to play 'Buck Adams' in this situation. . . . I said, 'Cal, get this through your thick head. You don't have a right to go over and shoot your girlfriend. You don't have a right to go over and beat her up. You don't have a right to go hurt anybody. I mean, if you are so desperate to hurt somebody, go out in the street and shoot yourself.' "

Buck Adams sucked in his breath and averted his eyes. A tense silence hung in the air. Then, he took up the story once more. He had put Cal on hold and dialed Jill's number. He told her, "Whatever you do, drop the phone. Don't look. Just run out the door." Then he clicked back over to Cal, who said, "Thanks a lot, Buck. I really appreciate the advice." And hung up.

Soon after, Jill heard Cal's car pull up outside. Clutching a cordless phone, she ran upstairs and, for reasons that escape her now, hid in the bathtub like the victim in *Psycho,* pulling the curtain behind her. She heard the phone ring and ring, but the portable phone she was holding was not charged. After five minutes, she heard a loud pop and thought Cal had broken a window. After a while, she crept downstairs, then out the door, then down the steps. At the foot of the steps, in the gutter, he was lying on his left side, his body slightly twisted. A light rain fell. Drainage water from up the street ran down the gutter and bathed his arms and face. Jill was sure it was a joke, just the kind of thing Cal would do to get attention. "Cal, get up," she said, with a nervous laugh. "C'mon, Cal." Then she began to scream for help.

————

AT THE 1995 ADULT VIDEO NEWS AWARDS, Michael Ninn's film *Sex* was the equivalent of *Forrest Gump* at the Oscars, nominated in sixteen categories and winning nine awards. The story is told in flashback by a sort of modern-day Ancient Mariner, a stooped service-station attendant who pumps gas at a godforsaken spot in the wind-whipped desert. As a young man of twenty, he pumped gas in the same place until he fell in love with a beautiful girl, played by Sunset Thomas. Then he went off to the city seeking a glamour job because, he told her, "I'm just a guy who works out in a gas station in the middle of nowhere. My fear is—my fear is you'll wake up one morning. You'll want more than I'll be able to offer you." He is recruited by a power-mad businesswoman, played by Tyffany Million, who molds her pretty boy into a supermodel. But the transformation wrecks him. "I'm on display like a goddamn piece of art in a museum," he tells Million, and in the next scene he writhes in agony before the pulsating TV monitors that surround him. He nearly over-doses on sleeping pills, and eventually returns to the abandoned gas sta-tion, the fame and the girl gone. He was nothing, one of the characters testifies; just "a busted-up cowboy." He "had no power," the voice-over narration concludes. "This he found to be one of life's supreme truths."

———

CAL'S FUNERAL WAS HELD at the Eternal Valley Memorial Park & Mor-tuary, a heavenly or horrific name for a graveyard, depending on your view of spending eternity in the San Fernando Valley. The church was jammed with men in sunglasses, weeping. The casket was open, which seemed ghoulish, given the way he had died. But it made a certain brutal sense: if there was one thing Cal might have wished for in his final appearance, it would have been to be viewed.

The minister knew nothing about Cal. He delivered a pro forma ser-mon about "the person that he was," and how that person was "a very unique and special man." Only two family members spoke, Cal's brother Brett and his mother. Jill was too shaken to talk and had someone else read her remarks. Brett told the room that his brother was "very com-petitive" and "not a quitter." Cal's mother, Jackie Potes, said that her son had been "a performer since he was two years old. He always wanted to be a movie star. He wanted to buy me a Cadillac."

Afterward, we stood around on the steeply sloped lawn overlooking the wide valley. Ron Jeremy worked the crowd, urging everyone to watch him in an upcoming HBO movie. "It's a big thing," he said, "with O.J.'s girlfriend." The male talent stood in small, tight groups, and the talk was mostly of men broken by women. There were mutterings about how the industry should "boycott" Jill Kelly.

A producer who had worked with Cal stood in the back during the funeral and watched all the sobbing men with a dry and dubious eye. He had seen how the male actors cut each other's throats every day to get jobs. "The comrades-in-arms thing just isn't there" was his comment. Out on the lawn, one of the men had approached the producer. "He said, 'It's a shame, isn't it?' And I said, 'Yes, it's a tragedy.' And he said, 'He could be any of us.'" And the producer said he'd thought to himself, So that's what this is all about. Already, Cal had been forgotten. "It's all past," he concluded. "A year from now, people will bring up his stage name, and it will be, 'Cal who?'"

Cal's mother told me that the day her son died, he had left a message on her answering machine saying, "My wife is ruining my life." Jackie Potes didn't know if that was true, but she knew one thing. "He wasn't a woman, and you know, women are the thing. They don't sell men. They sell women."

ONE EARLY AFTERNOON a couple of months after Cal's death, I was sitting in the main room of World Modeling when a tall young blond man in a black wide-brimmed rancher's hat, an Australian outback coat, and cowboy boots walked in. Brad, the "talent coordinator," told him to take a seat. The stranger asked me not to identify him except by his trucker's handle, Cowboy.

He was from Wisconsin, and he was trying to get out of trucking and farm work, he told Brad. Actually, he would tell me later, he was trying to save himself from bankruptcy court: he and a friend had unsuccessfully tried to start a trucking company in Wisconsin, and now creditors were in pursuit.

Brad gave him the usual discouraging new-guy speech. "This business is very, very tough," he said. "There are maybe fifteen guys total who make a very good living." Directors don't like new male talent, he said. The starting pay would likely be only $100 to $150 a scene, he said. A new actor would probably have to begin with gang bangs, he said. Cowboy took it all in, nodding, but said he still wanted to give it a try. Brad sent him to a back room with some pornographic magazines. When it was hard, just call out, Brad said, and they'd take some Polaroid shots.

Later, sitting on a couch in a side office, Cowboy told me it had taken him a long time, because he was nervous, and then, when he was finally ready, he had called out, over and over, but no one had heard him. "Finally, Brad came back," he said, looking at his boots, mortified.

Cowboy was raised in farm country near Madison. He didn't get along with his father, who owned a small farm-equipment business and so, from the time he was twelve or thirteen, he lived on a friend's farm and worked as a hired hand, haying, milking, building fences. That work has vanished now, he said. "The banks own more of the farms than the farmers do," he said. "Years ago, it was nothing to walk onto a farm and say, 'What do you need?' and go to work. That money is not there anymore."

So he came out to Los Angeles, looking for modeling jobs, escorting, porn, anything to pay back his debts from the failed business venture. But the escort services he tried said they didn't want men or weren't hiring. And now World Modeling wasn't exactly encouraging. "It's a lot easier in this business to get in as a female," he said. "Guys are a dime a dozen, and we pretty much put ourselves in that predicament." I asked him what he meant by that. "Because we've always kept women in back, held them down." Women found work displaying their bodies, he said, because it was all they could get—and the fact that women weren't part of the male workplace only helped make commercial feminine display more profitable. "Guys want to see what they can't see usually. They will pay more to see what's hidden." But now the male workplace was collapsing and the only employment realm that was prospering was female-dominated. "If you look back through history," he pointed out, "entertainment was always the thing that flourished during a depression—to take people's minds off how bad things are."

What would take Cowboy's mind off his troubles, I didn't know. But for now, Los Angeles held no promise. He was flying back to Wisconsin that evening, he said, returning his rancher's hat to his head, and he would figure it out, or not, from there.

———

WHEN CAL'S FORMER GIRLFRIEND Cameo heard that Cal had committed suicide, she couldn't believe it. "When I think of Cal, I think of somebody who was very, very ambitious. . . . And I never, ever thought he would be the kind of person who would kill himself. It's like Savannah. We never thought she would kill herself. They both seemed to care about themselves too much." But then she had an awful thought: Savannah had made the headlines in mainstream America when she died—the *Los Angeles Times, Rolling Stone,* tabloid TV. "I wonder if Savannah reached such a high level of fame after her suicide that he thought that was the way to do it." Maybe if he put a gun to his head, he'd be someone, too.

But maybe even more awful was the fact that in Cal's case not even a violent death merited public attention. In the weeks after his suicide, Cameo watched *A Current Affair* to see if his name appeared on the tabloid show, because, she suspected, "that's probably what he wanted." But Cal's demise passed unnoted outside the porn world. "There was no write-up. None. None." Even inside the industry, even among those who knew him best, there was no rush to memorialize Cal on celluloid. Buck Adams chose to make a film of Savannah's suicide instead of Cal's; women were more marketable, even in death.

Soon after Cal died, Jill Kelly was offered money for a photo layout to accompany a brief article about Cal's death in a porn magazine. Jill was going to do the shoot and turn the check over to Cal's family to help pay the funeral expenses. But then, she said, she thought better of it. "It wouldn't look right." And besides, she was booked solid for the next month with work. She didn't need the job.

DESTINATIONS

11

PARTING SHOTS
The Fighter Still Remains

ONE FALL DAY IN 1998, I could see a column of dense smoke rising from the Long Beach docks nearly thirty miles away. Concerned, I called Ike Burr. Was the shipyard on fire? Yes, he told me, but not to worry—the blaze was artificial. The shipyard had been turned into an action-movie set, and what I witnessed from my Hollywood window was merely a Hollywood disaster: a stuntman, in fact, smashing his car through the tinted glass of Building 300. Well, I said to Ike, if they were going to destroy a building, at least they chose the administrative Black Box and not one of the old craft shops where the real work was done. "Whatever," he replied, immune as always to silver-lining sentiments. "It's all in the past."

In the years since the yard's closing, Burr had been transferred a second time, to a Marine Corps base in the Mojave Desert. His job was "facilities manager," a fancy name for managing mostly custodial work. "You don't get that powerful feeling of turning a ship around," he said, but at least he had figured out a way to use his building skills: he was buying dilapidated town houses in nearby Twentynine Palms and refurbishing them to rent to marines.

Just as that ersatz firestorm swept through the gigantic edifices of the shuttered shipyard, so ornamental culture continued to engulf the

American man, whether he was a Citadel cadet fleeing the spotlight or a Spur Posse kid in a gimme cap making the talk-show circuit, an aerospace engineer clasping his company pin or a former insurance agent trying to expose the secrets of Waco, a grocer's receiving clerk trying to break out of the inner city or an underemployed carpenter whose masculinity was contingent on nailing women before the camera. In the summer of the last year of the century, as this book was readied for press, I caught up with some of those men and with others whose stories are in these pages, and heard of their recent accommodations and rebellions.

In the spring of 1999, Big Dawg had undergone a personal transformation of sorts. At the beginning of the year, his image was enshrined in the Pro Football Hall of Fame, after he and thirty other fans representing thirty other cities won a contest sponsored by Visa. His photo was displayed next to his fifty-word prize-winning essay recounting the highlights of his history as an ardent fan, how he had been a season-ticket holder for twenty-eight years, missed only a couple of games, and finally donned his basset-hound mask. Big Dawg had become a tourist attraction. In April, his mask would grace the cover of *Sports Illustrated*.[1] He spent the following summer anticipating the "return" of the Cleveland Browns. The new team boasted a $280 million city-financed stadium (with luxury suites leasing for $125,000) and a new owner, billionaire credit-card mogul Al Lerner, who had owned 5 percent of the old Browns and had helped broker the Browns' departure to Baltimore with his close friend Art Modell, on Lerner's private Gulfstream jet.[2] It looked like "the fans had sort of been used to make a profit," Big Dawg said, but he seemed to forgive both owners, exonerating them through a complicated theory wherein they stood tall against a "new guard" cadre of exploitative sports moguls.

"Art's move was to let the new guard know that the National Football League was about history, it wasn't all about money," Big Dawg asserted, adding that Modell "was motivated a lot more by principle" than by profit. How Modell had achieved all that by ripping up the historical roots of the Browns and making a lot of money in the process was unclear, but regardless, Big Dawg and his canine compatriots intended to be in their seats on September 12, 1999, opening day. In more ways than one, they were resigned to their new commercial status as fans. From the bleachers under the skyboxes, they would come not so much to celebrate their team's rebirth as to pretend it had never died.

Back in southern California, the former McDonnell Douglas engineers who were forced out of their outplacement center to make way for a company souvenir store had witnessed a final act of consumption.

The company itself became a retail bauble. In 1997, McDonnell Douglas sold itself to Boeing for $16.3 billion, the tenth-largest merger in American history. By then it had jettisoned 52 percent of its workforce nationwide, more than sixty thousand jobs. The company had shed its employees for the same reason an aspiring trophy wife might shed excess pounds—to attract a rich suitor. Chief executive Harry Stonecipher said as much in a company video. Asked for his thoughts on the security and well-being of the company's employees, he replied that McDonnell Douglas's duty was to "take very good care" of only two parties: its customers and its shareholders. After the merger, Boeing announced that it was eliminating three of McDonnell Douglas's four commercial aircraft lines and laying off more than eight thousand more employees, two-thirds of them from McDonnell Douglas's old southern California operations.[3]

The men in the Glendora Promise Keepers group came to suspect that the leaders of their national organization had similar priorities, and like Big Dawg they sensed that they were merely the object of someone else's marketing scheme. "The second year we went to the stadium conference," Martin Booker recalled, "the speakers were saying the exact same thing as the year before. It was kind of disturbing." By the third year, Martin and his fellow Promise Keepers were left with the sinking feeling that they weren't disciples so much as customers, being sold the same product over and over in a slightly new package. That third year, Martin said, "I remember sitting in the stadium in Anaheim, and I couldn't believe it—I was hearing what I'd heard twice before, *word for word*! It was very disappointing, because we realized this was all just a canned message. We wanted to participate, but we were just watching this pat, canned thing."

The Glendora Promise Keepers group soon began to crumble. The main activity that had held them together was the annual road trip to the stadium conference, and now most of the men didn't want to waste time going to a rerun. In the spring of 1997, Martin Booker asked to step down as the group's leader—his marriage was going through troubled times and he didn't feel comfortable directing the meetings anymore. No one volunteered to take his place. The men finally decided to take a "break" for the summer. In the fall, the group quickly dwindled to a trio who met occasionally, then not at all.

Meanwhile, Martin Booker's domestic life degenerated into what he woefully called "a bad Hollywood B-movie," and he had no group of men to turn to for help. His wife, he said, got involved with a coworker and left him. Then he lost his job at his evangelical ministry because "it wasn't politically correct to be seen going through a divorce." Finally, he had to sell the house. In the midst of all this mayhem, his wife suddenly returned home. About six weeks into their reconciliation, he said, the couple had a late-night argument about the television—she wanted to finish watching a program, he wanted to pray and go to bed—that ended in a violent struggle. Each accused the other of starting it. "I did slap her in the face," Martin admitted, but only, he claimed, after she had "smashed everything in the room and jumped at me." She called the police, and by the following evening, he was in jail. He eventually pled guilty to a misdemeanor, spent fifteen days in a halfway house, and agreed to attend a domestic-violence counseling group.

"I've lost my wife, lost my job, lost my house," Martin told me with a bleak laugh. "I guess I'm a poster boy for your book." He had found new work, "installing ceramic tile and marble in million-dollar homes." It was "kind of therapeutic," he said. "You're doing something with your hands and you can be proud of what you did." But when he got through decorating rich people's homes, he returned to his empty condo. "In this little snapshot of Promise Keepers you've looked at," he said, referring mournfully to his group, "I guess it's a pretty ugly picture."

It seemed that for some men, no matter how they tried, there was no winning for losing in a world where they had been taught that winning was all and losing less than nothing. A few men fled the scene entirely. Kershaun Scott's vigil in the desert town of Ridgecrest continued to century's end. Billy Shehan, the Spur with the most points, likewise retreated, so burned by his failed bid for fame that he preferred that the small town he moved to, a hundred miles from Los Angeles (where he lives with his wife and two children), and the unglamorous job he works at go unidentified. What Martin Booker and Big Dawg and their brethren didn't know was that the larger picture outside of their "little snapshot" wasn't much prettier, even for those who crossed the divide into the ornamental world and succeeded on its terms. You could be a paragon of the new masculinity, an icon atop the new hierarchy of men, and still be riven by the same dreadful doubts. There seemed to be no way out of the trap: you either retreated from the lens and were deemed an invisible man or you moved toward the light and saw your identity vanish in its blaze. Some among the "winners" in the ornamental sweepstakes tried to reverse direction, but the road back would prove just as daunting and disappointing as the road out.

Escape from Planet Hollywood

ON MARCH 13, 1996, the week of the twentieth anniversary of *Rocky*, Sylvester Stallone appeared at a press conference in downtown Manhattan to announce his prospective metamorphosis. Seated before a pack of entertainment journalists, the actor announced that his action persona had made him feel "very hollow." He was sick of being perceived as nothing more than a glob of muscle mass, a decorative embellishment on what he called the "Erector set" of Hollywood, in which "the actor is just moved from catastrophe to catastrophe."[4] He was intent on shattering the carapace of his own cinematic image. Four months from his fiftieth birthday, faced with the numbing, flattened sameness of his roles and the increasingly shaky status of the action genre, Sylvester Stallone could see the horizons of his movie frontier closing in.

His last two attempts, playing a futuristic supercop (a character drawn from a comic book) in *Judge Dredd* and a weary hit man in *Assassins,* had been domestic financial bombs, not bombshells. In the nineties, natural calamities, prehistoric animals, and invading aliens seemed the stars most capable of delivering a hit in the action universe. Even so, he also knew that the safest, most lucrative strategy for him was to stay with the old formula; Stallone had a sixty-million-dollar deal for three action blockbusters pending at Universal, and a multimillion-dollar obligation for more superheroics at Warner Bros. Still, Stallone wanted out.

With a new self and a new world of acting in mind, he did more than announce his intentions to the media. He fired his latest agent at ICM, who had only represented him for four months, and hired a new one, Arnold Rifkin, who had previously helped remake Bruce Willis by placing him in the occasional quirky part, most notably in Miramax Films' *Pulp Fiction.* Stallone was asking Rifkin to do the same for him, to find him grittier, "workingman's roles," ensemble dramas where he didn't have to do all the heavy lifting by himself.

So Rifkin had returned to Miramax Films in search of an "indie" art movie for Stallone (though Miramax's "independence" had been bought by Disney in 1993). The match pleased both parties: Miramax cochairman Harvey Weinstein would get the multimillion-dollar man at a bargain-basement price; Stallone would get his chance to rebuild from the cellar up. Soon afterward, at a Planet Hollywood appearance in Manhattan, an appreciative Stallone introduced Weinstein as his new mentor, "the man who did the impossible"; the portly Weinstein beamed and nodded from a corner, where he had positioned himself beside a glass-encased exhibit of Rocky's warm-up robe. "He became a huge international star and he got trapped into doing it for the audience as opposed to taking the gambles," Weinstein said to me later as we sat in the restaurant's private back dining room, where the two men had retired to toast their union. He wagged a huge cigar in Stallone's direction.

"There's many other things I want to do with him. Sly could've done *Get Shorty*—it would've been *brilliant*. Sly could've done *Pulp Fiction*. It's all about choice. Now he's at the point where he's gonna choose."

In the short term, Weinstein chose a part for Stallone in a modestly budgeted ensemble drama with Robert De Niro, Harvey Keitel, Cathy Moriarty, and Ray Liotta. It was, as Stallone announced at the time, his dream role. "I am not the centerpiece of this movie," he said. "It's something where I am just part of the machine. I am not *the* machine." *Cop Land* would be directed by independent filmmaker James Mangold, whose previous movie, *Heavy*, about an obese, loveless loser living with his mother, was the antithesis of an action flick. In *Cop Land*, Stallone would play a diffident, partially deaf New Jersey sheriff named Freddy Heflin, a sad sack shoved around by the big-city police officers who dominate his little town at the foot of the George Washington Bridge. Of course, Stallone had played underdogs before; that was Rocky's whole appeal. But though Freddy was to react valorously after an accident on the bridge brings the town to crisis, at least this underdog would be no greyhound. Not only would Stallone, as he said proudly, "keep my shirt on," but the flesh underneath would jiggle. Freddy was going to be fat. And with the avoirdupois, Stallone hoped, he might gain some unglamorized masculine heft. Stallone wanted to be loved for something other than being beautiful; he wanted to defy ornamental culture by making himself ugly.

———

IN AUGUST OF 1996, I met the actor for a drink in the bar of his habitual Manhattan lodgings, the Four Seasons Hotel. He lumbered in wearing a baggy Hawaiian shirt bunched up over a protruding gut, and shambled across the room with his eyes trained on the floor. His demeanor was only partly related to an effort to stay in the character of the hapless, overweight sheriff. He was also just plain embarrassed.

The first month had been the worst, he said. He was "cut down to the ground." He could barely stand to be seen in public with such flab. For weeks he was frantically "issuing disclaimers," as he put it. " 'This isn't me!' " he recalled telling people. " 'I'm doing this for a *film*!' I should've gotten a little sign. I started doing it with *strangers*. 'Hi, how ya doing? This isn't me!' "

A few days before at the hotel, Stallone said, "I was having breakfast here and the guy sitting next to me was doing *this* . . ." He pulsed a biceps up and down. "He was all pumped up. I guess the two other guys were trying to pitch him on exercise equipment or something. So I walked in, he was like"—Stallone dropped his voice to a Rocky-deep register—" 'How ya doin', Sly!' and gives me one of these." He showed a thumbs-up. "So now the whole meal, he's in this state of complete rigidity. . . . And I sit down next to him like this"—he slumped over— "and what do I order? Pancakes, french fries, and an omelette, and more french fries. And the guy is sitting there, the whole meal he's looking over at me like *this*"—a stare of utter horror. "He freaked. This guy is fucking *dying*. The whole meal he's talking to 'em, 'uh-huh, mmm-hmm,' and looking at me like, 'Oh my God! . . . So, Rambo is a walking greasy french fry?' "

In spite of the mortifying stares, Stallone was not sorry he'd put on the weight. The flesh, he felt, freed him from a more humiliating fate: that of a man forever before the mirror. "What I was doing was purely— I don't want to put down working out, it's good, but you become incredibly self-conscious. You are always aware of yourself; you are just *aware* of yourself. Do I look as good as I did yesterday? You are always looking for a reflection in windows and things. I don't think there's ever a moment, including when you are alone in your own house, when you are not constantly aware of every aspect of how you look."

He demonstrated by raising his arms over his head in a Mr. Universe-like pose, the drinking glass clasped in his hands like a tournament trophy. "Even having a conversation when you are in shape is"—he flexed his biceps again—"*everything* is a display." For decades he had believed that bulging pecs would be his masculine salvation, ever since that afternoon when a thirteen-year-old Sylvester had fled his unhappy family life for the dark comfort of the movie theater and found himself transfixed by *Hercules Unchained*. Steve Reeves's Hercules, oiled skin gleaming and roped with sinew, "changed my life." The young Sylvester went directly from the cinema to an autobody junkyard, where he proceeded to strain his scrawny arms lifting crankshafts. The weight-lifting regimen eventually installed him in the gym for several hours every day. But his middle-aged workouts only made him feel strangely static and dainty, encased as he was in his carefully sculpted muscle.

"The feminine mystique, be it in any shape or form, is apparent," Stallone told me. "You take a serious gym rat, a man who lives in a gym, it's like, what do you *do* with it? You've got it, but it comes out in this vanity thing which borders on the world of exotic dancing with women. You qualify for nothing—like the Chippendales dancers. . . . It's like the orchid; it's so gorgeous but it's a parasite. It lives off of everything but what it is." Even more humiliating, he observed, the gym-bred man was pursuing this overwrought "feminine" display at the very moment so many women were rejecting it. "The guy with the eighteen-inch arms, the thirty-one-inch waist, the male-model, chiseled, Calvin Klein–ad type of person, he is, for the nineties, the woman with the triple E. He's taking the place of the blond bombshell of the fifties. And the blond bombshell women, they don't even do that anymore! The woman on the street doesn't want to be Jayne Mansfield."

By gaining weight, Stallone said, he hoped to assume, at least on-screen, what to his mind was an older model of manhood. "These are guys who said unwittingly—they didn't articulate it, but they said: 'You know, I've got a fucking life to live, I've gotta bust my ass at the docks, or driving a bus, I gotta feed my three kids, I've got a wife that I don't spend enough time with. So when do I have enough time to go to the gym? If I'm gonna be married, hold a job, that's what counts. So I'm gonna put away this vanity and get on with my life. I don't even think about what I look like. I think about what I have to *do,* not what I *look* like when I'm doing.'"

Increasingly in action vehicles, all that was left for the actor to "do" was think about what he looked like. With computer animation, many death-defying feats could now be simulated. So action heroes found themselves confronting what was literally an invisible enemy: the four-headed alien, the fire-breathing monster, the exploding missile, the gigantic tornado were missing in action, to be plugged in later by a computer programmer sitting in a postproduction room. The action hero was just a "prop to move the story along," Stallone said, left gyrating in front of a blank backdrop known in the business as "the blue screen." Pretty soon, he said, the computer image of a performer would make the actual actor "disposable": "His imprint will be made and he'll be put in situations where he can literally be in two places at once. He can be at home and sick in bed, but his imagery in certain shots will be 'working.'"

At least playing Rambo, he said, "when you were chased by fire, you were chased by fire; it wasn't put in later on." In the new action productions, it was all shadowboxing. "For the performer, it's self-imposed sensory deprivation," he said. "The action film is no longer the action film. . . . It's more like what a farmer must've felt like, you know, a strong-backed real son of the earth looking at the industrial age, saying, 'Jesus, they don't need me anymore.'"

Stallone wanted to be in films where he was really working, not just dodging an imaginary threat on a blue screen. "To me, the ultimate movies are about the workforce. Everyday labor. Because labor, I think, affects everything. It gets at the core of our existence." In the previous generation's "action" films, the westerns and World War II movies, the male heroes played by men like John Wayne and Kirk Douglas and Steve McQueen were "part of a system," Stallone observed; they were "hardworking" and "indelible father figures" who "led an army." But Stallone's generation of action heroes were all alone, "the one-man army," as he called his Rambo persona and its knockoffs. "We're not fighting for America. We're just using the backdrop of this country or the American uniform, but it's personal. . . . The man, he's on his own. I have to be my own country. I have to be my own citadel. No one's gonna watch my back."

For some of those who had traditionally watched his back, Stallone's decision was baffling. "Sly has definitely always wanted to be respected," Ron Meyer told me one day as we sat in his spare, spacious office in the building known as the Black Tower on the Universal lot. Meyer had been Stallone's agent for nearly fifteen years and a trusted friend; his hardscrabble background was one Stallone felt he could relate to. When Meyer became president of MCA, which owns Universal, in 1995, he secured the lucrative three-picture deal for Stallone.[5] In spite of his elevation in status, Meyer remained unpretentious and direct. "Sly also has a need to work, a lot," Meyer said, a need he understood. When the two men met in 1981, as Meyer recalled: "We connected immediately. I clearly identified with his desire to succeed. Neither of us came from money and neither of us was picked likeliest to succeed. . . . I relate to his need for constant work. I get up every day and I'm afraid that people are going to take it away." But Meyer didn't understand Stallone's desire to flee the action field. "It's ridiculous, just ridiculous," he said of the decision to do *Cop Land* for so little money. As for Stallone's need to be respected, "We don't quite agree [on how to achieve that]. I don't think it means changing his image. He thinks it's good reviews. I think you can be respected with a successful action movie." All Stallone needed, Meyer believed, was to be a bit "more selective" about his starring vehicles. Of course, that was easy for Meyer to say; he didn't have to stand in front of people at the age of fifty with his shirt off and his chest oiled. But he did know what audiences loved most about Stallone: that he was the hero who came out of nowhere, "fired out of a box," as he put it. He seemed confident that Stallone would eventually stop fighting his destiny and give his fans what they wanted. After all, he observed, more than anything, "Sly wants to please his audience."

At the bar at the Four Seasons, Stallone and I were interrupted by a fan, who claimed to be asking for an autograph "for my girlfriend." Stallone signed a cocktail napkin and handed it to the man with a game smile. "As long as they don't call me Rocky, I don't mind," he told me.

In fact, he said, he had promised himself that from now on he would not acknowledge fans who addressed him by the moniker of his former celluloid self.

———

THE MOVIE TRAILERS WERE PARKED on a side street in Cliffside Park, New Jersey, a lower-middle-class suburban town along the Hudson River where time appeared to have stopped circa 1963. A production assistant in a headset stepped up to the largest trailer and discreetly knocked. It was time for the actor's first scene of the day. The door opened and a 210-pound sheriff with a fake bloody nose and a creased ranger's hat eased himself out slowly, hoping this morning to avoid the mob. It was hopeless, of course. They were already there. They were always there.

"Rocky! Yo, Rocky!" The teenage boys lunged forward, a yelping pack brandishing autograph books. Along the sidewalk, batteries of neighborhood moms were in their usual formation, shoulder to shoulder, their laser stares adoring and devouring at the same time. "How's the baaaaby?" one of them half cooed, half screamed at Stallone, and the chorus immediately took up the familiar cry. "How's that liiitttle baaaby?" "How's lii'l Sophiaaaa Roooose?" Their familiarity with Stallone's newborn child was based solely on a maternity-ward snapshot of his labor-weary wife, Jennifer Flavin, and newborn that had run in a supermarket tabloid. Stallone began the long plod down the hill through the gauntlet of fans, the police barrier marking the entrance to the set an endless block away.

"I know your name," a little boy clutching his mother's hand declared as Stallone pressed forward.

"No you don't," Stallone said.

"Yes I do!" The boy was adamant. "It's Rocky!"

Just before he reached the gate, a woman in a skin-tight halter rushed forward and, twirling around, presented her bare back to him. "Sign my back, Rocky! Sign my back!" she demanded. Stallone obliged. He always did. In spite of his vow a few nights earlier to spurn fans who called him "Rocky," Stallone, ever the dutiful idol, seemed incapable of turning away a votary.

As he passed, Pat Bertelli, the woman whose back had been inscribed, craned her neck to see what he had written. Her face fell. He had signed his real name. "I keep calling him Rocky," she told me. "Oh God, Rocky! That chest!" she said, oblivious to the fact that it was now enfolded in Freddy Heflin's flab.

In the scene being shot, Stallone was to approach the bossy wife of the town's kingpin cop to find out why she's depositing her garbage on another cop's lawn. Stallone shambled up to her, his shoulders stooped, his manner timid and deferential. After a couple of takes, the director Jim Mangold approached him. "I like what you're doing. It's just a little too—"

"Passive?" Stallone asked.

Mangold nodded. "Just a smidge. I don't want to discourage that, but"—he paused—"there's a way in which Freddy can be too vulnerable. One more time and deal with her a little more. Step up to it even more." Stallone said he'd try, but "asking Freddy to be tough is asking a lot."

After the scene was finished, Mangold came by Stallone's trailer bearing a stack of videos of a previous day's filming and a demonstration tape of the film's ending, shot with stand-in actors, to give Stallone a sense of how the director envisioned the last scene. Stallone groaned when he saw his fleshy self on-screen. "The noble turtle, the dork," he said, cringing. Then Mangold popped in the demonstration tape of the finale. The *Cop Land* story ends with Freddy taking on the entire town of bad cops in a gunfight and prevailing. Stallone watched the mock shoot-out in pensive silence. "Where's the crowd following me?" he asked when it was done. Mangold shook his head, not sure what Stallone was asking. "This is the lone man," the director said. "It's *High Noon*! The single man!" Stallone nodded glumly. He shouldn't have been surprised. He had read the script; he had known from the start that he would remain a loner, not a leader of men belonging to a society of equals. Even so, he was visibly disappointed. If Stallone had hoped for an ensemble drama of many male characters embedded in the life of a real community, by movie's end he would find himself back in that old Superman outfit, just another "one-man army."

Later that day, an entourage appeared on the set—a burly, bearded figure dispatching orders at top volume, followed by several fresh-faced young men clutching cell phones. Joel Silver, action-film producer extraordinaire, had arrived. The man behind the *Lethal Weapon* and *Die Hard* series, who had made a mint even when producing such lackluster Stallone vehicles as *Demolition Man* and *Assassins,* had come to see how the action star who had strayed from his gilded stable was faring. "God, I can't get over it," Silver said, casting his eyes on Stallone's corpulent figure with mock horror. His look of disgust needed no translation: what was the point of all this? As Stallone explained later, "See, Joel's a wildcatter. He's out there, and he's one-hundred-percent optimistic, and he's looking for that vein, the big one." It was the winning ethic that Stallone was trying to give up, but not without remorse.

"So why didn't you give *Conspiracy Theory* to me?" Stallone said, needling his former producer. *Conspiracy Theory* was Silver's latest action film, then in production, with Mel Gibson and Julia Roberts. "First of all," Silver said crisply, and I had the impression that they had had this conversation before, "it was written for Mel."

"Yeah?" Stallone said dubiously.

"The best script I ever had in my life, I gave to you," Silver shot back. He was referring to *Assassins,* the 1995 box-office disappointment.

Stallone shrugged. "I just want to play me," he told Silver, a hint of pleading in his voice. "Why can't I be me?"

Silver crossed his arms and said nothing. Stallone blew out an exasperated breath. They didn't speak for a moment. Then Stallone jerked his head in the direction of the set, where the next scene was about to get under way. "Wanna watch me get shot?" he asked. Silver nodded happily, glad to see Stallone back in his element. He settled into an empty director's chair to watch the gun go off and the squib of "blood" explode.

"Sly's been associated with so many of the big action movies that it's just hard for him to go in another direction," Silver told me. "But I don't think it's impossible." He just thought it was a waste of time. Why break out of success? "The guy's the biggest grosser of any movie actor in the business," Silver said. "Look at his movies, even the less successful ones have grossed more than this here . . ." He waved a hand disparagingly toward the work in progress.

When the scene was over, Stallone headed back to his trailer, Silver by his side, yakking at machine-gun speed about grosses and what Stallone was giving up. Kevin King, Stallone's assistant, met them at the door with a cell phone. Miramax's Harvey Weinstein was on the line. Stallone talked for a while, then hung up, triumphant. "Harvey raved about the dailies," Stallone said pointedly to Silver. "Harvey said, 'Whatever you do, don't do another action movie.' See! I love this guy."

Silver was not impressed. "Yeah, but what are you going to *make*? You know what *Assassins* made, and that wasn't even—"

"But when did you ever win anything at the Cannes Film Festival?" Stallone retorted. The blow wasn't even glancing; Silver clearly didn't care about such trophies.

"You see, that's the frame of mind," Stallone said to me after Silver left, as he paced back and forth in the trailer's narrow galley. "That ironclad fuckin' constitutional thinking is exactly what pervades every studio. I don't want to go back. I feel like when I do an action film, I've used one percent. And the rest is, it's all frustration." He stopped pacing and sunk into a chair, a look of defeat on his face.

Of all the forces lashing Stallone to the action mast, the greatest wasn't Joel Silver or an agent or the studios; it was the force whose representatives stood on the crest of the New Jersey hill, just out of the range of the cameras. Michael Bonacci, nineteen, and his friend Joseph Faris, sixteen, hovered anxiously, waiting for their chance. Bonacci had a boxed set of all the Rocky and Rambo movies—"I got 'em for thirty dollars at The Wiz," he said—and he was hoping to get Stallone to sign every one of them. Joseph Faris, who said he had "seen every Rocky movie like one hundred times," turned a blind eye to the new Stallone being created in his own neighborhood. "When I see him," Joe said, "I see Rocky." Michael Bonacci agreed: "Oh yeah, Rocky's like forever." He struggled to articulate why Rocky was so important to them. "There's just something about it. Everybody's been in that position at one time, where you felt like a nobody. And then to see somebody like that, just out of nowhere, just spontaneously come out and feel like they are on the top of the world! It makes you feel like it doesn't matter what the odds are, there's always a chance. . . . *Rocky*, it like makes you feel from *this big*"—he held up a thumb and a finger, a quarter inch apart—"to THIS BIG." He stretched his arms wide.

Michael Bonacci stared over at the movie set and gave a plaintive sigh. If only, he said, what happened to Rocky could happen to him. "That would be awesome," he murmured. "I play a guitar a little, and I sang at a talent show in high school. If someone were to call my house one day and say, 'I like your guitar playing or your singing, and you've been picked,' I'd just jump for joy. That would be *it*."

The odds, for these native sons of Cliffside Park, weren't promising. Michael, a year out of high school, had not been able to find a job. A promised contract with the air force to be trained for military-police service never came through. He was serving as a volunteer fireman while he figured out his next move. Joe was still in high school, but he didn't hold out much hope for employment, either. His older brothers, both graduated, now worked, respectively, at Grand Union and Pizza Hut. "My dad wants me to go into computers, but I'm not really interested in it," he said, and his reasons reminded me of Stallone's aversion to acting in front of the blue screen. "You're not *doing* anything."

At the end of the day, a chauffeured car arrived to take Stallone back to the Four Seasons. Shielded by his bodyguard, he made his way through a crowd of fans and climbed into the backseat. A teenage boy reached through the window and thrust into Stallone's arms a large portrait he had sketched and elaborately framed: it was of Rocky in the ring, his muscles glistening, his face bloodied.

"I feel like the fellow in *A Face in the Crowd*," Stallone said as the car finally pulled away. He stared down at the portrait on his lap and it stared up at him like a reflection in a fun-house mirror. Stallone had watched *A Face in the Crowd* a couple of nights before, not for the first time. The 1957 film recounts the career of a TV star who is destroyed by his own celebrity and ends up ranting maniacally to his own applause track, "Ten thousand miles away from home, and I don't even know my name." It seemed a cautionary tale. "I feel like the case of the Greek persona wearing the mask," Stallone said, still studying the portrait. "And he takes it down and you don't recognize who this person is." When Stallone removed the triumphal Rocky face, he thought his fans would see "the real me." Instead, they just saw a blank blue screen. "I don't exist. It's like people see right through me. I'm not real to them." He frowned out the window. "The bright side is, I realize that I don't need to have to vindicate myself, or vilify myself, or celebrate myself anymore. But the bad part is, the audience doesn't realize this. They couldn't care less. . . . So it's, 'Yes, Sly, you can be free. But not from *us*.'"

———

A YEAR LATER, *Cop Land* was released to polite reviews and tepid interest, and as it became clear to him that he hadn't made his great escape from action purgatory, Sylvester Stallone panicked. Not only hadn't he escaped, but it now looked like his return was going to be barred as well. "After I made *Cop Land*," he said in the late summer of 1998, as we sat at a banquette in Spago, the preferred dining spot of the entertainment industry's most powerful, "all of Hollywood turned their back." He looked around at the roomful of studio moguls, a few of whom nodded politely but not one of whom came over to say hello in the course of the afternoon. "I'm surprised they even gave me this booth," Stallone said, only half joking. "I'm like driftwood in here."

That spring, Stallone had begun to suspect that since *Cop Land* and the equally disappointing *Daylight*, his $60 million, three-picture deal with Universal was a dead letter. Universal was supposed to submit at least three scripts to him each year, he said, but the scripts offered had been insults. "One of them, *Shadow of Death*, I passed on it ten years ago!" One day, he said, Universal called him with what the studio executives promised would be his dream picture. "They said, 'The women are going to love this, and the critics are going to eat it up!' And I said, 'Lay it on me!'" The story, as he recalled it, cast him as an ex-boxer who runs a gym: "I'm approached by like Tony Galumphy, who says 'Man, the Tongs are out to kill one of their own and the father of the Tongs wants you to just get him safely back to China!' And I say, no way, but then I find out my girl doesn't have enough money to get into Harvard, so I go on this killing rampage so she can go to college!" Stallone said he handed back the project with the remark: "That's an interesting spin. Usually the girl needs a brain operation or a liver transplant, and that's why he needs the money. I'm killing for an Ivy League education?"

Then for a long time the studio offered him nothing. "They're gaslighting me," Stallone told me. Lawyers were brought in and negotiations dragged on. Stallone said that he was leaning toward an arrangement where he just made one action movie with the studio and called it a day—where "I say, 'Look, just give me half of what you owe me and just see you around. You *won*. You *beat me*." He was sick of sitting idle. "Three years without a script offer—that's a long time."

In this alarming downward spiral, Stallone lashed out for a time at his Hollywood "fathers." He fired Arnold Rifkin. ("He sold me out.") Miramax's Harvey Weinstein, he decided, was "the Don King of cinema," who just wanted to get Stallone's star power on the cheap. Instead of making good on his promise to cast Stallone in ensemble films, Weinstein had bought the rights to the *Rambo* series and seemed mainly to want to know if the actor would appear in the fourth sequel.[6] Stallone's doubts even extended reluctantly to his longtime supporter and protector Ron Meyer, a man about whom Stallone had once said, "There wasn't a wound he couldn't lay hands on and heal." When Meyer got his post at Universal, Stallone recalled, he said that even though he could no longer be the actor's agent, he would never abandon him. "I said to him, 'I'm gonna tell you, Ronnie. I'm no longer going to be at your side. I'm going to be in your way.'" Meyer repeatedly called during the year-and-a-half standoff between Stallone and Universal to assure his former client that he was still looking for a good movie for him, and Stallone wanted to believe him, but he no longer felt so sure.

By midafternoon, Spago was nearly empty. The moguls had returned to their offices. Stallone, for the time being, had no place to go. "I have not made a dime in two years," he said, and while he was obviously far from broke, it was that feeling of being laid off that seemed hardest to take. By trying to escape the role of the feminized muscle man, he had lost even that most rudimentary foundation of a masculine identity: the consolation of being the steady earner. "I see everyone else working and I'm not doing dick. I'm in a total limbo. I'm a man without a country. It's a scary thing to have all these accolades and then to have nothing." It was scary because he had plunged so suddenly, and who knew how much farther he could fall?

SEVERAL MONTHS AFTER THE DISPIRITING AFTERNOON in Spago, Stallone suggested we have lunch at his new redoubt, the Grand Havana Room cigar club in Beverly Hills. I arrived first and sat at a corner table, watching the other members, movie producers and executives, all male, making a painfully self-conscious show of being old-fashioned club men. They lit each other's cigars and talked portentously about their latest deals. It was hard to take seriously from a bunch of adult men who wore Armani jackets like team jerseys, with the sleeves pushed up, and topped their balding heads with baseball caps, the bills turned backwards. The owner of the club had tried for instant tradition: the walls were adorned with celebrity members' faces on mounted covers of *Cigar Aficionado* magazine, and each of the many cigar "lockers," built like a bank of safes into one wall behind a glass partition, boasted a personalized brass nameplate. But the most dominant totem, located in the dead center of the room, was a gargantuan wide-screen television, which at the press of a button rose slowly and magisterially out of its wood-paneled cabinet like the monolith in *2001*.

Stallone arrived with a spring in his step that had been notably absent in our previous meetings. Freddy Heflin had visibly vanished. Settling in his chair, he instructed the waiter to bring him water and a small piece of fish with no sauce. "This is my only meal of the day," he said cheerfully. "I'm down to three-percent body fat. I'm on a mission," Stallone confided. He was back to daily workouts in the weight room. "A spiritual rebirth. Well, a rebirth anyway. This is a gift, a new beginning." He had gotten an idea, suggested to him by the promised return of fifty-year-old former heavyweight champion George Foreman to the ring and seventy-seven-year-old astronaut John Glenn's return to orbit in the *Discovery* space shuttle. "If Glenn can go into space again, so can I. People thought I was an old guy in *Cop Land*. Well, I'm going to come back. And I'm going to blow people's minds." He was thinking about making another *Rocky*.

Stallone sketched out the plot he had in mind for *Rocky VI*. "Rocky is going against all common sense. He's fifty years old. He's past the family aspect and past doing it for his wife. He's not proving himself anymore. Now, his drive is completely spiritual, to sacrifice to give other people a chance. He's going to go back in the ring because he needs the money to build this community center for these young boys he looks after. He's doing it because he knows we need to build these institutions for the young, as safe havens, as launching pads. Adrian [Rocky's wife] will accuse him of a martyr complex and male menopause. And he convinces her, and the audience, that that's not it." How does he convince them? I asked. "He goes into the ring and he fights this young guy."

"And he wins?" I asked. My mind was flashing to a moment months earlier, during our chauffeured ride back from the gritty *Cop Land* set to glittery Manhattan. Stallone was then still consumed with his chances of rejoining a meaningful workaday world. In the dusk, the sleek sedan glided down the highway, approaching the George Washington Bridge. "See that?" Stallone said, pointing at the bridge's ornate ironwork. "The incredibly detailed work that went into it? That's *work*. That's when men had a real craft, when they really built something. Imagine looking out and seeing this and thinking, 'I *did* that.'"

Now, amid the smoke of the Grand Havana Room, he was Rocky once more, planning another comeback in the ring. "And he wins?" I asked. Stallone looked at me as though I'd inquired if the sky was blue. Of course he wins. If you were going to be a man at the end of the American Century, what else was there to do?

CHAPTER 12

REBELS IN THE KINGDOM

SOME JOURNEYS DEFY the map. To reach your destination, you must renounce the sextant and the guiding star and meander with the current. Six years ago, I set out to explore the American male dilemma. My hope, my guiding star then, was the thought that I might tackle the question that had plagued so many women, myself included: why do our male brethren so often and so vociferously resist women's struggles toward independence and a fuller life? Male resistance has been such a basic force driving women's distress and reluctance to engage in the world's affairs that, as a woman, I perceived that question to be foundational. Certainly, the masculine crisis playing out on the American stage seemed most visible, most noisily and violently demonstrated, in the battle be-tween the sexes. It also seemed evident wherever I looked in these years that men see women's advancement as a driving force behind their own distress.

But for the many men I've met in researching this book, that gender battle was only a surface manifestation of other struggles. The well-springs of their anguish were more obscure, and flowed through deeper channels. And so I put aside my prefigured map and set out to follow where they led. Lured from my intended course, I sometimes lost sight of the bright beacons and media buoys marking the shoals where men and women clashed, and also lost sight of that secure shore where my feminist concepts were grounded. So it was perhaps surprising, or at least surprising to me, that the journey men led me on ultimately led me back to feminism. With that return, I was struck all the more by how tragic it is that women and men find themselves so far apart. If my travels taught me anything about the two sexes, it is that each of our struggles depends on the success of the other's. Men and women are at a historically opportune moment where they hold the keys to each other's liberation.

Often, while writing this book, I've thought of the drawing of an artichoke that Craig Hastings, the youngest member of the Promise Keepers' Glendora group, once sketched for me on my reporter's notepad. He was attempting to delineate his struggle to peel away the layers of daily experience and draw close to male friends and to God, to diagram the hidden core of longing inside the opaque skin of things. But his drawing serves just as well to depict my travels with men, who suffered layers of betrayal, each of which concealed a deeper betrayal.

The outer layer of the masculinity crisis, men's loss of economic authority, was most evident in the recessionary winds of the early nineties, as the devastation of male unemployment grew ever fiercer. The role of family breadwinner was plainly being undermined by economic forces that spat many men back into a treacherous job market during corporate "consolidations" and downsizings. Even the many men who were never laid off were often gripped with the fear that they could be next—that their footholds as providers were frighteningly unsteady.

As the economy recovered, the male crisis did not, and it became apparent that whatever men's afflictions were, they could not be gauged solely through graphs from the Bureau of Labor Statistics. Underlying their economic well-being was another layer of social and symbolic understanding between men, a tacit compact undergirding not only male employment but the whole connection between men and the public domain. That pact was forged through loyalty, through a conviction that a man's "word" meant something in the larger society, through a belief that faithfulness, dedication, and duty would be rewarded in kind, or at least appreciated in some meaningful way—some way that "made you a man." Realizing that loyalty, whether to a corporation, an army, or a football team, no longer allowed a man to lay claim to male virtue—that it was as likely, in fact, to make him a pitiable sap—could be devastating to any man, but especially to those postwar men raised on home-team spirit, John Wayne westerns, and tributes to the selfless service of the American GI.

Even such a loss of loyalty, though, was not at the heart of things. Beneath it lay an even deeper and more private layer of male betrayal, as rabid football fan Big Dawg showed me. One moment, Big Dawg would be decrying the double-crossing NFL moguls who took his team away; the next moment, he was grieving the loss of the remote cane-wielding father he barely knew. From the start, I intended to talk to the men in this book about such matters as work, sports, marriage, religion, war, and entertainment. I didn't go to them originally to ask about their fathers. But they insisted that I do so. Over and over, the breakdown of loyalty in the public domain brought my male guides face-to-face with the collapse of some personal patrimony. Behind all the public double crosses, they sensed, lay their fathers' desertion.

This connection between the public and the paternal betrayals was sensed more than reasoned. The men I came to know talked about their fathers' failures in the most private and personal terms, pointing inevitably to small daily letdowns that were their most visible disappointments: "My father didn't teach me how to throw a ball" or "My father never came to my Little League games" or "My father was always at work." That they had felt neglected as boys in the home, that their fathers had emotionally or even literally abandoned the family circle, was painful enough. But they suspected that in some way hard to grasp, much less describe, their fathers had deserted them in the public realm, too. "My father never taught me how to be a man" was the refrain I heard over and over again. "I was not *guided* by my father," Jack Schat, from the domestic-violence group, said to me once, his voice full of anguish. Having a father was supposed to mean having an older man show you how the world worked and how to find your place in it. Down the generations, the father wasn't simply a good sport who played backyard catch, took his son to ball games, or paid for his education. He was a human bridge connecting the boy to an adult life of public engagement and responsibility. That was why shipyard worker Ernie McBride, Jr., took me to meet his father: Ernie McBride, Sr., had taught him "how to be a man," not by playing sports or bringing home a big paycheck, but by leading a meaningful life—by being the kind of man who would struggle against racism at a shipyard union local, a neighborhood grocery store, a public school; by being a man whose actions mattered to a society he cared about.

For centuries, of course, fathers have disappointed, neglected, abused, abandoned their sons. But there was something particularly unexpected, and so particularly disturbing, about the nature of the paternal desertion that unfolded in the years after World War II, precisely because it coincided with a period of unprecedented abundance. In the generation before the war, millions of fathers failed to support their families, and hordes of them abandoned their households, became itinerant laborers, hoboes, winos. But that was the fault of the Great Depression, not of its men. By contrast, the post–World War II era was the moment of America's great bounty and ascendance, when the nation and thus its fathers were said to own the world. Never, or so their sons were told, did fathers have so much to pass on as at the peak of the American Century. And conversely, never was there such a burden on the sons to learn how to run a world they would inherit. Yet the fathers, with all the force of fresh victory and moral virtue behind them, seemingly unfettered in their paternal power and authority, failed to pass the mantle, the knowledge, all that power and authority, on to their sons.

If only the fathers could have explained why. Because the men I got to know could have borne even their fathers' failure to bestow a legacy; they could have weathered the disappointment of a broken patrimony. What undid them was their fathers' *silence*. The sons grew up with fathers who so often seemed spectral, there and yet not there, "heads" of household strangely disconnected from the familial body. The nonpresent presence of paternal ghosts haunted long after the sons had left home, made families of their own. An aching sadness remained. Men spoke to me of waiting, year after year, for a sign, a late-night confidence, a death-bed confession, even—desperately—a letter delivered posthumously, for any moment that would decode the mystery of their mute fathers. "My dad was real quiet," Dennie Elliott, of the Glendora Promise Keepers, said to me one afternoon, his voice more mournful than bitter. "You could sit in a room and if he said half a dozen words in an afternoon, you were lucky. We'd always say, 'Wonder what Dad's thinking?'" Dennie would never find out. "In all the time I knew my father, he only told me, 'Always be good at what you do,' and 'Don't be late—always be on time.'"

As I was finishing this book, a new novel by sociologist and former antiwar activist Todd Gitlin arrived in the mail. When I had talked to Gitlin many months earlier, he had told me he was working on a father-son story that he thought might be of interest. *Sacrifice* turned out to be the tale of an adult son whose inexplicable and estranged father has just died, having either jumped or fallen in front of a subway train, the son doesn't know which. The father has left him an inheritance of sorts: a stack of diaries from "the abandonment years," in which he has inscribed, sometimes moment by moment, his innermost thoughts, yearnings, secrets. "He thought these materials were yours by right," the father's attorney tells the grown son. "He wanted you to have them." And the emotionally starved son devours them, not wanting the words to end. "Father, say more," he appeals to the dust-covered books, "I can take it."[1] The novel is the eloquent, mature reprise of a boy's fantasy, a fantasy shared by so many grown postwar sons: that salvation may come through paternal speech, by a father's silence broken at last.

That layer of paternal betrayal felt, for many of the men I spent time with, like the innermost core, the artichoke's bitter heart. The fathers had made them a promise, and then had not made good on it. They had lied. The world they had promised had never been delivered. But some of the men fathomed that there was yet one more level within, a betrayal deeper than that of personal or public male elders. It was a betrayal so all-encompassing that, as a few men understood, it could hardly be blamed on the fathers. Its tsunami force had swamped the fathers as well as the sons. Its surge had washed all the men of the American Century into a swirling ocean of larger-than-life, ever-transmitting images in which usefulness to society meant less and less and celebrityhood ever more, where even one's appearance proved an unstable currency. It wasn't that real work had disappeared or that men weren't still doing it, and it wasn't that men were no longer needed in their communities. But now even the most traditional of craftsmen and community builders lived in a world where personal worth was judged in ornamental terms: Were they "sexy"? Were they "known"? Had they "won"?

"Winning" was always a peculiarly prominent aspect of the American masculine quest, the source of much violence and bloodshed in our nation's short history. But men had generally been expected to win within a social context: they strived and wrangled to wrest a community out of wilderness; they "won the West" to build a nation. Dominance, for all its dark consequences, at least was harnessed to an objective, counterweighted by the summons to serve the needs of a growing society. The American Century, on the other hand, elevated winning to the very apex of manhood while at the same time disconnecting it from meaningful social purpose. Being first seemed to be all that mattered. The space program's opening decade was driven by such weightless imperatives, and because such moments of triumph, of firstness, had no larger significance, no social ballast, they had to be repeated again and again. It wasn't enough for John Glenn to make history by circling the earth three times; he had to go up as an old man and do it all over—and even then his achievement lasted only as long as the media coverage. Any lucky soul could win, but there could be no sense of victory because there was no object of victory.

If there was an enemy behind this cultural sea change, it seemed to most men to have a feminine face. Surely this ornamental realm of star turns, hair-sprayed media appearances, and retouched magazine covers was a pink-and-white girls' world, the dominion of the beauty queen. Men felt trapped in Miss America's boudoir. She was now their rival, not to be won over by a show of masculine strength, care, or protection, but only to be bested in a competition where the odds did not seem to be on the men's side.

But just because men have wound up in a beauty-contest world doesn't mean women have put them there. The gaze that plagues them doesn't actually spring from a feminine eye. The ever-prying, ever-invasive beam reducing men to objects comes not from women's inspection but from the larger culture. Cast into the gladiatorial arena of ornament, men sense their own diminishment in women's strength. But the "feminine" power whose rise most genuinely threatens men is not the female shoulder hoisting girders at a construction site, not the female foot in the boardroom door of a corporation, not the female vote in the ballot box. The "femininity" that has hurt men the most is an artificial femininity manufactured and marketed by commercial interests. What demeans men is a force ever more powerful in the world, one that has long demeaned women. The gaze that hounds men is the very gaze that women have been trying to escape.

Truly, men and women have arrived at their ornamental imprisonment by different routes. Women were relegated there as a sop for their exclusion from the realm of power-striving men. Men arrived there as a result of their power-striving, which led to a society drained of context, saturated with a competitive individualism that has been robbed of craft or utility, and ruled by commercial values that revolve around who has the most, the best, the biggest, the fastest. The destination of both roads was an enslavement to glamour.

Glamour is perceived as a feminine principle, but really it is an expression not of inherent femininity but of femininity's merchandised facade. Ornament is wonderful as frivolity, as something one adopts or discards for one's own fun and enjoyment. But when a mass commercial culture took over adornment wholesale, when women came to feel that beauty had been stolen from them as a pleasure and was being peddled back to them as a commodity, when women divined that they were being sold literally a bill of goods, they began to revolt. Revolt wasn't easy. Women quickly learned how protean and co-opting commercial culture could be; their struggle to define themselves separately from commercial dictates was soon met by flattering importunings to define their liberation in terms of Virginia Slims cigarettes and Charlie perfume, to lift their "self-esteem" with cosmetics and plastic surgery. But those women who struggled to keep the ornamental in its rightful place, to own it and enjoy it and use it instead of being owned and used by it, gained a new power, the power to stand back from the marketplace and see it for what it was.

Returning from a journey can sometimes make the familiar landscape of home clear, as if for the first time. When I returned to the old question of men's grievances against women, having witnessed the ways that men were betrayed by their culture, I came back understanding something else: what divided men and women could also unite them. Their common ground lay precisely in the concept over which they'd so often fought: feminism. For men seeking to struggle against their betrayals, feminism offers an essential key; in turn, men's success in their struggle may offer the key to feminism's revival.

Feminism and the Man

IN THE 1960s, American feminism reawakened from its slumber of almost half a century. Like other revolutions, the one for women's rights had come in waves. Past periods of feminist activism had concentrated largely on the ways women's rights were fettered by the courts, the church, the statehouse. They were sparked by revolutionary social and legal expansions of individual liberties that did not expand the liberties of individual women. The French revolution inspired Mary Wollstonecraft, and also enraged her by excluding half the population from its promised benefits; she wrote *A Vindication of the Rights of Woman* in indignant response to Talleyrand's "democratic" plan for public education, which excluded girls from school once they turned eight.[1] Likewise, in nineteenth-century America, female abolitionists went on from the emancipation of African-Americans to rally around the cause of women's suffrage. The feminist resurgence of the 1960s and 1970s, however, cohered around consciousness of sex discrimination in a very different realm — the commercial one.

Of course, the "second wave" of feminism, like its antecedents, challenged as well the older societal institutions of governance, religion, and employment — and went on to reshape profoundly the ways women are treated by the law, at work and school, in the doctor's office, and on the playing fields. But the starting gun in the postwar feminist campaign, Betty Friedan's 1963 classic, *The Feminine Mystique*, was a broadside almost exclusively aimed at the *commercial* mistreatment of women.

In hindsight, what likely provoked women's immediate and overwhelming response to Friedan's book was its single-minded focus on the way postwar American women were being strangely diminished and de-humanized by a new mass culture. As a twenty-six-year-old housewife from Lansing, Michigan, wrote (typically) to Friedan: "I feel like an ap-pliance. . . . My brain seems dead, and I am nothing but a parasite."[3] *The Feminine Mystique* identified an increasingly powerful yet largely intan-gible industry of household products, popular media, advertising, and pop psychology that was making women feel "dead," an industry that had created and then fed off what Friedan aptly called "the housewife market." The author described the moment she first truly glimpsed the source of women's oppression—her epiphany occurred while talking not to a lawmaker or a judge but to an adman.

> Properly manipulated ("if you are not afraid of that word," he said), American housewives can be given the sense of identity, purpose, cre-ativity, the self-realization, even the sexual joy they lack—by the buying of things. I suddenly realized the significance of the boast that women wield seventy-five per cent of the purchasing power in America. I sud-denly saw American women as *victims* of that ghastly gift, that power at the point of purchase.[4]

The "second wave" of the American women's movement was in large measure a response to this insight. From the first "zap action" of women's liberation—the famous protest against the 1968 Miss America beauty pageant—to the sit-in at the *Ladies' Home Journal* offices, from nationwide raids on apparel shows to campus-wide protests against vis-iting *Playboy* scouts, the prime suspect behind the modern woman's crisis was recognized as a mass-media and mass-merchandising culture. When the members of the Women's Liberation Front decided to invade the corporate inner sanctum, they didn't descend on the boardroom of an industrial titan; they chose the stockholders' meeting of CBS.[5] Likewise, the literature of feminism, from *Ms.* to radical underground newsletters to fiction, challenged the shiny surface of commercially packaged wom-anhood. In one bestselling feminist novel after another—Sue Kaufman's *Diary of a Mad Housewife*, Anne Roiphe's *Up the Sandbox!*, Sheila Ballan-tyne's *Norma Jean the Termite Queen*, Marilyn French's *The Women's Room*—heroines ensconced in consumerism's invisible showcase beat their wings against its Windexed glass. "What's the matter with you, Norma?" the husband, Martin, in Ballantyne's novel asks when he returns one evening to find his Pleasant Valley housewife half catatonic, staring at an ad for household appliances. "Do you want a new microwave oven?

Do you want a new kitchen floor? How about redecorating the bathroom?" No, she replies, "I want to die, Martin"—and he tries to snap her out of it with an extra $20 for the beauty parlor.[6]

With a sense of startled clarity, feminist social critics wrote of the problem that now had a name. "The mass media molds everyone into more passive roles, into roles of more frantic consuming, into human beings with fragmented views of society," feminist activist Alice Embree wrote in 1970. "But what it does to everyone, it does to women even more." In a consumer-driven world, she remarked, women are "doubly used as sexual objects to sell products."[7] Such observations quickly became feminist commonplace. As Lucy Komisar declared, typically, in a 1971 anthology of women's-movement essays, "Advertising is an insidious propaganda machine for a male supremacist society."[8] The implication of so much of the feminist critique of the seventies was that *she* was being controlled and being objectified by *him*. What was not then recognized were the ways in which men, too, were being controlled and objectified. As she was treated, so must he be. If she was expected to play the perpetually submissive and pampered housewife, then he was expected to be the perpetually dominant and powerful breadwinner. Men, subjected to this ideal of superdominance, could as little live up to or escape it as women could the ideal of supermodel glamour.

At century's end, feminists can no longer say of consumer culture with such ringing confidence that "what it does to everyone, it does to women even more." The commercialized, ornamental "femininity" that the women's movement diagnosed now has men by the throat. Men and women both feel cheated of lives in which they might have contributed to a social world; men and women both feel pushed into roles that are about little more than displaying prettiness or prowess in the marketplace. Women were pushed first, but now their brothers have joined that same forced march.

If the male march seems different, that's largely because it's been described, and thereby disguised, in "masculine" terms. The departure point of that march—the shutting down of places like the Long Beach Naval Shipyard—has typically been depicted as the loss of workplaces where men could exercise masculine brawn. But the more profound loss is of a world where men cared for each other and for the workplace society in which they were embedded. Likewise, the endpoint of that march—the world of superathletes, action heroes, and Viagra studs—is seen as a new horizon of amped-up virility, a technologically enhanced supermanhood. But it's really the rise of face-powdered vanity in another guise. This transit is a familiar one, previously traversed by women, a

historic westward march in which the Colonial ideal of the strong pioneer mother gave way to the commercial icon of the Las Vegas showgirl.

———

MY TRAVELS LED me to a final question: Why don't contemporary men
rise up in protest against their betrayal? If they have experienced so
many of the same injuries as women, the same humiliations, why don't
they challenge the culture as women did? Why can't men seem to act?

The stock answers that have been offered to explain men's reluctance
to break out of stereotypical male models don't suffice. Men aren't simply refusing to "give up the reins of power," as some feminists have
argued. The reins have already slipped from most of their hands, anyway.
Nor are men merely chary of violating sanctioned masculine codes by
expressing pain and neediness, as Promise Keepers and "wildman"-
retreat leaders have contended. In an era where emoting is the coin of
the commercial realm, it's unlikely that airing painful feelings would get
a man any further than a talk show. While the pressures on men to
imagine themselves in power and in control of their emotions are im-
pediments to male revolt, a more fundamental obstacle overshadows
them. If men have feared to tread where women have rushed in, then
maybe that's because women have had it easier in one very simple regard:
women could frame their struggle as a battle against men.

For the many women who embraced feminism in one way or another
in the 1970s, that consumer culture was not some intangible and impersonal force; they saw it as a cudgel wielded by men against women. The
mass culture's portfolio of sexist images was gender-war propaganda that
"contributes to the myth of male superiority," journalist Ellen Willis,
then a Redstocking Sister, wrote in her 1969 essay "Consumerism and
Women." In fact, she charged, liberal men who blame economic forces
for women's humiliating consumer roles just want "to avoid recognizing
that they exploit women by attributing women's oppression solely to
capitalism." Men, not the marketplace, many women believed, were the
root problem—and so, as Willis put it, "the task of the women's liberation movement is to collectively combat male domination in the home,
in bed, on the job."[9] And indeed, there were virulent, sexist attitudes to
confront. But the 1970s model of confrontation could get feminism only
halfway to its goal.

Because the women who engaged in the feminist campaigns of the
seventies were fighting the face of "male domination," they were able to
take advantage of a ready-made model for revolt. To wage their battle,
they could unfurl a well-worn map and follow a reliable strategy. Ironically, it was a male strategy—feminists grabbed hold of the blueprint for

the American male paradigm and made good use of it. They had at the ready all the elements required to make that paradigm work. They had a clearly defined oppressive enemy: the "patriarchy." They had a real frontier to conquer and clear for other women: all those patriarchal institutions, both the old ones that still rebuffed women, like the U.S. Congress or U.S. Steel, and the new ones that tried to remold women, like Madison Avenue or the glamour and media-pimp kingdoms of Bert Parks and Hugh Hefner. Feminists also had their own army of "brothers": sisterhood. Each GI Jane who participated in this struggle felt she was useful. Whether she was distributing leaflets or working in a women's-health clinic, whether she was lobbying legislators to pass a child-care bill or tossing her bottles of Clairol in a "freedom trash can," she was part of a greater glory, the advancement of her entire sex. Many women whose lives were touched by feminism felt in some way that they had reclaimed an essential usefulness; together, they had charged the barricades that kept each of them from a fruitful, thriving life. Women had discovered a good fight, and a flight path to adult womanhood. Traveling along the trajectory of feminism, each "small step" for a woman would add up finally to a giant leap for womankind, not to mention humankind.

The male paradigm of confrontation, in which an enemy could be identified, contested, and defeated, was endlessly transferable. It proved useful as well to activists in the civil-rights movement and the antiwar movement, the gay-rights movement and the environmental movement. It was, in fact, the fundamental organizing principle of virtually every concerted countercultural campaign of the last half century. Yet it could launch no "men's movement." Herein lies the bedeviling paradox, and the source of male inaction: the model women have used to revolt is the exact one men not only can't use but are trapped in. The solution for women has proved the problem for men.

The male paradigm is peculiarly unsuited to mounting a challenge to men's predicament. Men have no clearly defined enemy who is oppressing them. How can men be oppressed when the culture has already identified them as the oppressors, and when they see themselves that way? As one man wrote plaintively to Promise Keepers, "I'm like a kite with a broken string, but I'm also holding the tail."[10] In an attempt to employ the old paradigm, men have invented antagonists to make their problems visible, but with the passage of time, these culprits—scheming feminists, affirmative-action proponents, job-grabbing illegal aliens, the wife of a president—have come to seem increasingly unconvincing as explanations for their situation. Defeating such paper tigers offers no sense of victory.

Nor do men have a clear frontier on which to challenge their intangible enemies. What new realms should they be gaining—the media, entertainment, and image-making institutions of corporate America? But these are institutions, they are told, that are already run by men; how can men invade their own territory? Is technological progress the frontier? Why then does it seem to be pushing men into obsolescence, socially and occupationally? What kind of frontier conquers the American man instead of vice versa? Is technology not the frontier but the enemy? But if the American man crushes the machine, whose machine has he vanquished?

The male paradigm of confrontation has, in fact, proved worthless to men. Yet maybe that's not so unfortunate. Maybe, in the long run, it's a blessing. The usefulness of that paradigm has reached a point of exhaustion anyway. The women's movement and the other civil-rights movements have discovered its limits. Their most obvious enemies have been sent into retreat or defeated outright, yet the problems persist. While women are still outnumbered in the executive suites, many have risen in the ranks and some have achieved authoritative positions—often only to perpetuate the same transgressions as their male predecessors. Women in power in the media, advertising, and Hollywood have for the most part continued to generate the same sorts of demeaning images as their male counterparts. Blaming a cabal of men has taken feminism about as far as it can go. The intransigence of internalized and conditioned oppression cannot be as handily explained by such a simple and personal adversarial model. Other paradigms are needed to untangle the invisible skein of stubborn threads that restrains women and other subordinated populations. That's why those populations have a great deal at stake in the liberation of the one population uniquely poised to discover and employ a new paradigm—men. Men are so poised on two counts: First, by experience with their long confusion, especially (for some) their experience in Vietnam, where they more than other Americans faced a battle without battle lines and, if they were honest enough, got to confront their own culpability in their agony. And second, by need, because in their agony, the old approach offers them nothing; they must envision a new passage if they are to free themselves from their pain and their paralysis. By venturing from the conventional route, they may find a better way forward to a meaningful manhood. As the Reverend Gordon Dalbey said, in his defense of the prodigal son, "The rebel is closer to the Kingdom."

There are signs that men are seeking such a breakthrough. When the Million Man March and Promise Keepers attracted record numbers of men, pundits scratched their heads in bafflement—why would so many men want to attend events that offered no agenda, no battle plan, no culprit to confront? No wonder critics who were having trouble placing the gatherings in the usual frame of political conflict found it easier to focus their attentions on the reactionary and hate-mongering attitudes of the "leaders" of these movements, concluding that the real "agenda" must be the anti-Semitism of the Nation of Islam's Louis Farrakhan or the homophobia and sexism of Promise Keepers founder Bill McCartney. But maybe the men who attended these mass gatherings weren't looking for answers that involved an enemy. As Farrakhan's speech, chock-full of conspiracy theories, malevolent plots, and numerological codes, dragged on, men in droves hastened for the exits. "What was really fantastic about the day was just being together with all these men, and thinking about what I might do differently," George Henderson, a forty-eight-year-old social worker, told me as he and two friends headed out early. The speech wasn't so important. "You can just watch that on TV," one of his friends said, and they all agreed. The men weren't there to assign blame; they were seeking a place where they could start to think about their situation afresh.

The march and the rallies were perceived by their participants not as ends in themselves but as jumping-off points into unknown territory. The amassing of huge numbers of men was important not as a martial show of force but as a reassuring sign to individual men that they were not alone in their confusions, their sense of drifting, their desire to search for new ways of being men. Gathering together was a summoning of courage for the unmapped journey ahead. Lamentably, since those men returned home to pursue their journeys alone or in small groups, the lack of maps has mostly proved crippling.

American men have generally responded well as caretakers in times of crisis, whether that be in wars, depressions, or natural disasters. The preeminent contemporary example of such a male mobilization also comes on the heels of a crisis, though one outside the rubric of war: gay men's response to AIDS. Ironically, at the very time gay style was being co-opted to serve the needs of ornamental commerce, gay men were building a new society around the nurturance of men in dire need. Virtually overnight, just as the Depression-era Civilian Conservation Corps built dams and parks and salvaged farmland, just as the World War II–era Seabees built bridges, housing, and hospitals, so have gay men built a network of clinics and health-delivery systems, drug buyers' clubs, legal and psychological services, fund-raising and political-action brigades, shelters, hospices, transportation, home-attendant care, "Buddies" visits, meals on wheels, even laundry assistance. As Mark Senak, one of the original staff members of the Gay Men's Health Crisis, put it, they were just men who "overcame our fears and took care of each other when no one else was going to do it."[11] It was the sort of monumental social effort by ordinary men that would surely have stirred the soul of Ernie Pyle. Which may explain one unanticipated consequence of the AIDS epidemic. The courage of these caregivers has generated, even in this homophobic nation, a wellspring of admiration and respect. Their quiet and necessary heroism has humanized and *masculinized* gay men in the eyes of many of their fellow citizens. They had a job to do and they did it.

Half a century ago, Ernie Pyle conceived of a world where he and his fellow grunts were "all men of new professions out in some strange night caring for each other." His vision, tragically, occurred not at the advent of a century of the common man, but at the coronation of flyboy commercial celebrity. But Pyle's bugle call is still a summons for a generational transformation, waiting to be heard.

Social responsibility is not the special province of masculinity; it's the lifelong work of all citizens in a community where people are knit together by meaningful and mutual concerns. But if husbanding a society is not the exclusive calling of "husbands," all the better for men's future. Because as men struggle to free themselves from their crisis, their task is not, in the end, to figure out how to be masculine—rather, their masculinity lies in figuring out how to be human. The men who worked at the Long Beach Naval Shipyard didn't come there and learn their crafts as riggers, welders, and boilermakers to *be* masculine; they were seeking something worthwhile to *do*. Their sense of their own manhood flowed out of their utility in a society, not the other way around. Conceiving of masculinity as something to *be* turns manliness into a detachable entity, at which point it instantly becomes ornamental, and about as innately "masculine" as fake eyelashes are inherently "feminine." Michael Bernhardt was one man who came to understand this in his difficult years after he returned from Vietnam. "All these years I was trying to be all these stereotypes" of manhood, he said, "and what was the use? . . . I'm beginning to think now of not even defining it anymore. I'm beginning to think now just in terms of people." From this discovery follow others, like the knowledge that he no longer has to live by the "scorecard" his nation handed him. He can begin to conceive of other ways of being "human," and hence, of being a man.

And so with the mystery of men's nonrebellion comes the glimmer of an opening, an opportunity for men to forge a rebellion commensurate with women's and, in the course of it, to create a new paradigm for human progress that will open doors for both sexes. That was, and continues to be, feminism's dream, to create a freer, more humane world. Feminists have pursued it, particularly in the last two centuries, with great determination and passion. In the end, though, it will remain a dream without the strength and courage of men who are today faced with a historic opportunity: to learn to wage a battle against no enemy, to own a frontier of human liberty, to act in the service of a brotherhood that includes us all.

acknowledgments

THEY SAY MEN "DON'T COMMUNICATE," but the many eloquent men who were willing to speak to me for this book prove that a myth. My greatest debt is to them, for having the candor and courage to put their individual struggles into words.

The idea for this book began to take shape six years ago, during a John S. Knight Fellowship at Stanford University, and I'm particularly grateful to American studies scholar Jay Fliegelman, whose invented-on-the-spot tutorial on "masculinity" literature got me under way. Further down the road, I enjoyed the support of editors at *The New Yorker*, *DoubleTake*, *Esquire*, and *LA Weekly*, who published my early forays through embattled male territory.

My literary agent, Sandra Dijkstra, has been, as always, a source of much encouragement and an indefatigable defender. For assistance early on, I would like to thank Amy Leonard, Deborah Clark, and Jane Loranger. I am especially grateful to Ben Ehrenreich, whose meticulous fact-checking in the final stages spared me untold embarrassment. Religion scholar Paul Boyer, historian Christian Appy, and sociologist Todd Gitlin generously read drafts of chapters related to their fields and offered helpful advice. The book is graced with Jane Palecek's elegant design for the cover and interior.

William Morrow publisher Michael Murphy took this book under his wing and has been a generous and ever-on-call advocate. Also at Morrow, I'd like to thank Lisa Queen and Sharyn Rosenblum. My appreciation goes to Lynn Goldberg, for understanding the book and launching it into the world.

For aid and counsel, kindnesses small and large, I would also like to thank Sue Horton, Judy Sloan, Alyce LaViolette, Kevin King, Sandy Faulkner, Bob Black, Michael Bilton, Shirley Judd, Ira Levine, Tom Wright, Jonathan Kirsch, Larry Zerner, Susan Grode, Steve Oney,

Madeline Stuart, Liz Rymer, Dick Rymer, Callie Becker, Laura Pappas, Rob Faludi, and Marilyn Faludi.

There are still a few great editors in publishing, and I was blessed with the best, Tom Engelhardt, whose careful and caring editing has been invaluable. Finally, this book would not have been written without the nurturance, wisdom, and love of one good man, Russ Rymer.

notes

AUTHOR'S NOTE

Unless otherwise footnoted, all quotations of people appearing in the book come from author's personal interviews. In chapter 5, due to the intimate nature of group discussions, some of the men requested that their names be changed. In the Alternatives to Violence group, Michael, Paul, Carl, and Daniel are pseudonyms. In the Glendora Promise Keepers group, the following names are pseudonyms: Timothy and Nancy Atwater, Martin and Judy Booker, Jeremy and Glenda Foote, Frank Camilla, Howard and Libby Payson, Mike and Margaret Pettigrew, Craig Hastings, and Bart Hollister.

CHAPTER 1: THE SON, THE MOON, AND THE STARS

1. "An Echo Heard Around the World," *Life*, Aug. 22, 1960, p. 20; "A Different Drummer," *Time*, Aug. 22, 1960, p. 44; "Twinkle, Twinkle Little Star," *Time*, Sept. 19, 1960, p. 70.

2. "The Greatest Week in Space," *Life*, Aug. 22, 1960, p. 19; "Texts of Kennedy and Johnson Speeches Accepting the Democratic Nomination," *New York Times*, July 16, 1960, p. 7.

3. J. Fred MacDonald, *Television and the Red Menace: The Video Road to Vietnam* (New York: Praeger, 1985), pp. 111–121; Mike Benton, *The Comic Book in America: An Illustrated History* (Dallas: Taylor, 1989), p. 187.

4. John Taylor, "Men on Trial," *New York*, Dec. 16, 1991, cover story; Michael D'Antonio, "The Trouble with Boys," *Los Angeles Times Magazine*, Dec. 4, 1994, cover story; Lawrence Wright, "Are Men Necessary?" *Texas Monthly*, Feb. 1992, p. 82; Garrison Keillor, "Maybe Manhood Can Recover," *San Francisco Chronicle, Sunday Punch*, Jan. 10, 1993, p. 3; Waller R. Newell, "The Crisis of Manliness," *Weekly Standard*, Aug. 3, 1998, cover story; David Gates, "White Male Paranoia," *Newsweek*, March 29, 1993, cover story; "Men: It's Time to Pull Together," *Utne Reader*, May/June 1991, cover story.

5. Ronald C. Kessler and James A. McRae, Jr., "Trends in the Relationship Between

Sex and Attempted Suicide," *Journal of Health and Social Behavior,* June 1983, vol. 24, pp. 98–110; J. M. Murphy, "Trends in Depression and Anxiety: Men and Women," *Acta Psychiatr. Scand.,* 1986, vol. 73, pp. 113–127; Ronald F. Levant, *Masculinity Reconstructed* (New York: Dutton, 1995), pp. 209, 219–220; Andrew Kimbrell, *The Masculine Mystique* (New York: Ballantine, 1995), pp. 4–6; Darrel A. Regier, Jeffrey H. Boyd, et al., "One-month Prevalence of Mental Disorders in the United States," *Archives of General Psychiatry,* Nov. 1988, vol. 45, pp. 977–980.

6.   Yankelovich Clancy Shulman survey, 1986, described to me by Susan Hayward, senior vice president, Yankelovich; *The American Male Opinion Index,* vol. I (New York: Condé Nast Publications, 1990), pp. 17, 19, 29; Patrice Apodaca, "Cashing In on the Bad Boy Image, *Los Angeles Times,* July 2, 1997, p. A1.

7.   David Finkelhor, Richard J. Gelles, Gerald T. Hotaling, Murray A. Straus, eds., *The Dark Side of Families: Current Family Violence Research* (Beverly Hills: Sage, 1983), pp. 21–22; Richard J. Gelles and Murray A. Straus, *Intimate Violence* (New York: Simon & Schuster, 1988), p. 88; David Finkelhor et al., *Stopping Family Violence* (Beverly Hills: Sage, 1988), pp. 23, 24.

8.   Richard Slotkin, *Regeneration Through Violence: The Mythology of the American Frontier, 1600–1860* (Middletown, Conn.: Wesleyan University Press, 1973), p. 310; John Filson, *The Discovery and Settlement of Kentucke* (Ann Arbor: University Microfilms, Inc., 1966), pp. 49, 56–57.

9.   E. Anthony Rotundo, *American Manhood* (New York: BasicBooks, 1993), p. 13. The study of heroes, cited in Rotundo, is Theodore P. Greene, *America's Heroes: The Changing Models of Success in American Magazines* (New York: Oxford University Press, 1970), pp. 45–46; Vernon Louis Parrington, *Main Currents in American Thought* (New York: Harcourt Brace & World, 1930), vol. 2, p. 179. Also, see Slotkin, *Regeneration Through Violence,* pp. 554–555.

10.   Michael Kimmel, *Manhood in America* (New York: Free Press, 1996), p. ix; Parrington, *Main Currents in American Thought,* vol. 3, p. 16; Frank Triplett, *The Life and Treacherous Death of Jesse James,* ed. Joseph Snell (New York: Promontory Press, 1970), p. x; Filson, *Discovery and Settlement of Kentucke,* p. 81.

11.   Frank Norris, *McTeague* (New York: New American Library, 1964), pp. 8, 340.

12.   Boone wore the more highbrow beaver hat, though the confusion dates back further than Fess Parker: the actor cast as Boone in an 1820s play donned a coonskin cap when he couldn't get a beaver hat. The real Davy Crockett didn't start out wearing a coonskin cap, either; he adopted it after the look was already legendary—to keep up, in other words, with his mythmakers. Richard Boyd Hauck, "The Man in the Buckskin Hunting Skin," in *Davy Crockett: The Man, the Legend, the Legacy, 1786–1986,* ed. Michael A. Lofaro (Knoxville: University of Tennessee Press, 1985), p. 7; Margaret J. King, "The Recycled Hero: Walt Disney's Davy Crockett," in *Davy Crockett: The Man, the Legend, the Legacy,* pp. 141–143, 148; John Mack Faragher, *Daniel Boone* (New York: Henry Holt, 1992), pp. 335, 339.

13. Lance Morrow, "Are Men Really That Bad?, *Time*, Feb. 14, 1994, cover story.

14. Betty Friedan, *The Feminine Mystique* (New York: Dell, 1983); Eva Figes, *Patriarchal Attitudes* (Greenwich, Conn.: Fawcett, 1971), p. 12.

15. Herb Goldberg, *The Hazards of Being Male* (New York: Signet, 1987), p. x.

16. David D. Gilmore, *Manhood in the Making: Cultural Concepts of Masculinity* (New Haven: Yale University Press, 1990), pp. 46, 51, 163, 178, 187, 202–206, 230.

17. Robert Bly, *Iron John: A Book About Men* (New York: Addison-Wesley, 1990), p. 6; Robert Moore and Douglas Gillette, *The King Within: Accessing the King in the Male Psyche* (New York: William Morrow, 1992), pp. 214–215.

18. James Tobin, *Ernie Pyle's War* (New York: Free Press, 1997), p. 91; Bill Mauldin, *Up Front* (New York: W. W. Norton, 1995), pp. 42, 98–99.

19. Audie Murphy, *To Hell and Back* (New York: Holt, Rinehart and Winston, 1949), pp. 163–165.

20. Lee G. Miller, *The Story of Ernie Pyle* (New York: Viking Press, 1950), pp. 41–42, 89; Tobin, *Ernie Pyle's War*, pp. 18, 20, 30, 77, 132; Ernie Pyle, *Here Is Your War* (Cleveland: World, 1943), p. 117.

21. J. Fred MacDonald, *Television and the Red Menace*, p. 7; Tobin, *Ernie Pyle's War*, p.105; "Perspective on Greatness: GI Joe," *Hearst Metrotone News*, 1973; Ernie Pyle, *Brave Men* (New York: Henry Holt, 1944), p. 12; Ernie Pyle, *Ernie's War: The Best of Ernie Pyle's World War II Dispatches*, ed. David Nichols (New York: Random House, 1986), p. 306.

22. Pyle, *Ernie's War*, p. 195.

23. Alexander Feinberg, "All City 'Let's Go,'" *New York Times*, Aug. 15, 1945, p. 1; Frederick R. Barkley, "President Joins Capital's Gaiety," *New York Times*, Aug. 15, 1945, p. 3; "Victory Celebrations," *Life*, Aug. 27, 1945, pp. 21, 27–28.

24. Ernie Pyle, *Ernie's America: The Best of Ernie Pyle's 1930s Travel Dispatches* (New York: Random House, 1989), pp. 57–58, 103, 221–222, 338–339, 346–347, 369–371; Tobin, *Ernie Pyle's War*, p. 114.

25. Samuel Eliot Morison, *The Oxford History of the American People* (New York: New American Library, 1972), vol. 3, p. 306; Arthur M. Schlesinger, Jr., *The Coming of the New Deal* (Boston: Houghton Mifflin, 1959), p. 19; Arthur A. Ekirch, Jr., *Ideologies and Utopias: The Impact of the New Deal on American Thought* (Chicago: Quadrangle, 1969), pp. 107–108, 147–148; Franklin D. Roosevelt, "Commonwealth Club Speech, Sept. 23, 1932," in *Franklin D. Roosevelt, 1882–1945*, ed. Howard F. Bremer (Dobbs Ferry, NY: Oceana, 1971), pp. 100–106.

26. Henry A. Wallace, *The Century of the Common Man* (New York: Reynal & Hitchcock, 1943), pp. 5, 14.

27. John Morton Blum, *V Was for Victory: Politics and American Culture During World War II* (New York: Harcourt Brace Jovanovich, 1976), pp. 285, 288.

28. Ernie Pyle, *Brave Men*, p. 319.

29. Tobin, *Ernie Pyle's War*, pp. 61, 240.

30. Norman D. Markowitz, *The Rise and Fall of the People's Century: Henry A. Wallace and American Liberalism, 1941–1948* (New York: Free Press, 1973), p. 52.

31. Henry R. Luce, *The American Century* (New York: Farrar & Rinehart, 1941), pp. 22–23, 24, 37.

32. Wallace, *The Century of the Common Man*, p. 52; Markowitz, *The Rise and Fall of the People's Century*, pp. 305–306, 312.

33. Karl M. Schmidt, *Henry A. Wallace: Quixotic Crusade 1948* (Binghamton, N.Y.: Syracuse University Press, 1960), pp. 252–279; Curtis D. MacDougall, *Gideon's Army* (New York: Marzani & Munsell, 1965), pp. 248–283; Frank Kingdon, *An Uncommon Man: Henry Wallace and 60 Million Jobs* (New York: Readers Press, 1945); Markowitz, *The People's Century*, pp. 92–93.

34. Paul A. Carter, *Another Part of the Fifties* (New York: Columbia University Press, 1983), p. 25.

35. Studs Terkel, *The Good War* (New York: Ballantine, 1984), pp. 157–159.

36. Alexis de Tocqueville, *Democracy in America* (Garden City, N.Y.: Anchor, 1969), p. 627, cited in Kimmel, *Manhood in America*, p. 26.

37. "In New England, Busy Dad with Dad," "Pointers for Playful Fathers," special issue, "The Good Life," *Life*, Dec. 28, 1959, pp. 54, 125.

38. "Text of Kennedy's Inaugural Outlining Policies on World Peace and Freedom," *New York Times*, Jan. 21, 1961, p. 8; Norman Mailer, *The Presidential Papers* (New York: Penguin, 1968), p. 15.

39. *Moon Shot: The Inside Story of the Apollo Project*, prod. and dir. Kirk Wolfinger, TBS Productions, 1994.

40. "Five Key Groundlings," *Time*, March 2, 1962, p. 15.

41. Tom Lewis, *Divided Highways* (New York: Viking, 1997), pp. 89–91.

42. Robert A. Divine, *The Sputnik Challenge* (New York: Oxford University Press, 1993), p. 164.

43. Ibid., pp. xv–xvi; "Common Sense and Sputnik," *Life*, Oct. 21, 1957, p. 35; T. A. Heppenheimer, *Countdown: A History of Space Flight* (New York: John Wiley & Sons, 1997), p. 126.

44. Frederick Jackson Turner, *The Frontier in American History* (Tucson: University of Arizona Press, 1994), pp. 2–4.

45. When a 1966 Opinion Research Corporation poll asked Americans which, if any, federal program should be cut first, 48 percent chose the space program. William Sims Bainbridge, *The Spaceflight Revolution: A Sociological Study* (New York: John Wiley & Sons, 1976), p. 74; "Has U.S. Settled for No. 2 in Space?," *U.S. News & World Report*, Oct. 14, 1968, p. 74.

46. Neil Sheehan, *A Bright Shining Lie: John Paul Vann and America in Vietnam* (New York: Vintage, 1989), p. 719.

47. Associated Press, "Man Killed After Stealing Tank for Rampage," *New York Times*

May 19, 1995, p. A14; Kevin Gray and Jamie Reno, "The Road to Ruin," *People,* June 5, 1995, p. 65; Kelly Thornton, "The Rampage of Shawn Nelson," *San Diego Union-Tribune,* May 19, 1995, p. A1.

48. Tobin, *Ernie Pyle's War,* p. 120.

49. Ibid., pp. 115–116, 126, 159, 188–191, 206–207, 225; "Ernie Pyle's War," *Time,* July 17, 1944, cover story; Lincoln Barnett, "Ernie Pyle," *Life,* April 2, 1945, p. 94.

50. Tobin, *Ernie Pyle's War,* pp. 118–121, 212; Arthur Miller, *Situation Normal* (New York: Reynal & Hitchcock, 1944), pp. 1–2; Barnett, "Ernie Pyle," p. 95.

51. "The Greatest Generation," *Dateline NBC,* Jan. 15, 1999; Tom Brokaw, *The Greatest Generation* (New York: Random House, 1998), pp. 65–66, 112.

52. Garry Wills, *John Wayne's America* (New York: Touchstone, 1997), p. 157.

53. David Crockett, *A Narrative of the Life of David Crockett of the State of Tennessee,* James A. Shackford and Stanley J. Folmsbee, eds. (Knoxville: University of Tennessee Press, 1973), p. 194; Michael A. Lofaro, "The Hidden 'Hero' of the Nashville Crockett Almanacs," in *Davy Crockett: The Man, the Legend, the Legacy,* p. 54.

54. Norman Mailer, *The Presidential Papers* (New York: Penguin, 1963), pp. 52–53.

55. *Fallen Champ: The Untold Story of Mike Tyson,* prod. and dir. Barbara Kopple, Cabin Creek Films, 1993.

56. Gilmore, *Manhood in the Making,* p. 229.

57. Wallace, *The Century of the Common Man,* p. 18.

58. Thomas C. Reeves, *A Question of Character* (Rocklin, Calif.: Prima, 1992), pp. 58–59, 66–68.

59. John Kenneth Galbraith, *The New Industrial State* (Middlesex, England: Penguin, 1974), p. 50.

60. Robert H. Frank, "The Victimless Income Gap?," *New York Times,* April 12, 1999, p. A27.

61. Beth Shuster and James Rainey, "The North Hollywood Shootout: Officers Face Barrage of Bullets to Take Comrades Out of Line of Fire," *Los Angeles Times,* March 1, 1997, p. A1; Steve Berry and Scott Glover, "Bank Robber Bled to Death Unnecessarily," *Los Angeles Times,* April 21, 1998, p. A1.

62. Lynette Holloway, "The Fear Is Real Enough. The Gangs Are Another Story," *New York Times,* Feb. 13, 1998, section 3, p. 4; David Kocieniewski, "Youth Gangs from West Coast Become Entrenched in New York," *New York Times,* Aug. 28, 1997, p. B1.

63. Richard Lacayo, "When Kids Go Bad," *Time,* Sept. 19, 1994, cover story; Jon D. Hull, "A Boy and His Gun," *Time,* Aug. 2, 1993, p. 20; Barbara Kantrowitz, "Wild in the Streets," *Newsweek,* Aug. 2, 1993, cover story; Gordon Witkin, "Kids Who Kill," *U.S. News & World Report,* April 8, 1991, cover story; Michael D'Antonio, "Bad Boys or Bad Rap? Whether the Cause Is Emotional, Biological, or Sociological, the Fact Is That the Misbehavior of Boys Has Turned into a Scary Nationwide Crisis," *Fort Lauderdale Sun-Sentinel, Sunshine Magazine,* Feb. 19, 1995, p. 8; Brian E. Albrecht,

Debbi Snook, and Laura Yee, "Voices of Violence Series, Part One: Violence Is Their Language," *Plain Dealer*, Cleveland, March 6, 1994, p. 12A; Alison Carper, "Rough Boys," *Newsday*, May 2, 1993, p. 6.

64. "Youth Violence and Gangs," hearing before the Subcommittee on Juvenile Justice, U.S. Senate Judiciary Committee, Nov. 26, 1991 (Washington: U.S. Government Printing Office, 1992); "The American Worker Policy Briefing," *Roll Call*, no. 46, Oct. 5, 1992; Stephen Franklin and Carol Jouzaitis, "Bush Asks Billions for Job Training," *Chicago Tribune*, Aug. 25, 1992, p. C4; "1991 Defense Authorization Bill," hearing before the U.S. House of Representatives Armed Services Committee, Federal News Service, Feb. 6, 1990; Linda Rocawich, "Education Infiltration," *Progressive*, March 1994, p. 24; John Michael Kelly, "Inner-City Academies Offer Safety Nets," *Pittsburgh Post-Gazette*, April 21, 1998, p. A6.

65. Ann O'Hanlon, "New Interest in Corporal Punishment: Several States Weigh Get Tough Measures," *Washington Post*, March 5, 1995, p. A21; Jane Gross, "California Contemplates Paddling Graffiti Vandals," *New York Times*, Aug. 7, 1994, section 1, p. 5; Adam Nossiter, "As Boot Camps for Criminals Multiply, Skepticism Grows," *New York Times*, Dec. 18, 1993, p. A1; Laura Mansnerus, "More Courts Are Treating Violent Youths as Adults," *New York Times*, Dec. 3, 1993, p. A1; Ron Harris, "Kids in Custody: Part I: A Nation's Children in Lockup," *Los Angeles Times*, Aug. 22, 1993, p. 1A; Ronald Smothers, "Atlanta Sets a Curfew for Youths, Prompting Concern on Race Bias," *New York Times*, Nov. 21, 1990, p. A1; Jerry Gray, "Bill to Combat Juvenile Crime Passes House," *New York Times*, May 9, 1997, p. A1.

66. Richard Lee Colvin, " 'Hammer' Seeks to Keep Handle on Rise in Gangs," *Los Angeles Times*, July 16, 1989, section 2, p. 8; David Shaw, "Media Failed to Examine Alleged LAPD Abuses," *Los Angeles Times*, May 26, 1992, p. A1; David Freed, "The Only Agreement on Crime: No Easy Answers," *Los Angeles Times*, Dec. 22, 1990, p. A1; Sandy Banks, "The Legacy of a Slaying," *Los Angeles Times*, Sept. 11, 1989, section 2, p. 1; Mike Davis, *City of Quartz* (New York: Vintage, 1992), pp. 277, 280.

67. "State of the Union; President Bill Clinton's Speech; Transcript, Joint Session of Congress, Washington, D.C., January 26, 1994," *Vital Speeches*, February 15, 1994, vol. 60, no. 9, p. 258; Mike A. Males, *The Scapegoat Generation* (Monroe, Maine: Common Courage, 1996), p. 102.

68. Federal Bureau of Investigation, "Total Arrests, Distribution by Age," 1990–1997; Males, *The Scapegoat Generation*, pp. 104–105; Jerome G. Miller, "Juvenile Justice: Facts vs. Anger," *New York Times*, Aug. 15, 1998, p. A23.

69. "Once the poverty factor is removed," Males noted, " 'teen violence' disappears." Indeed, gang activity fell sharply in Los Angeles and across the nation as the job market improved in the late nineties. Males, *The Scapegoat Generation*, pp. 7, 107–109; Richard Marosi, "Killings by Gangs Take Big Plunge," *Los Angeles Times*, Jan. 1, 1999, p. B1; Matt Lait, "Los Angeles Homicides Plunge to 29-Year Low," *Los Angeles Times*,

Dec. 30, 1998, p. A1; Marlene Cimons, "Study Finds Murder Rate at 30-Year Low," *Los Angeles Times,* Jan. 3, 1999, p. A14.

70. Barbara Kantrowitz and Claudia Kalb, "Boys Will Be Boys," *Newsweek,* May 11, 1998, p. 54; Tamar Lewin, "How Boys Lost Out to Girl Power," *New York Times,* Week in Review, Dec. 13, 1998, p. 3; Michael D'Antonio, "The Trouble With Boys," *Los Angeles Times Magazine,* Dec. 4, 1994, p. 16.

CHAPTER 2: NOTHING BUT BIG WORK

1. Barbara Ehrenreich, *Fear of Falling: Inner Life of the Middle Class* (New York: Pantheon, 1989), p. 207.

2. The forty-thousand figure, from the Los Angeles County Federation of Labor, reflects heavy manufacturing jobs in the area lost to plant closings between 1977 and 1983. The accurate figure is likely to be at least double that number, according to Goetz Wolff, lecturer in urban planning at UCLA's School of Public Policy and Social Research and researcher for the Los Angeles County Federation of Labor, because the forty-thousand count included only larger plants and only jobs lost at the time when each of these plants actually closed, not jobs lost in the layoffs leading up to the plant closings.

3. Ann Markusen, Peter Hall, Scott Campbell, and Sabina Deitrick, *The Rise of the Gunbelt* (New York: Oxford University Press, 1991), p. 82; Mike Davis, "Chinatown, Revisited?: The 'Internationalization' of Downtown Los Angeles," in *Sex, Death and God in L.A.,* David Reid, ed. (Los Angeles: University of California Press, 1992), p. 30.

4. "Los Angeles County Employment of Major Industrial Sectors—1988–1998," Labor Market Information Division, California Employment Development Department, 1999; "Manufacturing Employment in the Los Angeles Area," Labor Market Information Division, California Employment Development Department, 1999; Lou Cannon, "Scars Remain Five Years After Los Angeles Riots," *Washington Post,* April 28, 1997, p. A4.

5. Gerald D. Nash, *The American West Transformed: The Impact of the Second World War* (Bloomington: Indiana University Press, 1985), pp. 62–63.

6. "The Case for the Long Beach Naval Shipyard," report of the Long Beach Naval Shipyard, 1954, p. 10, in collection of Long Beach Public Library; *Long Beach Naval Shipyard 1943–1997,* publication of the U.S. Navy, Long Beach, Calif., 1997; Neil Strassman, "A Long History of Service," *Long Beach Press-Telegram,* Feb. 19, 1995, p. A6; Lester Rubin, *The Negro in the Shipbuilding Industry* (Philadelphia: University of Pennsylvania Press, 1970), p. 43; Neil A. Wynn, *The Afro-American and the Second World War* (New York: Holmes & Meier, 1993), p. 16.

7. Charles F. Queenan, *Long Beach and Los Angeles: A Tale of Two Ports* (Northridge,

Calif.: Windsor, 1986), pp. 115–116; " 'Mothballs' for Navy Yard, Matthews Orders," *Long Beach Press-Telegram,* Feb. 8, 1950, p. A3.

8. Alexander Feinberg, "Mighty Carrier Roosevelt Commissioned by Truman," *New York Times,* Oct. 28, 1945, p. 1; "Text of Truman's Navy Yard Speech," *New York Times,* Oct. 28, 1945; Frank S. Adams, "Naval Might Backs President's Words," *New York Times,* Oct. 28, 1945, pp. 1, 31; Meyer Berger, "Seven Miles of Sea Power Reviewed by the President," *New York Times,* Oct. 28, 1945, p. 1.

9. *Long Beach Naval Shipyard 1943–1997;* "The Case for the Long Beach Shipyard," p. 13.

10. "Graving Dock Got Its Name from First 'King Bee of the Seabees,' " *Long Beach Press-Telegram,* June 12, 1986, p. O5; Donald W. White, *The American Century* (New Haven: Yale University Press, 1996), p. 54.

11. Chester Himes, *If He Hollers Let Him Go* (New York: Thunder's Mouth, 1986), p. 159; Gilbert H. Muller, *Chester Himes* (Boston: Twayne, 1989), pp. 20–21; Chester Himes, *The Quality of Hurt* (New York: Thunder's Mouth, 1972), p. 75.

12. "4000 Attend Formal Opening of Shipyard," *Independent,* Feb. 2, 1951, p. 3; "World War Two," *California's Gold with Huell Howser,* no. 409, 1993.

13. Dan Morgan, "Military Shipbuilders Procure a Windfall," *Washington Post,* National Weekly Edition, July 8–14, 1996, p. 29; "Navy Maintenance: Cost and Schedule Performance at San Diego and Long Beach Shipyards," United States General Accounting Office, Dec. 1992; Neil Strassman, "It's a Real Emotional Yo-Yo," *Long Beach Press-Telegram,* May 22, 1993, p. A5.

14. James W. Crawley, "S.D. Shipyards Offer Lobbyist Bounty If Rival Forced to Close," *San Diego Union-Tribune,* Feb. 26, 1995, p. A1.

15. Edmund Newton, "Tears Usher in End of an Era in Naval Town," *Los Angeles Times,* June 24, 1995, p. A1.

16. Ralph Vartabedian, "Pier Pressure," *Los Angeles Times,* July 14, 1996, p. D1; United States v. David Lee Bain et al., U.S. District Court, Southern District of California, grand jury indictment, criminal case no. 901051, Nov. 1988; Alan Abrahamson, "Ex-Shipyard Owner Pleads Guilty to Fraud," *Los Angeles Times,* Jan. 14, 1992, p. B5; Morgan, "Military Shipbuilders Procure a Windfall," p. 29.

17. Vartabedian, "Pier Pressure," pp. D1, D4; Chris Woodyard, "Navy Weighs Action Against Repair Shipyard After Judge Finds Fraud," *Los Angeles Times,* Sept. 23, 1989, p. 26A.

18. "Homicide in U.S. Workplaces," U.S. Department of Health and Human Services, National Institute for Occupational Safety and Health, Sept. 1992; E. Lynn Jenkins, Larry A. Layne, and Suzanne M. Kisner, "Homicide in the Workplace: The U.S. Experience, 1980–1988," *AAOHN Journal,* May 1992, pp. 215–218; Matthew W. Purdy, "Workplace Murders Provoke Lawsuits and Better Security," *New York Times,* Feb. 14, 1994, p. A1; Anne Ladky, "Unsafe Workplace Exacts Too High a Price," *Chicago Tribune,* July 19, 1992, p. 11; Dolores Kong, "Homicides Leading Cause of

Mass. Workplace Deaths in '91," *Boston Globe,* April 28, 1993, p. 24; Joseph A. Kinney, "When Domestic Violence Strikes the Workplace," *HRMagazine,* August 1995, pp. 74–78.

19. David E. Sanger and Steve Lohr, "A Search for Answers to Avoid the Layoffs," *New York Times,* March 9, 1996, p. A1; Daniel Howes, "Downsizing Pains ... Gains," *Detroit News,* March 17, 1996; Robert Trigaux, "Monster Mergers," *St. Petersburg Times,* Dec. 27, 1998, p. 14.

20. The estimate is from a 1992 report by the Los Angeles County's Aerospace Task Force. See Ralph Vartabedian, "Aerospace Cuts to Devastate Area," *Los Angeles Times,* March 17, 1992, p. 1A.

21. A. Russell Buchanan, *Black Americans in World War II* (Santa Barbara: Clio, 1977), pp. 17, 40–42; Gerald Nash, *World War Two and the West: Reshaping the Economy* (Lincoln: University of Nebraska Press, 1990), p. 77.

22. Vartabedian, "Pier Pressure," pp. D1, D4.

23. "Salute to a Civil Rights Pioneer," *Congressional Record,* Jan. 20, 1995, vol. 141, no. 12, p. E147.

24. Ibid.

25. The riots in Long Beach in April 1992, which received much less media coverage, produced the worst civil disorder in the city's history. One person was killed, 361 were injured, 1,200 people were arrested, and 345 fires were set, creating $20 million in damage. See Seth Mydans, "After the Riots: Tumult of Los Angeles Echoed in Long Beach," *New York Times,* May 20, 1992, p. A20.

26. Buchanan, *Black Americans in World War II,* p. 13.

27. The segregationist policies of such unions were finally broken after a prolonged legal struggle mounted by black workers and supported, after some foot-dragging, by the federal government. William H. Harris, "Federal Intervention into Union Discrimination: FEPC and the West Coast Shipyards During World War II," *Labor History,* Summer 1981, vol. 22, pp. 325–347; William H. Harris, *The Harder We Run: Black Workers Since the Civil War* (New York: Oxford University Press, 1982), pp. 119–122; Earl Brown and George R. Leighton, *The Negro and the War* (New York: AMS, 1972), pp. 11, 18, 24–27.

28. The integration of better-paying, skilled industries such as shipbuilding and ship repair was instrumental in reducing the income gap between white and minority workingmen in these years. After initial postwar setbacks, as black workers lost jobs at two and a half times the rate of whites, black male industrial employment again began to rise and, in 1951, the employment of young black men in their twenties reached a record high. But progress was short-lived; by 1960, black workers were further behind whites in wages, occupations, and unemployment than they had been at the end of World War II. Lester Rubin, *The Negro in the Shipbuilding Industry* (Philadelphia: University of Pennsylvania Press, 1970), p. 74; Harris, *The Harder We Run,* pp. 122, 128, 130–131; Susan M. Hartmann, *The Home Front and Beyond: American*

Women in the 1940s (Boston: Twayne, 1982), p. 5; Philip S. Foner, *Organized Labor and the Black Worker 1619–1973* (New York: Praeger, 1974), pp. 238–239, 269–270.

29. Queenan, *Long Beach and Los Angeles,* p. 116.

30. "The Long Beach Story," *Long Beach Review,* July 8, 1980, pp. 22–23; Ken Chilcote, "War Job Done, Douglas Plant Here Eyes Future," *Long Beach Press-Telegram,* Oct. 14, 1945; Richard DeAtley, *Long Beach: The Golden Shore* (Houston: Pioneer, 1988), p. 91.

31. D. J. Waldie, *Holy Land: A Suburban Memoir* (New York: W. W. Norton, 1996), p. 163.

32. Sherna Berger Gluck, *Rosie the Riveter Revisited* (New York: New American Library, 1987), p. 261; Cynthia Harrison, *On Account of Sex* (Berkeley: University of California Press, 1988), p. 5.

33. Waldie, *Holy Land,* pp. 33–34, 37, 62–63.

34. Erlend A. Kennan and Edmund H. Harvey, Jr., *Mission to the Moon* (New York: William Morrow, 1969), p. 241.

35. White-collar workers went from one-fourth of the total workforce in 1920 to one-half in 1970. Before World War I, about 200,000 men were "professional executives"; by 1970, their numbers were estimated to have risen to more than one million. Thomas C. Cochran, *Business in American Life: A History* (New York: McGraw-Hill, 1972), pp. 252–253, 271.

36. William H. Whyte, Jr., *The Organization Man* (New York: Touchstone, 1956), pp. 154–155; David Riesman, *The Lonely Crowd* (New Haven: Yale University Press, 1961), pp. 127, 139; C. Wright Mills, *White Collar* (New York: Oxford University Press, 1956), pp. xii, xvi, 74.

37. Theodore Dreiser, *Sister Carrie* (New York: W. W. Norton, 1991), pp. 3, 33.

38. Richard Matheson, *Collected Stories* (Los Angeles: Dream/Press, 1989), p. 89.

39. Ibid., p. xvi.

40. Richard Sennett, *Authority* (New York: W. W. Norton, 1993), pp. 88, 110.

41. Howard Banks, "Aerospace and Defense," *Forbes,* Jan. 7, 1991, p. 96; Anthony L. Velocci, Jr., "U.S. Defense Industry Must Change Ways to Stay Out of Financial Emergency Room," *Aviation Week & Space Technology,* Dec. 24, 1990, p. 16; "A War Machine Mired in Sleaze," *New York Times,* March 31, 1985, section 4, p. 22; Walter Isaacson, "The Winds of Reform," *Time,* Feb. 13, 1994, p. 12.

42. Julie Rees, "On Revolution," *Long Beach Press-Telegram,* Jan. 1, 1990, p. C1.

43. Richard W. Stevenson, "Battling the Lethargy at Douglas," *New York Times,* July 22, 1990, section 3, p. 1.

44. G. J. Meyer, *Executive Blues: Down and Out in Corporate America* (New York: Dell, 1995), pp. 190–191.

45. Herb Shannon, "Pep Talks Paying Off at Douglas," *Long Beach Press-Telegram,* April 10, 1977, p. B1; Ralph Vartabedian, "John McDonnell's Bumpy Ride," *Los Angeles Times Magazine,* Dec. 1, 1991, p. 18.

46. W. Edwards Deming, *Out of the Crisis* (Cambridge, Mass.: MIT Press, 1986); William W. Scherkenbach, *The Deming Route to Quality and Productivity* (Washington, D.C.: CEEPress, 1988); Daniel Niven, "When Times Get Tough, What Happens to TQM?" *Harvard Business Review*, May–June 1993, p. 20; Robert Heller, "Fourteen Points That the West Ignore at Its Peril; Failure to Subscribe to the Quality Management Philosophy of the Late Economist, W. Edwards Deming," *Management Today*, March 1994, p. 17; Jay Mathews and Peter Katel, "The Cost of Quality," *Newsweek*, Sept. 7, 1992, p. 48.

47. Vartabedian, "John McDonnell's Bumpy Ride," p. 20; Stevenson, "Battling the Lethargy at Douglas," p. 1; Mathews and Katel, "The Cost of Quality," p. 48.

48. Bruce A. Smith, "Competition and Tighter Budgets Push Aerospace Firms Toward TQM," *Aviation Week & Space Technology*, Dec. 9, 1991, p. 56.

49. Rees, "On Revolution," p. C4.

50. Meyer, *Executive Blues*, p. 190.

51. John Mintz, "Celebrating a Turnaround," *Washington Post*, Dec. 18, 1995, p. H1; Vartabedian, "John McDonnell's Bumpy Ride," p. 20.

52. Philip H. Dougherty, "Advertising: Campaign to Bolster the DC-10," *New York Times*, July 10, 1980, p. D15.

53. Dena Winokur and Robert W. Kinkead, "How Public Relations Fits Into Corporate Strategy: CEOs Assess the Importance of PR Today and in the Future," *Public Relations Journal*, May 1993, p. 16; James R. Carroll, "MD Under Fire for Billing Practices," *Long Beach Press-Telegram*, Oct. 14, 1993, p. A1; "Billing the U.S. for Trinkets," *New York Times*, May 24, 1985, p. A16.

54. McDonnell Douglas also charged the government $275,000 in one year alone for the coffee mugs, commemorative lapel pins, and other souvenirs it distributed at its fiftieth anniversary celebration, the government audit found. Another $23,650 went to buy fifteen thousand McDonnell Douglas auto windshield sun shades. Carroll, "MD Under Fire for Billing Practices," p. A1.

55. In 1990, having exhausted its purse, McDonnell Douglas secretly begged the Pentagon for a $1 billion loan. As an air force general scribbled down the company chief executive's plea in his notes that day: "MDC out of $ by end of oct. What can we do w/in next week?" The request, for once, was declined. Mintz, "Celebrating a Turnaround," p. H1; "McDonnell Payment Report," *New York Times*, Jan. 27, 1993, p. D2; Vartabedian, "John McDonnell's Bumpy Ride," p. 19; Bruce A. Smith, "Management Miscues, Delays Snarl C-17 Program," *Aviation Week & Space Technology*, April 12, 1993, p. 30.

56. Sherwood Anderson, *Perhaps Women* (New York: Horace Liveright, 1931), pp. 42, 44; Arthur Miller, *The Portable Arthur Miller*, Harold Clurman, ed. (New York: Viking Press, 1971), p. 38.

57. Sennett, *Authority*, p. 18.

58. Richard Matheson, "Clothes Make the Man," *Collected Stories*, pp. 33–36.

59. James S. Granelli, "Bias Complaints Unusually High at McDonnell," *Los Angeles Times*, July 27, 1997, p. A1.

60. Katherine Archibald, *Wartime Shipyard: A Study in Social Diversity* (Berkeley: University of California Press, 1947), pp. 216–217.

CHAPTER 3: GIRLS HAVE ALL THE POWER

1. Leslie Fiedler, *Love & Death in the American Novel* (New York: Anchor, 1992), p. 270.

2. James Gilbert, *A Cycle of Outrage: America's Reaction to the Juvenile Delinquent in the 1950s* (New York: Oxford University Press, 1986), pp. 34, 63, 75.

3. Ibid., pp. 66–70.

4. Ibid., p. 15.

5. Patt Morrison, "Farewell to Arms," *Los Angeles Times*, Dec. 5, 1993, p. A1; James F. Peltz, "As Defense Cuts Deepen, Southern California's Aerospace Industry Is Down but Not Out," *Los Angeles Times*, Sept. 26, 1993, p. D1.

6. D. J. Waldie, *Holy Land* (New York: W. W. Norton, 1996), pp. 7, 37, 41, 62, 158; "Birth of a City," *Time*, April 17, 1950, p. 99. See also Joan Didion, "Trouble in Lakewood," *The New Yorker*, July 26, 1993, p. 46.

7. Waldie, *Holy Land*, pp. 49, 176.

8. David Ferrell, "One of 9 Students to Be Charged in Campus Sex Case," *Los Angeles Times*, March 23, 1993, p. A1; Robin Abcarian, "Spur Posse Case: The Same Old (Sad) Story," *Los Angeles Times*, April 7, 1993, p. E1.

9. Janet Wiscombe, "Visit to a Shattered Home," *Long Beach Press-Telegram*, Feb. 3, 1994, p. 8; "Alleged Founder of Spur Posse Sentenced in Burglary," *Los Angeles Times*, Jan. 7, 1994, p. B2; Andy Rose and G. M. Bush, "Founder of Spur Posse Already Facing Numerous Charges," *Long Beach Press-Telegram*, March 21, 1993, p. A1.

10. Amy Cunningham, "Sex in High School," *Glamour*, Sept. 1993, p. 253.

11. "Posse Premiere," *Long Beach Press-Telegram*, April 2, 1993, p. A8; "The Spur Posse on TV," *Long Beach Press-Telegram*, April 6, 1993, p. A6.

12. *The Jenny Jones Show*, April 7, 1993.

13. Amy Cunningham, "Sex in High School," p. 254; Jane Gross, "Where 'Boys Will Be Boys,' and Adults Are Bewildered," *New York Times*, March 29, 1993, p. A1; Jennifer Allen, "Boys: Hanging with the Spur Posse," *Rolling Stone*, July 8–22, 1993, p. 55; "Sex for Points Scandal," *The Jane Whitney Show*, April 1, 1993.

14. "Spur Posse Member Killed," Associated Press, July 6, 1995.

15. Susan Faludi, "The Naked Citadel," *The New Yorker*, Sept. 5, 1994, p. 62.

16. Shannon Richey Faulkner et al. v. James E. Jones, Jr., Chairman, Board of Visitors of The Citadel et al., transcript of trial, volume 9, United States District Court for the District of South Carolina, Charleston Division, pp. 54–55.

17. Adam Nossiter, "A Cadet Is Dismissed and 9 Are Disciplined for Citadel Harassment," *New York Times*, March 11, 1997, p. A15.

18. Ronald Smothers, "Citadel Is Ordered to Admit a Woman to Its Cadet Corps," *New York Times,* July 23, 1994, section 1, p. 6.

19. Janet Wiscombe, "An American Tragedy," *Los Angeles Times,* March 22, 1996, p. E1.

20. "Sex for Points Scandal," *The Jane Whitney Show,* April 1, 1993.

21. Mark J. Henderson, "Civil Rights? Or Wrongs?" *The Brigadier,* Sept. 3, 1993.

22. James Gilligan, *Violence* (New York: G. P. Putnam's Sons, 1996), p. 64.

23. "Turner Turns Santa for 3 Schools," *Baltimore Sun,* Feb. 8, 1994, p. 2A.

24. *The Sphinx,* 1990, 1991, 1992, 1993.

25. Bill Hewitt, "The Body Counters," *People,* April 12, 1993, p. 34; Amy Cunningham, "Sex in High School," p. 252; Allen, "Boys," p. 54.

26. Waldie, *Holy Land,* p. 40.

27. Colyer Meriwether, *History of Higher Education in South Carolina* (Spartanburg, S.C.: The Reprint Company, 1972, 1889), pp. 69–71; John Peyre Thomas, *The History of the South Carolina Military Academy* (Charleston: Walker, Evans and Cogswell, 1893), pp. 13–19, 242–243; *A Brief History of The Citadel* (Charleston: The Citadel, 1994).

28. Col. D. D. Nicholson, Jr., *A History of The Citadel: The Years of Summerall and Clark* (Charleston: The Citadel, 1994), pp. 211–212; "Cadets Will March in Full Dress First Time Since '43," *News & Courier,* Charleston, Feb. 16, 1955, p. 14A.

29. Maj. Gen. James A. Grimsley, *The Citadel: Educating the Whole Man* (New York: The Newcomen Society in North America, 1983), p. 6.

30. Jack Leland, "Women Invade Citadel Classes First Time in School's History," *News & Courier,* Charleston, June 21, 1949, p. 16.

31. "Report to the President and the Board of Visitors of The Citadel," Special Advisory Committee on the Fourth Class System, March 16, 1968, p. 42.

32. Jim and Sybil Stockdale, *In Love and War* (Annapolis, Md.: Naval Institute Press, 1990), p. 471.

33. Ibid., pp. 470, 478–485, 488.

34. Waldie, *Holy Land,* pp. 63, 79.

35. Robert Feldberg, "Follies of '93," *The Record,* April 11, 1993, p. E1; "Tabloid Media: Paying to Get the Dirt," *Nightline,* April 8, 1993.

36. Gilligan, *Violence,* pp. 67, 110–111.

37. Rick Reilly, "What Is The Citadel?," *Sports Illustrated,* Sept. 14, 1992, p. 72; David Davidson, "Crisis at The Citadel: Lords of Cruelty?," *Atlanta Constitution,* Oct. 20, 1991, p. A16; Herb Frazier, "Ex-Cadet Describes Torment at Citadel," *Post and Courier,* Charleston, Oct. 10, 1991, p. 1A; Herb Frazier, "4 Ex-Cadets Invited to Talk to Investigative Panel," *Post and Courier,* Charleston, Oct. 30, 1991, p. 4B.

38. Reilly, "What Is The Citadel?," p. 72.

39. Herb Frazier, "Cadet's Father Confident of Citadel Probe," *Post and Courier,* Charleston, Aug. 26, 1992, p. 1B; Linda L. Meggett, "Racial Slurs Found in Citadel Room," *Post and Courier,* Charleston, Feb. 11, 1993, p. 1B; Linda L. Meggett, "NAACP Wants

Citadel Investigation," *Post and Courier,* Charleston, Jan. 5, 1993, p. 1B; "FBI to Probe Citadel Racial Hazing Incident," *Jet,* Oct. 22, 1986, p. 18; Michael W. Hirschorn, "The Citadel, Trying Hard to Shed Old-South Image, Set Back by the 'Incident,' " *Chronicle of Higher Education,* Feb. 4, 1987, p. 24; Sid Gaulden and Michael L. Field, "Racial Climate at the Citadel Questioned," *News & Courier,* Charleston, Feb. 26, 1987, p. 2B; Lee Aitken, "Racism on Campus: Beyond The Citadel," *People,* Dec. 15, 1986, p. 58.

40. "Report of the Fourth Class System Inquiry Committee," The Citadel, Dec. 5, 1991, pp. 6–8.

CHAPTER 4: A GOOD DAWG WILL ALWAYS REMAIN LOYAL

1. "Worker Displacement, 1995–1997," U.S. Bureau of Labor Statistics, Aug. 19, 1998.

2. "Median Usual Weekly Earnings of Full-Time Wage and Salary Workers, Annual Averages, 1979–1998," U.S. Bureau of Labor Statistics, 1998; "Employee Tenure in 1998," U.S. Bureau of Labor Statistics, Sept. 23, 1998; Kurt Schrammel, "Comparing the Labor Market Success of Young Adults from Two Generations," *Monthly Labor Review,* Feb. 1998, p. 3; Geoffrey Paulin and Brian Riordon, "Making It on Their Own: The Baby Boom Meets Generation X," *Monthly Labor Review,* Feb. 1998, p. 10; Peter Capelli, "Rethinking the Nature of Work: A Look at the Research Evidence," *Compensation and Benefits Review,* American Management Association, vol. 29, no. 4, July 17, 1997, p. 50; Bennett Harrison, "The Dark Side of Business Flexibility," *Challenge,* vol. 41, no. 4, July 17, 1998, p. 117; Sanford M. Jacoby, *Modern Manors: Welfare Capitalism Since the New Deal* (Princeton: Princeton University Press, 1997), p. 260.

3. Art Fazakas, "About Men: Don't Call Me Lucy," *New York Times Magazine,* June 19, 1994, p. 20.

4. Alan Snel, "A 'Matter of Pride' or 'Extortion'?" *Denver Post,* Nov. 24, 1996, p. A1; "The Stadium Binge," *USA Today,* Sept. 6, 1996, p. 20C.

5. Michael Oriard, *Reading Football: How the Popular Press Created an American Spectacle* (Chapel Hill, N.C.: University of North Carolina Press, 1993), pp. 36–37, 50, 191.

6. Robert W. Peterson, *Pigskin: The Early Years of Pro Football* (New York: Oxford University Press, 1997), pp. 103, 106.

7. John R. Tunis, *The American Way of Sport* (New York: Duell, Sloan & Pearce, 1958), p. 18.

8. Peterson, *Pigskin,* p. 195.

9. Michael Novak, *The Joy of Sports* (Lanham, Md.: Madison, 1994), p. 87.

10. Paul Brown with Jack Clary, *PB: The Paul Brown Story* (New York: Atheneum, 1980), pp. 40, 42–43.

11. Brown, *PB,* p. 47; "Massillon—City of Champions . . . City of Tradition," *Our Second Century* (Massillon: Washington High School, 1995); Howard Roberts, *The Story of Pro Football* (New York: Rand McNally, 1953), p. 101.

12. *PB,* p. 47.

13. Ibid., pp. 43, 45; Bill Levy, *Return to Glory: The Story of the Cleveland Browns* (Cleveland: World, 1965), p. 45.

14. Kent State bowed out before the end of the game after the Tigers had racked up more than fifty points, and Akron University, in a panic after the news of Kent State's humiliation reached its players' ears, canceled its upcoming engagement with the formidable Tigers. Brown, *PB,* p. 59.

15. Brown, *PB,* p. 47.

16. Donald L. McMurray, *Coxey's Army: A Study of the Industrial Army Movement of 1894* (Seattle: University of Washington Press, 1968), pp. 115–125; Writers' Program of the Work Projects Administration, *The Ohio Guide* (New York: Oxford University Press, 1946), p. 421.

17. Brown, *PB,* pp. 48–49; Carl L. Biemiller, "Football Town," *Holiday,* November 1949, p. 72.

18. "Massillon—City of Champions . . . City of Tradition."

19. As work lost its traditional aspect, psychologist Arnold Beisser observed, organized sports came to "increasingly resemble work in the arduous practice and preparation they require, in the intense involvement of coaches and athletes in the spirit of work, and in their actual economic productivity." Arnold R. Beisser, "Modern Man and Sports," in *Sport and Society,* John T. Talamini and Charles H. Page, eds. (Boston: Little, Brown, 1973), pp. 94–95.

20. Lewis Mumford, *Technics and Civilization* (London: George Routledge & Sons, 1947), pp. 303–305.

21. Jack McCallum, "A Mauling in Tiger Town," *Sports Illustrated,* July 1, 1985, p. 39.

22. WPA, *The Ohio Guide,* p. 420.

23. Lonnie Wheeler, "Father Football," *Ohio,* Sept. 1989, p. 19; Steve Doerschuk, "Paul Brown: Felled by Pneumonia," *Independent,* Aug. 5, 1991, p. A1; "Brown Built Massillon a Legacy of Excellence," *Independent,* Aug. 6, 1991, p. A1.

24. Tobin, *Ernie Pyle's War,* p. 29.

25. William Ganson Rose, *Cleveland: The Making of a City* (Cleveland: World, 1950), pp. 5, 975, 979, 1042–1043, 1059; Carol Poh Miller and Robert A. Wheeler, *Cleveland: A Concise History, 1796–1996* (Bloomington: Indiana University Press, 1997), pp. 138–139, 154.

26. Allen Guttman, *From Ritual to Record: The Nature of Modern Sports* (New York: Columbia University Press, 1978), p. 102.

27. See, for instance, Jim Brosnan, "The Fantasy World of Baseball," in *Sport and Society,* p. 380.

28. Murray Sperber, *Shake Down the Thunder: The Creation of Notre Dame Football* (New York: Henry Holt, 1993), pp. 109, 110–111, 112, 135, 285, 289, 466.

29. Michael Rogin, *Ronald Reagan, the Movie* (Berkeley: University of California Press, 1988), pp. 16–17.

30. Brown, *PB*, p. 7; Jack Clary, *Cleveland Browns* (New York: Macmillan, 1973), pp. 8–9, 14, 111–112; Jack Clary, *The Gamemakers* (Chicago: Follett, 1976), pp. 24–25; Tex Maule, "A Man for This Season," *Sports Illustrated*, Sept. 10, 1962, p. 32.

31. Steve Byrne, Jim Campbell, and Mark Craig, *The Cleveland Browns: A 50 Year Tradition* (Champaign, Ill.: Sagamore, 1995), p. 9; Wheeler, "Father Football," cover.

32. Clary, *Cleveland Browns*, p. 13; "Football: Brown Ohio," *Newsweek*, Dec. 30, 1946, p. 66.

33. Clary, *Cleveland Browns*, pp. 16–17, 21; Brown, *PB*, p. 106; Mike Shatzkin, ed., *The Ballplayers* (New York: Arbor House, 1990), p. 927; George Sullivan, *Pro Football's All-Time Greats* (New York: Putnam, 1968), p. 243; Paul Zimmerman, *A Thinking Man's Guide to Pro Football* (New York: E. P. Dutton, 1970), p. 363.

34. Terry Pluto, *When All the World Was Browns Town* (New York: Simon & Schuster, 1997), pp. 13–14.

35. Gerald Astor, *A Blood Dimmed Tide* (New York: Donald I. Fine, 1992), pp. 136–144.

36. Mike Wright, *What They Didn't Teach You About World War II* (Novato, Calif.: Presidio, 1998), p. 180.

37. Clary, *Cleveland Browns*, p. 112.

38. "Pro Football: All-America Conference Plays Its Opening Game in Cleveland," *Life*, Sept. 23, 1946, p. 91; Clary, *Cleveland Browns*, pp. 24, 28.

39. In the midst of the team's slump, more than 110,000 loyal fans turned out for the first two home games in 1956, causing Paul Brown to make the crack, "You might say seeing us lose is an attraction." Levy, *Return to Glory*, pp. xi–xii, 138–139.

40. Pluto, *When All the World Was Browns Town*, p. 88.

41. Guttmann, *From Ritual to Record*, p. 122.

42. Brown, *PB*, pp. 42, 54, 55–56.

43. Ibid., pp. 52, 54.

44. Ernie Pyle, *Brave Men* (New York: Henry Holt, 1944), p. 201.

45. Brown, *PB*, p. 148.

46. Ibid., pp. 16, 148; Clary, *Cleveland Browns*, p. 18; "Football: Brown Ohio," *Newsweek*, Dec. 30, 1946, p. 66; Byrne et al., *The Cleveland Browns*, p. 17; Maule, "A Man for This Season," p. 32; "Praying Professionals," *Time*, Oct. 27, 1947, pp. 55–56.

47. Clary, *The Gamemakers*, p. 32; Clary, *Cleveland Browns*, p. 19; Brown, *PB*, p. 15.

48. Clary, *Cleveland Browns*, p. 20.

49. Clary, *The Gamemakers*, pp. 33–34; Levy, *Return to Glory*, p. 111.

50. Clary, *The Gamemakers*, pp. 22–23; Harry Paxton, "Cleveland's Dream Quarterback," *Saturday Evening Post*, Dec. 1, 1951, p. 25; Pluto, *When All the World Was Browns Town*, p. 19.

51. Brown, *PB*, pp. 13, 19.

52. Levy, *Return to Glory*, pp. 136–137; Maule, "A Man for This Season," p. 39; Paxton, "Cleveland's Dream Quarterback," p. 126; Brown, *PB*, p. 157; Pluto, *When All the World Was Browns Town*, p. 30.

53. "Push-Button Football," *Life,* Dec. 1, 1947, p. 109; "Production-Line Football," *Time,* Nov. 22, 1948, p. 63.

54. "Aw Come On, Coach, Relax," *Collier's,* Dec. 10, 1949, p. 78.

55. Rick Reilly, "Browns Destroy Eagles, 35–10, in Huge Upset!," *Sports Illustrated Classic,* fall 1991, p. 15; Clary, *Cleveland Browns,* p. 7; Wheeler, "Father Football," p. 150.

56. Brown, *PB,* p. 157; Jim Brown, *Out of Bounds* (New York: Zebra, 1989), p. 69; Clary, *The Gamemakers,* p. 32; Clary, *Cleveland Browns,* p. 108.

57. Bernie Parrish, *They Call It a Game* (New York: Dial, 1971), pp. 30, 96.

58. Ibid., p. 96.

59. George Plimpton, *Paper Lion* (New York: Harper & Row, 1966), pp. 290–291.

60. Maule, "A Man for This Season," p. 33; "Aw Come On, Coach, Relax," p. 78.

61. Marshall Smith, "Sad News From the Campus: Nobody Loves the Football Hero Now," *Life,* Nov. 11, 1957, p. 149.

62. Parrish, *They Call It a Game,* p. 95.

63. Clary, *Cleveland Browns,* pp. 107–108.

64. Dave Meggyesy, *Out of Their League* (Berkeley, Calif.: Ramparts Press, 1970), pp. 7–10, 11, 153, 155, 181.

65. "Two Men Named Brown," *Newsweek,* Oct. 28, 1963, p. 88.

66. Jimmy Brown and Myron Cope, "Jimmy Brown's Own Story . . . My Case Against Paul Brown," *Look,* Oct. 6, 1964, p. 62; Parrish, *They Call It a Game,* pp. 36, 95.

67. Don DeLillo, *End Zone* (New York: Penguin, 1986), p. 54.

68. Zimmerman, *A Thinking Man's Guide to Pro Football,* p. 210; Brown and Cope, "Jimmy Brown's Own Story," pp. 64, 68; Parrish, *They Call It a Game,* p. 88; Pluto, *When All the World Was Browns Town,* p. 57.

69. Meggyesy, *Out of Their League,* pp. 47–48; Parrish, *They Call It a Game,* p. 99.

70. Levy, *Return to Glory,* pp. 160–161; David Harris, *The League: The Rise and Decline of the NFL* (New York: Bantam, 1986), pp. 35–36; Pluto, *When All the World Was Browns Town,* pp. 35, 36.

71. Harris, *The League,* pp. 35, 39; Parrish, *They Call It a Game,* p. 98; Pluto, *When All the World Was Browns Town,* pp. 47–48.

72. Brown, *PB,* pp. 262, 269, 285; Clary, *Cleveland Browns,* pp. 171–173; Pluto, *When All the World Was Browns Town,* p. 60.

73. Pluto, *When All the World Was Browns Town,* pp. 65, 67–68.

74. "A Team on Trial," *Saturday Evening Post,* Nov. 23, 1963, p. 86.

75. Marla Ridenour, "Modell Wants His Browns to Be Sharp for the RV Audience," *Columbus Dispatch,* Sept. 12, 1993, p. 10E; Benjamin G. Rader, *In Its Own Image: How Television Has Transformed Sports* (New York: Free Press, 1984), pp. 90–91, 121; Jim Duffy, Geoff Brown, Shari Sweeney, and Jay Miller, "Dagger of a Deal," *Cleveland Magazine,* Jan. 1996, p. 79; Byrne, et al., *The Cleveland Browns,* pp. 61–62; Randy Roberts and James S. Olsen, *Winning Is the Only Thing: Sports in America Since 1945*

(Baltimore: Johns Hopkins University Press, 1989), p. 126; Harris, *The League*, pp. 34–35.

76. Peter Alfano, "The Changing Face of Sports," *New York Times*, Oct. 27, 1982, p. B9; Rader, *In Its Own Image*, p. 205; "Notoriety Pays," *Atlanta Journal and Constitution*, Feb. 15, 1997, p. 14A; Bill Plaschke, "A High Price for a Championship," *Los Angeles Times*, Feb. 23, 1999, p. A22.

77. Robert Lipsyte, *SportsWorld: An American Dreamland* (New York: Quadrangle, 1975), p. 59; Harris, *The League*, p. 236.

78. Rader, *In Its Own Image*, pp. 79, 138–139.

79. Ibid., pp. 94–95, 193.

80. Michael Novak, *The Joy of Sports* (Lanham, Md.: Madison, 1994), p. 81.

81. Byrne et al., *The Cleveland Browns*, p. 154.

82. Miller and Wheeler, *Cleveland: A Concise History*, pp. 171, 178, 179, 180, 183, 188–189, 195; "City of Cleveland Receives 'A–' Rating from Standard & Poor's," PR Newswire, Sept. 26, 1989; Rich Exner, "Cleveland Emerges from Default, Burns Notes," UPI, June 26, 1987.

83. Jeff Hardy, "Kosar: 'I Just Wanted to Go Home,'" UPI, April 24, 1985; Christine Brennan, "Rozelle: Kosar Free to Choose," *Washington Post*, April 24, 1985, p. D1; Kevin Sherrington, "Black Days for Browns," *Dallas Morning News*, Nov. 23, 1993, p. 18B.

84. Sherrington, "Black Days for Browns," p. 18B; Bill Livingston, "Cleveland Was All Bernie Ever Wanted," *Plain Dealer*, Cleveland, Nov. 9, 1993, p. 1A; Douglas S. Looney, "There's a Love Feast on Lake Erie," *Sports Illustrated*, Aug. 26, 1985, p. 38; Mark Heisler, "Kosar Is Playing It Cool," *Los Angeles Times*, Oct. 18, 1985, section 3, p. 4; Hardy, "Kosar: 'I Just Wanted to Go Home'"; John Underwood, "The Pros Outweighed the Cons," *Sports Illustrated*, March 25, 1985, p. 20.

85. Byrne et al., *The Cleveland Browns*, p. 80.

86. Ira Berkow, "Man Bites Football Player," *New York Times*, Jan. 10, 1987, section 1, p. 49; Gary Pomerantz, "Year of Elway? They Won't Argue in Cleveland," *Los Angeles Times*, Jan. 18, 1987, section 3, p. 18.

87. Bonnie DeSimone, "Cleveland Getting a Football Fix," *Chicago Tribune*, Sept. 22, 1996, p. C1.

88. Byrne et al., *The Cleveland Browns*, pp. 80–81.

89. T. J. Trout, "The Desert Dawg," press release, 1993, in *Browns News Illustrated* collection, Berea, Ohio.

90. Brian E. Albrecht, "Few Have Zeal to Rise to Level of Super Fans," *Plain Dealer*, Cleveland, Dec. 17, 1995, p. 5A.

91. Tony Grossi, "Second Chances Cost Browns Little," *Plain Dealer*, Cleveland, Aug. 12, 1995, p. 1D; "Kevin Mack Granted Early Release from Probation," UPI, June 21, 1991.

92. "Turner Wants to Start for Browns After Holdout," *Detroit News*, Sept. 1, 1995; Mary

Kay Cabot, "Rison Expects to Join Browns Today," *Plain Dealer,* Cleveland, March 24, 1995, p. 1D; Mary Kay Cabot, "Rison to Challenge," *Plain Dealer,* Cleveland, Sept. 3, 1995, p. 1D; Diane Solov and Ted Wendling, "Browns' Woes Run Deep," *Plain Dealer,* Cleveland, Jan. 7, 1996, p. 1A.

93. Ned Zeman, "The Last Straw," *Sports Illustrated,* Nov. 22, 1993, p. 42.

94. Sherrington, "Black Days for Browns," p. 18B; Mary Kay Cabot, "Modell Calls ESPN Report on Contract 'Absolutely Untrue,'" *Plain Dealer,* Cleveland, Nov. 11, 1993, p. 4F.

95. Sherrington, "Black Days for Browns," p. 4F.

96. Letter from Peter B. Carden of West Chester, Ohio, to *Browns News Illustrated,* Jan. 21, 1995, in *Browns News Illustrated* collection.

97. John Underwood, *Spoiled Sport: A Fan's Notes on the Troubles of Spectator Sports* (Boston: Little, Brown, 1984), p. 23.

98. Leonard Shapiro, "For Fans, It's a Dawg's Life," *Washington Post,* Nov. 20, 1995, p. A1.

99. Luke Cyphers, "Fan Fright: Going to the Ol' Ballgame Has Never Been Scarier," *Daily News,* New York, Aug. 25, 1996, p. 87; Claire Smith, "In Philadelphia, Fans Are Penalized, Too," *New York Times,* Nov. 24, 1997, p. A1.

100. Frederick Exley, *A Fan's Notes* (New York: Vintage, 1988), pp. 134, 357.

101. Craig Neff, "Deboned," *Sports Illustrated,* Nov. 6, 1989, p. 20.

102. James Lawless, "As Game Approaches, Rabid Fans Are Barking," *Plain Dealer,* Cleveland, Jan. 13, 1990.

103. Brian E. Albrecht, "The No. 1 Fans," *Plain Dealer,* Cleveland, Dec. 17, 1995, p. 1A.

104. Brian E. Albrecht, "Family Dawg," *Plain Dealer,* Cleveland, Jan. 21, 1996, p. 1B.

105. Letter to Joe and Bud McElwain from Peter M. Arrichielo, Topps, May 23, 1995.

106. Hollace Silbiger, "Cable Host Dies in Fall," *Plain Dealer,* Cleveland, Aug. 10, 1993, p. 1B; "Children Lose Second Parent; Crash Kills Mother a Year After Their Father's Fatal Fall," *Plain Dealer,* Cleveland, Dec. 1, 1994, p. 1B.

107. Sperber, *Shake Down the Thunder,* p. 156.

108. Benjamin Harrison, "What Art Modell Wants to Keep the Browns Here," *Plain Dealer,* Cleveland, Feb. 13, 1994, p. 1A.

109. Peter King, "Down . . . and Out," *Sports Illustrated,* Nov. 13, 1995, p. 28.

110. Ibid., p. 35; Pedro Gomez, "Back in Baltimore," *Sacramento Bee,* Sept. 1, 1996, p. C1.

111. Paul G. Pinsky, "Maryland's Critical Turnover," *Washington Post,* Nov. 12, 1995, p. C8; Terry M. Neal and Michael Abramowitz, "Break Seen in Impasse on Stadium," *Washington Post,* Nov. 8, 1995, p. A1; Rudolph A. Pyatt Jr., "Modell's Unjustified Free Lunch: Executives Should Punt the Pitch," *Washington Post,* Feb. 1, 1996, p. D11.

112. Timothy W. Smith, "Owners Could Block Browns' Move to Baltimore," *New York Times,* Nov. 5, 1995, section 8, p. 53; Timothy W. Smith, "Bolting Browns Top NFL Controversies," *New York Times,* Nov. 8, 1995, p. B11.

113. Raymond J. Keating, "The House That Taxpayers Built," *New York Times*, April 15, 1998, p. A27; King, "Down . . . and Out," p. 32.

114. Jim Duffy, Geoff Brown, Shari Sweeney, and Jay Miller, "Dagger of a Deal," *Cleveland Magazine*, Jan. 1996, p. 76; Lester Munson, "A Busted Play," *Sports Illustrated*, Dec. 4, 1995, p. 64; Diane Solov and Ted Wendling, "Browns' Woes Run Deep," *Plain Dealer*, Cleveland, Jan. 7, 1998, p. 1A.

115. Miriam Hall, "Estate Planning as Motivation," *Plain Dealer*, Cleveland, Nov. 7, 1995, p. 7A; Leonard Shapiro, "In Cleveland, Color of Money Wasn't Brown," *Washington Post*, Dec. 12, 1995, p. D1; Solov and Wendling, "Browns' Woes Run Deep," p. 1A; Stephen Phillips, "Out from Behind Dad's Shadow: After Years of Waiting, Learning in the Wings, David Modell Emerges as Man in Charge," *Plain Dealer*, Cleveland, Dec. 24, 1995, p. 1B.

116. Bill Livingston, "Papa Art Walks Out on an Extended Family," *Plain Dealer*, Cleveland, Jan. 17, 1996, p. D1.

117. Smith, "Bolting Browns Top NFL Controversies," p. B11; "Browns Fans Suffer Loss and Brace for One More," *New York Times*, Nov. 6, 1995, p. C5; Steve Rushin, "The Heart of a City," *Sports Illustrated*, Dec. 4, 1995, p. 58.

118. Michael O'Malley, "Stadium Feels Like 'Dungeon' on Gloomy Day," *Plain Dealer*, Cleveland, Nov. 20, 1995, p. 11C.

119. Richard Sandomir, "Battle to Save the Browns Goes to Washington," *New York Times*, Nov. 30, 1995, p. B21; Steve Wulf, "Bad Bounces for the NFL," *Time*, Dec. 11, 1995, p. 64.

120. Bernie Kosar, "An Open Letter from Bernie Kosar to All Browns Fans," news release, Nov. 7, 1995.

121. "Professional Sports Franchise Relocation: Antitrust Implications," hearing before U.S. House of Representatives Judiciary Committee, Washington, D.C., Feb. 6, 1996.

122. "Antitrust, Monopolies and Business Rights Sport Franchise Relocation," hearing before U.S. Senate Judiciary Committee, Washington, D.C., Nov. 29, 1995.

123. Stephen Phillips, "Behind Revco's Doors," *Plain Dealer*, Cleveland, Dec. 10, 1995, p. I1; Bill Lubinger, "The Ripple Effect, Loss of Revco Likely to Reverberate Across Many Area Firms," *Plain Dealer*, Cleveland, Dec. 1, 1995, p. 1C; "Revco Rite Aid Merger Expected," *Plain Dealer*, Cleveland, Nov. 30, 1995, p. 1A; Marcia Pledger, "Rite Aid Drops Its Bid for Revco," *Plain Dealer*, Cleveland, April 25, 1996, p. 1A.

124. "Cleveland Browns Franchise Preserved in Cleveland: Mayor White, NFL Agree to Binding Commitments," news release, office of Mayor Michael R. White, Feb. 8, 1996.

125. Bud Shaw, "NFL Horror Flick Too Preposterous," *Plain Dealer*, Cleveland, March 9, 1996, p. D1.

126. V. David Sartin, "Boycott of Super Bowl Proposed," *Plain Dealer*, Cleveland, Jan. 9, 1996, p. 1B.

127. Tony Grossi, "NFL Says the Deal Is Done," *Plain Dealer*, Cleveland, March 12, 1996, p. 1A.

128. Vinnie Perrone, "Browns Bow Out, Fans Take Seats," *Washington Post*, Dec. 18, 1995, p. C1.

CHAPTER 5: WHERE AM I IN THE KINGDOM?

1. Steve Gushee, "The Promise Keepers," *Palm Beach Post*, Aug. 8, 1995, p. 1D.

2. Marie Griffith and Paul Harvey, "Wifely Submission: The SBC Resolution: Southern Baptist Convention and Marriage," *Christian Century*, July 1, 1998, p. 636; Larry B. Stammer, "A Wife's Role Is 'To Submit,' Baptists Declare," *Los Angeles Times*, June 10, 1989, p. A1.

3. "McCartney at Center of Controversy Again," *Minneapolis Star Tribune*, July 29, 1992, p. 2C; John D. Spalding, "Bonding in the Bleachers: A Visit to the Promise Keepers," *Christian Century*, March 6, 1996, p. 260.

4. Tony Evans, "Spiritual Purity," in *Seven Promises of a Promise Keeper* (Colorado Springs: Focus on the Family, 1994), p. 79.

5. Ibid., p. 74.

6. *New Man* eventually became independent of Promise Keepers. Robert V. Zoba, "The Unexpected Choice," *New Man*, Nov./Dec. 1997, p. 41. See also Rholan Wong, "Lessons from a Househusband," *New Man*, Sept. 1997, p. 58.

7. "Promise Keepers' Sample of 1994 National Survey on Men: Report on 1994 Conference Attendees," National Center for Fathering, March 1995, p. 6.

8. Sara Diamond, *Spiritual Warfare: The Politics of the Christian Right* (Boston: South End Press, 1989), p. 52; Bill Bright, *Come Help Change the World* (Old Tappan, N.J.: Fleming H. Revell, 1970), p. 97; Richard Quebedeaux, *I Found It! The Story of Bill Bright and Campus Crusade* (New York: Harper & Row, 1979), pp. 18, 91, 182–183; Colleen McDannell, *Material Christianity* (New Haven: Yale University Press, 1995), footnote 58, p. 302, n. 58.

9. Matt Campbell, "Promise Keepers Praised, Panned and Set for KC," *Kansas City Star*, March 24, 1996, p. A1; Bill McCartney with David Halbrook, *Sold Out* (Nashville: Word Publishing, 1997), pp. 84, 85–87; Bill McCartney with Dave Diles, *From Ashes to Glory* (Nashville: Thomas Nelson, 1995), p. 109.

10. Rick Reilly, "What Price Glory?," *Sports Illustrated*, Feb. 27, 1989, p. 32; Bryan Abas, "That Sinning Season," *Westword*, Aug. 30–Sept. 5, 1989, p. 12.

11. Abas, "That Sinning Season," pp. 15, 18; McCartney, *From Ashes to Glory*, pp. 51–52; Richard Hoffer and Shelley Smith, "Putting His House in Order," *Sports Illustrated*, Jan. 16, 1995, p. 29.

12. McCartney turned his wife Lyndi's despair into a sort of marketing tool for his second book; he brought her along on the book tour, where she titillated talk-show audiences with her tales of misery and bulimia. Ultimately, though, the airing of

domestic woes backfired when McCartney's pastor volunteered to the *New York Times* that the coach had also committed adultery. *From Ashes to Glory*, pp. 95, 197, 290–291; McCartney, *Sold Out*, pp. 48, 68–71, 104–107, 233–237; Laurie Goodstein, "A Marriage Gone Bad Struggles for Redemption," *New York Times*, Oct. 29, 1997, p. A17.

13. Sheldon G. Jackson, *Beautiful Glendora* (Azusa, Calif.: Azusa Pacific University Press, 1982), pp. 15–16, 52, 59, 61, 121; Donald Pflueger, *Glendora: The Annals of a Southern California Community* (Claremont, Calif.: Saunders, 1951), pp. 23–24, 199, 209.

14. Jackson, *Beautiful Glendora*, pp. 38–39, 64–65, 76, 78; Pflueger, *Glendora*, p. 231.

15. Neil T. Anderson, *The Bondage Breaker* (Eugene, Ore.: Harvest House, 1993), pp. 11, 57, 58.

16. Ken Abraham, *Who Are the Promise Keepers?* (New York: Doubleday, 1997), p. 39.

17. William G. McLoughlin, Jr., *Billy Sunday Was His Real Name* (Chicago: University of Chicago Press, 1955), pp. 8, 179; William T. Ellis, *Billy Sunday: The Man & His Message*, 1914, p. 204.

18. Charles Howard Hopkins, *The Rise of the Social Gospel in American Protestantism* (New Haven: Yale University Press, 1967), pp. 11–12, 19; McLoughlin, *Billy Sunday Was His Real Name*, pp. 27–28, 35, 37, 262; Roger A. Bruns, *Preacher: Billy Sunday and Big-Time American Evangelism* (New York: Norton, 1992), p. 130.

19. Gail Bederman, "The Women Have Had Charge of the Church Work Long Enough: The Men and Religion Forward Movement of 1911–1912 and the Masculinization of Middle-Class Protestantism," *American Quarterly*, volume 41, issue 3, Sept. 1989, pp. 432–465; Hopkins, *The Rise of the Social Gospel in American Protestantism*, pp. 296–297.

20. McLoughlin, *Billy Sunday Was His Real Name*, pp. 225–226; Hopkins, *The Rise of the Social Gospel in American Protestantism*, pp. 31–32, 177, 221, 224–225, 285–288, 291, 303.

21. Bederman, "The Women Have Had Charge of the Church Work Long Enough," pp. 432, 435.

22. Ron Stodghill II, "God of Our Fathers," *Time*, Oct. 6, 1997, p. 34.

23. Jim Zabloski, "Failure Is Not Final!" *New Man*, May 1998, p. 57; *New Man*, Nov./Dec. 1997, cover; *New Man*, Jan./Feb. 1998, cover.

24. Abraham, *Who Are the Promise Keepers?*, p. 7.

25. U.S. Census Bureau, Current Population Reports, Series P-60, 1998; "Five IOMA Studies Document the Effects of Gender on Compensation," *Report on Salary Surveys*, publication of Institute of Management and Administration, December 1996; "Background on the Wage Gap," National Committee on Pay Equity, Washington, D.C., 1998; "Women by Occupation, 1997," National Committee on Pay Equity, Washington, D.C., 1998; Karen Robinson-Jacobs, "When It Comes to Pay, It's Still a Man's World," *Los Angeles Times*, April 23, 1998, p. D1.

26. *Women Work, Poverty Still Persists: An Update on the Status of Displaced Homemakers and Single Mothers in the United States*, publication of Women Work: The National Network for Women's Employment, fall 1998, pp. 13, 21.

27. Caroline Walker Bynum, *Jesus as Mother: Studies in the Spirituality of the High Middle Ages* (Berkeley: University of California Press, 1984), pp. 113-117.

28. Barbara Welter, "The Feminization of American Religion: 1800-1860," *Clio's Consciousness Raised,* Mary S. Hartman and Lois Banner, eds. (New York: Harper & Row, 1974), pp. 137, 142.

29. Bruce Barton, *The Man Nobody Knows* (Indianapolis: Bobbs-Merrill, 1925), pp. vi-vii, 10-11, 12, 21.

30. Bynum, *Jesus as Mother,* p. 158.

31. Barton, *The Man Nobody Knows,* pp. 5, 85; T. J. Jackson Lears, "From Salvation to Self-Realization," in *The Culture of Consumption,* Richard Wightman Fox and T. J. Jackson Lears, eds. (New York: Pantheon, 1983), pp. 30-38.

32. Gordon Dalbey, *Sons of the Father* (Wheaton, Ill.: Tyndale House, 1996), p. 7.

33. Gordon Dalbey, *Fight Like a Man* (Wheaton, Ill.: Tyndale House, 1995), pp. 35, 90, 114; Dalbey, *Sons of the Father,* pp. 3, 6.

34. Dalbey, *Sons of the Father,* p. 20; Dalbey, *Fight Like a Man,* pp. 12, 25, 36, 103, 114, 117.

35. Dalbey, *Fight Like a Man,* pp. xii-xiii, 310.

36. Ibid., pp. 35-36.

37. Robert N. Bellah, *Beyond Belief: Essays on Religion in a Post-Traditional World* (Berkeley: University of California Press, 1991), p. 78.

38. Stephen Mitchell, *The Gospel According to Jesus* (New York: HarperCollins, 1991), pp. 19, 28, 30-31, 51; Matthew 23:9, King James Version.

39. Matthew 10:35-36, New International Version; Luke 12:53, Matthew 23:9, Luke 14:26, Luke 9:60, King James Version; Mitchell, *The Gospel According to Jesus,* pp. 44-45, 58.

40. John Dominic Crossan, *The Historical Jesus* (San Francisco: HarperSanFrancisco, 1992), pp. 299, 300; Richard A. Horsley, *Jesus and the Spiral of Violence* (Minneapolis: Fortress, 1993), p. 242.

41. Horsley, *Jesus and the Spiral of Violence,* pp. 232-233; Richard A. Horsley and Neil Asher Silberman, *The Message and the Kingdom: How Jesus and Paul Ignited a Revolution and Transformed the Ancient World* (New York: Grosset/Putnam, 1997), pp. 5-6, 10-11, 15-21, 77-78.

42. Peter Brown, *The Rise of Western Christendom: Triumph and Diversity, AD 200-1000* (Cambridge, Mass.: Blackwell, 1996), pp. 44-45; Norbert Brox, *A Concise History of the Early Church* (New York: Continuum, 1995), pp. 46-50; Charlotte Allen, *The Human Christ: The Search for the Historical Jesus* (New York: Free Press, 1998), pp. 59-61, 68; Erich Fromm, *The Dogma of Christ* (New York: Owl/Henry Holt, 1992), pp. 62-65.

43. William McLoughlin, *Revivals, Awakenings, and Reforms* (Chicago: University of Chicago Press, 1978), pp. 69-72; Ann Douglas, *The Feminization of American Culture* (New York: Avon, 1977), pp. 143-148.

44. Douglas, *The Feminization of American Culture*, pp. 160-161, 163.

45. Ibid., pp. 1-3, 162-163, 242.

46. Richard Quebedeaux, *I Found It!: The Story of Bill Bright and Campus Crusade* (New York: Harper & Row, 1979), p. 37.

47. Dean M. Kelley, *Why Conservative Churches Are Growing: A Study in the Sociology of Religion* (New York: Harper & Row, 1972), pp. 1, 21-25; Richard Quebedeaux, *The Worldly Evangelicals* (New York: Harper & Row, 1978), pp. 3-4, 14; Richard Quebedeaux, *The New Charismatics II* (New York: Harper & Row, 1983), pp. 90, 129.

48. Billy Graham, *World Aflame* (Garden City, N.Y.: Doubleday, 1965), p. 172; Quebedeaux, *I Found It!*, p. 57.

49. Quebedeaux, *I Found It!*, pp. 6, 8.

50. Bill Bright, *Come Help Change the World* (Old Tappan, N.J.: Fleming H. Revell), p. 80; Graham, *World Aflame*, p. 92.

51. "Promise Keepers' Sample of 1994 National Survey on Men: Report on 1994 Conference Attendees," p. 3.

52. Mark 15:34, King James Version.

53. Larry B. Stammer and Louis Sahagun, "Entire Promise Keepers' Staff to Be Laid Off," *Los Angeles Times*, Feb. 20, 1998, p. A1.

54. "Promise Keepers' Salary Controversy," *Washington Post*, Aug. 2, 1997, p. A8; Karen Auge, "Promise Keepers Founder Says He Wasn't Godly Man," *Fort-Worth Star Telegram*, Oct. 5, 1997, p. 14; Mary Winter, "Only McCartney Knows What the Future Holds," *Rocky Mountain News*, Denver, Nov. 28, 1994, p. 3D; John Henderson, "Mac Calls It Quits; CU Coach Seeks Times with Family," *Denver Post*, Nov. 20, 1994; Stuart Steers, "Under the Covers," *Westword*, Jan. 30, 1997.

CHAPTER 6: GONE TO SOLDIERS, EVERY ONE

1. Lawrence M. Baskir and William A. Strauss, *Chance and Circumstance: The Draft, the War, and the Vietnam Generation* (New York: Vintage, 1978), pp. 5, 276.

2. Clyde E. Jacobs and John F. Gallagher, *The Selective Service Act: A Case Study of the Governmental Process* (New York: Dodd, Mead, 1967), p. 110; Baskir and Strauss, *Chance and Circumstance*, pp. 15-16, 20-22; Alf Evers, *Selective Service: A Guide to the Draft* (Philadelphia: J. P. Lippincott, 1957), p. 110; Christian G. Appy, *Working-Class War: American Combat Soldiers and Vietnam* (Chapel Hill: University of North Carolina Press, 1993), p. 30.

3. The percentage in combat in Vietnam is likely less than 6 percent, the standard figure cited. That figure is based on a study in which the men were asked if they had ever "experienced" combat, a vague wording that includes the large numbers of noncombatant soldiers who found themselves in the line of fire inadvertently. I am indebted to Vietnam historian Christian Appy for guiding me through

these problematic statistics. See Baskir and Strauss, *Chance and Circumstance*, pp. 5-12.

4. Lawrence Wright, *In the New World: Growing Up with America from the Sixties to the Eighties* (New York: Vintage, 1989), p. 104.

5. Gordon Dalbey, *Sons of the Father* (Wheaton, Ill.: Tyndale House, 1996), p. 152.

6. John Wheeler, *Touched with Fire: The Future of the Vietnam Generation* (New York: Franklin Watts, 1984), p. 99; A. D. Horne, ed., *The Wounded Generation* (Englewood Cliffs, N.J.: Prentice-Hall, 1981), p. 96.

7. Jerry Lembcke, *The Spitting Image: Myth, Memory, and the Legacy of Vietnam* (New York: New York University Press, 1998), pp. ix, 6, 58, 73, 75, 77-78.

8. Horne, *The Wounded Generation*, p. 118; Lembcke, *The Spitting Image*, p. 53; Richard Stacewicz, *Winter Soldiers: An Oral History of the Vietnam Veterans Against the War* (New York: Twayne, 1997), pp. 4-5.

9. Bruno Bettelheim, "Student Revolt: The Hard Core," *Vital Speeches*, April 15, 1969, p. 405. See also Bruno Bettelheim, "Children Must Learn to Fear," *New York Times Magazine*, April 13, 1969, p. 125; David Dempsey, "Bruno Bettelheim Is Dr. No," *New York Times Magazine*, Jan. 11, 1970, p. 22.

10. John R. Coyne, Jr., *The Impudent Snobs: Agnew vs. the Intellectual Establishment* (New Rochelle, N.Y.: Arlington House, 1972), p. 188; Frank S. Meyer, "The Revolution Eats Its Parents," *National Review*, June 3, 1969, p. 541; K. Ross Toole, "I Am Tired of the Tyranny of Spoiled Brats," *U.S. News & World Report*, April 13, 1970, p. 76. Academics contributed book-length treatments of the Oedipal thesis, too. Most influential was Lewis S. Feuer's *The Conflict of Generations* (New York: Basic Books, 1969). Feuer, a philosophy professor who was teaching at the University of California at Berkeley during the early student revolt of 1964-65, maintained that even the shift in focus of student activism from civil rights to Vietnam was motivated by a desire on the part of the sons to find a more fruitful forum for unleashing their "aggressive impulses" against their fathers. See pp. 414-415.

11. Kenneth Keniston, *Youth and Dissent: The Rise of a New Opposition* (New York: Harcourt Brace Jovanovich, 1971), p. 275.

12. Robert Bly, *Iron John: A Book About Men* (New York: Addison-Wesley, 1990), pp. 2-4, 7; Keith Thompson, "The Meaning of Being Male: A Conversation with Robert Bly," *LA Weekly*, Aug. 2-11, 1983.

13. James Miller, *Democracy Is in the Streets* (New York: Simon & Schuster, 1987), pp. 181-182.

14. Nancy Zaroulis and Gerald Sullivan, *Who Spoke Up?: American Protest Against the War in Vietnam 1963-1975* (Garden City, N.Y.: Doubleday, 1984), pp. 65-66.

15. Samuel Lubell, "That Generation Gap," in *Confrontation: The Student Rebellion and the Universities*, Daniel Bell and Irving Kristol, eds. (New York: Basic Books, 1969), pp. 58-59; Seymour Martin Lipset, *Rebellion in the University* (Chicago: University of Chicago Press, 1971), pp. 80-81, 84-85.

16. Kenneth Keniston, *Young Radicals: Notes on Committed Youth* (New York: Harcourt, Brace & World, 1968), pp. 55, 59, 112–113, 116, 118.

17. Mario Savio, "An End to History," in *The Politics of the New Left*, Matthew Stolz, ed. (Beverly Hills: Glencoe Press, 1971), p. 134; Norman Mailer, *The Armies of the Night* (New York: Plume/Penguin, 1994), p. 144.

18. Peter Marin, "The Open Truth and Fiery Vehemence of Youth," in *The Movement Toward a New America*, Mitchell Goodman, ed. (Philadelphia: Pilgrim Press/New York: Knopf, 1970), p. 10.

19. Peter Berg, "A Founder of the Diggers Talks About What's Happening," in Goodman, ed., *The Movement Toward a New America*, pp. 13–16.

20. David Harris, *Our War* (New York: Times, 1996), p. 52.

21. Tom Engelhardt, *The End of Victory Culture* (New York: BasicBooks, 1995), p. 244.

22. Horne, ed., *The Wounded Generation*, pp. 185, 188.

23. "The Port Huron Statement," in Miller, *Democracy Is in the Streets*, p. 332.

24. Sara Davidson, *Loose Change: Three Women of the Sixties* (Garden City, N.Y.: Doubleday, 1977), p. 158.

25. Norman Mailer, *The Armies of the Night*, p. 271; Mark Gerzon, *A Choice of Heroes* (Boston: Houghton Mifflin, 1982), pp. 85, 96.

26. Marvin Garson, "The System Does Not Work," in Goodman, ed., *The Movement Toward a New America*, pp. 119, 122.

27. *The War at Home*, dir. and prod. by Chuck France, One Mo' Time Films, 1981.

28. Todd Gitlin, *The Sixties* (New York: Bantam, 1987), p. 256.

29. Theodore Roszak, "Youth and the Great Refusal," in Goodman, ed., *The Movement Toward a New America*, p. 86.

30. "The Port Huron Statement," *Democracy Is in the Streets*, p. 338.

31. Sara Evans, *Personal Politics* (New York: Vintage, 1980), p. 200.

32. Marge Piercy, "The Grand Coolie Dam," in *Sisterhood Is Powerful: An Anthology of Writings from the Women's Liberation Movement*, Robin Morgan, ed. (New York: Vintage, 1970), pp. 473–492.

33. Gitlin, *The Sixties*, p. 372.

34. Piercy, "The Grand Coolie Dam," pp. 483, 485.

35. Evans, *Personal Politics*, pp. 112, 160, 224.

36. Ibid., pp. 200–201.

37. Casey Hayden and Mary King, "Sex and Caste," in Evans, *Personal Politics*, pp. 235–238.

38. Evans, *Personal Politics*, pp. 189–192.

39. Gitlin, *The Sixties*, p. 373.

40. Seymour M. Hersh, *My Lai 4* (New York: Random House, 1970), pp. 39–40; Michael Bilton and Kevin Sim, *Four Hours in My Lai* (New York: Penguin, 1992), pp. 7, 98, 102; "Investigation of the My Lai Incident," report of the Armed Services Investi-

gating Subcommittee, Committee on Armed Services, U.S. House of Representatives, July 15, 1970 (Washington, D.C.: U.S. Government Printing Office, 1970), p. 6; "Investigation of the My Lai Incident," hearings of Armed Services Investigating Subcommittee of the Committee on Armed Services, U.S. House of Representatives, April–June 1970 (Washington, D.C.: U.S. Government Printing Office, 1970), p.61.

41. Mary McCarthy, *Medina* (New York: Harcourt Brace Jovanovich, 1972), pp. 30–31; "Investigation of the My Lai Incident," hearings of Armed Services Investigating Subcommittee, April–June 1970, p. 65.

42. Bilton and Sim, *Four Hours in My Lai,* pp. 143–144.

43. Hersh, *My Lai 4,* p. 59.

44. Ibid., pp. 49, 54, 72; Bilton and Sim, *Four Hours in My Lai,* pp. 113, 119, 122, 129, 140.

45. Bilton and Sim, *Four Hours in My Lai,* pp. 7, 24.

46. Richard A. Gabriel and Paul L. Savage, *Crisis in Command* (New York: Hill and Wang, 1978), p. 4.

47. Ibid., pp. 17–18.

48. Ibid., pp. 18, 117.

49. Frank Harvey, *Air War — Vietnam* (New York: Bantam, 1967), pp. 44–45.

50. James William Gibson, *The Perfect War* (New York: Vintage, 1986), p. 104.

51. Cecil B. Currey ("Cincinnatus"), *Self-Destruction* (New York: W. W. Norton, 1981), p. 130.

52. Gibson, *The Perfect War,* p. 156; David H. Hackworth, *About Face* (New York: Simon & Schuster, 1989), pp. 316–317.

53. Gabriel and Savage, *Crisis in Command,* p. 94; Gibson, *The Perfect War,* p. 23.

54. Gabriel and Savage, *Crisis in Command,* pp. 31, 55, 86–87, 94; Dr. Jonathan Shay, *Achilles in Vietnam* (New York: Touchstone, 1995), p. 13.

55. Douglas Kinnard, *The War Managers* (Wayne, N.J.: Avery, 1985), p. 174; Gibson, *The Perfect War,* pp. 442, 444.

56. Gabriel and Savage, *Crisis in Command,* pp. 32–33, 40–41, 54, 63–66, 77, 93–94, 96.

57. Baskir and Strauss, *Chance and Circumstance,* p. 3.

58. Gabriel and Savage, *Crisis in Command,* p. 31.

59. Joseph Lelyveld, "The Story of a Soldier Who Refused to Fire at Songmy," *New York Times Magazine,* Dec. 14, 1969, p. 32.

60. Hersh, *My Lai 4,* pp. 16, 18; Bilton and Sim, *Four Hours in My Lai,* pp. 50–52.

61. Hersh, *My Lai 4,* pp. 20–21.

62. Ibid., p. 19; Richard Hammer, *The Court-Martial of Lt. Calley* (New York: Coward, McCann & Geoghegan, 1971), pp. 55, 75–76; Tom Tiede, *Calley — Soldier or Killer?* (New York: Pinnacle, 1971), p. 50; John Sack, *Lieutenant Calley: His Own Story* (New York: Viking, 1971), p. 13.

63. Hammer, *The Court-Martial of Lt. Calley,* pp. 55–59, 76.

64. Hersh, *My Lai 4,* pp. 122–123.

65. Bilton and Sim, *Four Hours in My Lai*, pp. 83–85; Richard Hammer, *One Morning in the War: The Tragedy at Son My* (New York: Coward-McCann, 1970), pp. 98–99; Hersh, *My Lai 4*, p. 34.

66. Bilton and Sim, *Four Hours in My Lai*, pp. 79, 83, 92.

67. Gabriel and Savage, *Crisis in Command*, p. 76.

68. Lt. Gen. William R. Peers, *The My Lai Inquiry* (New York: W.W. Norton, 1979), p. 233; Hersh, *My Lai 4*, p. 19; Bilton and Sim, *Four Hours in My Lai*, p. 52; Sack, *Lieutenant Calley: His Own Story*, p. 30.

69. Sack, *Lieutenant Calley: His Own Story*, pp. 50, 57, 60–61, 75, 79, 138.

70. Ibid., pp. 67–69.

71. Ibid., p. 69.

72. Marilyn B. Young, *The Vietnam Wars 1945–1990* (New York: HarperPerennial, 1991), pp. 189–190.

73. Seymour Hersh, *Cover-Up* (New York: Random House, 1972), p. 10.

74. Sack, *Lieutenant Calley: His Own Story*, pp. 79, 83–84.

75. David Halberstam, *The Best and the Brightest* (New York: Ballantine, 1992), twentieth anniversary edition, p. 157; *Hearts and Minds*, dir. Peter Davis, Rainbow Pictures, 1974.

76. Bilton and Sim, *Four Hours in My Lai*, pp. 1, 182.

77. Gloria Emerson, *Winners and Losers* (New York: Harvest/HBJ, 1976), p. 65; *Winter Soldier*, Winterfilm, Inc., 1972; Hersh, *My Lai 4*, p. 81.

78. Hersh, *Cover-Up*, p. 15; Robert Jay Lifton, *Home from the War* (Boston: Beacon, 1992), p. 50; Bilton and Sim, *Four Hours in My Lai*, pp. 123–124; Sack, *Lieutenant Calley: His Own Story*, p. 117.

79. Bilton and Sim, *Four Hours in My Lai*, pp. 64, 71, 75, 77–79, 81–82, 92, 99.

80. Ibid., p. 79.

81. Ibid., pp. 71–72.

82. McCarthy, *Medina*, pp. 16–17.

83. Bilton and Sim, *Four Hours in My Lai*, pp. 135–136, 139–141.

84. Ibid., pp. 176–177, 181, 194, 206; McCarthy, *Medina*, p. 18; Gabriel and Savage, *Crisis in Command*, p. 205, n. 14.

85. Hersh, *My Lai 4*, pp. 46–47; Hersh, *Cover-Up*, pp. 101–105.

86. Richard Matheson, "Brother to the Machine," *Collected Stories* (Los Angeles: Dream/ Press, 1989), pp. 89–93.

87. Gibson, *The Perfect War*, p. 213; Gabriel and Savage, *Crisis in Command*, pp. 45, 48–49; Lembcke, *The Spitting Image*, p. 37; Howard Zinn, *A People's History of the United States* (New York: Harper Colophon Books, 1980), pp. 485–487.

88. Gibson, *The Perfect War*, pp. 210, 212; Baskir and Strauss, *Chance and Circumstance*, p. 143; Gabriel and Savage, *Crisis in Command*, pp. 43–44.

89. Hersh, *Cover-Up*, p. 31.

90. Gibson, *The Perfect War*, p. 111; John Balaban, W. D. Ehrhart, Wayne Karlin, and

Basil Paquet, "Carrying the Darkness: Literary Approaches to Atrocity," in *Facing My Lai: Moving Beyond the Massacre*, David L. Anderson, ed. (Lawrence, Kansas: University Press of Kansas, 1998), p. 93. Also see Emerson, *Winners and Losers*, p. 7.

91. Bilton and Sim, *Four Hours in My Lai*, p. 196.

92. Ibid., p. 197.

93. Ibid., p. 201.

94. William G. Eckhardt, Ron Ridenhour, and Hugh C. Thompson, Jr., "Experiencing the Darkness: An Oral History," in Anderson, ed., *Facing My Lai*, pp. 33–39.

95. Ibid., p. 39.

96. Ibid., p. 39.

97. Hersh, *My Lai 4*, p. 105.

98. Vietnam Veterans Against the War, *The Winter Soldier Investigation: An Inquiry into American War Crimes* (Boston: Beacon Press, 1972), pp. 2–3.

99. Eckhardt et al., "Experiencing the Darkness," p. 40.

100. Hersh, *Cover-Up*, p. 240.

101. Bilton and Sim, *Four Hours in My Lai*, pp. 321–322.

102. Hersh, *Cover-Up*, pp. 241–242.

103. "Americans Speak Out on the Massacre," *Life*, Dec. 19, 1969, p. 46.

104. Hersh, *Cover-Up*, p. 6; Bilton and Sim, *Four Hours in My Lai*, pp. 307–308, 323, 337, 339, 346, 355–356.

105. "An Average American Boy?," *Time*, Dec. 5, 1969, p. 25; Bilton and Sim, *Four Hours in My Lai*, p. 354.

106. Hersh, *My Lai 4*, p. 153.

107. Hammer, *The Court-Martial of Lt. Calley*, pp. 374–377; Bilton and Sim, *Four Hours in My Lai*, pp. 2, 340, 355; Sack, *Lieutenant Calley: His Own Story*, p. 15; Tiede, *Calley: Soldier or Killer?*, p. 16.

108. Sack, *Lieutenant Calley: His Own Story*, p. 21; Wayne Greenhaw, *The Making of a Hero* (Louisville, Ky.: Touchstone, 1971), p. 61.

109. McCarthy, *Medina*, p. 48.

110. Ibid., pp. 46–47.

111. Christopher Buckley, "Viet Guilt," *Esquire*, Sept. 1983, p. 68.

112. James Fallows, "What Did You Do in the Class War, Daddy?," in *The Vietnam Reader*, Walter Capps, ed. (New York: Routledge, 1991), pp. 213–215, 219.

113. Buckley, "Viet Guilt," p. 71; Edward Tick, "About Men: Apocalypse Continued," *New York Times Magazine*, Jan. 13, 1985, p. 60.

114. Tick, "Apocalypse Continued," p. 60.

115. John Kerry, "Vietnam Veterans Against the War: Testimony to the U.S. Senate Foreign Relations Committee (April 22, 1971)," in *Vietnam and America*, Marvin E. Gettleman, Jane Franklin, et al., eds. (New York: Grove, 1985), p. 458.

116. Robert Roth, *Sand in the Wind* (Boston: Atlantic Monthly Press, 1973), pp. 452–454.

117. Tim O'Brien, *The Things They Carried* (New York: Penguin, 1990), pp. 60–63.

118. Lembcke, *The Spitting Image*, p. 53; Baskir and Strauss, *Chance and Circumstance*, pp. 140–141.

CHAPTER 7: THE CREATURE IN THE MIRROR

1. Fred Turner, *Echoes of Combat: The Vietnam War in American Memory* (New York: Anchor, 1996), p. 63.

2. Marilyn B. Young, *The Vietnam Wars 1945–1990* (New York: HarperPerennial, 1991), p. 113.

3. Ronald Reagan with Richard G. Hubler, *Where's the Rest of Me?* (New York: Duell, Sloan and Pearce, 1965), pp. 112–121, 138; Lou Cannon, *Reagan* (New York: G. P. Putnam's Sons, 1982), p. 57.

4. Lou Cannon, *President Reagan: The Role of a Lifetime* (New York: Simon & Schuster, 1991), pp. 58–60, 486–488; Garry Wills, *Reagan's America* (New York: Penguin, 1988), pp. 147, 192–193, 196, 198–199.

5. Wills, *Reagan's America*, pp. 12, 16–18; Reagan with Hubler, *Where's the Rest of Me?*, p. 6.

6. Wills, *Reagan's America*, pp. 295–296, 314–319, 328–330, 336–337; Michael Paul Rogin, *Ronald Reagan, the Movie* (Berkeley: University of California Press, 1988), p. 33.

7. Wills, *Reagan's America*, pp. 319, 320–321, 332–333, 347, 350–354.

8. Rogin, *Ronald Reagan, the Movie*, p. 34; Wills, *Reagan's America*, p. 319.

9. Wills, *Reagan's America*, pp. 129–130, 460; Paul Slansky, "Reaganisms in Review: You Ain't Heard Nothing Yet," *New Republic*, Jan. 6, 1986, p. 10.

10. "Order of the Draft Drawing," *New York Times*, Dec. 2, 1969, pp. 1, 20.

11. Limbaugh also reportedly claimed at different times that he wasn't drafted because of "a football knee" and "a 4-F classification." James D. Retter, "Counterpunch: A Rush to Judgment on Limbaugh?," *Los Angeles Times*, May 25, 1998, p. F3; Paul D. Colford, "Limbaugh Told Short Version of Draft Story," *Star Tribune*, Minneapolis, Sept. 27, 1993, p. 1E; Kevin Sack and Jeff Gerth, "The Favors Done for Quayle: A New Look at Guard Stint," *New York Times*, Sept. 20, 1992, p. 1.

12. Fred Turner, *Echoes of Combat*, pp. 63–64.

13. Young, *The Vietnam Wars*, p. 213; Seymour M. Hersh, "What Happened at My Lai?," in Gettleman et al., eds., *Vietnam and America*, pp. 403–404.

14. H. Bruce Franklin, *M.I.A. or Mythmaking in America* (New York: Lawrence Hill, 1992), pp. xi, 3–4, 11–14, 48–49, 60, 93–95, 122–125, 129.

15. David Morrell, *Blood Oath* (New York: St. Martin's/Marek, 1982), p. 101.

16. Joseph H. Pleck, "The Theory of Male Sex-Role Identity: Its Rise and Fall, 1936 to the Present," in *The Making of Masculinities: The New Men's Studies*, Harry Brod, ed. (New York: Routledge, 1987), pp. 34–35.

17. Audie Murphy, *To Hell and Back* (New York: Grosset & Dunlap, 1949), pp. 10, 11, 272–273; Don Graham, *No Name on the Bullet* (New York: Viking, 1989), pp. 119–120.

18. Murphy, *To Hell and Back*, pp. 188–189.

19. Graham, *No Name on the Bullet*, pp. 190, 274, 278–279, 287–288, 300–301, 313–314, 320.

20. Ibid., p. 124.

21. Ibid., p. 327.

22. John Sack, *Lieutenant Calley: His Own Story* (New York: Viking 1971), p. 28.

23. Murphy, *To Hell and Back*, p. 269.

24. Peter Marin, "Living in Moral Pain," in *The Vietnam Reader*, Walter Capps, ed. (New York: Routledge, 1991), pp. 43, 48.

25. David Morrell, *First Blood* (London: Headline Feature, 1992), pp. vii–viii.

26. David Morrell, *First Blood* (New York: Armchair Detective Library, 1990), p. ii.

27. Morrell, *First Blood*, Headline Feature edition, p. 25.

28. Ibid., p. 17.

29. Ibid., pp. 8–9, 18.

30. Morrell, *First Blood*, Armchair Detective Library edition, pp. 55, 90.

31. Ibid., p. 77.

32. Ibid., pp. 172–173.

33. Ibid., p. 239.

34. Ibid., p. 240.

35. Ibid., p. iii.

36. Ibid., pp. 155, 224.

37. Ibid., p. 156.

38. Ibid., pp. 250–252.

39. Ibid., p. iii.

40. Vietnam Veterans Against the War, *The Winter Soldier Investigation: An Inquiry into American War Crimes* (Boston: Beacon, 1972), pp. 109, 167, 171.

41. *Vietnam: The Soldiers' Story*, The Learning Channel, 1998.

42. David Rabe, *The Vietnam Plays*, vol. 1 (New York: Grove, 1993), p. 89.

43. David Rabe, *The Basic Training of Pavlo Hummel*, in *The Vietnam Plays*, vol. 1, p. 60.

44. David Rabe, *Sticks and Bones*, in *The Vietnam Plays*, vol. 1, pp. 108–109.

45. Rabe, *Sticks and Bones*, pp. 166–167.

46. Ibid., pp. 153, 173.

47. Rabe, *The Basic Training of Pavlo Hummel*, p. 34.

48. David Rabe, "First Blood," unpublished draft, pp. 1–3.

49. Ibid., pp. 21, 100, 101.

50. Ibid., pp. 23, 26, 94–95.

51. Ibid., p. 102.

52. Pat H. Broeske, "The Curious Evolution of John Rambo," *Los Angeles Times Calendar*, Oct. 27, 1985, p. 32.

53. Graham, *No Name on the Bullet*, pp. 261–262.

54. Mary Shelley, *Frankenstein* (New York: Dover, 1944), pp. 93–94; Eleanor Flexner,

Mary Wollstonecraft: A Biography (New York: McCann and Geoghegan, 1972), pp. 251, 254.

55. Kevin Sessums, "Rocky Gets Real," *Vanity Fair,* Sept. 1990, p. 199.

56. Lester A. Sobel, ed., *Space: From Sputnik to Gemini* (New York: Facts on File, 1965), pp. 9–10.

57. Kirk Douglas, *The Ragman's Son* (New York: Pocket, 1988), pp. 417–418.

58. David Morrell, *Rambo: First Blood Part II* (New York: Jove, 1985), pp. 62–64, 235–236.

59. Gerald Early, *The Culture of Bruising* (Hopewell, N.J.: Ecco, 1994), p. 94.

CHAPTER 8: BURNING DOWN THE HOUSE

1. Stephen Braun, "A Trial by Fire in the '60s," *Los Angeles Times,* Dec. 18, 1995, p. A1.

2. Lloyd Grove, "Pat Buchanan, Sunny Side Up," *Washington Post,* Feb. 26, 1996, p. B1; Jeffrey H. Birnbaum, "The Pat Solution," *Time,* Nov. 6, 1995, p. 24; Michael Lewis, "Reality Bites: Journalist's Account of Pat Buchanan's Presidential Campaigning," *New Republic,* March 25, 1996, p. 23; Susan Faludi, "Pat Buchanan's Traitors," *LA Weekly,* Aug. 23–Aug. 29, 1996, p. 17.

3. Peter Carlson, "Vast Winged Conspiracies: Something to Worry About from the Pages of Paranoia," *Washington Post,* March 16, 1999, p. C1; Adam Parfrey and Jim Redden, "Patriot Games," *Village Voice,* Oct. 11, 1994, p. 26.

4. James D. Tabor and Eugene V. Gallagher, *Why Waco?* (Berkeley: University of California Press, 1995), pp. 1–3, 22; *Turning Point,* ABC News, July 13, 1995; "FBI News Conference, Waco, Texas," Federal News Service, April 20, 1993; "The Waco Hearings, Day 6, Part 6," CNN, July 26, 1995.

5. Richard Leiby, "Taking Waco on Its Own Terms: For the Hearings, Some Useful Words on the Lexicon," *Washington Post,* July 20, 1995, p. C3; Glenn F. Bunting, "Embers of Doubt Remain About Cause of Waco Blaze," *Los Angeles Times,* July 16, 1995, p. A1; Dick J. Reavis, "What Really Happened at Waco," *Texas Monthly,* July 1995, p. 88.

6. Starley McGuyre, "It Takes a Government," July 16, 1997, Info@waco93.com.

7. "Perspectives," *Newsweek,* Aug. 7, 1995, p. 17.

8. Jack Anderson, *Inside the NRA: Armed and Dangerous* (Beverly Hills: Dove, 1996), p. 116.

9. James Moore, *Very Special Agents* (New York: Pocket, 1997), p. 286.

10. Tabor and Gallagher, *Why Waco?,* pp. 42, 85–86, 101–102, 120.

11. *Waco: The Rules of Engagement,* prods. Dan Gifford, William Gazecki, and Michael McNulty, and dir. William Gazecki, SomFord Entertainment/Fifth Estate Productions, 1997.

12. Ibid.

13. Richard Slotkin, *Regeneration Through Violence: The Mythology of the American Frontier,*

1600–1860 (Middletown, Conn.: Wesleyan University Press, 1973), pp. 112–115; Christopher Catiglia, *Bound and Determined: Captivity, Culture-Crossing, and White Womanhood from Mary Rowlandson to Patty Hearst* (Chicago: University of Chicago Press, 1996), pp. 23, 45–52; Annette Kolodny, *The Land Before Her: Fantasy and Experience of the American Frontiers, 1630–1860* (Chapel Hill: University of North Carolina Press, 1984), pp. 10–11, 17–34.

14. J. Nils Wright, "Nationwide Leaving State Property/Casualty Market," *Business Journal-Sacramento*, June 7, 1993, section 1, p. 4; "Ex-Agents Suing Nationwide," *Business Insurance*, May 3, 1993, p. 2.

15. Richard Leiby and Jim McGee, "Still Burning: Was Waco a Massacre?," *Washington Post*, April 18, 1997, p. C1.

16. Also see Tabor and Gallagher, *Why Waco?*, p. 227; "Bulldozing of Site Decried; Lawyers Say Razing of Compound Prevents Unbiased Probe," *Dallas Morning News*, May 14, 1993, p. 31A.

17. "Basic Final Investigative Report of USS *Forrestal* Fire," Office of the Judge Advocate General, Department of the Navy, Sept. 19, 1967.

18. Ibid. Michael McNulty's footage can be seen in "USS *Forrestal*: Situation Critical," Discovery Channel, August 3, 1997, a television documentary on the disaster.

19. "*Waco: The Rules of Engagement*, Synopsis," promotional literature, SomFord Entertainment, 1997.

20. "Right-Wing Radio Station Burns Down," UPI, Nov. 30, 1997.

CHAPTER 9: MAN IN A CAN

1. Leslie A. Fiedler, *The Collected Essays of Leslie Fiedler*, vol. 2 (New York: Stein & Day, 1971), pp. 390–391, 394.

2. Col. Edwin E. "Buzz" Aldrin with Wayne Warga, *Return to Earth* (New York: Random House, 1973), pp. 6, 54, 86, 306.

3. Ibid., p. 10.

4. Ibid., pp. 257, 268.

5. Barbara Kramer, *Neil Armstrong: The First Man on the Moon* (Springfield, N.J.: Enslow, 1997); Matthew Purdy, "To the Moon: In Rural Ohio, Armstrong Quietly Lives on His Own Dark Side of the Moon," *New York Times*, July 20, 1994, p. A14; Al Salvato, "Out of the Moonlight," *Dallas Morning News*, July 24, 1994, p. 35A; "Apollo 11 Anniversary, Michael Collins: The Man Who Stayed Behind," UPI, July 8, 1989; Aldrin, *Return to Earth*, p. 278; Lawrence Wright, "Ten Years Later, the Moonwalkers," *Look*, July 1979, p. 22.

6. "How Seven Were Chosen," *Newsweek*, April 20, 1959, p. 64.

7. M. Scott Carpenter, L. Gordon Cooper, et al., *We Seven* (New York: Simon & Schuster, 1962), dust jacket copy and pp. 4, 10, 11.

8. "America's New Hero," *U.S. News & World Report*, March 5, 1962, p. 22; James Res-

ton, "Is the Moon Really Worth John Glenn?," *New York Times,* Feb. 25, 1961, section 4, p. 10; David Lawrence, "Man's 'Finest Hour,'" *U.S. News & World Report,* March 5, 1962, p. 108.

9. "Here Are the U.S. Spacemen: Mature, Married, Fathers," *U.S. News & World Report,* April 20, 1959, p. 112; "Space Voyagers Rarin' to Orbit," *Life,* April 20, 1959, p. 22.

10. John W. Finney, "7 Named as Pilots for Space Flights Scheduled in 1961," *New York Times,* April 10, 1959, p. 1.

11. Tom Wolfe, *The Right Stuff* (New York: Bantam, 1980), pp. 67, 191–192; Alan B. Shepard, "The Astronaut's Story of the Thrust into Space," *Life,* May 19, 1961, pp. 25–26.

12. Tom Wolfe, *The Right Stuff,* p. 64; *Moon Shot: The Inside Story of the Apollo Project,* TBS Productions, 1994.

13. Carpenter et al., *We Seven,* p. 71.

14. Wolfe, *The Right Stuff,* pp. 61–62, 78–89, 155, 158; Norman Mailer, *Of a Fire on the Moon* (Boston: Little, Brown, 1970), p. 47.

15. Wolfe, *The Right Stuff,* p. 151.

16. Carpenter et al., *We Seven,* p. 330; Wolfe, *The Right Stuff,* pp. 160–162; Brian O'Leary, *The Making of an Ex-Astronaut* (Boston: Houghton Mifflin, 1970), p. 79.

17. Donald Slayton, "We Believe They Should Leave the Flying to Us," *Life,* Sept. 27, 1963, p. 90.

18. Michael L. Smith, "Selling the Moon," in *The Culture of Consumption,* Richard Wightman Fox and T. Jackson Lears, eds. (New York: Pantheon, 1983), p. 194; O'Leary, *The Making of an Ex-Astronaut,* p. 231.

19. Carpenter et al., *We Seven,* pp. 23–24.

20. Ibid., p. 24.

21. Wolfe, *The Right Stuff,* p. 160; *Moon Shot: The Inside Story of the Apollo Project;* Slayton, "We Believe They Should Leave the Flying to Us," p. 90.

22. Carpenter et al., *We Seven,* pp. 93–94.

23. Ibid., p. 94.

24. *Moon Shot: The Inside Story of the Apollo Project.*

25. O'Leary, *The Making of an Ex-Astronaut,* p. 167.

26. Wolfe, *The Right Stuff,* pp. 74–77, 152, 202.

27. Aldrin, *Return to Earth,* p. 15.

28. O'Leary, *The Making of an Ex-Astronaut,* p. 102.

29. Richard Matheson, *The Shrinking Man* (New York: Berkley, 1969), front cover.

30. Aldrin, *Return to Earth,* pp. 54, 56–58.

31. Ibid., pp. 256, 260.

32. Ibid., pp. 180, 278–280.

33. Ibid., pp. 280–281.

34. Ibid., pp. 267, 289, 292–293, 299.

35. Ibid., pp. 23, 256.

36. Michael L. Smith, "Selling the Moon," in Fox and Lears, eds., *The Culture of Consumption*, p. 201.

37. Wolfe, *The Right Stuff*, p. 182.

38. Richard F. Shepard, "$2,000,000 Radio-TV Coverage Carries Story of Flight to Nation," *New York Times*, Feb. 21, 1962, p. 22.

39. "Applause, Tears and Laughter and the Emotions of a Long-Ago Fourth of July," *Life*, March 9, 1962, p. 34.

40. Raymond Moley, "What's Back of a Hero," *Newsweek*, April 9, 1962, p. 116; John P. Shanley, "Julie Harris, as Victoria, Wins TV Emmy," *New York Times*, May 23, 1962, p. 91.

41. "Applause, Tears and Laughter," p. 34; "Hero's Words to Cherish," *Life*, March 9, 1962, p. 4.

42. Wolfe, *The Right Stuff*, pp. 291, 293–294; "America's New Hero," *U.S. News & World Report*, March 5, 1962, p. 22.

43. Aldrin, *Return to Earth*, pp. 45, 206–207; "Off to the Moon," *Life*, July 4, 1969, cover; "Leaving for the Moon," *Life*, July 25, 1969, cover. The cover story chronicling the actual landing featured only the flag and the footprints on the moon's surface. "On the Moon," *Life*, Aug. 8, 1969.

44. Aldrin, *Return to Earth*, p. 45.

45. Buzz Aldrin and John Barnes, *Encounter with Tiber* (New York: Warner, 1996).

46. R. W. Apple, Jr., "Hollywood, D.C.," *New York Times Magazine*, Nov. 15, 1998, p. 40.

47. Sanyika Shakur, a.k.a. Monster Kody Scott, *Monster: The Autobiography of an L.A. Gang Member* (New York: Penguin, 1994), p. 100.

48. Ibid., pp. 6–7, 13, 52, 86–94.

49. *Eight-Tray Gangster: The Making of a Crip*, Thomas Lee Wright, prod. and dir., ETG-Saramatt Productions, 1993.

50. Ibid.

51. Shakur, *Monster*, pp. 110, 117.

52. Ibid., pp. 60, 72, 78, 84, 99, 110, 169, 178.

53. Malcolm W. Klein, *The American Street Gang* (New York: Oxford University Press, 1995), pp. 60–64.

54. Shakur, *Monster*, p. 56.

55. *Eight-Tray Gangster*.

56. Shakur, *Monster*, p. 5.

57. Léon Bing, *Do or Die* (New York: HarperPerennial, 1991), pp. 237–265.

58. William Broyles, Jr., *Brothers in Arms: A Journey from War to Peace* (Austin: University of Texas Press, 1986), pp. 171–172.

59. J. Glenn Gray, *The Warriors: Reflections on Men in Battle* (New York: Harper Torchbooks, 1959).

60. David Whitman, "The Untold Story of the L.A. Riot," *U.S. News & World Report*, May 31, 1993, p. 34; "Moment of Crisis: Anatomy of a Riot," *Nightline*, ABC, May 28, 1992.

61. Ted Koppel and Kyle Gibson, *Nightline: History in the Making and the Making of Television* (New York: Times, 1996), p. 417.

62. "Los Angeles Revisited, Part Two," *Nightline*, ABC, Oct. 22, 1992.

63. Amy Wallace, "Making the Monster Huge," *Los Angeles Times Magazine*, April 4, 1993, p. 16.

64. Ibid.

65. "Monsta," *60 Minutes*, CBS, July 31, 1994.

66. Miles Corwin, "Police Arrest Fugitive Gang Member Turned Author," *Los Angeles Times*, May 29, 1996, p. B1.

67. Ibid.

68. "Los Angeles Revisited, Part Two," *Nightline*, ABC, Oct. 22, 1992.

69. Nathan Irvin Huggins, *Harlem Renaissance* (New York: Oxford University Press, 1971), pp. 258–259.

70. Hugh Pearson, *The Shadow of the Panther* (Reading, Mass.: Addison-Wesley, 1994), p. 130.

71. Robert F. Williams, *Negroes with Guns* (Chicago: Third World, 1973), p. 46; Malcolm X with Alex Haley, *The Autobiography of Malcolm X* (New York: Ballantine, 1993), p. 245.

72. Susan Sontag, "Notes on 'Camp,'" in *Against Interpretation* (New York: Farrar, Straus & Giroux, 1966), p. 288; Esther Newton, *Mother Camp: Female Impersonators in America* (Chicago: University of Chicago Press, 1979), p. 103; Mike Phillips, Barry Shapiro, and Mark Joseph, *Forbidden Fantasies: Men Who Dare to Dress in Drag* (New York: Collier, 1980), p. 30.

73. Encyclopedia of camp cited in Andrew Ross, *No Respect: Intellectuals and Popular Culture* (New York: Routledge, 1989), p. 146; Sontag, "Notes on 'Camp'" p. 277.

74. John D'Emilio and Estelle B. Freedman, *Intimate Matters: A History of Sexuality in America* (Chicago: University of Chicago Press, 1997), pp. 290–291, 318; Allan Bérubé, "The History of Gay Bathhouses," in *Policing Public Sex*, Ephen Glenn Colter, Wayne Hoffman, et al., eds. (Boston: South End, 1996), pp. 187–220; Martin Duberman, *Stonewall* (New York: Plume, 1994), pp. 181, 193–195.

75. Duberman, *Stonewall*, pp. 188, 192–209; "4 Policemen Hurt in 'Village' Raid," *New York Times*, June 29, 1969, p. 33.

76. Duberman, *Stonewall*, pp. 183, 188–189, 191.

77. Charles Kaiser, *The Gay Metropolis* (New York: Harvest, 1997), p. 212.

78. Ross, *No Respect*, p. 163; Kaiser, *The Gay Metropolis*, p. 205.

79. *Gay Pride Day, 1973*. I am indebted to Martin Duberman for directing me to the video, and to Arnie Kantrowitz for loaning me his copy of the tape. See also Martin Duberman, *Cures: A Gay Man's Odyssey* (New York: Dutton, 1991), pp. 278–279.

80. D'Emilio and Freedman, *Intimate Matters*, p. 323.

81. Jack Nichols, "Butcher Than Thou: Beyond Machismo," in *Gay Men: The Sociology of Male Homosexuality*, Martin P. Levine, ed. (New York: Harper & Row, 1979), pp. 328–342; Seymour Kleinberg, *Alienated Affections: Being Gay in America* (New York: St. Martin's Press, 1980), pp. 146, 150.

82. In one notable instance, millionaire businessman David Goodstein bought *The Advocate* in 1974 and used his editorial columns to denounce gay activist "obstructionists" who were getting in the way of mainstream assimilation and acceptance. In the following decades, reader-supported gay magazines like *After Dark* were displaced by advertising-supported glossy publications that were thinly disguised consumer-marketing vehicles. In magazines like *Out* and *Genre*, mainstream celebrities claimed the covers and the young and fit accessorized and recreated on the inside pages. See Martin Duberman, *Midlife Queer: Autobiography of a Decade, 1971–1981* (Madison: University of Wisconsin Press, 1996), p. 74; Daniel Harris, *The Rise and Fall of Gay Culture* (New York: Hyperion, 1997), pp. 67, 73–75, 78–79.

83. Michael Wilke, "Gay Overtones Seen in Abercrombie Ads: The Duke's Descendants Star in 8-Pager Shot by Bruce Weber," *Advertising Age*, Sept. 16, 1996, p. 20.

84. Paul Tharp, "Devil's in Details: Condé Nast Bets on 'Swashbuckler,'" *New York Post*, May 16, 1997, p. 27.

85. Maureen Dowd, "Youth—Art—Hype: A Different Bohemia," *New York Times Magazine*, Nov. 17, 1985, p. 26; "Paying Attention to Details," *Newsweek*, June 3, 1985, p. 82.

86. Stephen Saban, "Conflict of Interest," *Details*, July 1982, p. 5.

87. Stephen Saban, "Karma Out of the Closet: A Luncheon Intercourse with Marilyn and Boy George," *Details*, June 1985, p. 78.

88. "It's a Man's World," *Details*, Aug. 1989, p. 155; Gene Krell, "Commentary," *Details*, Sept. 1989, p. 314.

89. Gene Krell, "Clothes for the New Depression," *Details*, Oct. 1987, p. 107; Charoline Olofgörs, "Dandy Lions," *Details*, August 1988, p. 135; Mick Farren, "Clothes Encounter," *Details*, March 1983, p. 32.

90. Allee Willis, "Some Like It Smog," *Details*, Oct. 1987, p. 148.

91. Kathy Kalafut, "Dangerous Liaisons," *Details*, March 1990, p. 147; Suzanne Huthert, "Commentary," *Details*, Feb. 1990, p. 162.

92. John Gabree, "Magazines: Details a Trendy Comer Among Fashion-Conscious Periodicals," *Los Angeles Times*, March 24, 1988, section 5, p. 5; Michael Gross, "True Brit," *New York*, March 21, 1988, p. 22.

93. Thomas Palmer, "Men: The Last Frontier," *Boston Globe*, March 18, 1990, p. A1.

94. Ibid.; Michael Garry and Henry Eng, "Men, Men, Men: New Men's Magazines," *Marketing & Media Decisions*, Sept. 1990, p. 38.

95. Geraldine Baum, "King James," *Los Angeles Times*, May 10, 1994, p. E1.

96. Chris Salewicz, "England Swings (By the Neck)," *Details*, Oct. 1982, p. 9.

97. *Details*, Sept. 1990, pp. 25, 26–27, 31.

98. "Clothed for Vocation," *Details*, May 1991, p. 14; "Stylin'," *Details*, Nov. 1990, p. 37.

99. Pat Blashill, "A Force of One," *Details*, Jan. 1994, p. 66; Henry Rollins, "Iron and the Soul," *Details*, Jan. 1993, p. 40. Also see Thomas Frank, "Why Johnny Can't Dissent," in *Commodify Your Dissent*, Thomas Frank and Matt Weiland, eds. (New York: W. W. Norton, 1997), pp. 41–43.

100. "Details," *Details*, May 1991, p. 39.

101. Pam Slater, "Men's Turn to Be the Clotheshorse," *Sacramento Bee*, April 18, 1997, p. G1; Christine Shenot, "Dressing Up: Men's Apparel Perking for Some Retailers," *Orlando Sentinel*, Jan. 15, 1994, p. C1; Julie Vargo, "No Post-Thanksgiving Hangover: Men's Wear Business Maintains Its Fast Pace," *Daily News Record*, Dec. 6, 1994, p. 12.

102. *Details* marketing book, spring 1990.

103. "Feat First," *Details*, March 1991, pp. 96–103.

104. "1996 Details Subscriber Study," MRI Custom Division, spring 1996.

105. James Patrick Melendez, "Letters," *Details*, May 1991, p. 8.

106. Keith Blanchard, "Pay for Play," *Details*, May 1992, p. 30.

107. Blake Nelson, "Straight, No Chaser," *Details*, Dec. 1993, p. 78.

108. Anthony Kiedis, "Whole Lotta Love," *Details*, July 1992, p. 34.

109. Ibid., p. 38.

110. Ibid., p. 34.

111. Memo from Roger Trilling to James Truman, Aug. 31, 1992.

112. "The Bad and the Beautiful," *Details*, March 1992, p. 104.

113. Anka Radakovich, "Love for Sale," *Details*, May 1993, p. 66; Anka Radakovich, "Voyeurvision," *Details*, Dec. 1993, p. 100; Anka Radakovich, "King for a Day," *Details*, June 1995, p. 83.

114. Chris Heath, "Flesh Prince," *Details*, May 1992, p. 86.

115. Blake Nelson, "How to Date a Feminist," *Details*, Aug. 1993, p. 46.

116. "*SICK*, A Paul Morrissey Film," *Details*, July 1993, p. 111.

117. Stephen Saban, "Tim-ber!," *Details*, Sept. 1990, p. 89.

118. Amy Spindler, "The Men's Shows Seek a New Hero," *New York Times*, Feb. 11, 1997, p. B9; James Ledbetter, "Sweating the Details," *Village Voice*, May 27, 1997, p. 43; Paul D. Colford, "Out to Get Their Man, Newcomers Vying for Male Readers," *Newsday*, May 15, 1997, p. B2.

119. "Opportunity Rocks!," *Details*, June 1997.

120. Harold Hayes, ed., *Smiling Through the Apocalypse: Esquire's History of the Sixties* (New York: Esquire, 1987), pp. xvi–xvii.

121. Barbara Ehrenreich, *The Hearts of Men* (Garden City, N.Y. Anchor, 1983), pp. 42–51.

122. Ads for Playboy products, *Playboy*, September 1962, p. 206; November 1962, pp. 158, 165.

123. "What Sort of Man Reads *Playboy?*" *Playboy*, May 1962, p. 45; "What Sort of Man Reads *Playboy?*" *Playboy*, Oct. 1962, p. 73.

124. D'Emilio and Freedman, *Intimate Matters*, p. 303.

125. Judith Newman, "Men Will Be Boys," *Adweek*, March 8, 1999, p. S44.

126. Richard Turner with Ted Gideonse, "Finding the Inner Swine," *Newsweek*, Feb. 1, 1999, p. 52.

127. Nancy Miller, "The F*#@ing Holidays," *Maxim*, Dec. 1998, p. 72; "Steal the Girl," *Maxim*, Dec. 1998, p. 50.

128. "The Triumph of Cleavage Culture," *Esquire*, Feb. 1999, cover story; "Because Beauty Has Something to Say," *Esquire*, Nov. 1997, cover story; "Rhymes with Boom-Boom," *GQ*, Jan. 1999, cover story.

CHAPTER 10: WAITING FOR WOOD

1. Michiko Kakutani, "Adolescence Rules!" *New York Times Magazine*, May 11, 1997, p. 22; Steven Stark, "Where the Boys Are," *Atlantic Monthly*, Sept. 1994, p. 18.

2. William L. Hamilton, "The Mainstream Flirts with Pornography Chic," *New York Times*, March 22, 1999, p. B9.

3. Brett Sporich, "Adult Revenues Jumped to $4.2B, Says Publisher, Adult Video News," *Video Business*, Jan. 26, 1998, p. 4; Joel Stein, "Porn Goes Mainstream," *Time*, Sept. 7, 1998, p. 54.

4. Linda Lovelace with Mike McGrady, *Ordeal* (New York: Bell, 1983).

5. Scott St. James, "This Dick for Hire," *Hustler Erotic Video Guide*, April 1995, p. 46.

6. Karen Thomas, "No Blues Over Blue Movies," *USA Today*, Aug. 19, 1991, p. 2D; Bill Zwecker, "Sheen Still Thinks Ex Is Fine," *Chicago Sun-Times*, Jan. 15, 1993, p. 17.

CHAPTER 11: PARTING SHOTS

1. Peter King, "Pick of the Litter," *Sports Illustrated*, April 19, 1999, cover story.

2. Leonard Shapiro, "Browns Racing to Get Ready," *Washington Post*, Oct. 6, 1998, p. E7; Vito Stellino, "Even If It's Not for Real, Bronco-Pack Rings a Bell," *Sun*, Baltimore, August 23, 1998, p. 14E; "Coveting the Browns," *USA Today*, July 28, 1998, p. 9C; "Background Player," *Plain Dealer*, Cleveland, Jan. 7, 1996, p. 1B.

3. Adam Bryant, "The Aerospace Merger: The Deal," *New York Times*, Dec. 16, 1996, p. A1; Elizabeth Douglass and Ralph Vartabedian, "Boeing Plans to Cut Nearly 6,000 Jobs in Southland," *Los Angeles Times*, March 21, 1998, p. A1; Laurence Zuckerman, "Boeing to Cut 8,200 Jobs By Year 2000," *New York Times*, March 21, 1998, p. B1; "A Conversation with Harry Stonecipher: Toward a Shared Vision," McDonnell Douglas Media Center, Oct. 1, 1994; John Mintz, "Celebrating a Turnaround: McDonnell Douglas, Once on the Edge of Bankruptcy, Is Blooming Again

Under New CEO," *Washington Post,* Dec. 18, 1995, p. H1; Stanley Holmes, "Boeing Will Keep 737 Work Here," *Seattle Times,* Dec. 11, 1998, p. A1.

4. "'Cop Land' Press Conference," Miramax publicity tape, March 13, 1996; Jeannie Williams, "Low-Budget Drama Is Sly's Next Move," *USA Today,* March 14, 1996, p. 2D.

5. Thomas R. King, "MCA's Meyer Is Already Thinking Big," *Wall Street Journal,* Aug. 9, 1995, p. B8; Anita M. Busch, "MCA Slips Sly $60 Mil Deal," *Daily Variety,* Aug. 8, 1995, p. 1; Claudia Eller, "New MCA Head Hailed as Nice Guy by Friends, Foes," *Los Angeles Times,* July 11, 1995, p. A1.

6. Robert Marich, "Miramax Thinks 'Rambo' Loaded," *Hollywood Reporter,* May 14, 1997, p. 1.

CHAPTER 12: REBELS IN THE KINGDOM

1. Todd Gitlin, *Sacrifice* (New York: Metropolitan, 1999), pp. 31, 33.

2. Alice S. Rossi, ed., *The Feminist Papers* (New York: Bantam, 1973), p. 29.

3. Betty Friedan, *"It Changed My Life": Writings on the Women's Movement* (Cambridge, Mass.: Harvard University Press, 1998), p. 23.

4. Betty Friedan, *The Feminine Mystique,* p. 208.

5. Carol Hymowitz and Michaele Weissman, *A History of Women in America* (New York: Bantam, 1978), p. 355; Marcia Cohen, *The Sisterhood* (New York: Simon & Schuster, 1988), pp. 189–194, 197–198; Flora Davis, *Moving the Mountain: The Women's Movement in America Since 1960* (New York: Simon & Schuster, 1991), pp. 111–114.

6. Sheila Ballantyne, *Norma Jean the Termite Queen* (Garden City, N.Y.: Doubleday, 1975), p. 75.

7. Alice Embree, "Media Images I: Madison Avenue Brainwashing—the Facts," in *Sisterhood Is Powerful,* Robin Morgan, ed. (New York: Vintage, 1970), pp. 201, 206.

8. Lucy Komisar, "The Image of Woman in Advertising" in *Woman in Sexist Society: Studies in Power and Powerlessness,* Vivian Gornick and Barbara K. Moran, eds. (New York: Basic Books, 1971), p. 207.

9. A Redstocking Sister, "Consumerism and Women," in *Woman in Sexist Society,* p. 484.

10. Letter in Promise Keepers letters collection, Denver, Colo.

11. Mark Senak, *A Fragile Circle* (New York: Alyson, 1998), p. 223.

index

abortion, 229, 230, 258–259, 415, 420
Abraham, Ken, 260
Academy Awards, 421, 445–448
Achilles in Vietnam (Shay), 321
Adams, Buck, 543, 544, 555, 566–568, 570, 574
Adams, Zack, 545, 547–549
adolescents, *see* boys, adolescent; girls, adolescent
Adult Video News Awards, 537, 538, 570–571
advertising, 7, 191–194, 204, 206–207, 220, 478, 517, 524, 528, 601, 602, 605
aerospace industry, 52–53, 56, 61–66, 74–91, 96, 97–101, 105, 183, 237, 238, 262, 263, 320, 432–433, 540, 578–579
African-Americans, 7, 42, 46, 56, 65–73, 93–96, 128, 139, 144–145, 175, 228, 376, 468–500, 596, 600
Afro-American Society, 128
Agnew, Spiro, 300
AIDS, 511–512, 606–607
Albert, Chris, 112, 113, 114, 141
Aldrich, Gary, 430
Aldrin, Buzz, 452–453, 459–468, 479, 483–484
Aldrin, Joan, 460
Aldrin, Lois, 465, 467
Allen, Tim, 466
Alternatives to Violence group, 7–9, 10, 31, 224–227, 237, 240, 244, 262, 282, 283
Ambrose, Stephen E., 225
American Century, 21–23, 24, 32, 33, 35, 37, 157, 188, 331, 332, 384–385, 593, 598
American Civil Liberties Union (ACLU), 120, 436
American Freedom Network, 427–428, 442–443
American Greetings Corporation, 214
American Manhood (Rotundo), 11
Anderson, Neil T., 242–243, 247
Anderson, Sherwood, 85–86
Andreotta, Glenn, 335
Angry White Male, 6–7, 407–408, 409, 416, 420, 445
Another Part of the Fifties (Carter), 23
Anselm of Canterbury, 264
antiwar movement, 295, 296, 298–315, 322, 343, 352–353, 355–356, 362–364, 368
Apollo Dream, The, 464
Apollo 11 mission, 452–453, 459–468, 471, 479
Apollo 13, 480
Apollo space program, 452–453, 457, 459–468
Apple, R. W., Jr., 468
Appy, Christian, 292
Arledge, Roone, 215
Armies of the Night, The (Mailer), 307
Armstrong, Neil, 28, 452–453, 462–463, 467–468
Assassins, 581, 587, 588
Athletes in Action, 233

Atwater, Timothy and Nancy (pseud.), 236–237, 238, 248–249, 268, 276–278, 280, 287
Authority (Sennett), 78–79

"baby boom" generation, 24, 27, 35, 134, 225–226, 232, 266, 300–301
Badger, Holly, 133, 134, 135
Bailey, F. Lee, 347–348
Balarezo, Carlos, 412–413
Ballantyne, Sheila, 601–602
Banks, Carl, 208
Barber, Troy, 231
Barbey, USS, 95
Barker, Frank A., 336
Barnes, John, 463
Barr, Bob, 430, 436
Barron, Mrs. Robert, 346
Barton, Bruce, 77, 264, 265
baseball, 105, 121–123, 133–136, 157, 166, 169, 175, 192, 211, 277
Basic Training of Pavlo Hummel, The (Rabe), 385–386, 389–390, 391
Bass, Dick, 471, 484–485
Battle of the Bulge, 175, 176, 188, 388
Baum, Geraldine, 513
Bayham, Michael, 408
Beavis & Butt-head, 531, 546
Beers, Edwin, 338
Behind the Green Door, 537, 546
Belichick, Bill, 202–204, 208
Bellah, Robert, 268–269
Belman, Dana, 107, 108, 109, 123, 132, 134
Belman, Don, 123
Belman, Dottie, 123
Belman, Kris, 104–107, 110, 111–112, 123, 132
Benson, Owen, 87–88
Ben Tre, destruction of, 29, 412
Beowulf, 126
Berg, Peter, 304
Bernard of Clairvaux, 264
Bernhardt, Arnold, 296–297, 298, 343–344, 351
Bernhardt, Dale, 350
Bernhardt, Michael, 296–298, 315–319, 322–352, 354, 355, 358, 362, 395, 607
Berry, Jean, 82
Bertrelli, Pat, 586
Bettelheim, Bruno, 300
Bible, 229–230, 233, 235, 238, 241, 255–256, 265, 268–270, 272, 273, 280, 559–560
Biddle, Francis, 20
Bilton, Michael, 327, 332–333, 339
Bing, Léon, 478–479, 482
Bishop, Jane, 117
black helicopters, 409, 413, 415, 444

Black Heritage Committee, 95–96
Blackman, Shad, 105–107
Blood Oath (Morrell), 375
Bloods, 479, 494
"blue collar" workers, 51–52, 56, 66, 79–80, 83, 88,
    92, 157, 158, 162, 163, 181–182, 185, 193–194,
    195, 199, 200, 204, 298, 543, 555
Blum, John Morton, 21
Bly, Robert, 228, 300–301
Bobbitt, John Wayne, 538
bodybuilding, 496–498, 583–584
"body counts," 322, 328, 330–332, 334, 337, 359, 376,
    379, 383, 392–393, 476, 494
Bogard, Gary, 512
Bonacci, Michael, 589
Bondage Breaker, The (Anderson), 242–243, 247
Bon Homme Richard, USS, 92, 433
Bonnie and Clyde, 478
Booker, Martin and Judy (pseud.), 237–238, 239, 241,
    242, 248, 249–250, 260, 261, 263, 268, 271, 282–
    283, 284, 286, 287, 579–580
Boone, Daniel, 10–12, 22, 38, 240, 452
Borgliatti, Barbara, 142
Bott, Paul, 65
Bouncer, The, 490–492
Boy, T. T., 549–555, 556
boys, adolescent, 102–152, 468–498
    African-American, 46, 128, 139, 144–145, 468–498
    anger of, 103, 112, 116–121, 123–125
    anonymity needed by, 124–125, 151
    "Bad Bad," 103, 114, 167
    boredom of, 109, 111
    control by, 113
    crime by, 45, 103, 134–135, 167, 470–481
    cultural influences on, 46, 47, 103, 149–151
    dating by, 118, 140–143
    employment of, 112–113, 114, 135, 136–138, 151, 152,
        485–489, 496
    fears of, 126–127, 138, 144, 146
    in gangs, 44–45, 46, 47, 328, 370, 468–498
    "Good Bad," 102–103
    homoeroticism and, 126–132, 145–151
    humiliation of, 125, 128–130, 132, 143–145
    media coverage of, 107–108, 110, 111, 112, 114–115,
        120–121, 123–125, 132–133, 141–143, 151, 468–
        498
    in military academies, 114–121, 122, 123–132, 136–
        140, 143–151, 297, 420, 578
    misogyny of, 107, 116–121, 124, 126–132, 145–146
    in postwar era, 3–5, 26, 102–103, 271, 378, 596–597
    privacy of, 124–132, 144
    rebellion by, 103, 104, 114, 167
    sexual exploits of, 103, 104–114, 116, 118, 121–123,
        132–136, 140–143, 150–152
    violence of, 43–47, 103, 107, 139–140, 143–145, 468–
        498
Brady, Jim, 416
Brady, Sarah, 415, 416
Branch Davidians, 42, 410–448, 578
brand names, 33, 110, 111, 132–133
Brando, Marlon, 103, 551
Brigadier, 119, 121, 124
Bright, Bill, 232, 233, 271, 272
Brinson, Claudia, 124
Brockington, John, 166
Brodie, John, 166
Brokaw, Tom, 35, 36, 225
Brooks, Zel, 245, 248, 249, 286
Brotherhood of the Rose (Morrell), 373
Brothers in Arms (Broyles), 479
"Brother to the Machine" (Matheson), 78, 336
Brown, Jim, 188, 189, 190, 192, 219
Brown, Paul, 158–191, 194, 195

Brown, Ron, 429
Brown, Sam, 306
Broyles, William, Jr., 479–482
Brunz, Wally, 177
Bryant, Richard, 146
Buchanan, Pat, 408–409
Buckley, Christopher, 352–353
Buford, Bill, 412
Bureau of Alcohol, Tobacco and Firearms, U.S.
    (BATF), 409, 411–412, 413, 414, 417–419, 428,
        435, 444
Burr, Ike, 73, 92–94, 99–100, 433, 487, 577
Buscaglia, Leo, 97
Butcher, Robert, 126–127
Bynum, Caroline Walker, 264

Cage, Nicholas, 513
California Organization for Public Safety (COPS),
    425, 428
Calley, William L., Jr., 29, 316, 318, 323–352, 379, 393
Cameo (porn star), 544, 556–557, 573–574
Camilla, Frank (pseud.), 239, 240–241, 287–288
Camp, Walter, 156
Campus Crusade for Christ, 232–233, 271, 272, 275
Cannon, Lou, 360
"captivity narrative," 419–420
Carden, Peter, 203–204
Carl (pseud.), 262
Carolco, 385, 404
Carpenter, Scott, 455
Carter, Paul A., 23
Caruso, Michael, 507–508, 528–529
celebrity, 35, 37, 39, 108, 110–114, 121–124, 132–136,
    141–143, 149–154, 191–192, 204, 209, 275, 301–
    303, 306, 310, 311, 347, 360–362, 432, 448, 451–
    498, 537, 540, 567–568, 580, 598, 607
Century of the Common Man, 21–23, 33, 38, 164
Challenger explosion, 466
Chambers, Marilyn, 546
Chapman, Alvah, Jr., 138
Charles, Ray, 470–471
Chavis, Steve, 234, 235, 236
Choice of Heroes, A (Gerzon), 308
Christian Coalition, 230, 409
Christianity, 241, 256–258, 259, 263–265, 272–273,
    274, 276, 284, 357
Christopher, Gary, 214–215
Churchill Society, 144
cigar clubs, 6, 40, 592
Cisneros, Henry, 94
Citadel Military Academy, 114–121, 122, 123–132, 136–
    140, 143–151, 297, 420, 578
Citizen Soldiers (Ambrose), 225
Civilian Conservation Corps (CCC), 20, 309, 606
civil-rights movement, 295, 309, 604, 605
Clancy, T. J., 131
Clary, Jack, 182
Clayton, Nelson, 413
Cleveland Browns, 155–156, 158, 164–223, 578
Cleveland *Plain Dealer*, 45, 196, 206, 209, 222
Clinton, Bill, 6, 39, 45, 298, 363, 408, 411, 415, 428–
    430, 447
Clinton, Hillary Rodham, 415, 416, 428, 429–430
"Clothes Make the Man" (Matheson), 86
coaches, 122–123, 161, 163, 171–173, 178–191, 194, 202–
    204, 209, 231–232, 234–235, 273, 285, 386, 387
Cobb, Lee J., 550–551
Colburn, Lawrence, 335
cold war, 19, 25–30, 36, 52, 79, 85, 184, 188, 279, 292,
    295, 452
Coleman, Larry, 231
Collier, Blanton, 190–191
Collins, Michael, 452–453

Columbia University, 302, 312
Communism, 4, 19, 22–23, 25–30, 32, 103, 188, 298, 331, 361, 388
computers, 102, 195, 214–215, 295, 320, 409, 415, 589
Condé Nast, 507, 508, 512, 514, 517, 523–524, 525, 528, 529
Conrad, Charles "Pete," 84
Conroy, Pat, 139
Conspiracy Theory, 587–588
consumer culture, 34–40, 85, 140, 217, 228, 229, 240, 258–262, 267, 275, 285–286, 304, 391, 451, 489, 504, 505, 511, 516, 526–527, 532, 565, 578–579, 599–602, 603, 604
Consumer Electronics Show, 537–538, 562, 563, 565
"Consumerism and Women" (Willis), 603
Cooper, Arthur, 512
Cop Land, 582, 585, 586–591, 592, 593
corporations, 26–33, 43, 52, 66, 73, 75–87, 153–154, 162, 179, 180–185, 225, 275, 292, 306, 319–322, 331, 354, 424, 541–542, 595
    as "families," 75–76, 81–82, 83, 96
Coxey, Jacob, 161
Crenna, Richard, 402
Crips, 472, 479, 486, 494
Crisis in Command (Gabriel and Savage), 319–320, 322, 327
Crockett, Davy, 11, 12, 22, 37
Crockett, Elizabeth, 96
Cronkite, Walter, 380
Crossan, John Dominic, 270
Cruise, Tom, 520
Culture of Bruising, The (Early), 405
Currence, Mike, 163
Currey, Cecil B., 320
Cyberella, 545, 546–549, 550
Cycle of Outrage, The (Gilbert), 103

Dalbey, Gordon, 250, 256, 266, 267–268, 281, 287, 293–296, 298, 301, 302–304, 305, 313–315, 352, 356–358, 378, 530, 605
Daniel (pseud.), 282
Daniell, Jim, 181
David R. Ray, USS, 92, 93
Davidson, Sara, 307
Davis, Ernie, 190
Dawg Pounders, 155–156, 169–170, 171, 196–223
Day of the Locust, The (West), 203
D-Day, 224, 296, 316, 332, 408
Death of a Salesman (Miller), 86, 363–364, 395
"Death of Captain Waskow, The" (Pyle), 18
Deep Throat, 537, 541
defense contracts, 52, 58–59, 60, 63, 69–70, 75–76, 79, 84–85, 87, 91, 319–320
DeLillo, Don, 188
D'Emilio, John, 504
Deming, W. Edwards, 80
DeMornay, Rebecca, 520, 521
Denver Broncos, 200–201, 205–206
Depeche Mode, 513–514
Depression, Great, 19, 20, 36, 85, 160, 161–162, 165, 195, 375, 389, 597
Details, 449, 506–529
DeVault, Jack, 410
DiCarlo, Rocky, 203
Dick, Harvey, 131, 138
Dirty Harry, 377–378
divorce, 86–91, 169, 239–240, 241, 357, 375, 428, 474, 559, 579–580
Dixon, Hanford, 196, 198
"Dr. You," 208–209
Dogma of Christ, The (Fromm), 270–271
Doines, Rennard, 324

Dolce, Joe, 507, 523, 524, 525, 529
Dole, Bob, 39, 364, 408
Do or Die (Bing), 478–479, 482
Doucet, Norman, 117, 128–129, 149
Douglas, Donald, 81
Douglas, James, 81
Douglas, Kirk, 399, 402, 585
Douglas Aircraft, 74–75, 77
Downing, Diane, 218
downsizing, 52, 60–66, 79–87, 153–154, 159, 216, 424, 562, 579, 595
Doyle, Clive, 419, 445
draft, military, 291–293, 313, 352–353, 356, 503
drag queens, 147–151, 500–505, 509–510, 513, 516, 518, 523
Drake, Steve, 536
Dreiser, Theodore, 77
Duberman, Martin, 502
Duchovny, David, 525
Duncan, Don, 384

Early, Gerald, 405–406
East, Nick, 540, 558–560
Eastwood, Clint, 284, 375, 392, 393, 447, 542
Ebert, Roger, 447
Echo satellite, 3–5, 25, 30, 34
education, 195, 322, 486, 534, 596
Edwards, Eric, 536, 540, 551
effeminacy, 126, 130, 132
Eight-Tray Gangster: The Making of a Crip, 476, 481, 490
Eight-Tray Gangsters, 472–485, 490
Eisenhower, Dwight D., 17, 39, 74–75, 456
Ekirch, Arthur, Jr., 20
Elium, Don and Jeanne, 46
Elliott, Dennie and Mary, 239, 261, 263, 597
Encounter with Tiber (Aldrin and Barnes), 463
End of Victory, The (Engelhardt), 306
End Zone (DeLillo), 188
Engel, Arthur, 59, 67
Engelhardt, Tom, 306
Enloe, Jesse, 410–411
Entertainment Tonight, 206, 400, 483
Entrekin, Morgan, 482–483
Equal Pay Act (1965), 262
Erikson, Erik, 125
Erwin, Vince "D. Dawg," 198–200, 204, 206, 207, 208, 219–220
Esquire, 353, 481, 512, 525–528, 529
evangelism, Christian, 272–273, 274, 276, 284, 357
Evans, Sara, 311–312
Evans, Tony, 229–230
Executive Blues (Meyer), 80, 81
Exley, Frederick, 205
Eyester, Ron, 131

Fairfax, Barbara, 137
Fallows, James, 353
Falwell, Jerry, 510, 541
fame, *see* celebrity
families:
    "corporate," 75–76, 81–82, 83, 96
    layoffs and, 63–65, 86–90
    men as heads of, 41, 227–232, 235, 239–251, 255, 259–265, 268–280, 285, 424, 444, 468, 495–496, 556–559, 564–566, 579–580, 597
    surrogate, 126–132
    values of, 10
    see also parents
fans, sports, 155–156, 158, 159–223, 468, 578, 596
Fan's Notes, A (Exley), 205
Fans' Rights Bill, 215–216

Faris, Joseph, 589
Farrakhan, Louis, 228, 606
fashions, men's, 507, 511, 512–518, 525
Father Knows Best, 24, 225, 557
fathers:
  abusive, 273–283, 382, 553–554
  authoritarian, 266–283, 375–376, 386–389
  betrayal by, 3–5, 26, 102–103, 271, 285–286, 294,
    301–306, 378, 382–385, 395–396, 595–598, 603
  biblical model for, 255–256, 265, 268–270, 272
  competitiveness of, 389, 396–400, 403, 405–406,
    516
  daughters and, 271
  ideal of, 171–172, 189, 301–303, 402–404, 405
  knowledge imparted by, 105, 123, 382, 385, 484–
    489, 530, 596
  son's relationship with, 3–5, 24–25, 27, 34–47, 105,
    123, 163, 168–172, 205, 221, 266–283, 356–358,
    366–369, 374–375, 382–385, 386, 391–396, 402–
    404, 515–516, 530–531, 595–598
  step-, 282, 370–371
  surrogate, 18–19, 35, 71–74, 81, 160, 179, 186–188,
    189, 196, 212, 275, 324–328, 337, 370, 371–373,
    399, 485–489, 495, 585
  "vanishing," 375–376, 407, 484–485, 596–598
  as war veterans, 5, 19, 22–24, 25, 35–36, 291, 299,
    303, 354–355, 366
Faulkner, Ed and Sandy, 119, 128
Faulkner, Shannon, 114–121, 122, 123–132, 136–140,
  144, 147, 149, 150–151
Federal Bureau of Investigation (FBI), 45, 411, 412,
  418, 426–427, 433, 436, 440, 441, 445
feminine mystique, 13, 40, 41, 583–584, 600–601
Feminine Mystique, The (Friedan), 13, 600–601
femininity, 38, 39, 126, 130, 132, 225, 259, 260, 300–
  301, 306, 451–452, 511, 591, 599, 607
feminism:
  gays and, 509, 522
  masculinity critiqued by, 9–10, 13, 16, 130–131, 228–
    230, 354, 595, 599, 600–608
  opposition to, 9, 13–14, 16, 40–42, 46, 89–90, 114,
    265, 413–420, 522–523
  "second wave" of, 600–601
  women's rights and, 13–14, 40–41, 42, 312–314,
    600
"Feminization of American Religion, The"
  (Welter), 264
Fiedler, Leslie, 102–103, 451–452
Figes, Eva, 13
Fight Like a Man (Dalbey), 250, 256, 266, 267–268,
  281, 287
Filson, John, 10
First Blood (film), 364, 367–368, 381, 385–386, 391–395
First Blood (Morrell), 367–368, 370, 371, 380–385, 386,
  389
First National Bank of Ohio, 206–207
Fiss, Galen, 175
Flanders, Annie, 509, 510, 511, 512
Flavin, Jennifer, 586
Florio, Steven, 529
Flory, Mike, 408–409
Flowers, Gennifer, 430
"flyboys," 16–17, 33, 39, 191, 362, 454
Fonda, Jane, 413
football, 105, 123, 155–223, 228, 261, 273, 294, 331,
  468, 596
Foote, Jeremy and Glenda (pseud.), 238–239, 248,
  249, 260–261, 281, 283, 286–287, 288
Ford, John, 179
Foreman, George, 592
Forrestal, USS, 433–434
Forstron, Jeremy, 124
Fort Lauderdale Sun-Sentinel, 44–45

Foster, Richard, 79
Foster, Vince, 429–430
Four Hours in My Lai (Bilton and Sim), 327, 332–333,
  339
"fourth-class system," 127–131, 136, 138, 139–140
Fox, Mitchell, 510
Francisco, Ben, 60
Frankenstein (Shelley), 395, 401
Franklin, H. Bruce, 365–366
Franklin, J. Ross, 345–346
Franklin D. Roosevelt, USS, 53–54
Freedman, Estelle, 504
Friedan, Betty, 13, 600–601
From Ashes to Glory (McCartney), 235
Fromm, Erich, 270–271

Gabriel, Richard A., 319–320, 322, 327
Galbraith, John Kenneth, 39–40
Gallagher, Hugh, 173, 174
gambling, 107, 134–135
gangs, 44–45, 46, 47, 328, 370, 468–498
Garland, Judy, 501
Garvey, Vaughn, 71–72
Gastineau, Mark, 201
Gay Metropolis, The (Kaiser), 502
Gay Pride Day (1973), 503–504
gays, 42, 147–151, 163, 229, 265, 498, 500–505, 507,
  508, 509–512, 513, 516, 517, 518, 522, 523–524,
  525, 604, 606–607
Gazecki, William, 425–426, 439–440, 446, 447
gender roles, 9, 39, 86–90, 149–151, 451, 500–505,
  516–518, 558
"gender wars," 115, 145–146, 594–595, 603–604
Gerder, Coolidge, 415, 416
Gersel, Bill, 88
Gerzon, Mark, 308
Ghan, Sally, 63
"ghetto stars," 472, 477–485
GI Bill of Rights, 23–24, 30, 75, 309
Gibson, James William, 321
Gibson, Mel, 375, 588
Gibson, William, 337
Gifford, Amy Sommer, 435, 436, 437, 438, 439, 440,
  441, 442, 445–448
Gifford, Dan, 425, 432, 434–442, 445–448
Gifford, Frank, 205
Gilbert, James, 103
Gilligan, James, 143–144
Gilmore, David D., 14–15, 38
Gipp, George, 157–158, 171–172
girls, adolescent:
  humiliation of, 118, 119–120
  in military academies, 114–121, 122, 123–132, 136–
    140, 144, 147, 149, 150–151
  power of, 106–107, 151, 152
  in sports, 122–123
GIs, 5, 16–24, 25, 29, 30, 32, 33, 35–36, 38, 39, 75, 157,
  172–179, 180, 183, 185, 306, 309, 595
Gitlin, Todd, 308–309, 311, 313, 597–598
Glenn, John, 26, 295, 454, 455, 456, 457, 461–462,
  592, 598
Glick, Phil, 159–160, 163, 164
God, 230, 234, 236, 242, 245, 250, 251, 254–255, 261,
  268, 270–273, 276, 280–281, 288, 356, 357, 378,
  432, 595
Godwin, William, 395
Goldberg, Herb, 14
Goldman, Stuart, 490–492
Golin, Mark, 527, 529
Good Morning America, 206, 215
Good War, The (Terkel), 23
Gore, Al, 430
Gore, Martin, 513

Gospel According to Jesus, The (Mitchell), 269
GQ, 512, 528
Grabinski, Ray, 58, 59
Grable, Betty, 459
Grace, Bob, 217
Graham, Billy, 271, 272
Graham, Otto, 175, 183, 184, 186
"Grand Coolie Dam, The" (Piercy), 310–311
Grange, Red, 219
Granger, David, 527–528
Gray, J. Glenn, 480
Great Depression, 19, 20, 36, 85, 160, 161–162, 165, 195, 375, 389, 597
Greatest Generation, The (Brokaw), 35, 36, 225
Great Lakes Naval Training Center, 174–175
Green, December, 117–118
Green, Ernie, 175
Green Berets, 25, 297, 363
Greenhaw, Wayne, 347
Gries, Robert, Jr., 170–171, 212
Griffith, Douglas, 79–80, 81
Grissom, Gus, 455
Groza, Lou "The Toe," 175, 185
Guadalcanal Diary, 18
guns, 414, 416, 421–423, 425, 427, 435, 439, 441–442, 444–445, 473–475, 499–500
Guttman, Dick, 465

Haber, Al, 310
Hackworth, David H., 320–321
Haines, William, 410, 412, 414, 416
Hall, Charles, 324–325
Hall, Donald, 169
Hamilton, Sara-Jane, 564
Hampshire, Russ, 542
Hanks, Tom, 480
Harasyn, Dan, 204
Harlem Renaissance (Huggins), 498–499
Harris, Daniel, 505
Harris, David, 305
Harry, Debbie, 523
Hartley, Nina, 541, 546, 555–556, 569
Hastings, Craig (pseud.), 280, 284, 287, 288, 595
Hatfield, Mark, 346
Hayden, Casey, 312
Hayden, Tom, 301
Hayes, Harold, 525–526
Hazards of Being Male, The (Goldberg), 14
hazing, 127–131, 136, 138, 139–140, 144–147, 148
Healy, Mark, 520–521
Hearts and Minds, 331
Heath, Chris, 522
Heaven and Earth, 388
Hefner, Hugh, 526, 604
Hemingway, Ernest, 373
Henderson, George, 606
Henderson, Oran K., 336, 339
Hercules Unchained, 583
"Herman the German" crane, 54, 55
Hernandez, Marty, 57, 58, 59
heroes, 374, 383, 432, 475, 484, 495, 500
Hersh, Seymour, 324, 332, 345
Hershey, Lewis B., 291–292
Hickok, Wild Bill, 11, 452
Hidden Keys to a Loving, Lasting Marriage (Smalley), 254
hierarchies, 66–67, 81–82, 91–92, 127–131, 136, 270, 388
Himes, Chester, 54–55
Hispanic-Americans, 56, 66, 67, 71, 72–73, 96, 487
Hitler, Adolf, 22, 185
Holley, Nathan, 69–70
Hollings, Ernest "Fritz," 138

Hollister, Bart (pseud.), 239, 241, 287
Hollywood, 17, 18–19, 32–33, 39, 296, 297, 308, 332, 359–406, 435–442, 542, 553, 577, 580–593, 605
Holy Land (Waldie), 104
Homans, John, 522
Hood, Robert, 84
Hornet, USS, 452, 453
Horsley, Richard, 269, 270
Horton, Scott, 411, 416, 420
Howard, Jeff, 108–109, 133, 135
Howard, Kevin, 108, 141
Howser, Huell, 55
Hubbell, Webster, 429
Huggins, Nathan, 498–499
Hughes, Howard, 54
Huh, Susan, 65
Human Rights Watch International Film Festival, 436
Hurlyburly (Rabe), 386

I Am Legend (Matheson), 77
If He Hollers Let Him Go (Himes), 54–55
immigrants, 65–66
Incredible Shrinking Man, The, 30–32, 78, 311, 497
Independence Day, 463–464
individualism, 38–39, 120–121, 123, 124, 187
Industrial Revolution, 137–138
In Love and War (Stockdale and Stockdale), 139
institutions, 29–30, 43, 78, 200, 284, 605
insurance industry, 424–425, 431–432, 444
Internet, 214–215, 412–413, 436
In the New World (Wright), 292
intimacy, 127, 131–132, 283–288
Intimate Matters (D'Emilio and Freedman), 504
Iron John (Bly), 228, 300–301

Jailhouse Cock, 563
James, Jesse, 11
James, Tommy, 163, 180, 186
Jammer, Cal, 537, 539, 540, 544–545, 555, 556–558, 559, 560, 562–574
Jane Whitney Show, The, 108, 123, 141, 142, 143
Jenny Jones Show, The, 108, 114, 141
Jeremy, Ron, 545, 546, 547, 548, 549, 562, 571
"Jersey" (drag queen), 500
Jesus as Mother (Bynum), 264
Jesus Christ, 77, 227, 233, 236, 239, 240, 242, 243, 255–256, 257, 264–265, 267–273, 274, 276, 280–281, 288, 358
Job, book of, 229–230, 280
Johansson, Mike, 569
Johnson, Don, 465, 466–467
Johnson, Larry, 91
Johnson, Lyndon B., 28
John Wayne's America (Willis), 36
Jones, Tony, 222
Jones, William E., 163
journalism, 468, 529
Joy of Sports, The (Novak), 193–194
Judd, Shirley, 63, 88–89, 97

Kadish, Mark, 348
Kahn, Ellis, 138
Kaiser, Charles, 502
Kakutani, Michiko, 531–532
Kassar, Mario, 385
Keeps, David, 515, 516
Kelly, Jill, 544, 555, 559, 563–570, 571, 574
Keniston, Kenneth, 302
Kennedy, John F., 24, 25–26, 39, 157, 164, 301, 302–303, 304, 322, 331, 355–356, 432, 506
Kerry, John, 355
Kersands, Billy, 498

Kiedis, Anthony, 518–520, 523
Kilmer, Frank, 36
Kimmel, Michael, 11
King, Kevin, 588
King, Mary, 312
King, Rodney, 480
Kingsley, Pat, 529
King's Row, 361
Kinkaid, USS, 57–60, 73
Klass, Philip, 373, 374
Klein, Calvin, 504, 506, 517, 523, 584
Kleinberg, Seymour, 505
Klum, Heidi, 528
Knapp, Katina, 556, 557
Knute Rockne—All American, 157–158, 171–172
Komisar, Lucy, 602
Kono, Morrie, 184
Koppel, Ted, 481, 494
Koresh, David, 411, 417–418, 426, 438
Korn, Lee, 437
Kosar, Bernie, 195–196, 203, 214
Koster, Samuel W., 336, 337
Kotcheff, Ted, 401
Kozoll, Michael, 394–395
Kroft, Steve, 483–484
Kubrick, Stanley, 455
Kuderna, Ed, 169, 197–198, 203, 207–208

Lake, Michael, 117, 144, 145–146
La Motta, Jake, 405–406
Landry, Tom, 179
LaPierre, Wayne, 414
Larkins, J. B., 94
La Salle Military Academy, 297, 345
Latimer, George W., 326
Laurie, Greg, 230
Lavelli, Dante, 173–179, 188, 193
LaViolette, Alyce, 227
Lawrence, James, 76, 83, 89–90
layoffs, 52, 55–101, 104, 137, 153–154, 159, 163, 216, 239, 243, 285–286, 424, 468, 562, 579, 591, 595
leadership, 318–319, 321–322, 324–325, 327–328, 333, 336–338
  see also heroes; marriage, spiritual leadership in
Lembcke, Jerry, 299
Leno, Jay, 111, 113
Leonard, Kurt, 59–60, 74, 91, 92
Lerner, Alfred, 210, 578
Leslie, John, 536, 544
Lethal Weapon, 375, 587
Levine, Ira, 543
Levine, Les, 202–203
Lewis, Jerry, 201
Lewis, Jerry Lee, 103
Liberty ships, 53
Life, 3, 19, 22, 24, 28, 185, 346, 376, 452, 454, 455, 456–457, 461–462, 463
Limbaugh, Rush, 363
Lime, Harold, 541
Lindbergh, Charles, 454
Lipset, Seymour Martin, 302
Lipsyte, Robert, 192
"Living in Moral Pain" (Marin), 379–380
Livingston, Bill, 196, 212
Lloyd, Murphy, 384
Lohn, Jule, 346
Lombardi, Vince, 179, 187
Lonely Crowd, The (Riesman), 76
Long Beach City College, 121–122, 133
Long Beach Naval Shipyard, 49, 51–61, 66–74, 75, 81, 86, 91–97, 99–100, 433, 471, 485, 577, 602, 607

"long-range reconnaissance patrol" soldiers (LRRPS), 323, 324, 332
Loose Change (Davidson), 307
Lopez, Chris, 231
Lords of Discipline, The (Conroy), 139
Los Angeles Police Department (LAPD), 425, 480
Los Angeles riots (1965), 380, 485
Los Angeles riots (1992), 68, 472, 480–481, 494, 495
Los Angeles Times, 58–59, 482, 491, 573
"Lost Boy" (pseud.), 108–111
Love, Kimber (drag queen), 148, 150
Lovelace, Linda, 541
Lownie (drag queen), 148–149
loyalty:
  company, 43, 63, 80, 154, 163, 200, 201, 219–220, 228, 273, 285–286, 595–596
  to parents, 269, 280, 285–286, 387
  to system, 225–226, 228, 387, 595
  team, 158, 163, 170, 175–176, 178–179, 180, 186–188, 191, 192, 199, 200, 201–202, 216, 219–220, 595
Lucas, Tom, 119
Luce, Henry, 21–22, 32, 346, 454
Luke, Steve, 160
Lychner, Joe, 465, 467
Lychner, Shannon, 465
Lynn, Amber, 566
Lynn, Ginger, 553

McBride, Ernie, Jr., 57, 58, 59, 67–68, 70–71, 596
McBride, Ernie, Sr., 67–71, 596
McCain, John, 433
McCartney, Bill, 227, 229, 231–236, 256–257, 275, 285–286, 606
McCartney, Lyndi, 235–236
McCloud, Austin, 560–563
McCloud, Dallas, 560–563
McDonald, Juanita, 489
Macdonald, Ross, 375
McDonnell, John, 80–81, 83
McDonnell Aircraft Company, 75
McDonnell Douglas, 30, 34, 43, 47, 52–53, 56, 61–66, 74–91, 96, 97–101, 104, 133, 154, 155, 183, 190, 225, 285, 320, 321, 578–579
McDonnell Douglas Outplacement Center, 43, 61–66, 82, 87–91, 97–99, 101, 154, 578
McElwain, Bud "Junkyard Dawg," 169, 197, 198, 202, 208, 218–219
McElwain, Celeste, 218–219
McElwain, Joe "Bubba," 169, 197, 198, 202, 208, 218–219, 220
McEnroe, John, 192
McGuyre, Starley "Mad Mac," 412
McMahon, Tom, 196–197, 208–209
MacMurray, Fred, 26
McNamara, Robert S., 320, 369
McNulty, Julie, 424, 427–428, 430–432, 443–444, 447, 448
McNulty, Mike, 413–414, 420–448
McTeague (Norris), 12
McVeigh, Timothy, 427
magazines, men's, 506–529
Mailer, Norman, 25–26, 37, 307, 456, 525, 527
Making of Masculinities, The (Pleck), 375–376
Malcolm X, 499
"male gaze," 204, 525, 527–528, 531, 540
Males, Mike, 45
management, middle, 29–30, 66, 73, 78–87, 92, 95, 156, 181–182, 190, 191, 193–194, 225, 252, 319–322, 325, 337, 360
Mangold, James, 582, 587
manhood:
  father-son relationships and, 3–5, 24–25, 27, 34–

47, 105, 123, 163, 168–172, 205, 221, 266–283, 356–358, 366–369, 374–375, 382–385, 386, 391–396, 402–404, 454, 515–516, 530–531, 595–598

military experience and, 5, 19, 22–24, 25, 35–36, 291, 298, 299, 303, 304–305, 307–308, 314, 315, 322–323, 352–356, 366

motherhood vs., 38, 96–97, 126–127

mother-son relationships and, 129–130, 131, 145, 169, 300–301

postwar, 3–47, 102–103, 271, 378, 596–597

promise of, 3–5, 169–170, 285–286, 348–350, 413, 594–600

rites of passage of, 5, 25, 39, 76, 129–131, 151, 187, 267, 298, 305, 313, 330, 349–350, 472, 476, 489

traditions of, 115, 116, 118–119, 127–131, 136, 140, 144, 156

see also masculinity

Manhood in America (Kimmel), 11

Manhood in the Making (Gilmore), 14–15

Man Nobody Knows, The (Barton), 77, 264, 265

Mansfield, Jayne, 584

Margold, Bill, 537, 538–539, 542, 543, 549–550

Marin, Peter, 304, 379–380

Marissa (drag queen), 148, 149, 150

marriage, 64–65, 81–82, 84–88, 90, 129, 131, 168–169, 225, 278, 282, 303–304, 416, 565–566

spiritual leadership in, 239–247, 249, 250, 251, 255, 261, 263, 264–265, 270, 271, 280, 579–580

Martin, Daniel, 419

Martin, Sheila, 418–419

Martin, Wayne, 418

Martino, Chuck, 570

Martinson, Chris, 231

masculinity:

alternative vision of, 41–42, 594–608

community and, 11–12, 17–23, 34–38, 74, 159–171, 173, 179, 258, 296–297, 308–314, 322–323, 351–352, 358, 480, 487–488, 584–587, 602–603, 606–607

crisis of, 6–16, 40–42, 47, 114, 407–408, 409, 416, 420, 445, 530–532, 594–608

cultural influences on, 14–16, 24–25, 34–40, 41, 46, 47, 103, 149–151, 226, 354–355, 420

femininity vs., 38, 39, 126, 130, 132, 225, 259, 260, 300–301, 306, 451–452, 511, 591, 599, 607

feminist critique of, 9–10, 13, 16, 130–131, 228–230, 354, 595, 599, 600–608

ideal of, 10–12, 16, 19, 20–23, 25–26, 37, 43, 44, 299, 304–305, 313–314, 342, 352–356, 359–362, 364, 366, 368, 412, 587

loner image of, 10–12, 20–21, 37, 44, 313–314, 364, 587

media coverage of, 6, 13, 41, 44–45, 46, 451–529

mystique of, 40

nurturance of, 38, 96–97, 126–132, 149–151, 160, 179, 296–297, 351–352

ornamental, 34–40, 83–86, 151, 262, 442, 448, 463, 470, 476–477, 502–529, 540, 577–578, 580–584, 591, 598, 599–600, 602

stereotypes of, 9, 12, 130, 603, 607

style and, 512–518

team notion of, 387, 391

"toxic," 42–47

usefulness and, 43, 55, 67, 80–86, 91–95, 101, 175, 182, 183, 261–262, 328, 407, 432, 448, 451, 457, 463, 468, 477, 488–489, 498, 518, 523

work ethic and, 52, 53, 55, 60, 64–74, 79–87, 94–95, 240, 276, 470, 477, 546, 569, 584, 593

see also manhood

Massillon Tigers, 158–164, 170, 172, 179–180, 182, 184, 194, 221

Mate, Ken, 308

Matheson, Richard, 77–78, 80, 86, 336, 459–460

Mauldin, Bill, 16

Maury Povich, 108, 112, 141–143, 281, 437

Maxim, 527, 529

May, Derrick, 94

Meadlo, Paul, 318

media, mass, 451–529

on adolescents, 107–108, 110, 111, 112, 114–115, 120–121, 123–125, 132–133, 141–143, 151, 468–498

football and, 155, 158, 164, 179, 189, 191–194, 204–209, 215, 217, 218, 222

on gangs, 468–498

on masculinity, 6, 13, 41, 44–45, 46, 451–529

space program and, 34, 452–468, 476–477, 479, 480, 483–484, 598

Vietnam War and, 344, 346, 352–353, 359

Waco siege and, 410, 411, 420, 426

women and, 601, 602, 605

see also television

Medina, Ernest, 317, 325–328, 332, 336, 339, 340, 347–348

Meggyesy, Dave, 187, 188

men:

aggressiveness of, 7–9, 10, 12, 31, 37, 43–47, 64–65, 88, 143–144, 224–227, 243–244, 250–251, 399–400

anger of, 6–7, 37, 60–61, 65–66, 89, 226–227, 243–244, 407–408, 409, 416, 420, 445

authority of, 16, 29, 36, 81–94, 158, 168, 179–186, 189–190, 225, 228–230, 243, 266–283, 310, 335–337, 343–344, 375–376, 386–389, 525

"bad" vs. "good," 417–418

bonding of, 126–132, 283–288, 322, 480, 535

as breadwinners, 13, 19, 23–24, 29–30, 42–43, 51–52, 82–91, 144, 153–154, 231–232, 238–247, 252, 262–263, 431–432, 470, 515–516, 595, 602

brotherhood of, 26, 131, 180, 258, 270, 283–288, 306–307, 313, 319, 321–322, 329, 595, 607–608

competitiveness of, 23, 183–184, 188, 211, 309, 330–332, 389, 396–400, 403, 405–406, 516, 593, 598

control by, 8–13, 15, 22, 37–38, 92, 156–157, 179–186, 189–190, 226, 239, 245, 309, 311, 455–458, 525

cooperation among, 17–19, 23, 26, 55, 73–74, 96–97, 131, 175, 183, 185

dependency and, 84–87, 96, 128, 131–132, 144

domination by, 9, 13, 16, 31, 37–38, 55, 56, 66, 92, 156, 180, 183–184, 185, 188, 190, 228–230, 270, 310–311, 423, 527, 598, 602, 603–604

emasculation of, 65, 68, 90, 144, 186–188, 257, 275, 342, 382, 507, 524, 529, 532

emotional expression by, 92, 232, 252, 286, 303–304, 403

"enemies" of, 32, 34, 38, 40–41, 46, 65–66, 118, 330–331, 358, 382, 409–410, 413–420, 442, 599, 604–605, 608

families headed by, 41, 227–232, 235, 239–251, 255, 259–265, 268–280, 285, 424, 444, 468, 495–496, 556–559, 564–566, 579–580, 597

fashions for, 507, 511, 512–518, 525

fears of, 78, 88–89, 240, 282–283, 373–374, 413, 557–558, 571

immature, 170, 171, 186–188, 300–301, 531–532

"invisible," 30–32, 78, 86, 311, 336, 337, 338, 459–460, 497, 580

loyalty of, *see* loyalty

macho image of, 17, 64–65, 158, 229, 310–314, 505, 525–526

movement for, 14, 15, 40–42, 228, 300–301, 603–608

"new," 451–452

men (continued)
  organization, 26–27, 29–32, 33, 43, 75–87, 153–154, 181–182, 331, 354
  responsibilities of, 19, 35, 38, 43, 55, 201–202, 226, 309, 322–323, 324, 343–344, 414, 444
  self-identity of, 43, 55, 59, 83, 154, 247, 254, 268, 412–413, 451, 591
  spiritual guidance for, 226–288
  status lost by, 30–40, 61–66, 78, 86, 87–91, 97–99, 106–107, 151–154, 186–188, 190, 227–232, 238–251, 268–280, 311, 336, 337, 338, 431–432, 459–460, 497, 502–529, 580, 599–600
  unemployed, 43, 61–66, 82, 87–91, 97–99, 101, 154, 578
  virility of, 25–26, 28, 451, 514–515, 546–547, 602
  as voting bloc, 6–7
  see also boys, adolescent; manhood; masculinity
Men and Religion Forward Movement, 257, 258
Mercury space program, 454–458, 461–462, 468
Metro, Alec, 535
Mexican-Americans, 66, 71, 487
Meyer, G. J., 80, 81
Meyer, Ron, 585, 591
Meza, José "Joe," 71, 73
Meza, Rick, 71, 73, 92, 99
M.I.A. or Mythmaking in America (Franklin), 365–366, 401
Michael (pseud.), 224–225
Michaels, Sean, 538
Midler, Bette, 504
militias, 289, 409–421, 424, 434, 436, 439, 442–445
Millen, Miles, 466
Miller, Arthur, 33, 86, 363–364, 395
Miller, James, 301
Miller, L. H., 415–416
Million, Tyffany, 536, 537, 563, 565, 569, 571
Million Man March, 7, 228, 605–606
Mills, C. Wright, 76–77
Miss America pageant (1968), 601
Missouri, USS, 343
Mitchell, Stephen, 269
Modell, Art, 155, 156, 188–194, 196, 198, 203, 209–213, 215, 216–217, 223, 578
Modell, David, 212
Monster: The Autobiography of an L.A. Gang Member (Scott), 472, 477, 481–485, 489, 492
Montana, Tony, 560–561
Moore, Bill, 231
Moore, James, 417
Moore, Jamie, 138
Moreell, Ben, 54
Moreell dry dock, 53, 54, 57, 58
Morgan, Jonathan, 545–546, 547
Mormons, 424, 441, 444, 446
Morrell, David, 367–368, 380–385, 386, 389, 404–405, 530
Morrell, Donna, 369
Morrell, George, 370, 371, 374, 376
Morrell, Matthew, 369
Morris, Felicia, 477, 492–493
Morrison, Cid, 552, 556, 558
Moss, Tim, 515–516
Mother Camp (Newton), 500
motherhood, 38, 96–97, 126–127
mothers:
  single, 263
  son's relationship with, 129–130, 131, 145, 169, 300–301
Motley, Marion, 175
Motta, Don, 63–65, 91, 97–98, 100–101, 190
Motta, Gayle, 64–65, 91, 98, 101
Ms., 601
"Mud Nest, The," 372

Mulk, Mike, 87
Mullen, Bill, 514, 519
Mumford, Lewis, 162–163
Murphy, Alan, 124
Murphy, Audie, 16–17, 371, 376–379, 381, 394, 395
Murrow, Edward R., 21–22
Myers, Gary, 155
My Lai massacre, 29, 315–319, 322–352, 393, 412, 413, 434, 447

Nader, Ralph, 217
Napoleon I, Emperor of France, 321
National Aeronautics and Space Agency (NASA), 26, 34, 79, 186, 453–463
National Association for the Advancement of Colored People (NAACP), 67, 144–145, 499
National Football League (NFL), 158, 183–184, 191, 196, 202, 211, 213–219, 578, 596
National Organization for Women (NOW), 120
National Promotions, 112–113
National Rifle Association (NRA), 414, 425
Nation of Islam, 7, 42, 228, 606
Nationwide Insurance, 424–425
Navigators, 271, 276
Navy, U.S., 53–55, 167–168
Nazis, 22, 25, 32, 300, 348, 360, 414
Negroes with Guns (Williams), 499
Nelson, Blake, 518, 522–523
Nelson, Shawn, 31
New Deal, 20, 79, 309
New Frontier, 25, 37, 331, 355
Newhouse, S. I., Jr., 512–513, 517
New Industrial State, The (Galbraith), 39–40
New Left, 301, 306–314
New Man, 230, 259, 260
Newman, Robert, 528
"New Mutants, The" (Fiedler), 451–452
Newsweek, 6, 44, 46, 108, 153, 462
New Testament, 269–270, 273
Newton, Esther, 500
Newton, Huey, 499
New York Jets, 191, 201
New York Times, 44, 46, 108, 117, 120, 215, 235, 405, 461, 483, 532
New York Times Magazine, 300, 353, 531
NFL Rocks: Extreme Football, 219
Nichols, Jack, 504–505
Nightline, 481, 493, 494
Ninn, Michael, 570
Nixon, Richard M., 157, 305, 345, 346, 366
Norma Jean the Termite Queen (Ballantyne), 601–602
Norris, Frank, 12
North American Model Boat Association, 468–469
"Notes on 'Camp'" (Sontag), 500
Notrica, Morrie, 485–489, 496
Novak, Michael, 158, 193–194
Novak, Tammy (drag queen), 501

obedience, 225, 231, 232, 280, 294, 324, 386–387, 389
O'Brien, Pat, 171
O'Brien, Tim, 356
Of a Fire on the Moon (Mailer), 456
Oglesby, Carl, 301
Old Testament, 229–230, 255
O'Leary, Brian, 459
Olsen, Greg, 326, 330, 339
"Once More to the Lake" (White), 303
On the Waterfront, 550–551
"Open Truth and Fiery Vehemence of Youth, The" (Marin), 304
Operation Giant Step, 453, 460–461, 463
Ordeal (Lovelace), 541

Organization Man, The (Whyte), 76
Oriard, Michael, 156
Oriskany, USS, 434
Ovitz, Michael, 483

Pacino, Al, 385, 393
Paper Lion (Plimpton), 184–185
paranoia, 184–185, 188, 409, 413, 414–416, 421, 428–430, 438, 446–447
parents, 269, 280, 285–286, 387
  see also fathers; mothers
Parker, Fess, 12
Parker, Herbert, 147
Parrett, Chris, 434, 435
Parrington, Vernon Louis, 11
Parrish, Bernie, 184, 186, 187, 188, 189
paternalism, 72, 81–82
Patriarchal Attitudes (Figes), 13
patriarchy, 13, 228–230, 270, 413–420, 444–445, 603–604
patricide, 300, 301, 342
Patton, George, 179
Paul (pseud.), 226
Paul, Saint, 229, 230
Payson, Howard and Libby (pseud.), 241, 250–256, 258, 261, 263, 278
Peace Corps, 295, 301, 302–303, 314
Penn, Arthur, 478
Perfect War, The (Gibson), 321
Perhaps Women (Anderson), 85–86
Personal Politics (Evans), 311–312
Pettigrew, Mike and Margaret (pseud.), 239, 241–247, 258, 261, 263, 278–280
Pfeiffer, John, 100
Phillips, Holly, 275
Phillips, Randy, 275–276
Pickering, John, 73, 99
Pickering, Robert, 128
Piercy, Marge, 310–311
Pitt, Brad, 542
Planet Hollywood, 464–467, 581–582
Playboy, 193, 526, 601
Pleck, Joseph, 375–376
Plimpton, George, 184–185
"Plinker, The" (Morrell), 374
Plum, Milt, 183
Pluto, Terry, 175, 178
politics, 58–59, 73, 95, 257, 258–259, 270, 503, 504, 511–512, 528, 540–541, 606
Pond, Greg, 515, 516
Poole, Roger Clifton, 127–128
pornography, 111, 152, 265, 287, 521, 532, 533–574
Port Huron Statement, 306–307, 309, 314, 343
Potes, Brett, 571
Potes, Jackie, 571, 572
Potes, Randy, *see* Jammer, Cal
Potter, Paul, 310
Povich, Maury, 112, 141, 142, 150, 151
Power and Control Wheel, The, 8, 9
POW-MIAs, 365–366, 368
Pracher, Rick, 482
Preiss, Bob, 440
President Reagan: The Role of a Lifetime (Cannon), 360
Presley, Elvis, 103
Procope, Derick, 507–508
productivity, 43, 55, 80–81, 83, 85–86, 91–95, 175, 182, 183, 261–262, 451, 468
Promise Keepers, 7, 42, 226–288, 293–294, 530, 565, 579–580, 603, 604, 605–606
"protection racket," 413–420, 427, 444–445, 556
Pulp Fiction, 581, 582

Pyle, Ernie, 16–24, 26, 32–33, 39, 75, 130, 157, 164, 175, 180, 362, 607

Quayle, Dan, 95, 363
Quebedeaux, Richard, 272

Rabe, David, 369, 385–393, 395
Radakovich, Anka, 521–522
Rader, Benjamin, 193
Rafkin, Jimmy, 105–107, 110, 136
Raging Bull II (La Motta), 406
Ragman's Son, The (Douglas), 402
Raising a Son (Elium and Elium), 46
Rambo, 229, 323, 364–369, 394–395, 398, 409, 466, 583, 584, 589, 591
Rambo: First Blood Part II (film), 364–365, 366, 367, 368, 394–395, 404–405
Rambo: First Blood Part II (Morrell), 404–405
Rambo III, 366–367, 368
Rambo IV, 369
Randolph, USS, 295
Rat Patrol, 478
Rauschenbusch, Walter, 257–258
Rawles, James Wesley, 434
Ray, Aldo, 78
Ray Briem, 467–468
Reagan, Ronald, 39, 63, 83, 157–158, 171–172, 195, 232, 359–362, 368, 394, 405, 407–408, 416, 429
Reagan's America (Wills), 362
Redford, Robert, 436
Red Shoe Diaries, 536
Reduction in Force (R.I.F.), 63–64
Reese, James, 478
Reeves, Steve, 583
religious right, 229, 230, 265–266
Rembert, James, 125–127, 131, 148
Reno, Janet, 415, 416, 436
Renshaw, Allison, 74
Republican National Convention (1996), 408–409
Republic of Texas, 410
Resister, 428–429
Revco, 216, 220
"Revolution Now" campaign, 232
Rhodes, Dan, 261, 263, 281–282
Ridenhour, Ron, 340–343, 344
Ries, Raul, 273–274, 280
Riesman, David, 76
Rifkin, Arnold, 581, 591
Riggs, E. L. "Al," 178
Right Stuff, The (Wolfe), 459
Ringo, Jim, 188
Rise and Fall of Gay Culture, The (Harris), 505
Risky Business, 520, 521, 522, 523
Rison, Andre, 202
Rite Aid, 216, 220
Rivera, Sylvia (drag queen), 501–504
Robinson, David, 108, 132–133
Robinson, Jackie, 175
Robinson, Jim, 297
Rockne, Billy, 172
Rockne, Jack, 172
Rockne, Knute, 157–158, 171–173, 209
Rocky, 364, 400, 466, 580, 585–586, 589–590
Rocky VI, 405, 592–593
Rodman, Dennis, 192, 532
Rodriguez, Lonnie, 112, 113, 114
Rodriguez, Louis, 58, 95, 96
Rogin, Michael, 361
Rolling Stone, 132, 573
Rollins, Henry, 515
Rollin' Sixties, 472–476

Ron Hunter Show, The, 436–437
Roosevelt, Eleanor, 69
Roosevelt, Franklin D., 20–21, 53–54, 69–70
Roosevelt, Theodore, 53
Rose, Damon, 534–536, 537
Rosenberg, Howard, 479, 482
Rosenthal, Terri, 55, 56
Ross, Linda, 137–138
Ross, Phillipe, 137
Rostow, Walt, 331
Roszak, Theodore, 309
Roth, Mike, 464–465, 466
Roth, Robert, 355–356
Rotundo, E. Anthony, 11
Rourke, Mickey, 111–112, 491
Route 66, 371–373, 374, 530–531
Rowlandson, Mary, 419
Rozelle, Pete, 191
Rudd, Mark, 312

Saban, Stephen, 509–510, 512, 524
Sabol, Bob, 66–67
Sack, John, 328
Sacrifice (Gitlin), 597–598
St. Croix, Steven, 538
St. Jox, Julian, 538
salaries, 66–67, 97, 153, 177, 191, 202, 252, 262–263
Salls, Duane, 213–214, 216, 217
Sand in the Wind (Roth), 355–356
Sands of Iwo Jima, 18–19, 24, 36
Saving Private Ryan, 35, 225–226
Savio, Mario, 237, 304
Savage, Paul L., 319–320, 322, 327
Savannah (porn star), 567, 573, 574
Scapegoat Generation, The (Males) 45
Scarpi, Bebe (drag queen), 503
Schat, Jack, 225, 226–227, 283–284, 596
Schell, Jonathan, 365
Schirra, Wally, 457–458
Schoditsch, John, 213
Schumer, Charles, 436
Schwarzenegger, Arnold, 35, 360, 466
Scoggins, Doyce, 60
Scott, Birdie, 470–471
Scott, Chris, 147, 148
Scott, Ernest, 470–471, 473–474, 475
Scott, Kershaun, 470, 473–477, 479, 480–481, 484,
    490, 493–496, 580
Scott, Kerwin, 468–472, 485–489, 495, 496–498, 505
Scott, Kody, 470, 472–485, 489–493, 494, 495
Scott, Vanessa, 495
"Selling the Moon" (Smith), 461
Senak, Mark, 607
Sennett, Richard, 78–79
service sector, 34, 38, 195, 262, 263, 488–489
Sex, 570–571
"Sex and Caste" (Casey and King), 312
sex objects, 482, 505–506, 514, 518–524, 527–528, 535,
    536, 545–546, 553, 554–555, 560–563, 572, 573,
    574, 602
sexual harassment, 88, 117–118, 125
Shadow of Death, 590–591
Shahid, Sam, 505–506
Shake Down the Thunder (Sperber), 172
Shakur, Sanyika, *see* Scott, Kody
shame, 125, 128–130, 132, 143–145, 312, 340, 352–353
Shamir, Yitzhak, 360
Shantery, Ed, 222
Shantery, Scott, 169, 197–198, 207–208, 222
Shaw, Bud, 217
Shay, Jonathan, 321
Sheehy, Maura, 519, 522
Sheen, Charlie, 553

Shehan, Billy, 47, 108, 110, 111, 112, 113, 114, 121–123,
    132–135, 140–143, 150, 151–152, 580
Shehan, Brian, 133, 134, 135
Shehan, Joyce, 133
Shelley, Mary, 395, 401
Shepard, Alan, 455
shipyards, 49, 51–61, 66–74, 75, 81, 86, 91–97, 99–
    100, 131, 530, 596
Shoemaker, Eugene, 457
Shrinking Man, The (Matheson), 78, 86, 336, 459–
    460
Siegel, Don, 377–378
Silliphant, Stirling, 372–373
Silver, Joel, 587–588, 589
Sim, Kevin, 327, 339
Simpson, O. J., 8, 98, 559, 571
Simpson, Varnado, 318
Sister Carrie (Dreiser), 77
Sixties, The (Gitlin), 308–309
60 Minutes, 430, 483–484
Slany, Kim, 74
slavery, 136, 600
Slayton, Deke, 455, 456–457, 458
Slotkin, Richard, 10
Smaldino, Dolores "Dee," 62
Smalley, Gary, 230, 254
Smith, Michael L., 461
Smith, Ron, 62, 65–66, 75
Social Gospel, 257–258
SoHo Weekly News, 509, 510
Solis, Joe, 72–73
sons:
    father's relationship with, 3–5, 24–25, 27, 34–47,
        105, 123, 163, 168–172, 205, 221, 266–283, 356–
        358, 366–369, 374–375, 382–385, 386, 391–396,
        402–404, 515–516, 530–531, 595–598
    "good," 225, 231, 267–268, 270–271, 275, 291, 294,
        296–299, 315–356, 379, 395–396, 405
    mother's relationship with, 129–130, 131, 145, 169,
        300–301
    "prodigal," 275, 291, 293–296, 298–315, 342, 343,
        352–358, 605
Sons of Liberty, 19
Sons of the Father (Dalbey), 294
Sontag, Susan, 500
South, Jim, 569
South Carolina Unorganized Militia (SCUM), 125
Southern Baptists, 229
Southwest Marine, 58–59, 67
space program, 3–5, 25, 26–28, 33–34, 191, 237, 295,
    331, 399, 452–468, 471, 476–477, 479, 480,
    483–484, 498
Speedie, Mac, 175, 185
Spelvin, Georgina, 546
Sperber, Murray, 171
Spielberg, Steven, 225
Spinelli, Mitch, 536
Spisso, David, 131
Spohn, Charlie, 72–73, 96
Spoiled Sport (Underwood), 204
sports, 47, 105, 121–123, 133–136, 144–145, 155–223,
    227, 228, 230–235, 261, 273, 277, 285, 294, 331,
    386, 387, 508, 532, 540
sports fans, 155–156, 158, 159–223, 468, 578, 596
Sports Illustrated, 144, 178, 183, 196, 210, 234, 578
Sprung, Emmett E., 2
Spur Posse, 44, 47, 104–114, 116, 118, 121–123, 124,
    132–136, 140–143, 150–152, 154, 158, 234, 311,
    420, 491, 505, 523, 578, 580
Sputnik, 27–28, 34, 295, 303, 331
Sputnik 2, 399
Stallone, Frank, 396–400, 404, 405–406, 407
Stallone, Jackie, 396–397

Stallone, Sylvester, 362–369, 395–406, 466, 530, 580–593

Stams, Frank, 198

Stark, Steven, 532

Steinbeck, John, 20

Stephen, Jack, 536

Stern, Howard, 111, 113, 114, 531

Sticks and Bones (Rabe), 390–392

Stockdale, James B., 139–140

Stockdale, Sybil, 139

stoicism, 124, 175, 387, 401

Stonecipher, Harry, 579

Stonewall Inn, 500–503

Story of G.I. Joe, The, 32–33

Stowe, Harriet Beecher, 271

Stracke, Win, 23

Students for a Democratic Society (SDS), 232–233, 301, 309, 311, 343

suburbia, 5, 23–25, 27, 75, 84–85, 94, 104–105, 140–141, 193, 236–237, 390–391, 398

Sullivan, Ron, 542–543, 550–552

Sundance Film Festival, 427, 431, 436, 439, 440, 446

Sunday, Billy, 256–257

Superman, 33, 366, 396, 406

Swann, Dennis, 72, 73–74, 94–96

Swindoll, Chuck, 229, 230

Swope, Bud, 550

Sylvia, Lorraine, 418

Tagliabue, Paul, 214, 218

Tailhook convention (1991), 84

Tarawa, USS, 94–95

Task, Seth, 170, 196, 198, 201, 217–218

Tavizon, Art, 122–123

Technics and Civilization (Mumford), 162–163

telemarketing, 112–113, 142

television, 5, 7, 12, 24, 34, 103, 105, 108, 111–114, 141–143, 158, 189, 191–194, 204–209, 215–218, 222, 225, 229, 248, 258–261, 274, 328, 332, 347, 361, 380, 392, 448, 459, 468, 476, 478, 481, 483, 492–494, 547, 559, 573

Teller, Edward, 28

Terkel, Studs, 23

Terry, Michael, 332

Testaverde, Vinny, 203–204

Theory of the Leisure Class, The (Veblen), 261–262

They Call It a Game (Parrish), 187

Things They Carried, The (O'Brien), 356

Thom, John, 75, 98

Thomas, Bob, 57–58, 59

Thomas, John Peyre, 136

Thomas, Paul, 536, 543

Thomas, Sunset, 545, 548, 549, 571

Thompson, Gerald, 165, 166–167, 168, 221

Thompson, Hugh, 335

Thompson, John "Big Dawg," 155–156, 158, 163, 165–169, 171, 187, 194–223, 578, 579, 580, 596

Thompson, Mary, 155, 168–169, 194, 207, 221

Thompson, Megan, 169, 194, 221

Thompson, Michelle, 169, 194, 221

Tick, Edward, 353

Tiffany (drag queen), 148, 149, 150

Time, 13, 22, 26, 32, 104, 181

Timken Roller Bearing Company, 159, 163

Title Nine, 122–123

Tocqueville, Alexis de, 24

To Hell and Back (Murphy), 16–17, 376, 394

Tonight Show, The, 111–114

Total Quality Management, 80–81, 91

Touchstone, Raven, 545

Trac Tech, 544–545, 569

trades, skilled, 67, 73, 74, 81, 85–86, 94–95, 539, 607

Treehouse bar, 147–151

Trilling, Roger, 514, 518, 519–520, 523

Triple Ought: A Novel of the Millennial Crash and the Second Civil War (Rawles), 434

Trout, T. J., 200–201

Truman, Harry S., 19, 22, 23, 53–54, 55, 70

Truman, James, 507, 512–514, 515, 517, 520, 522, 523, 524, 529

Tunis, John R., 157

Turner, Beau, 145

Turner, Eric, 202

Turner, Frederick Jackson, 28

Turner, Ted, 125, 145

Turner Entertainment, 463–464

Tyson, Mike, 38, 106, 553

Udall, Morris, 344

Ueberroth, Peter, 481

Uncle Tom's Cabin (Stowe), 271

Underwood, John, 204

"Unexpected Choice, The" (Zoba) 230

United States:

  economy of, 19, 42–43, 51, 102, 153–154, 195, 227, 246–247, 259, 262–263, 306, 348, 477, 488–489, 542, 595, 603

  frontier of, 10–13, 21, 26, 27–28, 30, 34, 40, 157, 240, 299, 305, 307, 328, 331, 360, 417, 418, 419–420, 437, 445, 452, 455, 459, 463, 598, 602–603, 605, 608

  industrialization of, 11, 34, 38, 51–52, 60–61, 136, 137–138, 139, 162, 257, 258

  masculine ideal of, 10–12, 16, 19, 20–23, 25–26, 37, 43, 44, 299, 304–305, 313–314, 342, 352–356, 359–362, 364, 366, 368, 412, 587

  religion in, 271–272

  Southern, 136

  as superpower, 22, 25–30, 157–158, 180, 184

Universal Studios, 585, 590–591

Unlimited Access (Aldrich), 430

U.S. News & World Report, 44, 300

Vajna, Andy, 385, 394

Van Damme, Branden, 466

Vanity Fair, 397, 505, 507

Vardell, Tommy, 198, 222

Varga girl, 525, 527

Vaughn, Vince, 508

VCA Pictures, 542, 545, 547

Veblen, Thorstein, 261–262

Vergnolle, Ron, 116–117, 118

Vesey, Denmark, 136

Viagra, 6, 15, 35

Vibe, 483, 507

Vietcong, 329–331, 334, 338, 409

"Viet Guilt" (Buckley), 352–353

Vietnam: The Soldiers' Story, 385

Vietnam Syndrome, 359–360

Vietnam Veterans Against the War (VVAW), 343, 355, 384–385, 433

Vietnam War, 25, 29, 82, 126, 139, 146, 195, 274, 276, 291–369, 376, 379–385, 393–396, 403, 409, 412, 413, 424, 433–438, 444, 447, 475–476, 479, 503, 605

Vindication of the Rights of Woman, A (Wollstonecraft), 600

violence:

  adolescent, 43–47, 103, 107, 139–140, 143–145, 468–498

  antiwar, 308–311

  domestic, 7–9, 10, 31, 88, 146, 224–227, 243–244, 250–251, 274, 277, 282, 395, 399–400, 417, 565–566, 580

  fan, 204–209, 221–222

violence (*continued*)
  film, 404–405, 478, 481
  gang, 468–498
  of war, 315–319, 322–352, 376–379, 385, 392
Vogel, Ron, 536, 544–545, 569
Vogt, Bob, 187
Vogue, 512–513
Voyeur, Vince, 538
voyeurism, 521–522, 532, 549

Waco, Tex., siege, 42, 407–448, 578
Waco: The Rules of Engagement, 420–448
Waco Whitewash, The (DeVault), 410
Wadsworth, USS, 72
Waldie, D. J., 104
Wallace, Henry, 21–23, 38
War at Home, The, 308
Warriors, The (Gray), 480
Washington, Desiree, 38
Washington, George, 164
Waskow, Captain, 18, 29, 35, 179
Way Back, The, 394
Wayne, John, 18–19, 36, 179, 305, 306, 316, 363, 368,
    392, 506, 585, 595
Webb, Marilyn Salzman, 311
Weber, John, 132
Weiner, Al, 122
Weinstein, Harvey, 581–582, 588, 591
Welch, Raquel, 459
Welter, Barbara, 264
West, Christina, 551–552
West, John C., 138
West, Nathanael, 203
West, Wallace, 139
Westmoreland, William C., 319, 336
"What Did You Do in the Class War, Daddy?"
    (Fallows), 353
Wheeler, John P., III, 299
When All the World Was Browns Town (Pluto), 175
"Where Have All the Sissies Gone?" (Kleinberg), 505
Where's the Rest of Me? (Reagan), 361
White, E. B., 303
White, Michael, 212–213, 218
White Collar (Mills), 76–77
"white collar" workers, 29, 66, 76–77, 79–80, 83, 88,
    92, 181–182, 185, 193–194
Whitney, Jane, 123, 142
Who Are the Promise Keepers? (Abraham), 260
Whyte, William, 76
Widmer, Fred, 327, 339
Wiggin, Paul, 182
"wild man" retreats, 228, 603
Williams, Paul Revere, 96
Williams, Robert, 499
Williams, Steve, 98–99, 100–101
Willis, Bruce, 581
Willis, Ellen, 603
Wills, Garry, 36, 362, 525
Wintour, Anna, 513

Wisniewski, Glenn, 75–76, 82, 87–88, 90–91, 97
Wolfe, Tom, 459, 461, 462, 525
Wollstonecraft, Mary, 395, 600
women:
  all-male bastions challenged by, 114–121, 124
  in antiwar movement, 304, 307–308, 310–314
  battered, 7–9, 10, 31, 88, 146, 224–227, 243–244,
    250–251, 274, 277, 282, 395, 399–400, 417, 565–
    566, 580
  discrimination against, 88
  empowerment of, 225, 240, 245, 247, 599–600
  equality of, 14
  fears of, 417
  "feminine mystique" of, 13, 40, 41, 583–584, 600–
    601
  as housewives, 26, 84–85, 228–230, 263, 601–602
  layoffs of, 61
  mass media and, 601, 602, 605
  movement for, 13–16, 29, 34, 40–41, 42, 89–90,
    225, 310–314, 354, 451, 594, 600–602, 604,
    607–608
  "problem with no name" of, 13–14, 15, 41
  "protection" of, 413–420, 427, 444–445, 556
  self-identity of, 154, 247, 253–254, 451
  as sex objects, 506, 519–521, 527–528, 535, 536, 545–
    546, 553, 554–555, 560–563, 572, 573, 574, 602
  vanity of, 39, 451, 583–584, 602
  wartime labor of, 26, 27, 75–76
  in workforce, 29, 60, 88, 154, 247, 253–254, 255,
    259, 262–263, 558
  see also feminism
Women's Liberation Front, 601
Wood, Bob, 466–467
work ethic, 52, 53, 55, 60, 64–74, 79–87, 94–95, 240,
    276, 470, 477, 546, 569, 584, 593
Working-Class War (Appy), 292
Works Progress Administration (WPA), 20, 76,
    157, 165, 220
World Aflame (Graham), 272
World Modeling Talent Agency, 533–536, 549, 552,
    559, 562, 569, 572–573
World War II, 5, 16–29, 35–39, 53–55, 74–75, 138,
    162, 172–179, 183–190, 213, 224–226, 240, 291–
    296, 299, 303–306, 315, 319, 321, 343, 351, 354–
    355, 358, 360, 366, 368, 371, 375–379, 388, 404,
    432, 584–585, 606
Wright, Lawrence, 292
Wright, Thomas, 481, 482, 490
Wyman, Jane, 78

Yankovic, Frankie, 175–176
Yeager, Chuck, 432
Young, Marilyn, 329–330, 359
Young, Philip, 373
"Youth and the Great Refusal" (Roszak), 309
Youth for Christ, 271
Yvonne (Vietnamese prostitute), 329

Zoba, Robert V., 230